Victim to Victor

"A . . . multifaceted exploration of truth, lies, victims and victories that moves far from an anticipated exposé format to probe the foundations of belief systems and how they operate in conventional and unconventional ways . . . [with] gritty examples . . . which simmer with hope, conflict, oppression, and revitalization . . . The result is a hard-hitting, controversial, raw examination that is highly recommended." —*Midwest Book Review*

"[A] poignant voyage of self-discovery where a path to higher spiritual enlightenment is beset by ill-fated relationships, broken friendships and the backbiting nature of various followers and leaders of the Unification Church. While dispelling rumors of the church being a cult, McKeon reveals the enigmatic bureaucracy that often stifles a devotee's growth in the church. He points out the positives . . . and the negatives . . . One of the qualities . . . is his resolve among an array of adverse life events . . . his willingness to divine more from life and to keep his world together is something many can identify with. At its core, McKeon's book will prove inspiring to more than a few." —*Manhattan Book Review*

"McKeon is intelligent and honest in his appraisal . . . The text has extensive, multiple examples of McKeon's experiences. However, it is his intellect and the sense of personal responsibility that he acknowledges that win the reader's attention and respect. The memoir is especially compelling . . . The book makes an intelligent statement about the importance of people feeling valued in ways that are healthy and the dangers of the alternatives." —*US Review of Books*

Other Books by Christopher McKeon

The Story of Life

Victim to Victor
Confessions of a Wrong-way Moonie

By (totally not a disgruntled)
Christopher McKeon
Tőteppit Press

Tōteppit Press
Rico, Colorado USA

www.toteppitpress.com

Publisher's Cataloging-in-Publication Data
McKeon, Christopher D.A., author.
Victim to Victor: Confessions of a Wrong-way Moonie / Christopher D.A. McKeon.
Rico, CO: Tōteppit Press, 2023. | Also available in eBook format.
LCCN 2023915240 (print) | ISBN 979-8-9864707-4-0 (paperback) | ISBN 979-8-9864707-5-7 (hardcover) | ISBN 979-8-9864707-6-4 (ebook)
LCSH: Unificationists–Biography. | Unification Church. | Moon, Sun Myung. | Cults–Biography. | Abused men. | Self-esteem. | Autobiography. | BISAC: BIOGRAPHY & AUTOBIOGRAPHY / Personal Memoirs. | BIOGRAPHY & AUTOBIOGRAPHY / Religious. | RELIGION / Cults. | FAMILY & RELATIONSHIPS / Abuse / Domestic Partner Abuse.
LCC BX9750.S44 A3 M63 2023 (print) | LCC BX9750.S44 (ebook) | DDC 289.9/6092–dc23.

Cover design by rebeccacovers
Text set in MinionPro

Information & Permissions
  Dedication page: Unification Church symbol (center circle represents God; four bars the four position foundation, the basis for all creation; the 12 rays the 12 gates to new Jerusalem (Revelations 21:10-14); circle arrows the universal give-and-take amongst God, Man, and creation (energy for action, multiplication, and maintenance of life)).
  Title page: Marble wall relief at the World Mission Center, New Yorker Hotel.
  All photos taken by or gifted without condition to the author except as noted: USCGC *Acushnet* courtesy Marine Exchange Alaska (contr. Robert Hurst) via NavSource Naval History (p. 58). *Golden Gate Seafood*, Google Maps (Jan. 2022; p. 67). *Three men boathooking a halibut*, Peter Thompson (aboard *Dues Payer II*, Kodiak), 2010 with permission (p. 204). *Moon, Kamiyama, Pak in Danbury*, Kiyoshi Nasu, Sept. 1984; caption quote by Bo Hi Pak (*Messiah — My Testimony to Rev. Sun Myung Moon Volume II*, University Press of America 2002, 165; p. 214). *New Yorker Hotel*, Michael McDonough, 2006 with permission (p. 235).

Let me dedicate this book
To all the Moonies on the hook,
Past, present, and future true,
T' Principle that changed their born blood's hue;
Tho' yet the glam they thought might come
From serving God's great chosen Son
Left them in a middle-aged lurch
Teetering in, then out, o' this thing called church;
They find, like me, the truth still burns
Like hot charcoal in th' soul's cistern,
Struggling to rise, to send airborne
The hopes and dreams o' these lonely forlorn
For whom the promise ne'er panned out
Of leaving Satan's hellish mount;
Who each their private course to burn,
Instead of peace, their hearts a-churned,
Impaled upon God's battlefield,
Their brethren 'ghast how they would yield
To th' fiery arrows of torment
That banish'd to their Lord's basement;
Wondering whether, near or far,
God's prickly ear'd note th' passing star
Of the Moonie who doesn't mind th' hook
But hates the poison that it took
To bring them up from Hell's death door
While crushing them 'pon the floor
'Neath the weight o' self-righteousness
Of smug interlocutors that make confess,
Then use it to condemn once more
And leave them wailing 'pon their moor;
O those mighty Moonies, saviors true!
Now such victims they doth rue
That e'er they found as though a specter
God's mighty Son—strangely—their exemplar victor.
— *Christopher McKeon 2002*

Table of Contents

Preface

The 2023 Edition

THE 2023 EDITION (DELAYED TO 2024; SORRY) YOU HOLD IN YOUR HANDS IS MY world as I wrote about it in 2003. Unification Church leaders, individuals, cultural references, and so on are from the decades leading up to it. I reedited the prose for style and clarity and added this preface and an epilogue from when I published it 20 years ago to a handful of friends for their response. They gave no accolades. Julian Sherry, as he's known in this book, advised me not to publish it at all.

"Well, that's disappointing coming from you, of all people," I said.

His tone came off cagey. "What you're saying . . . I don't think it's helpful for you or the church. You'll regret putting it out there."

Will I, though?

Then life sped up too much to carry it forward anyway, so through the cracks it went. In 2017 I discovered I'm an empath, a budding spirit medium and, according to my children, 'neurodivergently' ADHD and a high-functioning autistic besides. Altogether, it fired me down the barrel of my "healing through awareness" book *The Story of Life* (2022; sample at back), a revelatory Morphean red pill that's a "welcome to the real world" mind opener. After bullseyeing booksellers everywhere five years on, I realized this old manuscript's voyage through two decades of Moonworld, abusive love relationships, marriage–violence–divorce, and my inevitable Jabbokian confrontation with victimology carried its own healing power.

My account isn't an evil-Moonie-cult tell-all, a gory tale of domestic woe, nor an I-hit-rock-bottom-while-crying-in-my-beer journey of self-discovery that put me on the stairway to heaven. These have their place and offer their own kind of emotional experience. My story comes from scars, not wounds. If you were ever a Unificationist or some stripe of idealogue, a domestic violence victim or maybe a perpetrator, a near-suicide feeling crushed 'neath life's ironshod boot or love's heartless hate, or just can't stop shooting holes in your feet, this book might open your awareness to paralyzing, scapegoating victimism and a path of transitioning to your own life-giving victorism. It couldn't hurt.

The book comes out of my 1983–2003 journals, which Rev. Chung in his 1983 Berkeley, California God's Day (January 1) speech prevailed on me to start as a future testimony. It embues my story with the freshness of experiences thoughtfully recorded in the moment. It doesn't mean I didn't inadvertently misreport something or that another's point of view won't differ, only that I honestly put my encounters to paper as they happened instead of dredging them out of hazy memory years later. I didn't construct dialogue out of whole cloth but took it from my journals verbatim, paraphrased according to how I narrated the event, or reconstructed from memory in accord with my journals and honest reflection on the gist of what was said and my take on the speaker's personality and language. I compress some events that unfold over short periods into single scenes for clarity.

I make no attempt to accuse any person of villainy nor vengefully cast them in a bad light, but only to convey how I directly and indirectly experienced them and their effect on me. My tale isn't a manifesto on who or what they are. In some instances, I come off at fault or worse. As you read the acts of my play you may think I'm only venting or wreaking havoc, but my story is about *me*, not *them*; they're players reacting to or provoked by me in the context of situations I helped create. I don't know their motivating sufferings, struggles, or hurts nor how nice, kind, and beloved of others they are in different contexts. We all feel we're the hero of our own story; I think all concerned acted in sincerely righteous (if fanatical or deranged) belief and not with malice aforethought. And, too, people change with time.

In that vein, I change the names or characteristics of those who might not want their mad monkey in my circus because, to paraphrase Marty Rubin, I'm not so outrageous as to tell their tale. Where I haven't—I don't tell you which is which—it's because it would make the story too much a lie or confuse the narrative entirely. This especially is the case regarding Unificationists since, in nearly every situation, it was their position in a particular time and place that created the context and conditions for my incidents with them. I claim only my interpreted experiences and reactions as fact regardless how I narrate events.

I considered novelizing my tale but felt it would lose most if not all its healing possibilities. Besides, the American Unification Church is a story that needs an honest appraisal of its good aspects juxtaposed with its bad—benefit versus harm— which, so far as I can tell, no one's published. That said, I hope you have a positive experience with this book.

Christopher McKeon
Southwest Colorado, USA
August 2023

Prologue

I WAS FLYING HIGH WHEN I HIT THE GROUND. THE REVEREND SUN MYUNG MOON came shrieking through my hippiedom-bloated, change-the-world mind in the waning days of complacent America's tradition-shattering youth revolution midway through my first blackboard lecture on the coming of the second messiah. I couldn't understand from whence it came. Nobody had mentioned it. But there it was, a banshee panicking through my skull.

"Rev. Moon! *Rev. Moon!* Shit, it's the Moonies! Run! *Flee! Ahhhhhh!!*"

For just a tick I wildly eyed catapulting through the plate glass window not ten feet away. Then some 20 feet below I saw snow-covered, scalpel-edged granite and dead, spearpointed branches tearing and stabbing my soft body crashing headlong down the ironhard mountain. It soberly chained me to my folding metal chair two rows back from Ms. Forgettable droning through her book-in-hand lecture.

Here I was in a group of maybe 15 twenty-somethings looking hard into this new brand of Christianity for some sign of my future. I saw myself 'changing the world,' whatever that meant; ending war, poverty, injustice . . . getting rid of the world's arseholes is what all my pious talk was really going for.

What a double-take when my 'spiritual mother' who'd enticed me up to this rural, flower-mountain suburb in Nederland, Colorado grimly said, "Before you can change the world, Chris, you first have to change yourself."

"Whaaat?" *I don't think so.* "I want to fight evil, not be some holy roller."

"Just listen, okay?" She patted my knee. "You'll get it."

Hmmph.

In that simple contradiction lay the root of the most complex, controversial, and demonized love-hate relationship religious Americans have found themselves in since the righteous run amuck strung up Joseph Smith. On the one hand, we younkers wanted to follow Rev. Moon like the Pied Piper's rats.

"Following Father's direction is the core of our life of faith," Unification Church national pastor Michael Jenkins remarked near the change in millennium. "The direction he gives is not just a reaction to current affairs but is based on God's direct revelation and many years of preparation."

Being a good Unificationist is primarily about obedience. Theoretically, to Rev. Moon. But obedience regardless. On the other hand, and in spite of the holiness we imputed to him, we knew his oft-corrupt and vicious organization and our unexamined participation in it was ultimately leading us to some sort of doom we dimly perceived over the horizon but hoped wasn't really there. In these rose a tension between him, God, and us and therefore our obedience to his institution, its founder, and our own conscience . . . supposing, on the off chance, it survived.

My friend Miyako gravely gifted me this photo in Kodiak, 1983. I tearfully prayed with it for two decades.

He and his church are ever at loggerheads, its revelation and institution enmeshed in mortal combat. My conflicts involved my rooting around for a way to respond to his inspired direction in the context of an anti-inspirational institution. For all its lip service to his revelatory messianism, the institution shudders at the uncertainty and instability it creates. To ward off Rev. Moon's explosive spiritualism spreading unchecked, it relentlessly interferes with the natural development of Moonism in our members. Becoming like him, which he demands of us, poses a mortal threat to his Confucianly bureaucratic movement as an institution despite most efficaciously advancing his vision. This contra-dynamic has the simple effect of hammering a wedge twixt him and his church; he drives off in one direction, his church another, and we members pinball off this flipper and that toward the inevitable TILT. The net result is confusion, frustration, chaos, failed efforts, anger, blame, resentment, and a wholesale loss of devoted membership for quacks and scoundrels. And, naturally, Rev. Moon complains to deaf ears, his bullheaded own the most hearing-impaired of all.

Nevertheless, and powerless to stop ourselves because of an indefinable link to his core Divine Principle teaching, tens or maybe hundreds of thousands of young, middle-class Americans like me followed him through the interpretive lens of the church till our moral compasses were spinning in our own Burmuda Triangles that swallowed whole our patience, endurance, and self-identity. It turns out there *is* a primal connection between external accomplishment like changing the world and internal growth and development like changing myself. And evidently I couldn't do the former without first accomplishing at least some of the latter.

Damn, that's some bullshit.

And the church spins on like a bald tire in Georgia red-clay mud throwing up a lot of *stuff* but getting nowhere except in its own mind. Rev. Moon and his church foolhardily created for themselves a nasty, insoluble conundrum that, as it did me, breaks down members' trust in and sacrificial devotion to ostensibly *the* Messiah anointed by Jesus Christ Himself and hounds them to their fetid graves.

Despite the persecution I bore at the hands of ignorant and arrogant church leaders and eventually my choking, sucked-in-breath recognition that they'd been showing me the door for most of these 21 years together—kicked out or urged to stay away a record-setting 12 times—I don't look on those years as a loss, waste, or failure. And I don't view Rev. Moon as the Pied Piper . . . or the Angel of Death, for that matter, nor the engine of my impoverishment. Rather, it was a chosen voyage of enlightenment mostly (unfortunately) through howling storms and brutal seas that pummeled my little ship of life onto heartless rocks.

Wrecked; oh, *fuck* yeah.

But alive. And still on my journey . . . if I wanted to continue.

After 21 years of sincere, fingernails-scrabbling-at-rocks toil to fit in with and please Rev. Moon and his insatiable church, I expected more outward success and inner happiness in the end. I wasn't ready for a sort of Heideggerian nothingness, my faith and devotion hanging by a thread for want of its creator's touch.

I envisaged my talents and capabilities well used by him at his organization's top echelons in the way Mom once said, "Your father and I always thought you were smart enough that, if you'd joined the priesthood, you'd have ended up at the Vatican."

"Ha!" I'd rebutted, feeling pejorative. "They don't allow marriage and I'm not going through life a monk. I'd only wind up with some lonely troubles in the nunnery . . ."

For me, this is the man of holy faith he ever was regardless future trappings.

She didn't reply but I caught an *Oh, Chris* headshaking sigh in her eyes.

Regardless rank, I at least expected Rev. Moon and his vaunted leaders to take me in earnest as a meaningful participant. Why not? I wasn't anybody's chopped liver. But I wasn't the pliant organization man they demanded, either. Instead, I took him and his call to be like him as gospel; an out-of-the-box innovator that ended up a pain in the ass maverick, an enemy of their institutional state. *Oops.*

"You tired, you poor, you wretched 'B'-member bastards yearning to breathe free—donate ten percent to our better world and go worship with the Baptists."

Leaders quietly rejoiced imagining their persistent blackballing bringing my attendance of their Messiah to a lonely, sad, ignominious close. Notwithstanding the real carnage wrought by so-called cults, their greatest crime is filling followers with a vision while blocking them from realizing it. The frustration in not achieving a deeply held conviction—the agony, says Maya Angelou, of bearing an untold story—is worse than death.

Burdened by a parentally loving God ardently preached but only desperately dreamed of while slip-sliding through 21 years a Moonie that spawned the cruelest sense of victimization, was it possible to experience happiness much less Real God before I punched my own ticket? If I didn't want to yank the flusher on God's noble gift, I'd have to teach myself to steer *my* course off rock bottom by following *my* instincts and confronting the sea on *my* terms and nobody else's. That's the only way to handle a howling wind like Rev. Moon and a treacherous, unlighted rock like the Unification Church: take the bull by the horns and put it down.

Act I

Meeting the Moonies
My Axial Moment

I was a sour young man of 21 when I separated from the United States Coast Guard along the end of December 1980. Crippled in my right knee from a line-of-duty accident exacerbated by ineffectual care in the federal government's Public Health Service, I'd just had a real doctor slice a broad happy face across it. He flushed out the "ground hamburger" of dense, floating bits of medial meniscus and scraped smooth the scored-up backside of my patella. A horse needle of morphine in post-op oddly hurt worse. I'm largely immune to painkillers, so it struggled just taking the edge off though calmed my violent trembling. After a year on crutches and no follow-up rehab, I'd ambulate four more on a cane. But for now, five weeks later, I hobbled across the wintry street—eyes peeled for hidden ice—from my older sister Mona's Denver apartment to the 7-Eleven for candy bars and chips on a darkening February afternoon, 1981. *Star Trek* was about to grace her TV and I was in a hurry to get back with snacks.

She lightly stamped her feet outside the store holding something in her hand and sized me up as I passed. A cardboard box balanced atop the trash can beside her. I'd never noticed folks loitering at storefronts with a ravenish air, eyes seemingly x-raying my pockets. I thought the sight odd but shrugged it off. This was America after all and weirdness abounded.

"Hello," she said pleasantly to my curious look.

An absent "Hi," and I beelined for the snacks aisle. Exiting five minutes later, she pounced.

"Would you like to buy a scroll?"

I gave her and it a once-over. "What's that?"

"It's a Chinese tiger scroll." She modeled it higher up.

Boot camp at 19. TRACEN, *Alameda* CA. *Feb., 1979.*

"I don't know . . . looks kinda—"

"It's bamboo." A broad, glowing smile. "It'll look great in your house."

My house. *Ha.* But, what a concept! "Does 7-Eleven know you're selling stuff right outside their store?"

"Oh, yes." She showed even more teeth. "I have their permission."

Huh. How 'bout that. It's a sure bet they didn't know she and fellow fundraisers-cum-proselytizers, so blithely permitted on their doorstep, were extracting customers from circulation piecemeal. I looked her over with a mildly yearning eye. Italian looking on the slightly emaciated side if you discounted her padded, thigh-length coat. Dark hair; kind of puffy, thick. Five-six or -seven barefoot. Big smile, nice straight teeth. I approved. She was from Brooklyn, I'd discover. She looked it.

"Well, how much?"

"Just five dollars," she cooed.

FIVE dollars? That seemed a lot of dough for some dumb looking cheap scroll with a tiger printed on it.

"Hand painted," she corrected me.

Still, it didn't cost $5 to fill up my 1970 Opel Kadette's gas tank. I really didn't like her buttonholing me for money right outside 7-Eleven, especially with a bag of junk food in hand because I felt guilty saying no. I was developing a pretty defensive attitude. "I don't have any money left over anyway after—well . . ."

"It's for a good cause," she purred, the smart, skeptical saleslady.

"What cause?" nibbling her bait.

"It's for a Christian group."

And . . . hooked like a fish sure the worm it saw was alive and tasty but not scoping the sharp, grabby point. It was easy getting her five bucks because, for the previous two years, I'd been searching far and wide for a church that embodied my idea of spiritual life. The Catholic Church I grew up in—*confirmed*, for Pete's sake—was so dead and boring I abandoned it altogether the second I was free of my parents in college to dig through Protestant ones. My Irish grandmothers would've sprouted horns and forked tails if they'd seen it.

But what could I do? Catholicism in the 1970s seemed a relic of Druidism: heavy on ritual, light on content. Watching the pious past their prime unable to recall the Lord's Prayer without the *Monthly Missalette* convinced me it was a cabal of hypocrites and lazy ones at that. How hard was it to memorize? My catechism teacher made us do it. What was *their* problem? Yet, my 2-year search in the Coast Guard found me no church I felt happy with. Each seemed wonderful till I realized no one cared about anonymous servicemen blowing two jiffies or three through their congregation. We didn't merit the effort. I tried some Catholic churches on the off chance but, no diff: shackled to the past, lost in ritual, thinking a folksong group—my family ran one in St. Jude's down the mountain in Lakewood, Colorado—would make them relevant and interesting.

Well, for a while I'd given up. After my discharge I wanted to return to college but, for the life of me, couldn't figure out what I wanted to *do* in life. Geology with its chemistry and molecular constructions was beyond me; I'd proved that at Western State College in Gunnison, Colorado. Oceanography, which really appealed to the

2

wandersman in me, didn't look possible, either. Too much math like everything I liked except art, and what money was there in that? Still living on Daddy's nickel, how would I even pay for it? For the moment, none of it mattered. I was shacked up in my sister's waiting out the long days healing by reading, watching *Star Trek*, and playing guitar. The life of Reilly. Well, a painful Reilly. Crutches weren't my thing and I'd well and truly wearied.

My soon-to-be 'spiritual mother' was eyeing her mark with an inviting smile lighting her face. What an irony that she, too, was once—but are you ever really *not?*—Catholic. I couldn't say no, almost compelled to fork over my last dregs of cash. It didn't matter which Christian group it was going to and I didn't ask. She'd made the claim and that was enough. Who'd lie about that? Boy, howdy.

I went for the tiger scroll. She handed me a new one in a box. I hung it on my sister's wall where it probably drove her as crazy as my incessant guitar practice.

"How many times are you going to play that Popeye tune, anyway?" she said. "It's getting pretty annoying."

"Till I learn it." *What else?*

"Well, learn quieter." But it was a small apartment.

I felt sort of taken by this woman who now stuck her hand out and said, "My name's Ginny."

We chatted over an hour, our steamy breath wafting away like *Star Trek* and her sales numbers, just the two of us shivering under our hanging words in the icy twilight outside a cookie-cutter 7-Eleven. Sometime after dark a boxy Detroit van crunched into the snowy lot, inside faces aimed our way.

"My ride's here." That was unexpected. I'd supposed her car was in a parking space. "I have to go. Can I get your number?"

Well, yeah. Not often a woman asks for that. I scribbled out Mona's and curiously eyed a few men climb out of the van, gather up her goods, then all wave goodbye.

"That was weird." I languidly crutched for Mona's lamenting *Star Trek*.

~

IT WAS THE beginning of a new life unknowingly eschewing college, a 'normal' career, money, and social credibility. That didn't matter in my young twenties. The world was my oyster. Old age and responsibility seemed impossibly far away.

Though snagged, the hook wasn't set. I still imagined my life hadn't reached any defining moment—its proverbial fork in the road—and was comfortable hobbling home to Sis. The next day I plopped into her sofa for another round of *Star Trek*. Then, of all things, *she* calls in the middle of the show. What gall! How could I keep a conversation going with one eye on Captain Kirk struggling with reprobate aliens, pulling on his boots after a commercial-break roll in the futuristic hay, saving the universe from evil, and me gobbling down Gene Roddenberry's great vision for what human society could be if it wanted? If there was one thing that really caught my attention it was visions of a peaceful, caring future that saved the world from the bucket of hell it was. I wanted to save humanity. I was a superhero.

In junior and senior high school I crouched on the commode daydreaming of defending Earth from invading aliens with futuristic tech I'd found secreted on a remote island by dead, good-guy aliens. I recruited top fighter pilots from the world, even the irascible USSR, and sent out emergency calls when aliens showed up. We flew out for battle around the moon, over cities, hand-to-hand on teeming sidewalks, or crashing afire in jungles. My hands were swooping, jinking spaceships landing, taking off, and visiting the US president as I whispered film dialogue and soared far through imagination. What fun! At the height of my adolescent writing career I'd clacked it all out on Mom's ancient, cast iron Royal into a 300-page adventure yarn, the triumphant future novelist. I hadn't yet happened on *Star Trek*, but thought I was clearly on Roddenberry's wavelength when I did.

My mind was naturally lost in the vast reaches of the universe when taking in *Star Trek*. Carrying on a phone conversation had me trailing off into babbling as I lost track of where the hell I was. We managed some sparse talk before she gave up with a laugh. She oddly rang the same time over several days but it was apparent I had an attention deficit. We agreed she'd call back when I wasn't slugging down alternate realities.

We got pretty friendly the next two weeks. She let me gripe over the sorry reality of my post-service, pre-college, no-clue life to let free my soul-sight lurking within. It felt good and didn't occur she was telemarketing her church. I was just a 21-year old cripple a nice girl was courting . . . so long

Me, Blair, & Mom at home on North Turkey Creek. Summer, 1978.

as *Star Trek* wasn't sifted out.

I finally agreed to her "Christian organization's evening program" invite for Thursday night. "It's just a dinner and a presentation on what we do. I'm pretty sure you'll like it after all you've told me."

"Well, why not?" Mona watched me go with sly eyes. "Back soon!"

I parked my faded green Opel along a snow-crusty street at 1440 High, a 3-storey, early twentieth-century brick home the other side of a glaciated, winter-dead lawn in a quiet Denver suburb. The foyer, living, and dining rooms seemed altogether cavernous when I stepped inside. Scattered across the connected rooms were cheap tables covered in white like some Bohemian café. Stairs led to a primal darkness.

"Oh, you're Chris?" said the young woman bolting the freezer door behind me. "Wait here, I'll fetch Ginny!"

Lungs huffing frost on shifty feet, my skin was hot. I sensed everyone giving me a foxy once-over, sizing me up like a plated chicken. After I'd gone all in I realized each was passing judgment on their mate's new catch, wondering if I was worth reeling in although, in those days, anyone breathing was worth a pull . . . well, except blacks. At or near the bottom of desirable converts, they had to work hard to join; really want it. Something about "debased spiritual character" had American whites—clinging to a vestigial authority in the church—and racistly worse Japanese leaders steering blacks clear of their cozy heaven on earth. Rev. Moon had a different (at least, public) attitude:

For the white members, I warn you to be nicer than anyone else to the Negro people when they come here. You must be humble to them . . . It happened a few days ago, that one of our members encouraged a Negro woman with a baby to be seated in the rear, and she was hurt and left. And I thought that she could instead have taken care of the child, babysat the child, and let the mother hear the speech. (*How To Be a Leader* 1973)

My former best friend Jerome recounted through a strained laugh how his 1970s New York City Unification Church center loudspeakered each morning, "Good luck to everyone witnessing today . . . and remember, don't bring any blacks."

West Indian black himself, he saw it a delicious irony that he got the same picky admonition as if white; a convoluted equality, to be sure. I never encountered it on the early '80s West Coast, but many American and African blacks bitterly complained to me over the years of the racial obstacles placed in their way. In qualified fairness to the church, its public attitude toward blacks rotated one-eighty by the late 1990s because—I might be as cynical as Jerome here—practically the only group listening to Rev. Moon's message by then (and especially by 2003) *were* blacks. With or without whites fearing blacks spiritually muddying their waters, the Unification Church remains the white man's worst nightmare because, try as they might, the Asian hierarchy never trusts them with real authority in anything and emasculates them like Roman slaves. But they're the puppets they made themselves, ever choosing never to aspire higher than the subordination they wanted blacks persistent enough to join to accept as their own white-puppet status. One disfranchised group disfranchising another. Even Jerome conceded this sorry reality was a tastier irony than his own fish-out-of-water days.

I handed over my coat and Ginny padded up to greet my fidgeting self. *Whew*. Now in the clutches of someone I 'knew,' my nerves eased and muscles relaxed. We tossed some small talk across our table and then a 'waitress' served our dinner. Simple chicken and veg, nothing fancy. I noticed one table using actual crockery and wondered why I was eating off paper. But it was small potatoes, hardly registering in my mind. Those resentments wouldn't come along for a couple more years. In the meantime, I was enchanted. Everyone was friendly, eager to please. My service-inspired cynicism was beginning to feel so *déclassé*. I decided it could just stay in its room for the evening lest I wind up looking pathetic; nothing's drearier for a cynic than being surrounded by optimists.

A warm glow pervaded me. I lit up as the center of attention. Other guests were getting their share but, for the first time in years, I felt someone caring about *me*, *respecting* me. The military robbed me of all that dignity.

IN THE LATE 1970s the service was emerging from the Vietnam War a changed, all-volunteer institution. Recruits had fancier educations, bigger egos, and flying expectations. Low-end enlisted demanded more respect. Several I knew insisted subordinates *and* superiors address them by their proper rank.

"Don't call me 'Chief,' " we got tongue-lashed one day. "I'm *Master* Chief."

"Don't call me that," a plain vanilla third-class scolded our mustanged executive officer. "I'm not your son. I'm Petty Officer Jones."

That was great. The power of human equality. I was all for it. Yet, in the casual enlisted world, it grated my nerves being subordinated by titles. I was too low on the totem pole for respect-by-rank to be empowering at all. As much as I demanded personal dignity from others, I refused to be institutionally demeaned. If that meant diluting or refusing the respect they also demanded, then so be it. Seaman First Class—practically a steam bucketeer—was demeaning all on its own.

I'm so much better than that, and capable of so much more. Hell, I had 1-½ years of college when few enlisted had any. That made me as good as any officer or NCO, dang it, regardless my short time-in-service. If I hadn't been crippled up, I'd have made first-class petty officer by the end of my first tour but most likely entered officer's candidate school (OCS) for a commission. I tried on my boss' scrambled-eggs headgear one day when he stepped out of the office *sans chapeau*. I dare say, it sat damn nicely all squared off and pulled low on my brow. By that standard alone, I made a great officer. I admired myself in his mirror before hurriedly vacating his space. I wasn't entirely fearless.

My career dreams were cut short on a hot Mississippi night June 30, 1979. Some blasted idiot managed to stall his car *sideways* in the divided four-lane paralleling the beach in Biloxi, Mississippi. I couldn't see it in the midnight darkness till the brake lights on the car passing me lit up and I flew past him scanning the seemingly empty black road.

Shit! White letters in a jet field leapt at me. I flew down the gears on my Honda CB750–4 motorcycle, stomped the rear brake and squeezed hard on the front. The bike nosed down. My weight shifted heavily onto my hands.

Sand glittered in my headlights and I caught my breath. Turning tight enough to make the 90-degree, 20-foot exit to the service road and avoid the heavy American cruiser just on its far side looked impossible. The last thing I wanted was to drop my bike and guillotine my legs twixt car, road, and bike. I was now aimed straight for the front wheel and instinctively knew it wouldn't give an inch when my bike accordioned against it.

Damn. If only I could tighten my turning arc just another foot I'd clear his front bumper and crash in the sandy side median. But the road grit wouldn't play ball. So many clear thoughts shot through my mind in less than a second. *How fast a person thinks!* Memories played a slide show even as I analyzed my impending doom hurtling larger and furiously clawed straws.

When I'd first noticed the inky vehicle materialize in my low beam, its white passenger door lettering lighting the impression of a police car I was just too dumb to crash into, I was clocking 60 MPH. I calculated the distance to the car, my stiff deceleration, and the time to collide all fairly instantaneously and with no algebra skills at all. The result: out of time. My best course was to get the hell off the bike before I went through the handlebars. I rocketed off the footpegs with all my strength. I figured I'd sail over the handlebars to land agreeably in the beachy patch between the roads and roll to a nice, safe stop. All good.

But a half-second too late. The bike slammed into the car's front wheel at 30 MPH or better. The wheel snapped 90-degrees right. Handlebars whipped round. The rubber throttle handle jammed my pubic bone mid-jump, fortunately just above the family jewels I hadn't yet had much opportunity to polish. The grip's rubber burned down my corduroy to my inside right knee. It promptly hyperextended and ripped the medial meniscus, changing what would've been a maybe graceful swan dive into a crazy, elliptical spin. Passing over the car's hood, 'Taxi' in white atop the roof rotated through my field of vision. I dimly wondered why I hadn't seen it before. A wave of relief I hadn't busted up a police car swept through me.

Then I plopped into the worn-mattress earth like a well-baked potato. I rolled only once but my face shield roughly shoveled sand deep in my mouth. Choking and sputtering, I shed my helmet and eased onto my back to catch my gritty breath. A roadside motel perched over the service road. Its languishing patio guests, trying to beat the oppressive heat of the night, followed my spectacle. These folks now swirled around me. I tried to sit. Pain roared up my leg.

"Gah!" I groaned.

In a chorus they advised me to lie back. "The ambulance is on its way, buddy," somebody hollered in my pain deafened ear. "Don't worry, you're gonna be okay."

"Am I?"

A cadaverous black man in black slacks and a sleeve-rolled white shirt jogged up. White rag in hand, he loudly proclaimed his innocence. "That's my car you hit! You didn't see me waving this? I was flagging you down! Ain't my fault, man."

News to me. And so was the late '70s Deep South. I didn't appreciate he was possibly concerned over mowing down a white man. He was just a dude to me. Then the medics sirened up and clustered over me. They slipped a new-fangled but leaky air cast mandating reinflation every few minutes over my right leg.

Traveling to the local clinic I said, "Why no siren? Don't I rate that?"

"Don't need it," one said.

"I just wrecked my bike! I'm in pain. And you're stopping at red lights?" I'd been 20 years old 30 whole days now but thought I was pretty big stuff. They laughed and chatted amongst themselves. *Pfft.*

Like a lot of events in my life, this one had its quixotic moments. Along with its driver, the taxi was a deep, unreflective black, invisible till my lone headlight landed on its white door lettering. How'd the other car see it first? The real joke was crashing in Biloxi and flying over the city line into Gulfport. My wrecked bike a smoking heap on Biloxi pavement, me broken and spitting Gulfport sand.

The cops didn't know who should take jurisdiction to write the report. Ultimately, Gulfport's police chief approved a version blaming me for following too close. *A stalled car.* He was one of those beefy Southern cops flaunting a '60s buzz cut, bull neck, a barrel for a chest, and forearms like Popeye.

"The car was sideways before I even arrived, Chief, not to mention invisible in the dark." I slumped over crutches supporting my ankle-to-hip plaster cast since he didn't keep a chair for mere citizens in his brown paneled office. "And how could I be following a *parked* car anyhow? If you submit that, the insurance won't pay."

"That's what the investigation shows, young man. The report stands." Gruff eyes shot to the door.

I rolled my own hard enough to break after turning to shuffle out; I didn't know, he might've locked me up for that. Respect, right? The first real injustice of my life was incensingly bitter on my palate. *I'll have to pay the damages myself, thanks to this mulehead*, I silently groused.

THESE EVENTS RATTLED through my head listening to Ginny at our faux café in 'High Street house.' They formed my character, influenced my responses, dictated my behavior. My experience following the accident dead soured me on authority figures and unearned respect. Unearned from *me*, that is. A person can spend their life earning credibility but if, in their encounter with me, they fail to inspire or just piss me off, I don't give it. I *can't* give it. Ironically, I often feel hurt and offended when people don't automatically respect *me* based on my past accomplishments or title, such as it is. This condition, which I call hypochondriatic hypocrisy, was probably one source of my problems in the military as well as in the Unification Church. But I comfort myself that it was only a mild form while my persecutors seemed wholly given over to its pestilence.

Christmas & crutches at 7,500 ft. in 1979.

As I finished up dinner enjoying the warm glow of Ginny's attention, her authorities went into action. We gathered in the living room, the old wooden pocket doors trundled closed, and Bruce Grodner orchestrated a short video or slide show. He looked younger than his likely late-twenties in black hair over Jewish-looking features; another Catholic Italian from Brooklyn, I thought. He amused me with a coffee mug a member gave him with 'In Grod we Trust' emblazoned on it. Ten or so years later, when nearly all I'd ever owned besides my precious Fender guitar had been lost, stolen, or sold, I noticed he still had that cup. I admired his fortitude holding onto his prized possessions better than I ever did.

His presentation was electric. They screened photos of their various global organizations teaching peace while helping the great unwashed. The basic points of their guiding principles—which name they adroitly avoided—rested on typical Christian values I recognized and approved.

Impressive. This is a happening group. Going places. Changing the world. I like it! Young, energetic, idealistic folks devoted to their cause. *Committed.* They obviously had money, manpower, and a guiding philosophy. *All they need is me!*

My heart was humming with positive energy for the first time in three years. The shattered wreckage of my failed engagement to Diane, my first true love in college, was breaking loose. My injuries, pain, crutches, evil executive officer, inattentive commanding officer, the incompetent Public Health Service, its indescribably lovely and doting Vietnamese nurse Bùi who fell in love with me till she found out I was only 20 . . . all these spiritual aches and pains misted away and retreated from thought. I was alone with myself and surged with a lightness of being I'd all but forgot. I was galloping with wild abandon down this exciting road when I heard "special workshop retreat in the mountains for a weekend seminar."

Whoa! My reverie screeched to a halt. "I think I need a little time to think on it," I said to Ginny.

"Of course. No problem at all. I'm so glad you came." She smiled deeper. "Can I call you again?"

I considered her request already knowing my answer. "Sure, why not? I really like what I heard. I dig your group. Seems like a breath of fresh air."

"Because we are."

Nerves jangled, though. I felt crowded. A little *too* cared for. I needed bracing arctic air, the sight of my own breath in this world to ground me. I wasn't afraid of them. It's just my debacle in the Coast Guard was a bloodsoaked horse's head I couldn't shake. I trusted nobody. Even so, my thoughts were giddy with anticipation. A sense of purpose and direction budded in my heart's polar valleys.

I motored home to my sister's quiet and contemplative but racing under the hood. I mulled it over a couple days, then decided to attend the workshop. Their global perspective and laser focus on "Restoring the world," whatever that meant, captivated me. I didn't know it was the Unification Church. I'd never heard of it nor Rev. Moon but, even if I had, it wouldn't have dissuaded me. It was an exciting event in my otherwise morose life. Who needed a name? I'd never heard of cults, their alleged threat, wacky Eastern religions, or demonic, messianic wannabes. It was enough that Ginny called it a Christian group. There were a million of them out there. What difference did it make which one?

Their personalized attention enamored me. I was a 'guest' worthy of effort. After two crushing years in the service, that kind of appreciation was an aphrodisiac. Pure night and day. I came out of cold, heartless rules-and-regulations to meet warm, loving 'heartisticness.' And it crawled with icingly beautiful, unattached girls. What could be better? God *and* women. I was surely no monk. My college Dear John over freshman summer was a gaping wound dying for a suture.

I DIDN'T KNOW then how fantastically hidebound the Unification Church was or would even more so become. In those days, there were so many Americans in leadership positions that the Johnny-come-lately Japanese who'd later rule it under a stiff, hobnailed boot were constrained to a somewhat hands-off policy toward American methods and attitudes in reaching out to their countrymen. Those joining up were the cream of the hippie crop who'd survived drugs and free sex with a mostly sound mind and STD-free body; the most socially aware, change-the-world brigade the United States had fronted since our wigged Founders stomped all over monarchy and good form and Yankees crushed genteel, slaving Southerners underfoot.

Unfortunately, all that changed about the time I joined. Rev. Moon handed the Japanese a whip they cracked across Americanism in a vain attempt to transform our movement into their mindless, hierarchically bureaucratic, amoral, WWII Japanese Imperial Church they thought perfectly suited God's top-down ideal. Flush with seeming victory over American economic hegemony in the mid-'80s coupled with our presumedly irreversible political and cultural decline, Japanese Unificationists saw Americans as the crap of the crop. Yesterday's story. Plus, I think older Japanese wanted payback for the war. They certainly made a person feel that way.

The funniest example of it was the day Mr. Sato, Colorado's senior church leader, got a dose of Brooke Shields modeling Calvin Klein's *haute couture* on television not long after I'd joined and moved from High Street to the Boulder center. Brooke was coyly purring through Mr. Sato's television, "You wanna know what comes between me and my Calvins? Nothing," when his ears burned off from her pornographic insinuations. He banned blue jeans from his church centers.

"What the hell are we gonna wear?" I wondered of Julian Sherry, Boulder's center director and a growing friend. "Who of us owns anything *but* blue jeans?"

We all agreed Calvin was a rake and Brooke maybe a step away from a skin flick, but this was our American uniform Mr. Sato was messing with. I complained long and loudly of the stupidity, arrogance, and futility of his order.

Julian finally said, "Okay, I'll talk to Mr. Sato and let him know that Calvin Klein jeans aren't the same as Levi's and Wrangler."

"You have to *explain* that?" *Puh-leeze.*

He laid a gentle hand on my shoulder. "Just cool it. I'll let you know."

"Fine. Okay."

What was left of the free-spirited, liberty-minded idealists I'd met early in '81 would be exterminated by 1984 at the hands of vicious Japanese feudal lords like Mr. Kamiyama who were determined that immoral, ungodly American members would walk, talk, and eat like decent, upstanding, moral Japanese (hence, I learned to use chopsticks . . . but they did introduce me to curry rice; *yum*). And gutless, faux Christian Americans made it easy for them.

I foresaw none of the psychological warfare the Japanese would unleash on the American congregation, and 1981 seemed a watershed in Japanese–American relations. One reason was the hauntingly fresh memory of the Korean-Japanese Moonie combine smashing the United States Senate's craven hatchet job to deport Rev. Moon; jailed, if they were lucky. Minnesota Democrat Senator Donald Fraser accused him of spying for the Korean Central Intelligence Agency. Colonel Bo Hi Pak passionately rebutted the charge to a packed Senate chamber.

Until the later 1980s the Korean side of the church felt largely veiled from us rank-and-file Americans. We knew they were there but, like fantastical overlords, most of us had never met let alone seen one. We could rightly imagine them phantasmal high priests never deigning to set foot outside their holy of holies onto soiled American ground. The Japanese had day-to-day operational control, demigods to me who knew it and reveled in it. I never thought anybody could give them orders but, evidently, they interpreted them in some fashion from our super-god Koreans.

Colonel Pak's performance before the Senate subcommittee was released in book and video as *Truth is My Sword* for multiple, mandatory elucidations in every church center. I can still see the old boy tensing over the heavy wooden table in the ornate chamber, the room behind him packed, the floor in front smothered under photographers. The single microphone on the table boomed his passionate, tear-stained defense of Rev. Moon as a man of God. A real fuck-you to Fraser. "You nailed Reverend Moon's name and the Unification Church to the cross. You have crucified us . . . you are being used as an instrument of the devil . . . You may get my scalp, Mr. Chairman, but never my heart and soul [which] belong to God."

Heady stuff. I wondered why our most senior executive styled himself *colonel*. The church explained that during the Korean War he was at the Korean Army officer's school and desperately thrown into the fray. He survived a tank unit the communists had decimated. A casualty, he listened as they traipsed the battlefield shooting the wounded. He avoided their notice and survived the war, rising to colonel. With such exploits providing credibility and awe, everyone addressed him by his military rank, maybe because Korean Unificationists in those days could count on one hand those with even a wisp of social standing. We Americans weren't privy to Korean and Japanese leaders' holy first names and it was certainly a *harakiri* offense to use it if we were, so they were whatever title Rev. Moon bestowed.

Colonel Pak.

Realizing the Japanese and Koreans required that we address them as mister, reverend, doctor, or colonel while they addressed us only by our first names was my first conscious encounter with racial elitism, probably because I mostly grew up in the Nordic Rockies where we never got our chance to participate. Unless one was a senior leader or joined rich, any title predating church life was irrelevant unless it served a public relations purpose. If I'd joined with a PH.D. or a senior commissioned rank, I'm pretty sure my career in the church would've been agreeably different.

Joo Chon Choi, the Korean leader of church-owned International Seafoods of Alaska, said when I earned my ordination in 1985, "You are arrogant to think your title of reverend means anything." Well, titles *after* joining didn't rate. Unless it was a church-sanctioned PH.D. Or it wasn't me.

Going off to the weekend workshop would've been unthinkable if I'd had the slightest inkling that I'd be later telling these stories. At High Street, I'd seen only Americans, which is to say, whites; no asians, hispanics, or blacks. That experience would repeat at the weekend retreat in yuppie Nederland.

～

I BID MY leery sister goodbye and motored north to Boulder, then west up Boulder Canyon. I arrived handily by early evening through snowpacked dirt roads and parked on the shoulder where a quick getaway (if needed) was most efficaciously had. Goosebumps ran up and down under my coat outside my car. I shivered and took in my surroundings. Snow sparsely covered the ground where the weak sun landed strongest. In the greater shaded areas there was still a couple of feet.

I'd switched out crutches for a cane to give mobility a try and limped down the short, dirt driveway, negotiating the snow and ice with difficulty and a near fall; my cane could've used a spike tip. I was weak and often tired from surgery. My chest seized at the thought of retearing my knee in a breakneck tumble into the small parking area some 12 feet below grade where they'd erected a volleyball net alongside a large, modern, multi-storey wood-sided home bird-nesting on a vulturous slope. I nervously rapped on the heavy door and hove a long breath to calm down.

11

A thick clutch of strangers milled inside but the crowd eased my tension. Ginny latched onto me and got me feeling comfortable and looked after. Our first shared meal was built around some alien chemistry that was horrifyingly centerstage for breakfast, lunch, and dinner. Literally. Years later when haters were insisting that Moonies lured unsuspecting recruits up to their 'retreats' for a diet devoid of brain food, I laughed at their studied ignorance.

"Just what in the heck is this weirdness, Ginny?"

"Technically, bean curd. It's called tofu."

"Beans, you say? Green beans, lima beans, what kind are you talking about?"

"Forget it. Total protein and nutrition is all you need to know. They say it's better for you than meat. You'll love it."

"Better?" I was feeling harpy. Food matters. "What do you take me for?"

"Hungry. Now, eat up."

I came to loathe this ubiquitous, unknown gelatinlike 'food' over the weekend and the following two weeks I ended up giving them. I was a meat-and-potatoes man, a western-states American through and through. For breakfast, we shared it with hot oatmeal. I tried valiantly to chew and swallow the gooey stuff but couldn't get that horse feed down my throat for love nor money.

"It's normal American food," she sternly laughed. "Why're you complaining?"

"Okay . . . but I've never had it before. Must be the blandest, most tasteless gruel to ever insult my tongue. Shouldn't it taste like oatmeal cookies?" I drizzled yards of sugar and cinnamon to no avail. "How 'bout cold cereal or eggs?"

"Ah, sorry," one of the house leaders piped up, "we don't have any."

"Quit bellyaching," Ginny said, good-naturedly nudging me at our Japanese-style floor table. I'd stretched my bad leg out beneath it and tucked my (for the moment) good one under my thigh, my spine doing the work of a chairback but failing in sharp fire under gravity. "Didn't your mom—?"

"No." I slit-eyed the brown, gloppy pool of death with tight lips and exhaled heavy air through my nose. Ginny tucked in eyeing me sidelong. I mourned my empty pockets and considered pulling the ripcord on this adventure but . . . *nah* . . . seemed petty. It turned out Colorado Moonies were just church-mouse poor and giving their best. Tofu was cheaper than meat and who didn't like oatmeal? They boiled, broiled, fried, baked, grilled, or served the firm blocks raw for each veggie meal. It was all so very Asian—for me, hippyish—but as yet I had no inkling Asia had a part in this play. High in protein or not, my body wasn't metabolizing it. Several days and my hands were jumping beans and my legs rickety twigs. I was 21 and a rangy six-feet-six and needed solid cowboy feed to heal.

"Ginny," I eventually said, "You know I'm recovering from surgery. I need meat, eggs, potatoes, cereal—that sort of thing—or I'll have to leave. I'm literally ready to fall down and stay down."

Not sure if liability or recruitment ranked first for her. "Okay, okay. No need to leave. I'll talk to . . ." and she went to bat. A bodybuilder's tub of protein powder, whole milk, cereal, eggs, and periodically even meat materialized like magic just for me. While suckers gummed down goop and grout I chewed good, solid American cuisine. Boy, did I chuckle over this when the bigots said, "Obviously, they were depriving you of protein and contact with others without you knowing or they couldn't have brainwashed you into joining."

"They did have interesting lectures, you know." Didn't matter. They'd already brainwashed themselves.

My next two hurdles were getting off the unyielding, morgueish floor that we 'brothers' curled up on for a paltry six-hour rest that was far too short. Neither could my wracked knee take stretching out for long. Yet, bending it to roll on my side brought new pain to my hips. My surgery craved copious sleep and I just couldn't stagger up at 7 AM like everyone else and still function. Lack of rest was the second cause of my shakes. I wore out quick as an infant. That was my story anyway. With all my granny grievances they secluded me in a basement storage room where I could sleep on a thick, soft pallet through the noisy wakeup but rise in time for my special breakfast, protein shake, and the first lecture at 10 AM.

I was probably the most pampered Moonie recruit ever seen in this country before or since. One of the happier records I hold in the Unification Church.

Act II

Joining Up
The Ideas That Grabbed Me

Many joined the Unification Church through these weekend workshops because they melted in its happy, loving embrace. Detractors called it "love bombing;" it certainly leveled emotional walls. The fact is, many Americans felt a palpable lack of love, the archetypal loss of our species. We were seeking happiness, clarity, or deceitless love at a time when the hippie movement's easy passion and no-frills crusade was closing down. When we encountered 'the Family' in the '70s and early '80s, we *were* love bombed. In a big way. Nuclear detonations. It was overwhelming and life transformative. It's the psychology of gangs, isn't it? A person with no sense of family, love, appreciation, care, or just longing for a weapon to avenge their suffering heart invests with a sense of uniqueness in—and a plain Jane out of—the group; special, respectable, *accepted*. A new family. Armed against a cruel world run by crueler sonsabitches.

"You mess with me," they can say, "you mess with my *family*!"

It protects, envelops, liberates, *empowers*. I felt that way. So did perhaps most of the tens or hundreds of thousands of Americans who test drove the church since the mid-'60s. Where did it get the power to captivate and convert a generation of intelligent, educated Americans? In a nutshell it was, on its face, a welcoming, highly energized family of friends coupled with a new and exciting understanding of God and history inspiring us with the inevitability of a happy, peaceful world through Divine Principle. Hegel's dialectic transposed in God.

This was in stark contrast to Americans' disenchantment with government, war, peace, politics, and our own culture. We didn't just think a better world was possible. We knew it. This attitude showed up in a 1980s cartoon in the internal church newspaper *The Unification News* of an old Moonie regaling his grandchildren.

Eyes wide with amazement, they said, "Is it really true that Satan was in the world when you were young, Grandpa?"

"You bet! It was a dark place before True Parents."

In a generation, fallen nature's defeat and the kingdom of heaven on earth in full bloom. I thigh-slapped the absurdity but, deeper down, imagined it *could* happen if we embodied the Principle and Rev. Moon's inspired leadership. Utopian, eh?

Much humble pie later, I realized it's the same methodological belief in the impossible as magical thinking, an unarmed but not benign totalitarianist ideology differing little in essence from all the other isms besmirching the twentieth and now 21st century. Ideologized humans simply produce no other outcome regardless lofty idealism. *That* inevitability discredits their effort. Yet, I saw in Rev. Moon's self-sacrifice and unconditional love Gandhism, Martin Luther Kingism, American libertyism; human impossibilities like rocketing to the aloof moon and coming home alive. *That* validates the effort. The church both discredits and validates itself but, like all engines of historical change, inspires while alienating its most ardent adherents until only the ruthless, fanatically undevoted remain.

Over its 30-plus American years the church excelled only in abnegation, not affirmation. The horse's ass flings blanket accusations like "Brainwashing!" in the face of its massive success winning converts in the '70s and early '80s. That it couldn't hold onto them wasn't brainwashing wearing off but a different, altogether anti-American, anti-Christian, Imperial Japanese indoctrination that wouldn't take. As with any religion, it felt laundering our selfish, egocentric, sexually deviant, sinful brain was a good idea and a net benefit to society. We, the converted, agreed. Unfortunately for most of us, our leaders used our scrubbed-up brains for a collective bedpan. Their flatulence polluted our souls more foully than any of us ever managed to do on our own through what our Japanese *überMitglieder* (supermembers) derisorily stereotyped as sex-drugs-and-rock-n-roll Americanism.

Abnegate and validate. A stupid, self-defeating habit.

Already at this early stage of life I was adamantly suspicious of any behavior that reeked of 'love.' I wanted it; daydreamed of respect, opportunity, a chance to prove myself, to contribute, trusted with something meaningful. But the world's disguised hatred and deceit offered up in the guise of 'love' had gutted me young. I was initially open at Nederland's workshop. Then I threw up byzantine heart walls and thorny mind skeins. *Don't get too close, I'll spring like a rabbit.*

Fear and cynicism attracted me to the content of the lectures but palmed away the socializing enthusing my peers. My personal dichotomy was a reflection of the first public schism to rock the American Unification Church beginning in 1979–80. The West Coast branch, largely influenced by Sang Ik 'Papasan' Choi, one of Rev. Moon's early Korean missionaries, emphasized the social experience and deemphasized brainy truthiness. The result was the *choo-choo-pow* member expecting a happy environment over the Principle's stern reality. East Coast missionaries emphasized the Principle and deemphasized the social. The result was the process-over-content member holding Law paramount. East Coast members glared contemptuously askance at West Coast members appalled by their eastern brethren's ruthless spiritual brutality. A Unificationist version of Pharisees and Sadducees.

"This isn't the church I joined," said West Coasters transferred into East Coast-organized mobile fundraising teams (MFT).

"I quit!" East Coasters now in unPrincipled West Coast free-for-alls said.

Smack-dab in the middle, Colorado appeared to embody a fluid compromise between these polar Unificationisms that waxed and waned according to whichever leader held greater sway. Papasan Choi alumni ran my Nederland workshop and emphasized love-bombing and *choo-choo-powing* around a volleyball net over and above Divine Principle itself as the means to reach the aching depths of potential converts to bring out his or her dormant Moonie.

Obviously, I couldn't play volleyball. During activity breaks and love-bombing I lounged around shooting the breeze with Ginny, reading the lecture material, napping, or just vegetating. Despite my fears, the Principle they were teaching me was jabbing my guts and jerking my mind. I liked the challenge and the folks I met. I elected to stay for the additional 7-day workshop and then a repeat the week after that, which counted in their training regimen as a 14-day training. No car-dealer tactics pressured me but they didn't have to. I voraciously spooned down this 'new truth' if not so much the saccharine environment that packaged it. I was practically ready to buy. I only needed to pull the trigger.

Ginny said one day, "Do you have an older brother, Chris? Because I dreamed about him last night."

"Whaaat?" I tugged her by the forearm to a set of chairs. "When did I tell you about a brother?" I was sure I *hadn't*, so she'd instantly captivated me.

She recounted her dream. "He said he's really glad you're involved with True Parents"—that bombshell had dropped in Sunday's final lecture; I'd intuited Rev. Moon and the church just before the lecturer's big *ta-da!* that pull-started a full-blown panic attack—"because he met the church some years ago and could've joined but didn't. He said he's glad you're getting involved with the Family instead."

I perched immobile on my chair. My skin tingled. "Well. That's a thunderclap. But . . ." *Certainly the most self-serving story I'd heard.* Even if it was, I couldn't shake the fact she didn't—couldn't possibly—know I had an *older* brother, so I gave her story some weight. No, a lot of weight.

"I'm not trying to trick you into joining my church. Just ask your brother."

"Sure will." Never did. I forgot. I didn't think I'd off-gassed any vibes that dreams were anything more than fun and interesting, mine always some colorful adventure rarely marred by the prophetic or scary. "But it's something to think about, at the end of the day." One among many weights I scaled to balance up my experience.

I CALLED MY sister Mona the end of my first week. "Are you coming back, Chris? I'm definitely getting a weird vibe. Who are you mixed up with?"

"Don't worry. I'm fine." I hadn't considered that disappearing into a mountain retreat with a denomination and people I barely knew was something 'normal' Americans thought strange, even frightening and dangerous. But if I had concerns, I'd dismissed them. A premonition said, *Don't mention Rev. Moon.*

"You're sure? I can come get you if you need me to."

"No, no, everybody's nice. I'm having a good time." I was sure of it.

Except my days were punishing in my recovering condition. Although I rolled off my pallet late, the lectures and reflection sessions where we wrote down what we thought of the content and how it was affecting us dragged past 10 PM into midnight. I'd wash out and nod off against a wall or slip down to my storage room. Yet, it was so powerful that what I learned in those 17 days about God, humanity, society, Jesus, religion, history, the Family, and spirituality effectively carried me through (though partially induced) my next 21 years of toil and trouble with its very teachers. It was a solid foundation of inspiration and commitment to a cause and vision I still haven't—indeed, refuse to let be—shaken off my soul. I want a world of peace, prosperity, and freedom . . . a global republic. I think that dream is really the unspoken, unconscious American dream. That's why we're not just unrelentingly generous and fair but feel deep pangs of guilt when something reminds us, like the 9/11 attacks, that we're somehow remiss in our attention to it.

The '70s and '80s Unification Church was so wildly successful in America—more so, even, than Japan and Korea—because Rev. Moon's vision was the missing jigsaw piece in the American Dream. What's the crux of that if not the nation as a historically restorative beacon on a hill spreading peace, prosperity, and individual liberty into Earth's oppressively darkest corners? We young Americans in the '60s, '70s, and early '80s were desperately seeking solace in the ways and means of building the better world our parents and hippies had botched. We're blowing up Afghanistan and Iraq not out of revenge—a crass effort any two-bit nation could accomplish—but because we feel compelled to march into their hellscape as the Global Messiah bringing on the heels of our death and destruction for the wicked the peace, prosperity, and freedom deserved of the righteous. The Statue of Liberty doesn't ask the world to send us its best and brightest but its humble, unwanted oppressed.

It's a uniquely American mindset that, till the early '80s, fell like a ripe mango into the arms of Rev. Moon's radical view of America's historical, global, and messianic responsibility. He illustrates this last point simply:

> Because the Indians are of Asiatic origin and were sacrificed for the founding
> of America, this nation had to indemnify that by shedding blood for the sake
> of Orientals. Long before the Korean War was fought I felt this had to be true.
> (*Abel's Right Path From The Providential Point Of View* 1979)

If America fulfills its responsibility to unselfishly serve the world, the victims of its soul-sucking sins wouldn't hold them against it because they'd have been committed fulfilling albeit not a part of God's providence. The pained and resentful could set them aside if they saw America humbly uplifting the world similar to France letting go our collateral damage evicting the Nazis as not just a greater, but a more desirable, good. If America didn't do this, he warned, every sin it ever committed would boomerang till the last resentment was satisfied through indemnity. No one of us wanted to live through that harrowing possibility. It motivated us to pray, repent, and work like nervous rats scrabbling out of deepening waters.

NEDERLAND'S SEMINAR TOOK off with Chapter 1 in the green *Outline of the Principle, Level IV* study guide. Among our lecturers was Barbara Beard, Blessed (married) to High Street center director Michael, whom I found weird. I recall him around six feet with dark hair topping a thin, not particularly manly, frame.

"And *yet*," I told friends, "he can be such a popinjay!"

Living at High Street after I'd joined, he commanded we sprinkle holy salt—Rev. Moon's version of holy water—atop our heads before entering rooms showcasing his first Blessed baby. It was humiliating thinking we unBlessed members so despicable that we needed to purify our sinful bodies before approaching his divine progeny. This, despite Rev. Moon advising us that holy salt

> does not separate human beings from satanic dominion. Fundamentally it will not internally purify a person and should not normally be used on oneself when entering the center. (*The Tradition: Book One* 1985, c8)

He's an early example of leaders ignoring Rev. Moon for their own invented dogmas forcibly or deceitfully applied in their feudal domains with epicurean gusto.

Mrs. Beard seemed new to the lecture circuit. She read her in-hand *Level IV* apparently verbatim while striving to sketch out its diagrams on the blackboard. If there's one thing I don't do well, it's listening to often poor readers and I was chomping at the bit to move it along.

"Why," I tartly queried Ginny in a low tone, "must I sit in this uncomfortable metal folding chair for an hour and a half listening to this lady stammer through the book when I can read the entire chapter thrice in a quarter of the time and comprehend it twice better?"

"*Shhh!* Listen to what she's saying."

"She's not saying, she's *reading*. Give me a book. Let me read it on my own. You must have more than one."

"No,"—she matched my disdain—"you do need to sit here in this uncomfortable chair and listen to the lecture." Ginny was nobody's fool. "She says many things that aren't in the book, and you'd miss out on those. They're very important to your overall spiritual understanding."

"Like what?" I legitimately wondered. "It looks to me she's reading word for—"

She leaned whisperingly close. "Not everything's in the book, you know. She might emphasize something you wouldn't and you'd miss it." She always looked so satisfied setting me straight.

"Well, is she going to get to that part?"

"*Shhh!*"

Ohmigod. I wasn't one to play argumentative jerk, so I did spineless schmuck and sulked in my chair slugged weary by the deadening lecture. My thoughts smoldered but I made sure to crinkle eyes whenever Ginny checked my mood.

She flew wingman for my 3-day and two 7-days. A vacay treat from storefront trashcans and tiger scrolls, were it me. I thought her nice and perhaps interested in me, but later realized her intense care and personal focus was merely the conversion process keeping me on the straight and narrow. She weaned me off her love and attention in the months after I joined. I didn't understand yet that church girls were *verboten* before marriage. But her attention wasn't all nefarious. I had questions to which I wanted immediate answers and she provided them or found someone who could. Besides, it was very comforting to be gathered in for what I already wanted to pursue by someone I 'knew' in a sea of strangers.

Regardless Mrs. Beard's life-denying methodology, the content was heart-racing. Chapter 1 discussed why we were here in the first place. How we fit into the great scheme of the universe. That everything constitutes of complementary *yin* and *yang* opposites like *positivity* and *negativity*. Male and female, stamen and pistol, protons and electrons, the plus and minus energies of atoms and molecules . . . all were 'positive' and 'negative' in Subject–Object relationships.

Many of the American women in the audience were uncomfortable with or flat out hostile to 'negative' and especially 'object' being applied anywhere near them. Hands raised ahead of pointed questions.

"It's important to understand," Mrs. Beard said, "that positivity and negativity don't refer to 'positive' and 'negative' in the philosophical or ethical sense."

Someone said, "What does that mean?"

"That women are not 'negative' in any value sense." And I presumed she ought to know. "They're merely one half of a larger whole that includes a positive and negative aspect, like a magnet."

"Ohhh . . ." some 'sister' mouthed. A new term for *girl*.

"So, we're just objects then?"

"No, no, no." She tucked her *Level IV* under an arm. "It just references one side of a give-and-take relationship, like God and Mankind, or teacher–student . . ."

"That still sounds like—"

"I know, but it's not." She pulled her book out and flipped it open. "We'll get to that. Just be patient. It's not what you think, I promise."

They didn't all look copacetic but I wasn't a *sister*, so what did I know. The church somewhat proved Mrs. Beard's point through its half-hearted though still better than average embrace of female pastors, state directors, team leaders, fundraising captains, and whatnot since the 1960s. Nevertheless, no woman ever ascended to the rigidly all-male Korean regional leader cadre nor the extra rarefied, exclusively Adamic continental directorship. Only the barely tolerated Mrs. Moon eventually looked down from her messianic clouds on her barely-tolerable manservants.

Their teaching was all pop science but catchy and made a fair amount of untested sense. It seemed discernible in the world around me, so my buy-in was easy.

REV. MOON'S ESSENTIAL primer, *Divine Principle*—'DP' to members—is in its second English edition as of 2003. The first was in 1977 and pretty awfully translated. It inspired me, so no complaints. A makeover published in 1996 was its editors' hope for a more erudite, philosophical work worthy of doctoral study and respect. I was a seminarian when Professor Andrew Wilson and fellow student Jae Gil Kim unexpectedly posted chapter drafts on a bulletin board. I was breathless to discover their unannounced effort. For years, Americans complained of the childish 1977 edition and deplored its embarrassment to our faith. Now, before my very nose, The Book was being rebuilt from the original Korean. *Wow!* My feet were floating.

Pulse racing, I tore through the pages hanging off the bulletin board on thumb-tacked strings and devoured each chapter cover to cover. I raced unthinking across the circle drive out front and clattered into the old Catholic abbot's 3-storey home on the other side. It was a run-down, mixed-use apartment version of its former elegant, stately residential self in the throes of a cheeseparing restoration. Indoors was dusty, unkempt, and cluttered with children's toys, homeless junk, and construction scraps. The aged, grand porch in the rear overlooking the trees and mountains of our beautiful estate was, for a long time, hanging on the verge of collapse and off limits. For all that, I loved being in and around its architectural beauty.

I found Jae Gil Kim upstairs in a tiny room crammed with desks and chairs and panted, "Hey, Jae Gil. I saw your chapter drafts on the bulletin board! I had no idea you were doing this! Can I be part of your team? I really want to help on this!"

He looked me over, probably wild eyed like I'd seen Godzilla on the horizon. "Sure, I could use it," he measured out. "But I have to ask Dr. Wilson first. I will let you know after that."

"That's terrific. Thanks a lot, man! I look forward to hearing."

Massena House at UTS *where I discovered* Divine Principle *being quietly retranslated.*

I promptly scooted off in search of Professor Wilson to personally make my case. This was too big to leave with Jae Gil. He might be lackluster and fuck it up. I got a yes and for the remainder of the project contributed to the revised text and consulted on some historical issues. For a moment I was on the edge of the cutting edge. My merely (rusty) conversational Korean and lack of knowledge in some areas hampered me and frustrated my acute need to be a bigger part of this august team. *Ah, well.* I'm satisfied I made the effort and dropped some nuggets into it.

Once published, *Exposition of the Divine Principle* quickly debuted in Dr. Wilson's classes where we impious and impudent students lost no time savaging its translation errors and historical inaccuracies however substantially reduced from 1977's edition. If he'd advertised for more help earlier, we concluded, he'd have done a better job. We often got him sufficiently riled to snap at us. But, what good was our school if we couldn't roundly attack everything just to see how well it could be defended?

Divine Principle comes in two sections. The first deals with Christian theology such as creation, the Fall, eschatology, the purpose of the messiah, resurrection, predestination, and general Christology. The second covers interpretive biblical history, theoretical history, and the second coming of the Messiah. Creation, the Fall, and Jesus' purpose were a heavy slap upside my head at Nederland. Other chapters vindicated many of my long-held views. I finally had questions sensibly answered that I'd been nagging Dad and the Catholic Church with since I was five. I asked him one of my characteristically out-of-the-box conundrums in eighth grade while helping install sheetrock on a downstairs wall of our under-construction Box 201A (Star Route) house on North Turkey Creek Road in Colorado's Rockies.

"What happens if I go to heaven and you and Mom and the family go to hell?"

"I don't know, son," he'd grunted, roughly sawing a hole for an electrical box.

"But what does the church say about it? Don't they have an answer?"

"None that I ever heard." *Saw-saw-saw . . . break!* "Ye gods and little fishes!"

I brushed aside his bungled cut. Blurted, "Well, what if you all go to heaven and I go to hell? Won't anybody be able or allowed to help me?"

"Chris, I don't know. The church doesn't really have answers for questions like that. You just have to have faith that things will turn out the way they should."

The way they should? What kind of creepy answer was that? I wasn't much of a fan of Catholicism by then anyway and his replies only more firmly nailed that door shut. Faith as a substitute for knowledge? No reasonable answers? *Pshaw!*

But Divine Principle? Boy, did it answer questions. Its response to *that* question was that no one stays in hell a trice longer than wanted. People end up there because it fits their state of heart. Rev. Moon claims God created hell as a favor to fallen humanity because when the sinful 'breathe in' God's atmosphere of perfect love it feels as if literal, incinerating fire is flashing through our lungs in searing, excruciating torment. In hell, we can repose without the added torment of His perfection.

Imagine! As my heart changes, so does my venue. I'm not eternally condemned! When we overcome temptation and sin, our ancestors and others spiritually hanging around us—oft-influencing us to give in to it, the bastards—are liberated from their own fallen nature through our efforts, if they want it. Through us, their heart rebirths to inch ever closer to God's. Everyone needs Restore their fallen nature inherited through Adam and Eve before heaven can even exist in the first place. No unending lake of fire for God-dogs and S'mores. *I knew it!*

The Principle's perspective rang eminently true but, more importantly, cogently resolved my confusion and nagging fear. Damnation was just a total crock the Church, hell-bent on control through fear of punishment-punishment-punishment, had been shitting down our throats this whole time. If its barbarism emanated from God, then He was a cosmic ass I wanted nothing to do with. Divine Principle had me humming on crack. Once shot-up, I couldn't have cared less about my social environment, *choo-choo-powing*, volleyball, or even my bum knee. Suddenly aware how thirsty I was for real knowledge and truth had me slaking my parched mind with every drop I could read, hear, and talk up.

Come on, my heart shrieked, *feed me!*

PART 1's perspective on humanity's fall from grace naturally flows out of the Principle of Creation in Chapter 1, then introduces salvation as *Restoration*, the messiah's purpose, clarifies death and resurrection, and a Christology focused on Eden's reversal. How can we understand God's Old Testament lamentations and endless efforts to forgive without comprehending He created humanity as a real parent to each individual as the fountain of His love in the world? We weren't created or evolved for no purpose but to experience the deepest affection from God, to paint our unique portrait of love upon it, then send it merrily back. While liberal theologians cry there's no order in the universe, that humanity exists simply as the highest order of animal, that our lives are random and unpurposed by an uncaring God—if He even exists—and conservative theologians demand unflinching obedience to our Divine Spiritual Master—nothing like a good slave ideology—the Unification Church was propounding the earth-shattering concept, at least to me, that God is a keen, unconditionally loving parent we can profoundly know within the context of family. On top of that, it's not God controlling our tormentous grief and sorrow in some devilish lab experiment teaching us heavenly manners, *we are!* And because of that, God is a being of tears and heartbreak since the Fall of Eden.

A Catholic and dabbling Protestant, I staggered intoxicated by a concept of God mirroring Jesus stumbling from his tomb but recognizably slinking up to his grieving followers on the road to Emmaus with a startling, "Whassup?"

We're in control? God and Satan can do nothing absent our voluntary *yea*? If this was the Moonies' vaunted brainwashing then where was the problem? It not only made sense and gave me hope but unshackled me from divine fear and clerical tyranny, too. With a *chance*. It reordered my world in a way incomprehensible mere weeks before. Turning over my new vision of God in Nederland, I was Wimbledon chin-swinging from Catholic–Christian theology as I understood it to this startling Unification one. *Eeny, meeny, miny, moe, catch a tiger by the toe, if he hollers let him go, eeny, meeny, miny—*MOON! A no-brainer. *I choose the loving, parental God tearfully leading me to understand heart, Restoration, and happiness.*

Thousands of Americans hearing these lectures agreed, falling back overwhelmed not from *choo-choo-powing* but the Principle revealing a workable solution beyond sin irremediable outside grace to a fallen nature they could change. Rev. Moon noted circa 1988 that members weren't leaving the church because of intrinsic problems with him or Divine Principle, but because they rejected his organization corrupting their conscience from which they presumed *him* corrupt, too.

"The Principle," to paraphrase him, "will always pull their heart toward God and True Parents. They can never truly let it go. This determines its real truth."

This was when he was vainly encouraging leaders to reach out to part-time 'B'-members (me, before toppling down each level like sharp steps to the bottom) and the rapidly growing cadre of ex-members rather than endlessly witness to new recruits needing training from scratch but who'd eventually leave anyway for the same reasons. Full-time 'A'-members were a famine of effort reclaiming 'B'-, 'C'- and 'D'-members let alone wholly unPrincipled, apostate 'X'-members.

PART II covers God's original pattern for reversing Eden's fallout, Moses setting the pattern Jesus later followed, and history as an expression of God's providence working through the Fall's many problems. It introduces *indemnity* whereby a person, family, tribe, society, or nation takes actions designed to separate from Satan's accusation so they can move forward with God's plan of Restoration. Indemnity is the key to understanding how the Unification Church organizes its corporate life and interacts with self and others although, ignoring the Principle, it blames others for what befalls it. Jesus castigated the Jews for this attitude in pointing out how falling scaffolding that killed and injured many wasn't from their sins and no one should blame the victims. Unfortunately for the church, its attitude rampantly siphons energy from its Cain–Abel Restorational methodology to justify it.

Unificationists understand Cain and Abel as real people whose lives *symbolically* represent Satan and God. The Fall was a misuse of sex, thus love, first with Archangel Lucifer (God's servant) then Adam (Eve's intended spouse). As sex with Adam was less unPrincipled than with the archangel, first-born Cain represents Eve–archangel whereas Abel represents Eve–Adam. Thus, Abel represents God's side in His struggle to Restore the Fall; He looks to him to as His champion. Same with Cain vis-à-vis

Satan. Abel's murder ended God's effort to quickly restore Mankind to before the Fall; their dynamic ended up the pattern for human conflict. The danger here is that one can easily imagine symbolically representative individuals as literally Satanic and personally evil or Godly and intrinsically good in and of themselves.

The church made itself a Cain-Abel subculture dividing members into Cain-type (independent, disobedient, complaining, rational, thinking, riled by institutional injustice) and Abel-type (codependent, obedient, unthinking, irrational if faith wills it, adopting institutional injustice, agreeable). Contradicting leaders and elders makes one instantly a Cain-type *mondai kyodai* (Japanese; 'problem member'). Yet, Americans are automatically Cain-type and Japanese and Koreans Abel-type... in America. In Korea, all Japanese are Cain-type and, in Japan, all Koreans are Cain-type-*Abels* because, despite their traditional enmity, it's tough for Japanese members to disparage Rev. Moon's view of Koreans as God's chief Abels thus our master race. Naturally, I early on hankered for a Korean bride.

Pushed into my first church rebellion in 1984, I penned a 7-page essay in 1985 influenced by our loquacious American Founders and seventeenth- and eighteenth-century philosophers titled, *A General Discourse on the Symbolic Relationship of Cain and Abel, Regarding its Theory and Misapplication in the Unification Church*. With a Publian flourish, I signed it *Cassius*, a Roman jurist I thought embodied truth and fairness. In the dead of night, I 'nailed' my Lutheran poke in the eye with big ass thumbtacks to the front door of every San Francisco Bay church center.

I quoted *Divine Principle* chapter and verse to prove Cain–Abel a symbolic vehicle to remove fallen nature, sin, evil, grief, and resentment. Rev. Moon assiduously teaches how Cain comes first for the true Abel even at the cost of his own and his family's life. Alas, the Japanese running the American church, steeped in pre-war feudalism and confidence in their Imperial Way, saw everything through master–servant (senior–junior) eyes. So, too, our Korean leadership and Americans losing their republican way. After 21 years and despite his high-blown rhetoric, I'd say Rev. Moon also forgets it in relying on a messiah–disciple dynamic.

That blind obedience to leaders must unfailingly usher in the kingdom is the oft-cited *mea culpa* for the master–servant, Abel–Cain structure. I wrote,

> this infers that, since the Kingdom of Heaven is a place of perfection, we shall become perfect simply by following our leaders... since that action *alone* can bring to pass the Kingdom... Since there are no questions... no answers, and no need, therefore, to really garner an in-depth understanding... Man is not free, and therefore, not responsible, and becomes a slave to ideology... be it God's or anyone else's. Therefore, Man becomes the slave ruler of an enslaved universe, each person in absolute obedience, rightly or wrongly, with no cognizant reasoning, to a person "superior".... all the way up to God... the slave master... [and] a slave, since Man is created in the image of God.

My essay blew up the Bay Area church, if only for a heartbeat. Weirdly prescient suspicions left me *persona non grata*. The reaction to my rational, philosophical, and temperate essay hurt. Later, I wore their *mondai-kyodai* moniker with pride. A few years on, a stoop-shouldered friend outside a Sunday service discovered I'd authored it. He yanked a dog-eared copy from his leather shoulder bag to my gaping eyes.

"I've carried this with me every day for inspiration," he beamed. "I was stuck on MFT *seven years* and you literally saved my spiritual life with this!"

"How'd your center director take it? Did you—?"

"No way." He flipped the pages back and forth. "He'd have burned it. But I made copies for members I trusted."

"You're saying there's even more of 'em out there?" He shrugged. I stammered, "Man . . . I can't believe you've been carrying it around with you all this time. I mean . . . holy cow!" I'd made a positive impact after all.

CHAPTER 2—THE Fall of Man (The Human Fall in the 1996 edition)—is a behavioral noun in church circles by asserting Adam and Eve fell through corrupting love via sexual relations before spiritually, emotionally, and divinely matured according to God's plan. A 'Chapter 2 problem' is a Moonie's quintessential sin.

Everywhere in the church conversations whispered, "That Joe is so Chapter 2."

"I really struggle with Chapter 2," someone confides in their leader.

A sister says, "Don't you have Chapter 2 feelings for me? I do . . ."

"Be careful you don't fall," a brother warns. "Chapter 2 is the worst."

Or weeping in judgmental terror, "I'm so sorry! Please forgive me! I fell with this brother when we let our Chapter 2 feelings get out of hand."

On. And. On. There wasn't a worse opprobrium to saddle a Unificationist. It declares one literally Satan and unfit for Principled society. The accusation befell me although I didn't feel I deserved it since I'd never shacked up while an 'A'-member with a sister (or brother; just saying) or 'outside member.' But, once someone butters your reputation—lies, half-truths, innuendo—it's your *nom de guerre*.

Japanese but sometimes Korean leaders went to great lengths to metaphorically castrate members who fell while pretzeling the Principle to avoid rendering an official verdict he or she was guilty of a *bona fide* 'Chapter 2 mistake.'

"Did he penetrate?" they'd maybe pruriently ask. "So, you didn't actually fall."

Or, "How far did you go in? Just an inch? Only one stroke? Did you repent right away and stop? Okay, pray 40 days and fast for 3 . . . and stay away from that sister!" This sometimes went hand-in-hand with sudden transfers.

And worst, "You went all the way? You orgasmed?" This always preceded one's kick-out, disappearance to another state, or straight home to the auld country.

Americans ran afoul even of our own secular culture still dripping with Jesus' admonition, "If your eye causes you to sin, pluck it out." We privately castigated and detested ourselves, seeing no way out of our transgression. The Japanese had an easy understanding of sin so long as it didn't involve disobedience (that was mortal). If our cultural Christian guilt could accept it, moving on was easier. Their culture is far earthier than American and makes us look like worse prudes than Europeans do, in my experience. Perhaps that's why Chapter 2 tends to be more rife amongst Japanese and Koreans, especially their freewheeling leaders.

When Rev. Moon was fresh off the boat in 1971, he found sexual shenanigans rampant in his American church and ordered members segregated by sex. Sunday services had brothers on Abel's right-hand side and sister's on Cain's left. They were never to sit together. At the communal dinner table, brothers took one side and sisters the other; no food could be shared plate-to-plate between the sexes. For Matched or Blessed couples yet to 'start their families'—churchspeak for approved sex—any touching at all was felonious. The Church morphed into an asexual gulag, everyone's rampant mindscape frighteningly conscious of their sexuality while in the guarded church centers it posed and fretted the wrong side of the other gender's razor wire. It was hell. If the public only knew the rigorous, monkish existence we endured they might've had more respect and possibly sympathy. We practiced the age-old art of devotional self-denial and repentance through penance, but folks viewed the church through a lens scratched by dangerous cultist Jim Jones and Rolls Royce sex guru Bhagwan Shree Rajneesh.

Our high-minded center director Julian Sherry rented 1981's *The Eye of the Needle* for a 1983 movie night at San Francisco's Judah Street center. We coalesced in our living room, brothers and sisters jamming every inch of furniture and floor space and electrifyingly touching each other's tensely warm bodies while pretending not to notice. Then up popped a cunnilingus-cum-bareassed trip to poundtown that was so sexually charged I was sweating to see it onscreen. I supposed Julian took the 'R' rating for harmless murdering not perilous sex. We innocently expected a typical Hollywood segue from tasteful sexcapade to bloody action adventure.

Instead, that son of a goat Donald Sutherland slurped and tongued his merry way over Kate Nelligan's delicious breasts then down her quivering abdomen till wetly frenching the crux of her clambaked thighs, transfixing us years-long sex-starved monastics in a paralyzing, lickerish tension. Mouths fell open. Sisters were quietly breathing harder and shallower and some of us forgot altogether. Any brother worth his salt chastely squirmed with trouser pressure. Julian at last roused himself and sheepishly apologized for bringing such a satanic movie into the center. He fast-forwarded past what should've been the best part and we settled down to catch our breath over some perfidiously wholesome butchery. I think all of us went to sleep that night with visions of *something* rhythmically dancing in our heads.

Rev. Moon fostered in his ex-hippies and spiritual sojourners a rejection of extramarital sex that was the mainstay of our lives. "[T]o my mind . . . it is a custom / More honour'd in the breach than the observance," as this mindset on the heels of a pragmatic Matching bedevils many a couple's satisfying marital sex with the notion that certain charms or times or purposes unrelated to conception is unPrincipled, a fallen act regardless one's Blessed bed. His comment tantamount to, "Your Blessed wife should be chaste in public but a whore in the bedroom" fell on mostly deaf ears even as we longed for its liberated reality. Such contradictions are fundamental. Relationships with my few girlfriends while outside the church were marred then ruined by my deep-seated belief in the evils of unBlessed sex, guilt, fear of falling, and sense of irresponsibility toward true love, the suffering world, Rev. Moon's messianic mission, and God's cruelly broken heart.

"There is not in the world so toilsome a trade," to bastardize Jean de La Bruyère, "as the pursuit of God's love through self-denial." 'Tis happiness' death knell.

CHAPTER 2 CLEAVED my core. I'd been intimate with four girlfriends by that point. One used me for a couple nights before announcing her bigger plans. The second was my ex-fiancée, whose breakup scarified my heart and packed me off to the Coast Guard to drown her memories at sea. Ms. Legs in Gulfport, Mississippi was my not-so-divorced-as-I-thought fourth I went head over heels for after a weeklong night swinging our feet off a pier till the sun marched over a humid horizon.

Lover the third happened between my fiancée's mid-summer dump and my January enlistment. We met in the doldrums of my summer job before my third Western State semester and fell in love . . . it might've been a rebound. I was newly 19 and never heard of condoms. Back then, you had to ask for a box from the oft-female cashier; what self-respecting man would do *that* in public? Then we mutually ended our sexual relationship because our Christian guilt was chewing us up. Five weeks later she realized she was pregnant and rang my dormitory. I gasped and sweated through her life-altering words, my ever-averting eyes landing on my choking future and Dad's slow-burning visage.

At the Nederland workshop, my still-grieving thoughts were more on my beloved ex-fiancée than my now 2-year old son's mother who'd canned our agreement on adoption in the maternity ward. Perhaps my shame getting her pregnant then not tying the knot blocked her from conscious consideration. I was certainly appalled enough to hide it from my parents till court papers sniped me: my father mistook *Christopher* for *Charles* on the envelope and popeyed his son's brave new world.

Spellbound in my ass-kicking metal chair in Nederland by God's profound wound from His trusted archangel betraying him in seducing his daughter, who then turned the same intent on her brother, my mortifying guilt was a nest of spiders crawling through my soul. I cast back to my relationships and cursed myself for abandoning my virginity. My sin ate me alive. *Yuk.*

Besides my genuine sorrow for God, regret being a second-class citizen in the Messianic Age of Restoration was a foul aftertaste. When Rev. Moon Blessed the first 36 couples in Korea 21 years earlier, he'd ranked the virgins highest amongst their cohorts. Presuming no one lied, the first 12 were pure; the second 12 sexually experienced but unmarried; the third 12 married, the least among equals. When I'd been a couple years in the church, I realized I had big plans for myself in this organization and it crushingly pained me to see how far from his venerable standard I stood. I was only 21 when I heard Chapter 2 but thought my life already done-in by my own hand. Little did I know what an amateur I still was.

One of the biggest church mantras is that fallen humanity is deprived of love, desperately seeks it, equates it with sex, and strives for both at all costs. Without doubt, I've desperately chased love and acceptance all my life. I've never been comfortable with one-night stands and luckily dodged the risk, yet still screwed up my love life plenty. I didn't dabble. Sex arose only in serious feelings edging into marriage. Even here in my 'old age' I haven't found contentment in love or sex. My grand vision of marriage dissolved when, years later, the woman I thought sent by God was instead, according to big banana Yoko Kobayashi, "sent by Satan."

I foresaw none of the emotional destruction I'd suffer as a result of poor choices in timing and women. During the Chapter 2 lecture and for weeks afterward I was pensive and introspective, reverse engineering my life to restore and rebuild a fresh start now I knew the Second Coming was here to lead my idealism to victory.

The workshop's head *choo-choo-pow'*er remarked to our clouded mugs, "The worst thing you can experience in your life is regret."

"Well, that's just terrific," I said to Ginny. "Mine is losing my purity."

"You'll be fine. We all have past mistakes to indemnify."

Were it my only one! I corner-eyed her. Now I'm unsure I've learned a thing about sexual purity these past 21 years despite sedulously studying the Principle, soaking in Rev. Moon's words, and withering in the church's Puritanism *because I feel so goddamned starved for love.* Still, I broadened my mind from local to global and developed a penetrating intent to grow and change till I *am* a decent, pure man shameless in my Divine Parent's presence. *That counts for something, right?*

ANOTHER WORKSHOP PARADIGM shift was historical, which fascinates me. I dreamed all through high school of studying how great nations like Rome ceased to exist. My school didn't say much about it beyond, "You can study it in college," but never clued us in to Gibbon's *Decline and Fall* at the public library. I don't think I understood how whole countries disappear till the Soviet Gojko-Mitic-muscled Union up and pitched over dead in 1991. I wondered if Unificationists didn't ever dread their own thousand-year Reich just one day falling off the map from its ponderous moribundity. They never did because they couldn't imagine it would eviscerate its membership—by 2003 no more and probably less than a few thousand in the USA—or cross schismatic swords while *Thelma and Louise* racing for the edge with its own Roman–Soviet fall in the rearview, totteringly hoping to salvage what was left into a new order. Thus in 1998 Rev. Moon dispensed with Holy Spirit Association for Unification of World Christianity (HSA-UWC) for Family Federation for Unification and World Peace (FFUWP), later rejiggered to FFWPU.

In 1981 *Divine Principle's* Parallels chapter—relying on biblical and historical scholarship maybe suspect or downright wrong—enthralled the history buff in me. It divides recorded history into three 2,000-year segments: the age of Adam to Abraham, Abraham to Jesus, and Jesus to the Second Coming. Heavily into numerology, it extrapolates numbers derived from God's creation and the Fall to segment each indemnifyingly repeating major period into six minor ones.

For example, in the age of Abraham to Jesus there's the period of slavery in Egypt, the Judges, the United Jewish Kingdom, the divided kingdom, Israel's exile to Babylon and return, and the preparation for the Messiah. Each lasted according to Rev. Moon's rounded calculations 400, 400, 120, 400, 210, and 400 years, respectively. Then, in the age of Jesus, there's the persecution in the Roman Empire corresponding to the period of slavery under Egypt, regional church leadership corresponding to that of the Judges and, similarly, the Christian empire under Charlemagne, the divided kingdoms of east and west Franks, the Papal captivity and return, and the preparation for the Second Coming that begins with Martin Luther.

This aspect of Divine Principle enthralled me. It laid out the sweep of human history not as randomly crappy conduct but a consistently woven fabric of divine purpose and idealism. If there's one positive thing the Unification Church did for the Americans cycling through, it was to vindicate the existence of and necessity for idealism. While realists struggle to coerce idealists into knuckling under, the

Parallels dramatically demonstrated to me that idealism is the glue binding history's generations into a coherent story. How else can one explain the existence of hope in the most hopeless circumstance and the fresh blossoms of goodness at the close of unqualified depravity and madness? Why *doesn't* evil uncontestedly rule when it revels in coercion and good is rarely motivated to fight? Why *don't* bad people forever crush the good? I thought it's because good individuals, infused in some way of God, refuse to abandon hope and idealism and evil can't cope with either any better than Oz's Wicked Witch of the West could water.

From the ashes of China's great wars arose a united civilization that remained till Communism burned it to the ground. Yet, Chinese civilization continues its march toward a better future in spite of Mao Tse-tung's homicidal psychopathy because of its, and America's, idealists reviving its flagging hopes. Christendom's bloody pugilism, culminating in the world wars and Cold War, nevertheless made way for the era of the 'peace dividend.' And as 2003's world slides into the new chaos of Islamic fanaticism, America continues pressing forward its idealistic albeit increasingly ideological quest for a meritocratic society guaranteeing dignity and hope through (for now) individual liberty.

In many ways, America is idealism writ o'er the face of the Earth. If it didn't exist and someone argued its possibility, realists would scornfully laugh it off the planet. America is idealism's home base. Americans are the world's ultimate optimists ever perceiving idealistic possibilities our 'wiser' cousins ever attempt to distill out via 'healthy realism.' Because of this character, the Parallels struck one of America's deepest chords and led the American Unification Church to initial heights of success unduplicated in other nations because Americans uniquely resonated with Rev. Moon's idealistic message in a way other cultures can't and don't.

As it all sunk into my consciousness, my worldview changed and evolved. No longer could I envision myself merely a geologist for the USGS, a successful corporate employee, a workaday business owner. I'd irrevocably morphed from my youthful, naïve view of the world as primarily a *local* scene where I built my own privately happy life to viewing myself a *global* citizen filled with responsibility and obligation and all the world my stage. Graduating from my first 2-½ weeks in the Unification Church, I knew I'd never go back to my small, local, insipid existence. That Chris expired in Nederland. My resurrected mind now focused on global humanity, the sweep of history, the end of war, poverty, suffering, and the rise of global prosperity, common cause, and true human happiness. Was I brainwashed?

THE WORKSHOP WAS its own brand of crazy yet dramatically altered my course in life because the Principle painted a fresh portrait of a world I'd only dreamed of vaguely. I could segue out of biblical Christianity as it was scented with death. World War I and II were *Christian* wars. Slavery, then recently ended segregation, were *rejections* of Jesus. Rev. Moon's vision of a sinless society steeped in unconditional love lived unselfishly for others woke things deep in my heart I hadn't noticed. He captured my imagination and convinced me of his sincerity through his tearjerking poem *Crown of Glory* penned early in his mission from Jesus which, for him, seemed every day in every way suffused in *Christian* betrayal and denial:

When I doubt people, I feel pain / When I judge people, it is unbearable / When I hate people, there is no value to my existence.

Yet if I believe, I am deceived / If I love, I am betrayed / Suffering and grieving tonight, my head in my hands / Am I wrong?

Yes, I am wrong / Even though we are deceived, still believe / Though we are betrayed, still forgive / Love completely even those who hate you.

Wipe your tears away and welcome with a smile / Those who know nothing but deceit / And those who betray without regret.

Oh Master! The pain of loving! / Look at my hands / Place your hand on my chest / My heart is bursting, such agony!

But when I loved those who acted against me / I brought victory / If you have done the same thing, / I will give you the crown of glory.

You know I wanted that crown of glory, whatever it was. I cherished the kind of personal victory I sensed Rev. Moon was seeking in his poetic desperation. I wanted to stand before God and feel His hand on my back and a "well done!" in my ears. The stanzas surged through me a tidal force, washing away everything I'd held important and believed. It wasn't just the Principle invading my intellect that turned me from normie to Moonie. It was my real strife as a betrayed yet selfish victim striving for the unselfishly loving victor I saw Rev. Moon pursuing in such deadly earnest from his sixteenth year when all I was thinking about was girls, hobbies, and school.

I was impressed.

Gravely shook.

And *motivated*.

Idealism is the strong suit of youth. The young want to remake and save the world from itself. The older and 'wiser,' often having failed themselves, discourage it. Yet, those crazy kids persist. Every generation marches off on its own idealistic quest, crusade, or *jihad*. After a couple weeks of Principled preparation from Ginny and workshop leaders, I was out of boot camp and primed to march off on mine. I had a rocky start, though, beginning with my local leaders throwing a big, fat lie in my face and the realization I'd fallen for it and, worse, would let it slide.

Act III

Indoctrination
Learning the Ropes, Seeing the Warts

I cycled out of Nederland into High Street then to Boulder's residence-cum-witnessing center on a large lot at 777 Broadway, a square, gymnasium-sized two-storey building with stacked roof peaks lending a mercantile air. In a previous life it housed a University of Colorado sorority. Next door was a field where we often played softball. I pleasurably finger-picked my guitar on the gentle grass slope between house and backstop that served as bleachers where we gathered co-ed to cheer the action and admire our sexier brethren. Several years later I'd help construct a children's playground atop these fond memories, each posthole jab their deepening grave. The second floor's spartan, open rooms segregated by gender housed us in sleeping bags on the floor, cots, foam pads, and scrounged whatnots; a typical residential arrangement. As a lover of architecture and buildings, I explored every inch I had or snuck access into.

I had no idea whatsoever the sort of organization I'd joined by simply not leaving. Driving out of Nederland I had a 3-day and two back-to-back 7-day workshops cinched under my belt. To build on this, our center director Julian organized a 21-day workshop to bring us up to speed on church life, deeper aspects of Divine Principle, and what our leaders expected of us rookie full-timers. Ideally, a new member goes through a 3-day workshop then a 7-, 21-, 40-, and finally a 120-day workshop. But this was reality. A few 40- and 120-day workshops happened at the national level, often in New York City replete with graduations and class photos featuring Rev. Moon that carried enormous prestige, but they were irregular at best and I never got the opportunity.

Beyond my limited formal instruction in Boulder, it was just me and my DP. Julian presented us our own *Divine Principle* in this workshop. He signed my endpage with, *The way of the righteous is a life of overcoming. —SMM.*

"Originally, Father said *conquering*, not *overcoming*," he said.

"Why didn't you write that, then?" *I'd misconstrue it?*

"I think it's too confrontational. The press misquotes him 'conquering' the world."

"Literally? Like some Korean Genghis Khan?" He nodded. "Pssh! Unless there's an armory in the basement, that's total bullsh—crap. There isn't one, right?"

My DP 'Bible' with Julian's personal message was the Hope Diamond in my hot hands. Later, I found he'd signed everyone's with a message he thought *apropos* to situations and characters. Oh, well. We hit it off anyway and we've more or less been friends since, perhaps because he was college educated to which I aspired in my wide reading and command of English but never knew how I'd ever manage to finish. He stood slightly hunched seven years older at about six feet with sandy brown hair and all-American nordic features sporting a military bearing. He explained some backstory.

"When my dad was a colonel at the Pentagon during Vietnam, we were all protesting there and I burned my draft card right on the top step."

My Fender in Boulder's dining hall.

"Of the Pentagon? Like . . . you lit it on *fire?*"

His laugh was quixotic. "I had no idea how hard my father would take it."

"What, did he punch you out or something?"

"He resigned from the service."

"Wow. No kidding? That is taking it hard. He might've made general."

"I've always felt so much regret over it. I didn't expect he'd do that."

I guess he made it up to him since they seemed on happy terms all the years I've known them both. A couple years later at San Francisco's Judah Street center, his folks were the first nonmembers I'd met since joining. Two decades later, we still have fond memories and occasionally I visit them.

With his Rev. Moon quote, I could tell he surmised I desired the righteous life but that it would take a lot of overcoming. He was pretty blasted perceptive. Over 21 years later, I'm still trying to achieve that level of self control.

We stood chatting while I leafed admiringly through God's new gold standard. He said, "I'm wondering when your 'spiritual birthday' is. Do you know your first day with the church?"

"When I met Ginny or went to the High Street dinner program?"

He was shaking his head. "When you first heard the Principle . . . the second coming of the Messiah lecture and then making the decision to join."

"Well, shit—er, heck—that was over the whole weekend." I thought through the whirlwind. "I guess March 14, give or take."

"We'll go with that, then, but I'll double check with Ginny. Consider your spiritual birthday your baptism into Principle. It's your real age."

"Pshaw! You mean I'm just an infant to anybody who heard the Principle first? That's gonna be pretty hard to bear. Dang. Really?"

He barked a laugh followed by a jarring shoulder clap. "Don't worry, if you die I'll put flowers on your grave."

I think my mouth fell open as he disappeared to another task. That remark was his all-purpose pink slip to a conversation.

A PERSON'S PHYSICAL birthday has less relevance in the Unification Church than his or her *spiritual* birthday. You could be 25 but joined at 18, hence *seven* years old in the church. Quite an advanced age in those days. Members that ancient were Yoda sages. Or you could be 40 but *one* year in the church so, regardless, you didn't have the clout of a seven-year old. Spiritual age typically trumps physical age unless you're dealing with Japanese and Koreans, leaders, or folks with social standing outside the church like pastors with a congregation, PH.D.s with a classroom, or commissioned officers; anything that might give the church a societal leg up.

Physical age was vital for Japanese. A difference of a day automatically canceled strangers' camaraderie for hierarchical relations. Japanese friends said this was a cultural norm and children even beat up schoolyard peers if they didn't get the social etiquette they expected. In America, bullies beat you up for raw power and lunch money. Respect was only a side effect making their next theft easier.

It all sounded weirdly ridiculous. I figured I'd have got beat up a lot in Japan. A fair amount of my trouble with older members and leaders was for the same reason, I suppose. No doubt, it's why the institution ultimately relegated me to the undesirables bin. I expected people to demonstrate respectable behavior if they wanted my respect, not simply demand it off something as arbitrary as age or position. I'd had my fill of that in the military and was indisposed to more of it in a *church*. I so begrudged the Coast Guard botching their care of my knee and leaving me a gimp on a cane for five years that I sometimes went out of my way to prove to church elders just how unafraid I was of shitting on their expectations.

In 1984 I was enjoying an unexpectedly happy, collegial chitchat with a Japanese brother in Kodiak, Alaska's church-owned seafood company's mess hall.

And then he said, "When are you born?" Like any American, I didn't give it a thought. "So . . ." he was calculating it. "Ah. You are six months after me."

And just like that our conversation went from equal to what I can only describe as master–servant. In a blink, he took nothing I said seriously and his shift in tone made it clear I should accept his opinions and especially his directions regarding work and spiritual-life without argument.

I ostentatiously checked my watch. "Oh! Gotta go. Nice talking. See ya," *never if I can help it,* and jumped out of there fast.

My birthdate transitioned to a Soviet state secret, a church vow I kept till safely out of its Asian cultural clutches. Unfortunately, American and Western members adopted this attitude in struggling to fit their culturally Christian, square selves into a round, messianic Asian movement constantly drumming in the message that Western society was fundamentally Cainish and that, "You must challenge your old concepts." *We do, apparently. You damn sure aren't.*

Julian was one of the very few members I ever felt any consistent respect for. There were only three in these early years whom I believed warranted any real respect at all. One was Rev. Moon, of course, who'd unquestionably impressed me with his quality of thought and consistently saintly behavior which I took over and above his foibles that handicaps everybody. I'm not talking a Mother Teresa or St. Francis of Assisi saintliness. More that of St. Peter, Stephen, and Paul. Rough and rowdy sinful men indescribably committed to their heavenly mission and vision who took every lump along their way. That's how I saw Rev. Moon and deeply respected it. In a way, I loved him for it. Not only because he was doing those things, but because I wanted to do them too and knew how hard it was for me just to manage the baby steps that Rev. Moon had already accomplished in his youth.

I've always seen respect as an attribute of love. There's the simpleton's kind of respect where you salute an officer because, if you don't, they throw you in the brig. Or you respect the schoolyard bully's ability to put a pipe wrench through your skull. Or you respect the authority of the police through compliance. Or you respect the president of the United States because a majority fairly elected him. But that pedestrian feeling isn't what I think of as *respect*. Real respect is fearlessly ceding authority and control over your own person to another because you choose to. You serve or defer to them, salute them, and so on simply because you love and admire them and can't help yourself. *Respect* denotes our action of expressing nonromantic love for a person or institution. In the absence of that kind of love, a person goes through the mechanical motions of 'showing respect' for one reason or another—say, fear—or withholds its tokens.

My nature is to withhold when I can't develop a genuine love for a person or their deeds beyond my basic consideration of his or her human dignity. I may not respect them but I'll be courteous and benevolent unless otherwise warranted. For example, in Judah Street a few years later I was shambling upstairs cane-in-hand for the van keys to unblock a visiting leader's car. My fanatic Anglo-Indian spiritual elder Christine's fierce dark eyes blasted me not even halfway up the first flight, fingers whitened against the black-lacquered redwood banister.

Her hiss was frantic. "*Hurry!*"

"Why?" I said with a bit of *harrumph*.

"He's a *leader!*"

"So?" *Jeez, did she really just say that?*

Her mood hardened. "You need more—"

"Can't you see I'm rushing?" I'm sure there was a lilt I didn't quite tamp down.

I cut my hobble speed in half to prove my point and spent 15 minutes relocating the van when Christine wanted it done in two. That leader said nothing about rushing and he would've, so I didn't. This is one example of church members unilaterally assuming a responsibility not theirs to enforce respect or obedience for third persons who may or may not even care. Dictatorships are built this way. With an implacable sense of righteous grievance I resisted it all my years in the church.

The third person I deeply respected was Masahisa Kobayashi, whom Rev. Moon transferred in 1983 to replace Julian at Judah Street. He was the first and the only member or leader to take the time to explain Divine Principle to me in detail, to answer all my questions no matter how ignorant, outrageous, complicated, stupid, or controversial and treat *me*, the person, with respect. I really appreciated the man and considered him my spiritual father over Julian. Members often mistook me for a 'Jap-hater'—some spit it in my face—because I criticized their behavior and attitude in our *American* church. Not having an opportunity to be around Korean leaders for a couple more years yet, my venom targeted the Japanese and turncoat Americans adopting their arrogant, abusive attitudes. Members were usually surprised—more commonly unbelieving—when I let them know that Mr. Kobayashi was one of only three people I truly loved and respected in the church.

One Korean, one Japanese, and one American. Funny how it worked out that way considering the critical importance Rev. Moon places on Principled relations like Cain and Abel between these cultures. I think he had an opportunity there but didn't notice. I'd have to wait years for my best opportunity to capitalize on it.

I had no high hopes when I'd joined the church. Perhaps my self-esteem was trounced from my military tour. But I hauled up short in Judah Street's dining room when a Japanese sister tipped me off to how others were seeing me.

"You are ambitious person. I can see."

"Whaaat? Pfft! Nah, no way. I'm just a regular member."

"No . . . you have strong mind. Very ambitious. It true," she said in the much-mocked *itt-a-tuu-rue* Japanese accent.

In those days I equated ambition with venal, cutthroat greed, something only politicians and shitbirds in principle thirsted after. Her insinuation I was *that* was a cold dagger at my throat. *My God!* I couldn't defend my honor enough. Thinking her words over today, I can only shake my head. She was right as rain is wet.

∼

I SETTLED INTO life at Boulder center. My last formal Divine Principle workshop before 1995 in our learn-on-your-own, sink-or-swim church rolled up its doors soon after we arrived off Nederland's mountaintop. Various speakers presented the same information but in greater detail. For instance, we received in-depth, extrabiblical information on the life of Jesus. One detail stood out.

As every Christian knows, Mary was miraculously with child for a virgin birth. Perhaps it was easier to imagine it 2,000 years ago since the most educated men of the day were the one's flagellating their audience with it. In our modern culture awash in secular science it's simply a matter of faith. I never really liked that term, *faith*. That's what my parents, priest, and Sunday school teacher sternly said I needed more of whenever pushing off one of my insensitive questions. Faith seems to mean the emotional acceptance of the logically ludicrous when it doesn't mean hope. Christians accept the premise because it's a logical corollary to the God–man Jesus. Postulating his conception through something as dirty as sex is a harder Divine Christ sell when all things human are taken as irredeemably impure.

I listened amazed as Jesus' life unfolded. Unless I chose fanaticism, it was hard for Divine Principle's profundity not to sweep me off my Catholic feet. Here were age-old questions finding answers in clear, lucid, biblical arguments. When Julian dropped the bombshell that Mary conceived Jesus with Israel's high priest Zechariah, you could hear a pin drop as ten or more new members, some devoutly raised Christians, vapor locked. Yet, he articulately argued the Principle's contentions and, frankly, it made hella more sense than Christianity's vestal incontestables. Nobody walked out, anyway. This workshop gripped my heels and shook out all my loose feelings and spare credos for a whole new currency.

Ken Sudo was a guest lecturer. A sixtyish bantam Japanese having a delicately boned face under a high, balding forehead, he was gracious to a fault. I never got any condescension from him and accordingly rather liked him. He was known as "the man with no sleep" because, legend had it, he taught the Principle night and day without sleep till falling unconscious in the middle of a sentence. I imagined him keeling over at his podium and cracking his fine skull. I think he earned his reputation in Japan, so he was probably cross-legged on the floor. One story was when a severe illness confined him to bed. Unable to face his own imposition and suspension of his anointed teaching mission, he had it lugged to the lecture room and taught on his back to forestall certain exhaustion.

Listening to Julian recount it I said, "Man, that's dedication!" while rethinking what I wanted out of life.

"I don't know if he really did those things. I wasn't there. But he's practically a living saint *here*. I'd say he's earned his reputation."

I'd later experience his saintliness for myself. For now, Julian's 21-day *tour de force* trailing Nederland's appeal fleshed out my dry bones like the army Ezekiel raised up from the dry, dusty desert. It's a cliché, but I felt I was the dead coming back to life. My parents didn't yet know what I'd got myself into; I still think I wisely kept it from them. Of course, the church institution turned out a real albatross but Divine Principle set me free to understand God, inspired a personal vision embracing the globe, and awoke a capacity in me for reason in the midst of faith. Yes, although I reject the notion at face value, I naturally recognize the presence of an unknown and unknowable knowingness within. This is faith in its traditional sense, strange as it seems. But I arrived at it through reason and knowledge rather than superstition and illogic. The little I did know I felt I really *knew*, just as Plato read between the Oracle of Delphi's lines that he was the wisest of all.

Indeed, it's a fine line between certainty of knowledge and plain old arrogance, and I might've been a victim of the latter more than a beneficiary of the former. I should probably be happier if I stuck to what I truly did know, which is that I knew practically nothing, at least about God. Alas, I'm a man of passion. Once convicted, twice—nay, *thrice!*—stubborn. Yet, voraciously absorbing the Principle via lectures and my one book I began realizing the knowledge I was validating was a baseline for my faith in the rightness of my developing worldview, Rev. Moon's claim to fame, and his messianic mission to all peoples and religions.

I suppose that's the kind of faith I'd come to eschew in my critical rejection of the Catholic Church. Unlike Catholicism, Unificationism wasn't indoctrinating me into a liturgical dogma. The root of a Moonie is the simple belief in the Fall, how to reverse it, and Rev. Moon as Jesus' long-awaited successor. The rest is icing on the cake. Our lecturers presented a straightforward biblical history to clarify its mystical questions and historical controversies. Conclusions were certainly offered by any and all members but were hardly necessary. Every person hearing the lectures and seriously contemplating their message ran the numbers in their own head and naturally altered their perception. That was me. Nobody had to twist my arm. It made sense and answered the questions it raised. So, no shit it revolutionized my view of the world, my place in it, life, history, God, especially myself, and my duties thereto. Julian's workshop changed my life. There was no going back.

You might've guessed that, from the very start of my sojourn with the church, I was crossing swords with persons and institutional behaviors over daily behavior, work, participation, leaders, relationships, and so on. It seemed such a dichotomy to be so absorbent of the fundamental message of the church yet so consistently at odds with its expression in the institution. I didn't develop this tendency on purpose. In truth, I suppressed it. Strangled it at the root for conformity's sake. But it flowed insistently from my American cowboy heritage. My dichotomy's radiant brand was so obvious and depraved in the eyes of brothers and sisters that I might've had the mark of Cain seared into my forehead STARGÅTE SG · 1 Teal'c style.

The 21-day workshop put meat on my spiritual bones. It was all very exciting. I discovered a deep love for learning I still carry today. In junior and senior high I was a mediocre student preferring to socialize, write novels, and paint fine art over book learning. I wasn't much better attending Western State, either. Once I'd fallen madly in love with my eventually ex-fiancée, school barely registered. My GPA plummeted to something like 1.6, a 'D' average. *Ouch.*

Over the outdoor pay phone Dad said, "Your grades are a disgrace, Christopher. I'm pretty disappointed you'd let things get this far."

"I know, I know, I'm sorry. I just—"

"That's enough of that. If you don't bring them up to at least a high 'C,' for starters, I won't pay your tuition next semester. At this point, your mother and I are just throwing good money after bad."

"Yes, sir."

"See that you do." And *click* went that conversation.

Well, it was probably no surprise to him or Mom. They'd been all but speechless when I'd sprung my college plans and then more so that Western State accepted their math-dunce of a son as a geology major. But a college has bills, eh.

Mom's earfuls from my high school counselor never went down well. "Bone up on your schoolwork or I don't see anything but ditchdigging in your future."

"There's a lot more than ditchdigging for a high school graduate, Mom."

"Wait'll your father . . ." and *blah, blah, blah.* Nothing I hadn't heard before.

Sometimes, I think they see me even today as a ditchdigger merely doing other things. I carried the blithe expectation that somehow I could and would succeed at whatever I had a mind to. I still believe it despite all demonstrable evidence to the contrary. Lucky for me, hope (and opportunity) springs eternal.

MY IMPRESSION TILL now was the Moonies were an educational institution, not a church at all. Since joining I'd enjoyed only workshops, interesting conversations about God, society, and life during meals, then sleeping well (if not long) after senior members came home from . . . wherever. My utopia ended one dark early morn. An older brother roughly shook me awake.

"Hey, sleeping beauty, time to get up for morning service."

I rolled over groggy. "Morning what?"

"Morning *service*. You're supposed to attend regularly from today." He sounded like he'd been chomping the bit for this. "Hurry up! Don't wanna be late."

"Well, *dang*."

Two things grabbed me. First, I wasn't too hip rising and shining at the crack of dawn for *church*. Fanatics did that. You see, one of my problems with church is attending it. I love its theological side and practicing personal spiritual disciplines that naturally developed within, but I was pretty soured on organized worship even at Mass in high school. Not only was it boring as hell, I thought I could do a better job. Second, and ominously, was the rankling phrase, "you're supposed to." I thought I'd left that behind in the Coast Guard. But once accepting an organization into your life, it's human nature to please it. As it entwines your innermost sanctuaries, you find that placating it is more important, more personally rewarding, and more empowering of your self-righteousness than gratifying much less protecting yourself. With the added benefit of a hierarchical, dictatorial structure you can blame for most anything, it produces the option of a faux guilt-free lifestyle, too.

I dressed sleepily before slow-walking downstairs to the lecture room where all 50-plus members closely gathered on the floor. We belted out Holy Songs written by early Koreans and Japanese melodiously translated into English. They were beautiful, filled with love for God and His for us, but also images of sadness, pain, suffering, sacrifice, and duty. Rev. Moon himself wrote and set to traditional melodies some of them during his early travails. I love singing them even today. Then the brother or sister leading us prayed aloud and someone delivered a 20–40 minute sermon. Rev. Moon often spoke four, six, ten, or twelve hours, often chastising us when our squirming, youthful butts couldn't take the hard concrete another minute; he squatted when his knees couldn't stand a second more. Leaders limited morning service to an hour or less so we could bathe before breakfast at 7:30 AM.

My first morning service was pretty standard by my reckoning until it came to the end and the speaker said, "Please join me in unison prayer."

Unison what? I cast a wary eye and *Oh. My. God.* It wasn't five seconds before all those mouths launched into praying *aloud*. I'd never heard the like. A mini-auditorium of the faithful cried out to God, tearfully hollering storm-driven winds of atoning sorrow at failing to live up to the ideals and standards of God and True Parents. Moonies never pray this way anymore. They're too spiritually defunct, especially at Unification Theological Seminary where, at least 1995–98, its president allotted a 2-minute window for it during mandatory service. It rarely rose above a nervous whisper lest a calculating soul use it against us. But members in these vernal days sloughed off their worries with reckless abandon. Some cried crocodile tears to be sure, especially the Japanese who—mainly brothers—tended to zealotry, often beating themselves with their fists or open palms. They were the de facto standard for the penitent believers we iniquitous Americans longed to be. Many imitated their strident demeanor . . . both the good and, unfortunately, the bad.

This morning I was a staid, backslid Catholic shocked by this blatantly Baptist display. I tried to pray but couldn't focus. Booming voices ransacked my head of every thought. The cacophony rose slowly over 10–15 minutes in a cresting wave till it hit a crescendo of passion. Then it fell off over the course of another 5–10 till gently lapping at my ears. In these days, no one stopped unison prayer at a preset time. It went till the last person had wrung out their heart and fell into whispers then silence, after which everyone kept a prayerful posture as tears and emotion washed out to form tomorrow morning's wave and a respectful interval had passed. The leader softly crooned a peaceful, one-verse Korean ditty called *Tongil* (Unity), a lovely tune I sang over and over day and night as the mood struck. Service concluded when everyone in due course joined in with a final round in Korean then English. We jumped out at our new day pumped to kick hell out of Satan and any members imprudently showing his influence.

Unison prayer was awesome. But my first few mornings completely overwhelmed me in emotion and noise that tangled me in swarming confusion. I felt rising waters in a darkened compartment drowning my reason. The tumultuous babel wasn't just deafening but threatening. My mind was agony, the rude assault vicious.

I have to quell it! Stop! Stop! STO—OP!

I imagined whipping out an Uzi and spraying the room into blessed quietude. Several times I only barely restrained myself jumping to my feet and shrieking for some considerate silence. I wallowed in these murderous scenes for days while unexpectedly evolving an immunity to the racket. Eventually, I *was* the crowd crying, shouting, whispering, meditating. What an empowering source of energy! No longer did it suck out my thoughts. It simply blended into background noise, a binaural beat before it was popular. Unison prayer in the '80s, before the church self-destructed, was the best prayer experience of my life.

There were all kinds during unison prayer besides screamers. Not everyone felt a need for lung-busting fervor, though there seemed an unspoken competition for Most Pious. I did notice Moonies weren't praying personal needs but ardently that religious and national leaders made the right decisions, that God's Will Restoring humanity came to pass, for a world of love, that their personal failures didn't hinder human salvation, that today their personal mission was more productive, more successful, less sinful. Global things. Not shibboleths but their grave focus.

"Is this a daily thing?" I wondered of Julian. Unison prayer was ice water on my educational delusion and that I'd undeniably joined a *church*.

"Every day. Hence, we call it *morning* service."

My disappointment was crushing. "What about weekends?"

"What do you think, Chris? God's a 24-hour business, come on. And there's always Sunday service." He caught my look. "Don't worry, if you die I'll put—"

"Dang, Julian. You're practically a Catholic order."

"And me an old Jesuit, too. Food for thought."

"I don't know . . . maybe it's not for me." He cornered his mouth up at that. "Darn it, though, I really dig the Principle *and* the Family."

"That's what it's all about. I guess you could try it in the outside world."

I crossed arms. "Nah . . . I reckon if I've joined a real church I'll suck in my gut and get over my resistance to organized religion." He clapped my shoulder.

Maybe in retrospect it was an exercise in bad judgment, all things considered. Yet, in my short time exposed to Rev. Moon's thought, I admired and respected it; I wanted to associate with it. His comprehension of God, humanity, and spirituality seemed a viable path to a better planet. I couldn't see humanity mending itself any other way, least of all with existing religion. Even after the treatment his charismatic lunacy and cranked-up leaders gave me the last 21 years, I feel so.

MR. SATO (NOT balding Mr. Sudo) was lord of the central USA fief. I didn't know in 1981 that the American Unification Church had, by the late '70s, blindly begun a process devolving it from a free, open, people-oriented, God-fearing organization to a totalitarian, closed, feudalistic, leader-justifying one. Like Germans, Unificationists fell under the sway of a totalitarian mindset for the greater good. It was quiet but implacable and we got our own Imperial Roman emperor, prestige-hungry yet powerless senators, and a rabble ever distracted by emergency providential events and at each other's throats over failures. It sowed the mid-1980's church implosion and meltdown. Rev. Moon said it was splintering because members waxed arrogant and self-righteous after he'd told us to forgive and unite in the wake of poleaxing Senator Donald Fraser in his thankfully limited McCarthyist witch hunt.

I disagreed with his larger analysis. He was probably reasoning from the dark, as he often must, since his trusted leaders often misinformed him lest they lose power, prestige, salary, or their heads. I used to think he was practically omnipotent. That even in the absence of truthful information he'd just know a situation's reality. Didn't he speak with God, Jesus, Buddha, Moses, Muhammad, and others? Wouldn't he get accurate reports from them? Over time, his foolish and stupid decisions drained even my nearly limitless reservoir of credulity dry.

No, the arrogance and self-righteousness that might've provoked our crisis was embodied in the Japanese–Korean machine slowly but surely exerting its iron grip on power, choking off every shred of American independence, Christian values, and freedom of conscience. I woke up in 1984 to realize it had divided my nation into fiefdoms, each with its all-powerful feudal lord often at odds with the others. For example, Rev. Moon frequently called on a domain to send x members hither and yon for some grand purpose. These leaders commonly refused in roundabout fashion because manpower, like vassal serfs of yore, were a tangible asset that, once parted with, permanently depressed the financial and prestige coffers. This left Rev. Moon holding the bag and unable to mobilize the manpower or funds to successfully accomplish his goals. Leaders lied about their numbers to bloat accomplishments, deflate coffers, and pled membership poverty for their anointed tasks.

I saw these fiefs evolve into today's twelve regions each with its all-powerful regional director. Like the primacy the Roman bishopric foisted on protesting Christendom till it became the papacy, the regional director headquartered in New York City became, through sophisticated maneuvering and Rev. Moon's patronage, the chief among equals, the Regional Director of regional directors, the wonderful, all-knowing, all-seeing, most merciful and compassionate *Continental Director*.

In the late '70s and most of the '80s, the feudal lords were exclusively Japanese. As Koreans exerted more control under Rev. Moon's hand and the Japanese kingdoms evolved into regional directorates, he sent these top bandits—I'm being cavalier; not all deserve infamy—back home. The primary locus of power and authority in all matters ecclesiastical and temporal within America's Unification Church passed firmly and exclusively into male Korean hands. Eventually, he appointed a token white in the mid-'90s named Bill Stoner to one of the more backward regions. The other eleven all but ignored him. It was comical seeing him excluded from their meetings as if he didn't belong; I guess he didn't. Even when allowed to show his flag, their confab—more crucially, their political backdooring—was in Korean and to my knowledge he hadn't learned his Lord's soon-to-be-global lingo. From their perspective, it was expecting Jesus to grok Latin for pagan Roman convenience. Translating was an imposition on God, effectively sinful. Plus annoying.

In any case, it wasn't *our* self-righteous arrogance that did in a church enjoying explosive and logarithmic growth into the early 1980s. During the Fraser hearings, Rev. Moon boasted the church had 30,000 American members—he might've been lied to about that—all within about 15 years of its founding and seven since he'd arrived in the United States. Well, there *were* a lot of members. Many centers were teeming tenements. Bunk beds expanded floorspace in some and were quite the cushy novelty despite a 4-inch foam mattress. The rank and file generally cocooned in sleeping bags on uncushioned floors in the '70s and '80s. Brothers and sisters packed themselves on their segregated decks like sardines. I had the foresight in the Coast Guard to splurge $120 on a high-quality sleeping bag, a lavish outlay in 1980. And thank God. The smelly public bedrolls a center sometimes provided gave me the creeps. I slumbered in my red mummy bag a good ten years before shifting to covers. One nice thing about floorboards for a bed, it's never too short.

The real reason the church imploded was because leadership forsook its Christian God and Divine Principle for a neo-feudal, Confucianist, True-Parent nepotism merely wrapped in the Principle's spiritually egalitarian values, a Unificationism more diametric and imperial than the papacy. By then no member could freely travel center to center without their current and destination leader's permission plus a good report and expect to be a member in good standing. If you didn't like your providential duties or location, you could no more transfer at your own initiative to something more to your liking than a soldier could their billet without orders. The absolute feudal power of the upper- and mid-echelon leaders got so overbearing that even Rev. Moon chastised them for arrogating so much power to themselves. In an effort to remind members who the chief of the boat was, the church publication *Today's World* printed a speech in 1984 where he baldly compared his leaders to out-of-control servants and rightly asked why members were giving greater authority and credibility to the master's servants than the master himself. That same year at his Belvedere estate in Tarrytown, New York he said,

> The true leaders of the Unification Church are those who practice the Principle to their bones—to the utmost level . . . The most important determination among people is not some external sort of Cain and Abel position. Rather, the important characteristic of a person is if he serves more than anybody else, if he truly wants to live for the sake of others. The one who does that is Abel, regardless of anything else. A leader is the one who works harder and practices this principle more than others. Leadership does not mean receiving respect or admiration; it means working harder. (*True Way of Life* July 1, 1984)

Members like me welcomed his castigating words, yet they fell on mostly leader-idolizing ears. Leaders needed to unbrainwash then retrain the global membership to live up to the Master's words . . . a nonstarter. The natural consequence is a church slowly suffocating its spiritual and internationalist sentiment already divided atop rocky cultural and ideological platforms and sliding into civil war. In many ways, Rev. Moon was thoroughly sidelined by a hypocritical leadership that agreed to one thing face to face with their Messiah, did the opposite or nothing in the field, then lied their way out in the next face-to-face. Though some members engaged in forlorn internecine warfare to uphold the spirituality of the Family over their leaders' crass temporalism, more followed conscience-driven feet out.

As I wound up my 21-day Boulder workshop in April 1981 the church still appeared—in some cases, actually was—dynamic, extroverted, exciting, expanding, holy, Principled, moral, and credible. Everything I was looking for.

A NUMBER OF us were gabbing in the fireplace conversation pit along the Boulder center's south side. We often congregated in its comfy, collegial setting to chat over the Principle, complain, and watch the outside world motor by on Broadway. In some respects I was already feeling isolated from society. Not because the organization encouraged it but because I was spending so much time indoors engaged in lectures and other duties that, like the service, kept me to a small circle. I was ragging on our daily regimen. I despised dragging body and soul out of my comfy 6 AM bedroll after dropping off near midnight, swilling lectures, and the awful Actionizers Team. The latter's purpose was to give us newbies the opportunity to put action to the classroom by proselytizing along our college town's byways to invite any willing body to our daily evening program. My poison ivy.

I reflected our majority when I said, "We call it the Agonizers Team."

After more negativity, Ginny fell short on patience. As my 'spiritual mother,' she had to say something in front of disapproving pals. "This is how the church is, Chris. We witness to spread Principle to the world. Why else would any of us be here? The great food? You should quit complaining and do what you joined up for."

Her public chastisement smarted. I deadpanned, "Not sure I knew what I joined up to do. Maybe I should leave. I'm not really sure it's for me."

"Go ahead, why don't you? If all you're going to do is complain, you're more trouble than you're worth. Who needs you around anyway? We don't need you in our life to be Restored, we've already found True Parents. Maybe you *should* go, maybe you're just not ready, yet. Not everybody is."

Well, shit. She'd squared up. I was tasting crow. "Who said I wanted to leave?"

"Pfft! You did."

Man, was I feeling hot under so many edgy eyes. "I was just talking about how I feel about some things. It's a free country." Maybe on the other side of the property line. Frankly, I didn't want to leave. What was out there for me? Unemployment? A stumbling life on a cane? Back to living with my sister who didn't really want me there in the first place? Doing stupid shit for *me* instead of big things for the world? I loved Divine Principle. It truly caught my vision and I wanted to pursue it. If only it wasn't wrapped up inside a goddamned church.

As if to punctuate that she said, "'I recommend you pray more."

I dropped eyelids for a private roll. One thing about Ginny, she's an in-your-face Brooklynite who doesn't mince words. When I didn't toe her line, she let me know it. I appreciated her even though straight-talking women exasperate me if they don't know when to quit; I secretly love the trait so long as it doesn't come with a side of crazy. If nothing else, I know where I stand. Ginny was one of those rare women whom I liked a great deal *sans* romantic inclinations. I felt a great freedom in that. No stress from unrequited love, just friendship. Unfortunately, years later she forsook her 'parental' relationship which ended our casual affection. I suppose I really was more trouble than I was worth. It would hurt deeply but was one of those life lessons that yank you back into the reality of human nature and remind you that, idealism and altruism aside, you're solely responsible for keeping your own boat afloat and making your own self happy. It's all so tiresome.

MY FIRST FEW months in the Unification Church were a whirlwind of new sights, sounds, and smells. Oriental ones, in particular. I'd never eaten Asian food . . . except a yukky crunchy-noodle Bird's Eye horror at a friend's high school party across the mountain from my house in the Rockies. The American Unification Church developed a much tastier staple in Asian curry rice and Korean *kimchee* (pickled cabbage). I was a meat and potatoes man and platefuls of rice was a mind-bending innovation. Since forks were for losers in the church, I quickly mastered chopsticks. Tired hands for a while, but eventually pincered up whatever I desired.

The Japanese have a host of rules governing chopsticks. Some months after transferring to San Francisco, the center director's wife Yoko Kobayashi gaudily rebuked my chopsticking a piece of food to another's plate.

"It is very terrible," she said. "We use special chopsticks to pass the bones of cremated people during funeral ceremonies."

"Oh, well, okay, then."

"Yes, very bad manners." Not two minutes later her own chopsticks snapped a delicacy off her husband's plate. Hypocrisy lives in the smallest actions.

"Spoons are easier," I muttered. "No dumb rules."

Nattering in Boulder's commercial kitchen, I spun on my heel to leave and was startled to find *below* me a sister from Okinawa under four-feet-nine. Less than 100 pounds, her head barely touched my sternum. I teased her how I was taller sitting than her standing. Yeah, I was pretty barbaric in those days. So many things were new and exotic that I couldn't help playing the wide-eyed hayseed. Without realizing it, I think I insulted plenty (if not all at one time or another) of my Asian brethren. I probably deserved a lot of the shit the Japanese dished out. Tottering and flapping my arms to avoid crushing half her bones under my 190 pounds, I contemplated the shock and terror in her upturned face. Her spine arched frozen waiting for the skyscraper to collapse. I saved myself, but the whole thing left me red-faced. It had to look ridiculous. Afterward, she seemed skittish around me. I often felt a fish out of water because of my size and sometimes wished I could shrink—not my mouth, methinks—so I wouldn't be such a bloody sore thumb in the *Matryoshka* doll that was the Japanese church inside the American one inside the Korean.

How depressing bumping into short Japanese around corners, hogging elbow space at crowded tables, needing more stretch-out space to sleep. In many ways it seemed I'd found a warmly welcoming home, something I'd never experienced in the Coast Guard. Yet the nagging, long-dodged reality was that I didn't belong—more precisely, wasn't wanted. Americans are a novelty for Japanese; something to behold, politely laugh at, quietly remind themselves how thankful they are to be superior, civilized Asians, a delicately refined people a long chalk above boorish America. I think I mostly lived down to their expectations. But the Unification Church obsesses over numbers. It needs Americans. Vacuums them up. Nevertheless, once charmed into this Asian belfry it lets go your rope.

From the '70s through some of the '90s the Japanese were galley slaves airmailing hundreds of millions if not billions of dollars to the American church to fund a majority of Rev. Moon's American and global ministry. They derived a pride of place and a powerful sense of ownership from the effort, even those who'd barely if ever fundraised in Japan before shipping out for overseas duty in America, their generation's Manchukuo. I'm stereotyping, but that's how I saw it back then. Rev. Moon chastised Americans for not better reaping the Last Days' harvest to beat Japan's fundraising. He used it as a humiliating club to motivate us.

"Don't you Americans feel ashamed . . . Japanese members, your former enemies, are working night and day to send money to support your American church?"

"Isn't that just long-overdue war reparations?" some of us quietly said.

"Seems patently unfair," said others, "since it's hardly *our* church;" mere worker bees with no executive authority nor strategic participation whatsoever. It was Japan's colony before the Koreans stole it. Both looted our messianic inheritance. "Why *shouldn't* they support it? It's *their* operation."

Japanese in America proudly identified with the heroic money wars back home and broadcast their sacrifice in our cultural wasteland over tart waves of arrogance. I suppose I shouldn't speak too fast. Americans are an exceptionally proud people. If there's an enduring stereotype, it's the gum-chewing American ever pissy over his or her God-given rights and national accomplishments. But, still.

THE CHURCH TRANSFERRED me to San Francisco some months after joining. I lived relationships and activities in my years there which cleared my eyes to life with folks from other cultures, languages, and religions. I began comprehending the world's offense with the 'ugly American.' We're not a particularly arrogant, cruel, or selfish people. America is probably the best nation to show up in humanity's long, vicious march. But we oft come across that way because, in our geographic oddity amplifying our confidence in superior American ideals, we're simply ignorant of foreign sensibilities. Our center brimmed with the major cultures and their daily litany on our shortcomings. What an education that was.

The unwavering truth of Unificationism is its culturally Asian, philosophically Confucian hierarchy that denies members the pursuit of Divine Principle's vision within that very community. One might say it's more a problem of Asians intensely concerned with form and Americans function: behavior over performance, style versus results. Church goals here in 2003 still sprawl headlong over it.

Coming out of an unhappy military life, the worst thing the church could foist on me was rank and obligatory respect. I was a 19-year old naïf overawed of authority when I enlisted. Boot camp indoctrinated me with a required respect for superiors, but upon graduating chief petty officers only that morning berating me to sling to attention and shout "sir," slandering me in high-volume talk-downs, or ordering me to "Drop and gimme twenty!" were now all smiles.

"Just relax and call me Chief." Some offered up first names like best grog.

What. The—?

It was a habit that died hard. When it did, I avoided calling *anyone* 'sir.' Somehow, the word came to associate in my mind with subservience and inferiority. That not I but my 'superiors' controlled me hilt to point and I could just suck it.

After my knee injury, I more forcefully expressed these feelings as I gradually lost all respect for superiors who'd allowed its further damage from substandard medical care piling on restricted-duty so deathly tedious that a Coast Guard career became anathema. Sitting guard duty with equally gimped best friend Billy in our barracks' foyer onboard US Coast Guard station Group New Orleans—wholly superfluous; command considered doing nothing there preferable to nothing elsewhere—some cheesy-face Academy lieutenant strutted through the door. He stopped hard, eyes fixed on Billy and me as if seeing his first female Coasties half-dressed.

"You don't make attention when an officer enters?"

"We're injured and on special duty." I waggled my crutches to illustrate. He'd astounded because, for one, we were obvious leg injuries and making us hop up anytime an officer strolled past was medically contraindicated.

"Come to attention, you two, and right now. Crutches don't excuse proper military etiquette. Move it!"

And two, basic training strictly taught us not to rise to attention except when the commanding officer enters the space. I cast it in a modified light. "Er, we were specifically ordered to stand only for the base commander and, well, considering our leg injuries . . ."

That boot camp wasn't relevant was irrelevant to us goldbricks. Our swollen and mostly unworkable right knees were wrecked with as-yet unidentified and untreated cartilage tears and I was stalking our base on bored crutches till a much friendlier lieutenant snagged me a desk in the Vessel Traffic Safety office. Sitting and standing took loads of energy I didn't have and no small amount of pain, besides.

"You forget how to address an officer . . . what's your name?"

"No, sir. Of course not, sir. But we're injured, sir. Special dispensation, sir."

He was still a good 20 feet away and hadn't even moved. "Get on your feet, sailor! Or, by God, I'll have you at mast."

Alright, alright. No need to get mean. Somebody did send me to Captain's mast in a similar foyer encounter for quietly mumbling "asshole" into my shirt unaware I was Broadway projecting. My $100 fine never came out of my paycheck, so I knew our captain was a fellow traveler.

I chuffed a heavy sigh in preparation and staggered to my feet painfully groaning, taking three times longer than needed to settle armpits to crutches to impress on him the trouble he was putting me to just so he could feel like an officer instead of a person. I hung heavily in my too-short props so it was clear that standing me up was some form of UCMJ violation. Hunched over like the old man of the sea instead of the proud, ramrod straight Coast Guardsman he was hoping for, he stumped off in wordless disgust and paid us no mind again.

I gave Billy a thumbs up. "Mission accomplished."

"What a fucker that guy was."

"I'm talking to Senior Chief. We can't be doing this shit every time some hot officer waltzes through here. We'll both end up with amputations!"

"Good luck with that." He didn't seem very motivated.

The Unification Church doesn't consciously frustrate members from spiritually growing and developing. It achieves this result unconsciously as much as the Coast Guard ruined instead of fixed my knee. It's a product of the Confucian hierarchy and its total distaste for all things American, especially its people and our specious notions of equality, mutuality, and individual liberty. It came as no surprise to learn years later that, circa China's Warring States period, all of Mencius' known books were burned and his philosophy forbidden. What so scared Confucianists? Mencius taught that responsibility must flow down from rulers to the people just as obedience flows (Confucianistically) up. He said this was a function of love, which ultimately meant that rulers were the same as people. *Equality! Ye gods!*

I saw Mencius a natural disciple to Jesus. An opportunity for China to walk the democratic road of individual liberty 1,500 years before Europeans imagined it and Americans embraced it. Then China would've truly been the center of the world instead of a linguistic pretense. The Unification Church had the same opportunity to champion God's highest aspirations for us but chose the same reactionary course. Older members rarely lost a chance to clarify they didn't need us newbies for their salvation and only tolerated us as a necessary evil. A strange attitude, considering Rev. Moon says that without a family of 'spiritual children' one can never enter heaven. More bizarre, it's usually Westerners making these outrageous claims.

The irony of American Unificationism is that like Communism, Socialism, and Leftism generally, it turns Westerners against their culture and Christian heritage, even more so those selected into leadership. I'd been forcibly run out of the Unification Church twelve times by 2003, and two-thirds were by American leaders acting on their Asian superior's will or their own Asian envy.

MY FIRST EXPERIENCE with the importance of hierarchy in the church was Ginny disapproving me greeting a fundraising team captain with his first name. Larry Krishnek was an ex-hippie. An early '70s photo showed an outback wildman lost in thick, bushy hair and lush facial shrubbery vainly masking his broad, happy grin. I liked the fellow in that picture. Even though he was now clean shaven and army cut, he attracted me as a kindred spirit though we rarely traded words.

When he walked into the kitchen I blurted, "Hi, Larry!"

He greeted me affably but Ginny pounced. "You mustn't call him Larry."

"Why not? What am I supposed to call him?"

"You should call him *Mr.* Krishnek."

"Are you crazy? I'm not calling him mister. I don't even call Julian mister."

"Which you should."

"Pfft! I had enough of that crap in the military. I'd sooner never speak to him. Why should I call him mister, anyhow?"

"Because he's a leader, that's why." Her one and only rationale. She meant, *He's an officer and you're not.*

I had three semesters of college and a well-educated command of English when I joined the service. I'd toyed with applying to the Navy and Coast Guard academies in high school but didn't because, even though Dad knew a congressman who'd recommend me, their curriculums were heavy on math and I was a lightweight. Nevertheless, I resented being forced into an inferior enlisted status just to serve my country. I certainly didn't accept officers as *superior* to me; they were merely work supervisors. I acted out this mentality when stationed aboard *Acushnet* in Gulfport, Mississippi. My closest friend was a Christian lieutenant (j.g.) who invited me to his house for dinner, weekend Christian concerts, and church events. It was technically against regs, so we kept it on the down-low. I preferred him over the enlisted because we had more in common culturally, educationally, and professionally.

For example, I was arguing with our deck division's second-class bosun's mate over some task-related thing, and he threatened me with punitive action.

"Well, that's your prerogative."

His voice growled. "What'd you call me?"

"What?"

"What. Did you. Just call me?"

"Ummm . . ."—*fuck if I knew*—"prerogative?" Instinct was telling me not to define the word for him.

"Don't be calling me shit and think you'll get away with it, McKeon, you dumb disrespectful fuck, or I'll teach you a thing or two you'll really—"

"Yeah, yeah, totally. I'll just turn-to."

"See you do. I'll be talking 'bout you to . . ."

I rolled my eyes out of the compartment thinking, *He's my superior?*

My first-name relationship with my lieutenant friend was strictly shoreside. On board, he was *Mister* and *Sir.* I had no problem with that because our friendship fostered a mutual respect regardless rank. I never felt demeaned or inferior in any way. The military has strict rules about officer–enlisted fraternization but, in my case, it improved my mental condition, perhaps because I considered myself officer material and meant for a commission. In my mind's eye, I *was* an officer, a square commission in a round enlistment. I planned ocs at my earliest opportunity.

It's ironic I went from a fish out of water in the rigidly hierarchical military to the same thing in the Unification Church. But the military's code of conduct protected the low from the high by mandating responsibility and accountability à la Mencius, to a degree. The Unification Church encouraged leaders to shun responsibility and accountability and winked at abuse. I wasn't satisfied holding low enlisted rank and damn sure not a rank-and-file, abuse-me-please Moonie. The moment I discovered Unification Theological Seminary (uts) and Rev. Moon's insistence his future leaders arise only in its graduates, I resolved to attend. If he was raising an officer corps for his war against Satan, then I'd shoot for General.

Ginny's demand I call leaders of any stripe *mister* offended my egalitarianism, reignited bad memories of hierarchical Catholicism and the military, and reinforced my feeling of others forcing me into positions of inferiority to block my skills and creative genius. Even then I believed I could fulfill my destined potential only when I had the freedom to act on my own conscience off my own plans. Fired up with Rev. Moon's vision, I now dreamed of working side by side with him, sharing his vision till instinctively, automatically putting into action the very things he was thinking about. I concluded after three years of internal struggle that my thinking and vision indeed harmonized with his however less developed.

For instance, I often shared with friends what I thought he or the church should do next or how we should think about or react to some topic or event, only for them to deride me, laugh, pronounce me incorrigibly arrogant, or studiously ignore it. Then days, weeks, or months later he'd come out saying damn near what I'd said.

Yet no one ever said, "Gee, Chris, you were right. Shoulda listened."

It was like I'd never said it. Successfully predicting his strategy and opinions was fair cause to believe his unwillingness to take advantage of me set back his own goals; failures, by the way, he loses no time scapegoating.

NEAR THE END of my 21-day workshop Julian said, "You're joining the Actionizers Team. Only those Mr. Sudo and I consider ready for action are being chosen."

"That sounds cool," I said. "What do we do?"

"You'll learn witnessing."

My heart fell. This was totally new and immediately I had misgivings. "Going out on the street, flagging down strangers and witnessing to them about the church? I'm not really given to preaching my beliefs uninvited, Julian." It was abhorrent and filled me with trepidation.

"Be a good boy and do what you can." *Yessir!* And off I slogged to the front.

We grouped around our leader in downtown Boulder with flyers. "Your job is asking passersby if you can *briefly* tell them about our church. Then invite them to the evening program. Don't forget their name and number if they agree."

"Like the one I went to," I sighed, bracing Ginny. "Well, you did it, so . . ."

Most passersby only wanted to pass us by.

"Don't mention the church's name," our Actionizer leader said. I hadn't known its name at my 3-day Nederland workshop until the last lecture but figured out it was mighty unpopular in no time.

"Isn't that lying?" somebody said.

"Just be circumspect about revealing we're affiliated with True Father."

"Yeah, but why?"

"It'll make them negative about True Parents for no reason thanks to the nego press. We can't cheat them out of maybe their one and only opportunity to hear Principle. If they're gonna be negative anyway, at least they should get that chance so they can't accuse us in spirit world."

Nods all around. Ginny added her two cents. "We don't know how hard their ancestors worked to get them to meet you, Chris, just like yours did to get you to that 7-Eleven when I was there. You could've come earlier or later, right?"

"Yeah, I reckon." I hadn't considered that serendipity much at all after Nederland's day-three big reveal. Other irons, I guess.

"What if you'd heard all the negativity and blew me off? You talk all the time how you love DP. You'd have missed out on it. What would you be doing now?"

Chomping chips over Star Trek? "Yeah, yeah, good points." I disliked not being upfront, but the specter of losing people to Satan chilled our tongues.

"We're a Christian group with a message about God and the times," our leader continued. "If they insist just say, 'I can see you're not interested. Have a nice day.'"

"But—"

"Approach somebody else . . . or tell them. See what they say if they won't take no for an answer. Your call. It's their responsibility if they're negative after that."

Ugh. I could've lost my breakfast, but did lose my fear after a year or so. Right now, I was just a quaky new recruit filled with a burning desire to advance Rev. Moon's awesome Divine Principle because, ultimately, it was all about that, not him. He was the gateway to God and the Principle his roadmap. Dammitall if I'd have potential members unfairly judge him out of ignorance and send themselves to some dark spirit world. What a burden we thought we carried.

It didn't take long to realize 'actionizing' wasn't for me. Out on that sidewalk, I was a naked fat man, ugly and repulsive. I felt truly cut off. Life was moving along 'out there' without me, now segregated into a world of apocalyptic visions nobody wanted to hear. This blasted dichotomy plagued me from early on right up till now. Rev. Moon's galvanizing vision had me by the throat from the get-go, my new maxim his Restored world of unselfish love for the sake of others my adopted norm, not the exception. All the same I missed the 'real' world—my old world of sin, Christians say. I felt so in the Coast Guard, too, when our boot camp band played weekend concerts in local parks and me a shorthair in a sea of longhairs. But I could go anywhere and do anything off duty. The church had no such mode. I couldn't just walk off for whatever. No one would've physically stopped me, but they'd definitely wonder what I was up to and question my commitment as a member, to the Principle, and True Father as the Messiah. Peer pressure, baby.

The public's fear the Unification Church brainwashed innocent victims to use them against their will is definitely shite. I saw leaders all over America ask or order members to leave; they forcibly kicked or pushed me out repeatedly. I wasn't the only rookie giving them grief, either. During this time an attractive sister, who'd joined after me, habitually dressed quite obviously *sans* brassiere.

After a few hints, Julian caught up in the dining area. "Look, Mr. Sato says you need to wear a bra because you're making it difficult for the new brothers to overcome their fallen nature and reach a higher spiritual level."

"The heck? No! That's rude and outrageous! I'm perfectly clothed and it's more comfortable. That's their problem, not mine."

"I appreciate your feelings, but we're a church, not the university. You know Chapter 2 is a real problem for some people. We want members to be free of that struggle inside the center. Wouldn't you prefer it that way anyhow? Do you really want brothers gawking and making it harder by exposing your sexuality?"

"That's ridiculous . . ."

"If you're really serious about God and Principle, how would you feel if some hunky brother was always shirtless or in tight shorts? Would you really appreciate always having to fight your attraction? If you were serious about God?"

Her face reddened.

"Anyway, this isn't jail. If you can't accept that, Mr. Sato thinks maybe you need to consider finding spiritual enlightenment elsewhere."

She *harrumphed* off, but her next foray downstairs was in a bra. I think some brothers secretly regretted Julian's piety here . . . we all felt he used Mr. Sato only to deflect our aggravation. Unlike her, some reached a climax in their soul searching and chose to get off the bus. I wouldn't for another 10 months, but then only jumped deeper in for 20 more tempestuous years. *Yay, me.*

The Actionizers Team was supposed to funnel a steady stream of prime member candidates melded with on-the-job (OJT) training. The Moonie's day-to-day staple is witnessing, education, and fundraising. Rev. Moon declared that to qualify for the kingdom every member needs fundraise 3-½ years and witness another 3-½: the *Formula Course*. Its purpose was training members in the spiritual disciplines of living for the sake of others, self-sacrifice, paying our way, spreading DP, and so on. Cynics and haters took it for one more nefarious way he shoveled up millions off the backs of slave labor. It's true his methodologies earned millions to billions for his ministry including his family and lifestyle, but they're still wrong. Religious communities need support their primary albeit net-negative witnessing mission, so there are always those tasked with paying the bills. Jesus' disciples organized this way. St. Stephen was the first fundraiser for Christ.

I don't remember our Actionizing Team being particularly successful. I sure wasn't. The church experienced a drastic decline in membership from the mid-1980s because our local failure was nationwide. The cycle began in witnessers failing to transition meetups to guests to members who began their fundraising duty cycle, which members graduated to witnessing, which members started families and new missions. It was a good plan if it had worked. But too many self-destructive habits got in the way even the Prophet Mormon couldn't have slugged through.

Members got trapped fundraising 5, 7, 10 years often without permission to start a family and long after they'd mentally cratered into burnt out, cynical, self-hating, ineffectual husks and next-gen producers. Leaders cannibalized witnessing for fundraising because intractable bills made worse by graft and stupidity trumped all else. Church centers divided their time between fundraising—mortgage, food, gas, utilities, clothing, health care, etc. were local duties—and witnessing because, without the latter, why do the former? Plus, national headquarters taxed centers to pay its mission expenses. Those hotshots weren't about to peddle laser prints and peanut brittle on weekends to the disrespectful masses like us plebs.

Of my good and bad memories from Boulder, two stand out happy and fond as if only yesterday. One was my first experience with our Korean-derived Holy Day (holiday) celebration tradition. The other set the standard by which I judged the spiritual energy of the church . . . and usually found it wanting.

To prepare for Unification Church Holy Days we set up a Korean style table draped in white about 3×6 feet and 18 inches off the floor in the dining area. We separately stacked as high as two feet apples at each end and, in between, stacks of pears, oranges, grapefruits, bananas, hard candies, tootsie rolls, lollipops, and other goodies. The poorer the church center, the humbler the event. Members trickled in at the cold crack to prepare in silent meditation and prayer.

I thought getting up every day for Morning Service was a burden. Ending my first week of these crack-of-dawn services, a brother now more roughly shook me at *four-thirty* Sunday morning, even the military's traditional sleep-in day.

"Get ready for Pledge," he said.

"Huh? What's that?"

"It's at five. Don't be late."

Same story, different day. Pledge was a condition indemnifying Peter's renunciation when the cock crowed. Our traditions and activities reflected Rev. Moon connecting us one way or another to reversing the process and motivation of the Fall and providential events flowing from it to erase God's grief and sorrow. Pledge takes responsibility for

Typical local offering table.

Peter's, therefore humanity's, betrayal of Jesus. In the Principle, no providential person's actions are ever merely individual. Anyone God uses toward reversing the Fall is standing in for the whole devil-to-demigod universe. We very much saw ourselves representing our nations, races, families, and lineages all counting on us to pull their butts off hell's hearth. Few of us accepting Divine Principle's veracity saw daily life solely in personal terms. Every molecule of our being was living for the greater whole in the context of our individual needs and purpose.

Not purely individual in the world I accepted Pledge on Sunday, the first of the month, and Holy Days. The 12 disciples represented humanity, but Peter was Jesus' chief disciple. His failure wasn't his own personal problem but every future central figure's till indemnified. To symbolically rectify his mistake, we pledged our eternal commitment to God in place of his failure at the most crucial moment.

Pledge centered on the ranking member sitting Korean-style on the floor at the head of the room before a photo of Rev. (and sometimes Mrs.) Moon. On most days, his 3×4-foot pinup relaxed on a polished brass easel at the head of our dining area. It posed at the offering table on special holidays, too. Late the night before a member laid glossy, 6×8-inch cards printed with our pledges across a cleared floor. Members filtered in to an empty card spot right up to and even after 5 AM.

Precisely at five the leader in his (but sometimes her) kneeling position said, "Pledge service for [month, day, year]. Please rise and bow three times."

We stood, placed our left hand palm out against our forehead then our right palm out atop it, bent at the knees till kneeling, and bowed head-and-palms to the deck. We held this position a few seconds then stood for twice more, fingering up our Pledge card at the end. The leader called out the number of each pledge and we read it aloud. The really devoted memorized it. Afterward the leader prayed a representative prayer usually in his or her own language. Some foreigners and fewer Asians considerately used English, as they recognized this was AMERICA.

Prayed out, the leader said, "Please join me in unison prayer." We dropped to knees tucked under butt. The room erupted in soulful, tearful, brassy voices. In Boulder, 50-plus members said Pledge on a good day—thunder scale. We used Principled periods such as 12, 21, or 40 minutes for prayer, 21 the most popular.

Pledge of the Families (this came later as Blessed members increased):

> We families, the center of the cosmos, brothers and sisters, vertically connected and flesh and blood of the True Parents before the new heaven, pledge and swear, before the True Parents to become worthy of possessing the glory of victors by maintaining our position in responsible activities and by observing the family laws and traditions decreed by heaven.

My Pledge (original version for everyone; *Father* references God):

1. As the center of the cosmos, I will fulfill our Father's Will (purpose of creation), and the responsibility given me (for self-perfection). I will become a dutiful son (or daughter) and a child of goodness to attend our Father forever in the ideal world of creation (by) returning joy and glory to Him. This I pledge.

2. I will take upon myself completely the Will of God to give me the whole creation as my inheritance. He has given me His Word, His personality, and His heart, and is reviving me who had died, making me one with Him and His true child. To do this, our Father has persevered for 6,000 years the sacrificial way of the cross. This I pledge.

3. As a true son (or daughter), I will follow our Father's pattern and charge bravely forward into the enemy camp, until I have judged them completely with the weapons with which He has been defeating the enemy Satan for me throughout the course of history by sowing sweat for earth, tears for man, and blood for heaven, as a servant but with a father's heart, in order to Restore His children and the universe, lost to Satan. This I pledge.

4. The individual, family, society, nation, world, and cosmos who are willing to attend our Father, the source of peace, happiness, freedom, and all ideals, will fulfill the ideal world of one heart in one body by Restoring their original nature. To do this, I will become a true son (or daughter), returning joy and satisfaction to our Father, and as our Father's representative, I will transfer to the creation peace, happiness, freedom and all ideals in the world of the heart. This I pledge.

5. I am proud of the one Sovereignty, proud of the one people, proud of the one land, proud of the one language and culture centered upon God, proud of becoming the child of the One True Parent, proud of the family who is to inherit one tradition, proud of being a laborer who is working to establish the one world of the heart. I will fight with my life. I will be responsible for accomplishing my duty and mission. This I pledge and swear, this I pledge and swear, this I pledge and swear.

I especially cherished *sowing sweat for earth, tears for man, and blood for heaven, as a servant but with a father's heart.* The leader concluded softly singing *Tongil* so as to not unduly interrupt those still at it. The racket diminished till everyone was cycling its single Korean verse to English. *Tongil* concluded every unison prayer ever prayed in the Unification Church although in 2003 it seems a dying tradition in the USA, much to my sorrow. Unity is a concept Rev. Moon perpetually speaks to the skies. Unity of one's mind and body—separated and made enemies by the Fall—is the most important precursor to achieving anything for God and humanity. Then there's unity of members and leaders; Koreans, Japanese, and Americans; their nations; humanity with God; love with unselfishness; the world politically, culturally, linguistically, and spiritually. There are endless forms of unity that concern him and members. I adored singing *Tongil* particularly for comfort. I close my private prayers with it. Somehow, this song bound us disparate, frequently warring members together for that timeless moment. It bound us to God, True Parents, humanity, and the incredible concept of a world conceptually one that could be so in fact. This was our Principled responsibility to make happen. Here's *Tongil* in English:

> *Our cherished hopes are for unity, even our dreams are for unity. / We give our lives for unity, come along unity. / Unity saving the people, unity saving all nations. / Come here quickly unity, come along unity.*

A simple song with an easy tune. I misheard verse two as "come on all unity," and sang that. It carried a lot of weight for us and marked the formal end of Pledge.

Our leader faced us. "Please, sit."

He or she sermonized us, passed on news about True Parents, the Providence, something big the church was doing, some inspiration, and any special instructions for the day before dismissing us. We mostly plopped straight into bed till *church* service at 10 or 11 AM. Lots of religion Sundays. Had me longing for Mondays.

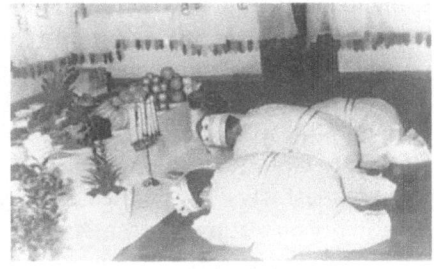

Kyum bae: *full Korean bow. Rev. & Mrs. Moon bow to God and True Parents' role.*

After Pledge on a Holy Day, the leader and helpers traipsed behind the offering table, scooped up handfuls of fruit, candy, and whatnot to let fly at the crowd with varying velocity. I gaped my first time, chastising my lying eyes and head-swiveling through the wild rain of goodies until flying apples, bananas, tootsie rolls, twinkies, hard candy, wrapped cookies, and whatever intersected my noggin and rang up stars. We took a huge delight in this. Throwers sometimes put some real muscle behind it, creating dangerous projectiles. Obviously, some of the fruit was ruined but nobody cared. We were kids jumping and clawing downrange of a machine-gun piñata, throwers aiming to cast a fair amount in all directions. No one duked it out the way they might've at a boozy Mardi Gras parade, and we shared the way we did as wee tykes calculating Halloween hauls.

The offering table's fruit and candy stacks washed the room in bright colors. We snapped photos and there was always a hefty banner on the wall commemorating the Holy Day. The church is big on commemorative banners, especially in old-school Korean heavy on Chinese characters as English is for no-hopers. Then, days or weeks later, our leader passed out similar treats he or she'd caught off Rev. or Mrs. Moon's own offering table if lucky enough to attend. These items were manna from heaven and not regifted lightly. In many ways, we members were humble farm folk delighting in some of life's homeliest pleasures that sophisticated city folk deride as simpletonism. Well, fuck 'em. I found it endearing. It might've helped pull me back into associating with them despite all our conflicts.

My second great Boulder memory was the day several church centers visited and formed my sense of how our movement ought to be. Well over a hundred of us sardined into our dining hall belting out hymns from our church songbook. I was one of five guitarists. Two were whacking 12-strings. The good vibrations we thrummed out was soul-stirring. We played our hearts to heaven, maximizing every ounce of volume short of snapping strings. Early member Dan Fefferman's—barely carries a tune but never let that stop him—1971 epic *Generation of Righteousness* was the centerpiece for me. It's a powerful song about a new generation—*ours!*—rising up from the sinful world to take responsibility for resolving historical sin and Restoring the world to Eden. It marked me for life. We sang with king-sized gusto. Grand Canyon smiles stretched every face.

In the early 1980s the spiritual energy of our movement was frighteningly intense. Members prayed and sang Holy Songs like passports to St. Peter. Groups of brothers—Americans; it was rare an Asian would stand out in the crowd—spontaneously united to harmonize the melody, pump fists, and grunt slogans such as, "Hey! Hey! Heeeey–hey!" Our whole bodies tunefully animated. Such antics arced through our souls and blessed our caroling holes. I never tired of singing. Especially the live concert kind.

Quiet, deeply tearful to strong, vibrant, shouted Holy Songs elevatored me straight to God. Rev. Moon wrote a number of these himself in some of his darkest and happiest days. He penned *Song of the Spring Breeze* during his stint of daily Korean prison torture to recant his faith, recalling the coming of spring and the hope it brings to those frozen in winter's deathly grip. He wrote *Grace of the Holy Garden* in rapturous joy at long last discovering the secret behind the Fall of Man. Japanese members wrote others in sublime spirit during vicious persecution over the 1950s and '60s. Some used traditional Christian tunes or lyrics from Korea repurposed to Unificationism. Contrary to popular belief, Rev. Moon profoundly loves Jesus and expresses it in speeches or Holy Songs he selected or wrote.

In my early days, leaders reminded me that before earning Messiahship—the only one of 300 candidates to survive—he was first loved and saved by Jesus, the first Messiah and only true Son of God. Although we accepted him as the second coming of Christ, we never considered him the Son of God in the way we traditionally did Jesus. This is because, according to the Principle, God very specially set up Jesus' birth over many thousands of years. When Jesus' death nullified the effort, God was unable to set up the same kind of birth for a second Messiah because of Satan's 'invasion' of the Providence that first needed someone to indemnify it. The second Messiah was left on his own to separate himself from Satan just to get where Jesus was at birth, at which point Jesus commissioned him at 16 to fulfill his mission left unfulfilled by the cross. I accepted this because I didn't see any incongruity despite its "there can only be one" *Highlander* overtones.

Naturally, one can see this story as a self-serving example of Rev. Moon's greatness or simply a true enough account of his agonizing early life pursuing his fundamental conviction. I chose the latter interpretation as it's less cynical, thus sensible.

Perhaps revealing Rev. Moon's own doubts, Julian related a story that displayed our Messiah's unconventional sense of humor. He's quite capable of keeping church members in stitches when he wants to. An old Korean with barely passable English making Americans laugh themselves silly is quite the accomplishment.

"Leaders were at a meeting in Tarrytown"—Rev. Moon's Belvedere residence—"and Father was looking out this huge picture window across the grounds. The sun was streaming through the clouds with this spectacular sunbeam effect. Father was just quietly watching the scene, standing at that big window like he does. He said, 'You know . . .' and everybody whipped out notepads and pens because he was about to say something important. You know how he is."

"Yeah, yeah." I'd seen some videotaped leaders' meetings.

"Everybody's perched like birds, just waiting to scribble down whatever amazing thing he's gonna say. Anyway he says, 'You know . . .' and he pauses, looking out the window, 'If Jesus comes on the clouds . . . we're *all* in a lot of trouble.'"

I barked a laugh. "What?!"

"Everybody freezes, pens hovering till it sinks in. Father was watching us with that twinkle in his eye and then the room exploded. Chris, it was hilarious."

"What a mixer. Man's a menace." I laughed for days thinking about it.

Many stories about his suffering also made the rounds. Some of them rang in the ear as purified horse hooey but others carried more fact and sounded plausible. One of the gut-punchers was the Pyongyang police—at the behest of Christian pastors, of all people—arresting him in 1946 for teaching false ideas and corrupting the youth, the same charges (including sexual allegations) they reiterated in 1948 for which the communists sent him to die at hard labor in Hungnam prison. The North Koreans fiendishly tortured him, binding his wrists behind his back then securing them to a high pole so his body weight wrenched his arms backward and up. They beat him in that position with truncheons on the chest, abdomen, legs, and knees, shattering his kneecaps. I wondered if those pastors expected, or knew, that would happen. Some real dirty shit just for being a 'false' Christian by witnessing their congregants away. They made medieval Catholicism proud . . . then ended up in the same pot.

"I stiffened my muscles as long as I could to protect my organs until they broke down to nothing," I recall him saying. "Then I had severe internal ruptures." He sometimes squats speaking long hours when his knee pain gets distracting.

Well, the police realized they were beating a corpse. They cut him down and tossed his shattered body into their snow-covered backyard. Like a good concierge they called his followers to bury him. He claims God met him at death's door.

He recounted Him saying something like, "You've done all you could, my son, and I'm proud of you. You did your best and I welcome you to your place."

Instead Rev. Moon said, "No! I am not done, I can do more! I *will* do more! Your providence must not fail. I will never let myself die before accomplishing my mission." Or words to that effect.

His smart, dedicated church sisters nursed him back to health over about six weeks. His devastated body never fully recovered, to which members who've spent meaningful time with him attest.

Older members told these stories to help us understand he wasn't simply the rich businessman we were now seeing but a devout, impoverished, even starving spiritual man who'd suffered grievously for his faith. Naturally, such tall tales inflated him in our eyes and created the impression he was a martyr to the cause, that his wisdom and plans were unquestionable. I generally accepted them, authentic or not, as valid testimonies to a life I was even then seeing worthy of respect regardless rumors of sexual shenanigans because, ultimately, his life led to Divine Principle.

That stands on its own merits and matters more to me than a Messiah whose only real role in my life is teaching it and Blessing me in marriage to reverse my fallen blood lineage. That's the basic teaching anyhow. Do Christians reject the Bible over mendacious popes and charlatans of the faith? Not as much as you'd think.

I took much of what he said as gospel but never felt compelled to defer to any promulgated infallibility as others did. It was a never-ending source of antagonism twixt me and a church leadership always reinventing itself in his shadow, concluding their own life stories of suffering and hardship rendered them just as infallible and unimpeachable in word and deed.

"If you obey True Father," they collectively said, "then you must obey me, his appointed leader, the same way. This is Principle!"

Yeah . . . no.

"Father lives by Principle," Rev. Moon said. "But if I deviate from it, you must not follow me. Do you understand?"

Leaders always fogged over that part. Of course, they did.

The aforementioned Big Lie now casually reached up and popped me in the eye.

Act IV

California or Bust
Processing Fish, Searching for Truth

he Boulder center's leadership unhappily discovered its expensive former sorority house could literally fall down around our ears.

"It seems the original builder used substandard specifications for the beams and joists holding up your roof," our rental engineer said after his thorough inspection. "A heavy snow could bring your roof down around your ears without any warning at all."

"It's really that dangerous?" Julian said.

"Well, yeah. I mean, one minute you're fine, maybe sleeping at night, and the next you're . . . well . . . you get what I'm saying."

"Yes, I get it just fine."

"No warning at all."

Julian had to see it for himself and scrambled through the attic access with a flashlight. *An adventure!* I pined to get up there, too. Oh, God, I begged.

"I can't, Chris. It's a liability issue, and Mr. Sato would never . . ."

Oh, spare me Mr. Sato! That excuse was pure effluent. Round one: Julian.

Back down to my tapping foot he said, "Damn, Chris, I could *hear* splintering and cracking sounds from the snow load! I can tell you, it scared me. This is bad." He gave me a knowing eye. "I guess we'll have to follow Mr. Sato's plan after all."

Such a complex roof couldn't be replaced in a few weeks nor with people living under it. The Plan was to evacuate a thousand miles to San Francisco. Seemed like overkill to me but a cooler adventure than the attic so, why not? I did boot camp on Government Island in the East Bay and dug the oceanfront locale.

It was a big undertaking. Our leaders decided we'd make the trek by van and rental truck. A call went out for licensed drivers. Well, I can't stand not being on the command deck of an operation. I spent as much of my off-duty underway time as possible on USCGC *Acushnet*'s bridge where I made upper-echelon friends and wrangled OJT on radar, navigation, radio, helmsmanship, and charting. My theory was the more I knew the more valuable, hence promotable, I'd be. The rating I settled on before choosing OCS was quartermaster (navigator). Before trashing my knee, I'd received all the materials necessary for advancement to petty officer third class. The best thing about spending time on the bridge was developing working relationships with the ship's officers, especially the captain, who was on the buddy-buddy side of me. I often visited his quarters for sea stories and good advice, which aggravated our feral XO. As a future officer, the opportunity to observe command was priceless. Most exciting was tracking or preparing to board a suspected smuggler.

USCGC *Acushnet. I barfed aside my captain.*

We'd monitored a suspected marijuana smuggler throughout the night, running darkened ship—no visible lights—a mile or so aft waiting for dawn. On the bridge, a lookout noticed we'd been spotted. Our captain rubbed his jaw and rejected a night boarding. Wait till first light was the consensus.

"It seems to me," I said apropos of nobody, "they can throw the dope off their boat and we'll never notice."

"That's a good point, sir," said our deck division chief bosun.

"How would you deal with that, Chief?" Our deck boss shrugged.

"What if we rig up lights port side," I rather quietly said to my lieutenant friend, "and steer starboard their wake? We'd catch any bails floating by and can snag 'em off the water with a boathook."

Mr. Big Ears officer of the deck said, "Ha! That's stupid. What're you even doing here, McKeon? You're not on watch. Clear the bridge."

"Aye, aye, sir." *Sigh.*

Not 30 minutes later my friend Billy stuck his head through the forward crew lounge hatch. "Hey, man, they're actually rigging lights out there like you said."

I jumped up. "Port side? That figures. Didn't I say it would work?"

"Guess whose idea." I was blank-faced. "Chief's. Takes credit for everything."

"And there ya go," I huffed. This was my first but certainly not my last good idea somebody stole for their own. Maybe I'm an easy mark. I don't often blow my own horn; try not, anyway. I'd long ago taken to heart Jesus' admonishment to do my good deeds in secret, though his holy counsel is golden shit when it comes to career building. We clambered topside where Chief was hollering at this or that schlep on the fantail. Lights rigged high up lit a 40-yard swath of 3-foot seas off our beam and there, floating by like grassy turds, were a series of bails.

Billy punched my shoulder. "Called it."

JULIAN SAID, "WHO'S ever been to San Francisco?"

My hand shot up. "I've driven into it once or twice and have a good mental picture how to do it." True enough, but when we got there my mind went blank on Bush Street and then I was the guy who'd lied on his resume.

"Okay. You'll be one of the drivers. Have the office sister Xerox your license."

My brain high-fived. I was a driver *and* a navigator. Now I had a good chance to avoid being human baggage stuffed in the back of a van. Precious little legroom in those boxy things. The Big Lie started with Julian having me shave my beard.

"That's the standard, Chris. New brothers picked to drive did this morning."

My expression reeked of skepticism. "What difference—"

"It wouldn't be fair if I gave you the privilege of driving while keeping your beard when other brothers who aren't have already shaved theirs off. Consider it a new start for you, like Abraham."

He buttered it thick. That I was screwing them out of something pressed me. The Unification Church was a clean-shaven outfit. No beards, mustaches, or over-the-ear locks. These styles were from our fallen life. Holding onto my beard was tantamount to Abraham refusing Isaac's sacrifice. That one didn't need to change his or her life to be saved but that the Church need absorb the fallen world into it was a total abomination. Such people were no better than Lot's wife. 'Holding onto your Isaac' is satanic, therefore, taboo. In all the videos the church shot during the hippie era, especially during its massive 1976 *God Bless America Rally* at the Washington Monument, every clean-shaven brother is in slacks, button-up shirt, tie, and short hair; sisters suited up in modest dresses or pants suits. This had a lot to do with Rev. Moon's own conservatism. But I think most of our dress code resulted from our controversial movement trying to look unthreatening to mainstream

Getting instructions for our San Francisco road trip.

America the way early rock and rollers donned business attire when unconventional groups were often scruffy, drugged-up hippies and half-naked, sex-crazed gurus. Probably it just made Americans wonder all the more what kind of brainwashing Moonies were using on their ex-flower children to force a traditional dress code when their own parents had struck out.

In sooth, I prefer smooth skin yet razors scrape and nick me bloody. Now I'd joined a stuffy church, a beard was a Sailor Ripley "symbol of my individuality, and my belief in personal freedom." I preferred it over lockstep. Shaving it *now* was a dangerous precedent for my '70s rebel at heart. In the '80s, only our seagoing cousins in Ocean Church rated facial hair. I guessed beardless fishermen lacked a symbol of maritime plunder in the eyes of 'outside members' and Moonies ever aim to impress. Permission to grow a beard symbolized you weren't subject to the stultifying rules foisted on hapless Americans by ultraconservative Asians who barely mustered a real beard between them and their Western lapdogs. It set you apart from the sheep, enhanced your manly sense of stature, got you noticed. You were a bad ass who told leaders how *you* were going to rock; more so, that you were *American*. A goddamn swashbuckler. Some Japanese sisters swooned in the presence of our virile, unJapanesed men. Yeah, man, members like me dreamed of beards.

Being a conscientious lad who appreciated Julian's point on fairness, I bowed to the pressure and traded my lovely, red-flaked beard for a scabby, red-chipped face. And then what happened? Those bastards in charge of the vans wouldn't let me drive after all. They'd already formed a clique. Team captains selected their best buds and blew off Julian's driver plan, at least along the lines he'd promised me. Plus, I was new and newly beardless and not a trusted part of anybody's brotherhood.

This tendency to ignore leaders is a defining personality of the Unification Church in America and certainly its most self-defeating habit. It affects the efficacy of Rev. Moon all the way down to the lowest team captain and group sergeant. Leaders, thereby members, did as they pleased regardless orders or promises. The all-Asian top dogs were the ugliest offenders. They lied to Rev. Moon so often that, absent direct communication with the Almighty, he couldn't possibly know what in hell was happening inside his organization.

They piously beat their chests. "Yes, Father, we will certainly do as you ask."

"Yes, Father," after implementing their own plans (if any) back in their fiefdoms, "we followed your directions exactly."

And when their ivory tower schemes inevitably went to shit then, "Satan invaded through members lacking faith, obedience, and hard work, Father."

Rev. Moon was sympathetic because he routinely laid the same censure on his global disciples not to mention Christianity's faithless haters. A realist, he barked a Rottweiler's lunch in leaders' meetings anyway, but it made no difference. His church self-operated at the molecular level and a fix was now too late.

The bad press brought on Rev. Moon by these independently acting local leaders is astonishing. Stories of 'heavenly deception' in the 1970s and '80s haunted his ministry for years when, contrary to his explicit directions, local Bay Area leaders instructed members that, since Satan deceived Adam and Eve to create the fallen world, it was Restoration to use any means regardless legality—a satanic concept anyhow—to reclaim its evil-got money for the heavenly purpose of reestablishing God's Ideal. This was nothing more than a financially convenient interpretation of his teaching that, to restore the Fall, humanity needs walk a path to reverse it. And what's more reversed than claiming fraud and deceit are a truthy, good faith defense against the dark arts and you'll thank me later? Like any religion, Unification theology is wide open to misinterpretation and misapplication masquerading as special communion with God. Unscrupulous leaders took full advantage of Divine Principle's theological ambiguities, decontextualized speech quotes, and sketchy institutional oversight to advance their cause however they saw fit.

Even more astonishing, those most responsible for this insubordination were the _über_ pious Japanese and Koreans whom Americans were least likely to suspect and, accordingly, their easy fall guy. After all, we were disobedient Christians while Asians were monolithic, hierarchical, consensus oriented, uninfected by Judeo-Christian sin, and (more importantly) obedient. _Not._ A little history straightened me out, as it's equivalent to Japan's Imperial Army dragging its unwilling civilian leadership into its China war then a Pacific one. This habit results in individual members feeling justified copying it for the greater good in ways that best advance their own agendas with mere lip service to the glory of God and True Parents. What a mess.

A friend recounted his experience at a leaders meeting in the mid-1980s that illustrates the tribulations befalling a church ignoring its own teaching and chain of command for expediency. In the 1970s, Rev. Moon created independent fundraising units called Mobile Fundraising Teams. MFT was one of the worst jobs you could get—flagellators thrived—because you fundraised shop-to-shop, house-to-house, bar-to-bar, parking lot-to-lot . . . any place of money to another circa 7 AM till 2 AM. A team captain dropped a member off at x, picked him or her up 5, 10, or more miles down the road in the evening, then rinsed and repeated through other venues till the last saloon exhaustedly bolted its door. Grueling work.

"There was this new member," he said with a laugh leading up to his leaders' meeting tale, "who somehow ended up on MFT. He hated it so bad he chucked all his flowers the first day and used his own money for his supposed result, then reported he'd sold out when he really spent the day skiving."

"Jeez, that's . . . what happened to him?"

"His captain caught him out, saying it was evil what he did since the whole purpose of fundraising is about Restoring fallen money back to God. Using his own money like that was totally fake, so, unPrincipled."

"That's cold." Having by then served on MFT, I felt his pain. "Wonder how long he'd have kept it up before going broke."

"Dunno. I think he ended up leaving. But it was one or two hundred bucks."

Rev. Moon had strictly ordered MFT captains to be good Abels and take care of, love, serve, and live for their (Cain) members' sake. He'd especially charged their teams with setting a good example to the public to avoid more bad press. Captains drove their team around and did the books. It was a great job. They didn't have to get out in every inclement weather to sell merchandise to semi-hostile customers who might brandish knives or brass knuckles for a better deal. The Principle strictly prohibits violence because only unselfish, sacrificial love can remove sin to change evil behavior. This is why Rev. Moon strives to unconditionally love Satan, so that he voluntarily repents to naturally, heartistically return to God.

"Anyway," my friend continued, "an MFT brother named Påvel fell on his captain's bad side, who decided to set an example and beat some motivation into him." Like the army, team captains have to answer for their team's result. They can have tough monetary goals (depending on their local director) that's multilevel marketing on methamphetamine. Hulking institutional let alone salvific pressure weighed upon these captains to perform and I suppose some cracked. "So, while he punched, slapped, and kicked this brother his team members were just sort of milling around watching it all . . ."

"The heck!"

"Too scared, I guess—"

"More like too obediently sissyish."

"—to stop it. I mean, the other brothers could've, one against—"

"Probably figured he was their *Abel* and whatever he did was Principled and Cain deserved it. God, I hate this kind of stuff."

He leaned in. "Thing is, the *cops* saw it. Driving by, I think. They stopped him."

"Whoa! Was he arrested?"

"It was a big stink but I don't think so. Påvel didn't press charges."

I stood up, too antsy to sit. "What a dumbass. I mean, come on . . . ehh, never mind. I guess I get it, the Principle and all."

"Exactly. So, Father gets the story at an MFT leaders' meeting, and he yells at this captain to stand up and then runs him through a cheese grater for it, hollering about the bad press, that he'd set the Providence back ten years all because he couldn't control his temper, put him and everybody in the crosshairs, gave Satan an opening to invade MFT . . . pretty much the works."

"Yet, never makes a difference, eh." MFT captains, center directors, state, regional, and other leaders acted more or less however they wanted with near impunity. That's how the early 1980s American Unification Church devolved into a feudal institution replete with bound serfs, internal passports, and a kind of internal security service fully at odds with Rev. Moon's vision and God's Divine Principled Ideal. Your only way out of an unhappy situation was to leave the church.

I can't blame all this tragedy on leaders, though. Rev. Moon created a command structure with no enforceable rules of right behavior. It's heavy on Confucian ethics of duty and obedience flowing up the chain of command but light on Mencius' ethics that need to flow down, too. I found Mencius a hallmark of General Patton's style that perhaps explains his battlefield success and everyman popularity. Maybe Rev. Moon is the kind of leader so interested in results—he is, but not at his ministry's overt expense—that he turns a presumptive eye to their means.

Beyond duty and obedience is the vacuum of unaccountability. Scratching our heads till bleeding we hotly eyed him promote serial failures, thieves, and scoundrels to even higher, more responsible and powerful positions ever more awash in *cash*. Lack of accountability provided a perfect soil for leaders obsessed with control and personal glory along with a pleasant, it's-only-what-I-deserve lifestyle mimicking their Messiah's. This gradually crafted out of the free-wheeling '70s American church a rigid feudal system that quashed the complaint box till itchy feet voted *en masse* after 1982 and defied every stubbornly deficient future effort to curb it.

BEARDLESS, I SQUEEZED into one of the vans for the long, late spring drive across the western United States to foggy San Francisco. It was a cramped ride. These were ordinary American passenger vans with two front bucket and three rear bench seats. They looked big on the outside but crammed with people, luggage, food, drinks, and knickknackery it was a sardine can without the lubricating oil.

Like clockwork I said, "Hey, okay if I drive awhile?"

"No," my van captain said. "Maybe later."

Bitching to Julian at rest stops only got a sympathetic shrug. "Just suck it up. I'm sure you'll get your chance. Anyway, if you die back there, I'll put flowers—"

Shut. Up. Julian. My motorcycle was packed in a moving truck and I couldn't get it out to ride. That was a real oversight and I was stuck. I sat in my sardine tin quietly stewing over being lied to and screwed. I was mad the whole way.

"You totally tricked me into shaving my beard," I said, still rubbing my scratchily unhappy skin. "Why didn't you just tell me point-blank to do it instead of dangling a driver job? Was that so hard? Did you think I'd bite your head off?"

"You're overthinking it, Chris. Mr. Sato initially gave me the responsibility of setting up drivers, but I can't control everything."

"If feels like you stooped to waving a phony carrot for something as simple as shaving my beard!" I envisioned tearing through the van like a berserker. Really giving them a what-for. And I made sure to vent on Julian at each stop.

He said, "Getting madder isn't going to make it any better. Mr. Sato gave the van captains control. He switched me just to oversight."

"Pfft! Why don't you oversee, then? Every time I ask it's always no, no, no."

"Just pray and keep your cool. It's a pretty small thing, Chris. We'll be there soon enough and we can all move on."

"Says you. *I* feel lied to and cheated."

"Well, that's your fallen nature talking. You look better without a beard anyway."

"Oh, for God's sake, Julian!"

"No beard is the standard. You chose to join, just like me. Roll with the punches, you'll feel better."

"I didn't choose to be lied to. Or used."

He shook his head. Slapped my shoulder. "Yeah, I get it. But life isn't perfect."

I slumped. "Ahh, you're too much."

Julian was an MFT commander before his big promotion to center director. He told rollicking stories of the early '70s. Practically a week or month after joining you could rise to MFT captain, assistant leader of something, center director, even state leader. Almost anything was possible because the church was new, growing fast, spreading through a vast, unMoonied land and desperate for bodies.

He said, "The more I looked at my Japanese leaders back then, the more I saw a sort of colonial lifestyle. Members worked their butts off like old-fashioned natives and leaders lived a kind of high life" dining at fine restaurants, visiting the cinema, playing golf, whatever struck their fancy. "When they made me an MFT captain, I naturally adopted my leaders' lifestyle because . . . why not?"

"It must be Principled if Father isn't stopping it?"

"What's sauce for the goose is sauce for the gander, is how I looked at it."

This is how consistently poor leadership razes Rev. Moon's ministry. The irony is the posh life he lives is the real role model for his leadership cadre. Although he was by then closing in on sixty from the impoverished, Spartan lifestyle of his first 40 years in Korea and Japan, he and fawning disciples were elevating him to new levels of elder privilege in America. Instead, he should've demonstrated an unambiguous example to his second-rate leaders who were then and now clearly having trouble discerning their duty to the church and obligations to members as they keenly nitpicked through every aspect of his lifestyle to justify their own.

Julian continued, "While my team was out fundraising, I'd get bored and pass the time doing fun stuff. I loved going to this shooting range for target practice since Father always said we have to be ready for anything. Sometimes I took my whole team over the border into Mexico on a day trip to eat, hang out . . ."

"Dang, Julian, I never would've figured you for such a—"

"I wasn't the only captain doing that. Some teams spent days carousing over the border instead of fundraising, then lied about their lack of result."

"Son of a—"

"I paid my indemnity. Mr. Kamiyama found out what I was doing and tore me a big new one. He furiously threatened me with regular MFT. I never saw him so mad. He said I'd better just forget all my satanic, aristocratic colonial notions."

"Boy, that kills me." Takeru Kamiyama was long Rev. Moon's right-hand man in America. Son of a Christian minister, he rarely appeared to have more than a passing acquaintance with such notions as agape love, compassion, fairness, and integrity. Vast numbers of American members imagined his grim visage adorning Public Enemy № 1 posters even as they blindly executed his orders like sensible North Korean apparatchiks. "Well, you had it coming. I'm kind of surprised he was so right on the money considering his reputation. But . . . I have to wonder how it would've gone if you were Japanese." A host of variables to consider.

"Don't get me started, Chris."

"But, come on, man. Considering you now, you were some, ehhm, less-than-righteous disciple before I knew you. I'm seeing you in a new light."

We chuckled, but his was more a stammer. "Take it as an object lesson. Anybody can be corrupted even when they think they're not. I never thought I was doing anything wrong because I saw it in my leaders and ran with it."

Maybe so, but his compelling stories made me wish I'd joined up in the wild and woolly 1970s, too. So, it's the greater problem of fallen nature. A lot of people don't know it, particularly most of today's Unificationists, but when Rev. Moon sent the first Japanese to America they arrived with a certain amount of humility. Considering their follow-on abusive arrogance, I found the claim hard to believe. But the way Julian and older members explained their experiences, American members arrogantly abused them first, putting them to cleaning toilets, sweeping floors, being quiet on the sidelines, and knowing their place in the *American* church.

Rev. Moon intended Americans accept them as spiritual elders if not necessarily operational superiors. A critical concept for him is that Korea, Japan, and America constitute the Abel, Cain, and Archangel 'Allies' in Heaven's war against Satan. It's therefore imperative they bury their colonial and Pacific War hatchets to live and work as one family. Sending waves of Japanese to America in the 1970s and again in the 1980s and 1990s was more than importing bodies solely to fundraise and carry on the ministry. It was making a spiritual condition to overcome the past, bring unity, and defeat Satan's efforts to divide and conquer God's army.

Accordingly, he was grinding his teeth realizing how American members treated these early Japanese and reversed the reins of power. They then ran our church with Koreans quietly operating without portfolio and Americans their drudge. True story or not, the Japanese indisputably controlled it by the early-'80s with a vengeance to Imperially remake us by stamping out our independence, individualism and, unfortunately (perhaps inadvertently), our Christian sensibilities.

It may be that Mr. Kamiyama in the '70s was still infused with the Christian principles possibly learned on his father's knee. While he appeared to exercise them on some personal level in the 21 years I off-handedly knew him, many felt they rarely sneaked an official peek from under royal skirts. But a well-chastened Julian grew into a thoughtful, worthy leader in my eyes. I think he was in the minority.

As a young member in the early '80s, I didn't know much about the '70s church and how it impacted the development and behavior of the church in the following decades. But I'd get a crash course in it after relocating to San Francisco.

～

ARRIVING IN THE Bay Area, Julian finally settled me in the driver's seat of our lead 28-footer. At last, I'd got my druthers: legroom for a squealing knee and a steering wheel to helm our caravan across the East Bay and Bay Bridge into the city itself.

He japed about it. "I was saving your strength."

"As an accordion. I knew you were lying, but the small favor thanks you."

Shoulder clap with grin.

Groaning up a gas-guzzling hill in our olympian rental I was unexpectedly hazy on getting over to Bush Street. I needed merely a 2-second glance at the road map. Instead of that, my team captain ordered me out of the driver's seat to plod half-speed himself through the map gripped to his steering wheel.

"You petty bastards are too much," I muttered. "I've every mind to grow it back."

"I heard that." *But what'll you* do *about it?*

By afternoon, we'd double-parked at Bush Street center across from a hospital's multi-level parking garage. Originally a physician's home, its red brick façade reached three floors out of a basement and fairly deep in its lot. We crowded in through its spacious front door set back in an outdoor foyer right off the sidewalk. It bustled with members. Sidelong scrutiny was clarifying our quality of welcome, but they dug up some floorspace. I was discovering a sleeping bag on the floor was the best one could expect in this church. Lower level leaders slept on the floor, too. Center directors and up had their own rooms with beds. Asian leaders didn't join us on the floor from any sense of religious humility, it was merely their cultural norm. I got so acclimated to this style of living that I stuck with it another decade before getting a bed. I've slept on everything: steel, concrete, wood, gravel, dirt, you name it—so fun for a corrupted knee crying for any scrap of horizontal support. I was 21 years old waking up stiff, sore, and tired. Something was wrong with this picture.

Some confusion not unsurprisingly reigned as to our purpose. It may be the local powers realized The Plan wasn't so smart as they'd thought or our higher-ups hadn't even told them. That was frighteningly possible. With time they found us billets across the bay in a relatively new church business, Golden Gate Seafood (GGS). It occupied 6 acres at 1815 Williams in a San Leandro industrial area. Older, white, single-storey admin offices fronted the street. It rose to a 2-storey section housing a fish production line, massive drive-in refrigerator and freezer, plenty of junked equipment, wooden pallets, oddments, and rubbish scattered around its overgrown back area with loading dock and a centrally situated cavernous, angled-roof warehouse near-on three storeys. My sense was of a bankrupted fish production and wholesale operation coming back to life under new management.

In the 1980s Rev. Moon hadn't yet developed a hefty American business presence. What he had mostly plied their trades in and around national headquarters in New York City. Developing GGS and International Seafoods of Alaska (ISA), for which I'd later work, was part of his grand strategy to not only improve his cash position but to substantiate his belief that the oceans were the future of human food production. With seafood development he pushed innovative (crazy, I thought) programs like shark jerky and fish powder as a third-world flour substitute.

He has three broad visions for the oceans. First, working on the sea builds out character and spiritual discipline—the last unspoiled frontier, after all; survival of the fittest. An avid fisherman, he insists ocean members feel his fisherman's life up close: rise at 2 AM, out before dawn on a 28-footer built in his Master Marine factory in the 'East Sun Building' near the projects (a member shot and crippled despite out after dark a no-no) in Queens, NYC, then fishing into the evening. An onerous regimen. He seemed to burn through energy to spare (with patchy naps) but ordinary mortals staggered to their sleeping bags like the walking dead.

Rev. Moon held annual tuna tournaments out of Gloucester, Massachusetts, the national headquarters for Ocean Church and home to his first commercial seafood ventures. He endured massive protests and angry confrontations with locals as in Bayou La Batre. Enterprising members won over the opposition or tamped it to a grumble not because townspeople discovered Moonies weren't ravenous baby stealers, though it helped, but because he pumped boatloads of (probably Japanese) money into their economy. Who wants to look a gift horse in the mouth? Cash, and lots of it, is often his personal lord and savior when it comes to defusing controversy. Hence, MFT's pressure cooker.

Second, many have died at sea, their bodies ever unrecovered. He says these folks are restless in spirit world, unable to happily live their new spiritual lives. Our duty as Restorers of humanity includes not leaving them out of salvation's loop. He primarily founded Ocean Church as a means to put Divine Principle to sea and restore these pitiable souls back to God through education. Who's ever thought of that? or ever worked to remember and save those who perished at sea in storm and war? or sets spiritual conditions through the difficult seaman's life to restore every circumstance of their Fallen demise? Well, it convinced me. My heart thumped hot for his Ocean Church motivation. With beards, it had me from *Aarrgh, matey!*

Third, Ocean Church trains its members in fishing and seafood. As he segued from Ocean Church to commercial fishing, these mainly American members were a pocketful of Japanese for him. Unfortunately, he seems to place only moronic, inexperienced Koreans and Japanese in charge of these ventures who doggedly run them like church centers, inevitably draining bank accounts and headcounts. Some brothers secured their master's licenses to swagger on deck as Unificationism's first boat captains. They cut teeth running 28-foot 'Good-Go' sport boats then graduated to 240-ton commercial trawlers also clapped together by Master Marine without much concern for internal watertight integrity, not that boat builders anywhere cared. Rev. Moon values these officer-class boat captains and generally treats them well, although he seldom spares the rod; he grinds down leaders more than us blue-collars. Well, perhaps *grind down* is too negative a perspective. One can just as well argue he trains the former more rigorously than the latter, hardly different from the military or varsity sports. Seldom does it seem to pay off, however.

The GGS mission, as best I could discern, was wholesaling seafood to remit cash to the church. The biggest monkey wrench in that plan was the very nature of a

Unification Church business. It wasn't enough for us to work 18-hour days for no pay. We also needed fuller indoctrination. Leaders accomplished this in two primary ways. First, company executives operated as center directors who treated us, their 'employees,' as missionaries. Second, team leaders supplemented by our executives and dignitaries like Mr. Kamiyama dosed us with daily lectures.

These were diverse: theology and biblical history, sex, the importance of not swallowing semen because, as Mr. Kamiyama drilled us one day, our bodies develop antibodies to kill the foreign material that'll leave sisters sterile. Odds are it's never happened in human history, so he was talking

Golden Gate Seafood.

shit to maybe put a damper on his anxiety over any oral–anal runarounds to the Principle's strict no-fall policy in our lax business environment. I didn't know but took him seriously. Infertility is a no-go in a church that glorifies marriage and family as the holy God–couple pact (infant adoption is a sterile Blessed couple's workaround) that determines whether we glory in heaven or wallow in hell.

I never figured out if he was talking to sisters or us brothers, too. As explicit as he waxed over heterosexual lapses, he left homosexual mischief aggravatingly vague. If underpenetrating a vagina isn't *really* sex, therefore 'the Fall,' then is a male blowjob *really* gay or worse than sucking up a Slurpee? Beyond personal preference, we just didn't know and knowledge was everything in this Divine Principle business. Our routine lectures were interesting, informative, and felt vital to our spiritual lives. But the material some of our leaders spouted had them looking unhinged.

To fully appreciate how destructive it is for company executives to treat us 'employees' on the job like church members in a center, you have to remember how authoritarian and feudal the church had got by the first half of the 1980s. A leader's word wasn't just law, it was *Principle*. Top brass generally ignored complaints up the chain of command even if your object of grievance was American and his boss Korean or Japanese. Like doctors, cops, politicians, and Catholic priests, they never break ranks unless a problem threatens a higher-up.

This sop mindset in a business environment where 'employees' have specific functions to perform erodes our ability to accomplish our duty for the good of the business. Top leaders often sabotage a company through their penchant for arbitrary and uninformed decisions based on theological interpretations and seat-of-the-pants thinking as well as a thorough disregard for the advice—regardless how informed by knowledge and experience—of regular (particularly American) members.

Take the demise of Sun Tours, a bus firm the church started in New York City in the 1970s. It developed over ten years through great hardship and the personal sacrifice of all involved, and was one of the few successful church businesses in America. It profitably rented tour buses to everyone except the Unification Church, which rarely if ever paid its bill. Disregarding many of its members' salient but proletarian advice, its leaders drove it into bankruptcy obstinately pursuing their 'providential duty' to support the transpo needs of its messianic welsh. The mindset was that Rev. Moon would never stand for one of his companies failing from doing its providential duty to subsidize the church with buses, but he proved them wrong. The saddest part was the members who, through no fault of their own, lost paying jobs in a church community abjuring any charitable system of help.

GGS went through its own trials and tribulations—fundraising teams spent years paying down its debts—and survives as of 2003. It frustrated me working a business lacking a clear demarcation between religion and work. Even so, we increased its operational tempo delivering fish to customers. Our tripartite setup consisted of a 91-foot trawler, a factory, and a marketing man. The Bayou La Batre-built, 240-ton *Green Hope* was one of the church's first ocean-going vessels but left out the one thing I consider nonnegotiable: watertight doors and bulkheads below the waterline. There was no law requiring it on fishing vessels, so the industry didn't bother. The deficiency was glaringly highlighted in the mid-1980s when these vessels moved from the staid gulf coast into Alaska's fiendish waters.

Matthew—later killed, I heard, his body lost at sea—skippered *Green Hope*. In 1981 it slipped at Sausalito, a small hippie-cum-yuppie hamlet anchored near the Golden Gate. Intent on developing my skills and usefulness to Rev. Moon, I grabbed every opportunity to learn. I mastered the forklift as the plant's operator and unloaded the flatbed when it arrived with pallets of fish, ran the loading dock area, and handled odds and ends. Getting stuck on the fish line, gutting and chopping all day long on a cane, wasn't for me by a long shot. As in the Coast Guard, I made every effort to forge working relationships with managers to net every leadership role I could. Forklifting was definitely blue collar, but I had more authority (thus, free time) on the shop floor than general laborers. Had to start somewhere.

Bored with all that, I pressed for truck driver in my portfolio. GGS taught me to drive our 20-gear, twin-axle flatbed and offered me 18-wheeler training. I rumbled our forklift on it north whenever Matthew radioed his imminent arrival. His crew offloaded and I zipped $4 \times 4 \times 3$-foot plastic fish tubs across the pier and hoisted them onto the flatbed for the better part of a day. Late-afternoon I'd cruise an hour or two out of Sausalito via the Dumbarton Bridge and south through the East Bay's heavy traffic to San Leandro alone with myself warbling John Denver tunes.

Young as I was, I could try anything awhile for a net benefit, but truck driving wasn't how I envisioned my life. I remembered Mark Twain's alleged advice to Jack London when he was aching to be a great novelist: "Go out and experience life." Here I was, taking that advice to heart. But it wasn't only broadening my experience and improving my general skills that I loved. It was the freedom of my own company. No one ordering me about, telling me how to think. On the freeway I was my own man making my own decisions alone with my thoughts. Not like other members invariably under this or that leader's thumb, glued to some hated job, reviling the shit they were taking with positive energy. I could do multiple, essential jobs and escape by truck for most of a day. I had to rush the fish so they didn't spoil under the hot afternoon sun despite their ice beds, but mornings I took my own time heading north. The more time to myself the better, I'd come to think.

The Coast Guard worked a theoretical 8-hour day with the other sixteen to myself (especially in port, if I'd lived ashore). In Unification Church businesses, I worked 14–18-hour days, participated in mandatory morning and evening services, Pledge, and a Sunday service mercifully shorter than a church center's to get us back to work all the sooner. Dad had insisted we attend Sunday Mass and Holy Days of Obligation and were heathens if we didn't, but the Vatican couldn't have cared less either way. Up till the Moonies, that's as religious as I got.

It was during these highway treks that I noticed the road signs getting harder to read. *What in hell's wrong with my eyes?* I kneaded and squeezed them.

I remembered my ophthalmologist in high school opining, "Growing six inches in one summer is too much for anybody." My 20/10 Mark 1 eyeball wasn't keeping up with its socket. "You're probably headed for myopia and maybe astigmatism, but I don't see the need for glasses at this point unless you really want them."

"Nope!" Perish the thought. I promptly forgot about it.

My oldest sister Senna wore glasses. Gazing from the passenger seat along North Turkey Creek Road back in 1973 or '74 I said, "What's blurry vision like?"

She explained something about unclear and dark, but it was too surreal.

"You see two of something? It's all smeary?"

"Something like that."

"How's that even possible?" Imagination failed through my twice better than average acuity. I had the vision of an eagle.

"Just be glad it's not you."

Now, my growing headaches and fatigued eyes prompted GGS to send me to an eye doctor. I darkly walked out with dilated eyes behind black plastic-and-cardboard sunglasses and shiny new John Denver spectacles in hand.

"This is awful," I grumbled, slipping into my new vision on the loading dock. A hammer punched between my eyes. "Owww!" The world shot through my brain with a fierce clarity. I staggered. Yanked them off. Squeezed my eyelids hard enough to break. How viscerally bright and painfully intense the sunwashed green leaves and colorful flowers! My eyesight had gone like Senna's so gradually I'd never noticed. I shook my brains. Sucked a humid lungful. Eased it out. "Right, let's try this again." I shaded my eyes. Now the ground seemed to move, curving upward at the edge of my corrected vision. I took a few steps and tottered, alternately putting my foot down on air and planting it on concrete sooner than expected. The world felt off, an optical bowl. "This sucks ass!"

I would've cursed the sky but didn't want any stray members reporting my Navy language. I bemoaned my fate and imagined how I'd be grist for the mill in a post-nuclear dystopia if I ever broke my lenses. I wore them only driving and even then only when a throb kettle-drummed up. Now they're on every bloody minute.

I PARKED EACH truckload at the back of the plant where I deftly unloaded the pallets of still-cold fish onto the loading dock and used a hand-push forklift to carry them inside to the waiting processing line. As they filled up the freeze trays, I forklifted them into the freezer. All in all, I was having a good time at GGS.

A goateed Louisianan maybe in his 40s handled our marketing effort. With some gravity he said, "I'm the legendary pirate Jean LaFitte's direct descendant . . . and the first one in my family to have never murdered anybody."

"Holy shit!" somebody said.

My artsy friend said, "You have my attention, sir."

"Did they reject you for that?" I said.

"Let's just say it was a rite of passage, and they weren't happy."

"Crime family politics," my friend joked outside his office in low tones.

That same somebody said, "You think it's really true?"

I shrugged. "That would be a pretty scary family. Who's the lucky lass Father Blessed him to? Maybe some scary Russian, ha ha!"

"Think he'll tell her?"

"Is he even Blessed? Does anybody know? I didn't see a Blessing ring."

"Maybe it's just his way of impressing us with the no-fuckery policies he enforces around here."

"I'm listening, you mokes. Don't make me come out there." We gave him a wide berth. Mr. Kamiyama had nothing on this guy.

He decided GGS needed a new logo after we arrived and commissioned any of us who could draw. I tried my hand but was rusty and not much of a logo creative anyway. My artsy friend who'd joined up with me created a cowboy riding a roped wild tuna in a splashing sea. He surrounded it with the ubiquitous red *yin-yang* arrowed circle used by virtually every Unification Church business. It denotes give-and-take action and circular harmony. Prodigious with Divine Principle. His first version was a realistic nineteenth-century cowboy with a wildly flowing handlebar mustache. It looked fabulous. But our reformed pirate of a marketing guru wanted something more cartoonish. My friend retooled it and GGS adopted it for its official logo. The company was still using it as of 2003.

GGS logo on my hat, 1981.

In the end, GGS didn't compensate him a promised dime, urging him to donate his work to the company, "Like a good member." Well, it was *our* company very loosely speaking and we put our blood, sweat, and tears into it. We were usefully young, impressionable, and idealistic. We believed with little scrutiny most of what our leaders told us. Some wised up sooner than others, but all of us fairly early on came to realize, somewhat cynically, I have to admit, that the church and its businesses were nothing so noble as we'd thought. Still, most stayed because of Divine Principle's power in our hearts, Jesus' suffering, and our deep desire to see God's salvific work accomplished on Earth. Maybe to score a spouse.

Many 'outside members' are surprised to learn not only how much Rev. Moon loves Jesus, but how much he communicated that to us lambs. His sermons during the '50s and '60s are filled with Jesus. And not just his personal love for Jesus, but the incredible value and sacrifice of his life and ministry. As big a screw up as Rev. Moon appears to me in 2003—his messianism notwithstanding—I've never questioned the sincerity of his faith in God and Jesus. His and our leaders' failures and foibles weren't something most of thought should erase the Principle's beauty and goodness nor discount its truth any more than the failures of Christianity over 2,000 years invalidate the gospels and the sacrifice of the faithful.

Green Hope caught and delivered our fish, I trucked it to the plant, and our LaFitte family reject organized the look and feel of the company and successfully marketed our products to wholesalers and retail consumers. All in all, we were successfully getting it off the ground and I felt more or less excited to be a part of it. All the same, I felt separated from the religious roots that had catapulted me into the church, had infinite questions about the Principle I had yet to hear answers to, didn't like the authoritarian nature of our leaders or their businesses, and was beginning to bore with the work. Soon, these feelings would come to a head.

When we'd moved to GGS from Bush Street, we needed a place to sleep. Having no room in their local center, GGS graciously allowed us to sleep in their warehouse. I didn't know how legal that was, but it was certainly interesting. Centrally located in the building, it was maybe a hundred feet square under a three-storey, angled roof of metal girders. Banded stacks of unassembled cardboard boxes, some as high as a couple storeys, occupied a large section. Somebody had forklifted these giant towers of cardboard to forge a right-angled corridor about three feet wide that led into a central courtyard surrounded by these overarching cardboard buildings. It was here we brothers bivouacked. Against one warehouse wall a stairway led to a large room on the second floor overseeing the warehouse floor (though not our courtyard) and that's where the sisters bedded down in comfort. If there's one constant in America's Unification Church, it's that sisters get the best living quarters, no questions asked. We slept in the cold, drafty warehouse surrounded by cardboard. They slept in a heated, carpeted room. Who says chivalry is dead?

In days, I decided sleeping on bare concrete like a Tsarist peasant was for the birds. I needed something befitting my self-importance. Eyeing my options, I carted my belongings up the sheer, 11-foot face of a cardboard mountain. On top, a two-pallet section formed an alcove maybe 4×8 feet. Stacks of cardboard rose up another storey on three sides. My view overlooked our courtyard and cardboard jungle. I laid out my sleeping bag, used an empty box to create a bookcase—Bible, *Divine Principle*, my growing multi-volume *Way of Tradition* collection, various odds and ends—and surveyed my domain. It was the only space of its kind.

Julian disapproved. "Suppose you roll off in the night? How would that look?"

"I'm a Rocky Mountain boy, Julian. I'm not falling off anything." I waited for the inevitable shoulder clap and his jovial *If you die, I'll put flowers on your grave*, but not this time. "Come on, don't worry. It'll be fine."

He grudgingly accepted my *fait accompli*. Round two: Chris.

I happened to have carried with me, of all things, my two fencing foils stuffed into my Coast Guard seabag. I hooked their tips and pommels as crossed swords behind the metal bands holding one of the cardboard pallets together overlooking the only egress to my aerie. I was the envy of the brothers, although being closer to the ceiling of a non-air conditioned space was much hotter over the summer than the courtyard. Such was the price I happily paid for my special, leaderesque digs. In the colder months, I thought it was a bit warmer than the concrete even with cardboard laid down to insulate sleeping bodies from the cold floor. In these early church years, nothing was more important than a properly established berth. Sleeping bag. Bookcase. Location. Had to have 'em all or it just wasn't home.

LIFE AT GGS went pleasantly on through summer and fall of 1981. Mr. Kamiyama periodically cycled through to impale us on lectures covering sexuality, gender relations, church standards of behavior, Rev. Moon's great sacrifices for us all, secular and biblical history, current affairs, and so on. The history was especially interesting and enlightening to me, though we all sometimes had to juxtapose his church perspective with reality so we could tell when the lectures faithfully represented *recorded* history versus remolding it to suit his viewpoint.

I got more sex education at GGS from Mr. Kamiyama and friends than ever in my life. His co-ed sex lectures often had me pretty uncomfortable; hell, downright embarrassed. Graphic descriptions of penises and vaginas offended some American sisters who made their displeasure known. Japanese sisters shyly giggled and lowered their faces while sometimes cutting eyes to nearby brothers. He usually spoke in Japanese while Peter Spoto or someone else translated to English. We had to patiently await translation while the Japanese were laughing their guts out over something ribald. I'll hazard the translations failed to match his words. Five minutes of Japanese in 30 seconds of English seemed flatly unrealistic, especially with the Japanese in stitches while we Americans weren't even sure we'd heard a joke.

One thing about these Japanese, they could wax unabashedly visual. Maybe they picked it up from Rev. Moon. He can be crudely vivid about sex. But I think they're just less culturally delicate than Americans. His 1990s sexual purity teaching went by *Absolute Sex* when it was *de rigueur* in American politics to chant abstinence. But he'd unequivocally denounced 'free sex' all through the sexy '70s and STD '80s, educating us on the true, God-ordained function of our sex organs, how precious they are, and how carefully we should use them. He was supposedly famous for dropping his trousers—not the full monty—to emphasize the salient point in earlier speeches. I'm not sure members know anything about that reputation these days. For us, Rev. Moon was the most sexually liberated prude we'd ever seen.

Ostensibly, the reason for leadership's perennial sex lectures was twofold. First, an unPrincipled love relationship between Eve and Archangel Lucifer that culminated in sex precipitated their Fall. Lucifer was God's servant but Adam His son. God destined them to marry only with spiritual and emotional maturity. The reason is the life-altering power intrinsic to popping your cherry that can derail the power of Principle. It affects everything about you, primarily your heart's ability to give and receive Godly love. I could easily believe this because it had already happened to me; perhaps any ex-virgin can attest to this truth. Sex outside a heavenly blessed marriage before internalizing Principled love renders one's desire for it a selfish pursuit and is how Rev. Moon characterizes fallen relationships. Our miserably screwed-up world arose in Eve corrupting her Principled love in wrong sex with the household help, then turning deceitful tables on Adam to save herself.

Second, leaders were preparing us for the Blessing of Marriage, the crux and fulcrum of our spiritual life. It's necessary we comprehend our personal, familial, and public responsibilities before our awesome transformation . . . not that any of us grasped even a tenth of it. Yet, it's the most sacred event in a member's life. The ceremony infuses spiritual and physical ritual that 'changes fallen blood lineage.' More than roping a spouse, we'd be stepping above and beyond the highest threshold ever attained by fallen humanity—even Jesus—into a hitherto unknown realm. Such unprecedented milestones are more gravely significant to Rev. Moon than our merely getting hitched. Notwithstanding our heartfelt awe as a part of something humanity's dreamed of since the Fall pitched us out of Eden, securing a spouse who'll (presumedly) never dump us is easily one's paramount life event.

Rev. Moon calls Blessed couples the highest state of existence in the universe. It reverses the age-old supremacy of angels over mankind and Restores us as God's literal children and His true heirs. This motivated Lucifer's treachery in the first place. He couldn't stand Adam more beloved of God than he, the brilliant, first-created archangel. Behind our bawdy lectures lurked Rev. Moon's potent pining that we not throw proverbial spanners into his fragile world Restoration machinery by fucking around with unPrincipled sex.

He said, "If you fall after receiving the Blessing, that is the absolute worst. Do you understand? God can never forgive such a betrayal. You cannot undo such a mistake. Satan himself will be restored before God even thinks about forgiving you breaking the Blessing."

"Why?" many wondered, affronted. "Satan's the worst betrayer and Adam and Eve fell when they were pure."

"Because they did not know Principle. You do. Falling after knowing Principle is worse than their sin in the Garden."

Seriously terrifying, that. Each of us silently swore we'd keep our sex organs firmly zipped in except with our spouse, when—*if*—we ever got one. Unfortunately, some members forgot their oath and his grim warning till the next morning.

Aside from lectures and work, I sometimes got into spats with my bosses, though it would be six more months before a member struck me for it. Like most, I steered clear of contention with Monsieur LaFitte after he dished his buccaneering family's tea because, who could say when heritage would trump common sense? In late summer or fall he decided our non-murdering if somewhat piratically homey church wasn't for him and split. I heard he later changed his mind and returned in glory to GGS. In these days, members came and went with some regularity, especially in the looser business environments. Contrary to the sensational press, the Unification Church never forced anyone to stay. It not only encouraged undesirables to beat it but outright forced some out. Sometimes, like me, in the arms of an escort.

Before departing Boulder for the Bay Area, Julian and I had been chatting about care and consideration and how I perceived its lack was making us all a bunch of in-n-out burgers for God. I said, "I don't know, man, sometimes I think nobody cares if I stay or leave, especially Ginny."

Julian lightly thumped my knee and sat back. "There was this one time I felt totally wrecked when this brother I really cared about left the church in New York. I went out literally all day looking for him, hoping I'd persuade him to come back."

"That's seems pretty extreme."

"His spiritual life was at stake. I prayed and prayed but never found him."

"What happened?"

"I was all upset with Mr. Kamiyama about it. I said I'd try again in the morning."

"Did you?"

Julian's lips whitened. "No. He said, 'Don't worry, he made his choice. There are some lineages that God doesn't want Restored. You need to let him go.'"

"What! He really said that?"

"Yeah, I was surprised, too. He said, 'Julian, some people have ancestors who've done such terrible things to God's providence and His champions that God prefers their lineage dies out.' I took—"

"What if they repent? What if this brother came back? Would Mr. Kamiyama—?"

"Of course, not. God told the Israelites that if a person turns to Him with real repentance, He forgives everything. But if not . . . then not."

"Everything's so life and death around here. This guy ever come back?"

Julian shrugged. "When a member chooses to leave the church and turns their back on the Messiah, God's ultimate champion, then God withdraws His mercy and forgiveness and leaves that person to his chosen fate."

"Jeez." Later I realized he was quite likely talking about me.

PETER SPOTO WAS a fast-rising star in the Japaniverse. I was amazed to see him understand Mr. Kamiyama's Gatling-gun lingo. I'd never seen a Westerner speak Asian and found it interestingly weird. It occurred that I, too, needed Japanese if I wanted to enter the upper echelons like Peter. By now it was crystal clear who had the power in this operation, and it wasn't Americans (Koreans were the power behind the Japanese throne, but I'd yet to see one in the flesh).

The Orient was mysterious. My experience was limited to that one Bird's Eye freeze-dried Chinese noodle dish I'd choked down in high school. Exactly why the world mocks American provincialism. But, hell, I grew up in the Rocky Mountains. Scandinavia West. Colorado is roughly old West Germany's size but its population was 96% smaller and a seventh New York City's when I first moved there in 1971. Unlike Germany, surrounded by similarly populated nations gabbing a multitude of languages, only sparsely populated English-speaking states with a side of Spanish surrounded Colorado. I thought it snobbish of Europeans to chide our intercultural deficiencies. Where in hell were we going to expand our horizons without hauling ourselves 1,000–8,000 miles? The best we could do out West was Spanish or hang at the rez . . . except neither was in my vicinity. Until 1979, only one black ever lived within a noticeable distance and I'd never seen an Asian. So, yeah, I was a bumpkin except I read a lot and my parents were globe-traveling sophisticates.

In addition to opening my eyes about God, Jesus, and Christianity let alone the major religions, the Unification Church sucked me into an international organization filled with alien languages, foods, cultural sensibilities, and attitudes. It wasn't easy getting along. Asians, black and white Americans, Europeans, South Americans, Africans—practically every culture on Earth paraded through my church life. We had a few Europeans at GGS. The rest were white American and Japanese.

One morning at breakfast I slung into a chair at an oblong conference table we'd set up as a front-office mess hall. I tucked into a bowl of cereal and milk. A catty-corner Japanese brother chopsticked down a lump of cold, white 'sticky' rice with a raw egg he'd scrambled in under an icy hunk of breaded fish from last night. I didn't say anything but I was thinking and it was, *Blech, how's he stomaching that?*

My face or vibe may have betrayed me. He eyed my innocuous Kellogg's through thin slits down his nose and jabbed his chopsticks at it. "How can you eat *that*?"

"How, indeed?" I swallowed my opinion with a dripping Raisin Bran chaser.

I WAS FEELING unhappy in the church and toiling away at GGS on no clear track. I needed to get away. I talked it over with Julian, and he talked it over with his leader. They tried talking me out of it but my ears were palms pushing them away.

"I just feel the need to leave. Maybe I'll come back after I think things over." But that was only a sop to shut them up.

"You know how to reach me," Julian said. "Don't be shy."

"Me? Pshaw! Nah."

What I was feeling was a need to validate the Principle in real life and reconsider my future. I couldn't do that surrounded by my object of analysis whispering its glory in my ear. Loathe to give up an exit door outside Colorado I might later want, my Honda CB750-4 was on its kickstand in a quiet corner of the plant. Without it, leaving San Leandro would've been a chore although I was certain Julian would've had GGS fork over bus money. I checked the oil and tire pressure, tightened the chain, and gassed up. My seabag went tightly lashed to the backrest. I bungeed my guitar case to it atop the right passenger footpeg like a Rubenesque smokestack.

"See you, Julian. Let's keep in touch, anyway." I gripped his hand.

His face seemed etched. He squeezed my right shoulder. "You bet. And if you die on that thing, I'll put flowers on your roadside grave."

"Ha!" But I imagined he was feeling New York City all over again.

I waved, goosed the throttle, and bounced. There's nothing like a road trip. I adore the open road. If Russia ever gets its act together, Americans by the tens of thousands will flock there on bulging wallets for the fabulous road trips to be had from Moscow to the Bering Sea. On the highway I felt freedom cut through me, liberating me in severing some invisible bondage. Maybe I'd been in one place too long. I'm the sort who dreams of what's over that next rise and ever hopeful it's better and more adventurous than the flypaper holding me now. Sometimes I think I'd drive to *nowhere* so long as I was leaving *somewhere*.

"You're a true *wandersman*, Christopher," Dad said. "Just like your father."

"You? Huh." But he'd lived round half the world. I reckoned so.

I rice-burnered through the Sierra Nevadas and dropped into the Great Salt Flats east of Elko, Nevada. That frying pan is so crosswindy I had to lean 20–30 degrees into it just to shoot a straight course down the road. When an upwind truck blasted by in the opposite direction, the wind disappeared and I'd careen for it. I had to be careful I wasn't taken unawares or I'd end up minced meat 'neath their 18 wheels. The first 25 miles or so was calm. I settled back on my seabag, boots cocked up on the highway pegs and hands occasionally clasped behind my helmet LA-Z-BOY style. I steered by gently shifting my hips in a slow-mo *haole* hula. Then winds kicked up and managing my bike got as onerous as punting a skiff through heavy seas. The last 60 miles to Salt Lake City left me slumped and sleepy.

Scenery's the whole point of my road trips, so I shunned interstates to ride the two-lanes. East of Salt Lake and high up in the Rockies on US 40 I ran out of steam around midnight; the last thing you want to do on a motorcycle is fall asleep at the handlebars. There was no such thing as all-night gas stations out here in 1981, so I decided to rest before my engine coughed dry. On the graveled shoulder, I cozied up to my ticking engine and dozed fitfully till morning for a nearby mom-and-pop to open up. November was biting hard at 8,000 feet. I shivered awake in cycles, giving up as dawn barely lit my surroundings. Stomping to warm myself, mom or pop finally flipped their 'Closed' sign. Gassed up, I blatted on.

I stopped at my college friend's 6,500-foot high winter A-frame in small-town Dillon for a few days, then headed for my parents in Ft. Collins. I wasn't sure what I was going to do with myself. I'd been recovering from knee surgery when I'd joined the church only months after my discharge. So far, I hadn't considered much.

What do I want to do with my life? What's my vision? My dream? How might I pay rent? How will I eat?

I had no idea and worried this bone my whole 1,200 miles. I'd planned on Coast Guard OCS with a 20- or even 30-year ride if it was worth it. My pileup ended the dream. I had to move on. Home with my folks in late December 1980, surgery in late January, recovery at Mona's in Denver, joining the church over February–March, and now back in Colorado for November had been a whirlwind but a circle from nothing to nothing. I'd been intent on college but couldn't figure out my major. I'd surrendered to geology. The bloody science was too harsh. I wanted to write and do fine art but couldn't see how I'd ever make a farthing outside Park Avenue's advertising, which doesn't do *art*. I dropped it almost as soon as I'd reconsidered, keenly recalling how one comic strip rejection slip from the *Rocky Mountain News* in seventh grade had discouraged me despite craving to be an artist and writer since elementary school. I figured I'd hang out with the folks to think it through.

I savored my full-throttle freedom. Yet I felt unhappy, even uneasy, away from the church. I blasted Japanese Holy Songs from my tape player. Maybe it was the novelty of the language, but I found them particularly beautiful and listened every day. Baby sister, now back from Holland for college, was a bevy of snidery.

"Sounds like a bunch of mindless babble to me."

"You think it's any better than Dutch?"

"Duh."

"That's 'cause you speak it. But it's guttural and uglier than Japanese to me."

"Pfft. You don't know anything. Turn it down or off. It's grinding my ears like grunting animals." However annoying the Japanese, here I was defending them.

What was it about the church that kept my mind on it? It wasn't 'brainwashing,' whatever that was. No, it was something shifting my heart. The story of humanity itself that Rev. Moon so unambiguously larded on my mind. Of fabled Adam and Eve, immature with hearts of innocent goodness corrupted by a self-serving swindler whose only aim was destroying God's family. Of a saga potted in blundering mistakes corrupting love and perverting our collective sense of place in the world. I resonated with their joy of ideal life and despair in reality. I'd lost my own true love in college, my sense of self and place forever altered, even corrupted. *Could I truly love again? Ever be untainted?* Two brief girlfriends since, but I'd ached for my lost fiancée and helplessly compared them to her. *How pathetic my self-defeating rut!*

I needed to begin life anew, direct myself to some higher purpose. No mere sinecure built of straw or sticks inside an idyllic white picket fence but a life well lived in brick. The more I reasoned it, the more attractive Divine Principle appeared. It was a way of looking at the world, history, and especially our future that wasn't only desirable but eminently sensible. It seemed to give me a directed sense of place in life. Through it, I'd found inspiration and motivation to rise above my ignoble self for something greater than physical needs and wants.

Hanging around my parents' condo, I closely observed my nearby family. The church taught us the Principle wasn't a local dogma applicable only amongst us members, but universal. Whether or not we know or even like it, we're all of us subject to the Principle because it describes reality acting in our lives since conception. It isn't the opinionated theology of one more Christian denomination. No, Rev. Moon plugged away at us, it's the actual story of God, Creation, His ideal, mankind, the Fall, and Restoration. It explained human reality, the process and methodology by which we live and die, love and hate, achieve greatness or descend into darkness. I'd mainly left GGS because I needed to find out on my own, in my own way, if it was true without them breathing down my neck. I needed some me-time.

The Principle's description of human nature is as true of Unificationists as it is of 'outside members' and I'd never heard it so topically analyzed. Catholic catechism didn't teach that we exhibit a nature other than 'sin,' religion's catch-all term for every behavior it disapproves. Rev. Moon got specific, explicating our four 'fallen natures'—failing to take God's viewpoint, leaving our proper position, reversing dominion, multiplying sin—stemming from Adam and Eve's Garden experience before, during, and after the process and motivation of the Fall. It was cohesive.

MY REVERIE SCRUTINIZING my family for the fallen dynamics I'd learned in the church lasted a couple months before events caught up with me. I was twigging to aspects I hadn't recognized, to be sure. The more I observed them, the more sense the Principle was making. I detected its narrative all around me. It progressively persuaded me it was a valid teaching I ought to incorporate.

The time spent at my parent's condo was the last freedom from Unificationism I'd get for 36 years. I'd satisfied my own mind that Rev. Moon was a *bona fide* spiritual leader and resolved to reverse myself and return to the church. If meeting the Moonies was an axial moment, my reflection period was its culmination. My path in life wasn't fated. However,

Home from GGS, my pen-and-ink of Turkey Creek house on the wall.

as with all gifts from God, my past need rise up and bite me in the ass before finding my higher plane. Repentance and restitution afore redemption. No shortcuts. *Sigh.* One afternoon I returned to gag on Dad's expectant air in the living room.

"Chris," he ominously said, "going through the mail today I accidentally opened a letter meant for you."

"Um, okay..." My mind did a Formula One lap through his pregnant pause, wondering what axe might fall.

"Do you have a child we don't know about?"

Oh, God! My heart rocketed to my stomach which leapt into my throat. *That axe!* Here was Mistake Numero Uno home to lay a sulfurous egg.

In early summer 1978 my college fiancée Diane dropped me like a rotten potato in a Dear John headshot through my future. My inconsolable tears were the headwaters to my river of sorrow. With my usual secrecy for private business, I'd confided in none but my best friend, Lance. When a cutie-pie named Monica hired on a month later at the Denver real estate firm I summer-jobbed for as a receptionist, a beguiling attraction rebounded me into her arms and a quiet love affair. I didn't reveal her, nor the impolitic four years she had on me, to my parents for quite some time.

We enjoyed a wonderful summer. But I couldn't help comparing her to Diane. It was practically axiomatic. That I couldn't move on to embrace another woman on her own terms without regret gnawed my soul. Sure wasn't fair to Monica. Yearning for Diane colored my relationship with her.

Once, I truthfully answered her curiosity. "Well, if Diane did come back...I don't know, I think I might feel compelled to go back to her." I was such a heel.

Then in late summer she said, "It's well after ten. You want to stay over?"

I squeezed her hand. *Hell, yeah!* But before we could deep dive I said, "I told my dad I'd be back before midnight. Last time I got home later than promised he chewed me out for making him worry. So, I better—"

"Sure. It's the right thing to do. No problem."

He picked up on the second ring. Probably waiting by the phone. "Hi, Dad. I just wanted to let you know I'll be home a bit later than planned. I met a friend and we're gonna hang out awhile longer."

It didn't take him a second to add two and two. "I don't think that's a good idea, Christopher. You'd better start home now if you're going to make it by midnight."

I pressed Monica's phone to my ear hunting fleeter words. Here I was, 19 years old—man enough to vote and kill in our next throwaway war—and Dad's demanding I hie home lest I fall into sin. Besides his prescience so obvious to me *now*, it may seem comical *then* at the tail end of hippiedom's sexual revolution that I was deathly afraid of him. Still am, in some ways.

"But—"

I felt his headshake on my end. His tone wasn't fucking around like I wanted to. "No buts, just come home. It's the right thing to do. I'll expect you in an hour."

Damn. I dumped her phone in its cradle. My ears burned with frostbite. She took my lame explanation in good humor. "See you next time, then. Drive safe."

"Yeah. Goodnight." *Chaste kiss.* I cranked my Opel to life. Driving away, the invisible bond now anchored to her bed tugged hard.

My father notwithstanding, we consummated our feelings and carried on quite happily a couple months. In September 1978 I got cracking on Western State's third semester 300 miles west of Monica. Diane did, too. It wouldn't be the first time I stupidly wedged myself between one woman I truly cared for and another I adored. I spent considerable effort failing to woo her back. A sickening image, now. 'Winning' a lost lover seems an arrant folly. I'd learn a woman who gets out doesn't want back in. Move the fuck on. Why pine o'er my fount of rejection? I may as well suck cyanide for the almond flavor.

In tenth grade my supreme mistake as a jealous boyfriend pushed away my girlfriend. It's possibly the most futile emotion I ever caught myself up in. It's naught but trouble and despair and turned me the mean fool. Learning my lesson and ravaging its spirit, I never caught it twice. I take the hint she's the wrong woman or I'm the wrong man. I'd only accomplish killing myself in one way or another. I now agonizingly discovered the fronds of this bitter truth with Diane. I had to move on. Despite my lesson, profound grief at losing her cut harsh. She was my first head-over-heels love. I prized her as

Budding artist. Leopard, 1978.

the jewel of my soul. I'm not sure I've ever loved another woman with the passion and abandon I felt for Diane. If truth is the first casualty of war, trust dies in failed romance.

You can't ever love like it's your first. Friends said it's always this way. Later, I saw it as God's way of ensuring the strength and vitality of love and marriage. Two people experiencing their first passion together builds a powerful bond not easily broken. I felt it with Diane. I'd loved my twelfth grade girlfriend. Goofed away my virtue my third week of college. But 'first love' was bound up in Diane. Emotionally, I'd given her my virginity for a persistent pull to her barbed-wire heart.

Jumping lovers breaks down the restraining nature of 'first love,' yet engulfing emotions endure. It seems the worst surrendering your deepest vulnerability to one who's lost theirs, as he or she abandons you with little emotional effort while, for you, it's a holocaust. Diane gave her 'first love' to me, yet transcended our bond to please her church. I'd tried all summer and fall to 'fix' us. At one point, I thought she'd fallen back in love and spread my *joyeux noëls* to my closest friends. Alas, I was fantasizing. It was a bitter pill and a blistering lesson and ran me off to sea to escape my torture in the tentacles of our happy Colorado memories.

My second year at Western State, competing emotions for Diane and Monica were pulling me apart. I'd placed myself in a pickle. Without my parents' knowledge, I periodically commuted weekends to Denver to bed Monica. In October, our mixed feelings came to a head in a heart-to-heart where we decided that, since both of us felt impaled on guilt over unwed sex, we'd keep it celibate till marriage. One last roll for the road and I twisted home through the mountains in lighthearted song buggering the speed limit. I'd dodged a bullet. Feelings bobbed on a calm sea as steely bands of fear fell away to unbarrel my heart. My chest was big sky country as all things Denver faded in the rearview. Sanguinity pursuing Diane's return thumped harder as I closed in on Gunnison. Unfortunately, our timing sucked.

Monica phoned my dorm room in November. "Chris, I'm pregnant."

"Uhh . . ." *Stunned* can't convey the earthquake tearing through me. An iceberg at my desk, eyes riveted unseen schoolwork only a second ago my biggest concern.

Our disaster sledgehammered my heart, mind, and soul down through my ass, the floor, and deep into Hades to Vulcan working his fiery forge. This was 1978. Free sex may have swept the land but 'respectable' folks weren't making babies out of wedlock without shame, trauma, and castigation. No way in hell could my parents know. I was resolute I'd handle it myself. Like the man I was.

I confronted my choices: marriage, adoption, abortion. The courts had legalized the latter and Monica was 24. But killing the baby to solve our conundrum was anathema. We instantly ruled it out. For all my regrets, at least I don't carry *that* guilt. The growing cadre of Blessed members had questions. Rev. Moon finally published his stand on the issue in Rev. Chung Hwan Kwak's 1985 liturgical guidance:

> God personally attends the creation of new life . . . The mother's womb grows only the spirit base, not the spirit itself. Abortion destroys that spirit base; therefore, the Unification view is that abortion cuts the relationship this unborn child has with God and God's divine love . . . We do not have the authority to interrupt the physical order of the cosmos based on lack of finances . . . [nor] if couples feel that their relationship at the time of conception was not very loving . . . The life of the mother is considered more precious because she does possess a spirit . . . we do not view abortion as a sin, as it relates not to a violation of the spirit self but the physical life . . . [and] is appropriate if the child was conceived through rape, incest, or any circumstance involving a break in the spiritual order. (*The Tradition: Book One*, c19)

If true, I presumed it was God's way of ensuring spirit world didn't fill up with deformed, unsurvivable, or convenience-aborted fetuses who'd never be nurtured in the soil of the physical world to develop eternal life the Principle claims essential to God's ideal. Abortion didn't consign a child to a purgatory of unconsciousness. It was death, total and final. Rev. Kwak at first appeared to place Rev. Moon squarely in line with abortion advocates, which surprised the hell out of me. But he clarified he wasn't, exactly, by limiting it to "a break in the spiritual order." His caveat seemed a thin tightrope to juggle for a balance bar.

Back at her place in Denver, Monica unhappily and somewhat angrily listened to me say, "I don't think God wants us to marry each other."

"Why? How can you say that?"

"I've been struggling so much with our relationship, even before we decided to be celibate . . . it's not only my sense of God's way. Sex was feeling wrong because I kept feeling pulled away. Who, but God? I'm sorry, it's hard to explain."

"*You're* sorry. *Phhh!*" Air huffed through falling locks.

I'd thought long and hard over my choice. I couldn't shake something telling me she wasn't the right woman, that it wouldn't turn out well. I attributed these deep, inexplicable feelings as the voice of God. For once, I obeyed it. I don't think she was ready for a baby, either, though she was certainly ready for marriage. Supremely disappointed with my decision, she seemed to face it with equanimity and stoicism; we were civil and caring throughout the process. We agreed in writing to split the $12,000 hospital cost and adopt out our child. I was at sea with the Coast Guard earning my share of the bill the day he was born. I don't regret not marrying her. But when I did get married with children, I realized how much I'd lost walking away and regretted losing my chance to raise our son. In any event, she'd rejected weekend fathering. For her, it was all in or all out.

Following Dad opening my letter she said, "I don't even want you around him anyway. That so-called church of yours is an evil cult. They'll tell you to steal him away for it and you would! Because you're brainwashed just by joining."

"That's your Midwest fundamentalism talking, Monica. They're not like that at all. And I'd never do any such thing anyhow."

"So you say."

"If you knew anything about me or my church, not to mention how up-and-down I am with them, you'd realize the last thing they'd ever want is *two* of me."

Her head was nonstop *no*. "Pay your support and stay away from my baby."

"Damn, Monica." My first run-in with Moon Derangement Syndrome.

I'm glad he wasn't adopted, though, because she built a relationship with Mom. They visited often and I never lost track of him. Today, we're working at a relationship over rocky ground which never would've happened had she followed through on our bargain. At the time, I just didn't know what to do over an out-of-wedlock pregnancy with a woman I sensed God was rejecting for me. Religion can be a useful and comforting thing, but often it severely limits one's ability to arrive at sensible, practical decisions for fear of heavenly punishment.

STANDING BEFORE MY inquisitorial father, my throat vice-gripped and a Nazgûl ringwraith's icy blade in my gut, I felt cheated by her decision to keep our baby when the nurse plopped him on her breast. We had a deal! The envelope my father had opened could only be Monica demanding money. Every muscle trembled through hot flashes. *How am I going to explain this?* My father was thunderbolt-chucking Zeus. I was moments from being a lightning fritter.

"Well, Dad," I said uneasily, striving to think fast through chilled molasses, "it's like this. Remember Monica? In Denver that summer after Western State?" His face flushed with, *Okay . . .* "We decided we didn't want an intimate relationship so we could be more in keeping with, you know, our Christian principles."

"I'm still not hearing an explanation."

"So, we chose to be celibate . . . but, we made a mistake. It turns out that a week before our commitment she'd already got pregnant and we didn't know. We'd agreed to put the baby up for adoption, but now—"

Mom sparked. "Adoption!"

My eyes flitted her way a second then back to roaming. "I guess she decided to keep it." Bullets of sweat oozed through my shirt.

"How'd you even pay for it?" Dad said.

"We split the cost and—"

"That's why you went into the Coast Guard?"

I needed some breaths here. "Yeah, I mean, I guess. Because Diane left me, really. But I needed a steady job."

"Oh, for goodness' sake!" They'd toiled wheedling me out of military service.

"I had to do something!" And I was glad I'd ignored them, regardless.

"Why didn't you tell us?" Bushy brows rose with pity in a plea to heaven.

"Because I—"

He glanced Mom's way. "Maybe we could have helped."

"Helped?" *You mean with the cross or the nails?* But he wasn't looking angry so much as perplexed. Hard to tell. He could've been charging up a thunderbolt. I scanned the letter. "Oh! It's not a lawy—*damn!* It's a child support order!"

"We know."

I stomped a circle while Dad pondered and Mom played distracted cheerleader from the sidelines. My *written* deal with Monica had released me from *ever* having to pony up cash. I slapped paper to tabletop.

"Fuckin' lawyers," I mouthed. "Some dirtbag helping a woman who didn't even keep her agreements screw me for keeping mine." *Hell, she's four years older than me . . . who should've known better, here?* I was just as poor then as now and feeling scandalously cheated and undone by her. "How can she do this to me?"

I still lacked any appreciation for the profundity of bringing a child into this universe. At the time it was more a problem of a unilaterally broken covenant, not a responsibility I bore. I wasn't feeling paternal because I'd never met my son. Monica's maternal instincts and single-mom pregnancy were absent in me. I felt disconnected as men usually are till pre- or postnatally experiencing their baby.

"How old is the child, Chris?" Mom said.

Math was radioactive. "Uhh . . . 'bout two and a half, I think."

"So, for—"

"I didn't say anything to you and Dad because I was afraid of your reaction. I mean, I felt totally ashamed, like I'd disgraced you." And I did feel ashamed. My eyes were on the floor, walls, ceiling, glass door . . . anywhere but Dad's face. Shit, I was scared of what he was going to do after he'd worked up to it. I couldn't even pace. My feet were entwined in the rug that fought my urge to flee.

As usual (and to my invariable chagrin), he surprised me. His voice dropped an octave of energy. "Well, your mother and I thought all along she was just looking for a husband. Getting pregnant is a woman's way of convincing a man."

"Really?" Was he defending me? *Understanding* me? My mouth shuttered with amazement, both from his calm attitude and that a woman would stoop that low.

"We never thought you should marry her," he continued, sympathy and softness in his voice now. "We agreed she wasn't right for you." Mom's face said, *Yeah.*

Holy shit! Stick a finger in your ear and dig out the wax, man. What a reprieve. My panic faded. I could swallow. My heart wasn't snapping at my ribs. The adrenalized trembling eased. I was cautiously feeling a *man* talking things over with my dad. It felt so odd. Zeus wasn't somebody you just chatted with. *Wonder if a thunderbolt's burning his back pocket, though?* It was hard not thinking it.

Zeus was speaking again. "What's your plan? You'll have to get a real job now."

"Good question." What *was* my plan? I'd only just determined to return to the Moonies. How could I do it with child support obligations? Would they even take me back, being such a sinner and all? If there was one thing the church was a stickler about not happening, it was sex outside the Blessing. I think this was the beginning of a pattern of previous behavior derailing future success. *She really torpedoed me, dammit.* My plans were birds on the wing, now.

Before a person receives a gift from God, wrongful behavior needs restoring. The church calls it *indemnity*. If God provides a gift to the undeserving, the unrepentant, the *unreconstructed*, Satan can accuse God of violating his own Principle. A person, who for St. Paul is always undeserving, must pay a price to avoid Satan's accusation. In my case, leaders would argue I couldn't be a member without restitution for my sexual sins and bastard child let alone the greater apostasy of rejecting True Parents and GGS for Satan's world. How might they take my mea culpa?

I called Julian, still toiling away at GGS. "I've had a lot of time now to think things over and observe Divine Principle in my family, Julian. I'm convinced. I want to rejoin the church, if that's possible."

"Oh, wow, that's great!" I caught his bubbling excitement. "I'm happy to hear you coming to your senses."

"Ha ha. But, look, there's a fly in the ointment." I gulped a lungful. "I just found out I have a 2-year old son from a surprise court order for child support."

Silence. "Ohh, man. What?" He blew a heavy breath. "I'm stunned. How—?"

"Don't make me explain the nuts and bolts, Julian. It was before the Coast Guard. She was supposed to adopt him out. I'm as shocked as you are."

"Are you, though?"

"Come on, man. You saying it's impossible?"

"No, no, I'm just . . . never mind. I'm sure the church will cover it since you'd be a full-time volunteer. It's not something that comes up much. I have to confirm with Mr. Kamiyama. I'll call you back. Hang in, there, Chris. Things are looking up."

Yeah, up and up. "Looking forward to your flowers." He was chuckling when I darkly tossed the wireless phone across the sofa.

Some hours later I was pulling hair and griping at the TV when the phone trilled. Julian said, "You ready for the news?"

"Just tell me, for God's sake." He's such a cheeky—

"Mr. Kamiyama says you can return to the church and he'll pay your child support." He sounded triumphant.

"Wow. How much persuasion did it take?"

"He knows you're a good member, Chris, regardless your latest mess. I just reminded him, is all." Maybe I *was* still one of his favorites.

"Well, then. In like Flint!" Alone in my folks' condo, I sank in their plush living room sofa. I'd been dreading his callback because no news is quite often bad news. I imagined Mr. Kamiyama telling me to go to hell like that New York City brother—I bet Julian thought I'd forgot about that—although his *yes* was likely on account of the movement's fanatical proselytizing. It's all about bodies and fodder's fodder. Head and shoulders melted into the soft cushions, my body curling into peace with—

"There's just one condition." My heart fibrillated. *Ugh, here it comes.*

I tried for airy but snarked, "Which is what?" My mouth was sand.

Rev. Moon's concept of paying indemnity allows no room for 'special conditions,' at least in my vulgate world. The Unification Church offers no free lunch even if leaders fix their own. If there's one soul-chilling hammer of death in Unification theology, it's indemnity and its inescapable dread. After all, every person desires free forgiveness of sin. No conditions. No payback. God's pure grace. Christianity's modern take on Jesus' sacrifice is God's forgiveness of sins past, present, and future with no more required than basic repentance atop the pillar accepting Jesus as one's personal Lord and Savior. Easy-peasy heaven.

But sin is a convoluted mass of worms gnawing the roots of a person's heart, corrupting his or her ability to love and live unselfishly, eternally severing Man from God. How could mere repentance and acceptance of Jesus or even Rev. Moon resolve such inner corruption? Impossible. Repentance is merely the first step that makes the following ones possible. First, you repent. Then you *act* to undo the spiritual chaos your sin created. That's the rack of indemnity. No doubt, in Mr. Kamiyama's view, I'd sinned in leaving True Parents in the first place, not to mention the spiritual trouble I'd got into since. I was a sinning apostate.

"Mr. Kamiyama doesn't think it's fair for you to come back to GGS"—as LaFitte's privileged family reject got to—"and live with the brothers and sisters here after you just walked out of the church." If Julian has one talent, it's temporarily masking the pain of bigger bad news with a smaller shiv in the spare ribs.

"Isn't this really just a sort of vacation, though? Like a sabbatical?"

"Funny. He feels you need to make some spiritual conditions to properly get you into the spirit of the movement."

"Exactly what condition is he proposing, Julian?" No airiness now.

"The indemnity kind. Your favorite." He was selling an oil-burner to a tire-kicker and making me pull teeth for it. I was circling my index finger till he meandered to the punch line. "He says you can come back and he'll pay your child support obligations but wants you to work MFT in Los Angeles."

"MFT!?" My ribs caved. I jumped, swallowing my tongue. *Shit.* Shit! *Shiiit!*

Everybody knew fundraising teams worked like dogs day and night, pressing people for money like Buttercup's Sicilian when death is on the line. My orders to MFT were a mule cart to Islam's Saharan salt mines and the very last thing I wanted to hear. Mr. Kamiyama couldn't have picked a better tool to divide the sheeps and goats in my heart. What a crafty motherfucker.

Mom and Dad's sofa was a bed of nails, now. I hopped up and paced. Even so, it didn't take me two seconds to decide. "I want to live Divine Principle with True Father and that's my absolute bottom line, so . . ." MFT couldn't be any worse than the Coast Guard, could it? *Think of it like the Army without all the noisy bullets.* ". . . okay," my bravado the last chip bouncing on a Vegas roulette wheel. "How bad could it be? It's fine. I'll do it."

"I knew you would," he said, maybe a little too smugly. "I told Kamiyama that, too. I said you'd agree because you're one of the best who's joined in a long time."

That was some unexpected praise . . . and a verbal K-Y for this MFT backdoor action. My eyes fell on my walking cane. "Wait. What about my knee? Will I get to fundraise from a stationary spot? You know, like sitting in a chair?"

Julian was dead air. "Well, Chris, you're kind of lucky Mr. Kamiyama is willing to take you back. I mean, *you* walked out on True Parents, not vice versa."

Well, fuckity-fuck. *That* did not sound good. Maybe I was too optimistic about my circle of hell. How could I fundraise on a cane? I'd only further destroy my knee plus add my now-involved hip, spine, and shoulder to the casualty list.

"In all honesty, you should be grateful for the chance to start over. I'll tell them about your knee, but you shouldn't expect any special treatment. I mean, this *is* an indemnity course for you." This wasn't Julian my friend but Julian my *boss*. And if there's one thing about the spiritual path his Jesuit soul firmly esteems, it's that hardship is good. He chuckled. "You should expect to suffer."

Another of his famous one-liners to buck us up. He let loose with it all the time in the old days, always ending with his signature, "Don't worry, if you die I'll put flowers on your grave, ha ha." And so he did here.

"All right. I'll give it a go on those terms. But I'm not crippling myself, either."

"That's fair. And I won't let 'em cripple you, either." He laughed. "Remember, you joined under me. I've got your back."

If that was an admission of care and concern, I had my doubts how far it would go. It was something, anyway. I hoped he meant it. He explained how to pick up my plane ticket to Los Angeles and we hung up. I put down the phone with a growing nervousness taking over my body.

"Man, Chris . . . what are you getting yourself into?"

Was this another mistake, like joining the Coast Guard or sculling through Monica's bed? I wished for a crystal ball right then. Thank God my parents weren't there to hear my compact with The Cult. They'd have only heard me stupidly joining the French Foreign Legion just to pay my bills. They certainly didn't applaud.

MFT aside, casting the die to resume my church life somehow worked to calm my soul with a sense of following Jesus' footsteps through the sand. It may be true I'm incorrigibly earthy nor a featherweight screwup either, but the right spiritual path was ever heavy on my heart.

Well, I wasn't sitting around to second guess. Immediate preparations to leave got me busy. I annoyedly met with *secretary* Monica and her *boss* the attorney—now I got it—and negotiated a more practical

Boulder, changing my '70 Opel's speedo cable.

$300 per month. Then my beloved Opel Kadette and Honda CB750 went on the block. I donated the $1,500 proceeds to the church.

"It's only fair," Julian said, "since the church is paying your child support."

"All of it?" *That's five months'* I'm *paying for!* "How 'bout spending money?"

Heavily, "It's a spiritual offering, Chris. An indemnity condition. And you don't need spending money where you're going."

"Not liking the sound of that." He snorted. I caught my flight to LA and the storied Teams for a new, if scarier, life.

Act V
On the Mobile Fundraising Teams
Money and Lies

My flight was a bore. I flipped through the in-flights and gazed across the dry, unfruited plains then later marveled at the absurd magnitude of *El Pueblo de Nuestra Señora María la Reina de los Ángeles de Porciúncula*—LA, to us modernistas. I was born and best bred out west in rural America. My first time seeing Old Shaky was after Coast Guard basic training when I'd flown in from Denver, where I'd been visiting my folks, to visit my sister Senna. It seemed hardly five minutes after the pilot recommended we *ooh* and *aah* out the right side of the aircraft down Las Vegas' glittery cleavage that LA's lights rolled over the horizon. Maybe 30 more twinkling-'neath-our-wings minutes to LAX. An alien world, a forbidden planet. Denver seemed a petite cowtown.

Shirley met me at LAX. I remember her as faintly rotund in her mid- to late twenties. She was an MFT captain—*my* MFT captain.

In our phone call Julian said, "Can you work for a sister as team captain?"

I'd rolled my shoulders. "Why not? I had—*hmm*—one female supervisor in the service. Rank and competence matter. Don't care if they're girls."

"Okay, good. Some brothers don't handle it well. Some flat out refuse."

"Like Japanese?"

"Well . . ."

The public never seems to know these tidbits about the church, only wild-eyed cultic tales. The Unification Church was a marvel in the 1970s and 1980s because it put women and what few blacks it let join into positions of—granted, lower—authority. In an age when women had only just shucked their Catholic *mantillas* at Mass and the Mormon Prophet, on the heels of America's tardy civil and voting rights acts, had a revelation that blacks should participate as full members in the Mormonverse, the American Unification Church was already a national leader in the realm of gender neutrality and equal rights . . . such as it was.

Shirley was happy and friendly. I liked her right off. Blondish hair lightly hung at her shoulders, curled up at the ends in that *avant '70s* curling-iron fashion. When we'd climbed into her blue Ford van in the dark parking lot, I rolled down the window first thing. It was a warm, humid night and I was simmering.

Speeding down the highway she said, "The other members aren't going to feel hot like you, so make sure you roll up your window when they get in."

"Why?"

She seemed genuinely surprised. "*Because*, you're used to colder weather. But for everyone here, this is a cold night. They're used to hot weather."

"Cold?" I was incredulous. "It must be better'n seventy!"

"That's hot to you, but cold to us." She was polite, I gave her that.

"Okay." I was stupid but got the hint just fine and laboriously cranked up my tall window. The interruption of cool air over steaming skin left me in hot flashes.

Yuk. LA's gonna suck.

Our *tête-à-tête* was typical of Shirley. She was an understanding woman; kind, considerate, and gentle. I liked her but felt put off by the sense of authority and command that swirled around her . . . like an *officer*. I had no trouble working under her, regardless. Whatever my shortcomings with authority, an inability to work for women wasn't one of them. Unlike stereotypical men, I never had to *learn* to work with women. It came natural. My only female superiors had been the woman owner of a bonded courier service I carried cash for in Denver and a Coastie third-class. I couldn't find any reason a woman boss would be problematic unless *she* made it so. I rather preferred women anyway. They weren't usually into manly putdowns and violent threats, and were a helluva lot better to look at. If I was going to spend time around a boss, better a sensuous woman than a manly man.

Not that Shirley was necessarily voluptuous. But I preferred her over the male captains often infused with a need to demonstrate they were gloriously zealous and in charge. Nope, a motherly touch wouldn't produce an inferiority complex in me. And if abused, my reaction wasn't of a woman abusing me, a man, but my boss abusing me, her human equal. I don't see the *gender* of authority, only *authority*. With Shirley, I didn't see myself working for a woman but a position filled by a woman. Whatever conflicts I had with her I took as conflicts with her position. If it was personal, as with some of the male captains, it boiled down to her exercise of authority as with any man. I thought I'd started MFT on good footing.

A quasi-military organization, the sometimes hundreds of Teams were a weird anomaly in our church. MFT expected absolute obedience. Ecclesiastical love was suspended. You might forget you were in a church altogether. Your business was making money, not hounding salvation; your pious work did that. The hierarchy denoted itself by military rank. Team leaders were *captains* and we rank-and-file were expected to all but salute them. In Japan, we'd probably be in uniform.

"Why you say captain first name?" a Japanese brother said, collaring me in the center after overhearing me with Shirley.

He's chiding me? "Why not? She's my sister."

"No. She is captain! You disrespect her and team member."

"What, you think you're in the army? Last time I checked—"

"Yes! This is MFT! We—"

"—it's a *church*."

"—are True Father army! You call her 'captain,' now."

I peered down from my (happily) God-given vantage. "You call her captain"—*and can suck it*—"and I'll call my sister Shirley, and my brothers—"

"You Americans. Always so full . . ."

But I'd tuned him out. A Julian shoulder clap that wouldn't knock this flyweight over but still rattle his chains and I bustled off to something else. Enforcers like him stuck their heads in everybody's business. I discovered not everybody likes Mr. Egalitarian, but I didn't care. Well, I did, but not really. I followed Shirley's orders and that was my duty. The rest was ego. I'd made every effort to address my Coastie superiors in the least militarily respectful manner possible, avoiding every use of *sir* and rank possible while avoiding accusations of insubordination. This wasn't disrespect but my insistence on respect for my own self as I saw myself. And this church would be no different. Nobody was hectoring much less menacing me into obeisance. Simply because it *was* a church demanded a familial collegiality even while recognizing levels of responsibility to accomplish tasks as a team.

I've always made fine distinctions that help me fraternize with my superiors while not compromising their authority or my duty. I reckon it's not most folk's forte, hence the rules and regulations militaries (and churches) impose to maintain good order and discipline. Maybe this Japanese brother needed *captain* in his mouth to crowd out what he really wanted to say.

Above team captains were *commanders* managing squads of teams like army platoon leaders or company-grade officers. Before I'd met Julian in 1981 he'd risen from the rank-and-file to team captain, then to MFT commander. Because of that experience he was, at the very least, well aware of what he'd put me into.

Next up were divisional staff controlling territories. At the top of the heap sat Mr. Kamiyama controlling the entire MFT organization. National in scope, each MFT command operated in their assigned territories. Periodically, these characters raided across boundaries either because their territory was burned out (over-fundraised) or just to piss off the invaded region's general leader by lapping his money bowl.

The church operated two types of MFT commands, urban and cross-country. Urban teams limited their operations to a particular city. In my case, Los Angeles. We never left the metropolitan area. That's not saying much, I suppose. It's darn near 100 miles north–south by 80 miles east–west. Cross-country teams hit the road for weeks at a time, traveling small town to small town. These crews left one bench seat for mostly awake members behind the driver–passenger seats. Behind these they built a multi-tiered, honeycombed plywood structure holding fundraising product and 'Tokyo capsules' for members to sleep like worms.

Cross-country MFT vans were probably the most unsafe vehicles on American roads during this time, though Ralph Nader never cared. In a crash, the interior of the van was a deluge of flying objects from heavy boxes of pictures and wooden frames to buckets filled with water, crates of flowers, personal effects, unbelted human bodies, and all manner of bric-a-brac. An MFT crew was 6–7 members and vans were cramped to bursting. The captain drove. The next honcho got the passenger seat as navigator, relief driver, and deputy captain. The bench seat behind held three shoulder-squeezed Americans or four Japanese if rib to elbow was okay and 1–2 ass-dying on deck or coffin-bound in back.

MFT policy forbade the navigator sleeping while the van was moving. The rule was two people awake and alert at all times to prevent the driver falling asleep and killing his or her crew. This was the number one cause of MFT accidents owing to the long hours: 5–6 AM till 2–3 AM six days a week including reveille, preparation, religious services, and so on. Sunday was usually reduced work though still exceeded 12 hours. Like frontline soldiers, we catnapped whenever and wherever possible. I knew members who'd survived van injuries and rollovers, though none who died. But brothers and sisters did die: crushed, thrown, lacerated, mangled, dismembered, decapitated; accidentally or purposefully run over, dragged, smashed; maliciously raped, beaten, shot, stabbed, strangled, disappeared. Not many, considering our numbers, but each one hurt. Members drove too fast or inexperienced, sleepy, praying not paying attention, yelling at the kids in back, ignoring red flags; ordered or stupidly going into dangerous areas, stepping into traffic, expecting God to nullify recklessness; or in other nonconscious ways brashly asking for trouble. And we all carried wads of cash with the media's bombsight on our back.

The only way in or out for those in Draculine repose was through the rear doors. I tried it once. Besides a poor fit, I got so claustrophobic with safety worries as to abjure it forever. I suppose if I'd trusted the driver like I did Mom I'd have fretted less. But images of rolling off the highway in a flaming van trapped in a plywood coffin collapsing around me as the van crushed and flung its guts to the heavens was too much not to dwell on. Strap me like a buck to the roof if need be.

These two MFT types came about because of the financial structure of the American Unification Church. The major source of money for operations came from fundraisers. Japan was a secondary source but most of this funded national headquarters in New York City, Rev. Kwak's World Mission Department, floated businesses or new acquisitions like the *Washington Times*, and bad debt. We plain folk never saw a dime of the Japanese loot Rev. Moon made a big deal about to the media (while excoriating our lackluster American work ethic for lackadaisically falling behind his cash masterclass) as a way to show how much salvation he was pouring into America when nobody else was stepping up. To be fair, Japanese capital funded tax-paying businesses serving his ministry such as the *Washington Times*, the New Yorker Hotel, and religious, scientific, and philanthropic organizations whose purpose was to spiritually succor the world from an American tit. The *Times* is the most obvious example, pushing his conservative thinking into our leftist-propagandized public consciousness to restore America's Godly greatness.

The fundamental financial framework of the American church was a bit like America's local-state-federal corpus. Local churches were responsible for their own support while providing a percentage of their take to their state headquarters. This housed itself in a local church center which had the dubious honor of providing for both its own needs and the headquarters staff and activities. State headquarters provided some kickback to the local churches on a case-by-case, as-needed basis while forwarding a sizeable chunk to national headquarters for administration, operations, national activities like Blessings (mass marriages, though members still had to cough up fees), national ministerial outreach, lobbying, business operations whose profit was pledged to the church, kickbacks to state headquarters on the same case-by-case as-needed basis, pocket fill, palm grease . . .

MFT accordingly established two primary operating methodologies. National MFT—the aforementioned cross-country teams—traveled the nation or discrete regions and sent their money straight to national headquarters. MFT restricted urban teams to metro cities like LA, Chicago, New York, Houston, Dallas–Fort Worth, Boston, and others. A percentage of their money went to the local church or state headquarters as payment for using the local fundraising area that was always in danger of burnout. A good analogy here is farming. You can only till a field so much until exhausting the soil and needing to leave it dormant a season or so. A farmer takes his property and divides it into fields that are active or fallow. In addition, the farmer may also determine soil productivity, kinds of soil, which crops are best suited to which fields, and the like.

The church divided a city, for instance, into multiple 'fields' that fundraising crews (urban MFT or local members fundraising on weekends and holidays or as full-time local MFT for their local center less their up-bound quotas) then farmed. Beyond dividing a jurisdiction by which crew would use which area, we further divided it by demographics. Shirley showed me my first fundraising map.

"See here?" She pointed to handwritten labels. "This neighborhood is 'humble,' this one's 'arrogant white,' this one 'wealthy.' Here's 'black humble,' 'black dangerous,' 'hispanic,' 'white but OK,' 'worn out,' 'off limits.' Like that."

"How'd you figure all that out?"

"We fundraised it. Members figure out who's who and what's what. Then we put it on our maps."

I whistled at the detail. "That's some work. You know exactly where to put who for what product."

"Yeah," she laughed. "So, I know where to put you."

If Mormons were expert proselytizers—we Moonies admired and envied their recruiting superpowers—Unificationists were expert fundraisers. When the public wonders how Rev. Moon got so much money in the '70s and '80s, they can be confident it was scientifically applied superior—in Japan, quite often fraudulent—business acumen in the best traveling-salesman marketing tradition of America. Cynical for a church, maybe. But effective for its ministry.

My assignment was urban MFT. Product went in the rear cargo area and our crew of six shared two bench seats. Darlene was a kind-hearted black sister in her early twenties, like most of us. We got along and shared happy conversations. She was narcoleptic. Often at the end of the day when she was tired her eyes drooped, head nodded and, even in the middle of a sentence, her chin dropped to her chest; out like a light and drooling down the front of her shirt. One, five, or 30 minutes later she jerked her head up wide awake, picking up at the precise point in her sentence when she'd dropped off. In a moment, she'd realize the awful truth and redden enough to see. It was pretty hard for her, and we were sympathetic. Even so, it was our van's Johnny Carson skit.

Margarita was an extrovert beaming smiles and kindness 24–7. True to her Spanish heritage her dense, wavy black hair framed her attractive face and golden laugh. She was from LA and, unlike me, felt comfortable in the city. She often wore cute dresses with puffy, lacy shoulders common to school uniforms, knee socks, and saddle shoes. A total cutie in my eyes. She was right out of my own late '60s early '70s fashion-verse. Her sweeping smile of broad, gleaming teeth formed a beautiful contrast with her dusky olive skin and jet black hair. Her gregariousness seemed a bit at odds with the prevailing norms of the church. The fear of touching the opposite sex was palpable on my team, as with much of the church during these years. As far as most of us could tell, Rev. Moon had eradicated extramarital sex and casual making-out from the average member's lifestyle. We were now living through an extreme Victorianism, a monstrous upheaval for Americans used to the public excess of the sexual revolution. Margarita didn't have that hang up and freely tapped, brushed, stroked, nudged, palmed, and poked my shoulders, arms, hands, and knees more than I was used to. Maybe she was attracted; I never asked. While I agreed with the necessity of building a firewall between the sexes to mitigate the destructive drama of love affairs, the human need for touch is as powerful as for sex. Margarita was a breath of fresh air in our airless church. She made me feel human amongst humans again. I never felt myself falling in love or sexually fantasizing. I appreciated enormously her familial casualness and loved her for it. I felt like *her* brother, not just a church brother.

I knew Betsy from Boulder. She was ex-hippyish and often sported tie-dyed garments usually to her ankles. Modest and chaste for a hippie, she hailed from Vancouver and was always fun to laugh with. A lot of hippies joined the American church. Pre-salvific photos were often wildebeests of long hair and scraggly beards or no bras. It was remarkable how they changed lifestyles from hearing the Principle. In many ways, Betsy embodied the finest attributes of the hippie movement: kind, generous, world-oriented, concerned with human happiness, open to new ideas, willing to sacrifice personal success for a positive change in our world, upbeat, energetic, happy with herself, and outgoing. I admired her like Jesus Christ's sister if she'd been a bobbed blonde with draped, straight-cut dresses that camouflaged buxom curves. She was an intellectual and we pitapatted through many a noble discussion on life, love, God, and the universe. Unlike the sex and pharmaceuticals that decimated the credibility, utility, and health of the hippie movement, Betsy was a naturally pure soul. We spent months exotically undressed divided by a screen at a San Francisco acupuncturist the church vainly paid to fix our jalopied bodies.

Young Soon was a lovely young Korean sister with bright eyes and a narrowed moon face. For a Korean—my first encounter with one—she was open and talkative if not exactly gregarious in Margarita fashion. She was earthy and familial and seemed to feel at home around us. I certainly felt at home around her. I don't recall any cross words except her darkening face and sisterly aggravation when I teased her as 'Choo-wah-wah' or 'Choo-choo-wah' and sometimes 'Choo-choo-pow' after she described her parents renaming her to Joo Hwa to change her fortune. She eventually changed it back and maybe not a little because of my Americanist wordplay. Oh, well. All's fair between brothers and sisters in the trenches. Well, mostly.

Months of working day and night with these sisters and I discovered I loved them even more than my own. Contrary to what I may have thought was my fate, I didn't find myself falling in love with or sexually drawn to any of them, a liberating air only the drowning can know. Not because they weren't attractive or downright beautiful but . . . well, I suppose it was our vibe though, at the time, it seemed God was helping me get a break from my loneliness and loss it seemed only a woman's arms could ease. Our penetrating bond as real family welled in me and lit my heart and lightened my load. Despite our exhausting work, the pleasure of my team's company made it all bearable. Sentiment engulfs me just writing about them.

I'd be proud and grateful had Rev. Moon Matched me to any of these unstinting workhorses. I was the only brother on the team and, in our early days, their hardcore grit sometimes put me to shame. MFT formed our team from its semi-invalids which, as it turned out, were only sisters. The church didn't want to take them *out* of MFT, that would impair the bottom line and reduce their opportunities for the serious indemnity only MFT could provide. All of us one way or another took it for a huge blessing in the same vein as Jesus teaching us to turn the other cheek.

> . . . do not resist an evil person. If anyone slaps you on the right cheek, turn to them the other cheek also . . . If anyone forces you to go one mile, go with them two miles . . . love your enemies and pray for those who persecute you, that you may be children of your Father in heaven . . . If you love those who love you, what reward will you get? . . . what are you doing more than others? . . . Be perfect, therefore, as your heavenly Father is perfect. (Matt. 5:38–48)

That's indemnity. The world mocks Moonies stupidly slaving over Rev. Moon's personal prosperity while taking for a blessing, *exactly as Jesus preached*, the public's rock-throwing, jaw-smacking, sometimes murderous molestations. Yet, Christians denounce their own faith and savior in deriding ours. Some of our money went to his fancy pants and, yeah, we cared but not really. God mattered. Divine Principle mattered. True love mattered. We sufferingly sacrificed not for a *man* but our faith in a better world through his *teaching*, as have 2,000 years of Christians following Jesus. If he stole our sacrifice for a better quality soup, that's on him.

MFT saw more sense cobbling its cripples into one team. The only difference between us and normies was that we shaved a few hours off the day, working 8 AM to midnight give or take. Julian and maybe Mr. Kamiyama in a fit of Christian charity had been watching out for me after all, and I prized their consideration. Kindness in degrees, I reckon. Or they expected me to earn its continuation.

～

SHIRLEY WHIPPED FROM the airport around LA picking up team members. She introduced me as each one stumbled inside to unexpected stranger danger. They were friendly and welcoming. I felt uncritically accepted, at home on their team even while dreading the indemnity ahead of me. When I joined the church, selling was the farthest thing from my mind. I've never liked the drudge of acquiring money, just spending it. Gazing out my window, I now felt thoroughly lost. No clue where I was in this urban Serengeti. Around midnight, Shirley idled up to a lit house in a hushed neighborhood called Anaheim. She clunked the gearshift into PARK.

"MFT rents this house, Chris, and we have to be mindful of our neighbors. They're regular families and don't like us much."

"So . . . what's that mean for me, exactly?"

"It means, please don't make any racket or create any issues with our neighbors. They already complain enough as it is. They don't like so many people coming and going all hours in their family neighborhood."

"Okay, I get it." I scoped out the few members moving around outside. I could see our activity at this late hour shaking folks out of bed to dial up trouble.

"Not the police, so much. Zoning. And the landlord. The house is packed with members and we run MFT out of it without a business permit."

"You need a permit just to live here?" She nodded. "Well, how many—?"

"Fifty, up and down. And some of the Japanese have expired visas. You see what I'm talking about?"

Packed and expired. It was TV news on bugaboo illegals just waiting to air. "Yeah, I reckon. Don't need a bulldozer coming through, eh." I flashed a smile.

"No, we do not. We basically have good relations and nobody's reported us." I was nodding. "Okay, that's my spiel. I don't know you, so don't take it the wrong way, but please, *please* be mindful."

"Promise. Cross my heart. No worries."

She eyed me even as she twisted and popped her door open. "Good. Help us get our product inside."

I watched her click her door shut. *Aye, aye, ma'am.*

An 8-foot cinder block wall ran along one side of the house, separating us from that neighbor. A concrete sidewalk ran inside its length and terminated at a sliding glass door opening into a modest, classroom-sized living room devoid of furniture except a couple of plastic chairs and a blackboard affixed to the far wall. A small garden–patio area reposed on the door's far side where members organized their flowers, water buckets, and other product after their 2 AM return and before their 6 AM wake-up. I greeted a Japanese sister.

"Shhh!" she squelched from dark eyes, pointing next door. It was difficult not projecting. "Please, no talking this place. Neighbors."

"Right. Gotcha." I gagged myself to admire a high-trunked, fluffy tree across from the sliding door.

Shirley whispered, "Our holy tree for prayer." To battle, then exhausted sleep.

Our schedule was fairly routine. Awake by 6 AM, occasionally showered but definitely shaved by 7 AM. No easy task in half a Roman century with one bathroom for brothers and maybe two for sisters. As usual in the American church, sisters scored the best sleeping and bathing arrangements while private-room leaders expected us brothers to rough it. Well, sexism wasn't dead (maybe only reversed?) in the church after all. Long live sexism.

Before breakfast, we sometimes had morning service. Most see MFT as front-line combat duty to piously avoid at all costs. As Rev. Moon notes,

> MFT work is difficult and troublesome, isn't it? Only a handful said no, so the rest of you must agree with me. When new members come and are getting assigned to missions, they often hope they aren't put on MFT. The important

point is whether people just want a free ride and an easy job or really want to take responsibility . . . When I was at the communist concentration camp at Hung Nam, the prisoners had to do forced labor. Some duties were easier than others, but the amazing thing was that the prisoners who tried to be smart and get the easier jobs were the ones who never lasted. They all died . . . Some people would rather have an easier mission than MFT, but eventually they will leave the Unification Church . . . [for] an easier life . . . Here you are reshaping yourself to resemble me . . . Money is a secondary goal; most important of all, MFT is the best possible training you could get, (*To the MFT*, WMC 1980)

which in my judgment, and although we took him seriously, vastly understates our fear and loathing. Church members attended morning and often evening service every day, plus a major one on Sunday. MFT had no time for that kind of nonsense. At our Anaheim house, Sunday service was unknown. A short morning service on Mondays inspired the troops for another seven trench-footing days.

"That seems kind of dumb, Shirley," I said. "I mean, we need regular spiritual food for this, don't you think?"

"I hate to break it to you, but we're pretty much on our own on MFT. You have to take responsibility for yourself."

That caused me to realize I'd got used to leaders spoonfeeding me. I made a show of looking over a few bustling Japanese I'd already pegged as anti-American zealots. "Well . . . it doesn't seem like it's working all that well."

"Everybody has their problems, Chris. Don't judge what you don't know, yet." I dropped my eyes at her merited dig. "Anyway, each team does its own kind of morning service in their vans. Our spiritual life isn't neglected."

"So, survival of the fittest?"

"Now you're getting it. We still need to take care of each other, though." And somehow she read Rev. Moon's words, sermonized, and prayed passionately all without railroading a tree. It seemed positively miraculous at times.

I didn't know why we didn't have a normal, all hands Sunday service. I supposed it was a good fundraising day and maybe Monday wasn't. Result couldn't be thrown aside for spiritual nourishment in a time-consuming service. Wasn't "MFT . . . the best possible training [we] could get?" On Mondays, we all gathered in the furniture-less living room and sat on (perhaps once carpeted) bare, corpsy concrete packed nearly shoulder to shoulder. A cruel joke to glutes and spines. The center director, usually but not always the MFT commander, ran the service. It consisted of some limited reading from some of the thousands of quotations from Rev. Moon's various speeches in the *Way of Tradition* books. I collected the whole multi-volume set of this gem of a pocket book. Burgers gulped in a vegan world.

Julian once said, "Publishing these books is one of the worst mistakes our church ever made."

"I don't see why. I get a lot out of them. Who can trudge through all Father's speeches for the gold?"

"Because, they take Father's words out of context. The whole speech is important to understand any part of it. Snippets only add to members' misunderstandings and our enemies' ammunition to paint him as a fringe lunatic and cult leader."

He forgot to include leaders using it to wholly misconstrue and misapply his teachings as a means to justify their own. "It seems Father would've caught that."

"It was Mr. Kamiyama's thing. Father trusted his judgment."

"The heck? I thought Father commissioned the books."

Julian squeezed his shoulders and puckered his mouth, brows furrowed. I wasn't sure how to read that. Regardless, we loved these books and it was *très en vogue* to collect them all to fill our flapping sails.

After reading some quotations with a spin, our commander might brief us on Rev. Moon's activities, the latest on God's providence, our center's financials, testimony from members or other inspiration, and HQ's ever-present cry for more munitions before moving on to unison prayer. We were fervent, weepy, and loud in 1982. The service leader often shushed us lest we bring down our neighbors' wrath. It was nerve-wracking living under a Damoclean sword, but prayer was the most inspiring part of our day, our moment to connect to God, our inner spirituality, and inspire ourselves. Passion was next to impossible in a van.

The Japanese sisters running the kitchen served my team's breakfast 7:30–8 AM after any morning service and the regular teams departed. Breakfast was often a mix of American-style scrambled eggs with Japanese-style vegetables, spam or some other cheap meat, and always rice. I suppose I should clarify the egalitarian nature of the church I was so proudly trumpeting. It was somewhat egalitarian for Western sisters. It was not so in the slightest sense for Asian, particularly Japanese, sisters. I never knew how they ran things in Japan, but in America they were most every center's unofficial house Negroes. If there was a servile job to be done, they caught the assignment. I didn't know if this was Rev. Moon's Korean heritage crudely getting back at their 40 years of colonial excrement, his idea of Japan as the 'mother' Eve nation whose duties included mothering American church centers (we all know Mom's our slave), or just how Japanese brothers preferred it.

The primary nations in God's Providence of Restoration are Korea, Japan, and America. Korea represents Adam, the father. Japan, Eve. America the good, pre-Fall of Man and the evil, post-Fall of Man Archangel Lucifer. Since the Principle accuses Eve for initiating the Fall, she's the one who needs endure the greatest indemnity on her way back to her unfallen state. The Bible gives great import to Godly men living as 'servants of servants,' meaning, in the traditions of the day, humbling themselves as far as necessary. And what's more humbling than that? If a servant is nothing, then you're less than nothing. Jesus, too, insisted the first among his disciples should be the humblest servants of their assembly.

So it is with the Unification Church using the Japanese sisters as the ultimate slave labor throughout their time in the American church, from joined at the fundraising hip to chained in the kitchen. Even in Rev. Moon's homes, most of his personal servants aren't Koreans but Japanese sisters. They do his cooking, cleaning, laundry, and child-raising. Since they arrived in America, Japanese sisters have truly been the servants of servants. As I understood their lot, my heart went out to them.

Like Montezuma, though, our Japanese sisters in Anaheim had their revenge. Most of what they fed us was Japanese. Outside Korean circles, Asian curry and rice was the number one food of the American Church and one of my favorites. Once in a while they served us hamburgers or spaghetti, their idea of traditional American fare. Otherwise, I was a tourist in mealtime Japan.

We mixed breakfast with product preparation for the day's selling. It wasn't unusual to see even Japanese scuttling about with food in their hands and mouths while doing team chores. This, despite Rev. Moon mocking Americans for eating on the go along the time-ne'er-waits-on-the-hungry streets of New York City. I scored some respite from this hurly burly hobbling on a cane. Sometimes, I thanked my lucky stars I'd been crippled but for the pain. Our team still prepared each morning like the others. We moved vexatiously aged in our hoary youth, generally pulling away from the dock as other teams were probably pulling up to their drop zones. We sold through sundown and moonrise till slipping home midnight–1 AM depending on how we felt . . . generally like shit, but teeth gritted to stay the holy course.

"Of course, we understand your physical situation," our leaders periodically cautioned us through Shirley if not in person, "but not all brothers and sisters do. So, don't create tension in the center."

"What's he really saying, Shirley?" I said, slit-eyed.

"We can't slack off *too* much or other members will feel like we're not pulling our weight. And we're not here for that, anyway."

"What, they think we're lying? My cane is fake?"

"Don't take it so negatively. People are people. Not everybody likes MFT, and special treatment, real or not, just creates Cain-type feelings."

"So, they're jealous. They should try feeling—"

"Shush, Chris. Satan invades through that and tears us all down."

Jeez. I can't be myself because I'm damaged, and because I'm damaged I can't be myself. A Yossarian-worthy catch-22. "Okay, Shirley. I understand where you're coming from. I don't want to make anybody's life harder than it is."

"Good boy." I kind of missed Julian's follow-up shoulder clap.

Good politics dictated we not return or leave too early or late. We could always goof off in our workday when only God could observe. After taking care of our product, we met around the garden's 'holy tree'—my overloaded hand ached fire in my cane's saddle—for five minutes of prayer to close our day. Sisters went off to carpeted comfort. I unrolled my sleeping bag *sans* pillow over our seen-better-days living room's concrete. Unless dreaming the dead, the bulk of our fundraisers' racketous return startled me awake circa 2–3 AM. I routinely woke head-to-foot sore, particularly my knee despite makeshift support. That stone floor was a death knell between my lower back, left hip, right knee and shoulder, and hand. In no small way it contributed to my rapid decline in physical health.

I MAINLY SOLD laser photos and foil etchings shop-to-shop along LA's unending commercial strips. I footslogged morning till night and it seemed I was treading the same horizonless block, at the same stores, crossing the same streets, the same every *Groundhog Day* thing. Shirley dropped us at locations she'd selected off her map with a time she'd cruise by to pick us up. Since we couldn't tell how far we might get, pre-arranged pick up points didn't work because then we might short our daily gross. Shirley rode the road in hopes she'd spot us. It could be hit or miss.

This work terrified me. I had no experience prancing into some hard-working body's store not to buy *their* products but sell them *mine*. Would they throw me out? have me arrested? humiliate me? Not knowing made it worse. Shirley dropped me off and I stepped tentatively into my first store. I saw the likely manager and approached. The shops were small along these infinite avenues. Big-box superstores didn't yet dominate. Most were moms-and-pops and their owners or managers easily approached. In most cases, they were receptive to our request to sell to their employees and customers. It seems odd in our hyper-greedy post-*Wall Street* world but, since we visited a store only once or twice a month, I suppose they didn't feel threatened. I could stroll into, say, a shoe store and ask the manager's permission to sell, and then everyone inside was all the same to me in pre-uniformed commercial America. Our laser prints and metal etchings were a novelty. Their beauty captivated the eye. Shiny and bright. The most radiant colors ever seen.

"That's too much money for this ol' thing," folks said, suddenly uncaptivated.

"Totally, right? But it's a donation for my church"—*Christian fellowship, religious group*, or just, *'Sorry, that's the price;'* whatever was apropos to the demographic—"so we have to ask more to cover our costs." Or some such thing.

"Oh, I see . . . well, maybe this once . . ."

Cha-ching!

In 1982 most of us thought it reasonably safe for local members to openly sell as Unificationists. When doing so, I approached a person in a shop and said, "Hi! I'm selling some items to raise money for my church." Ofttimes no one even cared *which* church. They were happy to donate money to *any* church, especially Hispanics. "Could I show you some samples?"

Some were more curious . . . or suspicious. "Yeah? Which church?"

"Unification Church." I might've obfuscated with HSA–UWC or some variant if that seemed wiser but never lied, and Shirley never demanded it.

They often tossed it with an eyebrow flip. "Okay, just wondered." Out came cash. Or a choleric double take. "Get the holy fuck outta here or I'll call the cops!"

"Yessir! God bless you. Have a nice—"

"*Git!*"

These kinds were a minority in my experience. Our method of raising money was still new and dewy-eyed in the United States and we Moonies its pioneers. We also peddled boxed peanut brittle and other candies person-to-person in parking lots and mid-level jewelry home-to-home. Thinking back, it's a wonder my teammates never suffered a street hit, what with our small black cases loaded with thousands of dollars of silver and gold. Some did now and again but it was rare that street-level members heard of it. The church didn't exactly trumpet the hot tip that, besides transforming our fallen nature to Restore us to God, fundraising might accidentally and through no fault of its own *kill* us.

Revealing our church ties was more the exception than the rule, I think. I didn't always sell my products this way but determined case-by-case how a person might react to discovering I was a Moonie. Most of us weren't oblivious to the risk of getting beat up. It certainly happened. But if someone asked me flat out, "Are you a Moonie?" then I felt ethics-bound to come clean. The church generally encouraged us *not* to reveal we were selling for the church but for a business, often as a student. Later working local MFT for my San Francisco center, our team captain pointedly enjoined us from mentioning the church. It was then up to each of us, alone on the scene, to choose our road according to circumstances and moral fortitude.

Cross-country MFT rarely, if ever, admitted they were Moonies. They traveled under entities such as One World Products that were just fundraising shell companies so members wouldn't have to lie about their receipts going *directly* to the church. What OWP did with it wasn't their concern. This bothered many of us and formed the core of Moon-the-Charlatan denigrations despite the disconnect between him and Mr. Kamiyama's operational realities on the ground. On the other hand, we appreciated the practicality as well as the added safety. And the name of the game was cranking out spiritual war matériel, not soft-selling the church.

Fundraising scandals arose with regularity in Japan where 'heavenly deception' got hopelessly out of control. I believed it was Sang Ik 'Papasan' Choi, a flamboyant, now elderly Korean leader and one of three original missionaries to America, who invented this notion. He'd successfully missionized Japan, so Rev. Moon sent him hither to repeat his magic. He was fruitful in California, though got so delusional that Rev. Moon forced him into retirement partially on the heels of a scandal I brought to light. Heavenly deception is a modified religious version of 'turn-about is fair play.' It reverses Satan deceiving Adam and Eve to steal the created world from God in order to Restore "all things" of the fallen world (like corrupted money) out of Satan's false ownership. In practical terms, it meant never admitting selling products for Rev. Moon and his church, but to 'deceive' the public into buying maximum product by making it easy for them. Just a straight-up business deal. No muss, no fuss. Rev. Moon took a more black-and-white approach.

> These are the major three rules of spirit world. When you go out on MFT training, all the money you make is for the public fund and for that reason you should return every penny you make. But at the same time your doing that makes you a public person, and anyone who is nasty to you and slanders you is violating this law and they will be chastised. Because you are a public person, because every bit of what you are doing is for the sake of God, fund raising is not stealing, not at all. Some people try to criticize us by saying that Unification Church members lie and justify it by calling it heavenly deception; I never taught you to do that and I was very angry at hearing such a thing. We don't have to lie. We must be totally honest. (*My Life*, Belvedere 1978)
>
> Some members try to hide the fact that they are members of the Unification Church, and that is absolutely no good. Wear your ID and show to the world that you are a member of the Unification Church and that you follow Reverend Sun Myung Moon. Go forward proudly in that capacity and let people contribute to this cause. (ibid)

Whether he believes it is immaterial. He said it to *us*, so the ball was in our court. In reality, some of us transitioned to pleading our religious cause if a potential customer wouldn't buy, because it was the sale that really mattered. And why not? Switching to a hard sell actually made us more honest. The heavenly deception tactic gained widespread notoriety and many church centers eventually dropped it. It was largely a West Coast stratagem. Midwest and East Coast churches—in practice if not in theory run independently of the other—didn't much apply the tactic. California's foolishness still hounds the national church.

While some MFT practiced heavenly deception, it didn't sell deceptive wares in America. Our products were honest: laser prints, foil etchings, candy, terrariums, wood roses, and luxury items presented to buyers as just what they were.

In contrast, Japan's heavenly deception not only kept the buyer in the dark as to the entity selling and profiting from their products, but the truth about the product itself. For example, the church raised gargantuan returns selling (Korean, I think) porcelain vases—tens of millions officially reported—purportedly having spiritual powers. Members showcased videos of spiritual flames coming out of vase tops, miraculous healings of buyers, golden promises of wealth and happiness, *ad nauseam*. We observed these stories and videos (with some minor credulity) in befuddled amusement. It reinforced our general belief, adopted in the face of the practices and results of Japanese leaders running the American church, that Japanese were scoundrels and idiots. They fraudulently sold phony products to suckers who paid thousands to sometimes $10,000 per vase with nothing more than anecdotal testimony and crocodile assurances. I guess Americans buying network marketing and televangelist products are just as gullibly dumb, but we didn't know how stupid we were in the early '80s when forming our critical opinions of the Japanese.

One of Japanese MFT's methods for selling these vases, besides house-to-house and shop-to-shop, was to dress sisters in navy blue clothing that looked suspiciously like police uniforms replete with white hat and gloves. They stationed them along roads and highways and used police hand signals to flag down traffic to the side of the road where, instead of a fine, they audaciously pitched a 'prosperity vase.'

"What absolute brilliance!" marvels P.T. Barnum in his jealously spinning grave. Japanese consumers may have been moronic but their MFT was bold and innovative. It was monstrous, but we had to give credit where due. They made untold millions before their amoral government investigated and scandalized the church. Many if not all the questionable tactics used in America were direct imports via thousands of Japanese shipped in to handle American MFT. Mr. Kamiyama, let alone Rev. Moon and the rest of the Asian hierarchy, considered Japanese MFT experts and go-getters and Americans lazy, unsporting novices.

"I am sorry to say that the American MFT record is far behind that of the Japanese," Rev. Moon said often enough to nettle us while ignoring the considerable conflict from Japanese thrusting their brazen tactics down our resisting throats.

Americans had an oft-quoted retort: "You can't do that here, you'll get arrested."

Experienced with handling Japan's corrupt police, bureaucrats, and politicians, they laughed presumptuously in our faces. "You too much worry. God will protect us. *We* can do! You need more faith and you can do, too. This is Principle."

"You have no idea." We shook our heads and waited for the shitstorm.

I'll be the first to admit that Japanese MFT was the hardest working cabal I ever met. They're zealous, fanatical, single-minded sonsabitches absolutely obedient to their leaders in a way we'd never seen outside them resisting US Marines, or Nazi stormtroopers. A tyrant's wet dream come true working any hours, selling any product, going anywhere, doing virtually anything for the cause. Now I saw how tyranny and war-crime madness had once been so easily nurtured amongst them. And, yet, they had scruples after all. They could've secretly earned whopping, maybe literally uncountable, monies prostituting for God and True Parents all those fabulously beautiful, exotic, starry-eyed Japanese sisters here, there, and everywhere. It wasn't unthinkable to Imperial Japan but I guess it gave even Japanese MFT pause. It was probably never imagined except for the moment it occurred to me writing this paragraph. Somebody would've talked. Right?

The heavy Japanese presence on American MFT was a terrific tension builder. As a stereotype, they were inescapably alien in thinking patterns (reversed), sense of logic (didn't have any), attitude toward True Parents (mindless zealots), faith (completely uncritical), eating habits (public masticators), food choices (plated fish with head, tail, scales, *eyeballs*), and their indoctrination seemed of a wholly different *Divine Principle* than what we had in America. To top it off, their leaders heavily propagandized America as the land of barbarians caring only for money and drugs and sexually assaulting Japanese sisters given half a chance. In short, that we're depraved, unPrincipled thugs, an opinion little changed from World War Two. Not only did they land like colonial masters revisiting fond Korean memories, they were infuriatingly arrogant, condescending, and stupefyingly ignorant of our country and people . . . the same mindset that imagined their Pearl Harbor strategy a slam dunk. It might be we were tasting our own colonial medicine but it rankled all the same. From my point of view it was undeserved. I never colonized anybody.

"They own us whole hog now," some said.

"We only *thought* we won the war," said others bolstered by grim economics.

Maybe their Unificationist arrogance *was* bolstered by Japan's powerful economy. To all appearances it was steamrolling America's sagging '80s fortunes under its rising-sun's sod. They were certainly proud of Japan's new muscle and contemptuous as ever of the Great Satan now declining in their sainted shadow.

My MFT team was all-American except for Young Soon—Koreans seemed a tastier kettle of fish—so I only contended with Japanese in our house. That was enough. We were outnumbered Spartans. They certainly made a jumbo contribution to the growth and development of the American church in the 1970s, '80s, and perhaps the early '90s. Even in 2003, they're the primary witnessing agents for most American church centers now so few Americans remain. But they wrought a veritable wasteland in the hearts and minds of Americans who, like me after discovering my Japanese worship was a fraud, only wished 'the Japs' would leave. The only Japanese really a pleasure to have around were those who, defying all orders and indoctrination, Americanized . . . or, as I prefer to say, *universalized.*

HOW MUCH MONEY could we make selling this stuff? You'd be surprised the cases of peanut brittle we could move in parking lots. During my time in LA, I made $7 per laser print, two for $10. It was a high price for a low wholesale of maybe fifty cents, but justified as a religious donation. I didn't consider it sinful, shameful, or unethical. It's the same way a plate of spaghetti goes for a ripoff at swank events then and now. I might sell 5–20 pictures per day. Not a lot, really. But for me it added up to $50–$150 per day. That means our team produced $350–$1,050 each day. Weekly, it might be $2,400–$7,000 or more. Holidays and special dates like Mother's Day always spiked sales. We operated maybe ten teams out of our Anaheim house. That made its take $24,000–$70,000 *per week*. Monthly, it ranged $96,000-$280,000 and annually, $1.1 million–$3.3 million. Even subtracting our meager expenses it's a good haul. Did you think fundraising was a lot of work for chicken feed? Shit, we practically printed money. And we were only one house.

I was a lousy fundraiser because I was under-motivated. My knee was a swollen, stiff, throbbing, sharp bone-on-bone wrack and ruin that sometimes went out from under. My shoulder satchel, anchored down by laser prints and metal etchings, aggravated my spine, right shoulder, and left hip from walking off-kilter on my cane. Mile after mile it turned my palms fiery, sore, and raw. As I age, my hip and back paralyzingly ache from my umpteen miles of hiking, forever hauling my damaged body and its load of 2-for-$10 salvation. Did Mr. Kamiyama, our ultimate overseer, ever thank me or MFT in its thousands for our long hardships? Not that I recall. He rolled his Big-Wheel life through the Messiah's cheese shop as we lived our Edwardian downstairs station. Oft demoralized, I sat on bus benches an hour here and there bemoaning my fate, wondering why in holy hell I'd acceded to his punitive conditions. But that was sometimes, not always. I could've quit but didn't.

"Goddammit," I harangued myself. "This *is* the life I want! But why must it be so haaard?" Then my Divine Principled conscience pushed me to my feet.

Our commander hammered into our heads why we fight. "You are fundraising for the sake of God's providence, not to make True Parents or church leaders rich. This is God's will and our sacred duty to Restore the world!"

"It doesn't seem very sacred dragging my leg down the road," I said to Shirley. And she understood, as did my beloved van mates. Maybe the only people in the world who ever truly, heartistically, felt my pain. I hoped they were feeling it back from me. I wasn't always so sure in my self-absorption.

She said, "We're all struggling, Chris. Our bodies are weak, yeah, but our—"

"Spirit is willing. I know. And mine is. I'm just . . . it sometimes seems so . . ."

"How can God make headway in this world if His champions are impoverished? How much could Father do for the Providence back when he was poor in Korea? He would've failed to teach you Principle just like Jesus failed."

I hadn't forgot Jesus' pain. "Must be an easier way, though."

She laughed and squeezed my forearm.

Our commander said, "When we are fundraising we must remember our duty, why we are out there. Not lose hope. Not give up. Not give Satan power over us."

The Japanese shouted, "*Hai!*" But me? "Easier said than done, I say."

I supposed he wasn't any different from company commanders just a few years earlier in Vietnam reminding their unenthused troops what they were fighting for; of their duty to God, country, and fellows to defend the free world from murdering communist psychopaths or die trying; of not goofing off in the field but attacking the enemy with verve. The church presented our struggle in the military light of fighting the enemy Satan and his army of darkness. We saw ourselves soldiers of God, fist-pumping through holy songs like *Song of the Heavenly Soldiers, Unified Soldiers,* and *March of the New Age* that resoundingly forged the metaphor into reality. Our day-to-day suffering on MFT and witnessing teams were combat wounds to the soul. We couldn't let the enemy spiritually and sometimes physically kill us when there was so much righteous conquering for God still to do. We had to persevere. We had to live. We were on *jihad*.

To combat my demotivators, I set goals like getting five blocks before taking a break, selling my first picture, or making my first $50 or $100 before resting, enjoying an ice cream, or downing a cold beverage to ease the blistering sun. Shirley was instrumental. My honesty gave her insight. I freely admitted goofing off when too tired, sore, or aggravated to fundraise more than a token. She patiently recognized my physical, mental, emotional, and spiritual limitations because she recognized her own. She made the effort to nurture me, to develop my commitment and ability. My sense of duty transformed. I saw myself a real heavenly soldier fighting to win—*Restore*—a core aspect of the Fall from the hand of fallen humanity so it could be put to cleansed use in God's providence. She was my blessing.

In truth, our whole team was 'lousy' in the sense we didn't produce the kind of return the healthy ones did. We were tired, sore, in pain, some on MFT already far too long and plumb burnt out. I never asked what the earnings ratio was between my team and the others, but I imagined we did 50–70% of their revenue. Those team members were *insane*. Stoked. Absolutely committed to THE LIFE. I observed so many (especially Japanese) brothers approaching their team captains cap in hand as though real army, practically snapping to attention for their awesome leader.

He spake and they respondeth, "Yes, Captain!" "No, Captain!"

I rolled eyes and hiked brows with astonishment and disdain. What were they going to do about me sauntering around yakking first names—our commander was still *mister*, being scarily Japanese—besides kick me out of MFT? I could only laugh. These servile numbnuts were the very epitome of boot camp etiquette and, when they inevitably left the church, threw stones at everybody but themselves. It was hair-raising. Unlike real *jihadis*, I suppose we impressionable youngsters were lucky Rev. Moon was a life-or-death unconditional, sacrificial, non-violent agape love bomber and never imagined us wearing Semtex.

One Monday I was nodding off in morning service exhausted from my efforts the previous week and poor concrete-sleep catching up. My well-worn cane lay across my lap. My back hunched and bent as our commander regaled us.

A brother noticed and roughly pushed me. "Wake up!" he hissed.

"Yeah, right. Thanks." *Where's a lazy American when you want one?*

Minutes later he roughly punched me. Voice clipped, "Yeah, yeah, okay."

My head drooped yet again. He socked me in the shoulder with angled knuckles that jabbed deep to the worn out bone. It sharply hurt. Got me plenty mad. I bored my best optical drill through this pugnacious bastard's eyes to his pea brain.

Hushed but deliberate, I leaned into halitosis range to ferociously inflect. "I'm exhausted with a wrecked knee and back. Touch me one more time, I'm going to *break. Your fucking. Arm!*"

I'd had enough of these brainwashed goons taking it on themselves to mush me into faux military line. *Been there done that, thanks, and you're not the boss of me.*

Our commander could yell at me from his poop deck if he'd a mind to, not this prick. Body language shouted, *Fuck with me one more time and I'm wreaking some biblical wrath!* The tenor of my voice and look in my eyes that he'd be first in berserker line got through his cloudy mindset. He backed off a startled rabbit. I tried paying better attention but nodded in and out of the rest of the service and cared not a whit. My spiritual life was wrapped up in Shirley's van now.

One of religion's odd contradictions is its ever-present tendency to love your neighbor through violence. It's no wonder the Spanish Inquisition was so willing to exalt Torquemada and the *autos-da-fé*. His zeal, like that brother forcefully keeping me awake, falls well within the hallowed traditions of organized faith. Although Unificationism preaches Abel giving himself up for Cain's sake, its Mr. Hyde side generally preferred a 'tough love' that freely employed verbal abuse, punishment, threats, guilt, delayed acceptance, and ostracizing over care and compassion. Hardly beyond the pale of traditional, obedience-minded religious orders, but we expected better from our new-way faith.

These fanatics were effective fundraisers and that's what mattered. Do-or-die 18-plus hours a day seven days a week. Except for Sunday, they averaged 3–4 hours sleep including the brother who'd punched me. My team averaged 4–5. They moved a lot of product and took no (overt) pay. I respected their zealous commitment to our worthy cause so long as they didn't overshare their peculiar ways and means of accomplishing it. The church cooked up delicious food if you liked Oriental, a place to sleep if you didn't mind bare concrete, a battlefield triage healthcare, and a place in heaven if you enjoyed the one we were getting a taste of here on Earth. To hear Rev. Moon talk nowadays, we need jump through a fuckton more hoops to earn our place than we ever imagined from reading *Divine Principle*.

WE FUNDRAISED SHOP-to-shop during the day and I turned expert. I lost my fear and intimidation at the prospect of confronting people for a Godly piece of their wallet for my cheap products. I walked from midmorning till 7, 8, or 9 PM hitting up every kind of shop you can think of: shoes, grocery, clothing, music, auto repair, electronics, pizza parlors, burger joints. Nothing was off limits.

The first time I walked into a pizza place to sell to the fellow behind the counter, my eyes tracked up and up . . . and up. I was transfixed.

He eyed me like burnt toast. "Can I help you?"

I actually leaned over the counter to see if he was on a platform. "How tall are you?" This was once in a lifetime. I'm sure my tone was knocked for six.

He blew a laugh. "Seven-feet-one."

"Wow! You're the first guy I ever saw taller than me." Not exactly, no. But my dormmate at Western State was only a scant six-eight. Rookie numbers. This dude was next level. And the more I shop-to-shopped the more I sprained my neck. I met more men forby six-six in LA than anyplace in America. "It's so weird looking *up* to a person for a change."

"I wouldn't know. So, whaddaya want?"

MFT allotted us $2 a day for lunch and Shirley thumbed it out each morning. It seems laughable in 2003, but two bucks was an effective lunch in 1982. Naturally, we could tap our fundraising result if our scruples didn't mind. Now and again I heard some did, from Coca-Cola to strip clubs. Inventory control in the church was no match for pilfering members, at least to a degree. You could easily claim you were robbed, lost the money, or had to sell for half price in a stingy neighborhood. I figured it was infrequent since our captains and commanders never lectured us for it, and they damn sure would've if they'd seen a trend. My result bought a few sodas, ice cream, and potato chips and my conscience minded its own business.

"It's not unPrincipled if you spend a dollar or two for water or other 'urgent' needs," Shirley early on schooled me on Mr. Kamiyama's tacitly blind eye.

Worded like that, a strip club kind of qualified. Money in the Unification Church is serious business, moral and otherwise. It considers all money public because members raise it for the greater good of the church and God. Shirley's words and our conscience undisturbed by snacks notwithstanding, all us of viewed using public money for private purposes a criminal undertaking. The church forbade it.

> When you go out fundraising on MFT, maybe you have two pockets. One is the Church pocket and one is your own pocket. Some money goes in the top pocket and some goes in the bottom pocket. Yes or no? I'm sure some people may not do that but they think, "I'm earning much money today. I deserve some, because I worked very hard." That's a logical, Western way of thinking. I'm sure some people think like that. Those who did think that way in your heart, repent right now, today! (*To the Crusade*, Lancaster Gate Church 1978)

Nevertheless, it happened with some frequency. Professional-level theft was a higher echelon scourge anyway. Team captains sometimes swiped money for a movie, strip club, book, magazine, or whatever caught their lightweight fancy during the tedious hours their crews were sweating out sales. Of course, a strip club was far greater trouble than a movie. *How* one spent purloined funds was often more important to the church than the fact it *was*. Captains and commanders used members' result for shooting clubs, Mexico day trips, gifts, and personal aggrandizement. Rev. Moon was unambiguous about the sacred role of public money.

> Public funds, particularly Church funds, are a fearsome thing...The worst judgment comes to those who misuse public funds. When you go to spirit world, this is the first thing you will find. (*My Life* 1978)

Yet, some of the biggest scams and embezzling operations happened right under his nose by top leaders appropriating money for luxe food, cars, homes, clothes, $3,000 violins and top-end tuition for their Blessed *wunderkind* . . . maybe Swiss accounts for a rainy day; any and all items they felt deserved in their role as leaders.

It's no surprise that stories about it raised a ruckus amongst the hoi polloi who no longer saw a dollar bill as a slip of scrip but a sweat chit soaked in their own blood and tears. Cash in hand is memories plowing through endless LA boulevards to get it. A currency of anguish. When embezzlers behold money, they see it only as what they want; vampires feeding greed off our carnage and torment whom some members wanted to lynch only gradually with piano wire.

My day over or product depleted, I thudded onto a bus bench to wait for pickup. Sometimes Shirley caught me earlier than expected hoofing down the street or emerging from a shop. Once, relaxing on my bus bench faithfully awaiting her arrival, it slowly dawned she wasn't coming. Hour after hour piled up creeping fears and hot feelings. I considered hiking home but LA is a *big* goddamn town.

"Where in hell is she?" I badgered myself.

Around 9 PM, finger poised over a pay phone's dial, I realized I didn't know the number for our house. I'd never asked and Shirley hadn't offered. We must've thought it unnecessary. I called information but, in that moment, couldn't even recall which of greater LA's more than 300 towns our house or I was in. I knew nothing of the city beyond its byways to forever. Each day I jerked awake, rode a desolate street with no name, and dropped into sleep.

"I am such a fucking moron!" I whacked the receiver into its cradle hoping to satisfyingly shatter it, but Ma Bell built bullish.

At long last, information dug up a number for a church center somewhere. I slung in coins and the operator dialed. Unfortunately, the only person home was *Janglish*, a broken-English Japanese. She didn't get much of my story nor had our house location or its phone number. I tried an hour or so to find somebody who could come for me, but in the end was left to my own devices. Thinking it over, my best course was to wait here for Shirley. A good call. At maybe 10:30 PM tires barked to a stop like the city's namesake landing hard.

I fell into the empty van. "Oh, my God! I thought I'd be spending the night out here! What happened?"

"I'm so, sooo sorry I'm so late! I drove up and down looking for you. I wondered if you got mugged or arrested. By then, I was late for everybody else. I had to pick them up, get them dinner, and drop them off at their night spots."

"You're here now, that's all I care about."

"How on earth did you get so far? I never, ever thought—"

"Just lucky, I guess. It was a productive day, anyway."

"Well, I got you dinner." She pointed to a hot bag of burgers. "Just ride around with me tonight and rest."

"God bless you, Shirley." Small favors make the world go round.

When things did go right, she picked us up near 8 PM for McDonald's or cheap local. We often ate as she freighted us to our next area joking, laughing, storytelling, basking in family. Evenings we sold pictures house-to-house and apartment-to-apartment. We'd heard stories of residents willing to buy a member's whole kit for sex—sometimes homosexual—but I never got propositioned.

But what if somebody did *do that on a lonely, depressing day?*

Thankfully, I never had to find out. One of our brothers rapped on a front door that opened on a man in a towel who promptly dropped it with the sales pitch and offered to buy it all plus a tip for some play time.

"I got the heck out of there," he said, "and went somewhere to pray awhile!"

We hoped it was true. It made us wonder how many times somebody, somewhere stepped in with a leer . . . because, loneliness.

What a world, we thought.

"Would that result be tainted?" we queried our leaders. "Can God use tainted result?" We tied ourselves in knots trying to figure out such things.

Not our leaders. "Yes, it is unPrincipled result. But God can use it with indemnity conditions." Of course he can.

When it got too late to bang on doors, we shifted to bars and nightclubs. This was difficult because we were interfering with people's fun who sometimes made us the butt of their jokes. Roses in a bar was easier than pictures because folks were half in the bag and not thinking straight, or a man might consider you a godsend for a woman he wanted. Having no taste for alcohol, I detested bars. Until I landed on MFT, I hadn't seen a bar since my best buddy Billy got me drunk on crutches aboard Group New Orleans. I tailspin-puked hourly till the weariest dawn ever.

Members got robbed especially nighttimes at fist, club, knife, or gunpoint. Attempted (male or female) rape seemed few and far between. No one I knew was, but it happened. Rev. Moon was ruthless in his views: it was the woman's fault, period. Not for provoking it, that was on the man, but for not ending it.

> You must determine, "Even if I give up my life I must not give up my chastity, my purity" . . . even if you have to use razor blades you must protect yourself. This is quite contrary to the common concept of Western men and women. A permissive, promiscuous life make[s] it impossible to be considerate of such things. (*Preparation for the Blessing (1)*, Lancaster Gate Church 1978)

> [O]ne Korean girl . . . gave a testimony of how she barely escaped being raped while fundraising. She had been constantly warned not to go out after 9:00 p.m. . . . [America is] more dangerous than Korea. But she was so eager to get a better result that one night she went by herself to a certain area and was grabbed by three strong men who forced her into a car. They tried to rape her there . . . she never gave up; she kept fighting them . . . [homeowners] called the police. This was how she narrowly escaped . . . I felt very proud of this little Korean girl who fought so bravely. Would you American women fight like that? Perhaps you would give in, thinking, "Why should I endanger my life to fight off these men?" That would be a pragmatic approach, but it would not be the right one . . . You are engaged for three years and keep yourselves absolutely pure . . . [people] assume you must be brainwashed by Rev. Moon . . . But you know the value of purity and that Satan would make you his victim if you let him. (*True Parents and Our Responsibility*, Belvedere 1981)

Death before dishonor. Discussing a Korean sister's rape, Mrs. Moon said that before losing her purity a sister should kill herself or fight hard enough her attacker does. Not doing so is tantamount to fallen Eve's desire for life above what matters to God and her ancestors' salvation: sexual purity that reverses the Fall.

Ludicrous, some thought.

Others said, "That's pretty severe."

"Ignorant, too," I said, since she wasn't talking from experience. "If a sister survives a rape, it seems she better clamp her mouth and work it out privately with God than risk a worse calamity with her Unification family."

Occasionally, sisters and brothers too came home bloody or black and blue from robberies. It didn't happen often and thank goodness. It would've box-cuttered morale let alone revenue. When it did, the media sensationalized it. We saw these unlucky members as heroes confronting Satan in his hometown and surviving his best effort, paying indemnity for us all. Through their suffering the whole MFT command spiritually benefitted. They hadn't died but were martyrs all the same. Any of us felt ready to risk or suffer abuse and (maybe) death in the house of evil, but their bodies had hit the actual chopping block for God and True Parents. I felt our leaders made a serious effort to prevent danger, so we weren't as perilous as Islamic bombers. If it occurred then we admired and, to a degree, venerated the person suffering it. But the risk was intrinsic to the business.

I suspect if bars were open all night then MFT would've crafted 24-7 fundraising operations. The law shuttered them at 2 AM, so fundraising halted. My team quit at midnight, plus or minus. We put away our flowers, product, prayed, and made bed by 12:30–1:30 AM. The others returned 2–3 AM depending how far away they were at closing time. Their arrival filled the room with chaos, energy, and noise that spooked my sleep almost nightly. Thankfully, they wasted no time bedding down.

REV. MOON DEVISED a plan he thought would structure the church in such a way to keep a steady flow of both money and recruits: the *Formula Course*. It consists of 3-½ years fundraising followed by 3-½ years witnessing. One's 7-year service was the qualification to start a family with a Formula-Coursed spouse. It was a grueling plan and none too welcomed by members. Seven years of penal servitude before the church allowed us marital relations. If you *had* a spouse.

The Formula Course made perfect sense. The Principle teaches humanity is fallen because its original ancestors got lost in sexual love while immature—the rationale for later blocking me from 1982's Blessing—and without God's approval. It was the self-interestedness of the Fall's three biblical characters that made it what it was. Adam and Eve sexing it up in unruly passion wouldn't have been much of a Fall at all. It was God's plan anyhow. Rather, Eve had a (spiritual) sexual relationship with Lucifer who selfishly manipulated her to confound God's plan. It corrupted Eve and set her on a path to egocentrically manipulate Adam into sex solely as a means to undo her Fall with the archangel. According to Heung Jin Moon (Rev. Moon's dead second son who spoke from spirit world through medium Cleopas Kundioni that's transcripted in 1992's *The Victory of Love*), Adam was so wrapped up in his own egocentrism that he couldn't have cared less what befell Eve and ignored all the warning signs. When Eve lured him into her 'tree of good and evil,' it was a reverse cowboy wrongness because their actions were predicated on selfishness rather than God's intended unselfish, wholesome love.

The story may seem fantastic, particularly to Muslims and traditional Christians, but had substantial repercussions in our day-to-day church life. I saw the 'servant of servants' Formula Course, rooted in the Cain–Abel dynamic that separates thus reclaims one from Satan, emanating directly from Rev. Moon's faith in the Fall. It was his contention that if he allowed a church couple sex willy nilly without first making indemnity conditions, their sexual love would be just as corrupt and tainted as Adam and Eve's in the Garden, fail to separate Satan, and nullify their Blessing of Marriage altogether, which is Divine Principle's *raison d'être*. He said,

> [F]or the first three years you do not engage in the physical relationship of married life. You live a spiritually married life and restore spiritual children, at least three each. After three years you unite as husband and wife . . . and have

> your own children . . . by the time the seven-year course is over, you will have restored both. Spiritually, Adam's family will be restored, and yourself, with your own children, will have reached perfection. (*To the Crusade* 1978)

Hence, he brought together a practical and spiritual need into a handy, one-size-fits-all policy benefiting church and member alike. He taught us our basic responsibility to Restore the created world and humanity from Satan's ownership. Money, because it represents the external, physical world that Satan stole through the Fall, and people, because they represent the spirit world and fallen Adam and Eve. While he required no monetary amounts be earned, he did require each member restore—recruit into the church—72 spiritual children before they qualified for the Blessing. He selected this number because it corresponds with Jesus' 72 disciples.

"Ugh," I later said in San Francisco. "This means I'll *never* get Blessed."

Julian said, "Quit griping and selling yourself short. Try! You'll be surprised—"

"I sure will! I can talk DP all day but I hate witnessing it." Why? Hard to say. Anxiety? dread? fear of rejection? didn't care?

"Find a way to do that, then."

"On the street? How?"

His full-torso shrug said, *You're a big boy, Chris; step up and figure it out*. He could be so aggravating.

But I wasn't sure I wanted to. When it proved impossible for most everybody, Rev. Moon cut the number to three with the caveat the whole 72 needs be earned before death. Then he allowed members to get Blessed and start their families if they simply *pledged* at least three spiritual children in the future. Living with a spouse was an epic, knock-down drag-out *Mad Max* cage fight in the church.

In practice, his Formula Course was a flop of monumental proportions despite there being "no such thing as retreat; first go over the MFT mission and then on to something else greater." The church didn't consistently implement it and anyway damaged morale. Some worked MFT the mandated 3-½ years. Others segued out after far less or got spiderwebbed 7–10 years. I met some of them and trembled at their despair, umbrage, and gall. They showed up to their forties with no job skills beyond touting trinkets streetside and place-to-place. Though enabling their own servility to MFT, leaders nevertheless signed off on starting their families before menopause regardless their lack of meaningful earning power to support them beyond poverty to low-income against Rev. Moon's rosy prognostication that,

> Once you women are seasoned on MFT, supporting your own family will be no problem . . . you are fund raising under adverse conditions, but in ten years the world will know what we are doing, and with community and media support you could certainly do more than you do now. Then raising family expense money and Church money will be simple . . . No one can take away your ability to gather money, and . . . you will be able to support and educate your children and grandchildren. (*To the* MFT, WMC 1980)

To add insult to injury, he eventually reneged in the midst of long-range financial mismanagement woes on his implicit and sometimes explicit promise to take care of full-time members. He announced that everyone was now responsible to provide for themselves and should look to their own devices for survival.

"God, what a slap in the face!" somebody said, face hardened in betrayal. "We did everything..."

Many of us reflected, "I gave all my best years because he promised us statues in our hometowns and a pension. And, now what?"

"Then you were just being selfish," the hardier said. "That's why Father has no money anymore and you can't get your precious reward. Is that why you joined? To get something instead of serving God's providence through True Parents? Where's your heart? All you Cains: stealing one way or another through no result."

"Screw you," a hefty chunk said in dripping disgust.

"You're Satan! You failed, so Father failed. Leave! We don't need you."

Irrespectively dismissing decades of obedience to Rev. Moon and his leaders *as they'd required of us* was our Fort Sumter. His realpolitik in misfortune gutted us. Although some persisted as nominal members via Sunday service (because, Divine Principle), their nursed grievances defeat the very purpose Rev. Moon founded his church on in the first place. They're better off, spiritually and economically, spewing all their fury and bile in a shrilling siren of broken promises and abuse. The hope is Rev. Moon takes corrective action. If no one speaks up then discontent lives on to insidiously defeat his lifetime of spiritual conditions and church ministry anyway. For the institution, that's the very crow now come home to roost.

"How can God love our church when members violate every law of His heart?" I said to Shirley back in LA's present, my blood hot from pesky Japanese brothers pushing me around and our commander pushing us ever meaner. His compassion for our crash-car bodies seemed an ever more thinly veiled suspicion.

"Remember Paul in First Corinthians, Chris," Shirley said.

"The Bible?" *So, what was it he said? If I give all I possess to the poor and surrender my body to the flames, but have not love, I gain nothing?* "So, you're saying rest on unconditional love or I'm the same as them. Like the Sermon on the Mount."

"Like True Father. Every satan falls through the power of love without strings."

"I think the church is too busy banging its gong."

She tilted her head like her neck was tired, her lips a moue. "Word to the wise: don't make its problems your story."

I didn't yet see it under Shirley's motherly hand and my own naïveté, but that sums up the story of the American Unification Church. It sacrifices itself to bring millions to the Blessing, witness to Christian ministers it fêtes in Korea, and raise money to pay for it all while its putridly blindfolded bureaucratic process spiritually murders and devours its own members, spitting them out like broken sunflower hulls... very much like Communism and Leftism generally. The irony is crushing. The church gained nothing over the years uncaringly practicing lovelessness. It necessarily declined into fantasy where each great victory is only a precursor to some nebulous future triumph or happens only in the unverifiable spirit world.

The hoped-for Mormonesque Formula Course structure laid over Unificationism ended up creating a social inequity instead. Rev. Moon blamed its failure on lousy witnessing landing too few recruits to replace veterans. Members who'd completed their 3-½- or 7-year service couldn't rotate into witnessing or babymaking, the heart and soul of Unificationism as with Christians called to spread the Gospel and be fruitful. For the church, you can't progress past the simple individual growth intrinsic of MFT until pouring your heart and soul Ezekiel-like into raising up your own spiritual children from the fallen world's dry bones. But recruiting failed because the church metamorphosed into a totalitarian feudal society anathema to American sensibilities. Members socialized into a love and appreciation for the Principle held on the longest. Those who didn't or came later got disgusted faster and left sooner. Herein lies an excellent lesson for any church: practice what you preach.

ABOUT FIVE MONTHS after my arrival in LA we heard Mr. Kamiyama's wife had become an IW, a so-called *itinerant worker* traveling place to place like a circuit judge doling out spiritual guidance and comfort (sometimes judgment and penance). Our commander announced her pending arrival.

"You should prayerfully prepare to meet her to discuss any spiritual concerns." We nodded, trying to gauge this state of affairs through his inscrutable nonexpression. "But her purpose is not to change situations."

I scrutinized him saunter off stage. "Was that aimed at us, Shirley?"

She sighed. "Don't worry about it."

Some time later, she pulled us in early one evening. "Great news! We're meeting Mrs. Kamiyama tonight. We'll get dinner then head home."

Bam! Had I prayerfully prepared?

We crowded into a boxy, dark-paneled, measly sized room I thought must be our commander's fabled private stall. I admired its lamplit warmth and especially the wound-round rope-style rug over padded wall-to-wall carpet cushioning my ass maybe permanently flattened from barebones stone. A soundproof quality suffused the space. Icebreaking chit-chat quieted our nerves.

Mrs. Kamiyama came across pleasingly pleasant for a standoffish Japanese and seemingly concerned for our spiritual welfare. I approved. *At least someone in the Kamiyama clan cares.* In her early fifties was how I read her: pre-war and petitely Lilliputian. She'd cut her black, slightly graying hair short and permed to a curl like Mrs. Moon's. Her delicate face was a waxy brightness promoting reddish cheeks smiling down upon us children, sagely grandma in for tea from the plantation's big house. A fragile package, she nonetheless moved easily from standing to sitting on the floor and back again while the rest of us, probably 30 years her junior, struggled down let alone back up. Especially me with my recalcitrant knee.

We'd heard a slew of thrilling coast-to-coast stories of her rescuing members circling their desolate drains that buoyed our hopes. I'd been on our team now about six months. Our work schedule had wrought havoc on all our health. My back, shoulder, hip, and knee agonized through my days marching gold-paved streets on a stooped cane and sleeping it off on bare concrete without so much as a medieval peasant's straw pallet. I longed for a hay barn.

I know what I want to say. I glanced at Shirley feeling Mrs. Kamiyama's holy, unyielding power. *But how to broach it?*

Then through a burr in her throat a sister said, "Mrs. Kamiyama, I feel so broken, and we're all just physically falling apart."

Thank you, I silently mouthed her way.

"Ehh?" Surprise lit Mrs. Kamiyama. "What do you mean?"

Ball rolling, we let out like a yardful of mangy, baying dogs choking through our maladies and peppering her with our woes.

I said, "I'm not sure I can take this life anymore—"

"I can't," said maybe Margarita.

"—because some days I feel like I'm going to literally fall down dead."

"Me, too," Betsy and Darlene echoed. Young Soon was naturally more restrained at Mrs. Kamiyama's august feet.

"The pain is almost unbearable and getting worse," I continued. "I'm afraid I'll end up in a wheelchair."

A lichen of shock spread across Mrs. Kamiyama. "I was told you had some physical issues, but . . ."

Shirley said, "What can you do about our situation? We're dedicated to God and True Parents, but we've reached our tether. We need help."

I think she'd never encountered what tumbled out nor the passion of our sorrows. Some sisters were wiping tears. My own burned hot and wet, my throat a raw pit.

She said, "I understand your feeling and will see about your situation"—sit-chi'ay-shon in the typical accent—"and get back with you." She scanned our beseeching, and my possibly skeptical, features. "I promise. Please, trust me."

We nodded and mumbled our understanding and thanks for her visit.

"Do not worry. God will work. Keep your prayer."

And that was that. We filed out excitedly if pessimistically replaying our meeting through each other. In a church chockablock with healthy, sprinting youth we were a Houston-we've-got-a-problem oddity. I suppose our feelings were hope swirling through cynicism. But at least we'd got to speak to someone besides our fanatical, crockpotted commander. Someone with Lord Kamiyama's ear firmly pinched twixt forefinger and thumb. We hoped.

A few weeks later Shirley said, "Guess what? We're getting a new mission."

We all of us gaped. *What? Really? Where? How?*

"We're going to pack up our van with all our things and drive to San Francisco." We traded wide eyes and shit-eating grins while Shirley explained. "There's a new mission there. Some kind of experiment. It's just starting and we're part of it."

"But what is it?" Betsy said.

"Does it involve fundraising?" I said.

"It's supposed to be a witnessing center, but for crippled and injured members like us. Otherwise, I don't know any more than you do. We'll find out there."

"Who?" Margarita said. "How?"

Shirley looked to be thinking over how much to tell us. "Well, I *heard* that, apparently, Mrs. Kamiyama was furious with Mr. Kamiyama over our physical situation and insisted he give us a different mission in keeping with it."

"You think he even knew?" Betsy wondered.

"He knew about *me*," I said. Shirley didn't have a peep for that but her face said *I don't know, maybe, probably, yeah* all at once. I breathed, "Always so cryptic between conscience and Principle!" But my heart gushed over Mrs. angel-of-mercy Kamiyama. No one but Rev. Moon could've moved our mountain to Muhammad.

On our last legs, we were beginning to recognize the unpleasant truth we'd have to leave the church to save our health. "But, San Fran's good enough for me!"

Not only me. Our collective joy was a soaring energy bounding through us. We whistle-cleaned our van for sleeping bags, pillows, blankets, clothes, toiletries, books, and all the detritus of human life somehow along on our combat tour.

∼

FUNDRAISING IS AN integral aspect of Unification Church life that's saturated in spiritual meaning and the Restorational (salvific) process. Rev. Moon says,

> When you come into the movement, you go out to MFT, fundraising movement, by which you discipline yourself under hardship, and under adverse conditions you restore the things of creation for a period of two to three years. Then you move on to witnessing. Witnessing is another level. Adam was lost; you are going to restore that by finding spiritual children . . . First you go through restoring all things of creation through fundraising. You must restore your spiritual children through witnessing. You must win the Cain and Abel struggle by serving them, so that you elevate yourself to the parents' position. By doing so, you will form your own family, heavenly character, heavenly heart, and ultimately heavenly citizenship. (*To the Crusade* 1978)

> [You] must contribute not only material but also men, and give them with God's heart . . . centering on love. (*Persecution and Blessing*, Belvedere 1980)

Funding the church is a need coterminous with the unavoidable side effect of gilding Rev. Moon's lily along with his toadies' lifestyles. Despite its tons of businesses, each local church center needs be self-supporting. There was just never any will to venture into sensible, high-volume cash flows—say, gas station–convenience stores or garbage collection—because they served no flashy providential purpose and anyway fundraising has a visibly high gross margin.

Even so, many of us felt inspired and closer to God through our fundraising regardless, and maybe because of, its difficulty. It could be drudge duty, to be sure, but a slight change in attitude could make the effort a spiritual bonanza. Part of any religious life is overcoming oneself, which brings Julian to mind. It involves not just sexual urges and criminal tendencies but also one's sense of limitation and unwillingness to live for others or just something greater than ourselves. When people choose to work for God they're choosing to do the unusual, which often leads to hardship plus criticism by their community, as with St. Francis.

Unification Church fundraising was indeed a business, pure and simple. No sentiment was ever lost pursuing its financial needs. But MFT was the perfect place for megalomaniacs to spiral out of control because the usual self-correcting mechanisms of a spiritually-oriented atmosphere were virtually nonexistent. What mattered was result, not one's sensitivity or spiritual needs. In this way, MFT really was an army at war. What commander could possibly care more about his men than winning the battle? But we needed an equal consideration for both, the emphasis on the one or the other case by case. Because we *weren't* an army at war.

I hated fundraising as exceedingly boring and beneath me. A leader, strategist, and organizer, I was wasted in the trenches and knew it. All the same, I found huge personal satisfaction fundraising for my next-up, local center in San Francisco. Unlike MFT, my connection to the money I brought in and its ultimate use was powerful and immediate, especially since every month $300 of it settled in Monica's lap (after my $1,500 donation mostly covered me on MFT). But Los Angeles was a wasteland for me. While I failed to develop much spiritual growth on MFT, I did develop a great sensitivity to the sufferings and sorrows of church members and resolved to make a positive difference in their lives.

How controversial it was in the great enslaving cultures of Greece, Rome, Islam, and the New World suggesting that slaves more productively and happily work with one day off per week and a reasonable number of work hours per day. Mr. Kamiyama and his coterie of overseers saw little practicality in such leniency and, predictably, MFT suffered those empires' fate. It ultimately died out as a department of the church which itself is dying out as a spiritual venture here in 2003.

$\sim$

LITTLE LOVE WAS lost and no sentimental tears shed as we wedged ourselves amongst clumps of stuff and each other's bodies. Shirley rocketed us due north to San Francisco for what I envisioned a candy-appled life of personally meaningful contributions to Rev. Moon's ministry and God's Providence of Restoration.

Unfortunately, waiting for me was possibly one of the most megalomaniacal leaders ever to afflict the American Unification Church.

Act VI

A Falling Out

Organized Violence, Bureaucratic Indifference

Our two-row van did a yeoman's job carting the six of us with baggage hauling luggage north up the I–5. In spite of church prohibitions on touching the opposite sex, we foxholeers squeezed embryoblastically into every nook and cranny. Somebody else was often our pillow for comatose, war's-over snoozing. Our journey was the happiest and most congenial time I ever spent in the church . . . maybe my life. We chatted, joked, giggled, guffawed. I felt they loved me and I loved them. We could've been contented 5-year olds on a functional-family excursion. It was liberating, too, because our interplay (from my viewpoint) lacked all the romantic attraction, unrequited love, and sexual tension I usually feel around the fairer sex. I drifted off on Margarita's shoulder, Betsy's chest, Darlene on my arms, Young Soon my knee and felt at perfect ease as if curled up with Mom. I can't speak for them, of course, but my libido was in neutral. I was cheery and serene. In these conditions the cramped, 12-hour trek (with stops) was heavenly. I wished it would never end. *Accepted at last! Only Shirley's benevolent thumb. Fallen nature dead and buried. I should be so lucky.*

We coasted sidelong a newly purchased, 3-storey Tudor home on Judah St. at Seventh Ave. in the Inner Sunset on San Francisco's ocean side. For sure its strategic seat at Biblical and Providential (seven arising in four plus three representing completion in the Principle) enthralled some leader

Judah Street center, 1982; 3rd FL. L–R windows: Julian, office, prayer room; 2nd: brothers' room, sisters' bath/rooms/porch; 1st: living, entry, dining, porch.

to ante up the downpayment. Numerology counts big in the Mooniverse. It controls time periods and timing of events. For example, the 36-couple Blessing, Rev. Moon's first at age 40, derived from 3 sets of the Principle's 9 stages of human growth times the Four-Position Foundation, the basic building block of the Godiverse.

Rev. Moon also uses numerology to establish time periods for *spiritual conditions*, a term for activities devoted toward accomplishing some spiritual or providential purpose. Members do conditions to help achieve spiritual, intellectual, and other pursuits. For instance, at Denver's High Street house I practiced rising at 5 AM (corresponding to Peter betraying Jesus) to wash last night's kitchenware, then read ten pages of *Divine Principle* each night for a 40-day period, all kept private as Jesus recommended. He established 3, 7, 21, 40 and 120-day membership training cycles, each an important Biblical number. Fundraising conditions are usually worked over 40-day periods, as are witnessing and prayer campaigns. The massive 1976 Washington Monument Rally was conceived and put into preparation only 40 days in advance. His own life and ministry unfolds via 7, 21, 40, and 70-year periods, and he counsels us to establish 21-year life plans over three 7-year blocks. He extensively teaches members his own principles of success, though it isn't much use when we can't operate independently of him or the church.

Fanatics whipped up all sorts of conditions to test themselves and spiritually grow. A popular one—in some places in the early '80s, peer-pressured—was the cold shower condition for 21 or 40 minutes over 3, 7, 10, 21, or 40 days. It wasn't easy by a long shot, especially where winter cooked up an excruciating iciness. I tried a few and quaked shivers 'neath a Siberian stream shouting song and prayer or taking the pain clenching teeth. I admired these brothers and sisters' strength and commitment but thought they were a bit on the fringe if not the teetering edge.

'Strong' conditions weren't unknown to me. I did 40-minute prayers at 5 AM or midnight for 21 or 40 days indoors or the wintry outdoors. In 1984–85 I climbed Twin Peaks in San Francisco (a church Holy Ground) rain or shine for daily 40-minute prayers at 5 AM atop the puny flat rock lying at the summit of the tallest of the two. Gale force winds once blew me off the crest and halfway down its slope like a paper cup, fingers ice-axing purchase in the scrabbly soil. Impossible to walk up even crouched, my clawing hands and dug-in toes pushed me hands-and-knees to the peak. I did this condition about a year and never missed a day. In the 1990s I did several 120 full Korean bow conditions that left my kneecaps bloody tatters and my joints and muscles in trembling fire. Many of us viewed the hardships and rigors of fundraising itself as a powerful condition grinding out spiritual growth and development. I appreciated this view. In future, living on my own, I oft-fundraised weekends for my local church center and handed over all my result to walk my own path of indemnity. Nevertheless, after awhile I felt only malice for it. Both MFT and local fundraising in San Francisco permanently satisfied my sense of duty for raising church funds. Higher levels of responsibility called me.

Besides endless prayer conditions such as all-nighters that rotated center to center, fasting too was a major religious devotion. Everyone fasted three days at least once. Then Rev. Moon required seven days as a Blessing qualification. I was attending City College of San Francisco during my first 7-day fast. So busy and distracted, it passed fairly easy especially after the third (hump-) day's hunger pangs. That was the worst, when folks most often gave up. Day four dawned downhill all the way. Ultimately, I did three 7-day fasts. I knew of several who fasted 40 days to emulate Jesus. Leaders discouraged this. They closely monitored us and, if our health seemed dubious, ordered a stop or a juice fast conversion.

"When True Father ordered the first 7-day fast as a condition for our Blessing," a 36-couple Korean said to me in our dining room, "we all thought we would die."

"It was bad as all that?" This was after I'd done my own.

"Ohh, very bad. We lay in our beds aaall day praying, loud suffering noise, crying to God for our miserable situation."

"Wow." What else could I say?

"I'm sooo amazed how easy it is for you young members now. You fundraise, witness, and work like nothing is different. You take no extra rest, even. For us, it was very different. Much more difficult."

"Well, it's probably just our attitude more than anything. We *think* it's relatively easy whereas those first members, the early church, believed it was virtually—"

He was waving a fast palm back and forth. "No, no, no, no, no . . ."

"—impossible . . . what. You don't think so?"

His head wagged. "You do not understand. No one had done such fasts before. There was no spiritual merit for us. We had to build it from nothing. Now, through all these years, Korean and Japanese members have built so much merit. That is why it is now easy for you in America."

"Hmm." That was a not uncommon 'merit of the age' argument, which stole our personal thunder. "You don't think it's just from us having seen it done and—"

A smile split his face. He took my pontificating hand in both of his, squeezed, and tottered off. *Well.* Inscrutably, he'd neither agreed nor disagreed. How diplomatic.

Despite the 'cult' moniker the press and Christianity ruthlessly lavished on us, most members were serious about their religious and spiritual lives. Their monkish flagellations, which the majors celebrate, proves it. Some are fanatical, and others abusive egomaniacs but, in fairness, they're still more or less pursuing the ideal until they aren't. Leaders didn't permit conditions they thought might medically harm our bodies, overly discourage us, or break our faith else I suspect some members—*cough, cough: Japanese*—would've whipped themselves into a whirling dervish.

Experiences and feelings like these paraded through my thoughts as we drifted to a halt at 198 Judah Street, faces pressed to glass for a glimpse of hearth and home. Most of all, relief soaked and gladdened our hearts that Mr. Kamiyama had sent us to the 'sick member' house from fine-fettled MFT. Judah Street center was a lovely single-family built in 1911 for about $4,000. Its entirely redwood bones came by ship from the big logging areas in America's northwest. Sadly, forty-some layers of white to gaudy to battleship grey paint insulted its beautifully stained and oiled redwood. I later spent considerable time restoring our woodwork to its shellacked beauty. Our new home sat just down the hill from University of California's medical center and a bit over a mile from the Pacific Ocean. Two blocks north was delightful Golden Gate Park that we frequented to witness, picnic, and play.

In mid-1982 Rev. Moon was attempting to cross dress MFT with witnessing. Members knew us as the one and only MFT–witnessing center. Our mandate, simply enough, was to witness while fundraising HQ's bills. The latter meant hitting the highways and byways of the Bay Area every Friday evening through Sunday as well as holidays and special days and, eventually, in Nevada, too. I think the idea was members could follow both halves of the Formula Course at the same time in one center before starting their families and other missions.

Julian surprisingly transferred in from Golden Gate Seafood across the bay as our center director. We inherited Anglo-Indian and top MFT fundraiser Christine along with Katie, a cheery and more grounded Betsyish Canadian hipster who'd both arrived earlier. During the 1970s and '80s, MFT headquarters annually awarded special lapel pins to that year's *crème de la crème*. Christine was a frequent recipient. Fundraising junkies avidly competed for them. I never won any . . . not surprised, are you? Christine was somewhat famous for being run down and dragged by a car when flower-selling an intersection.

Her doctors didn't sugarcoat her future to the church reps and MFT commander. "There's nothing more we can do. She'll be dead in hours."

Then, "We expect her to pass this evening . . . prepare yourself for sometime tonight; certainly before morning."

But she was a barnacle on life. "We've revised our prognosis, but you should plan for tomorrow . . . the day after tomorrow . . . well, we're now expecting it won't be until . . ." she didn't. Surprising her medical masters, she held on till Rev. Moon himself praised her "iron will" and her body mended out of the grave.

She and I were the odd couple of the house. We confided in and very much liked each other yet couldn't help fighting like feral cats in a bag; the real litmus for kin. Once, I'd taken a break from the remodeling Julian later had me doing to veg on our TV. She swooped into the living room a huffy force of nature.

"Why are you sitting here in the middle of the day when brothers and sisters are all out working hard for True Parents?"

"I'm just—"

"And with the TV on! Like you can do that."

"Relax, Christine, I'm resting my knee. I'll be back on the job in a jiffy."

She was a ramrod at the coffee table's corner. Hands on hips, her Anglo-Indian regency splashed all over me. Eyes practically bulged. "You can read *Divine Principle*, then. Turn it off. We don't watch TV in the day."

"Well, I do. This is my break."

Her hand frog-tongued the remote control off the table and she'd aimed, pressed, and killed the TV before I could blink, eyes never straying a tremor from mine.

Blood boiled. *Flame on!* For a guy with a cane, I was on two feet in a split tick. The remote disappeared from her hand into mine. The TV flashed on, its babbling bouncing around the room. Eyes locked. "Come on, now. Don't be—"

Mid-sit, thinking I'd won, she wrenched the remote from my supposedly tight grip and the TV blacked into silence. "Off!"

We did this a few more times, artillerists dueling to quell the other's guns first. Good thing nobody happened by. My eyes were seeing red and I couldn't muster up any words that wouldn't get me tossed out the front door on my ear. I stalked out and stumped as best I could up the stairs mumbling and muttering everything I wished I could've said straight to her face, except this was a church, she was a sister—*older* was all the same to me—and, dammitall, I liked her. I paused on the second landing where she couldn't see me and tapped feet a beat, then bent down and peaked through the railings. The living room was empty. Off reading her DP, maybe. I slunk back in and switched on the TV . . . at a much-reduced volume.

"She needs to realize I have my own schedule," I muttered.

When *Christine*, a demon-possessed, blood-red '58 Plymouth Fury flattening any irksome body hit theaters in 1983 I bought the ominous *Watch out for me – I am pure evil – I am Christine* promotional bumper sticker. Her name in satanic red atop hellish black, I thumbtacked it over my floor pallet to remind me who it was I was sometimes dealing with. Yet, somehow I loved her. Now, that's demonic.

The church gave us a couple of Japanese sisters to cook our meals, though all the sisters rotated through kitchen helpmeet. They provided sack lunches whenever we fundraised around town. Betsy once thought little 'tween-bread messages of encouragement would inspire us in the nadir of our day. I sank hungry teeth into my sandwich one noontime and out came a 3×3-inch soggy slip of paper. Barely legible through the mayonnaise and tomato juices, runny ink incredulously read, "God loves you! You're doing a great job. *Mansei!*" (Korean: *10,000 years* but, in the church, mainly *victory* or *hooray*. And now, *yuk*).

"I thought you'd like it," she said, scuttling round the kitchen largely unperturbed, "and appreciate how much we care about everyone out on the front lines."

"Yeah, sure, but why don't you just drop the note in the bag instead of between the bread? It kind of ruined the sandwich, all I'm saying."

I got a shrug and a gen-yoo-wine Betsy eye-lit smile, which was ordinarily invigorating. But now, I thought it just meant my words had only whiffled twixt her ears. She always looked for ways to inspire and comfort with an enormous, if unconventional, mother's heart even bigger than Shirley's. I was irked, but cross was impossible. I did get vexed when she spatulated a pile of chocolate chip and M&M pancakes onto my plate. Quite the experimental hippie, she was.

We spent an abundance of time fundraising our bills (including the $250,000 mortgage on the house) in and around the San Francisco Bay Area and farther afield in Nevada. Julian cruelly placed me on a recently arrived national MFT brothers team that steered me all through the California–Nevada Sierras and Nevada's high-altitude deserts in the fall and winter of 1982–83. I sold flowers and pictures off a folding chair all around Lake Tahoe's 'metro' area with snow flogging in sideways and across sometimes wind-whipped, small-town desert Nevada. Considering my time in college, the service, and MFT, I was naïvely provincial.

A frailish woman in her 80s marched up to my spot outside a yokel desert post office. She loomed over me. "Who are you selling this stuff for, young man?"

I eyed her diminutive frame and the briefcase-sized purse clutched across her chest like it harbored gold bullion. "One World Products, ma'am."

"What's that? Some kind of regular business?"

I laughed. "Is there another kind of business?"

"Don't get sassy. So . . . you ain't one of them Moonies?"

Gulp! What? "I'm a student"—of *Rev. Moon*, but never mind—"selling these pictures to raise money. Would you like to get one? It would really—"

"Well . . ." She tossed her eyes around. I wasn't sure if she was concerned or waiting for backup. "I guess it's a good thing you ain't one of them damn Moonies, then. If you were," she patted her purse, "I'd have whipped out my thirty-eight and shot you on the spot." She harrumphed.

Judah St. MFT. *Nevada. Dec., 1982.*

The heck? "Uhh, well, then, thank goodness . . . In that case, would you—?"

"Oh, hell no. You have a nice day, young man." And off the anachronism pitter-pattered.

Our team captain had said, "Sell your product as college students under OWP." Now I knew MFT thus our commander weren't bullshitting us just to stem the potential loss of sales to bigots who didn't want a clutch of beautiful fresh roses, a scented wood rose in a vase, a framed hi-def laser photo, or a peacock of a metal etching for their wall. It was the evidently real specter of dead Moonie blood pooling on all that unsold product.

When she'd tetchily blasted the post office to perdition she pulled up and said, "What religion are you, anyhow, young man?"

"Born and raised Catholic, ma'am." I wondered if she'd now reveal her Ku Klux Klan affinities.

She stiupped teeth. "Well, could've been worse, I suppose."

"It could?" I shuddered what it meant to be a *black* Moonie in Nevada. I grew up rural, but the Rockies had nothing on the whitewashed desert mind out here.

"Sure, it could!" She smiled like an angel. "What if you'd lied? I can tell."

She drifted away. I smiled and waved. In another town, the sheriff rolled up late morning and barked his tires in the angled parking off to my right. Shorty boots dropped to the ground and out he climbed, springs bouncing up in creaking relief. He slammed his door and ambled straight for me. I watched the approach.

"What are you doing here?"

"Selling flowers, sir."

"I can got-damn well see that, young man. Don't be mouthing off."

"Yessir."

"What's your relig—what church do you attend?"

Since when does a cop quiz you on your church? I expected he'd demand my sales permit. Nevada was full of surprises. I considered asking what business it was of his, or lying, but knew the rathole either one ends up dragging you down. "I go to the Unification Church," like it was on par with the local Protestants.

He nodded. "Moonies, huh? Thought as much."

"Well,"—may as well try—"would you be interested in—?"

"You getting out of my town is what I'm interested in. Where's your vee-hikkle? I'll help you pack it all up."

Shit. You learn something new every day. "I don't have a car, officer."

"*Sheriff*, got-dammit."

"Yessir. My friends are picking me up later."

"More Moonies? Not here, they ain't. You git out to the town line and meet 'em on the *other* side, or you can walk to the next town if you've a mind to."

"How far's the next town?"

"Thirty, forty miles, give or take."

I choked. "You expect me to walk there?"

"I don't 'spect nothin' 'cept you leavin' *here*. Right now."

"There's nothing but desert out—" He rested a hand on his gun butt. "Well, could I just sell till my van gets here and then never come back?"

"No. You can go to the town line or go to jail. Up to you."

I squinted up at him. "I don't get it, Sheriff. There's no law against selling flowers or having a certain religion. How come—?"

"You're disturbin' the peace and that there's agin the law. Had some complaints." I hadn't. "You sayin' you prefer jail an' a judge?"

"No, sir." I ostentatiously handled my cane in case his cop eyes missed it.

Eyes slitted. "Now, where'd you get that, boy? You old enough for 'Nam?"

"The Coast Guard. Line of duty."

He paused a beat. Glanced around. Eyed his patrol car. Head nodded. "Tell you what, I'll give you a ride to the town limits."

"Can't I wait in the library? I won't sell anything."

"You figure that's inside or outside the town limits?"

Man, this guy hates Moonies. "I appreciate what you're saying, Sheriff, but it's cold and my van won't be here till evening sometime."

"You seen service. I'm sure you can handle leavin' my town. Now, up."

His town. Like medieval private property. He hoisted my two 5-gallon, water-filled flower buckets—like I was supposed to hike the highway lugging *them*—as I folded my chair, shouldered my book bag, and exaggeratedly hobbled on his heels to my one-way ticket. He shot scree pulling off the town-line's roadside. I waited cold and stomping till our MFT van found me at dusk.

"I'm really sorry, Chris," my team captain said. "We haven't had trouble in this town before. But, it's been awhile." He scratched it off his map.

"Yeah. Glad I could clarify it for you." His peace offering was a hot chocolate.

In San Francisco we fenced a running battle with its public eye zealously arresting all our members for fundraising despite its absolute legality. With each arrest Julian phoned the city's district attorney in righteous indignation. He helpfully tore his disinterested police chief a new asshole as a prelude to ordering our member's release. I then traipsed downtown to the courthouse jail to pick up our felon. They mostly nabbed Japanese sisters who couldn't speak English, hence, protest.

I was downtown in the Financial District near Market and Pine picking up a Japanese sister when a cop double parked his squad car. "You know peddling without a license is illegal? I'm gonna have to write you both up."

"Get in the van," I told the sister. I finished loading her 5-gallon buckets in the back of my van and slammed the doors closed.

"You hear me? And I'll be needing those buckets for evidence."

I looked down on him from my divine height. "How do you know she was peddling? You weren't even here."

"Because I'm not blind."

"She's fundraising for our church, and that's not illegal. Call the city attorney's office. They'll tell you."

"So you say. It's illegal peddling if I say it is. And I'm saying—"

"You can say it all day and the city attorney will still chew you out for unlawful arrest." By now, we'd moseyed our discussion to my open driver's door. "Anyway, she wasn't selling anything. She was just getting in our van before you even arrived. You can't charge her with anything."

"I saw enough. You resisting?"

I was on the seat, door closed, and lock punched down before he reacted. He grew a couple feet. "Open that door right now and exit the vehicle!"

I cracked my tall window an inch. "You're acting illegally and beyond your authority. I'm not talking to you. Call your supervising sergeant!"

He sputtered. "Open up before I smash the glass and drag you out!" The fact he already hadn't meant he knew damn well he had no authority for it.

"Call your supervisor or I'll consider myself free to go. Go on! Call him!"

He stared daggers and mouthed all manner of threats before I rolled that inch closed, dropped the van into DRIVE, hit my left turn signal and pointedly looked over my shoulder for traffic and his possibly leveled sidearm.

"I'm leaving now," I shouted through the glass. "You calling your sergeant? Well, you have my license plate if you need me."

I slowly, lawfully pulled off the curb. I'd figured some words from the district attorney had filtered down the ranks or he'd have been dramatically more aggressive. The police chief probably advised them to arrest us only if we didn't resist. It was a calculated risk. My Japanese sister eyed me like God and Satan all rolled into one. She knew enough to know you didn't get away with shit like this in Japan. Over there the church had to (and did) grease every skid beforehand.

When the cops arrested our members, though, their flowers were always a write-off, as they refused to return the 'evidence' for the 'crime' the city DA had already ruled was not. We fundraised, the DA put screws to the cops for false arrest and harassment, and they made up their own laws to arrest us for violating. Absolute bastards following their chief bigot's illegal orders. But they were pissing in the wind so long as the mightily lawyered Unification Church needed fundraisers.

On the domestic front, our 4-storey house included an unfinished dirt-floor basement that was useless. We lived on the second floor. The sisters moved into the best room in the house with an enclosed porch and a hallway bathroom. We brothers made do with a bay-windowed corner room and hiked a flight for the undersized bathroom next to the small office and Julian's private quarters overlooking both streets through two leaded, lattice-paned triple bay windows.

Privacy in the church is a figment. Like the open-seat aft enlisted head on the Navy's WWII Fletcher-class destroyers, we used the commode while another one showered and more occupied the sink and mirror shaving, brushing teeth, primping, whatever. We third estate lived this way most everywhere in the country. The church expected a public life where nothing was hidden similar to Rev. Moon's early Korean pastoral (and marital) life in his one-room church–residence.

> You are not a private person. (*My Life*, Belvedere 1978) . . . public life runs so contrary to the prevailing American system . . . incredible . . . hardship must be overcome to achieve it. (*God's Warning to the World II*, "Public Life" 1985)

He wasn't kidding. Time alone in the bathroom was a scarce, therefore prized, privilege and I avidly timed it. I was reposed on the can unwinding a fistful of tissue when Julian barged in and gave me one shuddering look.

"That's not how you do it!"

"What?!" I practically barked in disbelief.

"You're using too much. You have to conserve, the world is overwhelmed by waste. You don't need that many sheets."

He was my spiritual leader and boss. And I was literally butt-naked. What could I do? "Fuck off," howsoever humbly worded, was out of the question in those days. I swallowed my humiliation. "How much is enough, then?"

He thrust his hand out. "Here, let me show you . . ." He pulled off three sheets of toilet tissue—*three goddamn squares!*—and handed them over, a big yuk-yuk grin on his face. "This is all you need. And it'll save us money, too."

He handled that episode as a man born to royalty without the slightest expectation his will would or could be challenged. I meekly accepted his proffered sheets like the theoretically good Moonie I was and resolved to never shit behind unlocked doors again. Ironically, his outrageous assault on my dignity did teach me conservation. Thereafter, I used far less tissue than ever before. Not *three*, for damned sure, but not an impenetrable handful, either.

We'd heard rumors for a year about a movie Rev. Moon was producing. He envisioned a whole celluloid empire starting with a slam-bang war story about MacArthur's liberation of Seoul in the Korean War. *Inchon* (1982) was his first foray onto the silver screen. It was evident to those of us who let our brains do our thinking that neither he nor those he put in charge (particularly Mr. Ishii, a seasoned member but an unremitting naïf) had the slightest idea how to craft a film.

Local leaders wined and dined us on tales of Mr. Ishii cruising Hollywood and Japan with a suitcase of cash, throwing it like confetti and buying up what he thought was all the top talent his movie could ever want: Laurence Olivier as MacArthur, David Janssen (scenes cut after unexpectedly dying), Japanese heavyweight Toshiro Mifune (my personal favorite), Jacqueline Bisset, and other 'A'-listers. We marveled at the wads of magical mammon our church had to spare for this spectacle—MFT's bloodstained loot (ours or Japan's)—while we struggled to fundraise our expenses let alone the gargantuan mortgage we'd no hand in negotiating. Ultimately, Mr. Ishii spent something like $48 million on the most soul-strangling movie to ever shred eyes. Moonie haters like Steven Hassan alleged that Rev. Moon ordered us to uncritically sing its praises, but I never heard that happening anywhere. We *expected* it to be great and felt no compunction lauding it beforehand. It was the most expensive film ever made at the time and its slick advertising foretold Oscars. How could it *not* be awesome with all that treasure and talent? Little did we know how effectively money plus stupidity can fuck up anything.

General MacTurkey.

Boxfuls of full-color posters and letter-size flyers arrived. We dutifully dished them out all over town on windshields, in mailboxes, and into hands of irritated passersby to excite fans to flood the box office. The posters looked fabulous, although MacArthur–Olivier's image looked as if his manly chin had melted down under a glaring paste-up face job.

"Where's the virility?" I wondered aloud to Julian. "He looks like a weasel."

"Hush up! Don't be negative. This is *True Father's* movie!"

I didn't shut up but did fly my jaundiced eye below his radar. Our promo goodies included cases of a 10-page, full-color behind-the-scenes booklet about the movie, war, and Rev. Moon. The marketing was first rate even if the film was a dumpster dive.

I'd had misgivings early on. Mr. Ishii hired the author of *The Green Berets* and *French Connection* to co-write the screenplay. How in hell could that bag of crackers ever imagine Robin Moore writing him other than a potboiler about valor, heroism, self-sacrifice, and freedom for cash instead of commitment? I excitedly cracked his *Oh! Inchon* advance book with a heady expectation . . . until the first few pages. Then I threw up in my mouth.

What a hack job. "We was robbed!" I thundered to all.

I was distraught by the boorish prostitution, deceit, cowardice, failure, and vice painting South Koreans dissolute and little else. It reeked of pretension. Churning through it was a bout of diarrhea. I threw it down in disgust. We all trekked to the theater for a midday screening and sang Korea's anthem in line, a native flopping out her window to join in. An audience barely qualifying as sparse trickled in.

"It's the middle of a weekday," I said to a flit-eyed Julian. "I'm sure it'll buck up with a few word-of-mouth weekends."

"I'm sure it will, Chris. It's going to rock." For all his bravado, he didn't look especially convinced. More than I did, though.

Unlike the book, the movie began with old newsreels of Kim Il Sung making his deal with the Moscow Devil. I heard that last-minute change alone cost hundreds of thousands and secured Rev. Moon a screen credit. It roared downhill from there.

We stumbled dazed from the theater. I harped a gaudy displeasure. "Oh, my *God* that sucked. It's literally the worst movie I've ever seen!"

Feeling goaded he admitted, "It's not what I expected, I can say that."

"Come on, Julian. You need to let some reality in."

"Shush. Don't be negative."

"Dealing with reality isn't negativity. It's just accepting what is."

"What *is*, is our faith in True Parents. Focus on that, okay?"

I shoved hands deep in pockets and blew a heavy, head-shaking sigh.

Even blindly loyal Japanese were prattling on with frowns and tight words. They never called it a turkey but merely, "Disappointing," and "Maybe not so good."

I couldn't recommend even seeing it free and thought few did. How could we? The film was so bad—practically booed off screen at its Washington, DC premiere— it lasted one heavily recut week and grossed a mere fraction of costs regardless a last-ditch, million-dollar give-away to lure in the unwilling. When the trauma wore off, most of us collectively flushed it from our minds. We dumped left over promo like used porno though I kept a copy of each on the off-chance it might have historical value one day. Rev. Moon *was* the Messiah after all. The film never even made Blockbuster's old-shoe shelves or I'd have bought a copy for a keepsake. I recently saw a poster for $25 on eBay, so there was something to that idea.

The fiasco was sorely disheartening and not just because we wanted Rev. Moon's *cinema paradiso* to succeed. He'd gleefully preached God's vision for an epic Jesus flick giving the Principle's perspective that he didn't come to die. Boasting a mini-Jerusalem film locale maybe for a future theme park and hunting for the right lead, he foretold the incredible impact his saga would have on global Christianity.

"I'm already moving ahead with developing a screenplay," he gloated.

We all clapped and shouted, "*Mansei! Mansei! Mansei!*" Yeah, baby.

Inchon flopping like Midway in '42 popped his bubble. He postponed indefinitely his conquest of Hollywood after washing a river of our money through a cauldron of incompetence and probably embezzlement. Mr. Ishii squandered obscene sums on food, meetings, salaries, parties, bungled shoots. I wagered the Korean Unification Church siphoned a cut for 'logistical support.' Leaders smugly (till it misfired) extolled Mr. Ishii's bulging briefcase of banknotes whacking 'A'-list doorknockers for reputations willing to bet "Hello, 'B'-list" big.

We thrilled to this 1951 vision in Korea's war clouds snapped by an American pilot in 1943 Europe.

Aged Olivier was frank. "People ask me why I'm playing in this picture . . . Money, dear boy."

Now seeing what is as it is Julian said with weary disgust, "These people agreed to do Father's movie only out of greed."

"Well," . . . *duh*. "It's Hollywood." But I didn't have the heart to pile on.

"They knew who fronted it, but the cash was too good." He was disjointed. "Playing their parts but leaving their heart and soul home with their integrity."

Or something like that. We blamed greedy actors though many of us understood the script itself was spoiled fruit. Nobody Mr. Ishii hired could create shit.

LIFE IN THE church went on. Leaders stuck us right in. No chance to recuperate from MFT. My pain and short-fuzed energy made my days a raspy chore. I settled into witnessing less fundraising Friday–Sunday, holidays, and 'consumer' days. Most worked chairs in deference to broken health. What a pleasure to hawk bucketed tall-stemmed roses seated instead of schlepping pictures. It was relatively easy and we made money. I also escorted Christine's suitcase of jewelry she sold on ships.

I met many an entertaining lunatic waltzing up to hand over $20 bills saying, "God said to give you this." Obese street rats panhandling $60 a day sometimes threatened bodily harm if I didn't vacate their turf. One afternoon, three such misfits at a downtown subway entrance promised me skeletal disarray for handing out Rev. Moon flyers. I wondered on which one my walking cane would shatter if they forced me to defend myself, and if the end would be jagged enough to shove through the next guy's belt-busting belly. They satisfied themselves literally masturbating against Rev. Moon's photo—he sure collected colorful enemies—then went to scare up some just desserts from passersby. Without doubt, I preferred innocuously vending flowers to controversial flyers. Who doesn't love a sweet-smelling rose?

With Dad at Newport Beach, '82.

I accompanied Julian to the San Francisco Flower Market in Friday's wee hours to buy bunches of roses, carnations, fern stems, and dandelions. Roses cost 70–90¢ per bunch of 25. We sold 3 for $5, 6-for-$10, and a dozen for $20. I thought our price ruinously high until I meandered into a florist and gaped at a dozen just like ours going for an eye-watering $70. I anticipated the weekly market visit because it got me away from the church and into 'real' society as a buyer, not a seller. I enjoyed the energy and sense of freedom even though I felt out of place, a stranger now in a strange land.

Friday mornings we repackaged our flowers into plastic-wrapped units of 3, 6, and 12. That way we could whip them from bucket to customer with a minimum of fuss on our part and reconsidering on theirs. When ready, everything went into our Ford behemoth. Julian hard-charged us to our drop-off points. There were many days he had to all but drag me out of that van, having lost all mind for fundraising. Had my fill. Shell shock, if you like. However, time stumbled on till I achieved a chaired-up street veteran and senior housemember status so very unlike MFT. I discovered a comfort with it till my whining dried up.

An MFT crew with national aspirations worked out of our house for awhile. "Too gung-ho for me, though," I said to Julian. "They're as fanatical as special forces. Their captain . . . well, Shirley rocked."

"Sounds like just what you need, Chris."

My guts gelled. "Come on. That guy's a tyrant, all pushy and, if you ask me, on the edge of psychosis."

"Luckily, I'm not. You'll thank me. More, traditional MFT is good experience."

I'd heard his pious confidence already. "We worked at High Street and I don't relish his memory, Julian. Let me do something else that won't tear up my body."

His head wagged uncompromising Jesuit eyes. "This is better for your spiritual life." He deviously slated me to accompany them and I rapidly fell in hate with it.

Months later, so disgusted with my whole lifestyle, I climbed out a third-floor window and shimmied up the fire escape ladder. Plopped on the metal platform bolted to the roof peak, I followed them antlike hunting me down. My team captain, Julian, Christine, and others calling my name echoed up to my eagle's nest. I'd be damned if I was coming off my perch until the fundraising van abandoned me.

Then Julian had the presence of mind to walk into the small courtyard separating the main house from our free-standing garage and, hands on hips, look up. A hand shaded his eyes. And there I was, the mouse atop the house. *Well, fuck.*

He shouted up. I wouldn't come down. He had to climb the ladder and squeeze in beside me on the platform for a face to face. "This isn't good, Chris."

"None of it's good, Julian."

"I'm not at all happy you're pulling this."

"Have you even been listening, though?" We stared, silent, across the rooftopped city. "Anyway, I'm not 'pulling' anything."

"Yes, you are. But"—*sigh*—"I guess I can see where you're coming from."

"Well, that's something."

"Watch it, eh." He considered all our situations awhile. "The house has a lot of problems and lots of junk lying around. What do you say to maintenance and cleanup, see where that goes?"

I took in his greenish eyes and well-meaning face. We shook hands. He was unhappy with my escapade, to put it lightly. But I won some respect standing up for what I didn't like. It wasn't that I unremittingly despised fundraising or lazily refused to financially support the very house I lived in. The main problem was it continually degraded me. While I chafed at the bit for an opportunity to do more responsible work and utilize my talents and experience, leaders pressed me into mindless grunt work; a patrician in a pleb world. Well, I'd done

My usual Mr. Maintenance, 1983.

enough of that in my disabled condition. The Formula Course be damned. Six months on MFT and all my other fundraising at this or that center was enough in my view. Unaspiring members aplenty could take my place. Let me move on and up. Follow my talents. Not bury them like Matthew 25:18's hapless servant.

This was the greatest bother in the American church: precious little room for Americans to advance. We weren't Sunday Christians. This was frontline combat locking horns with Satan and a hostile, fallen world. Julian often waxed poetic for the golden days of the '70s church when a person could join and weeks later rise to MFT captain and higher in a year or less. The church had been rapidly expanding across a large country, turnover was a constant problem, and many were needed but few choosing. I longed for those opportunities to make a public difference.

The church had spread across the nation by the time I joined in early 1981 with fewer and fewer open positions. Still, good team captains, witnessing leaders, center directors, local (versus national) regional leaders, and even competent state leaders were always in short supply. But so many roles were filled only by Rev. Moon or top leaders' direct appointment instead of on-site managers that it was nigh impossible for a member lacking high-level connections to gain responsibility. The system guaranteed the near hopelessness of ditching patently incompetent and abusive leaders . . . and being American was an automatic demerit.

Regardless our purported mission, we operated in a twilight zone for awhile and mainly fundraised to support the house. Julian was our team captain. I retailed flowers by chair and bucket at downtown venues, beachside areas and, my favorite spot, the famous Cliff House. It perched along the Pacific's high edging where the sea penetrates the Golden Gate and sported the worst weather in the city. It sometimes blew so fierce the rain lashed me laterally or else froze me solid. I sold through ship-sinking gales from a protected alcove at the popular restaurant's entrance. Quite often I made my best money on its worst days. Beats me.

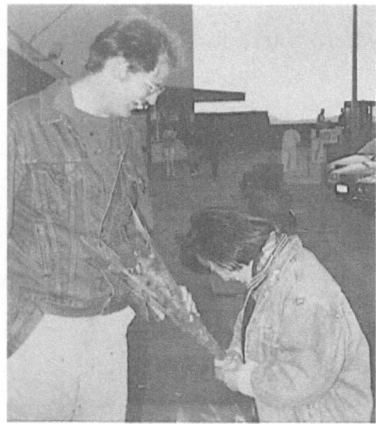

Judah St. fundraiser. Cliff House, 1987.

These were the days Julian touted me his best fundraiser owing to my (now) uncomplaining attitude and can-do spirit regardless inclement obstacles. I appreciated praise on the heels of my less than stellar fundraising reputation and enjoyed working with him. He was one of the best members I met in my 36 years service to the church. Unfortunately, he'd turn against me in a power struggle involving our local Korean despot, but that low blow was yet to come.

Dwayne, an ex-Marine, indulged himself telling 'classified' tales and demonstrating how to render us unconscious in under ten seconds by compressing our carotid. His manly torso often sharing my renovation chores shirtless prompted complaints from some of the sisters that he was overcharging them with sexual tension. Up went the dress code à la Mr. Sato. For such an earthy guy, he once stumbled home in shock from an underaged lass propositioning him in a diner.

" 'Trashing out,' she called it. What the hell is that? Trashing out?"

I said, "It's a weird take on sex for sure, but hardly more apropos considering the Principle's take on it."

"Yeah, totally fallen. Such a cute girl, too. Probably from a good family."

"Ha! Maybe. Maybe not." Then I reconsidered. "Bet her dad was a preacher."

He was a funny mix of right-wing fringe lunacy and conservative Christian mores. "It's disgusting. I couldn't do it even if I wanted to."

Could I? If I wanted, I supposed. And that was the difference.

Then he up and disappeared. Was nice knowing you, Dwayne.

MANY MONTHS OF this routine and Masahisa and Yoko Kobayashi arrived from Japan to take over from Julian. We became Rev. Moon's next experiment: *Asian Church*. Somebody had reported up the chain a scuffle in our third-floor bathroom between psycho MFT and our witnessing team. He decided their fight nixed a critical spiritual condition of unity that crashed our fabled MFT–witnessing program. He disbanded it and chased MFT out of our house. *Buh-bye, psychos.*

Ostensibly, our new mission was witnessing to Asian-Americans. In practice, the largely Japanese work force the church sent in to augment our job preferred Japanese tourists. They never understood (or cared) that tourists go home when their visas expire and are no use to the American church. If they stayed, they only put themselves and the church at risk. Immigration and Naturalization (INS) hammered this home one midnight, smashing through our front door in a coordinated, Bay Area anti-Moonie campaign to snag visa scofflaws.

"Holy crap, Julian, lookit! I gotta replace the doorknob and bolt lock assemblies, not to mention all the woodwork. How come we have to pay for it?"

He blew off a heavy breath of unspoken agreement. "Just take care of it."

"They could've surrounded the house and knocked. Dang! We a cartel? Total freakin' cowboys. And who'd they bust? Nobody!"

"Well, Mr. Kobayashi says the East Bay residences weren't so lucky."

"Did you have any clue what a major trafficker in Japanese the church is?"

He fisted hands over his sternum. "Just suspicions, I guess. At my level."

"Real geniuses running this operation." I rolled Marty Feldman eyes.

Japanese members flooded the American church intending to overstay their visas. A legal no-no. We heard Congress later approved a 2-year missionary visa that legalized our Asian imports and mostly took us out of INS' crosshairs. Immigration trouble was a direct result of our failure to retain Americans. And the more Japanese and Koreans washed ashore and self-indulgently Asianized our church, the less Americans wanted any part of it. A predictable cycle of doom.

Mr. Kobayashi was a munchkin-sized early forties. Close-cut thick black hair framed a baby face. He had a habit of gruffly responding in chuffy grunts and multiple, crisp head nods, leading a fella to infer that he either understood or agreed, neither of which was usually the case. His was a distinctively Japanese response wholly lost on straight-talking Americans. I liked him and enjoyed his stories as a 5-year old

Our Judah Street crew circa 1983. Call me Mickey.

during the Pacific War's last year and our occupation of Japan.

"My most vivid memories are the night a bombing raid exploded our house to pieces, then gum-chewing Americans stomping through in muddy boots."

"My boots always came off in the Rockies, so I appreciate that."

"They ruined our expensive, precious *tatami*." Stuffed-straw floor mats.

"I guess we looked like real barbarians."

"My parents were very angry. But"—he shrugged—"nothing we could do."

Rev. Moon Blessed him to Yoko, heavier-set and similar in age. She had a pleasant singing voice and often sang us Holy Songs. In their baggage train came small children and Shiori, a young, moderately attractive if heavily *maquillaged* sister I took for mid-twenties and somewhat disowned for joining the church by her illustrious house of top imperial servants at Tokyo's palace. She spoke no English and showed no intention of learning it. She was here strictly as the Kobayashi's personal attendant and never deigned consort with us worker bees. When we said "hello" and "good morning," we were ghosts: unseen, unheard, unacknowledged. We thought her a total weirdo, the frothy whipped-cream of the crop.

Her stony silence had Christine wax louder in a slow, Chris Rockian *Rush Hour* cadence. "Can you ... understand ... the words ... coming out ... of my mouth?" She hilariously retreated step-by-step as Christine advanced with her voice rising in a vain (let alone aggravated) belief volume eventually trumped ignorance.

I tried befriending her because, weird as she was, I saw something kind and appealing. Maybe I was just her kind of weirdo. At a group outing on the beach I observed her digging around the shells and crabs in the wet sand with her toes. Her vague, almost normal humanity struck me. It was a fateful decision on my part. I never expected that seven years later we'd end up condemned by the Kobayashis, Kamiyamas, and all the highest toadies if not Rev. Moon his own bloody self.

I was now carting our team around the Bay Area to dentists, doctors, groceries, errands, fundraising, and witnessing. I journaled,

> I had to pick up Margarita from the dentist, bring Shiori out fundraising, and I lost most of my energy in the driver's seat ... So, the van blew a radiator hose, the Mexican roses we bought for .45¢ each were 90% all dead, it rained, members were frustrated I was so late ... all-in-all it was an exhausting 7-½ hours of straight city driving [plus roadside repair]. (Feb. 8–9, 1983)

I disliked witnessing, though less so than MFT ... perhaps some fear of rejection or sense of guilt at dragging unsuspecting souls into our spiritual maelstrom. A growing Japanese–American chaos pushed away my many ready-to-join spiritual children. It takes real salesmanship to persuade someone out of closely held beliefs and I never felt comfortable browbeating folks into jettisoning theirs for (growingly dysfunctional) mine. I was happier giving God back-office support.

I was seeing myself doomed to the trenches like many a haggard older member flitting through and resolved to climb out one way or the other. My first opportunity came when my rooftop tantrum over psycho MFT dovetailed with leadership realizing the house needed substantial repairs and renovation. Brothers like Dwayne and I shared most of this work but, as they one-by-one quit the church, Julian noticed my skills with ever more clarity. Second-string all the way, dammit.

Mr. Kobayashi emphasized Julian's witnessing–fundraising routine, then moved to employ Japan's successful strategies. His first step was imitating its flourishing video centers harvesting recruits by the thousands. These were a bevy of televisions wired to video cassette players (VCR) in headphoned cubicles where guests imbibed VHS Divine Principle lectures, soulfully scored biographies of Rev. Moon's life, and introductions to the plethora of non-profit groups he'd founded all crying out for donations and volunteers like *you*.

Regardless my construction background helping Dad build our house in the Rockies, erecting one from the footers up in a year-long high school Building Trades practicum, let alone my repair work around the center, Julian imported a brother named Steve from the New York church to build our video center. This really peeved me. I knew damn well I could do a high-quality job myself.

"Nobody takes me seriously," I complained. "I want to be included."

"I don't know, Chris. I'm not sure this is your thing."

"You've seen my work around here, not to mention my experience in Colorado. Come on. Give me a chance here."

"It's not what Mr. Kobayashi wants."

I barfed a laugh. "You mean Mr. Sato." He shot me a queer eye.

Plenty of carping later he said, "Okay, I'll put you in as Steve's assistant."

Better than nothing, I guess. "Thanks, Julian! You won't—"

"He's in charge." He gripped my shoulder, his face commanding. "Just do what he needs done."

I spread my hands. "You expect I'm gonna drop his body in the bay?"

"Just don't make me regret it with Mr. Kobayashi."

"Man, it rankles you disregarding me. Fella's gotta fight tooth and nail . . ."

Steve had his problems with me but we hit it off and worked well. He wasn't *too* bossy or fanatic. He took my input on the video center's design and we built it from beautiful oak and a quality Formica on the desktops. We chose the brothers' second-floor sleeping room cornering the street intersection. Five half-height, carpeted wall cubicles with oak trim went up along the Seventh Street wall. Against my passionate advice he walled up the

Video room, beloved bay window walled up.

fabulous cornered bay window. Light curtains that we'd never again touch disguised the blank wall behind the glass, maybe to fool prowling city building inspectors. No architectural integrity at all. *Sigh.*

We ripped out the wall-to-wall closet for a control room housing a bank of five cutting-edge, compact VCRs that piped our tapes to each TV. We hid them away because Mr. Kobayashi and Julian didn't want guests fiddling with our expensive equipment or maybe substituting porn; apparently, that wasn't unknown in Japan. It was quite the high-tech setup for the low-tech early '80s. I designed it and installed wall-to-wall oiled wood shelves—interrupted by a boxed, vertical plumbing run—over a Formica counter to house our video collection. I screwed a 4×8-foot dry marker board to the wall separating the video room and permanent-markered a schedule template where members could reserve cubicles for their guests. Another video center took shape in New York City after we'd started ours and we fiercely competed to be the first to operate in the United States. We won. Barely.

Julian rented home movies for us to watch for entertainment or as Principled instruction he thought worthy along with documentaries like 1962's *The Truth About Communism* narrated by Ronald Reagan. We copied all these videos on our fancy equipment for members and guests and built a couple-hundred tape library. This took the better part of 2 years, long after Steve had returned home.

AFTER COMPLETING THE video center, Mr. Kobayashi decided to remodel our dirt basement to give the brothers some decent sleeping quarters. We'd dormed in the room that was now his glitzy headhunter pot—I woke one 2 AM to a gearhead redlining his motorcycle at the intersection only to realize it was a brother snoring a few bodies over whom I couldn't wake nor shove over to shut off his *vrooming* mouth—and reduced to nomads in our own house.

"You want the job?" Julian said.

"Finally! You ask me *first*." He stared, brows up. "Yes, yes! It'll be great."

That began a 2-year remodeling and maintenance career. To my knowledge, the powers never applied for permits for the massive work we did on that venerable old building inhabiting the historic register. It ultimately included a complete rewiring and installation of new lighting, finishing the basement with a full bath, a video center, two classrooms, and a 15-person bunkroom on the third floor extending into the attic. But, whatever. This was God's business.

I poured concrete and rewired. Ultimately, we decided I may as well do the whole house. It was running juice through singled cloth wires and porcelain insulators installed in 1911. As with everything in the church, Mr. Kobayashi goaded near-impossible deadlines. I often went without sleep for three days at a time, once so groggy I couldn't wire up a simple light switch. My knee, back, shoulder, ankle—I fell down the stairs and cracked the same one I'd torn up in college—degrading my health encouraged poor practices. I was hot-wiring a wall sconce in the first-floor living room we now used for services because I was too lazy, tired, and sore to hobble down then up the narrow basement stairs to

My usual Navy dungarees, '83. toggle the breaker. I touched the wrong wire. Twenty amps of 120v built through me and then I was airborne like a no-name *Star Trek* extra. I crashed into the exterior (brick) wall and plunked onto my tingling ass where I sat dazed a few trembling minutes, legs splayed and thinking over my choices.

Christine ran in wide-eyed at the buzz and thump. "Pretty stupid," she said of my chattery explanation, helping me up once I had muscle control. "I thought you were dead! Don't do that again!"

"I'm sorry . . ."

Julian flew downstairs, shook a despairing head. "Really, Chris?"

"At least I didn't break the wall." Christine rolled eyes to the side.

"Don't make me cart your corpse out of here. And don't tell Mr. Kobayashi."

I chuckled, flexing the last tingles out of my fingers. "If I was a betting man—"

"You'd be your bookie's favorite customer. No more corner-cutting on safety."

"Aye, aye, mate." I remained a fan of hot-wiring without keeping him in the loop, but was a damn sight less cavalier about what I touched and when.

Prepping the basement dirt for concrete under clip-on work lights was like working a mineshaft. I bought books on remodeling and building codes that covered everything from electrical and plumbing to cabinetry and finish work. I divided the basement into a spacious sleeping room, a bathroom, and my own work room where I custom-built a complex of 2×4 plywood shelves and work benches. We carpeted the sleeping area and *presto!* it was the hottest property in the house.

I built the bathroom from the dirt up. The only work I farmed out to a professional was the sloping concrete shower deck; didn't want to screw up drainage. I built an enclosed toilet with an oiled wood louvred door and a magazine rack custom built into the wall. Next door, through another louvred door lined on the inside with plexiglas, was a 7-foot square shower. I tiled the floor and walls in beautiful red-blues and the strongest exhaust fan possible. Two expensive, multi-phased shower nozzles and bath pipes on one wall with short plastic stools and bathing bowls created a Japanese bathhouse effect. The shower built a heavy steam behind the plexiglas for a sauna-like experience. Negos slandering me as a 'Jap hater' never recognized my effort to give Japanese members a sense of home. Par for the course, really. Two sinks, a broad plate glass

Top: *the basement as I found it;* bottom: *sleeping area construction.*

mirror with plenty of lighting, and a door for indoor access to my work area finished it off. It was drop-dead gorgeous. Talk about comfort. We might have been the most pampered non-leadership brothers in the church.

I loved the work and honed a fair skill. But my injured body made it wearyingly difficult. I had to push myself through gut-wrenching physical tribulations. Then, in the finished basement, the ghost of MFT past jerked my spine into the grave in a wrestling match with Julian. I couldn't move. He dragged me to my sleeping bag and doubled-up wool blanket pallet atop padded carpet. It took days to stand then walk. Mr. Kobayashi sent me up the hill to the university doctor.

"There's nothing wrong with your spine we can see."

"Except it goes out and I can't move for a friggin' *week*. Just that."

Thumb and forefinger stroked a wise if unbearded chin. "Well . . . probably just muscle strain. Rest when it happens and take painkillers as needed."

"That's it?" *Shrug.* "Thanks, Doc. You're a real comfort." Lower back freak outs followed for years. New pain multiplied by old to the square root of bullshit grated my nerves, rendering me all the more an irritable man.

Eager sisters on Julian's grand basement tour greenly ogled Cinderella's ball gown. It didn't take long before they asserted our lap of luxury was a privilege reserved to sisters amongst the American enlisted. One dark morning Mr. Kobayashi announced after morning service, "The sisters will be taking the basement as soon as K'risu renovates the prayer room to accommodate the brothers, plus room for more."

"We're getting kicked up to the third floor?" No one was more put out than me.

"Yeah, sorry," Julian said. "I argued against it but . . . sisters."

"It feels like I fixed a hungry meal only for the dog to gulp my plate." He laughed. "I'm a great believer in female equality, Julian. That means they don't live better than me on account of their sex. I built that room for us disenfranchised brothers."

"Come on, don't take it so hard." *Yeah, but I see the wistful gleam in your eye.*

"That'll be your swan song one day. I'm pretty . . . vexed and cranky they get it on the strength of tears it's too barbaric to step into the second-floor hallway to their next-door bathroom. They've had the best rooms—"

"Put it away, Chris. Negativity drags you *and* the house down. It's done."

"I bet Christine led the charge." In blood red letters. He didn't say no.

With a months-long sigh and in no particular rush, I constructed dark-stained, oiled bunk bed frames three levels high (similar to my USCG cutters) off four posts anchored floor and ceiling in a room a quarter the basement, left of the stairs and next to the small, center-room office. We once caught a guest on the verge of joining wildly banging his girlfriend here, splayed in front of Rev. Moon's holy photograph. Julian was beside himself with sputtery indignation and summarily threw them out with hardly a moment to zip up. Another time, a guest made his way up and stabbed Rev. Moon's photo over and over with a pen.

Julian cradled the desecration. "I can't hardly fathom it. It feels like Father's own murdered body. It's a real attack. The spiritual consequences could be just as grave as if he'd physically stabbed him." We all soberly felt it.

Top: *finished basement sleeping;* bottom: *door to the luxury bath.*

"Reckon we gotta stop letting even trusted guests wander unsupervised."

Each bed in its 3-tiered rack hinged up. Below, a storage compartment lined with Formica held clothes and personal items. It slept 15 plus floor space for visitors. I discovered an empty void behind what I'd thought was the exterior wall meeting the steeply sloping roof 5 feet off the floor. Using my nautical mindset for maximal space, I sawed out the plaster and lathe and built 15 stained, hand-oiled cabinets between the rough-cut redwood studs. These fit hanging suits, shelved books, and stored effects. Behind them, I floored and sheetrocked the void for storage space not to mention good hideouts. I broke open the ceiling in two places, bolted vertical wood ladders in place, and finished it out with three sleeping spaces on a carpeted floor. I moved my pallet into one. I rewired the lot, a nightmare crawling through the tiniest slots and threading electrical cable along impossible channels.

Cinderella's clock bonged and, to our sisters' delight, we brothers disappeared to our less-refined albeit more comfortable and sunnier pumpkin penthouse. We'd lost our fabulous bath for our old one-sink and stall-shower, but at least we stretched out on beds with *mattresses*, something the sisters didn't have. Small victories.

A steady stream of visitors hummed in the video center and we used the first-floor dining and living rooms for meetings and post-video guest debriefings. In the meantime, I set upon the second floor's now empty rooms with woven, cloth-like wallpaper, a fine, thick carpet, and easy-on-the-eyes color schemes. In one room, I hung a 4×8-foot blackboard. The other, street-side room I decorated with quality chairs and coffee tables. These took over as the center's official teaching spaces.

In early 1983 Betsy, Katie, and seven others shifted to Hearst Street house over the bay in Berkeley, then to the International One World Crusade (iowc). Katie stayed with the Blessed child nursery till she ran off at summer's end to live in sin with her Blessed husband down south. I missed her. The nursery was in chaos and I drove the kids to school for awhile. With the Kobayashi's visiting Japan, Mrs. Kamiyama ran it for a month. I frequently visited her. Joo Hwa transferred but we kept in touch via Korean letters Mr. Kobayashi helped me edit. My knees, back, and shoulder worsened and degraded my health. I needed naps and half or whole days off to get through the next several days' work. This caused no small resentment and persistent conflict with the sisters

My built-in cabinets.

and some brothers who judged me an unMoonielike slacker. Mr. Kobayashi via Mr. Kamiyama authorized medical interventions, including full physical rehab. "You're our toughest case, yet," they said, rebuilding me with vicious, agonizing exercise and re-teaching me to run, a privilege my body had forgot. In about a year I set my cane aside for setback days. But that was then. This was now.

In keeping with Rev. Moon's dictum that we all learn Korean, I'd spent the better part of six months teaching myself from Mr. Kobayashi's *Learning Korean* by Andrew Sun Park while he drilled my phonetics and vocabulary. He'd taught himself and claimed a 60% comprehension of Rev. Moon's speeches. I admired that and wanted it. Eventually, I couldn't teach myself past my level. I needed a Korean.

"With Joo Hwa gone," I said, "would you be willing to get me a tutor?"

He thought it over part of a day. "Yes, if you promise to study hard and practice."

"Whoa! Yesss!" He set me up with young and pretty nonmember Kyung Mi. Brothers and sisters sarcastically resented my special doodad from public money.

"Anyone can go," he said. "Just organize it around everything else."

"I'll help anyone who wants it." Yet, none came. Wouldn't be the first time my peers begrudged my initiative heeding Rev. Moon. He says Korean is humanity's next global language—the world would've spoken Jesus' own—to capture his heart and deepest expression. Americans laughed away it supplanting English as another entertaining eccentricity, and years later I found it a dumb choice for software engineering. Few members learned enough to find a commode. Julian assigned me to teach the Japanese English and everybody Korean. A more defiant clutch of students I never saw. The Japanese had no use for either beyond the minimum to command Western barbarians and move product. The rest didn't care.

Kyung Mi was pleasant. I looked forward to her twice-weekly visits with great anticipation to finally comprehend my true mentor, Rev. Moon. She was the first 'outside member' I'd met outside work and witnessing in a very long time. It was refreshing to converse with a 'normal' person' I wasn't trying to recruit or sell who anyhow had no interest in joining or buying. She got too busy at some point and substituted her younger brother Woon Jae, with whom I also got along. We stayed friends for some years until I moved to New York City in 1990 and lost track of their family, some of whom returned to Korea. I got to know them all. Her mom was always happy to spend a few hours chatting. She spoke no English and we cycled between Japanese and Korean, which I could halfway speak. When I got stuck in one, often I knew the right words in the other. It was a lot of fun. She fed me like a malnourished king. It was a mistake to eat before visiting because she'd compel me anyway. She cooked up huge meals, even if I was the only one at her floor table. I wondered if she might be softening me up for Kyung Mi, but later realized that was a presumptive conceit. Rev. Moon often (maybe) joked that Koreans are the lost tribe of Israel. Kyung Mi's mom sure acted the Jewish matron.

San Fran's Castro District Halloween Perversionary with Kyung Mi after my first Kodiak season, 1984.

A paltry five-six yet topping Mr. Kobayashi, she was a strong and muscular runner and gymnast. I thought her heavy-breasted for an Asian but she wore them well, if that's a thing. Plus, instant attraction. I can't imagine why he thought pairing me with an 'outside sister' was a good idea, considering the Fall and the badgering loneliness the church pickled us in. He might not have known my dream to marry a Korean . . . in my headier moments, one of Rev. Moon's daughters. I felt anything was possible if only I could work with him.

But she was hands-off. After my course took a sharp left downstairs in 1984 when the Bay Area's big cheese ran me out of Judah Street, we fell in love—well, I did— and carried on a torrid affair in 1985. Even my parents liked her; a first. Finally, I proposed proposing.

She said, "I can't marry outside my race."

"Korean's a race? Don't you love me, too?"

"Yes"—*kiss, kiss*—"and it would be nice, but . . . my boyfriend is waiting there from before I came here."

A fist shattered my ribs and flattened my heart over a pulped spine. I slumped with the jolt. "A boyfriend? I'm . . . your boy-toy?"

She squeezed my hands. "No, no, that's not how it . . . My family doesn't know about you and me. I'm so sorry."

"But your mom loves me!"

"As my friend. Never for my husband. She expects me to marry my boyfriend when I return home to Korea. Everybody does."

"Return to—? My God!" I might've been dizzy but too drowning to notice.

"It's not something . . . I could never—. No, that's not . . . but . . ." Hot rivulets slithered down her broad cheeks. At least she was hurting, too.

I despairingly cried months till I was dry. Morose winds rattled the voids.

A couple years later we met up for coffee. I chewed my lip driving her home. She said, "You were right, Chris. He's very—I wish I'd married you. I regret . . ."

With pangs, it was now me squeezing her hand with warmth. "It's okay, but thanks for saying that. I'm sorry you're having a rough time." Her longing eyes climbed out of my rusty Beetle and life. I never would've fallen for her had Mr. Kobayashi not derailed the most significant event in anybody's church life.

By late 1982 I'd been chaste several years, eyes on the Blessing prize that Rev. Moon now announced for July 1 in Madison Square Garden (MSG). Leaders sent their recommendations to the Blessed Family Department (BFD) in New York City. Its job was keeping track of Blessed couples and children, sexual status, those not qualified, and interviewing candidates. No haphazard operation this, but organized with the soulless efficiency of the Mormon missionary department. Julian as house manager provided his own recommendations to Mr. Kobayashi who then winnowed his chaff.

Each Blessing embodies Rev. Moon's numerology. The event at MSG would Bless exactly 2,075 couples. It was the logical progression from the 36-couple Blessing—same year he wed his third wife, Hak Ja Han, aged 40 and 18—to the 72-, 120-, the 430-, 777-, and 1,800-couple Blessings. Numbers built off preceding ones (not including one-offs). He holds them at unspecified but sudden intervals. Often, it's years between Matching and Blessing. In this case, couples are engaged but forbidden to touch. In some Japanese-run departments of the era, couples weren't even allowed to communicate regardless eventual consummation.

My ideal woman, armed and patriotically ready in Golden Gate Park.

Candidates travel to New York City where Rev. Moon centers himself amongst hundreds of brothers and sisters to spend sleepless days and nights Matching them up. He stands two members for a once over, sometimes sitting one or both down. He injects a lot of levity into the proceedings as well, asking a shy brother if he prefers a taller wife or a red-faced sister if she wants "a brother with big equipment." Matchings go quick enough, but sometimes he's stumped or concludes a spouse hasn't joined yet and he or she needs await the next one. Witheringly disappointing. Tails between legs, these outcasts stumbled home to Blessed centers.

Leaders said, "You should never expect or desire, even dream, of being Matched and Blessed. It is a great honor and indemnity condition. So, you must approach it with ruthless seriousness, and never without a 7-day fast, prayer conditions, and a very humble attitude. Satan invades through arrogant expectation."

Rev. Moon Blesses members as surrogate Adams and Eves to experience God's creational heart and Restore the Fall in holy sex that restores the family Satan destroyed back to God's side. It's the crux of Unificationism and our Moonie life. You aren't 'saved' (Restored) nor a true member without it, just an apprentice, a novitiate, a probationer. It was so crucial to our identity that Blessed members discriminated against the unBlessed. It got so bad, I changed the subject when asked my status. They sank sharp, Blessed talons atop their rigid hierarchy. Very demoralizing.

After being Matched, a couple left the room to decide if they'd accept it. The church forced no one even if peer pressure and personal morality oft-dictated the outcome. If a couple agreed, they reported their acceptance to the BFD. If not, they returned to the Matching room and staff informed Rev. Moon they'd rejected it. Some members had difficulty deciding either way because, for example, so many Japanese–American pairings lacked a common language and translators were ever in short supply. Probably 95–99% of Matched couples automatically or after some stunted conversation accepted their Match. Some ballsy brothers rejected theirs because the sister's hair was too long or the wrong color or she wasn't pretty enough, and so on. It didn't end well for these clods.

Sometimes Rev. Moon said nothing. Sometimes he stopped Matching or paused mid-sentence with a hard eye on their reasoning. He threw the brothers rejecting their Match over looks and hair out of the Matching.

He said to the room, "Come back when you are more humble and ready to listen to Rev. Moon." Then hissed, "He should be grateful she has a hole! He doesn't even deserve that!" Defeating Satan and Restoring the harsh, evil world we live in is serious Restorational business and he didn't abide cowards nor fools.

One couple sheepishly said, "We're sorry, Father. We can't accept your choice."

"Why?" he snapped.

"Well . . . we don't really know exactly," the brother nervously said. "It just doesn't seem right to us. Something's off."

He looked them over a minute, then cracked a knowing smile. "Sure! You sit down. No problem. I'll find you someone else!"

"The difference here is their attitudes," Julian explained. "If they're humble and unselfish, Father does his best to Match them to someone they're happy with."

"That's reassuring," I said.

"I agree. But if they're arrogant or selfish, he won't Match them, or he will to someone closer to their spiritual level to minimize struggles in their relationship. Sometimes to someone spiritually higher who might pull them up."

"That has to suck for the spiritually higher person."

"Maybe, but not necessarily. You have to consider why you're even attending the Matching. Motivation matters."

"Hmm." I thought that over. *How would I handle it?* I didn't want struggle, just love. Acceptance without qualification . . . or bribery.

Julian said, "He does that when he senses a member is capable of growth, or maybe just worth the chance."

"Otherwise he wouldn't throw their innocent Match into that fire?"

"What do you think? He's not Mao. He considers everybody's situation, but he never deviates from Principle, either, even in that. He doesn't Match people lightly, Chris, like some common matchmaker."

"I'm sure." And yet there was a lot of talk about just how well he could Match anyone. Most of us believed he had 'spiritual eyes' that saw our situation and could accordingly pick an appropriate, non-destructive spouse. He said,

> I have a philosophy of balance in matching — a harsh person needs to be balanced with someone softer. A weak, soft person needs someone strong . . . a pretty woman and a handsome man together may lose everything and leave nothing behind . . . I try to make a permanent base . . . from the viewpoint of central true love. Sometimes my methods look strange, or labyrinthine, and

you can't see the light at the end of the tunnel. But if the end result will be true love, I will go that way. (*True Love Vol. 1*, c5 1989)

Julian said, "During the Matching, all our ancestors in spirit world line up behind us so Father can spiritually see not just how two candidates click, but how their entire lineage interacts."

"What, he can literally see them in long rows disappearing into the distance?"

He quick-flipped a shoulder. Mouth-shrugged. "Something like that, I guess."

"So, like if they're fighting? Hating each other? Have to Restore their historical resentments, like World War Two?"

"Exactly. Your Blessing is a historical, ancestral event. It's not just you getting married. You need to keep that firmly in mind."

"Oh. Right. Yeah, of course."

Even more daring and audacious than those rejecting their Match for superficial reasons, some members declared their own choice to Rev. Moon's face or worked it out with a senior leader having his ear.

When he'd stand them up they'd say, "Would Father please consent to . . . ?" and then spell it out. These were older members. Instead of a flippant "No," he might go over each person's life, history, lineage, consider their nationalities and ethnicities, consult senior leaders for backstory, and so on. I imagined he didn't want members pulling this trick very often.

One time he said, "No, he has a difficult, dark spirit world. If I Match you, it will only cause spirit world to kill one or both of you later."

These were words to the wise. Supremely crestfallen this couple said, "Yes, Father. We'll accept your choice, then."

Others didn't take it as well and, deeply in love, determined to marry their own choice come hell or high water. They usually left the church to effect it, as no center tolerated a member living in unBlessed sin. Dissatisfaction with a Matching often ginned up extramarital affairs, or one or both Blessed members leaving the church to marry outside it. Responding in part to these scandals Rev. Moon said,

> Everything is not accomplished just because you received the blessing. The blessing is conditional . . . There are some who fall, and after the fall want to be blessed again. How can there be another blessing? . . . the blessed families who fail will become nourishment for worms. (*The Ceremony of the Declaration of God's Eternal Blessing*, Seoul 1991)

> The persons responsible for family breakdowns cannot be forgiven . . . [going] to the most fearful hell among hells. (*Blessing and Ideal Family*, c4 p4 1998)

"Breaking the Blessing is worse than the sin in the Garden," Julian said, "because we know the Principle whereas they didn't. God can *never* forgive such people."

"What an absolute crock of—!"

"Chris . . ." He disliked my occasional coarseness. Got his Jesuit up.

"I don't swallow that for a second. It contradicts his own teaching that every person must be Restored before heaven can even exist. Ergo . . ."

"Yeah, I admit it opens a can of worms. I think he's using hyperbole here to really hammer home how terrible it is to fall after the Blessing. That's what you need keep in mind." He was big on recognizing Rev. Moon's verbal jujitsu. "Just take it with a grain of salt. He's only making a point."

"Hmm, yeah, okay. Fine. I can see that." I suppose I lucked out with a mentor like him who, in his own way, encouraged critical reasoning instead of uncritically swallowing whatever jizzed our way in our strobe-lit leader fetish. Not that I'd have characterized our church life to him that way.

"He just means that God will only forgive Blessed members who fall *after* Satan repents, not before, which is the chance he's giving us."

I let go a heavy breath. "I reckon it's his way of pushing us to not fu—mess around since the consequences are tragic. If not eternally then in the meantime."

"That's how I read it. I hope when you're Blessed you still do, too."

"Why wouldn't I?" I took a long gander at him. "What're you saying?"

"No, no, nothing. I'm just saying, because church life isn't for everyone. Members need to really think through their motivations."

"And I'm not?"

He leaned in. Hard. "Don't try to take it the wrong way. I'm. Just. Saying."

"Sure, Julian . . ." I was unsure where he was going with that. I imagined these conversations were on his mind when he contemplated my name for his Blessing recommendation. In hindsight, he might've had a good read on me. *Sigh.*

To scrape up 2,075 couples, Rev. Moon lowered the spiritual age requirement— time in service—from three years to one. I was a 1-½-year veteran by now and thrilled to be included in the draft. My heart soared with sugarplummed possibilities and Restoring my ancestors. Those younger than a year wailed and gnashed their teeth. It's hard to quantify the life-quaking excitement and sense of salvation we felt leading up to the Blessing. This was our moment to escape the Satanic world and return to the bosom of God who, through Rev. Moon's various ceremonies, forgave (conditionally) our Original Sin. This means, on the strength of Rev. Moon's conditions, Satan temporarily withholds his accusation we're sinful—didn't St. Paul say none are worthy?—thus lacking merit. He qualifies our qualification:

> How can you deserve such an extraordinary blessing? Only in the capacity of True Parents' children and in a relationship of love with them. There is no other way to qualify for the blessing of True Parents . . . If you have a fine, outstanding fiancé, you should feel: "I don't deserve such a person. Somebody else must have paid the indemnity for me so I could receive him (or her). Thank you, Heavenly Father." (*True Parents and Our Responsibility* 1981)

If he hadn't made a deal with God to dish it out on a conditional basis then the Providence of Restoration would've stalled and Satan won. We were prepared to troop to the Blessing for an eternal spouse with our general worthlessness and probationary status foremost in our minds. I supposed it was the same with any religion when you got right down to it.

Imagine my astonishment and life-wrenching disappointment when Julian said, "Mr. Kobayashi isn't recommending you for the Blessing. He feels you're too young and immature." I think he truly expected, *Oh, no sweat. Totally get it. I'll wait.*

Instead I said, "But I meet all Father's requirements! Members who aren't even a year old are getting special dispensation to go. How's that square?"

He watched me with a certain impassive detachment. A real son of his officer-class dad, he was. I could see he empathized with my plight to some degree, but the trooper and corporate man he was prevented him granting any reprieve.

"I understand how you feel, Chris. I originally thought you should go and tried to persuade Mr. Kobayashi to reconsider." He paused to let me register what he was saying, but my ears were thick with betrayal. "He's adamant that you're still too young and spiritually immature regardless your chronological ages."

"Yeah, sure. No, I understand. I'm not Blessing material."

Julian eyerolled and looked askance.

They were probably remembering me climbing the roof to escape MFT. From my perspective I wasn't any more stupid, silly, naïve, screwed up, or less mature than my brothers and sisters slated to go. I worked hard at my assigned tasks, did my duty, prayed fervently, assiduously studied the Principle, was the only western member in the Bay Area and probably one of a handful in America taking the initiative to learn Korean (let alone Japanese), and publicly joined at the hip with Rev. Moon. What more could I do? *Grow up, he says?* Even Blessed, actual married life was maybe seven years out (if I was lucky) when I'd presumedly be as mature as anybody else in this screwed up world. *Too young? immature?* It smelled lame.

Perhaps Julian really did argue my case. I found it hard to believe. He was looking more like one of those 'good' American leaders—Negroes of yore knowing their place, not making waves—who bite the tongue off their conscience to do as they're told through a shit-eating grin under bulbous white eyes. That they're often the only Americans who last proves the point. If you exercise a conscience, you're doomed in church leadership. They're the worst Americans, though, because they stupidly abandoned the West's great Christian heritage, nurtured over 2,000 years, that created the modern world premised on liberty in conscience. Our Christian heritage is to treasure, not cringe from under a cynically Imperial stare.

The Japanese taking over American church leadership seemed mostly devoid of any real Christian heritage. Those having religious training prior to joining the Japanese church were often varying brands of Buddhist or Shinto with a smattering of Christian—more in the Korean church—or, like Mr. Kamiyama whose father was a minister, grew up on a Christian knee. Most were culturally religious or irreligious and sometimes *bona fide* criminals. Joining the church in that milieu, which believes it's the Completed Testament Age, was jumping over 2,000 years of human spiritual development in God's central providence. In my experience, they largely lacked Christian empathy and virtue and thus were poor spiritual and operational—but great *Bushido*—leaders for culturally Christian westerners.

Julian was a decent leader in most respects: inspiring, smart, organized, capable, and concerned for his members' welfare. His good qualities broke down whenever he bowed too low to the Asians running our show. This was one of those times and I felt thrown under the bus. I was spiritually 1-½ and physically 23. Members younger than me in our house and elsewhere were going. They didn't seem particularly extra mature to me . . . just a helluva lot more uncritically obedient.

"I feel singled out for taking True Father at his word to study Principle and become more like him, an active doer not a passive follower. I bet it's my mouth not wanted at the Blessing! Because I might say 'no' to Father?" I was discovering how arbitrary the church was, its great Divine Principle notwithstanding. One leader does this and another that, mutually contradicting yet both considered Principled, therefore within their rights. It was ridiculous. This was *my* spiritual salvation.

Julian chuckled. "You do have a way of tossing monkey wrenches into people's gears. But, believe me, that's not the reason for Mr. Kobayashi's decision."

"Huh. Do I." *Just bend over Chris, it'll only tickle a minute.* "Are you sure there's no changing his mind? Look at the quality of people who are going! Am I so less?" Maybe he'd go another round or two for me.

"Chris, you just need to accept the reality that we all have different paths of Restoration unique to our own lives." Julian was being his conciliatory best. "Yours is not getting Blessed this time around."

"Hmmph!"

"There will always be Blessings so long as Father's alive, don't worry."

"How does anybody know how long that is? You don't. Meanwhile," fingers fast-drumming the tabletop, "I alone of literally everyone in the center need stay unBlessed and unsaved? And, as Father and Blessed members continuously remind us, not even be a *real* church member?" *Am I the only one taking this seriously?* Julian spread hands. Sometimes even he butted up against the wall of no answers. "I'll say this, Julian. Only True Father, the Messiah, has the right to open or close the Blessing to me. Church leaders seem to think they're on par—"

"That's wrong, Chris. Father can't deal with every single—"

"He does with Matchings! They're *all* there."

"He has to delegate. That's Mr. Kobayashi's job. Father appointed him."

"Well, he's not the Messiah. Father is. He can't make *this* choice. This is Father's decision because it's my eternal salvation. I mean, what if I die before—"

Back to head shaking. "This is why Mr. Kobayashi doesn't think you're ready."

"Yep. Too disobedient. That's what it's always about." I dropped my head heavily back on my neck and gave up. I grudgingly accepted my fate—no choice—but felt cheated out of the life path and wife that God may have very well wanted for me but for their interference. My whole soul heaved in mourning.

Still, members were only 'recommended.' Nothing was guaranteed. Rev. Moon was indeed the final arbiter. He always turned away some members for one reason or another. Others who weren't recommended would sometimes find themselves personally invited by him or some top dog to jump in at the last minute. But those lucky sods were *there*, in the city, in the building, not way out in the wilderness like me. Without permission, I'd never make it inside. If Rev. Moon himself said I wasn't ready, I was prepared to accept that. He was the chief, my spiritual master, a man I respected, the *Messiah*. But not some local kinglet who was fundamentally on the same spiritual plane as me, motivated by who knows what and about as knowledgeable of my spiritual reality as the postman.

The Blessing was intensely controversial, splashed across front pages the world over. Brides and grooms dressed alike in traditional Moonie wedding fashion: white gown and veil for sisters, dark blue suits, red ties, and white shirt and gloves for brothers. They dolled up catty-corner to the midtown venue in the New Yorker

Hotel at 8th Avenue and 34th Street, which in 1975 Rev. Moon purchased in near-condemned condition and still tottered on the edge. The 2,075 couples squeezed into its every pore and pimple. On signal, they snaked arm-in-arm two abreast across the intersecting canyons into the Garden. A literal traffic stopper.

A van of deprogrammers hired by pious parents zoomed out of nowhere and screeched to a close halt. Its side door banged open. Men boiled out. Two plucked a kicking and screaming bride from the line. Another muscled her husband-to-be out of range. Flinging her bodily inside, the van smoked tires and thunderously flew down the street, the bride not seen again till she'd renounced Rev. Moon. Her shocked groom, adrift in the street, eyed his future vanish round a squealing corner. Brides wept in disarray but the procession broke a leg and marched on.

Her kidnapping shockwaved through our faith. All of us steamed red. Bags of stories circulated of members abducted to remote locations or suburban upstairs prisons and basement dungeons by deprogrammers, paid by parents, who subjected them to emotional and psychological torture until they broke down and recanted their faith in Rev. Moon and Divine Principle. Some never cracked. A brother, John, had his clothes taken after an escape attempt. Desperate to get away from his upstate New York cell in the dead of winter, he climbed out a window late at night and shimmied down a drain pipe to the ground, then dashed barefoot and buff through foot-deep snow for hours. He found help, but local cops often conspired. We saw him a heroic figure of indomitable will even as we sensed our own danger.

I dreamed how I'd handle my parents snatching me. How I'd Singapore cane their deprogrammers, fending them off like Captain America. Or if captured, how I'd confound their deprogramming psychology the same way I confounded San Francisco's communists and my Unification Church leaders. Or, how I'd craftily make my escape through remote woods, freezing temperatures, and barbed wire. Daydreaming was great fun. Alas, my parents were too open-minded after my older sister Senna defeated them. They considered me my own man. Capable of my own decisions. Mature enough to sink myself if that's what I wanted. They decidedly wouldn't interfere . . . so determinedly they usually failed to give discussion and insight on decisions they thought I ought to reconsider. I'd have appreciated that. I guess I'm lucky hailing from red-blooded Texas drained of all my blue-blood dregs, but deprogrammers would've been a grand adventure.

The newly Blessed bouncing back to me leadenly waiting in our empty house were a freight train through my psyche. Over the years I wondered how life might've unfolded had Mr. Kobayashi sent me to MSG with my peers. What the right sister from Rev. Moon's hand might've meant to me and my future course in the church. What I'd missed spiked me hands and feet. I reeled, riven and hewed.

⁓

ASIAN CHURCH MOVED right along witnessing to hundreds of Japanese tourists who viewed our videos, heard our lectures, and shared our meals. Then they boarded their JAL flight home. Clueless or obstinate, our Japanese never accepted that witnessing to tourists was a useless exercise for the American church. Maybe they'd been secretly directed to send qualified candidates back to Japan as their 'real' mission. Secret orders from a closer chain of command contradicting those from a farther chain were hardly unknown in our church anywhere in the world.

With Mom and Dad at San Fran's Palace of Fine Arts. Jan., 1983.

We did manage to witness to Asian-Americans. Some of them joined part time. A few white Americans and a Navajo joined, too, and one fine day I all but crashed into a black US Navy Commander in his winter blues on our red-carpeted stairs. He, like many cycling through our center, had joined part time but I never encountered him again. All in all, it seemed to me our progress was nil. Membership increased mostly from Japanese church imports.

It was during this period I met Mr. Kamiyama in the flesh. I was swapping out light bulbs in the foyer's high-ceilinged chandelier when he pushed through Judah Street's sticking front door—remember that INS raid?—in a leaderly suit and tie. I knew his boyish face right off. Awe struck through me so close to a man who lived and breathed Rev. Moon's presence. Eyes pulled his face up my ladder. He studied me, light bulb in hand, eyeballing him back.

After this pregnant pause he said, "Ohhh. Someday, you will be president."

"I—what?"

With that, he jammed closed INS' handiwork, Mr. Kobayashi bounded down to bow and greet, and I disappeared in the mist. He visited numerous times, sometimes with Messrs. Sawamukai, Nakata, Tigumera, Sato, and others. He inspected my work on the house, missing few if any details. I never forgot his odd remark. It's as clear now as if this morning. I'd never thought much of myself up to this time, but his surprising prophecy opened a floodgate of pent up emotions and self-confidence I'd never accepted. For the first time, it seemed okay to believe I could do something meaningful, something great; that my vision of myself, shelved since I was four and Oswald or somebody brazenly murdered my hero JFK, was reasonable and achievable. Mr. Kamiyama might've forgot his words ten seconds later, but they've lived on as a validation that I was born to achieve historical greatness that forever altered humanity's course. What that meant was . . . well, a wink and a nod.

Several months after this epiphany, Julian advised us at morning service that an Ocean Church team would be joining our household. Rev. Moon created this department for those who'd died at sea. These lost souls can't be Restored through the efforts of the church on land because so many are spiritually stuck in their watery limbo from resentment, confusion, and so forth and unable to enter the spirit realm to move on with their lives. An effort was needed to reach out to these sufferers and that was Ocean Church's mission. With time, it forgot this founding aspect and devolved into nothing more than a seafood harvester and a waterborne version of land centers that took prospects out to fish and commune with nature on the high seas instead of plopping them in front of a blackboard or videotape.

He explained this was the first such team in the country. They'd bounced from center to center suffering disrespect, abuse, and persecution for being different, such as the only members allowed facial hair which they sported with élan. The rest of us had to scrape the blade so the world wouldn't presume us a variant of the wacky Maharaja Rajneesh or Jim Jones' Templars. Our clean-cut witnessing uniform was slacks, business shirts, and neckties. Funny how we always seemed to identify with Mormons. All we needed were the nametags. Sisters, of course, wore anything so long as it Victorianly sheathed cleavage and thighs from prying eyes.

Our commandment was elementary: love and embrace Ocean Church members like good Abels and treat them better than we treated ourselves. In this, we gained victory during their year-long stay in our house. They brought a 28-foot, twin-engine fiberglass 'Good-Go' sport fishing boat with them from our East Sun Building boatbuilders in Queens, New York. My new best friend Griswold, who went by Hemi, was a plank owner, having laid the fiberglass himself. I took many a joyride

Ocean Hope 1. *Alan shepherded our gaggle of* Ocean Hopes *to Alaska.*

with him and his free-bearded comrades on San Francisco Bay. If there's one thing I love, it's boats. Alan Hokinson and his band of brothers crewed up the *Mary D.* and *Golden Sea*, "along with our personal persuasive tools," to sail through pirate-, smuggler-, and communist-infested waters for Alabama. Six months later he was back with three new-built *Ocean Hope* trawlers on their way to Alaska. I wandered Fisherman's Wharf, sometimes with Steve, craving sea adventures.

Hemi and I shared a lot of traits, like our sense of humor. We hung out in our free-standing garage where he taught me knife throwing and we aired grievances. He reveled in his cultivated bad-boy image that mated with a lovely full beard he often slathered in baby oil just to freak out the Japanese. The sisters especially looked on him as the definition of uncouth with hardy feelings of envy and disgust, showing all the same confused contradictions in their attitudes toward Americans I later witnessed in Alaska. Our first thanksgiving dinner with Ocean Church plus Alan's crews had 40 members crammed into several rooms with multiple turkeys dominating tabletops. Hemi twisted the leg off the largest and gnawed it medieval style. This got a big laugh but really churned up the Japanese.

He was spurring in long stirrups. "I'm challenging their perceptions."

"Pfft. It'll never work. They're set on themselves."

"Eh." He tore a bite. Licked his 'stache. "They need to expand their horizons."

"Haven't got far. Pegged, judged, and packaged you in a New York minute."

Sigh. "Ya gotta start somewhere, Chris."

Weirdly, the Kobayashi's unobtrusively moved into a secret apartment. Julian refused to squeal because Mr. Kobayashi didn't want us coming over to talk (rant?). I didn't discover its location—right around the corner!—till after they'd departed with their servant Shiori to manage business finances at national HQ. Blessed couples and those in college then used it for a residence and quasi-church center. My future friends Jerome Trumpet and Joachim Baum were two of those. Joachim was a portly German in his thirties with close-cropped black hair flecked with grey, heavy jowls, and beefy, square-rimmed silver glasses. We shared many delightful conversations there, me gleefully annoying him with exaggerated, Germanesque parodies. Sadly, *Jägerschnitzel* with a side of heart attack took him out in the mid-1990s.

In the dining room with our new powers.

I hung out there whenever I could to escape the repression Judah Street fell into after the Kobayashis left and the macabre Mr. (apparently Mrs.) Uchiyama took over. They drove our center into the ground like a short kid in a tall car. Neither could stand me nor our new Korean city leader. I wondered if it was because I was a foot taller and a hundred pounds heavier and just scared him to death. On more than one occasion I was certainly ready to cinch him by the collar and belt and heave his arrogant ass right through our broad dining room window. Dreaming about it was a little masturbatory. He was a haughty man, adapting the powers of a medieval feudal lord to his clerical role. At one point, so perturbed with me and our city leader, he ceased coming downstairs for 5 AM Sunday Pledge and sent his wife instead. I interpreted that as a calculated insult with an attached message to us members.

When I first met Mrs. Uchiyama at the top of the third-floor stairs she slowly, deliberately looked me up and down like a cheap dress on the sophisticates' rack. Then a disingenuous, toothily face-swallowing smile parted her visage reminiscent of Hollywood's exaggerated, buck-toothed, coke-bottle-glasses 1942–45 Japanese soldier caricatures cackling while machine-gunning American good ol' boys.

In high-pitched Janglish she said, "Ohhh . . . big body, little head, hahaha!"

Well, fuck you, too, I poisonously smiled. She endeared me not a whit and set our tone. They tainted Mr. Kobayashi's unfathomable void regardless him razing my '82 Blessing. Best Japanese leader I met, bar none. Right up there with Julian. I valued and respected him as a spiritual parent . . . well, until Shiori. Once or twice a week we met cross-legged on the floor of Julian's former command bedroom overlooking Seventh and Judah to go over my impressions. I underlined everything of gravity in *Divine Principle*, jotting questions and comments in every white space. He answered each with a solid or theoretical response based on his overall knowledge or an honest, "I don't know." I respected that because it was so unusual for particularly Japanese leaders (as it is for cops on a traffic stop) to admit any lack of knowledge.

"This is how Father wants Principle taught," I enthused. "Father to son. Elder to younger. Passionately. Dynamically." Lectures were for ignorance. "I've learned the best Principle with a real truth-seeking guru!"

His head sharply nodded as typical. "Unhh. I think so, yes. A better way."

Jesus' mission lanced me. The Jews murdered him, so he'd only partly completed thus postponed his mission till passing it on to Rev. Moon. His family in particular refused his chosen bride and kept him unmarried in a marital milieu. From the Principle's perspective that the Messiah, in the symbolic position of Adam, must take a bride symbolizing Eve just to get his mission into first gear, his effort seemed doomed from the start.

"From the gospels and the Principle's assertion God had no assurance Israel would accept him, it seems more likely they wouldn't, and his family proved it. Yet, He called him anyway."

Sharp nod. "Yes, I think that is correct. Mostly, his mission was suicide from that and more."

"So, he knew that from a young age but still—"

"Even though unlikely, it was always possible he could find victory in defeat."

Sigh. "But didn't. God must've cried through the whole disaster." I came away from our dialogue thinking Jesus was *da bomb*. When I reflected on his tragedy in prayer, I sometimes wept in despair for him. I renewed my teenage love I'd let evaporate like smoke off an abandoned fire.

My aggravated mindset increasingly cowboyed up.

Responding to his messianic critics Rev. Moon said, "No person has loved Jesus more than me." Bombastic, but a truth I felt unfold over my experience with him. The Principle's poignant message and Rev. Moon's speeches about Jesus' life and mission vindicated his genuine commitment to him and God. He wouldn't have mentioned it otherwise when it could later undermine his claims, nor made it a conduit for members to so viscerally experience Jesus in a way that might overshadow himself.

Mr. Uchiyama's imperious, *yakuza*-flavored rule was a morale disaster. The house wantonly Japanized. Once in '84 my starving, construction-gutted stomach growled in joy over a gleaming plate—let's face it, Japanese sisters could rock the kitchen and rarely disappointed. Then a deep-fried fish rockin' head, fins, tail, skin, and bulging eyeballs chopsticked onto it. I gawped at the alien beastie. This was too much. Not only insulted by the arrogant presumption I'd accept a charcoaled, garbage-can reject as food in my own goddamned country because it was heavenly Japanese cuisine, I had no idea how to eat it without choking to death on its slivered, all but invisible bones. I tried, then excused myself to build a few peanut butter and jelly sandwiches. Now *I'd* insulted our cook and all Japan with American insensitivity. I muted Mr. Uchiyama's tongue-lashing in between satisfying bites.

With the Kobayashi's gone, our house appeared to declare independence from the church. Perhaps that's why the Big Man on Campus—Sang Ik Choi, one of the first three Korean missionaries to America—later brought us under his authority. The Japanese called him *Papasan*, as he was their original and greatly successful missionary from 1958. He began losing Rev. Moon's way when he came to America in 1965 (despite repeating his Japanese magic) through his *Principles of Education*, a mishmash of Divine Principle, philosophy, Asian religion, and ancient wisdom.

A member said to me, "He developed his own messianic complex early on."

"He thinks *he's* the Messiah? Shit, our church has competing messiahs?"

"His mother raised him believing he was God's chosen one. After joining the church, he got to thinking Rev. Moon was *his* John the Baptist making straight *his* way. That's why he's nuts."

My head bobbed. "Okay, sounds plausible, yeah."

"He's been nurturing this mindset for years."

"And, evidently, with not a little observable resentment."

He was nominally in charge of the Washington Street center in an upscale neighborhood that in the 1970s and early '80s was the scene of wild and woolly anti-Moon demonstrations. Locals hated the Moonie pod in their midst. But ol' Papasan was such a gregarious, garrulous, smiling, embracing man tripping slick compliments off his tongue that he soothed them into closeting their ropes.

Mr. and Mrs. Choi at their Tokyo church circa 1960.

By 1984, Washington Street was all but empty, not even a shadow of its old dynamism. July's Blessing followed with October's in Korea—Mr. Kobayashi denied me it, too—was a spiritual earthquake in the church. Adherents' strapping—*mature*—faith and surefire commitment suddenly melted away. Couples who'd accepted the Matching now wanted out of their Blessing. Rebellion against the Imperial feudalism of our Japanese overlords swept o'er the land. Many thousands mutinied and deserted. I pegged late '83, early '84 as the start of our American movement's long slide to the nethergloom. Rev. Moon attributed the upheaval to the spiritual chaos generated by 1982's Blessing events that goaded spirit world to shudder and roar as he separated the sheeps and goats. Cain-type members rebelled against the church, God, and His loyal Abels. He said Abel-types were supposed to reach out with love and compassion to Cain-types with soothing, comforting, educating love. Mostly they reached out with a spiritual cudgel in white-knuckled hearts to beat these satans till their obedience improved.

"Why are Americans leaving the church?" they reverently wondered till seeing the light. "Ahh . . . they made a base with Satan through their selfish, egoistic way of life. Through it, they are betraying True Parents." A sadly typical example of the willful ignorance by the self-righteous the world over.

The 'troubles' grew pronounced by late 1983. The church lost members faster than it recruited. *Poof!* went vast fundraising potential and institutional spirituality. Revenues plummeted. Rev. Moon called on local centers to transfer more funds to national HQ. Once housing 50–70 in its 3-storied glory, Washington Street was a 4-person shell: Papasan; 5-year Small Mike the asinine 'Italian Stallion' American; 13-year Matsumoto the Blessed Japanese; and a Japanese sister-servant-cook.

In 1983, I led workshops there on Rev. Moon's Victory Over Communism (VOC), his powerful lecture series detailing the roots, leaders, atheism, and historical role of communism in God's Providence. When I delivered Christine each week to our local grocery store in the Haight–Ashbury, I hung outside to practice VOC on the communist activists. They lurked near the front doors passing out lying flyers and spreading the totalitarian word. Arguing voc's perspective, I regularly confounded them. After a month of it they refused to engage at all. When we trundled into the parking lot, they scuttled into their broke-ass commie bus and made rubber.

"Wow, Christine, look what I did! I defeated communism!" *Empowered!*

"Good work! Load up the groceries."

Also, I gave Divine Principle training courses to new members and guests while teaching English and Korean to our very unappreciative, disinterested members. I cherished my expanding responsibilities however frustrating. *At last! I'm showing my chops and moving up.*

Best school friend Lance at sister Blair's wedding in Hotel Boulderado. Jan., 1984.

MY NEW BESTIE Jerome said, "Father sent me here personally to earn my bachelors and then my graduate degree."

"He sends people to college?" I felt an itch. "Does he pay for it, too?"

"Sometimes, but he isn't mine." He laughed as big and toothy as Mrs. Uchiyama but a damn sight friendlier, though I detected a hint of financial aggravation.

He was attending San Francisco State University when he trooped into our foyer in 1983. Born in sunkissed St. Vincent and the Grenadines, he close-cropped his African hair over strong cheekbones, a somewhat feminine face, and a sort of burnt umber skin tone—very reddish for a black man, I thought. About five-nine and muscular, he invariably attired himself in a sports jacket, white shirt, and dusty tie; poor, but rarely fashion casual. Blacks were largely unknown to me at this point. I'd met some in the Coast Guard that, to me, were usually a misbegotten stripe thoroughly discrediting themselves. Instantly, I saw Jerome was different. He was in college (something I aspired to finish but so far couldn't), spoke educated English without affectation, was flush with intriguing and unique theories and philosophies, and came off a brainy intellectual. I was captivated.

He'd got Blessed at MSG to Carol, a white American. Her brother practiced and taught Rev. Moon's Unificationist *Won Wha Do* martial arts brand. Jerome got fast-tracked to start his family after a 30-day indemnity period because, he said, she was in her mid-thirties and could lose her chance to conceive. Older members often got this dispensation regardless countervailing factors because Blessed children were all. Those in their twenties and early thirties had to wait the standard 3-plus years, depending on their leader. Then Rev. Moon declared an "emergency period" in 1983 and 'asked' Blessed members to postpone starting their families for an additional three years to save the Providence from shipwreck. Disagreers generally left the church, sometimes as a couple like Katie but often not.

According to Jerome, Carol laughingly cored his wide eyes after consummating their nuptials. "Now you can't divorce me, you can't get rid of me!"

She then belatedly informed him she was seriously ill with kidney disease and other undisclosed health problems, and unable to conceive. I liked her and we shared some pleasant conversations. Jerome went full-Krakatoa. I don't know why, he was infertile, too. Some childhood thing. Maybe it was her ailments or that she'd lured him in under false pretenses. He was a real stickler for things like that . . . yet must've misled the BFD, too, else didn't know, which I had reason to discount. The laughing contempt he saw in her eyes certainly stung. Regardless, once a couple consummates the Blessing, Rev. Moon only extraordinarily annuls it. The average member is stuck or must abandon the church. Many did on their way to divorce court. The rate for 1982's Blessings was appallingly high. Among those I counted, 65% broke up within three years. That was way above America's statistical norm the Japanese and Koreans derided as evidence of our detestable archangelism.

Jerome left her high and dry and eventually moved on to the second of his four (while I knew him) marriages. Carol and her brother never stopped hating him for dumping her, I think her brother most of all.

"I steer clear of him," Jerome said. "He does martial arts and might kill me."

Brows hiked. "Pshaw! Come on. Nah."

"You don't know these people, Chris."

"Still . . ." Carol expired mid-'90s and maybe that got him off the hook. Mildly distraught despite ever-boiling resentment, he keenly felt her departure. "That's pretty weird, Jerome. I thought you despised her." I guessed a first marriage holds as much sway over the emotions as first love and virginity's loss.

He was snappish. "You know nothing about it. You've never been Blessed."

"Okay, dude, whatever." *Man*. Sometimes, he was a prick.

His intellect drew me. We made fast friends and gabbed hours of philosophical and historical discourse, often hanging out at a Chinese restaurant at 9th and Lincoln Way next to Golden Gate Park. The owner worked his seven cute daughters in exchange for college tuition. We were all of us good friends in 1983 and '84. Meeting Jerome and his older-member roomies—as exotic to me then as Greek gods—is when I discovered the Kobayashi's secret lair was spitting distance the whole time. Maybe his young children was why our money went for his private hideaway.

I loved getting out of the center and operating on my own recognizance. My errand-running, jack-of-all-trades remodeling mission delivered a hefty flexibility. I scampered off to hardware stores, lumber companies, beaches . . . anywhere I wanted for real or pretend errands to escape the prison-camp conditions the Uchiyamas had brought like a venereal disease to Judah Street.

It wasn't long before Jerome and I ended up their whipping boys and Papasan Choi soon joined the fun. Until our Korean regional leader shipped those two shitbirds back to the trenches, Papasan tried running our center with a hardier iron fist. I drew a cartoon, much admired and circulated by the few Americans still clinging to the faith, of Papasan's foot stamped on a prone American's throat while evil safely murdered Rev. Moon. To me, it summed up the entire condition of the American church in 1984, as though *Man in the High Castle* Japanese were reaping vengeance for World War Two and the Koreans were co-prosperity sphering it all the harder. We were living under ruthless colonial masters. They lacked only a government's power to shoot dissenters. And thank God or I'd be pushing up daisies if, like the Imperial Army rampaging through Southeast Asia, they or their American lackeys could've *Bushidoed* budding counter-revolutionaries like myself.

Papasan's tyranny. Left: *his* New Principle *in pocket; members: "You're God, Papasan!" "Be my messiah!" "You know everything" "I love you!" "You're the greatest!" "Hai!" "Pull my strings!" "Yes, Papasan!"* Right: *Papasan (church leadership) sundering American flag, boot pinning Righteousness wearing star of heavenly law struggling to save Rev. Moon from evil's attack.*

JEROME'S AND MY kid-sized disagreements with Papasan Choi erupted in conflict-cum-warfare with some brazen violence at Washington Street. One April evening Papasan's exalted Italian Stallion, Small Mike, saw Matsumoto, a typically slightweight Japanese, clattering in the front door. Spoiling for revenge (or Papasan, like Henry II moaning to his knights that "not one... will avenge me of this one upstart clerk," had maybe raised a *what-if?* in Small Mike's small mind), he ordered Matsumoto to do some housecleaning. Naturally, he told Small Mike to go to hell. What Japanese took orders (especially to do women's work) from an American swine? Their verbal confrontation spooled up. Small Mike balled his fists. Laid into Matsumoto like he was tenderizing an extra tough cut of *Wagyu* for a picky eater.

Jerome and I arrived at Judah Street from somewhere. We bounced into the video center where we often watched videos and talked God, philosophy, and reprobate leaders. Matsumoto was screening a movie at a cubicle near the sadly boarded-up bay window. He tabled his headphones. Rolled his office chair off the desk. Spun his puffed and bloody visage to us. We stopped dead, faces practically slack. Cuts littered his face. His nose, eyes, and jaw were swollen over dark brown and black bruises. Dried blood spotted his nostrils, one eye half closed.

"What happened to your face?!" Jerome stammered. "A car accident?"

Sheepish, "Small Mike beat me up." His eyes were downcast but I could tell he was seething inside. In true Japanese Moonie fashion, he'd never show it.

"*What?!*" Jerome nearly shouted. "He did... he beat up your face like that?"

His head cut a short, single bob. "Because I wouldn't clean up some mess."

"This was over cleaning up?!" Jerome's voice was tart. Matsumoto nodded.

My head spun over this abrupt violence in our church, but Jerome was giving me insight on how he'd reacted to Carol. More, even. He was shaking in his shoes, trembling like a bird. Matsumoto was our friend—well, Jerome's. I'd deemed him fairly arrogant. Full of himself and judgy as hell. In hindsight, he might've been a bit of a mini-me, but no matter. What set him apart from the Japanese was that he'd thoroughly Americanized. He spoke fairly good English, took our freedoms and cultural norms to heart, and didn't play Japanese ball with traditionalist leaders. They despised him a traitor to his people like scurrilous blacks lambast pretentious house Negroes for cozying up to the anti-color.

151

Matsumoto's tempestuous relationship with Mr. Uchiyama and Papasan Choi would now energize the strangest affair to ever butt heads in the American Unification Church during the 1980s and maybe ever. The Japanese wholly turned on him and unreservedly cheerleadered Small Mike's violence. Who'd-a thunk?

Jerome said, "All right. What happened? Tell us the whole thing."

Matsumoto laid out Small Mike following him around Washington Street house like a naggy spouse squabbling over his attitude, his disrespect for Papasan—Small Mike worshipped the guy—his refusal to do his share of house work, and other complaints that buttered over the unspoken crux of the matter, his Americanization. Matsumoto didn't say it in so many words, but I gathered he'd been less than curt with Small Mike in true Japanese fashion despite his adopted Westernism, and did very little to forestall his ham-handed impetuousness. After enough of Matsumoto's disagreeable disagreeing, Small Mike let him Americanly have it.

"Did you call the police? He'll be arrested!" Jerome sounded almost giddy.

"No, I don't want to get the church involved in a scandal."

"You—what are you talking about?" I said, now irritated. "The guy just beat the shit out of you. He totally violated the Principle, True Parent's teachings, the law—everything! What's the matter with you?" I couldn't believe he was showing us all his victimized butthurt, then refusing to slap that dumbass into jail.

"I don't want to drag True Parents through more mud," Matsumoto explained, unconvincingly. True enough, though. Scads of members' dirt stained Rev. Moon's face, like that MFT captain who'd thrashed his crewman in front of the cops. "Besides, it'll only make Small Mike madder and get me thrown out of the house."

There's the real truth, like enough. I said, "Jeez, Mats, where's your sense of Principled behavior? What'd you come over here for, anyway?" He should've stayed Small Mike's pummel boy over there if he was just going to take it on his knees.

"Well . . ." he hesitated, eyes furrowed. "I wanted someone to talk to."

"You need to go to the police," Jerome matter-of-factly said. "You can't let him get away with this. It violates every single thing the church stands for." He paused, summoning up that great intellect of his. "If you let Small Mike get away with this, it'll become the standard of the church. Mr. Choi will use him like a whip against everybody he doesn't like!"

That was a lightbulb moment: I knew just who it would be. "Yeah, Mats," I quickly agreed, "he's right. He's a wild animal, always threatening Jerome."

It looked for a moment that Jerome had forgot that. He'd visibly paled at the memory because, muscular as he appeared, he wasn't a fighter by any stretch of the imagination. He was an academic, an ivory tower wannabe with a recliner plan.

A Japanese sister slid into the room curious about the hushed conversation she'd overheard in the hallway. She ox-eyed us seated in a circle with a misshapen, black-and-blue Matsumoto.

"Oh, excuse, please," and demurely closed the door. We all knew she was off like a shot to report our subversive activities to Mr. Uchiyama.

"I don't know," Matsumoto said. "I'll think about it tonight."

I said, "Where are you gonna stay?" It was a salient question.

"I'll go back to my room after midnight or so, when I'm sure he's asleep."

"That's dumb. What if he sneaks—"

"I don't think he will. All my things are there, anyway." Horses and water, eh.

Papasan Choi was out of town for this event, so we reported it to Mr. Uchiyama after leaving Matsumoto. Slit eyes telegraphed malicious intent.

"This not your concern," he said. "You must stay away from Matsumoto."

I said, "You're seriously telling us to let violence reign?"

"He is problem member. His situation will be dealt with."

"Apparently not with Divine Prin—"

"Is Papasan responsibility." Snippily, "Do not interfere." He eye-stabbed the two of us to reinforce his point, then ascended the stairs to his gilded cage.

We settled in for a week of high tension awaiting Papasan's return. Jerome had by this time got permission to swap his rental in the Kobayashi's old apartment for free Judah Street. The Uchiyamas and Japanese initially welcomed an elder Blessed member, but Jerome could have a grating nature. He was highbrowed (if not exactly cerebral) and knew it. He tended to look down on church members, nearly all of whom had abandoned or couldn't rise to higher education, and he hadn't even graduated yet. He'd accordingly made enemies of the Uchiyamas, Small Mike, Julian, the Japanese, and others. Next to Matsumoto, I was his only real friend in the house and, importantly for him, still more or less in Mr. Uchiyama's and Julian's good graces despite Small Mike agitating I show more respect.

With the Bay Area church community unwilling to declare Small Mike's violence unPrincipled and unacceptable, he felt more emboldened than ever. He seized on Mr. Choi's absence to make himself our de facto city leader, at least over our two centers. Bush Street, still a taut ship enjoying a solid American leader and a mission that didn't include us, ignored him as inconsequential.

Matsumoto was made of sterner stuff than I'd thought because the next morning he reported Small Mike's assault and battery.

"Unfortunately," one of two cops said on Washington Street's porch, "the 24-hour reporting limit has passed. It's not possible for you to press charges now."

"But he might kill me next time!" Matsumoto's voice was saturated in worry.

They clucked and scribbled. "If it happens again, don't wait. Or move out."

"Exactly," I said after he recounted it. "You should move here, where you're protected around members."

He was shaking his head, though. "No . . ."

I threw my hands up. Small Mike had hid and stewed while the cops investigated. Maybe it was out of respect for Matsumoto calling the cops that he didn't trounce him again. A great relief to him and us.

Some days later Jerome, a couple Japanese sisters in their sumptuous basement, and I were the only members home. Small Mike let himself in with a longish, heavy wood baton in hand. He clomped through the house snapping it down on tabletops, stair railings, and walls like an African tiger hunter driving his quarry into a trap.

"Shit," Jerome instantly said, snapping closed his textbook. "that's Small Mike."

"How'd you divine that?" But he was spiritually perceptive and 'saw' things.

His eyes were furtive. "Maybe he'll stay downstairs."

"Pish! If it is him, not a chance."

I couldn't stand Small Mike any more than Jerome or Matsumoto but went downstairs anyway to scope out the commotion. Hovering on the last step, I said nothing as he banged his baton on the dining room tables.

He caught me in the corner of his eye, his tone innocent. "Jerome home?"

Renovated café room windows where Small Mike tried intimidating Jerome.

"No," I lied. "Why don't you leave?" Instead, he swished by and up the stairs banging his stick. I followed. "The hell you think you're doing, Small Mike?"

He confronted Jerome seated in the café-decorated second-floor study room, stalking threateningly round his chair albeit making no move to attack. I presumed my presence put him off. To ensure it, I leaned in plain sight against the heavy wood railing wrapped around the stairwell. Spying on his tableaux, I was saying, *Two against one; your move.* Five minutes of cagey talk and balked baton swings and he clumped downstairs and outside.

Jerome was patently shaken. He breathed out taut nerves. "Did you see how he was threatening me? The violence he wanted to do? That damned stick of his?"

"What are you going to do?" Clearly, Small Mike was on Jerome's ass, not mine.

"We have to get Mr. Choi to rein him in as soon as he comes back."

That was the plan. A confusing man, Mr. Choi adopted Mr. Uchiyama's attitude. His loyalties were obvious: he'd allowed the Uchiyamas, Mayumi, and Julian to devolve morning service into plain-spoken accusations against Jerome and me, who made themselves mental or physical no-shows for our turns at the lectern.

Two Sundays earlier he'd said, "We must be rational and scientific, relying on proof to guide our wisdom." Two weeks later: "We must rely on our conscience to decide what to do," while denying our conscienced rebuttals and rejection of violence. His house 'debates' in front of guests—Americans never returned after a boisterous, hours-long Japanese songfest for Mr. Uchiyama's birthday—were ludicrous. In one, he had Julian argue free sex and Jerome chastity. Extremism was the only way to win. Julian won. Papasan concluded, "Yes, Julian did a good job, but Jerome's point of view is the correct one." Thus, authority trumps proof, conscience, and votes.

Now, we circled up in Washington Street's high-ceilinged, Victorian living room. He said, "Matsumoto deserves his situation; he is arrogant and disobedient."

All eyes swiveled to us. I said, "What. Now *we're* the baddies?"

"If you put it like that." Disobedient archangels daring to challenge Principled Abel. The self-satisfied smugness on their faces told the story. We were toast.

But violence is intolerable against a free people. We weren't about to go down quietly. Our neck of the church was on the verge of literal cultdom. Who knew what might come next. We got on the phone to national headquarters. Jerome personally knew our current American church president, Dr. Mose Durst, an affable if spineless former university professor. He'd taken over from Neil Salonen, who'd crumpled under the psychological pressure from the Korean and Japanese leadership in the early 1980s. Dr. Durst came on the line. We explained our problem.

"I really can't believe it," he gasped. "Are you sure you didn't misunderstand the situation? That maybe something else is going on?"

"Like what, possibly?" We traded eyes. Was he even hearing us?

"I don't know. I promise that," on the strength of his long-standing relationship with Jerome and my insistence, "I'll call Papasan and get to the bottom of it."

What even Jerome didn't know was that he was Papasan's spiritual son, joining the church under his tutelage. He therefore had a strong incentive *not* to rock the great missionary's boat, especially on account of his weak and tenuous position as titular head of the American movement. The same Asian blade that parted Neil's manhood was poised for a repeat performance on the Durst Jewels and probably no one more keenly knew it than he. In the highly politicized position of church president, one wrong move made eternal enemies of the senior, often vindictive, Japanese and Koreans. It was their obdurate animosity that led Neil to throw in the towel. When our phone call brought only Papasan's gentle rebuke for going over his head, we knew Dr. Durst had decided we were expendable. Things got ugly.

Judah Street went oil and water. Mr. Uchiyama loathed Papasan Choi. Perhaps he had a hard time overcoming Japan's historical contempt for Koreans or just hated any check on his gangsterism. The Japanese dutifully followed his lead and refused to work with Papasan at all. Ironically, his most ardent champions were Julian, Jerome, and me. We all liked him because (till now) he was likable, a breath of fresh air in the Uchiyama's noxious smokehouse. We certainly didn't want him losing power to them. But with our Principled let alone Christian stand against violence as a tool in the church and his astonishing support of Small Mike's force and intimidation, the house underwent a sea change. Suddenly, the Uchiyama's were his bosom buddies ready to march into hell to die at his stylish Italian oxfords. Members dutifully followed their vacillator-in-chief without regard to the Principle or even common sense. Jerome and I were now bad apples in Papasan's healthy barrel.

Julian lost his balls in the confusion. Apparently, safe aboard ship beat walking Papasan's plank. He threatened Jerome on several occasions. "Mr. Uchiyama is your central figure and wants you out of this house *today*. As do I. So, go!"

"I have every right as a Blessed member to stay here," Jerome said. "True Father himself sent me to San Francisco to get my college degrees. *He's* my central figure. No small-time leader has any Principled right derailing Father's will. My life and what I'm doing is Father's life and God's will!"

Julian spluttered but wasn't ready to cross Small Mike's line. He was still a good man, a righteous member however confused by a phony Principle of Obedience.

Julian, the Uchiyamas, and my closer 'siblings' warned me, "You need to distance yourself from Jerome and what's coming for him."

"Head-down for the apocalypse? No! I won't abandon conscience for obedience unless you convince me it's Principled. But you can't, can you?"

"Yes. Obeying your central figure, like Isaac did Abraham, is Principle."

I wrestled with it through painful days and nights, wondering if my analysis of the Principle and its proper expression was right. It was onerous. The church resolutely schooled us to never question nor disobey central figures. The Principle is supposed to be our standard for guidance. In practice, everything boils down to obedience to one's local leader as the fount of global authority. Even Rev. Moon felt obliged to complain in a coincidentally contemporary speech published in *Today's World* about members putting leaders over Divine Principle and Rev. Moon himself. His argument that members elevated the master's servants over the master didn't work for him, and it didn't work for us. I journaled on April 29:

> They all speak Japanese and don't want to speak English. Last night Mr. Choi said . . . all kinds of things that completely contradicted things he said before. I really can't figure that guy out—is he senile, or what? This house is so un-Principled and EVERYONE has fallen into that abyss. I, alone, with Jerome, am fighting against it; yet, how correct are we? It's difficult to think of oneself as the only correct voice crying in the wilderness . . . I see Divine Principle violated on a daily basis . . . Mr. Choi teaching his *own* ideas, rather than True Father's . . . a 13-year Blessed member beat-up by a 5-year unBlessed member [twice rejecting the Blessing] . . . condoned and even lauded. The Japanese all tell Mr. Choi they're glad Matsumoto was beat up and that he should be kicked out—which Uchiyama did. I see people living the most despotic and nepotistic lives . . . Mr. Choi do one thing and say another . . . constantly contradicting himself . . . exalting himself above Father, always praising himself . . . angry when not treated with whatever respect he thinks he deserves . . . unable to control his emotions. I see Father ignored and never talked about . . . [his] words never utilised until it's time to accuse and condemn . . . morning service turned into a three-ring circus where everyone just gives their own idea and condemns Jerome and me daily . . . no God or True Parents here, and I hate it.

Grappling with it was agonizing and possibly faith-breaking, thus Bay Area members avoided my widely cast net for advice. On May 12, I quit vacillating:

> To-morrow, I reckon, is when the big showdown will occur . . . this life here is a big lie. If I compromise my principles, I'll be completely invaded by Satan; my character . . . forever impugned. I shall lose my medical support . . . child-support . . . ability to go to Texas . . . if I follow this course, I shall lose everything; including my reputation . . . But I will NOT surrender! Never! Nuts! I am correct. If I go to hell, it shall be with my integrity (more-or-less) intact. What Mr. Choi is doing is a big lie. I cannot stand for it, though I lose my very life . . . [they say] this is a cultural problem, but that's a small part . . . Now that Jerome's kicked out all the stops are pulled. But he won't leave.

Small Mike lured Jerome into the foyer for a fake phone call. "Papasan kicked you out. Why are you still here? Move out *today* or something's gonna happen."

"You're not my boss. And you're a liar. Get lost." He started up the steps.

"If you stay then you attend Sunday service or you'll get what Matsumoto got. That boss enough for you, big boy?"

The next day Papasan called me to his fix-the-house Plan 'A' sit-down with the intent of teaching me the error of my ways. He was dead set on eighty-sixing my friendship with Jerome. We sat across a small table in our living room where Christine and I had so long ago clashed over the TV. What a kinder, simpler world that was! The middle of the day, most of our household was out fundraising and witnessing while I was home remodeling and maintaining the center. Papasan was a real smoothie. No wonder, masquerading as the Japanese Mr. Nishikawa, he'd so successfully missionized Japan. He sweet-talked and cajoled me through full-faced teeth into having nothing more to do with Jerome.

"As soon as he's out of the house," he crooned, "you'll go back to being your normal self. And this church center to its normal self."

"My normal self? What do you mean?"

"Jerome brainwashed you. You're not normal. You behave crazy."

"Brain—?" I huffed a laugh and lightly, nonconfrontationally said, "No, I don't. Jerome hasn't brainwashed me. He's just my friend—and my church brother."

"Yes, it's true what I'm saying. As soon as he's gone, you'll be happy again."

"Look, Mr. Choi—" I growled.

"Do not call me that! I am, 'Papasan.' That shows you do not love your central figure. You don't follow the right conscience."

"I'm not your little puppy dog you can pet and I'll just wag my tail." This kind of patronizing exasperated me.

He took a calming breath. Sipped his tea. "You know, you have this very arrogant, close-minded, hippie spirit. Listening to what you say is a waste of time. So, we're not here for that. We're here to correct your wrong attitude."

"The wrong attitude that beating up members you don't like is unPrincipled? Or the one using Small Mike as a *yakuza* goon to scare everybody into obedience?"

I guess he was exasperated, too. He slammed his fist on the table, jumping our cups and saucers and my heart. "You're just a stupid hippie!" he shouted, the worst anti-American opprobrium he knew.

Unthinking, I banged my own fist down right next to his white-knuckled own. "A hippie?" my voice incredulous. "How can I be a hippie? I have short hair. I'm a member of the church. I'm not out drinking, drugging, or screwing women. I have no hippie attitudes whatsoever. How dare you call me a hippie?"

Our conversation stopped dead, fast. We were at loggerheads. He thought I was under some voodoo influence of Jerome's and I thought he was a messianic wannabe perverting the church and ruining our lives.

"Yes! You are a hippie. That's your problem. I saw it when I first met you." His voice calmed, smoothed. "Even Mr. Kobayashi gave up on you because you never listened but did as you wanted." That body-checked me. Thoughts flailed. Later, Julian said it was bunkum. "But I wanted to help you, to raise you up."

"Listen, when you first came here all the Japanese hated you. Nobody liked you but me and Jerome. Not even Julian was all that supportive. We stood by you. Mr. Uchiyama was so full of hate he refused to lead Pledge. He sent his wife!" Papasan was quiet, maybe contemplating Uchiyama's insult. "It wasn't till Small Mike and Matsumoto that everything in this house turned upside down like it is now. I've done my job. All the work you, Mr. Kobayashi, Julian, anybody asked me to do. I've always listened to my leaders and obeyed them." *Mostly.* "But this is ridiculous. You're teaching violence is okay in our church while True Father says—"

"Don't talk to me about True Parents!" he thundered, his voice blaring and peeved. "True Parents are not your leader. I am your leader!"

My neck burned. "The hell you are. I didn't join *your* church. I joined True Parents church. This church center belongs to True Parents, not to you!"

157

"Then you should get out!" he hissed. "If you don't like it here, leave!"

"Why should I leave?" He and Mr. Uchiyama certainly worked off the same playbook. "This is my church, too. Don't you think I care about my church? That I want it to succeed?"

"You don't know what you're talking about," he said. "Jerome has you bewitched! He is unadulterated junk. Possessed. This is his fault."

"Let me tell you something, Mr. Choi. I really struggled with my conscience over this issue, and not a little bit, either. And to me, you're the one at fault, not Jerome. Why did you ever let Small Mike beat up Matsumoto?"

"Matsumoto is an arrogant bastard." I admired his command of English.

"Whatever. He's still a nice enough guy and a good brother. He didn't deserve Small Mike beating him up like some dog."

"Oh, yes, he deserved it. And so do you."

Oh, really? "Are you going to sic Small Mike on me? Because I'll tell you right now you might not get him back in the same condition." He leaned back. Muttered something in Korean. We were both tiring of this fruitless discussion. He'd realized I wasn't to be cowed. That maybe another tack was called for after all. Whatever my faults, this last month of forced introspection had pushed me to overcome an Everest-sized fear of authority. "I'll think about what you've said, Mr. Choi. I admit you had some good points about my blunders." I swear this old man rolled his eyes. It almost busted up a grin. "But if I can't reconcile with your ideas, I don't see how I can stay a member." I expected a threat like that to spur a rethink.

He laid a contemplative look on me as if eyeing Screwtape in the flesh and pushed back his chair. He silently rose and stalked out. Yet another thick, post-combat lungful sighed out of me. *Where the fuck am I?* A sense of rootlessness overwhelmed me. When I shakily stepped out of the dining room Christine, all big sister swoll, was hands-on-hips on the stairs, her tone a harsh shellacking.

"How can you talk to Papasan like that? I heard everything!"

I raised eyes to her stern, reddened face. "Why were you listening in, then?"

She descended till she was two steps up thus eye level. "He's your *leader*, Chris! How can you talk to him like some satanic, outside—?"

"He's no leader of mine." I flicked a hand in the direction he went. "You heard him tell me to ignore True Parents and listen only to him. Did you join Mr. Choi's church or True Parents church?"

"You're wrong, Chris. You're being totally unPrincipled."

"No, I'm not. You are, for not standing up to him. He has everybody around here terrified of disobeying their so-called central figure, and meanwhile they're disobeying every principle Father ever taught us. Especially about Cain and Abel and unconditional, sacrificial love for the worst person."

"Father always says that obedience to our central figure is Principled obedience to him and God. It's the path of Restoration. You're misreading—"

"Only if they're following Divine Principle! Not some half-assed, made up . . ." My body trembled hot with adrenaline and, yeah, fear. This was gut-wrenching shit. I let out a deep breath. "Everybody's so full of anger, Christine. Hate, violence . . . they want to kick us out so they don't have to contend with us anymore. And why? Because we said it was wrong to beat up Matsumoto. How's that make us unPrincipled? Or even controversial, for God's sake! How can any right-thinking person disagree?"

She was unconvinced and swept past me for the kitchen or basement stairs. I didn't look because I'd leaned on the railing and wearily pulled myself up.

That night I was working on a letter in our library room. Jerome arrived to pick up a paper I'd edited. At that moment Mr. Uchiyama, with or without Mr. Choi's knowledge—who knew at this point?—evacuated all guests and members.

Jerome's eyes went white. "Get ready for violence, Chris. They're emptying the center. There's going to be some blood shed tonight!"

"I hate to say it but, yeah, you might be right. Spoiling for it all day."

"I need a weapon to defend myself. Like Small Mike's stick."

I caught my breath. "Are you crazy? You can't do that! Don't walk that road."

"That only makes me vulnerable to their assault. I've already been struck!"

"Because you're in Abel's shoes. God's side always has the disadvantage with evil. The good guy never draws first. Even if he *looks* it, evil can claim self-defense."

"Man, you're setting me up!"

"Arm your mind, Jerome, not your hands. If we're on God's side, stay on it."

He listened, showing me he followed truth. I left. He settled in to pore over exams. I admired his pluck amidst chaos. Mr. Uchiyama and Hidetoshi came in to harangue him into leaving for about five minutes before giving up.

Descending the stairs an hour or so later in our noiseless, guestless church, strained voices and pointed laughter gusted up from the dining room. I lowered myself onto the landing where I couldn't be observed and stretched my ears.

"We must throw everything of his out the door," Mr. Uchiyama said. Hidetoshi's voice grunted agreement along with others.

Julian said, "We need to be careful. He wrote a paper for school that accused the church. If he does something like that, wouldn't he go to the newspapers?" Voices babbled. "We have to be cautious, is all I'm saying."

Said Yoichi, a 6-month member who'd helped me on numerous renovation projects, "Maybe we should invite him outside to . . . a picnic in a secluded place where we can more freely 'discuss' things. Perhaps bring his stuff in another car so he does not know . . . beat him up, even. Leave him there."

I dropped my mouth at that. They bantered his idea back and forth.

Darlene—yes, my beloved MFT sister; that's how corrosive it was—said, "We should contrive a situation that'll make them feel forced to leave." *Et tu, Brute?*

"I still think we should throw him out. This is our center, not his! Even in the Communist Party, when you don't toe the line they kick you out."

Purged was the word that came to mind. I'd never heard a member favorably compare our church to communism, though. *Off. The. Rails.*

"Jerome is crazy person," Mayumi said. Agreement all around.

A brother said, "I heard he's been crazy his whole time in the church."

"His bad reputation goes back as far as the day he joined."

"I think we should definitely have a meeting with him, but we shouldn't start off with conflict in mind." I stifled a laugh. *That's exactly their purpose in refusing to address his central issue, which is Mr. Choi unleashing violence.*

"Maybe it's better to take this issue to all the center leaders in the Bay Area. When they decide, they'll kick him out with whatever means necessary." No provision for Jerome to air his side, naturally.

A Japanese said, "They will sign a card of condemnation against him. That will be enough to remove him." A Japanese church tactic, I guessed.

"Why do they think we are all evil and wicked ones? He is crazy one!" Already punctuated by laughter, the room erupted at Mayumi's remark.

"There is only one solution, and that is to remove him from the center."

Julian said, "After they decide, then we'll . . . solve . . . this problem."

"Let's get Matsumoto over here," Hidetoshi said. "We'll get him to convince Jerome to leave. That seems more likely to work."

"Okay . . ." Julian warmed up to it. "We'll pressure him to let Jerome stay at his apartment. That'll give him an out so he doesn't feel like he's being kicked right out onto the street. It'll make a resolution easier, too." More agreement.

"Wait," a sister said. "Isn't he living with his wife? He won't want—"

Julian said, "We can pressure Kathleen to move into the center . . ."

"That is more Principled anyway," said Mr. Uchiyama. "They are living without permission." *In sin.*

". . . then he and Jerome can live together and learn to be friends." Which was weird. According to Jerome, he'd been friends with Matsumoto for seven years.

They were a lynch mob. I was appalled. A mouse on darkened stairs. Mouth hanging and head shaking as the cats planned dinner. This same day the US Supreme Court rejected Rev. Moon's appeal and ordered him to report June 18 to Danbury prison. I couldn't help seeing the connection in their jolly, unfazed scheming.

Midnight, Mr. Uchiyama and Hidetoshi filed into the library and menacingly encircled Jerome. Time to act on their impatiently unrefined Plan 'B.' I beat them to the closet as cavalry to spy. Julian was pointedly absent.

"Leave this house!" they each demanded. "Now! Get out!"

"I'm busy with—"

"No discussion! No dissent! We are your central figures. Obey!"

"You?" His voice lilted in laughter. "Father's my central figure. I'm not going anywhere. It's the middle of the night and I've got exams. Plus, you have no authority to force a Blessed member who hasn't violated Principle out of a church center."

"You do violate Principle when you don't obey your central figure. Your own words condemn you. Now, get out! Now!"

"True Father's very clear that only Divine Principle merits absolute obedience. If you were Principled, I'd obey you and let Small Mike"—he glared at the memory— "beat up whoever Papasan sics him on. But it's unPrincipled! Thus, I *am* being Principled in disobeying your satanic violence to oppress me and Matsumoto."

"That is absolutely—" But Mr. Uchiyama couldn't hold a candle to Jerome.

"Disobedience to you is obedience to God and True Parents and Divine Principle. Stop being satanic and I'll obey you." His eyes flitted between them.

Plan 'C': they grouped up to pull him to his feet by the arms to bodily drag him downstairs and toss him out the front door. He twisted easily out of their grip. That surprised me because Hidetoshi was tall and strong-looking. Julian might've been a good man but Mr. Uchiyama wasn't. He punched Jerome square in the face, maybe emboldened by his gorilla Hidetoshi slugging me from behind the other day. Before I could react, Jerome snatched him off the floor and pitched him across the room. I gaped from my vantage. I'd only dreamed it. He did it! Hidetoshi tried pinning his arms behind his back, presumedly so Mr. Uchiyama could have another go, but Jerome whipped his arms out of his grip and cocked both fists. Hidetoshi was a leaf quivering in the wind, his bluster shot. He only squeaked what he wanted to yell.

"My *chi* is strong," Jerome gloated. "If you were righteous, you'd wipe me out."

"Everyone hates and despises you here, Jerome! Leave!"

Mr. Uchiyama fumed climbing onto his feet. "Yes, you get out! Tonight! Now!"

"Be quiet! You are against righteousness and Mr. Choi has made himself the king of unrighteousness. You're nothing but a couple of hoodlums. Get out of here!" He stomped a lead foot and pulled back a fist.

"This isn't over. Papasan—"

I burst from the closet. They fled. "Holy shit, Jerome! I–I mean . . . fucking hell! I'm just . . . I'm . . ."

"You see them try to practically kill me? But they're weak women. No *chi*."

My library-room closet hide at left for Jerome's safety from Mr. Uchiyama.

"This is the last straw. Ol' Uchi-coochi's gonna get you one way or another."

"Him and his loco wife can go to hell." We both burped a laugh.

I crossed arms. "Maybe you should go back to the Kobayashi's old place."

"Too late for that. You gonna be awake? I have to study." I tiredly nodded.

Plan 'D': they avalanched upstairs to his sleeping area with Jerome on their heels and me spying from the stairs and scooped all his belongings into a pile to cart them downstairs and heave onto the sidewalk, likely imagining they'd lock him out when he dashed out to retrieve them.

Jerome said, "I'll throw everything you own out the windows if you do that."

They'd have to hike past the study room to do it. Jerome, and me now openly observing, was a waiting roadblock. The choice was all out combat (they now figured to lose) in the hallway or let him foil their plan. Must've forgot the windows.

Plan 'E': they gave up. A blown-out, dissipating storm.

But the die was cast. I could see Armageddon peeking round the corner. *Shit.* I missed my morally quiet life with my MFT sisters and Mr. Kobayashi. A day after this debacle, Mr. Uchiyama sat me down after some forgettable bluster.

"If you want to stay here, you must follow three points."

"Besides blindly obey?" I breathed deep. "Okay. What do you have in mind?"

"First, you must ask my permission before you do work on the centers."

"My job is maintenance." I laughed. "If you don't want it, just change my mission."

"I am not saying that. Also, from now you must pay your medical costs."

Now I prickled. "It seems kind of weird working for free *and* paying my doctor bills, especially since working for the church, for free, created them."

"That is the rule."

"How am I supposed to pay for it? Working for free and all?"

"You can fundraise at night, in your free time."

"That's crazy."

"You have enough for trouble. Use for fundraising. That is Principle."

"I'm not creating trouble! You are, preaching violence against members."

"You do not understand Principle. Like Matsumoto and Jerome."

My gut clenched. I eyed him hard. Leaned forward. "Is that a threat?"

"Nooo . . ." He'd obviously recovered from being Jerome's medicine ball. "Most important, you may only speak to Jerome in public. No private talking."

"Eh? Why not?"

"You and Jerome always plotting against us, against Japanese member."

"How would you know? It's Japanese who don't speak English reporting us."

"Only when another Japanese member is there can you talk."

"Well, we don't! And it's outrageous."

"I am center leader. You must obey if you want to stay here."

I'd have laughed if I wasn't so hot and trembling. "Who do you think you are, telling me who I can talk to and under what circumstances?" This was too much. It forced me into a worse situation than I wanted. The point of his intimidation.

He spread his hands. "Regardless. This is condition to be here."

"Just for me, though, it seems."

"Yes, just for you. Because you are problem member."

"How is that even Principled? You do whatever you want. Like a heathen."

"It is indemnity course for you. You need much indemnity."

"I don't think that means what you think it means, amigo." He cocked his head. "I think it's better I talk it over with Mr. Choi . . . maybe whoever's his boss."

His voice stridently rose to command level. "If you want to continue member of this church, then you obey. That is Principle! *Obey!*"

There was no middle ground for bullies like him. He needed Rev. Moon's 1984 speech shoved deep up . . . *sigh*. This was a good time to revisit my commitment to the church. Yet, I adored Divine Principle's understanding of God, Jesus, and human history. I loved and respected Rev. Moon and saw myself an intimate part of his ministry. Abandoning him again petrified me. *No, the church needs conform to its own teachings, which we're upholding in the face of corruption and organized violence.* I would not be cowed by calls to fake authority and phony principles.

"Well, in the meantime, I'll talk to Jerome whenever I like and that's that. Take it to the bank. America's a free country and you can't stop me."

I certainly can registered on his face.

Mrs. (Mamasan) Choi must've concluded Papasan dropped the ball because Plan 'F' was a household powwow in our Judah Street dining room she moderated. We chaired up in a room-sized circle and discussed Small Mike's violence and the many incidents in the house, the manner the center was run, and the bad American–Japanese feelings. She was having none of it. I wrote May 16,

[She] lambasted Jerome and me like we were criminals! Her words were very coy and seductive, twirling her confusion around my mind . . . after she called us about every terrible thing in the book . . .

At the same time, I penned Rev. Moon a letter that noted,

. . . even I felt myself turning against Jerome. My goodness! I was shocked at the hypnotic state she'd woven! She said terrible things . . . no leader should.

Maybe chastened Jerome said, "I want reconciliation, Mrs. Choi. I'm sorry I haven't controlled my emotions and let this problem get so general."

"After all you've done? You are only lying. Not a sincere apology."

"Well, it only became a general problem because, one by one, all the members chose to support an obvious evil."

"You are Satan!" She blasted him, and me his henchman, for a few minutes. "You are why members are not successful in their mission here."

I said, "Mrs. Choi . . . I get the sense that Small Mike and Jerome are already apologizing internally." I then intimately expressed my feelings as a member and an American. Most Japanese seemed overtly moved. I felt a shift in their mood.

There was a moment, maybe brought by spirit world, where everyone seemed ready to apologise to each other . . . even the Japanese.

I felt a lot of empathy for their struggle with a host of issues, including Small Mike's Korean-sanctioned violence against one of their own, which they dared not oppose. I felt our problems melting. When Mrs. Choi parted her lips, I was sure it was to spread a healing balm. How callow I was. Instead of a salve I got salt.

"Jerome is a worthless, violent criminal! Look how he treated his Blessing wife. I don't know how he's even here. I don't know about Father sending him to school. But you," her acid gaze dropped on me. "How long are you in the church?"

"A little over three years." I felt reconciliation puff away in her rude gale.

"I've been in the church thirty years! What makes you think you know the Principle better than I do? Have you lived and worked around True Parents? No? What makes you think you have any understanding of God or True Parents to challenge my husband who personally knows them?"

Wow. Unanticipated. I was tongue-tied, my thoughts jumbled. "Just because I'm only a young member doesn't mean I have no understanding of right and wrong." I trembled in my chair at contradicting her authority to her face. All eyes expectantly rested on me, Julian's in particular. "Violence is wrong, and especially it has no place in our church or used against members." I saw most members now agreeing with me. "That's the only issue that needs resolving. If Mr. Choi doesn't think so, then maybe he doesn't understand Principle." Gauntlet, and Julian's brows, raised. Mrs. Choi snapped eyes at my insolence.

Small Mike recovered from his dalliance with a heart. "You mind your mouth and listen to Mamasan. You, too, Jerome. You're the root of all the trouble here, and especially with Chris. You need to listen to your elders."

"Man, you can f—shove off, Small Mike! Follow your own advice."

"How dare you point your finger!" Hidetoshi said. "You're the problem, Jerome. Why don't you leave right now? Mrs. Choi obviously wants you to go—"

"Be quiet, Hidetoshi!" snarled Sonoko in Japanese, a crack in the wall.

"—like every person here. Follow Principle. Leave before you're struck down!"

Jerome laughed. "Like you already tried twice? And this fake Italian Stallion, too?" He sneered. "You have no power over me because you are a criminal and also immoral. Because you are unPrincipled. Your *chi* is dead like your soul."

"I'll take you right now, Jerome," Small Mike said. "You think you're so tough?"

I said, "Thirty years, Mrs. Choi? And you stoke this psychological violence?"

"This arises in unPrincipled Jerome, young man. He does nothing here. Not dishes. Not witnessing. Only study, like a nonmember."

"That's not true, Mrs. Choi," Julian at last offered. "Jerome has sacrificed his schoolwork on many occasions to help around the house."

"Many times I'm the only one cleaning the kitchen, Mrs. Choi," Jerome said. "I help the sisters move heavy stuff like rice bags. I guide and teach them witnessing. You know my result. I'm a top witnesser anywhere in the church."

"That's certainly true," Julian said. "He does go witnessing with members . . . there are many positive things about Jerome I think we should recognize here."

We'll talk about you later, she eyed. To me: "Do not presume to know—"

"I'm old enough to know the Principle is very clear about loving our enemies and sacrificing for Cain. That's *Father's* way. The Principle of Restoration. Where does it say we should strike our enemies?" Gauntlet slapped.

She volcanoed. "Jerome must leave this house immediately! That is the final word. You have no understanding of Principle. You need training. You need workshop!"

Do I, really. "This all sounds very Soviet to me . . . or North Korean." What could I say? Youth was pie in my face. All I could do was wipe out my eyes.

She said, "Matsumoto is a problem member," and slowly faced his downcast visage for a hard examination. "He does not follow Principle, he follows his own way. He caused this problem because he is arrogant. Not Small Mike, he is not the problem." He preened. Sat back. Kicked a heel atop his knee.

"It's okay to beat up members who are arrogant, sinful, or imperfect? That's True Parents' message you learned over 30 years? I haven't heard that anywhere."

"You don't know Principle." Then she explained Mr. Choi's weird concept of violence published in his book *Explanation of the Principle.* Rev. Moon declared it heretical, not to be followed. With confidence in her rectitude she said, "When a good man strikes a bad man, that bad man can change. He can grow and develop. It is good for that bad man to be hit, because it allows him to overcome his sin. But, if that bad man strikes a good man, then that bad man will be destroyed."

In a nutshell was her husband's premise for tolerating violence. He'd spied a bad member in Matsumoto. An arrogant, self-righteous, stuck up, Americanized problem child needing a lesson for his own good. Daring to contradict his exalted groupie that day at Washington Street was striking a good man. Small Mike was an inveterate brownnoser thus high on Papasan's great member list, maybe groomed for a headier power. He must've noticed; he'd appointed himself city leader.

Jerome and I thought Papasan's philosophy of beneficent violence was goddamn dangerous. It justified a whole range of abuse. It's a Nazi philosophy, a communist system of the State reigning supreme over the individual because, after all, who

164

identifies the 'good' and 'bad' man in any conflict? It's the antithesis of Americanism. If Papasan's principle is valid then only God—He's not around; therefore, his high priests—can infallibly know who needs a whuppin'. The notion is so dangerous a precedent for any society that Jerome and I believed confronting it here and now with Rev. Moon's same inflexibility for that MFT captain who beat his crewman was nonnegotiable. Otherwise, it would destroy our church and us along with it.

On Mr. Choi's behalf, Mrs. Choi was identifying me as a 'bad man' in need of a beating. Like Frederick Douglass, I damned sure didn't think so and wasn't taking it. If I had to wrestle down my 'master' or his Jabbokian Stallion, so be it.

"Mrs. Choi, what you're saying is a justification for violence." I shot eyes at most everyone in our circle. "It puts all us members in the position of never knowing when Small Mike or somebody will single us out to overcome sin through a required beating. Maybe y'all are okay with that threat, but I'm not. It's beyond wrong."

I finished with a sharp eye on Julian, but he was head-down contemplating. I didn't think he disagreed with me. It was an institutional problem he couldn't yet face. I wondered if any Japanese saw their dead end in Papasan's philosophy.

She and I were irreconcilable and she knew it. What had seemed a moment of reconciliation and recommitment to the Principle had rechasmed into division and enmity. She fixed me with a withering stare marshaling a comeback. I left-eyed her suck air and open her lips but nothing came out. *Well, naturally. Her argument's absurdly untenable.* We were stalemated because her intimidation wasn't erasing my long-steeped Christian sense of right and wrong.

She said, "Julian will you pray? Then a Japanese member." Our meeting ended. Her polarized house shunned us. I wrote to Rev. Moon that Mrs. Choi was

> more interested in defending the Japanese no matter what the cost, and she simply wanted to subjugate us. She . . . lied outrightly, she used trickery and falsehood. Finally, she used hatred and resentment, I could even perhaps say racism, to make sure Jerome was completely pushed out. These people are crazy! They violate everything they purport to espouse, they're violently attacking people, exalting those who use hatred as an instrument of policy, allowing violence to be used as a viable means of power-extension. They're completely out of control, with nothing to brake their behaviour . . . Is this *your* church? Is that what you're suffering for in order to establish? or is this *why* you're suffering? . . . You said when we're confused, to find a course and follow it absolutely. Well, I'm confused, so I've chosen the best course I know. I've already lost my spiritual life here . . . wherever I go, Mr. Choi will call ahead and condemn me, so I must take my leave for awhile, because no one would accept me . . . I shall work with Hemi Lanetta as a sort of "central figure."

I spent the next several days pondering my conscience and future with the church. *Am I right? How important to God or True Father is obedience, anyhow?* He relentlessly advocates it but qualifies it with an overriding obedience to the Principle, to Abel unconditionally loving Cain as the only path to Restoring the Fall. Obedience to leaders, even to Rev. Moon, never supersedes obedience to God, conscience, and Principle. That's what he preaches and it's how I was seeing it after my (in Mrs. Choi's view, paltry) three years in the church. Like her 30 had made any difference.

He later elevated conscience to the highest throne. I'd been on the right track after all. But in the early '80s these were death-defying conundrums. My eternal life was at stake. The pressure from minor deities like the Uchiyamas was eviscerating. Our Korean regional leader must've heard something because, within days of Mrs. Choi's roundtable, he summarily packed these two peas and their pod off to trench duty. A couple years later I found him a cook and her a waitress at the diner occupying the large, glassed 34th and 8th corner of the New Yorker Hotel's first floor.

I said to Jerome, "The day Loco Yoko took my order to ol' Uchi-coochi sweating buckets behind the counter, I remembered her 'big-body-little-head' bullshit. I was dying to say, 'Ohhh . . . big position, little future. Ha ha ha!'"

"Bastards got their comeuppance. I should go there. Did you, though?"

I sighed. "Nah. Maybe I didn't care anymore. It was enough seeing 'em slaving away to one of the few instances of poetic justice I ever saw in our church."

Papasan appointed our Japanese brother Hiro as center director. The comedown from the classy, erudite, caring, and Principled Mr. Kobayashi depressed me. Hiro joined only a year-minus ago. *I'd* taught him Divine Principle. We'd been friends until this fracas. He'd made no effort to disguise his hostility.

When he heard (probably from Christine) about my tête-à-tête with Papasan, he said something along the lines of, "You're the very spawn of Satan himself."

I Julian-clapped him on the shoulder. "A fox smells its own home first." He raised curious eyes. I laughed. "Figure it out."

After my noisy parley with Papasan, I'd suspended what little participation in church activities I had going. I slaved on the house and hung out with Jerome. A week later I said to him, "I've decided I can't in good conscience stay a member here. Life's just intolerably vituperative. I'm leaving. Going to my folks in Texas."

"Damn." He slumped and huffed. "I better go, too, before Small Mike . . ."

"I'm sorry. It's . . . too much." Four days after Mamasan and four days before leaving, Darlene castigated me over Pledge and morning service. Go figure.

I blood-stroked a 3-page letter of resignation detailing the abuse and blind folly overrunning the center since Mr. Kobayashi's departure. Mouthing a quick prayer, I moped my millstone downstairs into Mrs. Choi's hands in the kitchen.

"Here's my letter of resignation. I've decided to leave the church." As tough as I felt I'd got by then, I quaked in fear to speak those words to her unyielding face.

She seemed hardly shocked. Certainly not disappointed. "I'm sorry to hear that," she smoothly lied with all her husband's aptitude. "When are you leaving?"

The 64-dollar question. "As soon as I pack up my things and arrange airfare." She struggled to wipe away a flickering smile.

The day before my flight out Matsumoto said, "I'm concerned you're leaving the church with a bad impression and that it's somehow all Jerome's fault."

"No, man. Not at all. Uchiyama and Mr. Choi made it inevitable."

"Ah. I guess that makes me feel better. I'm coming tonight for the debate."

"Pssh! That dumb thing? Read my letters to Father, instead. I can't believe Papasan's making such crucial blunders. He must be daft." I took a beat. "You okay?"

"Yes. But nothing's fixed with Small Mike. Mr. Choi lied about that. I forgave him on my own. He still hates me, though."

"What else is new? People think they're perfect and above the law. Like Durst selling us out. I can't believe you don't leave." He shrugged. Six weeks to this.

⁓

I MADE MY way to the folks, then ten days later to Aunt Veronica in Denver, a Navy Reserve lieutenant. I hung around socializing into an American society I'd hardly experienced since January 1979 when I went into the service. As a brainwashing operation it hardly differs from the Unification Church except, unlike government, Rev. Moon never sent us out to kill his enemies, though Papasan was gravitating in that direction. Everything was so different: music, prices, social norms. I felt I'd popped through a time warp or back from a sojourn in Japan. A John Denver and Neil Diamond fan, I discovered modern rock on this new thing called MTV. But I bored quickly with my hang-out life. I wanted to do something.

I chose to backpack the Rockies over summer to ponder my future. I loaded up my army Alice pack, cleaned up my Lee-Enfield rifle I'd managed to hold onto, dug out my college-era mountain boots, then my aunt trucked me a couple hours' northwest. I trekked my gear into the Rawah Wilderness, losing one of two canteens in a swift stream my first day. The Veterans' Administration sent me about $65 a month for my Coast Guard disability and I thought I could live on that a few months. Surviving on canned tuna and pork-n-beans was harder than I thought. I hiked out of the mountains to Boulder. Impossible in 2003, I journeyed unmolested in 1984 through shopping mall parking lots, past schools, and clear through town with my rifle slung over my shoulder until reaching my 777 Broadway alma mater on the far side. Steve, my video center boss, was now living there. Time to visit and see what was post-Papasan what.

Ready to rough it through the Rockies after departing Choiville.

I tiredly leaned my rifle and Alice pack against the building at the kitchen's side entrance and stepped inside to meet him. As we chatted, cops rapped on the door.

"Who owns this firearm out here?" All kitchen eyes were flies buzzing me.

"It's mine, officers. Is there a problem?"

One of them read off his notepad and pushed his lips out. "Why's it out here?"

"Just visiting and wasn't sure they wanted me to carry it inside."

He nodded. "Well, our concern is someone swiping it. We saw it passing by."

"Oh . . ." I hadn't even thought of that.

"I ran the serial number so we know it wasn't stolen or used in a crime."

"Better you don't leave it lying around like that," mused the other.

"Yeah, right." Boy, I loved the peaceful American West in those days.

Mrs. Sato was Boulder's center director. I think her Blessed husband is Tateo Sato, who ran Ocean Church. She was glad to have my help on the playground Steve was starting to build. Rev. Moon had recently mobilized Blessed American church

167

members as itinerant proselytizers. *Pioneering*, he called it. Can't bring kids on a rough job like that, which could mean sleeping on park benches. They'd farmed them out to Boulder's makeshift orphanage. This was the latest in a time-honored church practice dating to the 1950s when he sent sisters vagabonding across Korea preaching his new Divine Principle. Following Jesus' orders to take only sandals and cloak, they'd put theirs into real orphanages or with relatives to traipse town and country 3-plus years. A grueling period in church history. Rev. Moon certainly expected no less from over-indulged Americans.

"You can see what we are tasked with," she said. Young children crawled the walls. "The center needs playground. Steve is now starting."

"I have a lot of experience with stuff like that."

"Steve says you are good member. You can stay if you help. Sooner is better for this, so your help is very appreciated."

Hungry for real food, I grinned. "That sounds fine! We'll build a beauty."

For a week she didn't find my presence odd. But in accordance with the internal passport system the Japanese had going in the American church she was obliged—an American might've let it slide with Steve's endorsement—to call up Papasan Choi for his report on me. He shocked her with some lurid tale, emphasizing I had no permission to travel the church or change centers. I was AWOL. Rogue.

She confronted me toot sweet. "I am change mind. So shock to hear you leave church. I cannot let you stay in this center as ex-member."

"I didn't leave the *church*, Mrs. Sato. Just his center. My issue is only with—"

"I am sorry." Her eyes slanted away. "Please go. Must not come back."

What did I expect? Steve took it hard and fruitlessly tried changing her mind. Then several days later he called my aunt's house. "Hey, Chris, good news! Mrs. Sato thought it over and had a change of heart."

"You mean she now thinks I'm qualified to enter her holy domain?"

"I understand, but don't be negative. She apologized for her hasty reaction and invited you back. She said Mr. Choi's report doesn't matter. After talking to me and maybe getting a better picture from others, she's decided you're a good member."

"She could reverse any second. Thanks, Steve, I really appreciate it, but the fish company up in Alaska offered me a spot." I chuckled. "And it pays money."

I'd been talking with Johnny McGurk, who I'd met a couple years earlier at Judah Street. He'd shown up after hitchhiking and flying his way down from Alaska with a shoebox of tinfoil-wrapped pistols to fake out the airport x-rays. You sure as shootin' can't do that now, but there his guns were and him not in a Canadian jail. He'd been fishing in Alaska for awhile and wrangled me a job. Feeling true to Rev. Moon's way despite the psychos running Judah Street, I didn't want to abandon our movement. I'd remembered Alan's many boats in San Francisco; Alaska's fishing business sounded like a great opportunity and an exciting adventure.

He said, "Oh. That's disappointing. Well . . . if you change your mind . . ."

"You bet. You're a great guy, Steve. I'm sorry I put you on the spot."

"Forget it. Good luck up there. Father loves fishermen."

International Seafoods of Alaska wired my ticket. I winged north on a seabag.

Act VII

On the High Seas of Alaska
Life, Death, and Poverty

Excited was an understatement. When the plane's propellers spun down, I disembarked onto Alaskan soil and entered a new world of adventure I hadn't tasted since the Coast Guard. Except this was better. No Uniform Code of Military Justice, only raw Alaskan freedom smashing headlong into Unification Church totalitarianism with no sure bet on the winner. Eyes gulped my first Alaskan after crossing the cloud-shaded tarmac and stepping through a smoky glass door into the terminal's bedlam. A youthful, short-cropped blonde squeezed into blue denim jeans and a tee-shirt highlighting her chest eyed me, her back and one knee-high black rubber 'cannery boot' casually against the wall. What jumped as genuine Alaskan was the hefty Bowie knife thrusting from the top of her right boot. *Wow, this is America!* Tough women.

Unlike most airports in 1984, the small terminal in Kodiak had virtually no security. Denizens sported all manner of knives on belts, in boots, jutting from back pockets. The only thing it checked for at the one metal detector was firearms. Having grown up mostly in the Colorado Rockies, I felt right at home. Armed to the teeth, the average Alaskan (like most rural Americans) posed little or no threat to anyone. Sober, anyway. Although guns were ubiquitous, Kodiak's biggest weapons problem was the lowly knife married to deep-pockets booze. Large blades or small, drunk fishermen got stabbed with some regularity in the dark parking lots of the local gin joints. They were mostly low-on-genetic-scale half-wits asking for it because who else takes a $2,000–$15,000 cash payout from their boat captain only to skip the bank for a beeline to the bar to get falling-down drunk? If the low end wasn't getting knifed and dropped into Kodiak Harbor over drugs and loan sharking, they were getting rolled. At least there was no street crime. And who'd do it? Folks bristled. The odds of a bullet over a wallet were at least 50:50. Hardly worth the risk. A good lesson for the lower forty-eight to ponder, I always thought.

Kodiak Island is a gorgeous set of highland peaks rising off Alaska's southern continental shelf separated from the Denali Peninsula by the rampageous, hell-raising Shelikof Strait. This body of water runs hard northeast by southwest and is a wind tunnel in stormy weather, churning waves into better than 65-foot mountains. I was struck by the land's complexion. *How much like Ireland it looks!*

My heart ballooned with ancestral sentiment. Then I realized why Kodiak is saturatingly green: it rains every goddamned day. Or seems like. Short, irritating cloudbursts most of summer and a drizzling damp in fall. But when the sun burns across a cloud-free sky, the island is majestic. Snowcapped peaks scraping azure skies lift off brilliant blue-green seas framed against infinite space. A few days going native and I concluded every American church member could use a summer in Alaska . . . especially the Uchiyamas now toiling in the furrows and gutters.

Kodiak, 1984. Bridge over channel (seaplane runway is L–R white line) under construction.

Kodiak town occupies a small plot in the northeastern tip of the island not far from the largest Coast Guard base in the world. Crammed onto a spit of land at the base of steep-sided, thickly green mountains, the burg looked as if it might tip in the water. The airport south of town has a large mountain at one end of the runway mandating a sharp, hair-raising turn on the heels of wheels up. It's such a small space only short-haul prop jobs used it. Snow, thick rain, and fog routinely closed it in the mid-'80s and forced townsfolk to ration food. One long string of heinous weather put such a crimp in imports that ice cream was all the local restaurants had left to offer. Many of us threw caution to the wind and jumped on the Kodiak Shit-weather Diet.

In summertime, daylight runs about 5 AM to midnight. It was tough getting used to. Our bunkhouse blacked out windows with heavy drapes and later I used a heavy wool shirt over my stateroom porthole. If I shuddered up at, say, 11 PM for some reason, I sometimes got awfully confused . . . *is it tonight? or tomorrow?*

Canneries rose in high-storeyed buildings along the water's edge off the small channel that severed Dog Island from Kodiak, then south along the banks of Kodiak Harbor. The bulk of the population worked the canneries, a large number being Filipino. The pay for unskilled work such as filleting fish on a conveyor line was pretty good in 1984 at $12–$15 an hour compared to the average minimum wage of a couple bucks and change. Overtime was never in short supply when the boats were in port and workers competed for its fabulous pay.

The channel between Kodiak and Dog Island did double duty as the island's main boat plane runway. Every day a steady stream of flying boats roared through the channel, passing trawlers and boats large and small before soaring into the sky carrying my imagination. Anytime a boat chugged out of the harbor into the channel, it was vitally important to slow for a look not only both ways for vessel traffic but *up*. No one wanted a planeful of gasoline immolating their decks.

Out in the harbor leaning drunkenly to one side sat a ponderous 600-footer that had lost power during a storm. Abandoned by her crew—many died anyway—it drifted derelict till the Coast Guard towed it to Kodiak where the US Marshals sealed it. A standing dare to sneak out and prowl its ghostly decks called, but no one of us ever answered. It was a grim reminder to all Kodiakans of our profession's dangers. The sea is a mean bitch when it's ready.

Man, I congratulated myself, *Kodiak looks like an adventuresome town!* This was already shaping up to be my best Moonie adventure yet.

I moved into International Seafoods' (ISA) bunkhouse on Shelikof Street, the main drag along the south-end's cannery row. The boxy 2-storey, prefab-looking tin pile maybe 125 feet long fascinated me because this was my first time living with brothers and sisters on the same floor. Moonies segregated hard. Sisters could've snored up in the moon for all we saw. The second floor was a wide passage with

July 4th midnight fireworks out in the harbor.

dorm-style rooms either side holding bunk beds to sleep four. One end of the ugly, black-sheet-divided paneled hall was brothers, the other sisters. Ostensibly, we used segregated stairways at either end but daringly ignored the rule for convenience. Downstairs were a couple of offices, a few rooms for supervisors, an institutional kitchen, and a large mess hall that doubled for church service and company meetings. The latter could probably seat 200 on the fold up, bench-style rectangular tables common in the public schools.

Besides the bunkhouse, ISA operated a private home to the north of town on quiet, dirt Bancroft Street, two canneries, a gaggle of 28-foot Good Go's from the East Sun factory in Queens, and its 240±-ton fishing trawlers *Ocean Hope 1, 2, 3,* and *Green Hope* which in 1981 had fished for Golden Gate Seafood when I'd worked it. Unlike the *Ocean Hope* series, it was built for the Gulf of Mexico not Alaska. Yet, it stood its ferine seas longer than *Ocean Hope 1* and *2*.

Japanese labor mostly managed and worked ISA. Many of its church members came straight from the motherland with limited or no English. They worked our cannery alongside as-needed local Filipinos. The church owned the former Pacific Pearl cannery across the street about 300 feet southwest of the bunkhouse. It was there we tied up our boats. Pac Pearl was deserted. The brass initially assigned me as the plant's OJT electrical engineer because of my experience rewiring Judah Street. I checked out numerous high-voltage electricity how-to books from the public library and began mastering its industrial systems. The goal was Pac Pearl in operating condition, but nothing came of it in the two seasons I spent on ISA's payroll. The building was outfitted with canning machinery from its shrimp processing days and I had a blast exploring its cavernous structure, tracing circuits, and cleaning it up.

It appealed to my logical, organizational, and restorational personality, I suppose. There was work to do but not a lot; plenty of time to hang out. The four of us were a marooned bunch of lads on our own recognizance. Just how I liked it.

The old Pacific Pearl on Shelikof Street.

Apart from the plant, I ran the forklift at the airport south of town. ISA operated a small operation up in Bristol Bay on the Bering Sea near Egegik River. A beachfront townette, Egegik was remote and dangerous. The hard-packed beach at low tide was its airstrip. Wide and flat, its expanse supported DC-3s and -6s. We paid a private outfit called Winky's Airlines to airlift our catches out of Egegik to Kodiak. I then forklifted the heavy plastic bins of fish out of Winky's DC-3 onto trucks bound for the ISA plant.

Winky was an authentic nut case. Wearing a pre-war leather aviator hat with goggles and a chest-holstered semi-auto, he was a smiling mass of self-confidence that made you feel you were in the presence of a Vietnam-era CIA bush pilot. Maybe he was; he had the crazy. With its minuscule rear wheel, a DC-3 deck angles 10–15 degrees downward nose to tail. It took a bit of skill to angle forklift tines through the tilted rear door to pluck out fish pallets without skewering thin aluminum skin. I operated under Winky's icy, baleful stare and periodic threats as he awaited the sound of puncturing metal and his chance to justifiably plug me.

While flying from Egegik, his late-'30s DC-3 once developed a life-threatening oil leak in one of its two engines. It rapidly lost altitude. In a last ditch effort to make it to Kodiak, he squalled a new plan at our onboard ISA rep.

"Get back there and heave all that shit off the plane!"

"What!" shouted the rep over the open-window props, contemplating tens of thousands of slimy retailed dollars falling o'er the land. "All of it?"

"Ya wanna crash instead?"

He surveyed the thousand-pound bins through the flight deck's passageway aft. "How am I supposed to push 'em out? They must weigh—"

"No, dumbass! Scoop 'em out the door."

The wind ripping through the open rear cargo door fish-tailed the plane across the sky as our unsteady rep sent thousands of pounds of salmon or pollock sailing into the void armloads at a time all the way to Kodiak. We laughed ourselves silly imagining natives running for cover from the falling manna.

Unlike nearly all church-owned businesses, ISA paid its members. I earned $300 a month in the summer of 1984 before joining the boats. Out of that, I paid a newly reduced $150 in child support to Monica as well as my mostly-subsidized room and board at the bunkhouse. Nothing but extra work was free with these people. I discovered Americans working the boats got to keep their money. The Japanese uniformly signed their paychecks back to the company that had just issued them. Payroll cost ISA the total of withheld taxes, but otherwise seemed a ruse to keep the Department of Labor off its back. One Japanese brother refused and ISA summarily billed him the airfare and sent him home in disgrace, an object lesson to the rest. I guess our Korean boss, Joo Chon Choi—not related to Papasan, thankfully—figured American members, a number former criminals like some of our pre-church Asian leaders, wouldn't go for it and let it ride, meager as it was. Perhaps more to the point, ISA expected us to survive the non-fishing winter on our own, so we banked earnings for that. The Japanese returned to their local church centers in the off season or joined the Alaskan or national MFT in the lower forty-eight for the winter when ISA paid only a caretaker crew.

As in all Unification Church businesses at the time, the Japanese toiled like Egypt's beloved Hebrews sunup to sundown. Time off was minimal. The church and ISA expected a 7-day workweek for God and balance sheet. In truth, we worked those hours because the fishing business often demands it, although at Pac Pearl we had an easy-to-bear laid-back schedule. When the boats motored in heavy

ISA plant on Marine Way.

with fish, it was all hands on ISA's deck round the clock till the last fillet slid into the freezer. Kodiak's plants seemed to prefer as many cheap Filipinos as they could import and ISA stuck out like a sore thumb with its Japanese (Moonie) workforce. But Filipinos were our cavalry over the hill during peak labor.

Personal sacrifice has always been a problem with church businesses because each is seen as an extension of the spiritual ministry merely earning, instead of serving, bread for the greater good. The church expected business members to sacrifice toward financial success the way it expected it for ministerial victory. If Rev. Moon wasn't skittish about pushing mothers and fathers into a witnessing wilderness, blithely suggesting they store their children in orphanages while hiking byways on the Lord's business, he surely didn't shy from expecting us to just as hardily sacrifice for the sake of the financial engine powering them all. From his point of view, it only made sense. Any family business expects their children to freely toil for everybody's sake. The church billed itself 'the Family' in those days and its businesses viewed themselves in the same vein . . . except we weren't a real family with parents concerned for our best future. There was a lot of advantage-taking of members (primarily work hours and pay). They themselves took advantage of the church. Followed a skewed conscience. Let Rev. Moon do the heavy Restorational lifting. Some of these practical issues got addressed as members produced Blessed children in the later 1980s and '90s. Until then, church businesses were sweat shops. Illegal in every sense of the word. ISA was no exception.

Americans and Europeans crewed the boats. Japanese with a smattering of Koreans manned the cannery. It chasmed ISA. We Americans were famous amongst the Japanese for representing the criminal element; gangsters, we were. Before the church, some boat members were petty criminals, armed robbers, car thieves, drug users or dealers, and whatnot. Hearing Principle radically changed them but it hadn't much altered their tough characters any more than it had our *yakuza* leaders. A number of boat members had drinking problems, more than once sneaking back shitfaced after midnight to an irate, shotgun-wielding skipper at the boat's weather door concerned the tepid footsteps heralded electronics pilfering. One of my later crewmates, shot twice behind the ear in Dutch Harbor likely by drug dealers—cops ruled it suicide, to his mom's outrage—caught syphilis from a prostitute. We damn sure kept this shit to ourselves, but the Japanese nonetheless saw us an unruly gaggle of disobedient satanists and rejected us.

This wasn't the face the Unification Church wanted displayed to the citizens of Kodiak. But it was impossible to crew rough-sea trawlers with our emasculated, feminized Unificationists. Boat members got a wide latitude in return for discretion and hard, underpaid labor. Even so, Boss Choi (to distinguish him from Papasan Choi) routinely castigated us Americans in the most vulgar terms during Sunday service. He was so vituperative, and once evidently making too much eye contact with the formerly lesbian, maybe 20-year old American sister with the Bowie knife in her boot, that she jumped up from the floor, gave him the 'up yours' salute with a fist, and stormed out loudly cursing him. She was later prattling with a Japanese brother in the mess hall who, belaboring the misconception prevalent throughout our Japanese faction that Americans hold their parents in contempt, made a comparative crack about her mother. Infuriated, she grabbed him by the throat. Pinned him to the wall in one smooth movement. Her fearsome Bowie knife pressed his carotid till the skin—and other bits—was just about to leak.

"Don't you never say no fuckin' word 'bout my mama again. Got it?"

He nodded hard, bulbous eyes down his cheeks at her lethal point.

She was the talk of the town for a couple weeks. Boss Choi was a breath away from billing her the airfare on the next plane out of town. Still stupidly ignorant, that brother asked me what he'd said wrong.

"Do not all Americans not care about parents?"

"You really believe that, don't you?"

"Well . . ."

Yeah. I'd discover the Japanese church did a real bang-up job indoctrinating its members with anti-Americanism. Our Alaska Japanese uncritically believed we were sinful, maybe irredeemable, crazy for (Boss Choi oft-proclaimed) sex, drugs, and rock 'n' roll, incurably individualistic, scornful of parents and authority, and unwilling or incapable of understanding God or Divine Principle. Sounded to us exactly like the mentality that seduced Japan into believing it could win the Pacific War decapitating the fleet at Pearl Harbor. How unfortunate for us.

"You can say a lot of things about an American's dad, but don't ever, and I mean never, insult their mother. He—or she—will fight you every time if you do."

"But Americans do *not* respect parents like Japanese."

"So? Are we Japanese?"

"They say all kind of bad thing about parents. Why they get so angry, then, especially that crazy lesbian sister?"

"She's not lesbian. She joined—"

"She acts like it. She looks—"

"—the church and follows Divine Principle."

"—like it, too. Huge!"

"Are you okay?" I leaned in close. "I mean, mentally?"

"I do not understand your meaning."

I sat against one of the mess hall tables. "Look, bub. Americans love freedom. As they grow up, they want to press for more and more of it, often in tension with parents who want to slow them down."

"Yes, but that is—"

"You listening? Americans might get angry with their parents, might even be so mad they leave home and quit talking to them awhile. But don't ever mistake that for hate or some magical, unJapanese 'disrespect' that *you* can dish on."

"I understand."

My lip twitched up at that all-purpose statement. "No matter how much we're mad at our folks, we'll always stand up for our mom. Take that to the bank."

"The bank?"

"And, you don't understand. But *that's* respect. Not whatever Japan is selling."

He grunted. "*Sooo, nehhh . . .*"

This simplistic if contradictory reality registered some amazement on his face. But he didn't get it. Too indoctrinated. My pat clarification wasn't going to wash away years of propaganda.

"Well, I admit that sister does not accept any . . ."

"Crap?" I humbly offered. "Bullshit?"

" . . . anything negative from anybody about her mother, even if she has so much negative mind about her." He contemplated it. "That is crazy."

"Bet you won't make that same mistake twice though, eh." Some inkling of respectability lay somewhere in that.

His face fogged. "Is she really lesbian, though?"

"The heck?" I rolled eyes heavenward.

Although Japanese mainly staffed the cannery, ISA's bookkeeper was a German-American named Frank who, in our view, took sadistic glee presenting paychecks to boat members—anyone, really—for zero dollars and zero cents after exciting them over all the money they'd earned during the last fish 'opening.'

Watching their face fall he'd say, "Well, now, you owe the company for"—*point, point*—"this and this. See? Then there's your room and board plus your phone charges, here." And, et cetera.

Some members lost whole paychecks to lower-48 phone charges. I learned quick what an asshole he was and, like Johnny McGurk and others, more than once said so to his face when collecting pay or paying the company store. We concluded he hated boat members for reasons of his own. Maybe he was secretly threatened by our unabashed gun-toting. We certainly threatened him more than once.

NOT LONG AFTER my arrival, Johnny and I were kicking back outside the bunkhouse like hayseeds watching sparse traffic slide by. A hulking truck mounting maybe a 15-foot long, 6-foot diameter cylinder rumbled by. Putrescence all but punched me out of my plastic chair. I gagged hard. Wrestled down my stomach.

"What in hell is that?"

"That's the offal truck, man."

"The awful truck? It damn sure is! But what's it carrying?"

He fixed me with head-scratching eyes. "Fish guts, what'd you think?"

It took a few weeks to discover he'd meant *offal*. New vocabulary. "My God, it stinks! I can't hardly breathe."

"That shit'll make you projectile vomit." Another new word. "Total evac."

When fish go through a cannery, all parts not filleted and flash frozen for sale are conveyored to a holding bin: the offal tank. It sits in it maybe a week, rotting and putrefying. The offal driver parks under the tank, drops its funnel into the cylinder's open hatch, and shot-glasses it in. A Japanese brother monkeying around pulled the chain release and dumped nearly a week's worth onto the ground. He and some unlucky losers wheelbarrowed the hellspawn back into the tank over a long, retching day. Not even masks blocked it. Weighty offal quaked by our bunkhouse at least once a day. Anybody rashly sucking air gagged or hurled.

I often scaled halfway up the mountain to ponder God, church, life, and love.

Head dingo Boss Choi was somewhat slender with a heavy head and pan face, his version of the rugged American if you pretended away his plush middle. His oft-reiterated motto was simple: "You must have a gun to be a man." He expected brothers to purchase at least one. I felt considerable pressure to acquire some ordnance from my peers *and* myself. It wasn't cheap. I had to wait a month for my first $300 payday. Draining my obligations but talking an advance out of Frank, which he duly noted, I scraped up enough for my first pistol. I was no newbie. I'd got my surplus 1942 Lee-Enfield rifle at Western State for $65 in 1977 and the Coast Guard rated me 'expert' with rifle and pistol.

Cruising Kodiak's gun store for the perfect buy Johnny said, "Hey, man, you shouldn't buy nothin' under a .44 magnum."

"I prefer forty-fives."

Short, sharp headshakes. "Kodiak has the biggest bears in the world. You meet one of those fuckers you'll wish you had a rocket launcher, ha ha!"

"Come on, a forty-five is huge. Denver cops swear by 'em."

"Won't penetrate, I'm telling you. Bounce right off its head. The only pistol that'll save you from one of those bastards is the biggest *magnum*."

"This Ruger Blackhawk looks like it'll do the job, then."

"A six shooter, heh-heh. You need a semi-auto with mags for a fast reload."

I dug out my cash wad. "Nah, six oughta do it." Love me a cowboy gun. "If I can't discourage it in six, what's a reload gonna do? If I even can reload."

"Yer funeral." I gave him side-eyes.

Bears were the real reason I even considered a gun necessary. They infested Alaska like rats, especially Kodiak Island. Its grizzlies grow biggest and most entitled owing to an abundant food supply thus a reduced hibernation.

"Just wait till you see one of 'em, Chris. It'll scare the pants off ya. They're absolute monsters. Eat you whole in a couple of bites."

"Maybe you'll be there to throw yourself in front of me like a good Abel."

"Not a fuckin' chance. That's why I carry a pistol *and* a 10-gauge with *slugs*."

Folks nicknamed one of Kodiak's two banks the bear bank because of the meaty, stuffed Kodiak brown looming in its lobby. Rearing high upon hind legs, paws outstretched, mouth snarling menacingly at the bank's patrons for a cunning memo not to diddle on their fees, it was a leviathan. I lumbered inside with Johnny and my new Ruger to open a checking account with the remains of my pay. I was so taken aback by the bear's gargantuanism that I

Johnny and me goofing our ordnance around the nearby islands we frequently visited.

pulled my pistol out of its box to double check I'd bought a .44 and not a .22 plinker. That hairy goliath made it seem an impotent peashooter.

"Huge, right? You top out at its elbows. Imagine it *alive*. And hungry."

"I don't know, Johnny . . . this looks like it's only gonna piss it off."

"Trust me, you'll be glad you have it if it comes to it. You can't outrun 'em."

"Well, hope springs eternal." A great comfort in the wilderness wondering if a surly bear might leap out claws first from some impenetrable alder.

Outside, we leapt for a ride to the bunkhouse in the back of a passing pickup truck. Crime of crimes, sprinting for the barely slowing tailgate my stainless steel single-action jiggled out of its cardboard box, slapped the pavement, and skidded across the road. I froze, blood cold, in my tracks. Goggled as it bounced and slid like my own manhood under a belt sander.

I flung an angry, sterile fist around and wailed, "My brand-new pistoo—ol!"

Johnny laughed and waved, legs dangling off the receding vehicle. Furiously cursing, I snatched it up. Painful scratches scored the cylinder and a half inch along the muzzle. Worse was a small corner triangle of the rosewood grip broken off along the strap. I found it on the pavement and dreamed of glue.

What a schmuck! I raged stock-still and red-faced, Johnny receding with the pickup . . . it wouldn't be the first time he'd leave me in the lurch. In the mess hall, Boss Choi expressed satisfaction with my weapons purchase, grunting admiringly at its size and heft while tut-tutting the damage. I was a little put out that ISA, whose policy very nearly dictated ownership, didn't pony up the cost. But the Coast Guard didn't, either; uniforms were only free in boot camp. And I wouldn't have to turn in my company gun when it was time to head south with the birds.

While the boats plied their trade, Boss Choi busily committed ISA to bad deal after bad deal. One of the ways the company made money was by contracting 'outside' boats. According to our captains, he resolutely inked deals with incompetent and unscrupulous captains who took big monies up front then often failed to deliver as promised. Try as they might, our skippers couldn't persuade him to write more advantageous contracts or fire the losers altogether and pay the same money and bonuses to us. We were more than willing to work 24×7×365 for what he was throwing down their shoddy ratholes. But, no. We were *members*.

This problem plagues Unification Church businesses. Why pay tons of money to outside vendors, many of whom only intend to cheat the hated Moonie cult, when you could pay the same—less actually, but a tidy sum for us—to church members who'd conscientiously deliver the goods and be grateful for the dough? It was a logical argument escaping our wisest Korean business minds. Boss Choi seemed convinced his best chance for success lay in paying vast sums to outsiders who continually underperformed, sometimes on purpose. His business acumen was so bad that by the end of 1984's season ISA was on the ropes, unable to pay its obligations for the winter. After five years of likely incompetence and possibly pilferage, Rev. Moon gave up subsidizing ISA and told him to sink or swim.

Rev. Moon visiting Kodiak.

I found it dubious he'd let ISA reach the auction block. If he disapproves anything, it's abandoning properties and businesses—though he did Sun Tours—as they carry providential and historical significance. Facing a shortfall of liquidity due to his bad contracts and poor judgment, Boss Choi did what any face-saving Unification Church leader would do: he sent Japanese sisters out to fundraise the winter. Their dire effort through its miserable weather kept ISA in the black till 1985's season kicked off.

His plan disgusted me. I noisily bitched, "It's totally disgraceful using Japanese sisters this way!" I'd worked many a shift with them boxing salmon roe in the cannery and now cared about them almost like family to the point of considering sharing their winter MFT . . . until Inouye (*"inoo-uay"*), a Japanese brother running a roe group shift, spat his version of *Not on your life!* I rattled on, "Boss Choi would do better listening to our boat captains who *understand* the industry." My righteous mouth for the silently acquiescent only made me his newest frenemy. Two Choi's under my belt, now. I was on a roll.

FLIRTING WITH BOATS coming and going, steel bellies teeming with fish, I said to Johnny, "I'm bored caretaking at Pac Pearl. I want something adventurous."

"Ask Jonathan. He's got an open berth on our boat." Yessir, his 118-foot (though soon-to-be-ill-fated) *Ocean Hope 3* was for me.

I tracked him down in July. We were acquainted, but I didn't really know him. "How 'bout it, Jonathan? I'm Coast Guard qualified." He offered. I jumped.

He's one of those New Yorkers you expect in a movie about The City. Looming six muscular feet with thinning, brown curly hair and loudly, obnoxiously, brashly, bullyingly, arrogantly contemptuous of non-New Yorkers, he could be a terror to his crew with threats of a thrashing or tedious tales of fights he'd won before getting religion. The Moonies actually calmed him down. Brought out his inner child to hear him tell it. But like all skippers, he could be a complete dick when it suited. He did know his stuff, however. I had unwavering confidence in his skills getting me home alive. And he did. Though not without a hiccup or two.

My first summer in Kodiak was naturally the last summer ISA paid crew shares to the boats so it might cut costs and save Boss Choi's bacon from Rev. Moon's now-sizzling pan of occasional accountability. A crew share is a high-incentive method to reward crewmembers a share of their boat's total earnings.

For example, suppose a boat earns $100,000 in an 'opening,' the period of time US Fish and Wildlife opens harvesting of a specific species in a particular area. In our case, ISA deducted the costs for fuel, food, water, paint, repairs, maintenance, and so on to divide the remainder by the number of crewmembers. If it lopped off $50,000 for all that then $50,000 was left for the crew to split. If the boat had five crewmembers, let's say, that

Ocean Hope 3 *passing the ISA plant, me at port stern.*

would be a $10,000 crew share. Each member of the crew was theoretically entitled to that much cash each. This constituted a *gross share*. However, different positions and responsibilities rated different shares. So, it was necessary to recalculate to get the payable *regular net share* based on that.

A captain typically took 1-½ to 2-½ regular shares as the boat's owner or operator. The first mate got a similar though smaller spread for his second most responsible position. The second mate, if a boat has one, the same but a smaller range. A regular crewman got one regular share. Anyone considered less than that, such as a new guy like me who'd only shipped on midsummer or in his first season or is less than a marginal worker, got a ½ to ¾ share. After adding up all these shares, the boat's (in our case, ISA's) money pot got redivided.

Say our skipper Jonathan got 2 shares, our first mate 1-½ shares, two regular crewmen 1 share each, and me a ½ share. One share now calculated to $50,000/6 total shares = $8,333. The skipper got $16,666, the first mate $12,500, the two regular crewmen (one being Johnny) $8,333 each, and the new guy, me, $4,166. That's from a single trip out of many over a season. *Sign me up!*

This pay system is amazingly lucrative if you catch a lot of fish. I knew folks making $30,000 *per month* for half a year's work. That wasn't even the high end. But ISA took a hefty cut. Unlike 'outside' boats, there wasn't all that much left to share. Still, it was big money to us. That summer's regular share was per season, not per trip, and worth about $15,000. Frank possibly led me on but that meant $7,500 for me. I was thrilled. I could live a winter on that. Then ISA divided it by the months I'd worked *on the boat* and paid me $1,500 less my first $300, on which Boss Choi buoyantly expected me to survive till 1985's season. When 1984's ended, I winged for San Francisco for survival and a MacArthuran return to college.

He wasn't happy. "I'm concerned school will tempt you back to a fallen life and away from God and True Parents."

"I understand that, but I can't go through life uneducated with a paltry fifteen-hundred buckaroos when Father keeps telling us to be like him."

"He didn't go to university. It's not necessary and anyway leads to arrogance."

"Nobody takes you seriously anymore without a degree. I'd say he went from rags to riches in a lucky time. Anyway, there's CARP." A Moonie campus group.

He sighed to emphasize his point. "*Saaa* . . . Okay, then. Good luck. So, you are welcome back next season. I hope to see you."

"You bet!" We shook hands. I saw his offer as mended fences and felt glad. I didn't like my growing list of sour relationships. MFT was hard, but real family.

~

THAT FIRST SEASON I met Nanami, an interesting friend and Blessed Japanese sister who later besotted me. Evidently, she'd carried on an affair with an American boat member and was now conscience stricken. She wanted to confess to someone but didn't know who'd keep her secret. Unificationists are well aware their God-fearing comrades will blab their every personal detail to the most judgmental leader. I still held the Japanese as models of perfection despite Judah Street. We Americans were totally subservient and Rev. Moon stonily scolded us over Japan and Korea's closeness to the heavenly ideal while our unPrincipled West was Satan's hellish toilet.

My starboard-side stateroom on Ocean Hope 3.

She said, "I decide to tell you my secret after checking all member in Kodiak, K'risu. Neh? You must be only person I can trust."

"Mum's the word. Honored, but . . . how'd you decide?"

"Simple talking. I say things to see how reaction. That is how I was sure you are so different. That I can trust you."

"Well. Aren't you tricky."

She broke the whole megillah while we perched on upturned 5-gallon buckets on *Ocean Hope 3*'s foredeck prepping bait baskets for an upcoming halibut opening far out in the north Pacific. I was coiling line and attaching hook lanyards when she'd climbed aboard. Helping me with the line, she shared in roundabout fashion her fall from grace.

When she ran out of steam I stopped work, hands in my lap. "That's . . . pretty shocking." I'd been celibate since 1979 and had a high opinion of Blessing purity. Her face fell. "But I totally understand. Our church creates so much hopeless loneliness. Anyway, you're not the only one. More banging on around here than the Navy."

Tears fluttered down her cheeks even as her face, darkened with anxiety, fear, worry, sorrow . . . visibly brightened. I don't know where it came from but I felt a terribly parental, fatherly heart for her.

"Your kindness so precious me, K'risu. I feel . . . more happy. Weight is less."

"I know you're terrified about telling anybody anything in this church, the way it crucifies people. But I think you need to confess it to some central figure just to get it off your chest. Then do whatever indemnity conditions are imposed."

"I want to! But . . . am scare. I not want to. And anyway, who?"

I looked over the harbor and pursed. "Well, Boss Choi is your direct central figure since we don't have any sort of church environment here."

"He might send me back. I not want go. I like America. I want stay."

"To Japan? Well, I expect he'll be upset you fell, but he seems a decent sort for a church leader. I mean, he hates us but you're Japanese. He's got a heart for you guys." She snickered. Formed a contemplative face. "You work an important job here and anyhow all you'll get is probably some fasting and prayer, maybe—I don't know—an indemnity condition . . . MFT, or . . ." It could be anything. His unpitying words aside, Rev. Moon is big on repentance through indemnity. Every member is precious and not merely for crass, pragmatic reasons. He loves God, thus us.

"Oh, my God, I am so nervous! My stomach is kill me."

"Awwhh. I wish I could take it away." She half-smiled.

Kodiak, not to mention its Unification Church and ISA environment, had a way of drawing out anybody's loneliness, which has always been mankind's greatest aphrodisiac. When fornicators got caught, the average Japanese unceremoniously headed back to Japan head down in widow's weeds and Americans cast off to the lower 48 if not straight out of the church. I hadn't picked up on that, yet.

"I really, really want avoid that," she said.

When she did tell him, he wasn't upset. He was livid. Then like the contemptible douchecanoe I belatedly realized he was, he publicized her confession to our entire colony and, circumbendibus, as Babylon's great whore in Sunday service. My heart was a black hole in my chest. I felt I'd plunged in the knife myself.

"God," I railed to the ocean from my high vantage on the precipitous slopes overlooking Kodiak, "these people are such bastards!" It was a rough, tiring climb but worth it. The quiet wind, twittering birds looping high above the harbor, and the island's drenching green was a poultice soaking into me. "How does the wonderful Divine Principle and True Father's preaching of unconditional love create so many Frankensteins?" This was fast becoming my life's greatest conundrum.

Afterward I said, "Were I older and wiser, like I am *now*, I'd have counseled you to swallow it like the paper hidden in a golem's mouth."

"Is okay. Is all out now."

"I really thought he'd react differently. I'm so, sooo very sorry, Nanami." I wished I could cry but felt too deadened by her pain and my remorse.

She flat-smiled under wet eye blinks. "Even life is very bad, internally, I feel better. I know God forgives me. I will get through it."

"That's what matters, I reckon. But it seems so unfair and unnecessary what . . ."

She squeezed my hand then hugged me hard.

Considering the mind-boggling stress Blessed couples were under, largely owing to hardly knowing their spouse plus forbidden to consummate their marriage or sometimes even meet till a leader or the Blessed Family Department (BFD) bestowed its plenary indulgence—remember, couples waited 3–6 or more years—it's a wonder even more lonely-hearts weren't rampaging through bunkhouse beds, Pac Pearl, Bancroft House, and quiet getaways. Certainly, their restraint—no one knew for sure how much sex there really was—was due to our great faith in the Principle's interpretation of the human Fall and fidelity to God.

Boss Choi's abuse of Nanami's confidence devastated her. He fired her from her managerial position in the plant, ordered a 7-day fast, officially informed the BFD she'd fell—it decreed an *additional 7-year* wait—dished to her Blessed husband and, after all that, exiled her to New York City (evidently a dumping ground despite being national headquarters) in public disgrace. At least it wasn't Japan.

When everything but her exile had come down like a demolitioned high-rise I said, "I am mortified beyond words, Nanami."

"You did nothing wrong, K'risu. I am grateful for you. This is all me, not you. I treasure everything you did. You were here for me when nobody was."

"Okay, but . . ."

"You still are."

My naïve, youthful stupidity in human relations and probably leftover Catholic guilt had advised her to confess when I could've *maybe* made *myself* her central figure for this purpose. Pioneered something different in our movement. The church places life and death in public confession and I accepted that. The reason is that a member can't confess privately to God for their sin because one needs satisfy Satan's conciliatory demands, not God's nor our own conscience. Much value is placed in confessing to one's providential central figure because he or she directly represents True Parents in the larger providence, who represent God. It wasn't necessary others know and I don't recall Rev. Moon advising public disclosure or even (as a rule) doing it himself. But it was vital one's central figure knew so the chain of command was properly notified all the way to God; one could be certain they were forgiven *in toto*, that via conditions of indemnity Satan had no ammunition to accuse.

I cared deeply for Nanami and searched her out during her fast. "I'm sharing the last three of your 7-day fast with you. Like a *real* central figure."

"You would do that? Is not necessary."

I smiled. "I know. I want to. We're in this together." She kissed my cheek.

The boats were all underway. I'd called out sick. We were home alone in the bunkhouse talking and cheering up. We broke our fast together (me, chili; her, miso soup) and luxuriated in our mini-vacay. Again, my body was sexually in neutral. And thank God. We could've easily repeated her mistake cuddled up on the loveseat under blankets watching TV and suffering our ravenous travails in one of the reserved first-floor rooms, happily touching and breathing each others' ardent air. Yet, she felt as much a sister as my MFT mates. I marveled and soaked up our ever so rare human intimacy. She was the best person I'd met in Kodiak. I mourned her public disgrace and ouster to New York City like my own. She was one of those Japanese who'd Americanized into human. Honestly, it was only a matter of time before some mistake, trivial or serious, gave the hierarchy the excuse it wanted to make her one more example to the rest of the Japanese: *do not Americanize!*

ABOARD THE BOATS I inherited their freedom from shaving and promptly grew my first church beard. Rev. Moon exempted Ocean Church from resembling clean-cut, responsible citizens unthreatening of the public welfare because he thought fishermen needed beards to meld with the manly traditions of the sea, not unlike the US Coast Guard and Navy's policies at the time. Now 25 years old, I was finally feeling a man. It wasn't the beard. That was merely its manifestation. No, it had to do with living on a rough trawler with big Americans like me who trusted I'd do my job without killing them as they slept through my watch. *At last! No more tiny, supercilious, hair-pulling Japanese.*

Freedom was short lived. In weeks ISA sent us Tamara, a gaunt Japanese pariah we quickly dubbed 'Tomorrow' on account of his general refusal to do anything today. He despised the boats, crews, work, being out of his bunk, and sharing words with us. So we teased him, the cruel satanic bastards we were, till he got permission to debark.

Salmon seiners. Bumble Bay, 1985.

We sailed on a number of salmon openings as a floating freezer. Fishermen operating 40–60-foot seiner boats brought their catches to us at the end of the day or whenever their holds filled up and negotiated a per-pound price. We offered ours in 2-foot red letters on a 4×5-foot white signboard lashed to our port and starboard foc'sle railings. Many boats insisted on cash because often they wouldn't see a bank for months. Thus, we carried as much as $200,000 every time we went out.

Well, that jackpot was mighty tempting for buccaneering bastards. Kodiak was awash in piratical gossip. Their modus operandi was creeping aboard after midnight when the crew was soundly snoring, cut their throats, steal all valuables but especially the cashbox, then open the sea cocks sometimes with fires to further obfuscate the crime. Vessels vanished to the murky bottom where dead men write no tell-alls.

Jonathan wasn't one to play with this threat. We armed up. Johnny and I joked how no pirate would ever disembark under his own steam. More than once at Pac Pearl's docks Jonathan greeted a crewman tiptoeing the decks after midnight with an eye-level double-barreled 10-gauge when they creaked open the weather door. I slept with my scratched but loaded .44 mag under my pillow. Johnny's .22 semi-auto went under his own with the magazine unseated and a .38 revolver in easy reach. Jonathan also had a 9mm semi-auto and an 1860s Springfield trapdoor rifle replete with a 2-foot bayonet. If we didn't know the boats tied alongside parked or offloading fish, we worked with sidearms. Nobody was taking us for suckers.

It was uncomfortable toiling away in the fishhold wearing iron under foul-weather gear. To ease our labor, we often hung our holsters on a peg out of sight of the main hatch. Jonathan, swinging fish bins between seiner and trawler with the hydraulic booms, wore his belted nine-mil for all to see. It was pure deterrence. A gunfight could go either way. He insisted on 24-hour watches when anchored out of port. We didn't disagree and stood 4-hour watches in the wheelhouse all night when most boats let their whole crew sleep. I stood mine armed and alert, Coast Guard style. My throat wasn't bleeding without a fight.

An incident with *Ocean Hope 1*—I think Alan Hokinson was captain—proved us right. As many coastal towns were dry, company policy had us fork over free cases of beer—soda, for Christian crews—as an incentive for boats to sell their catch to

ISA. We stacked a head (bathroom) deck-to-overhead with up to 50 cases. *Ocean Hope 1* used their commodious lazarette (after-steering compartment). One night its crew peacefully slumbered without a care in the world for their lives or Boss Choi's bulging cashbox. Unknown perps oared alongside, stealthily boarded, and off-loaded their entire supply of beer. Morning tea was a shock.

"All they left," one of them gibed, "was some empty cans."

"So they partied while they robbed you blind," Johnny laughed.

I said, "All I can say is, you dumbasses are lucky they only wanted to get drunk. You could be turning into Father's fish powder by now."

"Obviously not," same guy snorted.

"Obviously," Johnny said, "they were yokels not *pirates*."

Same guy kept his phlegmatic air.

"What he said," I said, thumbing Johnny. *Dumbass*. Of ISA's four boats, ours was still the only one sensible enough to maintain a watch at anchor. We heard of boats pirated and crews murdered, but no one torched us. Lucky, them.

Johnny's Blessed wife Takako, whom I knew from Judah Street, jetted to Kodiak for a prenuptial visit. He was showing off his .22 pistol in his stateroom. She playfully grabbed it as Jonathan passed by headed for mine. Seconds later she appeared at my door and pointed Johnny's pistol at Jonathan.

Flicking her wrist the way Ma Barker saluted feds she cried, "Oh! Communist! Communist! Bang, bang, bang!"

Jonathan all but crapped his pants in bug-eyed shock and fear. "*Jesus Christ!*" he hollered, whipping the gun out of her hands. Just then Johnny appeared, cool and serene. Jonathan, ever the gun-safety fanatic, pulled the magazine. "Damn, Johnny, this thing's loaded! There's even a round in the breech."

"Jeez, Takako, you almost shot Jonathan." Johnny was puckish.

Still laughing, she faced each in turn. "He's okay, I was playing."

"You need to teach her some common sense, man."

"Aw, she was just fooling around."

"Thank God the safety was on!"

"Sure, she'd never shoot you, Jonathan. Nothing to worry about."

Jonathan squeezed out past them, maybe to visit the head. Takako hung there giggling, not really getting the point of our conversation or how close she'd come to manslaughter. But Johnny did. He kept his guns out of her reach after that. It wasn't every day somebody threw the fear of the Lord into tough old Jonathan. Johnny and I got a lot some serious laughs out of Takako's folly.

Kukak Bay at dawn. Summer, 1984.

Alaska was wall-to-wall guns, especially aboard our no-pirates zone. We needed to grow an awareness for Japanese and European greenhorns who were barely fledgling novices with a firearm's picture yet thrilled to distraction by the real thing. One of *Green Hope*'s crew, a Frenchman named François, paid us a visit and took to admiring Johnny's other shooter, his much more powerful .38 revolver. His first experience touching a gun, he pointed it at the deck with a chartered grin and pulled the trigger.

Click!

This time Johnny showed some concern and mildly rebuked François, but he knew it wasn't loaded. Later that same day, however, François swung by again on some errand and picked it up without Johnny's permission.

He said, "Hey, look at me!" pointed it at the overhead, and pulled the trigger. "Don't! It's—"

BANG!

The report blew out our ears in Johnny's tight stateroom. François shot a hole clear up through the weather deck we had to patch. We were a lot more careful with guests on board our heavy cruiser after that. The last thing we wanted to explain to Boss Choi and the insurance company was a bullet hole through our *bottom*.

We worked numerous openings around Kodiak and the Denali Peninsula. Isa once sent us to the wrong place and we spent a week doing absolutely nothing all by ourselves in the mirror-finished waters of gorgeous Kukak Bay. One morning, Jonathan buzzed our skiff over to a box-truck crag maybe 75 yards away and stacked up 100 beer and soda cans all over its shelved face for target practice. When we hit one, the contents exploded or shot the can off like a rocket. We spent four days trying to shoot them all, covering our deck in hundreds of spent casings. Alaska's pristinely quiet beauty was positively shot to shit that week.

Heading west through calm seas and sunny skies for Dutch Harbor on August 27, 1984 and maybe 12 hours out of Kodiak, Johnny and I posed for photos on our main deck as we motored southwest through the Shelikof Strait. We expected a humdrum trip like all the rest and boredom tugged hard. Then all hell broke loose. Around 5 AM an odd *bonk!* reverberating through the hull

Shelikof Strait. Aleutian Range on horizon. Aug., 1984

jerked me awake. It was common to whang large logs and whole trees swept to sea by storms in Alaska's waters. By my reckoning, we should've been well out to sea and clear of such flotsam. Yet, it didn't sound like an echoey log hit at all. More like a heavy, thumping rock.

Are we grounding? Nah, not if we're as well out to sea as we should be. Besides, Jonathan must be on watch by now. For all his personality faults—top dog in the douchey dickhead category—he was an accomplished mariner I trusted.

It took only milliseconds to consider and dismiss all the not-rock possibilities. My instincts screamed trouble. I unzipped my sleeping bag to roll off my bunk. The boat pitched violently to port. Slammed me into the paneled starboard hull. With a horrifying grating noise of tearing metal and grinding stone, our 243-ton trawler jumped and bucked like a horse itching burrs under the saddle as we plunged full bore into—*what?* I clutched my bunk's wooden side rail for dear life and braced my other palm hard against the chilled, undulating hull.

We wildly careened through improbable rocks, our steel hull shrieking and groaning as it gave under the tremendous pressure exerted by the boat's inertia. The hull was 3/8-inch or better plate steel and buckled under the load. An adamantine gravestone momentarily caught as it bumped steel rib over rib, compressing our portside hull *Titanic* style in a sharp pinch as though sheet metal. Creasing its way to the next in line, this one reinforced by a 1/4-inch steel sheet welded perpendicular to the hull plating, it couldn't so easily compress this rib to pass on by. Our full 243 tons compressed onto a spot the size of a fist. The weight was more than the steel plate could bear. A 6-inch wide vertical tear following the rib-line split the hull about 25 inches upward from the forward engine room deck and downward a couple feet into a buoyancy void. One deck beneath my rack and several feet below our waterline, hundreds of gallons per second of glacial North Pacific roared into our vessel's innards, a horizontal Old Faithful.

Mere moments had passed. I lay moon-eyed in my bunk. Eyeballed Tomorrow ever ensconced in his. Puckered up to stave off a mass bowel evac, for sure.

How'd our master mariner bring us to this? Sometime after dark he'd said to George, our 21-year old Coast Guard reject and future Dutch Harbor statistic still running on more nervous energy than even I ever did, "Hey, you awake enough for watch on your own if I crash a few hours? I'm beat."

"Sure, sure," came his salty assurance. "Plenty of energy. I'm wide awake."

"Wake me for anything, got it? Especially if you get sleepy."

"Absolutely. I'm great, though. No need to worry."

Jonathan got comfortable in his captain's chair and conked out. Uncharacteristic, aye. But he hadn't slept much preparing to put to sea and it had been a long day and night. Now he was showing his developing trust in young George. Some hours later, nervous energy spent, George passed out chin-to-chest like narcoleptic Darlene on MFT. We sailed hours on autopilot with no hand at the wheel. A ghost ship. Jonathan *was* zonked. Many hours later we reached the point where

My top rack. 'Chicken head,' a nonmember punk rocker, racked below me in this shot.

a zigzag was called for: 45 degrees to port a couple hours, starboard 45 many more, then a few degrees port to our original heading. George didn't zig. We barreled headlong into a rocky outcrop about a day's sail from Chignik, a rustic frontier settlement far down the Alaskan Peninsula.

Our powerful 12-cylinder, 8-foot tall by 12-foot long Caterpillar blindly drove us forward and deeper into the rocks, opening more hull plating to hungrier seas. Our massive three-bladed, 54-inch diameter screw slashed the rocks, chopping out foot wide chunks of bronze till a third of each blade was mostly chewed away.

Later, dreaming from the vantage of the rocks, our *Titanic* blissfully plowed calm seas, lights ablaze, Jonathan and George dead snoring high up on the bridge, us in our trusting racks. Closer and closer, our prow rose up till our dark hull blotted my vision. The sound of stone tearing metal crashed through my ears. Crazy.

Jonathan convulsed awake the same instant I did, George not far behind, all of us wondering what that mysterious *bonk!* was yet, in the pits of our stomachs, knowing all too well. No time to react. Before Jonathan was out of his chair we were one with the rocks. Our boat threw itself violently to port, back to starboard, then back to port—dice in God's rolling hand. It was all Jonathan and George could do to fend off breaking bones... or necks.

As we lost way, Jonathan clawed his way to the helm and threw the engines into neutral. At least he might save our screw. The boat ground sickeningly to a halt and settled in the water. I leapt from my bunk. Jonathan or George must've killed the main engine because it was noisily winding down like a slowing turbine. I hoped that was it. Our boat fell silent. No machinery. Eerie.

I'd rather be found floating in clothes than underwear. Precious seconds went to dragging on Levis, pullovers, socks, and tall cannery boots. I burst from my stateroom facing our benched, U-shaped dining saloon. Johnny was already laying out bright orange survival suits across the 3.5 × 7-foot Formica-topped, rectangular table. Alaskan waters average a deathly 53°F even in August.

In Kukak Bay Jonathan had said, "Twenty bucks if you dive off the boom."

"Twenty?" Never one to dismiss a challenge, I leaned back and saw it was 30 some feet off the deck plus five or six to the water. "That ain't so high. Easy."

"Go ahead, then. Let's see it." Everyone's eyes goaded.

"How 'bout you? Put your guts where your big mouth is."

"For forty."

I chuffed. "Chickenshit." Then atop the slender steel structure, I balked. They were ants, the water hazy in the distance. "Damn. Feels way higher than it looked."

"Come down if you're too scared," he hollered. They egged me on, him the worst.

"Twenty bucks and your rep, Chris," I muttered and leapt into the void making damn sure I cleared the steel rail. I splashed down in a breath-sucking 51°F. I couldn't see

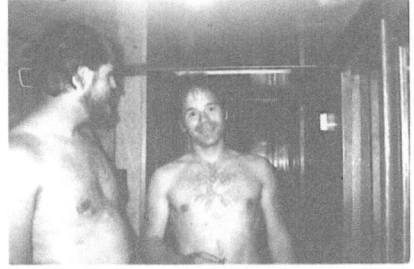

Jonathan and me in dining saloon after a 51°F Kukak Bay swim. Early Aug., 1984.

a whisker underwater from the glacial silt. Unnerving. Every swish and floating scrap against my legs had me in fits imagining some Alaskan monster yawning jaws for lunch. The crew jumped off the stern ramp for at least a minute of iced sea.

I lasted five before trembling up the transom rungs. "Pay up, sucker."

"You didn't *dive*. You *jumped*. Doesn't count."

"You're welshing? You lyin', fuckin' cheapskate."

"Rules are rules." He laughed pulling one over the rube. Top-dog douche.

Our survival suits on the galley table reminded me we might end up neck deep. We didn't yet know where we were or how deep the sea 'neath our keel. Would it sink under our feet, leaving us treading water and hoping against hope for rescue before drowning or freezing to death?

Johnny, ever the cautious fellow, eyed me. "First thing I thought about. Maybe we should put 'em on."

"Shit, I forgot we had 'em." *Glad the crew's delegating itself responsibility.*

"You don't want to forget these babies. They'll save your life."

"Let's not get ahead of ourselves. What happened?"

His tone shrugged. "Sounds like we hit rocks."

"Ya think? What about Jonathan or George? Weren't they on watch?"

Johnny was distracted and his nerves were showing. "I don't know. Must'a fell asleep. Nobody woke me up for mine, anyway."

"Hmmph," was all I managed to that. He hadn't even blinked to say it. Nothing rang worse in a Coast Guardsman's ear than asleep on watch. But how else could we hit rocks? After all his arrogant posturing and belittling of our abilities... "Him falling asleep on watch seems preposterous."

"How do you explain it?"

"We don't know what happened. Bet he's on the radio. I'll check for flooding."

"Good idea. I'll finish with these."

"Tomorrow's a ghost in his rack. Check on him later."

He brayed a dismissive laugh. "Fuck him. He oughta be out *here*." Johnny wasn't straying a foot from his neoprene messiah.

I spun away for the door to the weather deck and crashed headlong into George bounding down the wheelhouse steps to my right on his way to the engine room. His face was drawn, eyes dark with something. We elbowed through the galley door into the starboard anteroom where we kept a top-door deep freezer, foul-weather gear on pegs, and a head unusably crammed with beer. At the far end was the steel hatch to the weather deck. To its right on the inside was the 2-½ × 4-foot deck hatch to the engine room. George banged down its steel ladder one step at a time and I shoved open the heavy weather door and stepped out beneath the upper deck's overhang where we had a crude machine shop, various gear and, bolted to the deck, the wire rope winch controlling the booms and trawling net.

Dawn was just streaking through the sky, the early morning pitch beginning to dissolve. "At least it looks clear. Hope it stays that way. But, where the fuck are we?" I couldn't see much beyond our deck rails in the lingering darkness. It seemed the middle of nowhere. Almost a black void. Ocean maybe to the horizon.

That made it more imperative than ever to stem any flooding. We had to stay afloat as long as possible. I cracked then threw off a flush scuttle cover to our fish hold and dropped into its rimy, still darkness. Close to 50 feet by the boat's 26-foot beam, it was divided into ten fiberglass bins with a central 'courtyard' beneath the main hatch. Each bin opened onto a central passageway and could be closed off by sliding 1×8 planks into steel slots from deck to overhead. As the deck crew dropped fish through the scuttles above each bin, the fish hold crew shoveled powdered ice ('snow') on top from the central passageway to build a new snow bed for the next layer of fish. This ensured they properly layered and iced so their body temperatures evenly reduced to near-freezing without damaging the meat.

Switching on the overheads, I raced fore and aft carefully checking for flooding and other damage. None. Our hold looked tight. Back on deck, I locked down the scuttle, made my way aft, and descended into the lazarette. The last space at the stern of the boat, it held machinery to control the rudder. It, too, was dry. Things were looking good. Maybe our shipwreck was a mere glitch on our voyage. I reveled in a growing optimism. Everything aft of the engine room checked out. I headed forward to see how George was doing.

I slid hands-on-tubular-rails down the engine room ladder Hollywood style. My boots clanged the removable steel deck plates, loose and unsecured on steel framing over the bilge curving into the keel. An engine room deck is built this way for easy inspection and repair of what's below. Surveying the scene, the aft engine room appeared normal. I scanned for water rising through the deck plates under my feet but they were dry. Advancing forward past our 1-storey Caterpillar, a Niagara Falls roar from the forward engine room housing our hydraulic engine and other equipment pummeled my ears over the shattering racket of the sea crashing our hull against rock. Water was shooting under pressure through the port side. Over a foot of seawater sloshed in the port list then cascaded over the coaming of the bulkhead opening and down the 3-foot ladder into the lower, aft engine room.

I yelped, "Oh, shit!" and raced forward.

Seawater poured down my boot when I landed on the first step of the ladder up to the forward engine room. Colder than ice. Almost instantly numbing.

"Shiiit!" I hollered.

Wet socks were the last thing I wanted to suffer. It's funny how small annoyances in the midst of life-threatening disasters are so fixating. George was stripping off his jacket and trying to stuff it into the geyser. He'd already shoved most of our life jackets into the hull split but it only minimally slowed the inrushing seawater that kept blowing them out. I eyed our lifejackets with concern.

Half-seriously pointing, I shouted over the boat raucously pitching side to side, "What do we use if we go down?"

"Maybe the skiff."

"Oh, yeah. Good move, then."

We needed something to plug the hole *now* not later. What else was as stoppering as a lifejacket? Well, a mattress, if you could get it in the hole or, better yet, outside and flat against the hull. But we weren't a USCG cutter with fancy damage control stores. He looked to be in a mild panic judging by his now less-darker but wilder eyes. Likely his realization our shipwreck was probably totally his fault. I imagined him dreading Jonathan's beating for killing us all. After a minute dredging up Coast Guard damage control training and considering our options, I set to building a shoring brace to pressure some stuffing into the breach.

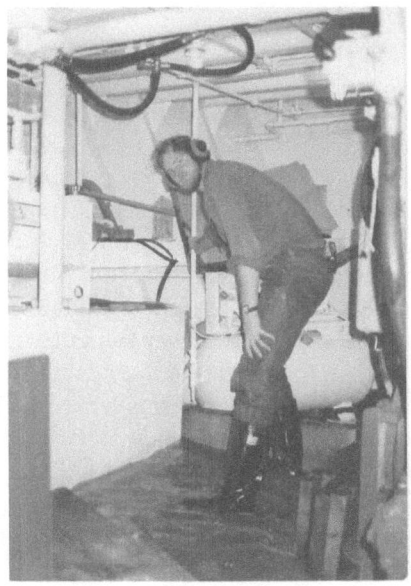

Wedged shoring stems the sea.

189

"I'll be back in a minute with bracing. Find a sledgehammer!"

He nodded understanding. I turned, jumped to the aft engine room deck, and clambered up the ladder. Without a thought for the rest of the boat now, I burst onto the weather deck. This was our main fish sorting area. Roughly 50 feet in length, 2-foot steel stanchions peppered it port and starboard. Rails welded on three sides of each took dropped-in, 5-foot rough-cut 2×12s that made ten sorting boxes, each one around a scuttle to a fish bin below. I hastily yanked these heavy, splinter-spiked planks from their slots and heaved them with rasping grunts toward the weather door leading to the engine room. Lungs protested my furious rush.

Ladder through open bulkhead to after engine room on damage control mission.

Collecting what seemed enough for a start, I piled them piece by piece into the overhang space then through the weather door, then again down the ladder into the engine room where they clanged deafeningly on the loose-fitting steel deck plates. I jumped down the ladder careful not to break an ankle on the caddywhompus boards then tossed them yon forward and, as before, moved them plank-by-plank into the forward engine room. Sweaty, backbreaking, exhausting, headrushing work on a thrashing, possibly sinking, deck.

George scared up a 10-pound sledge and we got to work. The Coast Guard had trained me in combat damage control. George hadn't got that far in his brief career, so I was the only one aboard with real training and knowledge to handle flooding. Most fishermen have little understanding how to save their boats in such an emergency. I thought deep water fishing boat construction should follow common sense regarding internal watertight integrity, but was notorious for having little to none. Used to a high level of compartmentalization aboard military ships, I was appalled by the casual construction of multi-hundred-ton trawlers.

Here we were living the perfect example with heavy flooding in our forward engine room separated from the four-times grander aft engine room by an *open* bulkhead. A watertight scuttle led from the forward compartment to a stateroom above and the hatchway from the aft compartment to the main deck. If we couldn't contain the forward flooding we had no hatch to seal it off from the after space. We might float with the smaller space flooded, but both? It didn't seem likely to me, especially with our belowdecks buoyancy void now flooded.

Knowing we couldn't save the aft engine room if everything went to hell, I placed the heavy 2×12s on end along the deck against the life jackets George put his bodyweight into holding against the inrushing seawater. With other planks perpendicular, I set up a wedge between the planks and the heavy steel mount for the hydraulic engine. My sledgehammering forced the perpendicular planks against those pressing on the life jackets in the torn hull and built pressure against the sea, forcing them into the breach. It significantly reduced the inflow. The tear in the hull was about two feet high, so I tried duplicating my shoring wedge atop the first. It failed for lack of an immovable back support above the deck-level motor mount. Oh, well. One was better than none.

The reason the hull split where it did was a 1,200-gallon hydraulic oil tank welded box-shaped to the hull, reinforcing it. As the rocks skidded down the hull, scoring a visibly deep crease in the metal and bouncing over each rib, they encountered the tank's vertical side welded alongside a rib. The steel plates could bend and crease under the pressure but here it was impossible to compress the box plate on its vertical axis. It held the rib firm. The rock caught. Our vessel's momentum weight split the steel vertically alongside the rib's other side like a wet paper towel.

Outside, the boat continued forward and the rocks slashed the 1,200-gallon hydraulic tank. It spewed oil into the sea which backwashed through the breach, making the deck slippery as wet ice. Then it carved about a 1.5×8-foot gash in our 8,000-gallon portside diesel tank, venting most of it, too. How very lucky. It could've opened the engine room. We'd have flooded out before George even got down to check. Maybe impossible to feasibly lock off the engine room hatchway or get off the boat in pants much less survival suits before it went down like a blown sub.

"Thank you, God," I repeated to myself.

I sent George to the bridge to make a report so Jonathan had some idea what was happening beneath his feet. Meanwhile Johnny had rigged our skiff, currently lashed to the fish deck, for a quick launch. He'd stocked it with food, blankets, suits, and other necessities in case we went down. He was a quick thinker, there. A real survivalist. When he'd finished, he dropped into the engine room to see what could be done with our machinery. He was our engineer and whistled at the (when all was said and done) $1 million in damage. Thankfully, Boss Choi probably back-patted himself, we were insured.

"Choi says they ruled it an 'act of God,'" Johnny laughed back in Kodiak.

"Ha! Poor God," I said. "Blamed for everything."

Under the hull, pipes formed a radiator to circulate freshwater from our engines plus the port and starboard generators. The rocks sheared them all away. The main engine and one generator then sucked seawater into the cooling systems, requiring an expensive overhaul by Caterpillar. As it happened, the running portside generator was feeding off the port tank when it vented to the sea and pulled seawater into its fuel system, totally fouling it. Our starboard one wouldn't run because of other damage. Johnny spent hours dismantling the port one's fuel system and cleaning out the seawater cylinder by cylinder. It was painstaking work and many hours before he coaxed it to life. Until then, we had lights on batteries.

The whole affair smelled like a scene out of 1981's German flick *Das Boot*, a WWII U-boat shoot-'em-up. As I built up my wooden shoring in the forward engine room the lights flickered on and off. Batteries sparked from seawater splashing under pressure through the air. The boat pitched violently side to side with loud, reverberating booms and screeching metal. Furiously laboring to stem the flooding, *Das Boot* feverishly unreeled through my mind. Inside my own drowning steel box, I caught how it might've felt depth-charged on a wartime sub. *Yuk.*

Struggling to keep my feet on the slippery steel deck, seawater almost topping my boots sloppy with hydraulic oil, the violent pitching threw me several times backward into the hydraulic engine. I spine-slammed its mounts hard enough for a permanent lower back injury already smarting from years on a cane (and MFT) that pains me to this day; no disability from ISA, naturally. Several hours later I'd reduced the flooding from hundreds to just a few gallons per second. My next task was helping Johnny figure out our unpumping bilge pumps and the engines.

Drenched in sweat, I first flew up two decks to the bridge. George was there in a foul mood, probably grinding teeth under Jonathan's ongoing and well-deserved tongue-lashing. I delivered a breathless report with military precision.

"Okay, here it is. There's major damage and flooding in the forward engine room, now substantially reduced. The sonar transducer gear below the hull is hung up. The hull plates around it are bending and warping under our pitching and twisting. It looks to me they're on the edge of imploding."

He clouded. Looked thoughtful. "That's not good." Johnny and I, mostly working on the wrong side of it and the Caterpillar from the ladder up, might not make it out. It left my mouth dry. "The tide will shift and it'll be less a problem, maybe."

I brightened. "Both generators are down with seawater fouling or else some damage we haven't found yet. Johnny's working that. The pumps are knocked out, too. The batteries were damn near compromised by seawater but it seems like they're out of danger with the flooding reduced."

"Make sure everything we don't need is turned off so they last."

"Aye, aye." I grinned. "The good news is the rest of the boat is tight and dry."

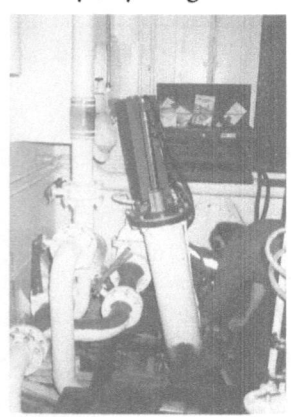

Transducer swung a 3-foot arc as if mounted in butter.

He nodded. "Well, no good news here. The long range radio is busted. Probably shook up by the crash. I can't raise the Coast Guard. I can't raise anybody."

"We're on our own?" *Wonderful.*

"I'm sending out our SOS by shortwave."

Eyes drifted through windows to our predicament. The boat had solidly rammed itself twixt two rock ridges about even with our main deck and twice our beam. A shallow sea surged within. Rocks led breakwaterish toward shore a few hundred yards starboard. A shadowy island in the misty distance astern marked the channel where George was supposed to zig but fucking snored. I said, "Well, besides the transducer, we're in no danger of immediately sinking, even if it was deep water. But, honestly, despite me shoring it up the engine room's gonna flood out eventually without pumps."

"Keep Johnny on that. Pumps, then generator."

"Yeah, but we need the generator to run the pumps."

"*Tscht!* You know what I mean. Just get it done."

"Aye, aye." Training dies hard. At least I didn't blurt out 'sir.' That would've just been embarrassing. Jonathan stolidly resumed his maybe 30-mile mayday. Later, a trawler miraculously caught it and steamed to assist.

"The fucking Coast Guard," he groused at my next report. "Once they found out we weren't in *immediate* danger of sinking, all they cared about was pollution."

"They're not coming?"

"They grilled me on our spills. I recalled that tank was low and hydraulic was minimal. I mean, 1,200 gallons? Please."

"What'll they do?"

He sniffed. "You know how big the fines are for diesel? Choi'll crucify me."

"That's some real fuckery from my old pals. Well . . ." I was thoughtful. He made eyes at George. "If they ask, it's all above my paygrade."

Johnny had a generator on line by late morning. Jonathan supposed our breach was possibly repairable now the tide was lurching the boat less, so we lowered George over the side on a bosun's chair with welding equipment. Even our lesser pitching bounced him all over the hull. Once we worked up a solution to steady him, we found our generator wasn't juicing the voltage the welder needed. DIY repairs were out while troubleshooting that. We hauled

Beat from 36 hours of crises, flooding, busted pumps. Rebuilt generator rumbling in back.

up George, and Johnny jumped ship to some nearby rocks for a view of our chewed-up screw and peppered hull. I was about to go over with a camera for a Kodak moment because he's nothing if not a photo hound, but Jonathan got nervous.

"Get back aboard!" he bawled off the bridge rail.

"Come on, Jonathan," Johnny said. "It's no big deal. What could happen?"

"I don't care. Don't go over the side again. Shit!"

Johnny griped himself aboard, then we forgot to shoot the hull and screw.

Two days later at peak high tide with our trawler savior stationkeeping off our stern, Jonathan spent several hours rocking our boat fore and aft with our vastly reduced-torque screw trying to free us of the rocks. We were heavy in the bow, listing to port 20–25 degrees. This made sufficient buoyancy difficult despite draining most of our freshwater bow tank to add lift. Johnny and I manned the engine room, nervously eyeing the sonar transducer tower wavering around like a drunk on parade as the boat struggled over the rocks. Nerve. Wracking.

Johnny said during a lull, "Hey, if that transducer blows I'm outta here."

"What if I'm stuck in the back? Aren't you going to get me out?"

"Man, if that thing blows, any one of us'll be lucky to get out of here alive. You know how much water will blow up through that hole? It'll be a foot around!"

"Well, shit. I don't like the sound of your every-man-for-himself philosophy."

"You do what you gotta, Chris."

"Do you?" The 3/8- or 1/2-inch steel bent and warped like modeling clay. "How's it not gonna break, though? It must be hot and soft as hell from all that twisting."

"If it don't, that's quality Master Marine construction," he said. "Hats off to 'em. You can write a testimonial."

The engine room revved to an ear-shattering din of jumbo Caterpillar as Jonathan fought us off the rocks. He violently rocked us forward and back like a fed-up car in a snowbank. The screaming engine, thrashing propeller, and grinding rock on steel blasted through our hearing protectors and split our heads. Talk was impossible. We hand-signed racing about tending each unfolding crisis.

I hauled topside. "Come on, Jonathan! The engine's gonna explode! Do a tow." His head shook hard. "The transducer okay? Yeah? Then get down there." "Dammit!" I pounded steel below.

Then, lo and behold, off we scraped. Our friends shadowed us in case we sank on our 30±-hour limp into Chignik. A peaceful hamlet, its Alaskan natives in quiet amusement watched our listing boat waddle in so far over as to rival the Riddler's crazy house from 1960s *Batman*. We forked our vittles off sliding plates.

Chignik was dry (no alcohol). Drunk natives frozen dead the next morning had some Alaskans seeing liquor too dangerous for grown adults to choose. And here our head was loaded for bear. Roads were boardwalks over mud traversed on three-wheeled motorbikes with bulbous, spongy tires. The only way in or out was by boat or seaplane. The mayor/police chief/fire chief/medic/pastor, wearing his vicar's hat, visited to ensure all was copacetic. We found flyers for church and Bible study all over the boat for weeks. Few of us attended our own Sunday service by choice, so he was preaching to a flat choir.

To Jonathan his cop hat said, "Keep all that alcohol aboard. *Capisce?*" Mayorally, he added, "And let me invite you to my home for dinner with my family. Okay?"

"Sure, honored," Jonathan nodded. Brass polishing brass.

State police seaplaned in from Anchorage for sinners chained to an Atlas-like steel pole bearing his vaulted living room and flew them home after time served.

Anchorage Bay. Chignik Bay beyond. Docked at right.

"Seems pricey and inefficient for petty crimes," I griped.

We got access to a working long range radio—no telephones in Chignik—to contact ISA, which hadn't known of our dire straits till a sister boat heard the Coast Guard's radio report that "*Ocean Hope 3* is now clear of danger and not expected to sink." *Ocean Hope 2* took on repair materials to get us shipshape and Bristol fashion for our return trek. It arrived in half a week.

In the meantime, we found ourselves running low on meat. Jonathan organized a hunting party. We shouldered weapons and hiked into the hinterlands huffing single file along rocky foot trails in search of an unlucky deer or two, eyes and ears honed sharp for irritated, surprised, or surly bears. Jonathan packed along his 10-gauge loaded with slugs in case some pre-mauling bone-breaking was called for. At the back of our slow-moving line Johnny, ever the practical joker, threw a large rock into the low trees and alder off to Jonathan's right. Who jerked three feet left, shotgun to shoulder. My heavy revolver leapt into my hand on pure instinct, cocked and aimed on autopilot. We froze, senses straining.

194

A moment of tense worry later, Johnny's quiet snickering filtered up the trail.

"Johnny, you goddamned motherfucker! Why you do shit like that?"

"Pretty funny, Jonathan, watching you shit your pants."

"Fuck you. Do it again, I'll shoot *you*."

More snickering. I let out my hard-drawn air. Decocked and holstered with a nervous laugh. "Fuckin' Johnny," I mumbled, giving him the dead eye. Then louder, "Very funny, dumbshit. You need a black eye to match yer fuckin' heart."

He didn't care. We shared a good laugh over Jonathan later. It wouldn't be his last practical joke, but bears were a true threat to life and limb and bore watchfulness. His jokes exacerbated our tension and decreased our situational awareness proportional to our irritation. Maybe he did us a favor, though we bagged no deer.

We tried patching the smaller holes with an underwater epoxy Dana off of the *Ocean Hope 2* applied using scuba gear, but it was of minimal value. After much preparation, we set sail under our own power for Kodiak. A day's travel later,

Off to hunt up dinner with soon-to-be-late George.

thumping vibrations forced Jonathan to kill our engines. Close inspection revealed our propeller shaft was bent and slowly mashing the bearings and shaft seals. Now we were taking water through the stern. We crossed our fingers we'd make it to Kodiak under our own power. Open-ocean towing is a dicey venture.

Unfortunately, whether from the boat's listy movement or delayed shock, I got good and seasick on our 3-day voyage home and barfed my guts out. Pathetic. We docked in Kodiak and many church members came down to greet our nearly lost souls. Tomorrow jumped the gap *today* and rabbited for the bunkhouse before we'd even thrown a line around the bollards to cinch in close. Maybe the riskiest thing he ever did. We never saw him on the boats again. Just as well.

"Good riddance . . . in a nice way," I called to his disappearing back.

I was so happy to put feet to familiar, dry land that I dropped to my knees and kissed the concrete wharf. I stood as a Japanese sister from the administrative office marched up. Stunning green eyes, so unusual for Japanese, set off angelic features. I expected a dazzling smile and a warm hero's greeting but, nope.

She half smiled and held up a paper. "This is phone bill. You must pay."

"It's only been two weeks!" Eyes narrowed. Brows scrunched. I gave her a pointed once-over. "Say, how do you say elephant in Japanese?"

"Elephant?" She considered it. "We say, *tzo*."

"Okay, then. From now on I'm calling you *tzo-chan*, because you never forget."

Her face darkened. She pushed the paper at me. "Overdue. Pay now." And off grouched her gorgeous green eyes and to-die-for physique.

To onlooking Johnny I said, "Back from near death and hit up for charges right on the dock like a common scofflaw." *These fuckin' people.*

"Maybe the finance office is worried your luck's run out."

"And now twice doomed. Collect before we fly the mortal coil." Head shaking, I shoved the bill in a pocket and turned to the boat. It was then I realized I'd had no fear throughout the ordeal. I'd handled every issue with professional aplomb. I felt pretty good about that, like I'd proved myself. But later, in mainland Homer for repairs, our shipwreck gave me the fright of my life.

Our first task getting to its tidal shipyard to make Seattle-bound repairs was to rebuild our notchy screw. Jonathan loaded it in the back of his straining pickup for a mainland shipper. Weeks later it came back good as new. It was now we discovered our freshwater cooling system missing and our Caterpillar and generators brining for a month. Shot through with rust, for sure. We made additional engine room repairs and readied to get underway.

Because of the vented 8,000-gallon diesel tank, it was vital we pull into Homer trailing not a lick of slick. Jonathan wasn't kidding about Boss Choi's wrath. Coast Guard fines can break a boat. I wasn't sure how we'd

Grizzly fam on patrol.

avoid it, but nature provided the answer. We sailed round Kodiak's headland, through the straits between Raspberry and Afognak islands, then north into the Shelikof and a savagely darkening sky. A storm was already kicking up the seas. By nightfall we plowed a raging typhoon. Seas whipped up 40 feet.

I banged down the engine room ladder with a death grip. "Hey, Johnny! This storm is just what our holey boat needs, ain't it?"

"Reckon it's shipyard or bust for Jonathan. Have yer survival suit handy."

Our plan was making Homer then a safe sail to Seattle for a fix and upgrades over winter. Therefore, not only were we carrying all our personal stuff, but ISA wanted us to ship cargo to Seattle. Our fish deck was covered in crates, machinery under tarpaulins, Jonathan's sleek black motorcycle, and other known and unknown odds and ends. We'd lashed everything to the deck with nylon rope which, when wet, tends to stretch. The storm's intensity ratched up 45–50 degree rolls. Jonathan noticed first his motorcycle then the cargo begin to shift. If it moved too much it could break loose or destabilize our equilibrium and capsize us, *Ocean Hope 1*'s 1998 fate. He detailed me to the weather deck to keep the cargo tightly lashed.

"While you're out there," he yelled in my ear over the rattling storm, "I want you to pour all that laundry detergent I bought down the port fuel tank fill pipe."

"That's what you bought all that for?"

"Yeah, it'll dissolve the diesel so we don't leave an oil slick in Homer." He pointed at the storm. "And this is perfect. It'll work like a washing machine agitator."

I shouted near his ear. "How am I supposed to get powdered detergent down a five-inch hole in this wind?"

"It's under the bridge deck." He clapped my shoulder like Julian. "It'll be fine." I made for the ladder below. "Be sure you pour it down the pipe when the boat rolls to starboard," he bellowed as an afterthought. "Otherwise, the water rushing back into the tank will blow all the air up the pipe and you'll get a face full of soap!"

"Why don't you ask Johnny or Jack to do it? They're earning the—"

"Because I'm asking you. Now hurry up with that cargo."

"I get all the shit duty!" But to the weather deck I sulked bound in cannery boots, green Helly Hansen foul-weathers, and the yellow Sou'wester I loved that kept my head drier than any hood. The boat rolled so far with each wave I could slide my hand six inches over the rail at peak roll and it was in the ocean. I glanced at the blinding halogen lights a good thirty feet over my boots bathing the fish deck in a yellow-white glare. In a trough, the waves disappeared above the lights into an inky night sky. Topping a crest, *Ocean Hope 2* and *Green Hope*'s deck lights pitched and rolled in a frenzy, then sank into the black sea without even a gleam to mark their spot, only to burst atop a wave like Poseidon seizing a star. With each roll of our boat, eighteen inches of seawater hurled across the deck, knocking me down and wetting me under my Helly-Hansens. I tightened the lines holding Jonathan's prized motorbike and large pieces of machinery, then drunkenly weaved under the bridge overhang and unscrewed the steel cap to the port fuel pipe.

Jonathan was dead serious about the air. It blasted up the pipe with a brassy, hollow *whoosh* chased by seawater rushing through the torn hull with each roll to port. Breaking open a 20-lb cardboard box of suds, I waited for the roll to starboard then hastily dumped all the soap I could into the black maw till the deck angle shifted downward with the roll to port. It took an hour to pour several of these heavy loads of detergent down the pipe. When I miscalculated, a face full of sand-blasted powdered detergent fell like snow to the watery, now sudsy, deck.

"Done!" I rested at last.

Ass firmly planted on steel under the protected overhang, legs stretched out in front, I held on as mad seas washed port to starboard and back again across the main deck afore me with each hectic, 45-degree roll. Not only did we wildly heave side to side, the boat struggled up each wave's 50–70 degree slope, a roughly 40-foot climb. Lurching over the crest, fully a third of the hull hung suspended mid-air. Our remade screw thrashed amok half out of the receding wave front. A moment of suspense and the bow dropped into the trough. Our weightless bodies floated on deck till the forepeak plunged through the surface and buried itself halfway to the wheelhouse. Trawlers in Alaska sport 18-inch and taller heavy-gauge steel 'breakwaters' welded to the deck that angle aft from the centerline in a 'v' to force green water off the deck before it pummels the wheelhouse to rubble. Each bow impact reverberated accordion-like aft through the hull, rippling through the decks and up our legs. Dully watching the deck inundated by yet another bone-cracking wave, I was beginning to wonder if we'd even stay afloat with all the damage we had.

How's that sonar transducer doing? popped into my thoughts.

Johnny was dry on engineering watch below. I paid visits to check the cockeyed transducer and the forward engine room. We'd left the hole heavily braced but it wept seawater and . . . who knew? Maybe the repeated shock of slamming into wave troughs would shatter my temporary repair and flood the engine room with hundreds or thousands of gallons per second, sinking us before even Johnny registered his mortal peril. We wouldn't be the first vessel to hit the bottom of a trough and just keep on for Davy Jones' locker. Hairy business.

A shattering *crack!* shocked me from my reverie ensconced under the protecting overhang. I blinked at the 30-pound grinder motor bolted to a $3/4 \times 18$-inch square plywood plate practically touching my right knee, having landed pile driver fashion from its resting place on the metal workbench directly above me.

"Thank you, God," I muttered, the wind snatching my voice over the side. "That would've smashed my knee to a pulp! Thank you, *thank you!*"

My wits were rattled. I was gills green, too, barfing till nothing was left then retching some more on principle. We sleeplessly endured the storm late afternoon through night. Exhausted near to a black dawn and more confident the cargo lashings would hold awhile, I collapsed in my stateroom, my body lifeless in the mattress. Each herky-jerky roller coaster had me worried I'd end up broken-necked on deck—some boats had seatbelted racks—but I only flopped limply in the confines of my high-sided bunk like a sack of taters. Suitcases stashed on Tomorrow's empty lower bunk athwartships (mine ran fore and aft) slid raspily from end to end, banging to a gunshot stop with each roll. It was aggravating as hell. I was too dead to do more than fall comatose to its *bang! slam!* rhythm.

Above Chignik after rope climbing up its water supply pipe.

I WOKE TO our main engine thrumming low at slow speed. The deck rode steady as a rock. I'd slept about six hours and bright noon sunlight streamed through my porthole. Somewhat refreshed, I peered out through smarting eyes on a sunwashed sea smooth as glass and a blue sky washed of clouds. My stomach rejoiced.

Homer reminded me of a wild west town. The ramshackle Salty Dog Saloon was our first sight ashore. We ducked through its five-foot-odd heavy-framed weather-beaten door, pistols on our hips, into a dim, hazy interior of sullen looking fishermen. If they'd spent the night in the same flaying sea, I understood their mood.

In a hush Johnny said, "Some of these Meskins look a little too ready to carve us white boys up with their switchblades and boat knives for my taste."

"They gon' cu' you for daaat," I japed.

He glared. "Startin' with you, dumbass. You got a megaphone in your throat?"

Damn. We didn't stay long.

After eating—all I managed for three days was plain scrambled eggs—we shifted to a pier the base of which was a heavy timber grid. As the 25-foot tide went out, our boat dropped till the keel rested on it. Insectoid workmen scurried making necessary hull repairs to get us safely to Seattle for our major overhaul and refit. They only had a few hours each turn of the tide. The job took nearly a week.

Jonathan said, "If they finish up today, we'll put out tomorrow."

"I could get used to sleeping on a *level* deck," Johnny said.

"Yeah," Jack said, "here's to our listing days being over."

Then late that night the keel buoyed off the grid with the rising tide and slipped to port. Our vessel smashed resoundingly starboard into wooden pilings. I flew off my bunk. *Oofed!* on hull steel. Doors racketed. Crockery shattered on the galley deck. Items elsewhere titanically banged across bulkheads. Fifteen seconds and we landed on the fish deck shaking in our socks. Having by now lived on a 25-degree port-listing deck damn near

Seattle-bound via the Inside Passage. Oct., 1984.

two months, the savage shift to a similar starboard one unnerved me. My walloping heart refused to downshift.

"What the hell was *that*?" I thundered.

"We sinking?" said Jack, jumping uphill and throwing wary eyes over the rail.

"We're almost on our side!" Johnny took in the pier rising in the gloom.

After a thoughtful minute Jonathan said, "Oh! I know what it is. Did I mention the yard last-minute sealed off that tank today?" We traded irked eyes. "I forgot to counterflood. We fell over when the tide popped the keel off the bottom."

"Oh, ha ha, joke's on you?" My jilted heart still palpitated. Our shipwreck hardly bothered me. *That* was a great piece of adventure. Scary as it could've been, I'd been too busy to worry. Now Jonathan was all shrugs and grins saying, "No big deal, don't worry, boat's fine," but this second crash left me quaking like a near-death.

"That's bullshit, Jonathan. How'd you forget something like that? What're you paid the big bucks for? That's two-hunnert goddamn tons of—"

"Shut up, Johnny. Go back to sleep."

"Pfft! Like I could."

At last we departed Homer and rendezvoused at sea with *Ocean Hope 2* and *Green Hope*. There was still no certainty we'd make it to Seattle on our own and ISA saw safety in numbers. Boss Choi certainly didn't want to lose our boat now he'd sunk so much into temporary repairs and travel costs. A rare smart decision. Near the northern entrance to the Inside Passage—the series of waterways and islands lining southern Alaska's and western Canada's coast—Jonathan felt a desultorily worse, then a steadily grinding *thump thump thump* from the wheelhouse.

He cut the engines. All of us jammed below to inspect the shaft and seals. "It's too bent now. No way we can spin it without reaming out the stern."

Jack said, "We're dead in the water?"

"What do you think?"

"Good thing Mr. Choi sent the 0-2 and *Green Hope*. Right, Jonathan?"

"You wanna ride one of them to Seattle? Then shut up."

Johnny confided, "Don't know what bug's up his ass. Ridin' me awhile now."

"Quit fuckin' with him, then," I said. "You know he's touchy as—"

"He needs to chill out. It's all our necks on the line, not just his."

"Johnny!" Jonathan hollered from the bridge. "Help Jack with the tow line!"

"Yowzah. Comin', boss."

I rolled my eyes. Sometimes, he was just looking for trouble.

Ocean Hope 2 hooked us up. We lounged several days in deck chairs, fishing off the rails, shooting plastic bottle caps tossed in the 9-knot current, and catching up on sleep. We stood 4-hour steering watches since our tow was doing all the navigating. Easiest underway ever. As good as a cruise ship without the stewards but Johnny's fine cooking and none of the racket. The silence of the sea was God's church.

The peaceful, heavenly Inside Passage off Canada.

We docked at a shipyard, unloaded ISA's cargo, and dropped in on our local seafood company a time or two. Jonathan unexpectedly forced me to attend Pledge service.

"You need it. Sisters are all over you. You're such a ladies' man."

"Shouldn't I be getting laid if that was so?" *Pah!*

"Better not be!"

I WINTERED IN San Francisco after October 25. My first thing was a job at Ace Hardware on Cole Street where I'd bought Judah Street's renovation supplies for a couple years. They knew me and happily took me aboard. I looked up Kyung Mi in my loneliness and alienation and ended up a dewhiskered one-lady man till she abruptly fluxed off to that Korean beau. In January 1985 I started City College of San Francisco. I'd swapped my youth hostel for a dining room in the house of a New York psycho and his skin-and-bones Chinese girlfriend at 1573 19th Avenue. He once burst in from the unsealed-up kitchen swing door when he overheard my deep sigh over life's many pricks and galls.

On my pallet, back against the wall, I jerked my eyes up. "Wha—?"

"Thought you were masturbating and just came," he said, eyes wild. "Guess not."

Deranged was a mite too complimentary. Would he laugh his head off or jump in for more if I was? Birds were nesting in my gaping maw before he imitated Sister Mary Stigmata back through the closing swing door.

"Men or women," I carped, "all I ever seem to find is weirdos."

At the end of April I arranged to wind up school to make Alaska for the start of the 1985 season. This year, I'd be a full crew member and qualified for a full share. Or so I thought. Instead, ISA cut out crew shares entirely for a flat $300 monthly wage. This was part of Boss Choi's smashing strategy to make up for all his previous bad decisions with a worse one. We were now the lowest paid fishermen in all of Alaska. Slaves . . . minus the whip. Right back where I'd started. And we moved boatloads of fish that summer. I'd easily have earned $30,000 over the season with crew shares. It was my college money, no different from the respectable suburban girls seasonally working the fishermen on their backs for a full-ride tuition. I felt sandbagged.

"I should join a non-church crew," I crabbed with Johnny.

"They ain't gonna hire you, man."

"Why not? I have good experience."

"Up here, it's who you know. Got any friends outside ISA?"

I threw my head back. "Fuck."

"You're a Moonie and folks know us. Just suck it up or go back to 'Frisco."

Anyway, I'd sworn I'd contribute *something* to Rev. Moon's ministry. Survival was key but I truly didn't want to fondle money (tuition, either) while doing nothing for the world. Like most of us on the boats, I resented Boss Choi's ego and corrupt largess for 'outside members' and his parsimonious greed gutting our pay, not theirs. He gave us less respect than his cannery members though we understood the business and supplied his treasured product withal.

Meeting the boat for season 2 at its Seattle shipyard. Early May, 1985.

Well, that's the reason, isn't it? Plain old ego stoking resentment of the competent. It's these kinds of leaders making it so taxing for Americans to keep the church dear. Every day some moral quandary bitch-slapped our conscience. Rev. Moon often said to us, "Challenge your concepts, and overcome your limitations." Sure, but when is flouting authentic moral belief absent a compelling rationale challenging our concepts and not just a moral dereliction? It was never easy to tell. Generally, church leaders taught us to err on the side of obedience to them and sometimes Rev. Moon; to put our conscience, if we had one, on low heat. From the mid-'90s he spieled on the sanctity of individual conscience but, in the '80s, it was a dirty word, a hellish trick, disloyalty and treason wrenching open a door to Satan's invasion. We struggled with our moral conundrums on the pragmatic boats and rarely found any inner peace no matter which side of an issue we came down on.

Fishing was a damn dangerous business. It proved its lethality each week across the fishing grounds in the deaths, dismemberments, injuries, and wrecked or sunken boats. We all felt Boss Choi was unfairly, even illegally, cheating us of our fair pay for this perilous, life-threatening work that Rev. Moon cherished. Did he know how Boss Choi was running his business? doing his members dirty? We believed he was providing Rev. Moon false reports for two reasons.

First, church leaders always lie away bad news. Like any autocrat, Rev. Moon can react unpredictably when he senses bad results in the incompetence or unPrincipled selfishness of those who should know better. Leadership's established tradition was to avoid the consequences of bad news by not reporting it. Second, we believed him a good man, fair and Principled, who wouldn't knowingly cheat us. Leaders' chicanery couldn't and didn't originate with him. I believe that sop less after all I've seen these 21 years but, for me in the 1980s, he could do no wrong.

I thought the crew share system about the fairest pay system in the free market. The money earned by a boat's company was divided equally by all, even if some merited more than others. No one seriously debated the captain receiving more than

an able crewman. It was his boat and his risk after all. He carried legal and moral responsibilities plus our lives on his shoulders. The first mate did more responsible work than a regular crewman. Yes, very fair. If all companies paid their employees like this there'd be wealthier workers and healthier companies. It once occurred to me how compensation isn't actually in cash but lifestyle. A secretary isn't expected to live like his or her boss. Earning $20,000 a year against an executive's $80,000-plus is a statement the role deserves a $20K diet, clothes, car, apartment, and so on. That executives can't effectively manage absent assistance is immaterial to the politics of compensation. Crew shares smoothed out this inequity very well.

Gulf of Alaska. Jun., 1985. Seasick at pivot point off watch in 9–15 ft. head seas; following & quartering seas no sweat. Johnny's Boston Baked Beans revived me after foodless days.

My second season started with a ravening shock I was worth a piddling $300 a month to ISA though we reaped it millions in fish booty. *Ocean Hope 3* held over 100,000 pounds of fish. In the summer of 1985, ISA paid 64¢ to $1.43 a pound for salmon off the seiners. King-sized, red-over-white hand-painted fo'c'sle signs shouted our current, sometimes hourly-changing, pricing for salmon. A bidding war ISA instigated to draw more boats to offload to our tenders got so pricey it nigh broke every cannery's bank in Kodiak, including ours.

Other boats sometimes squelched over the radio at the Moonies, cursing us and threatening harm. Jonathan often shouted right back, giving no quarter. One evening we'd docked at ISA's pier. I loitered outside on the main deck taking in the ambience. It was a lazy dusk. Quiet. Serene. Ghosting out of the twilight a soda can bulleted past my head, harshly clanging off the steel bulkhead next to me and blowing its contents. Heart seized, I turned to see a crewman on a passing boat in the act of launching another round. Infuriated, I ran inside to our alcoholic head, grabbed a six pack of beer, and semi-auto fired each one with every ounce of muscle I had. It didn't occur to me in that moment that I could do to his head what he'd just nearly done to mine. I was too mad to think.

Later that night the selfsame hellboat chugged by. Eggs plastered ours. We had to wash them off with haste because, once dried, we'd have to chip them off with the paint. Jonathan, *Green Hope*'s skipper Matthew, and about 15 of us decided enough was enough. We'd gathered multiple 48-egg flats on deck well after midnight when our nemesis got underway from the fuel dock. Their crew had got good and drunk waiting for their tanks to fill. As they coasted by our boat, we crouched behind steel bulwarks until they drew opposite. With a shout of *Now!* we leapt to our feet and flung every egg at hand. Hundreds peppered the enemy's superstructure all at once, splattering the faces and bodies of its drunk, beer-slugging crew sneering at the Moonie boat as they glided by. Talk about a surprise. They ranted and raved the coarsest language but, lacking ammo, couldn't do a thing about it. Our broadside forced those boozers to sweat their best stoned hours till dawn scrubbing hundreds of eggs off their boat. Never messed with us again, the snooty bastards.

SUMMER OF '85 rocked on. Anchored in Bumble Bay at Kodiak Island's south end, Jonathan nearly killed me when he jerked the boom cable I was holding. He'd under-calculated the tonnage of snow in our fish hold and ISA sent the independent *Mar del Sud* down to transfer ten tons from their hold to ours. We shoveled it by hand into a 4×4×3-foot plastic fish bin, hoisted it out of the *Sud's* hold with both booms which Jonathan deftly swung over and down into our hold where we shoveled it back out. Grueling, sweaty work in the frosty air belowdecks.

Snow and water sprinkled the deck planking around the 8×10-foot main hatch. I gripped the boom cable to hook up the bin. Jonathan bumped the hydraulic lever at the bridge deck control station overlooking the main deck. The cable jerked. Yanked me off my feet like a ragdoll. Slingshot me forward. I sailed catty-corner over the open hold and belly-flopped onto sloppy deck wood. A vertical steel deck divider filled with sharp angles and unyielding attitude reared up fast and hard. I knew it would split my still-blooming genius like a watermelon. A millisecond to death, both hands got palms out against my skull. They took the brunt. I ended up with bruised hands, a sprained neck, and a glaring, pissy, headaching disposition.

"Sorry!" Jonathan called down with his trademark shrug.

I rolled on my back holding my head. "Haah . . . Uugh . . . Aaah . . ."

Maybe Johnny down below caught me flying over the hatch, because this was when he finally lost his cool with Jonathan. He wasn't winning their shouting match. Spitting his fit on the fish deck he ranted, "You're such an *asshole*, Jonathan. I quit!"

"Walk off my boat in the middle of an opening"—kind of light-humoredly—"and I'll never take you back on." Because

Hiking above Bumble Bay. Jun., 1985.

it wouldn't be the first time Johnny ate crow off his threats. He Blighly gazed from his winch controls. "Think it through, now. Not half-cocked as usual."

"Fuck you!" He stalked inside and snatched his gear from his stateroom.

"If he leaves on your boat," he hollered to the *Sud's* impassive skipper, "he's never coming back. He's got till we're done here."

"I'll tell him, Jonathan. Don't get your hopes up."

"Pfft! Dumb fucker. Chris! Take Johnny's place in the hold."

"Fuck!"

Johnny hopped the gap to the *Sud* for a ride to Kodiak. He turned to wave before I dropped below then middle-fingered Jonathan. "See that, Jonathan? Fuck you."

This was so like him, never willing to take shit from anybody regardless the unthought-out consequences. He'd been going round and round with Jonathan since I showed up in Kodiak. If it wasn't verbal slugfests it was threatened fisticuffs he usually calculated he'd lose. Jonathan was muscular and tough. We all knew that, the Bronx street rat he was, he'd be devious and mean as fuck in a real fight. Johnny took retreat's lesser form of courage. This time, it looked like capitulation. Maybe Boss Choi would surprise us all and back him against Jonathan.

The boat felt empty after that. Johnny was my only reliably non-judgmental and non-backstabbing friend at ISA. I didn't get along all that well with Jonathan, either. He delighted in poking fun at what he considered my slow talk and slower thinking, a product of growing up in the laid back American West, perhaps. A frenetic New Yorker, he jabbered on like a 33 RPM record stuck on 78. Not as fast as a New York Puerto Rican but wasting no space between words, either. For me, it was nigh impossible to catch his staticky garble over the public address system he passed orders through to our fore and aft stations when tying up and getting underway. He talked too fast, the mic too close. The crackling speakers masticated it.

In conversation I often said, "What did you say? What was that?"

Visibly irritated and oozing sarcasm for the mentally retarded (or Japanese), he fixed me with a stare. "I. Said. You. Should. Clean. Out. Your. Ears. And . . ."

"Never mind."

We worked a few multi-week halibut openings in the long-haul Pacific that saw my last brush with death before the season wound down. Longlining in 20-foot seas aboard *Green Hope* (similar to but lighter and shorter than *Ocean Hope 3*), we rolled and pitched a chute-the-chute 24–7. Besides exhausting, it complicated plain old living. Try keeping your white-knuckled ass on the mechanical bull of a commode in the forepeak of a trawler in this rodeo. It's a wonder the bulkheads weren't splattered in piss and shit and blood. Spewingly smelled like it, though.

Three men boathooking a halibut.

Halibut are slimy. It takes two or three brawny men wielding boathooks to bring these 4- to 8-foot seagoing sonsabitches over the rail. Out of water, they launch into a full-body spasm. Connecting with a human often breaks bones. They're very dangerous to take aboard any boat let alone a small sportfisher like a church-built 28-foot 'Good-Go.' Crazy bastards are practically unkillable. If frozen fish breaks your toe in the grocery store, you can bet it's halibut. Boss Choi (and he wasn't alone) preached the tactical soundness of stunning it a few times with a .45 Colt or .44 magnum to the brain before hefting it over the rail into air and a tight Good-Go. This was where the screaming bone-breaking happened.

They're easy to catch, however. All it takes is a line about a mile long with a six-foot lanyard tied into it every fathom of its length. The lanyard's end sports a wicked hook curved like a fancy capital 'C' virtually impossible to pull out. We coiled our longline into 20, 30, or more plastic buckets about 24 inches across. As each one fills with line, it snakes over the basket top into the next basket's bottom. Fifty-some halibut hooks baited with chopped squid hook over the basket edges with attached lanyards running down inside the basket to the coiled line. On the longline's end is an anchor. With the boat burping along in the wide open sea, a crewman heaves the anchored end off the stern along with its top end attached to a buoyed flag pole and pennant so we can find it again. The fast-sinking anchor peels the baited hooks off the first-in-line basket rim as the longline flies out, an infinite garden snake on speed. The crew stands around the baskets sitting atop a roughly 7×15-foot heavy wood table and, as each one empties, swipes it out of the line-up and shoves the other baskets to the table's stern end.

Well, this is damn risky work. The most common accident happens from an incorrectly set hook and lanyard in the basket. As the line plays out at the velocity of the now-plummeting anchor plus the boat's way, the lanyards attached to it should smoothly pull each hook off the edge one-by-one in order. But if, for instance, a lanyard is laid under another lanyard or hook 40 is reversed with 45, then as it jerks away it pulls the hook and lanyard lying atop it along for the ride, which then pulls a bundle of intervening hooks out of the basket in a wild, unwinding clump. This sometimes causes a hook to wildly arc around the basket. If you're in range, it can snag your foul-weather gear. The more kinetic energy the deeper it digs. In the worst case it hooks a rib, hand, eye, neck, forearm, crotch . . .

If it happens, the line attached to the descending anchor inexorably pulls the ill-starred crewman off the stern into the water, then quickly down 60, 100, 200 feet. Even if he's managed to hold a good lungful all this time, his eardrums are bursting and his chest compressing under the pressure in excruciating pain and eventual blackout. If he's lucky enough to fumble out a knife and cut the lanyard or tear out the hook, he still has tons of water to swim heavily clothed up through. It's safe to say that once dragged over the stern you're as good as dead barring a miracle.

This happened when I was on the stern deck on a halibut trip, but we got knives to part the lanyard before it pulled our mate over. There we were, several of us impotently trying to slow his drag for the water, all of us frantically hunting a blade. Often it's cold, but always wet. We layered up under foul-weather gear. It's almost impossible to get through it for the knives on our belt in an emergency. We accordingly stationed colorfully handled knives around the basket table. It was during one of these emergencies before my time that Jonathan accused Johnny of jumping out of the way of his hooked shipmate so he wouldn't get dragged over with him instead of helping cut him loose.

Jonathan privately said, "That's one of the main reasons I don't like him. I know I can never trust him in a real emergency."

"That might've just been a shock reflex you can train out."

Jonathan resolutely wagged his head. "You should never make the mistake of trusting him, that's all. Mark my words."

I bore it in mind, thinking back to our shipwreck when Johnny was reasoning why he'd abandon the engine room with or without me. It never interfered with our friendship but, then again, he never had to decide.

On this particular halibut trip atop 20-foot seas I lost my footing on the halibut-slimed deck. The boat rolled hard to starboard and, unable to check my sudden motion, my boots slid over the ooze like wet ice. I was at the centerline with nothing to grab and no time even to throw myself flat as the deck tilted 15 . . . 20 . . . . 25 degrees. I hit the bulwarks—planking framed over a steel deck made it only as high as just above my knees—and cantilevered right over the edge. A blink in time. Eyeing the roiling water against *Green Hope*'s dirty steel hull, I saw rushing death.

Simply put, when you fall over the side of a massive steel vessel like a 240-ton trawler in heavy seas, it batters your body to a pulp against the hull in seconds. I wouldn't be thrown 20 feet from the ship, which would've afforded me the option of drowning in terror. No, I was about to plop headfirst into the water no more than a couple feet from the rising and falling hull. If the screw didn't suck me under, I'd still be upside down when the first wave bone-cracked my body into the hull that would've, at that moment, been moving *opposite* the direction of the wave. That's just how boats roll. It was all too grim even in that split second of realization.

I had no chance to call out. No one even noticed as they concentrated on their own job, footing, and safety. Pivoting over the side, my hands flailed for anything to grab. Luckily—providentially—*Green Hope* had 4-inch steel square tubing welded along the top of their bulwarks starting about midships the fish deck and running 10–15 feet aft, upon which they rested their huge steel fishnet wings. More out of the boat than in by this point, my right hand hit the tubing and instinctively deathgripped it. My left hand flattened against the inside of the flat steel bulwarks. Wicked strong in the torso from my work, this arrested my motion over the side. It was only then a crewmate noticed me struggling off the rail.

"Hey, you okay? Somebody grab Chris!"

Then the boat surged up and rolled back to port, and my boots—God bless 'em this time!—slid me right along the deck back the way I'd come.

I plunked onto something to rest my frayed nerves awhile. "I'm good. Now."

Later, when contemplating not working a third season to instead head off to Cyprus as a newspaper editor, Dad said after hearing some of these tales, "Your mother and I were talking it over even before you came back and decided we were willing to pay you what you'd have earned to not go back to Alaska."

"Crew shares or Boss Choi's slave wage?"

"Whichever kept you out of Alaska . . . within reason, of course."

I laughed. He didn't understand crew shares, methinks. At least they didn't want me to die a young and stupid death. That's love.

～

ALASKA WAS A fabulous experience. I thought every Moonie would benefit from a summer learning the manly arts, experiencing raw nature, and getting a taste of life on the edge. Not merely members. Leaders especially needed pulling off their fleshy pedestals into the teamwork of a crew at sea where an arrogant presumption could be fatal. Although for the most part the Japanese didn't like Western boat members because they couldn't shake their gangsterized stereotypes reinforced by church ideology, our manliness impressed them. To my mind, this accounted for the illicit sex between Japanese sisters and American brothers. The church was a stodgy asylum but hard, sweaty work seemed to break down the artificial social–sexual barriers that Rev. Moon and ever more fanatical leaders erected.

A Japanese sister said to me, "Japanese men are too . . . woman. Neh? They no have American muscle."

"Preaching to the choir, sister."

"Ha, ha! No bottom, no strong chest, no bushy beard . . . very small."

"So, *that's* what y'all are doing coming aboard for photos." *Holy mack—*

"Most important," she added, "they no have American manly feeling—"

"You mean virility?"

"—that you brothers . . . ehh . . . yes, maybe that is it."

This was shaping into the most revealing set of words from a Japanese . . . let alone a sister. They were sometimes unabashedly gaga over us Yankee brothers. Our frequent photo ops went straight home to mom and dad and girlfriends. All polite smiles and red-faced embarrassment to us, but their letters were ribald.

My head was wagging. "Man, I thought you sisters—"

"Back home," she said through a sneaky grin, "we tell a different story to our 'outside' friend than to member."

Now I was a little red-faced myself. "Like what? You Japanese are so—"

She laughed big. " 'See the wild American men I with? Are not they hunk? Oh, my God, I wish I had one! Maybe I will!' "

"Dang." I had to pick up my jaw. It wasn't just her. Several others said they wrote home the same or similar. Japanese men must be annoyedly wondering how to keep Sachiko and Tomoko happy in the patriarchy now they'd seen gay Amerikay. "No wonder Boss Choi's always ranting about us."

"Yes, he hate you *men*. Is desperate to keep sister far away. Japanese leader very angry when he send member home for Chapter Two."

"A fate worse than death." I remembered Nanami.

We stared over the darkening waters from *Ocean Hope 3*'s foc's'le—we'd just snapped some photos home—soaking in Alaska's majesty.

"Is very beautiful here, neh?"

"Every church member should see it once. That's my motto."

"Please, no wrong idea, K'risu. Japanese sister are very Principle member." That grin again. "Usually. Fall is very bad, but . . ."

I studied her leaning on the rail, unsure where she was going with that. Not below to a bunk, if that's what you're thinking. We were happy doing brotherly photo ops and made sure to wear our guns (if we didn't, they'd ask) so friends and family got the point. *We're manly Americans. Don't fuck with us.*

This tension built hostility between our American and Japanese brothers. Inouye, the aforementioned roe supervisor, disliked me

Japanese photo op aboard OH 3, 1984.

on general principles, but I think he just didn't like me around Japanese sisters. In port, I was often bored and lonely. To relieve it I volunteered at the cannery, usually late at night when they processed salmon roe (*sujiko*, in Japanese). Isa made a fortune selling it in Japan. It might've been the one area that Boss Choi's malingering business sense hadn't constipated ISA's earnings. Agitators leisurely cycled round circular, 6×3-foot stainless steel vats, the roe in constant motion. We scooped it into plastic-lined $15 \times 12 \times 5$-inch wooden crates for shipping. Japanese sisters, supervised by brothers, did the work. It exhausted their mostly slight physiques. These brothers displayed what I took as disdain for them, never stooping to anything considered women's work and, according to my eyeballs, never helping sisters in any aspect of their duties. I was beneath contempt for empathizing.

These sisters seemed mostly middle class Japanese who'd joined the church in or after high school or college. They'd never done physical labor outside housework or MFT in their life. Some were adept, but many seemed out of their league and pushing from duty. I always had a soft spot for Japanese sisters. In my early church years I was very attracted and hoped Rev. Moon Matched me with one if I struck out with a Korean. I was more than willing to do jobs they couldn't or didn't want to do. One was at the end of the production line, nailing hundreds of 22-lb crates closed and carting armfuls to pallets I'd forklift into refrigerated stacks.

They were grateful. I enjoyed being useful and appreciated for a change, and struck up friendships and happy conversation in mixed Japanese and English. I wasn't looking for side action, just familial company. For Inouye, I was American therefore a sinful, criminally minded interloper defaming Japanese men and deflowering their women. It was unfathomable any man would work late hours for women without pay except for an ulterior sort of remuneration.

As a shift supervisor he frequently marched up to argue, never failing to channel Mr. Uchiyama. "Get out! Go, now!"

"I don't work for you," I forcefully reminded him, "and I can help out my brothers and sisters if I want, so piss off."

I got away with that kind of insubordination because leaders like Boss Choi couldn't help operating their businesses like church centers. I think in their minds a churchy environment offered better employee control than a secular business model where members might mistakenly think they had some independence and rights. Our businesses rarely fired members and when they did he or she merely transferred missions. Throwing away able bodies except for absolutely, irredeemably (usually American) unPrincipled acts was too dumb even for them. After all of Papasan Choi's malignant condemnations, Boss Choi still took me onboard without any, "You better behave, or else." I gave him kudos for that. Running a business this way was good for us when we felt rebellious but a weak support for the bottom line which, in ISA's case, was growing plainly precarious. Accordingly, Inouye was powerless. Only Boss Choi could toss me out. But he wouldn't. I was improving efficiency thus the bottom line with no sisters shagged. Win-win.

Inouye's spats escalated till we eyeballed toe to toe, fists cocked and ready to fire. Five-ten, but I didn't see him packing any wallop. A supervising sister authoritatively calmed the situation. He stormed off like the petulant shit he was.

She said, "Maybe is better you try different hours to help out in *sujiko* room, when Inouye-*san* not here."

"That's your sage advice?" Which I took, by the way.

"Please. All sister appreciate your help."

REGARDLESS MY PERIODIC troubles with Boss Choi, Inouye, Jonathan, Frank, bureaucrats like *Tzo-chan*, and the church in general, I loved and adored its Alaskan iteration. But in 1985 ISA was in bloodcurdling financial straits, its red books more swiss-cheesed than *Ocean Hope 3* on the rocks. Rev. Moon was threatening to hold back his last subsidized nickel if it wasn't better run. It looked like another winter of fundraising discontent for the Japanese sisters. Par for our Moonie course.

Jonathan had early on promoted Jack, our crewmate and a sort-of friend—not in the least like Johnny—to first mate. Until then, we'd got along. It seems power often promotes personality over duty and Jack waxed arrogant, contemptuous of the lowly crewman, and a bit pompous and dictatorial. For example, one of our legally mandated jobs was washing down the hold with disinfectant after offloading fish. That meant shoveling tons of left over, half-melted, fish-stinking ice into bins to hoist over the side. It was onerous, muscle-wrenching toil we despised.

"It occurs to me," I said to Jonathan before Johnny jumped ship in Bumble Bay, "that it's a whole lot simpler if we shoot seawater over it through our fire hose till it melts, then just pump it over the side." *Without breaking a sweat*, I didn't say because we could do it on our butts sipping umbrella cokes and Jonathan didn't seem to consider that Principledly industrious.

"No, absolutely not. It won't work anyway and will take too long."

"Why would it take longer than shoveling? How about we just experiment? See how it goes? You never know till—"

"I don't want you doing it, period. Just shovel as usual. Have it all done by the time I get back."

Jack said, "Who's in charge?" Another way of saying, *I'm not shoveling, right?*

"You are. Make sure it's done like I said."

I traded eyes with Johnny—*since when did we need somebody in charge?*—and stared daggers into Jonathan's departing back.

Johnny shrugged. "May as well get started."

"Well, shit."

I trooped after him for picks and shovels. My idea was a good one. Jonathan callously shooting it down without even trying it on for size burnt my chaps because that closed-mindedness had so often cannonballed my good notions elsewhere. We resigned ourselves to more than a half day's arduous drudge. Sometimes shoveling ice seems awfully like breaking rocks on a chain gang, and this was one of those times. The formerly powdery snow was so hard from recurrent freezing and thawing that we needed pickaxes to break it up, watchful we didn't stab the fiberglassed deck. Instead of helping like he did as part of the crew, First Mate Jack Ass sternly babysat through the main hatch from the bridge deck with a Captain Ahab obsession for the great dirty-white shoveled ice. Then he disappeared into the boat's bowels.

Massaging my aching back I said, "You know what? To hell with this!" I marched up on deck, dragged out the hose gear, and plopped down with my legs hanging over the hatchway. Johnny climbed up to watch, clattering his shovel and pickaxe alongside. "Don't look so skeptical. This'll work."

"Jack'll tell Jonathan anyway and then he'll kick your ass."

"Nah, we'll have a nice clean hold in half the time."

I opened up the seawater and ran the hose an hour or so, watching in satisfaction as the pumps shot melted ice into the harbor.

Johnny said, "Pumps are loud enough to get Jack out here chewing your ass."

"Must've cranked up the TV or zonked out. Power makes you sleepy."

"Never knocks out Jonathan, ha ha!"

We wrapped up in two-ish hours, less than half the time to shovel and none of the aches and pains. The hold was spotless. It seems silly, but it took real guts to countermand Jonathan's order. This was the nature of the church. Leaders so thoroughly indoctrinated us with obedience to authority that doing our assigned tasks according to our own best judgment was a moral earthquake.

The fire hose incident made Jack our frenemy since, now detesticled, he'd sided with Jonathan. It was part of Johnny's tense quarrels with Jack that brought his running rebellion against Jonathan to a head in Bumble Bay the day he hopped *Mar Del Sud*'s rail. The following year Jack passed his Coast Guard captain's exam and took his master's license. I admired him for achieving part of my Coast Guard dream. He got permission to start his family with Masako and had a son.

He hadn't learned much as first mate and got even less seasoning. A few months into his captaincy in February 1989 Johnny phoned that he'd holed *Ocean Hope 2*'s engine room on Kodiak's jetty, flooded, then took out 85 feet of the fuel dock. He drowned his crew in March leaving shelter on the Peninsula to cross the Shelikof in a typhoon gusting 200 MPH stoking 65-foot seas. Reaching Kodiak means sailing abeam that weather (bow, to quartering, waves). They broached and capsized in a ruthless instant when he foolishly tried to come about for a rethink. Gone with nary a burp. Just a life ring, some flotsam, and an EPIRB blinking in the mad storm sending its stillborn *Help! I've sunk and can't float up!* to the Coast Guard.

I felt bad but could only shake my head at his novice mistake. I felt worse for bereft Masako and mailed her $50, which in my usual San Francisco penury was a near fortune. It was unusual when members died. We were young and invincible. His death shockwaved through our fishermen. I felt it talking to Hemi and instinctively the bottomless despair Masako had to be feeling with a newborn on the breast.

Jack had said, "When we first met, we had to share a hotel and no touching."

"That had to be stressful," I said, reflecting on my loneliness.

"Damn straight. I had to fake a bathroom break to relieve the tension."

I gaped. Belly laughed. "Shit! Oh, my God. That's faith, Jack. She deserves you." Whatever our later problems, I liked him and knew he saw Masako, as Johnny did Takako, his personal and providential *salvator*.

"She's the best thing in my life, Chris. I'm really looking forward to our family."

In Seattle Hemi said, "All he could think about was getting home to Masako and his new baby. Did you hear? Johnny said somebody talked to Tiger Park in spirit world. He saw Jack with Jesus and Heung Jin Nim."

"The welcoming committee, eh?" I laughed but not really. Took a beat. "Those fucking boats still aren't properly watertighted. Jack might've had a chance with actual compartments. I bet that new fiberglass 95-footer isn't, either."

"Bitch to Master Marine if you want. Nobody's gonna care. It's the industry." Breaths came heavy. "Man, Choi wanted me working on Jack's boat this winter."

"With your master's license? You'd be at each other's throats."

"I'd be fuckin' dead now, too, if I'd followed my central figure. I'm not going back, because they run the place like real jerks. I've had enough of their stupidity."

"Whoa." I blew my lips. "A real shame everybody's jumping ship over assholes. If you do get a boat, though, I'd be happy to crew with you."

"Right on, brother."

A few months later Jack came to Johnny in a dream. "What happened?"

"You're dead, that's what. How'd it happen?"

"We capsized. It all happened so fast, there was no time."

Johnny blew awake in terror having never dreamed the dead and immediately swore off alcohol. None of us were sure exactly how *Ocean Hope 2* went down till then. Our general suspicions seemed validated. After all, Jack coming to Johnny in a dream was the most natural thing in the world for a Unificationist. But it showed that despite what we learned in the church about spirit world plus Jack's ghost story, our hallowed Moonie place in it, and that medium's Tiger-Park tale, Jack was confused about his death and where he was. If we accepted it at face value, which I did, it seemed no one in spirit world, least of all God, had bothered to give Jack the score. That opened a few theological dilemmas I couldn't resolve.

Within a year, Johnny reported the church reBlessed Masako to *Green Hope*'s skipper, whose own Blessed wife had died in a car accident. This was the first time we were hearing about reBlessings. It caused a stir because it seemed to violate the notion the Blessing was eternal, one spouse forever. Rev. Moon partially explained it away as a "convenience Blessing" for human beings too weak and fallen to go through life without sex and companionship.

Well, *duh.*

Then he confused the issue deeming a child born to a reBlessing spiritually belongs to the husband, therefore his original wife. This terribly complicated things for me because, what about the parental love he holds up as one of the highest Godly natures? Was a child supposed to switch hearts in spirit world for another woman he or she never met during life on Earth? How was the reBlessed birth mother supposed to let her child go to the previous wife? If we live for eternity in spirit world, the reBlessing concept could only create chaos and anguish in people's hearts who'd spent half a lifetime or more with a second spouse. This was only the beginning of many years of his redefinitions that plunged us into turmoil.

By late September 1985, with practically no money in my pocket on account of sharecropping Boss Choi's fertile swells, I begged off one last halibut trip—wouldn't have got a penny more for working it—and Scooby-Dooed for City College.

Act VIII

Back to School
Persecuted by Moonies and Their Enemies, Too

*B*y the mid-1980s, America's Unification Church was weathering 1SA levels of stress throughout its many organizations. After the Madison Square Garden and Seoul Blessings in 1982, American members voted discontent with their feet. Thousands upon thousands vanished into the night like wise rats fleeing billowing bilgewaters. Leaders encouraged us to see this as America's failure, our capitulation to Satan's invasion in our lives because, as Rev. Moon ever notes, Satan only invades when a person makes a condition, a common base, for it. Some of us figured our leaders' unPrincipled conduct was more certainly hanging out the red lantern for his unwelcome arrival than us.

The US Government had put Rev. Moon in a time-out at Danbury's federal pen for tax evasion in 1984. This unfortunate event stemmed indirectly from the witch hunt launched by Senator Donald Frazer in the late 1970s that was only a recently concluded saga when I joined in early 1981. Rev. Moon remarked to members that we mustn't give in to anger and resentment aimed at Frazer for his douchebaggery toward him and our church, and especially that we need maintain a humble attitude. Apparently, we didn't get the message. He accused members of fulminating with arrogance and vindictiveness for our persecutors that reanimated the government's investigation (barely interred after Frazer's 1978 primary loss) out of its political grave to fang Rev. Moon with a 1981 indictment for tax evasion.

As Mr. Kamiyama—a discount roomie in his spiritual mentor's cell—related to me some years later, "The whole problem began with arrogant members making spiritual conditions for Satan to invade and attack True Parents."

"You're saying *we* attacked True Parents?" I didn't like where this was going.

He bobbed and wagged all at once, quite an accomplishment. "Many faithless members opened the door to make it possible. That is the direct cause of government members making a base with Satan that put them on the path to attack Father."

Jive talk. Nanami dialed me in February 1986. "Father's speech just telex into Japanese Office. He say Americans were Abel and Japanese Cain when they first came here. I am so surprise. Also, they are not problem: he went jail most because we Japanese *completely* mess up American church, destroying it." *Wow.* I'd been condemned for thinking it. Now *he'd* said it in a smothered speech.

I said to Mr. Kamiyama, "But they obviously found real tax issues. Right?"

He waved hands. "No, no, no. That is only a distraction. Father did nothing wrong with money. If anything, we did."

"You? What do you mean?"

"Never mind that. The problem is that Father was innocent of their accusations. He suffered Satan's blow through faithless members and satanic prosecutors digging into his situation for a hook, some way to grab him. They had to make it all up."

Danbury. L–R: *Moon ("I am here because of the providence of God. I don't have any enemies. I only feel thankful."), Kamiyama, Pak.*

Fresh off the boat, Rev. Moon had yet to incorporate the Unification Church. He'd banked monies in a personal account under his name. "We did not consider tax issues because it was not Father's personal money. It was public money. Church money. Father used it, of course. But for us, it was not Father's own money."

"I get it. He's the founder and CEO of our church."

"Yes. The Unification Church is *his* church."

"It's only natural he'd have access to his own organization's funds."

"The government said that was all a lie. It was personal income, like a salary, so he must pay." Echoing Colonel Pak: "They were conniving and unscrupulous."

"Did he even get a salary? Or just buy whatever out of the public fund?"

"No, no, the church provided a salary for him to personally use. About $20,000 per year, at the time, to support True Mother and True Children."

Mrs. Moon had recently achieved 12-child status around the time I'd joined. None of us knew about his illegitimate children. We assumed he was supporting only those with her plus from his two previous marriages, of which we did belatedly hear albeit knew practically nothing. He was tightlipped of his pre-1960 life.

"In 1972, right?" He nodded. "Well, twenty grand a year seems pretty reasonable to me . . ."—I'm earning only 20,000 inflation-adjusted dollars less in 2003—"a bit on the low side, even."

"Yes, Father never takes public money for private use. He is very scrupulous."

"The government didn't think so. They said a personal account meant personal money. And he didn't pay the tax." A mortal sin for Internal Revenue priests.

"Only $7,500 of owed tax, they said."

I whistled. "And they spent over $3 million prosecuting him for *that*?"

"Even IRS' own rules don't allow prosecution if it costs more than what is owed. They did anyway. Therefore, it is Satan's attack, not simple law issue."

The case glaciated through the system. Leaders harangued our prayers morning, noon, and night for the investigation to exonerate him. We had names of the judge, investigators, supervisors, lawyers . . . praying for each "to do the right thing." Then in a mind-blowing, gut-bursting bombshell of a charge, investigators discovered the church had fabricated evidence—so infuriated, Mr. Kamiyama recounted, they immediately filed charges that slam-banged the whole thing into court.

Pressing for what evidence the Royal We had fabricated, Julian at last said in my fourth year, "Don't spread it around. We don't need any more drama."

"I promise. My lips are sealed. It's just between you and me."

He sighed long and hard. Words seemed to catch in his throat. "Okay. So, Mr. Kamiyama told me that he and some top leaders created accounting ledgers and post-dated them to make it clear the money was exclusively church funds."

I fell back in my chair. My voice rose. "What? I mean, he—?"

"*Shhh!* You want to know or not? The government already knows, obviously, but this isn't for public church consumption."

"Okay, okay. Sorry. I'm good. But, come on, they faked the books? And thought they'd get away with it?"

Julian snickered a head shake. "Japanese leaders in the seventies had only a perfunctory awareness of American accounting rules, and anyhow were pretty lackadaisical about it. They operate under very different rules in Japan."

I sagely nodded like I had some inkling of it. In my fourth year, I knew a lot about a little. "They figured they weren't doing anything bad much less illegal?" Julian shrugged at that. "Just righting a wrong, then?"

"That's about it. They thought the government would see Father wasn't personally liable for income tax on church money passing through his bank account."

"Umm . . . that seems pretty stupid even to me, young and *immature* as I am." He ignored my still-smarting dig. We took a beat. Some version of good stories out of bad decisions ran through my thoughts. "So . . . how'd they figure it out?"

"For whatever reason—maybe some member talked; I don't know—somebody was skeptical of their authenticity. The FBI chemically tested the paper." Stunning even Moonies enured to leaders' bollixing stupidities, the FBI found the paper was newer than the dates written on it. "They were absolutely furious the church lied to them and slavered after revenge. And here we are."

They dupe and *that's* legal. "What a marvelous mess." My voice had a laugh to it, but still. "I can't believe it. These freakin' leaders!"

His expression was grave and altogether unamused. "For once, I agree with you. Mr. Kamiyama put Father right in their sights." He twiddled his fingers a minute. Slumped in his chair. "He said they sincerely believed that, since Father was in truth innocent of the accusations, God would protect them—"

"From the harm that might come out of their brazenly illegal—*immoral*—act?"

"Exactly. To the tee. Mr. Kamiyama said they were absolutely confident when they forged the ledgers. 'No problem,' " he imitated the Japanese accent.

What a fantastically cuckoo and witless rationale. Even so, this mentality was epidemic in the '70s and '80s because it often, if not routinely, worked so well in corrupt Japan and maybe Korea. The same mindset lay behind 'heavenly deception,' mainly West Coast leaders taking the position that since Satan deceived Adam and Eve to steal God's creation, His champions were justified deceiving the Satanic world to take it back. It justified lying to Americans about to whom and what their money was going to get more of it easier, but threw Rev. Moon under the bus. When it made the newspapers, the national church had egg on its face but Rev. Moon a neck-deep shitstorm with legs. Despite his orders to cease and desist, it sporadically marched on several more years under tone-deaf, low- and mid-level leaders.

Well, God didn't protect Rev. Moon nor Mr. Kamiyama from the revenge of the Justice Department. Regardless our months of fervent prayer (in near total ignorance of the moral and legal realities in play) that Judge Goettel would come to his senses and dismiss the government's cockeyed case or find him not guilty, he sentenced both to white-collar time at Danbury prison.

～

IN JANUARY 1985, some months after my first season in Kodiak when I'd rented the dining room from that batshit New Yorker and his emaciated Chinese girlfriend on 19th Avenue, I was back at City College struggling to achieve Jerome's level of education. My abuse at Papasan Choi's hands burned fresh in my mind. Two weeks before leaving Judah Street in 1984 I'd resolved to get justice from Rev. Moon. I thought it was possible he'd get a letter. Had to try. Yet, no reply to what I considered shocking revelations. I'd kicked off a weekly then daily letter campaign.

I started with a sweeping explanation of Judah Street's situation in typewriter English. A 7-page update went out on May 15. When I segued to Alaska, I switched to writing weekly in Korean. By January I was writing a short Korean missive every day. He'd called on members in December to write their experiences to him by January 31, yet no response to mine had landed.

"If you don't respond," I finally wrote, "I plan to come out to Danbury and sit down in front of the gate for a hunger fast until you address my complaint." Still no response. I included a self-addressed stamped envelope to thwart his last excuse. It was this last-ditch effort that got me results, though not from Rev. Moon.

A stern memo from the prison authorities informed me they didn't permit self-addressed stamped envelopes in prison correspondence. They called him on the carpet over who was sending him these mysterious daily messages in Korean and what the contents were. I guess he was forced to explain I was some lunatic follower who wouldn't leave him alone. He needed to find a way to shut me up because now I was causing him more trouble with the warden than he was himself.

In my shitbox of a room, the phone rang. On the other end was Peter Kim, a top Peter-to-Jesus Korean leader whom Rev. Moon had unofficially adopted. He introduced himself. "Is this Chris? Are you sending True Father so many letters?"

"Yes, that's me. Indeed I am."

My first letter to Rev. Moon, 8pp.
May 1, 1984.

"Well, uh, why are you writing these letters?"

"I want Father to know what's going on in his own church. And I want justice."

"Justice? For what?"

"For what Mr. Choi did. He orchestrated violence against members and when I complained, he threatened me with it, too. He kicked me out of the church."

"What do you expect Father to do?"

Huh? That stumped me. All these months demanding this or that action and now I couldn't think of a thing. But anyway, what was he saying? Wasn't what I expected self-evident? "I want him to put a stop to Mr. Choi's abuse. And I want him to give me a mission because, now I'm kicked out, I don't have one."

"I don't think Father can just tell Papasan what to do . . ." *Who's fucking church is this?* Peter was dissembling. The phone hissed in my ear. He was maybe working out a prevarication although I wasn't convinced. "What are you doing now?"

"I'm going back to college, trying to finish my education."

"What are you studying?"

"Well . . . I'd like to get a degree in Asian history and language. You know, I've been teaching myself Korean for a while, now."

He chuckled "Yes. Father is impressed that you write so much Korean." *Really? Cool.* "Father appreciates you writing in Korean, but even though it is very good, it is a little difficult to understand."

That surprised me. I felt I was doing a good job even if my grammar was atrocious. I've read some awful English by Japanese . . . eh, I guess he'd have a hard time with it. I was dedicated, though. I wrote in vertical lines right to left on traditional writing paper just like Koreans. It was fun. I felt not only proud of myself doing it, but accomplished. Me, communicating in a foreign language. It was awesome.

"Father appreciates your Korean effort, but asked me to ask you to please send him a detailed explanation of your problem . . . in English."

Now I chuckled. Couldn't help it. *Reckon he's not all that impressed after all.* "Okay, then. I'll do that. Right away. I shall explain everything." *Again.* "Then what?"

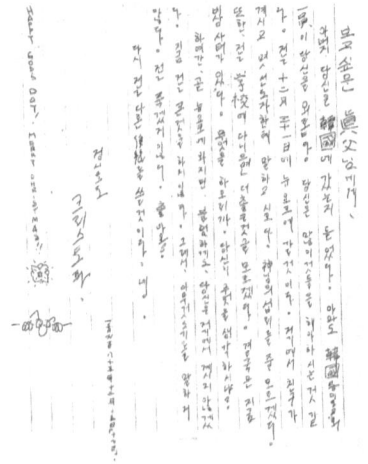

Weekly Korean, 1p. Dec. 15, 1985.

"Father will read it and he will make some determination about the situation. Papasan is a long-time church member. Father has trusted him very much."

I saw where this was leading. I was about to get a Durst Dismissal. Old Papasan would get a slap on the wrist, if that, and I'd be left out in the cold. A 'problem member' forever best forgotten.

"What about me, though? What should I do?"

"Father says you should do what you are doing now."

"Just go to college?" I was incredulous. I had to wonder if Rev. Moon really thought that far ahead into this conversation or if Peter was making it up as he went.

Probably the latter. Sigh. I didn't want to make my own decisions. Shit. The church had taught me several years by now only to obey, to not take initiative. I'd sucked at it, sure. But Rev. Moon was my general. I needed orders. I couldn't just self-deploy. "What about my mission, Peter? What about working with the church? I'm *persona non grata* around here! Nobody wants me."

"You should continue with your schooling."

I paced on my phone's short leash. "But I want to continue working with Father and the church! I don't want to just go off and do my own thing."

Thou doth protest too much, I felt Peter thinking. "Father wants you to continue what you're doing now. Don't worry. God will guide you."

Like he'd guided me right out of the church? to Mrs. Sato? into ISA and the arms of another lunatic Korean with the same bleeding name? Scraggily related, for all I knew. Anyway, top leaders were all very chummy; clubby. Members everywhere pre-knew me as if robed in atomic scarlet shame, the 'problem member' who'd confronted venerable Papasan. Unless Rev. Moon cleared me, praised my opposing Papasan's megalomania and violence, named me a Hero of the Unification Church, I'd be mud forever.

Cursed with a conscience and a deep, abiding respect for Christianity's two millennia of tradition and Divine Principle's call to a higher way, I'd finally spoken out against his corruption of Christian and Unificationist principles. I'd censured his slyly Marxist philosophy championing "restorative violence." Mocked his belief *he* was the true Messiah. That I owed *only him* total allegiance and Rev. Moon nothing or next to it. Exposed President Durst's corrupt refusal to uphold the dignity of True Parents and the integrity of the church over his mentor, Papasan.

Fuck me! Why did my parents have to fill me up with a conscience? Why couldn't I go along to get along in time-honored common sense? I saw the corporate types, the brownnosers, the institutional men and despised them. They invested their energy not in people, personal growth and development, nor God's providence of Restoration but in career enhancement, in power and control. And succeeded.

Goddammit! The Unification Church wields so much moral authority over me. Rev. Moon: the Son of God. His top leaders: Sun Kings. The Japanese: humanity's Mother Race. Koreans: the best thing since *before* sliced bread. Americans were shit and we knew it. Felt it. The spike hammered deep every day. Our conscience was suspect. Our morals and motivations crass. Our sexual nature contemptibly corrupt. Our societies, philosophies, religion, and politics all tools of the Devil fit only for consignment to the fiery pit. Nothing American was good. World trailer trash . . . though not *black* in a light brown Asian world. There was that.

Hell, Mr. Kobayashi took all our Japanese down to San Francisco's Castro District every Halloween night when the looniest gays burst forth in their craziest, almost illegal getups for a massive block party. The men of the West Coast's queer capital

Dear Father
care of Peter Kim,   San Francisco
                                                    March 10, 1985

Thank you for finally responding to my plethora of letters! I'm very sorry to have caused such a furor with the prison officials, and I hope no one is angry with you on my account. Now, I sent two letters to you way back in June, 1984, so, what happened to them? I assumed you never received them, though I could be wrong about that, and that's why I am now so determined to get your attention. Where do my letters go? I can't wait any longer, so please don't be offended by my pressing you so much. I am enclosing the original two letters, plus my resignation to Mr. Choi. Though they may perhaps be a bit emotional, I believe they are still essentially correct.

Father, let me first clearly explain that I am not writing to you in hopes of revenge against Mr. Choi, or for any other injustice I've suffered in this "church." Rather, to know my standing from you is my desire; to be vindicated(or not) by you, even privately, is enough, because I don't need the approval of church members for my life. What I DO need is to know whether or not my philosophy, my nature, my understandings, while obviously not perfect, are in the general direction of goodness and usefulness to God. I need to know what's true, and what's not. You're my only source, Father.

After all, Mr. Choi is your problem, not mine, except insofar as he causes, or his methods cause, my country to fail in its mission by forcing people to reject Principle because they see such a repulsive representation of it. I consider the events at Judah St. Church to be quite indicative of our movement as a whole, and that's why I took such exception to them. Chastising Mr. Choi is rather pointless without taking greater action. He is, after all, a product of his environment, among other things. Why is our church like a communist country, with such ruthless extermination of dissent, or even of simple questioning? Why do leaders wield such power to destroy the lives of others, and why is these abuses remain so consistently unchecked? I initially liked Mr. Choi a lot, but I cannot and will not support such unethical behaviour; and it is these methods, not any one person, which I loathe. I want to be very clear on this.

Obviously, you may do whatever you like about this problem. Given the history of our church, I certainly don't expect anything to change. However, all my suffering has made me "strong," and I no longer will accept these "leaders" telling me right from wrong - I know perfectly well. I have a brain;

Via Peter, 4pp. Mar. 10, 1985.

paraded in every manner of disgustingly wacky and perverse costumes from all-but-naked g-strings-and-a-thimble to full drag. Kissing, tonguing, groping in plain view. Proving in all their glory to staid Japanese the hopelessly depraved corruption that was Western 'Christian' society. They were all atittle for weeks afterward, reminding us of our impure heritage, barbarian culture, and satanic society. It was enough to make one puke onto both sides of the story.

I'd directly reaped this whirlwind from the East. I'd stood tall and flagrantly called Papasan and his cheap, anti-Christian hokum corrupt. Condemned his pompous mien as unPrincipled, destructive to True Parents' ministry and our lives. *Yelled* at him. Thumped my fist right next to his imitating his authoritative power. In short, cut my own throat. Turds like Papasan appreciated the gesture. Peter's message was: relax and bleed out. "Sorry," was his unspoken admonishment. "You

Handwritten English to Rev. Moon. My NYC events, 3pp. Jan. 12, 1986.

shouldn't have challenged the sacred cow. You shouldn't have held your Christian values over and above your sanctified leader. *You shouldn't have acted on your own conscience without permission!"*

"So . . . just keep going to school?" I said in defeat.

"Yes. Father will decide if something should be done. The best thing you can do now is finish your education. Father needs Americans with college degrees, too."

But does he want *us.* "Okay . . ." tenor and tone soft, "if Father says so." What else was I to do? I'd finish school but wanted to pitch in to his ministry as well. It seemed I'd have to figure out that path on my own. I didn't expect much from him—a harsh letdown, but there it was; *is this how Jerome got his college mission?*—but there was always hope. Aye, sometimes I lived on nothing more than its dregs.

"Yes, that's what Father says. You can do it."

"Okay, then . . ." He rang off. I worried my dog-bone future.

A power struggle amongst our top leaders followed Rev. Moon's incarceration. To counteract it, he'd declared Mrs. Moon a co-founder of the church in successfully completing her 21-year course of indemnity since their 1960 Blessing. But, it was outrageous a woman controlled the church and gave orders to Korean Adams. Something had to be done. A clique led by Colonel Pak—that fiery acolyte who'd vociferously testified to Rev. Moon's righteousness, excoriated the Frazer Committee's religiously motivated persecution, pledged his life to defend and support his spiritual master and mission—attempted to seize control. Since Rev. Moon wasn't dead but only in prison it fizzled fast enough although, for many months, conflicting orders issued out of national headquarters as members loyal to one side or the other disseminated their own directions to the field.

Mrs. Moon was only Rev. Moon's proxy. Quashing her authority was futile. *Wait until the man's dead. That's the obvious play.* But it was typical of our big-ego Koreans, many of whom secretly chafed even under Rev. Moon's messianic authority. One has to wonder the carnage they'll wreak lighting off a free-for-all power grab when he wings up to heaven. Billions in people and money ride on the outcome. Inevitably, I expect the Unification Church to splinter into factions. I see (in 2003) three main schools of thought, each seeking to reconcile Rev. Moon's charismatic authority as Messiah with the core truth of Divine Principle, the Christian tradition (conscience), and institutionalism.

One school sees the True (Moon) Family as the fount of all authority and truth. They're prepared to ignore the Christian tradition and even Divine Principle as necessary. True Parents' words are the embodied voice of God to be obeyed first and foremost above all else regardless contradiction.

A second faction views Divine Principle as the ultimate Completed Testament authority. They're prepared to ignore True Family if it contradicts the Principle's core teaching and to greater or lesser degrees Rev. Moon's speeches explicating it. While all members accept the Principle as the Completed Testament, only this faction is comfortable ignoring—perhaps denouncing—Rev. Moon, his words, much less his children if they violate or teach against the written Principle as they interpret it. Rev. Moon has, on occasion, championed this view.

A third camp views Rev. Moon, True Family, and Divine Principle as God's latest and greatest revelation to Christianity's 2,000-year tradition. While accepting him in the role of Messiah and the Principle in the role of conscience, they categorically deny any unearned role to his children. To be taken seriously, True Children need walk a start-from-nothing course of indemnity similar to their father's and earn the respect and loyalty of church members.

These factions provide a glimpse of the chaos to come when Rev. Moon finally buys the farm and the issue of spiritual let alone operational authority is contested. Succession and theological conundrums tore apart Christianity and Islam and, over a millennia later, bakes fratricidal hostilities to a crisp. All claims of greater righteousness to the contrary, the Unification Church will undoubtedly walk a similar path . . . if it even survives Rev. and Mrs. Moons' glorious ascensions.

I'D RUN INTO Jerome after hitting town in fall 1984 after my first season in Alaska. He was still at San Francisco State University. We began hatching big plans to pursue our dream of teaching the Principle and working personally with Rev. Moon.

He said, "I was ordained at nineteen in a storefront Baptist church in New York. You're born to the ministry, Chris. Like me. You should follow that path."

"I can be ordained just like that? I didn't even know that was possible."

"You're thinking like a Catholic. Any Baptist pastor has the authority to ordain ministers. And I know just the man for it."

"I don't know, Jerome." It sounded dodgy. "How is a degree not necessary?"

"Does a man need a degree to respond to God? Speak the Word? To preach?"

"I guess not." He made sense and it sounded alright. It was along my path anyway. In winter 1985 he taxied me in his shabby, outdated sedan over to Rev. Dr. Eddie Welbon's Sunday service. He pastored Pleasant Hills Missionary Baptist Church in a black–Hispanic neighborhood. Jerome worked hand in glove with him. Service over, he introduced me all around. We three clustered in the pews.

"Rev. Welbon, this brother Chris has the spirit. He's called by God to preach and I testify to that. He's wondering if you'll ordain him."

Dr. Welbon scrutinized me through dark eyes. In his fitted grey, three-piece suit over white shirt and loud striped tie, he had the look of a Saturday morning car salesman more than a pastor and preached like a smacked-up televangelist. My smarm alarm was *screeing*. I found him affable enough, so I hit snooze on that.

"So . . . you want to preach? You think you have the gift?"

The heck is a gift? This was Jerome's world. I was a prim Catholic howsoever sheathed in revelatory Moonism. "Yes, sir. I feel God is calling me to a teaching mission. Jerome agrees my ordination is an important qualification."

"Hmm, uh-huh, yes, I see . . ."

"What do you think, Rev. Welbon?" Jerome said.

He wasn't charging for it and quizzed me on the Bible and faith an hour or so upstairs over lunch for evidence I was legitimately experiencing a call to ministry. I was; no doubt. That's why I'd been a sucker for my spiritual mother Ginny's pick-up line that early '81 evening at a Denver 7-Eleven baited with, "It's for a Christian group." I felt dedicated to helping create a harmoniously loving world which meant dealing with the problem of sin. What other way than religion's? living and teaching the values of sacrificial love and unselfish devotion I'd learned from Jesus and now Rev. Moon? I knew I had a strong affinity for the ministry when I found myself devoting near on five years as a Catholic altar boy in elementary school. I 'said' every Mass every Sunday. Body shivered and knees quivered 'neath my black-and-white cassock the first time I stepped to the front of the altar as a living lectern for the priest to read his 20-lb Catholic Bible to our hundreds of faithful. Despite a banging heart and dizzyingly tight chest, I reveled in my newfound right-hand role.

My grandmothers naturally dreamed of me living the priesthood. A good Irish Catholic family should produce at least one priest out of six children. I was the only one who seemed interested. And I was. But even as young as ten, I knew I wanted to marry and even whom: the alluring Kimberly, my 1960's neighbor up the street in Bowie, Maryland. My friends dared me to kiss her on a hot walk home from the swimming pool. I laid a fast smack on her lips and she blew up with embarrassment. I was certain I wanted to marry her and felt no shame, only flustered in front of my friends on a dare. She agreed to marry at twenty. Alas, her family moved to Australia not long after and I was left holding an empty, broken heart. I briefly tried reinvigorating our relationship during my lonely Coast Guard years after tracking her down to the Appalachians where she worked as a veterinarian. She was divorced but had a boyfriend. *Sigh.* No, the celibate life wasn't for me. If the Church allowed married priests, I daresay I'd be causing my Red Chief brand of trouble for the pope instead of Rev. Moon.

"The Vatican is where you'd have ended up for special study and higher office," Mom said over one of my visits. "And I'm sure much happier than you are now."

"Sounds good on paper, Mom, but the church and service taught me I'm no company man. I'm pretty sure the Vatican lives and breathes obedience."

"You're more conformist than you think. You'd have done fine."

"Pshaw! Come on. I'm an out-of-the-box thinker. A status-quo challenger. I hate authority's undeserved perks. I thrive on developing new understandings of old beliefs and helping *people*, not . . . whatever."

"You might be overselling yourself, Chris. I think—"

"Why do you think I'm always in trouble with those fossilized Moonie leaders? I'm pretty sure I'd have stepped into the same cowflop in the Vatican or wherever I ended up . . . probably wouldn't be so quick to throw me out the door, though."

"You might've done better than you think. They'd have found you something like they always have with troublesome priests in the university."

"Ha ha ha. My 'special talents.' Some remote diocese, maybe, where I'd die of boredom. It's true my church doesn't care how remote a center is, though. The disobedient are unPrincipled therefore a threat." A satanic dagger hiding in the folds of membership aimed at Rev. Moon's heart. That's all it takes to warrant me cast to hell's cold fires. "But honestly, Mom, I don't see Catholicism much different."

She tut-tutted, chopping vegetables. Her face said I might've overstepped a little with that comment. "Your father and I think you shouldn't have anything to do with them. We feel you'll be much happier back in the Catholic Church."

"Yeah . . ." That was two lifeless steps back. "Nah."

Lunch over, Dr. Welbon accepted my spiritual *bona fides*. "As Jerome told you, our conference and my license permits me to ordain without seminary training."

He laid out a 6-month regimen of instruction and a preaching practicum in his church, interrupted by my second season in Alaska. He and senior clergy of the Bay Area's National Baptist Convention endorsed my certificate of ordination and certificate of license to preach in December 1985.

"It's pretty hilarious," I said to Jerome, pointing with a laugh. "Look here, one of these pastors is named Jesse James."

Professionalizing at last.

"Don't disrespect these people, Chris. You stand in a unique position now."

"How so? I'm just the newest dime-a-dollar preacher." He shook his head. "Okay, what?"

"Rev. Welbon said he thinks you're the first, or one of the first, whites ever ordained into the black church. It's a historical condition for black–white Restoration. It'll go over big with True Father."

"Is that why you brought me to Dr. Welbon?"

"We're historical figures, Chris. You have to change your attitude and start thinking that way. Nothing we do is unimportant in God's providence. Ordained by Rev. Welbon is critical to our mission."

I dug into his eyes and decided that's exactly why he set me up with Dr. Welbon. No one at Pleasant Hills knew for sure if I was their only white ordination but unquestionably treated me with that kind of respect and admiration. On the other hand, many (*religious*) whites and even blacks were ambivalent and sometimes downright hostile. Dad certainly thought my studies and ordination were worthless. He barked when I visited, "That was in a nigger Baptist church!" after which he froze in Liberal shock at his blurtation. I was a real crossover. Hated for it, often enough. Absurdly typical. But, right now, I was a full-fledged minister. *Hot. Damn!*

Besides any church recognizing my preachability, I was *Reverend* McKeon. My psyche buzzed. After my flopperoo in the Unification Church I'd now accomplished something! My first achievement since graduating boot camp. And, yet, convincing Moonies I could preach, let alone something worthwhile, proved to be Sisyphean. Christians took the integrity and competency intrinsic of my title and praised my sermons. Satisfaction's relaxing warmth in touching lives saturated me body and mind. I especially felt I was giving a service to the nation when blacks praised my frank honesty over the differences and conflicts twixt our races while knitting together a compelling (Divine Principle) vision transcending it.

I longed to carry my soulful heart to Unificationists languishing moribund. I reflected on the value of Rev. Moon's life-changing vision, amazing understanding of God's nature, purpose of life, root of human sin, God's Restorational history, and compelling vision for a unified, happy humanity. Our church was an inspiration for Christianity, not its enemy. It didn't deserve to die the death its leaders were riding it hell for leather into. With so much to say and offer, I oft-compared myself to Jesus weeping over stiff-necked, arrogant Jews seeing no value in him at all.

> O Jerusalem, Jerusalem, you who kill the prophets and stone those sent to you, how often I have longed to gather your children together, as a hen gathers her chicks under her wings, but you would not. Look, your house is left to you desolate. (Matt. 23:37)

By 1985 the church *was* desolate, a boozy hemophiliac hemorrhaging members. I had something to offer yet it rejected me on account of my unconventionality, my willingness to disagree with leaders, my out-of-the-box thinking. I didn't know how to subvert my basic nature to win its approval and wasn't sure I even wanted to. But I wanted its acceptance to participate. To contribute to Rev. Moon's vision and ministry. Be recognized as a person of value and worth however imperfect and prone to error. Loved by the people, church, and vision I loved.

I got none of it and turned to my Christian roots. Catholic up the backbone, I took a Baptist ordination because I saw no future in Catholicism over and above pew warming . . . ironically, my Moonie future. Still, Rev. Moon and his vision drew me. I couldn't shake it, couldn't live without it. My sense of global vision and desire to live for the sake of the world firmly rooted in him. One foot in the Christian church and the other in Unificationism generated constant flux and tension, never happy in the one nor accepted in the other. A dynamic of doom.

When talk of another Blessing came up, I wrote to Boss Choi in Alaska. "Will you recommend me to the Blessing Committee?" I also mentioned my ordination and how it inspired me.

He wrote back, "I won't recommend you since you're not at this moment working for ISA," and anyway I was too arrogant and uppity thinking my ordination would make any difference in my life or that anyone in the church would stoop low enough to respect it. "It is nothing more than a Christian title and has nothing to do with True Parents. You should not be so proud of it. Your pride is arrogance."

There's just no pleasing some people. But let me be a Christian pastor with a congregation and leaders would fête me day and night. For a new twist, I was feeling like the black man in the early '50s South slipping into an elevator arms loaded with packages. He's expected to remove his hat in deference to the whites around him but can't, so a white man silently takes off his hat and lightly drops it atop his load of packages. The black man wants to say *thank you* but can't, because that would imply the white man had done him a service. No white would so lower themself much less stand it insultingly implied. He can only stand with lowered eyes and the white man accepts his humility. *Go along to get along.*

That's the dynamic I felt going on with Boss Choi. His letter ignited a bonfire of determination deep inside. *Somehow, sometime,* I fumed, *I'll defeat these arrogant people by succeeding where they've only failed.* My passion raged fervent and furious for 15 years. In the meantime I was an ordained minister striving after my dream of a harmonious world centered around immutable spiritual principles.

PIVOTING IN LATE September 1985 from my second stint aboard *Ocean Hope 3* to the quiddities of higher education, I scared up a part-time job and jumped into the student government at City College (CCSF) with both feet. I met another albeit less unhinged New Yorker named Robert who never took no for an answer. We formed a new political party on campus called Action Party. He ran for president. I ran for council member. He lost. I won. The all-powerful Chinese Cultural Club (CCC) that turned out en masse every election to vote Chinese destroyed him.

When I ran for vice president then president, the same Chinese-American defeated me by calling on the CCC to flood the ballot box when I couldn't call on anybody— least of all whites, an electorally lazy and fickle bunch who split their votes into defeat when their candidates ran against the ethnic clubs. In my presidential run, Robert formed his own party and vainly ran against me in a 3-way as nothing but a spoiler. Many who'd have voted for me now voted for Robert while every single Chinese voted for my nemesis. I lost by seven votes and Robert by hundreds. *Fuckin' moron.*

Campus newspaper election coverage. May 1–12, 1986.

To combat the electoral power of clubs like the CCC, Black Cultural Club (BCC), and La Raza we requested student council permission to start a European Cultural Club—we'd have called it the White Cultural Club as an in-your-face counterpoint to the most aggressive ethnic clubs but knew they'd lynch us for it—to land the $50 club budget and a power base to motivate voters. In the rising bedlam of the council chambers, the ethnic racists running the Chinese, black, Hispanic, Vietnamese, African, and other ethnocentric ghettos shouted us down.

"*Racists!*" "*Imperialists!*" "*Fascists!*" "*White supremacists!*" "*Jingoists!*" et cetera *ad nauseam* were so many Molotovs hurled our way. And . . . *boom!* These violent, narrow-minded bigots posing as philosopher kings while using their clubs to brutally ethnize campus politics and club each other over age-old foreign grievances drowned us in a bucket. White was everybody's love-to-hate.

We'd really gamed it as an experiment to see what would happen. No whites would've joined anyhow because they were the most apathetic, self-loathing people on campus. You could hardly get them to vote at all never mind for anybody wearing their skin who'd only win if ethnically unopposed, despite the student council controlling $250,000 per year in student monies derived chiefly from its campus bookstore cut and taxes called fees levied on these selfsame indifferents. I want to say *fuckin' morons*, but that would be overusing it.

It's the same old shoe in our society then and now. Leftism-infected whites bend over backward to show how progressive and lovable they are by ostentatiously loathing their culture, history, color, and hard-fought personal accomplishments as a peccavi for racial sins, i.e., somebody else's history. And for what? Nonwhites revile them regardless. It's only tossing off the champagne with the cork.

This secular trend dominates the Unification Church. Few Americans defend our multi-ethnic culture, democracy, values, and Christian heritage because the Asians hatefully detesting Western, and above all American, culture as abusive, satanic, and corrupt vilify them. From the early '80s but more likely the mid-'70s, American members acquiesced in the face of hardcore Asian ethnocentrism and outright racism. Divine Principle's inherited Western and Christian values evaporated atop their hateplate with naught but totalitarianism and heathenism's dry grounds in its place. The church made itself into Ezekiel 37's spiritually dry-boned desert. That it must exsanguinate our American church was all but predestined.

CCSF's student council, within reason, controlled the campus police. Some years earlier there'd been big trouble in little Havana with gangs and drive-by shootings. The police instituted a series of campus rules for safety. One was frisking males albeit not females entering public events like dances. Their ostensible goal was excluding weapons but it didn't need a rocket scientist to realize your woman could tote your arsenal since the police philogynously pawed only their carry-on. I sponsored and organized a dance as a councilman, which paid all the costs. Entering the building its known sponsor, an elected official, and not meeting CCSF PD's gangbanger profile, the cops forced their near-cavity search on me regardless. Furious at their colossal affront to my dignity and liberty, I condemned the practice in open council and devised a plan that brought a vote prohibiting it.

Shortly thereafter the youthful, plus-sized police chief called me into his office for a conversation. "I'll accept the Council's recommendation if you keep your nose out of any more departmental affairs."

"Recommendation?" I snorted. "We voted the policy out. The Administration can't reverse that. Nor you. It's in our charter."

"That's—" I thought he might throw his coffee at me but proved he was a better man. "Listen here, our job is law and order on this campus. Students don't get to decide what that is."

"Well, I appreciate that, Chief. The Council isn't trying to interfere with your job. You just can't willy-nilly body search students at campus events any more without some probable cause. There hasn't been any gang violence or shootings here for years now, as I understand it. Regardless what's going on in the city."

Eyes scalpeled me to my inner communist. "Ain't how it works, young man."

"I'm going on 27 and a disabled veteran, Chief. What're you? Thirty? Forty?"

He leaned back. Made sure his shiny star sunk deep into my military pupils. "We'll see how it goes. The President ratified your vote, so . . ."

"Again, Chief, the President doesn't have a say. He's just being diplomatic."

"Is he."

"Well, yeah. He can't order you not to do your job, either. The position of the Council is, keep the peace but don't body search innocent-till-proven-guilty students anymore. That's all. Basic constitution. Right up your—"

"Okay. Get out."

"Yessir, Chief. And, thanks for your good work." Not like I hated cops. Just gropish pat-downs reminiscent of British colonial roadblocks.

"Don't make us meet again. And close the door."

That was a big moment despite my notoriety with the police. I felt *empowered*. I'd single-handedly changed a major policy affecting thousands of students. I went on to change, reform, and invent many other important aspects of the student government, from budget processes and financial management of clubs and academic groups to forging new relationships with the administration, prying the council out of the Dean of Students' despotic—kleptocratic, we thought—fingers, to rewriting major portions of the student government's constitution, writing a standard operations manual for it, and other things. All very exciting.

AS drafts new constitution; Special election planned

The Guardsman on my work.

For the first time I closely worked with gays. It was odd with my faith condemning homosexuality as opposite God's intention, thus only illicitly pleasurable. I was quite without humor for these practically alien 'guys.' An affront, they might say, to my dignity as a man. AIDS was painting hideous headlines. Only a couple years earlier San Francisco, awash in deaths, had herculeanly shut down potent gaydom's free-sex bath houses. My attitude was entirely negative owing to my unsettling mental image of anal sex and maybe the ruthless sexual harassment Castro District queers foisted on me selling Judah Street's roses (black, my bestseller).

How. Ever. I learned to work collegially with our one gay councilman. A Vietnam War medic now 43, he was the only one older than me. My biggest lesson from student government was that it's possible to work professionally, on good terms, with those I detest or live repugnant lifestyles. A reversed Ronald Reagan–Tip O'Neill: political enemies yet golf buddies. He tripped in his apartment and stabbed his temple on a coffee table corner, then improbably dropped dead a day after qualified doctors prophesied him fit and fettle.

I heard it in chambers. "What a ridiculous way to go after his tour in 'Nam."

"Seconded," somebody said.

I met Roxanne, a proud Jewish woman coming before council on some business. I scoped her five-nine, attractively blonde and shapely legged frame. The crow's feet developing around her eyes and mouth painted 'older woman,' maybe 32. Her bubbly personality shined pleasant through a coy smile. She instantly charmed.

Ostracized from the Bay Area Unification Church, I was on my own at school. I wanted to stay true to the Principle and celibacy for an increasingly improbable future Blessing, but was also feeling lonely and demoralized. After Boss Choi's casual rejection, I despaired any leader would ever recommend me. Hanging out on a white leather sofa at a fellow councilman's thronged posh house party one night, Roxanne scooted in next to me. Warm. Aromatic. We chatted amiably.

"Mind if I kiss you?"

I snorted my soda. "Kiss me! Really?" *This is one for the ages.*

"Yeah," she laughed, her big bright smile enveloping me. "You're not afraid of a little kiss, are you?"

"Umm . . ." *Kinda, yeah.* "Why would you want to kiss *me*?"

She snuggled in. I felt the life in her body. " 'Cause you're cute, dummy."

"Well . . . it seems innocuous enough. And pretty fun besides."

"Now you're thinking." She fell on my face. "Mmmm . . ."

The brush of her lips blasted my hormones into orbit. Spiritual resolve went right out the window into a dumpster, lid slamming down hard.

A slight hitch. Days before this party I'd somehow got involved with a Chinese-American cutie named Bernie who'd probably voted against me. Five-four, maybe five-five on tiptoes, she was pretty short but, playing for CCSF's volleyball team, was in tip-top condition—meaning sexy if a bit thick in the middle—with a round, oval face and booming smile. We were just friends, which is how I happened to be visiting her apartment. Her roommate was in her own bedroom with her boyfriend. We hung out on her living room sofa shooting shit and sipping sodas.

Then it seemed I was oozing up from a blackout drunk. The world filtered into my consciousness—hearing before seeing—and there I was on my back atop her sofa cushions now lined up on the cheap rental carpet as a makeshift bed, buck naked and Bernie in my saddle furiously spurring cowboy.

What the—? How'd I just go from couch to floor? Gabfest to sexfest? All these years and I still don't know. I have no memory whatsoever of the time between innocently conversing on the sofa to my sudden carnal awareness. *Maybe I'd revved up and forgot our hot hands?* My friends eventually wondered if she'd slipped me a Mickey. In the moment, however, I didn't know what had happened and other parts didn't care. I reached up for bodacious boobs.

The more I thought about it the more I realized that, in my whole life before and after, I couldn't recall a single moment I couldn't remember. The one exception was driving home under a clear, bright moon in 1976 on Colorado's North Turkey Creek Road when I found myself unexpectedly a mile farther down the twisting lane than I'd thought I was and no memory how. My watch showed no unusual time loss, so I figured aliens hadn't abducted me. Must've been daydreaming. Under Bernie, my mind was blank. A grey zone I couldn't pierce. And not only regarding unaccounted-travel like Colorado but our penetrating interactivity. It flummoxed me. Caught up in the moment, I set it aside for later.

Then with a sickening twist of despair she whispered, "*Unnhhh . . .* I didn't know a *minister* could do this!"

Oh, *shit.* Returning to base after making out with Roxanne, I backhanded myself to realize I was involved with one woman and now almost another. How would I explain myself to God much less the church? From a Divine Principle point of view, it wasn't safe to let me out of the basement. Not knowing what to do and too chickenshit to explain, I broke off Bernie's several-weeks with hardly a word. She was royally pissed. I ran into her a year later on campus and explained.

"I totally didn't mean to break your heart. Truly, I'm so, so sorry about that."

"Thanks, Chris. I really appreciate you finally telling me why."

"I'm . . . happy to see you again, anyhow." Good friends a year or so more.

I kept mum on her suspected Mickey Finn but, if she did date-rape me, my remorse hardly seemed appropriate. I just didn't know for sure. How could I accuse her? I let it go. No sense wracking my brains over what I couldn't even hazily recall, about which I had no way other than confrontation of discovering the truth.

"Just move on," I told myself. She'd been fun and no STDs turned up. I wasn't as devastated as a date-raped woman, maybe. But she'd shattered my faith and celibacy backing my protective ministerial bubble, which is why Roxanne's party dumpster might've yawned so wide for our innocuous kiss.

I SLEPT 1–3 hours a night fall 1985 through spring 1986. The main reason was my heavy responsibilities with and renovation of CCSF's student government. I chaired and reformed the important finance and constitution committees along with several others. Adding to this load was 18–21 credit hours of school work. It all kept me up well past midnight. My 4:30 AM alarm belled a shrill icepick in my eardrums every morning, seven days a week, to hustle me off to Holy Ground to pray.

In the mid-'60s Rev. Moon established a Holy Ground in every great city in each of the 50 states, a 6-week magnum opus crammed in a '65 Plymouth Fury station wagon. These grounds, sanctified through his founding prayer along with soil and stones packed in from Korea, are where our prayers more clearly penetrate the interference of Satan and spirit world so God hears them. Dedicated to the Principle despite my female foibles, I set hard spiritual conditions for myself. Besides my daily trek up to Holy Ground and periodic 3-day fasts, I conducted the 7-day granddaddy the church expected of all real members. It normally requires we do at least one weeklong fast to qualify for the Blessing. It's a touchstone for true membership. I hadn't yet done it when Papasan forced me out of Judah Street, so I did it on my own while proving my *bona fides* and value to church leaders.

I was then rooming at 1033 Ocean Avenue with Robert and Jerome over a Korean-owned deli/restaurant that often gave us free food. Those two got along like feral cats, particularly regarding Jerome's kitchen hygiene and Robert's unilateral art jobs on our rented walls. I slept on the floor of the streetside bay-windowed living room in my sleeping bag with my old army blanket friend for a pallet.

My individual efforts were a wasted exercise in church eyes. A 7-day fast not under its auspices wasn't considered a member fast. But it was real enough to me. I continued my normal routine: up at 4:30 AM for Holy Ground prayer, back down the mountain for my 8 AM class, all day at school and my job into evening, return home, do homework, write papers, and connive our church comeback with Jerome. By Day Three, I was desperately hungry and felt vitally weakened. On Day Four my body snapped back and I felt fine. Day Five, I easily chased the bus, traipsed through school, and handled my daily schedule and job as though eating. Day Seven, I broke my fast at midnight with a half-hour prayer and a bowl of steaming soup.

Fasting is a powerful spiritual condition. Secular people don't understand where the energy and power come from when you're denying your body food. If you're only starving you indeed lose strength; you're *involuntarily* going hungry to no purpose. All you think about is your cravings. When you fast, your mind isn't focused on food. You're aware of your hunger and your body covets food. But your mind is tightly focused on *voluntarily* going hungry for a spiritual purpose. I've starved for want of money and spiritual purposes. They're markedly different.

Starving consumed my stomach with a sensation of emptiness, burning, and pain. Legs and knees were weak, my body enervated. If I sat relaxed I fell instantly asleep from critically low blood sugar. Starving was a grueling hardship I weathered for several months a few years later at University of California at Berkeley. When fasting, my stomach burned painless a day or two. The first three days I got progressively weaker and fatigued, then burst forth with renewed zest. My days flew by. Maybe if you're looking at starvation you'd best start a spiritual fast before your food runs out. You'll endure the hunger better, improve your spiritual condition, and attract the good forces of the universe to help you.

In truth, I never would've fasted without the Unification Church training me in its value. I'd fasted once as a teenager to raise money for a youth center through my Catholic Church in Denver. But it was only 24 hours and anyway a crowded group effort. We spent it chewing gum, playing poker for pennies, and illegally smoking cigarettes in full view of our supervising priests. Moonies didn't fast for things but to pay indemnity toward spiritual development, spiritual conditions to advance God's providence through difficult periods, and relieving the suffering of others. I saw it in the best tradition of the Christian monks. My 7-day fast emboldened and enfranchised me as a *member* with every Moonie I encountered and to hell with their disparagement. *Oh, you didn't do a seven-day fast yet? I did.*

I wasn't Blessed—ever a black mark on my character and general holiness—but I'd *fasted*. Perhaps I waxed arrogant. But for all the heat church members were raining on me like poisonous frogs, I felt justified feeling proud of my no-support-group accomplishment in the face of all I was coping with.

When I began my Holy Ground condition, I had to take the bus. I was too poor for a car or even a bicycle. That meant walking the half mile to the bus stop, riding to the end of its route halfway up Twin Peaks, hiking its morning-dark trail to the paved road circling the twin mountaintop, then up the steep, rubble-strewn slope to the crest. A 2-shoe flat rock topped the peak. I stood atop

Twin Peaks. I parked along lower right guardrail, hiked up at left.

it and prayed no less than 40 minutes. I was quite the sight wearing an army field jacket under my Alaska foul-weathers in the colder, wetter months, my nifty yellow Sou'wester tied under my chin for protection against the cold, fierce winds and frequent lashing rains off a less-than-pacific ocean.

Sometimes, deep in prayer shouting into the winds of God, I'd feel the unusual presence of others. One morning, I realized the group I'd opened my eyes on clustered near my stone were Moonies. Despite knowing who I was—I recognized many of

229

them—their furtive glances told me they were afraid to acknowledge, socialize, or mingle let alone join me in prayer unless their leader did. Worse, they rarely invited me over, a pox to their God. Ignoring the *ex-*'problem member' was SOP. Dominating the mountaintop they saw as theirs yet ceding it to my satanic presence anyway, they circled off to one side to pray. One of my few Protestant victories over these Papist exclusionists. God had to be laughing through tears.

It was a clear indicator the church was spiritually sick, in mortal decline. I felt I had an important role revitalizing it and that wasn't just my ego talking. It was members reacting to my philosophy, my vision for the church, my heart for Rev. Moon and his messianic role. I keenly inspired some even as I alienated others, my words and deeds separating sheep from the goats. My prayer condition atop Twin Peaks' Holy Ground was my training period, my education. I was getting ready for God to call me back to His task. I couldn't falter.

Looking back, I can say it was to be or not to be. Certainly, powerful leaders opposed and sabotaged me at every turn. On the other hand, my own foibles stung and conflicted me and I felt I was my own worst enemy. Nevertheless, I ruthlessly held to my ultimate calling of restoring our church to its former spiritual verve, innocence, and sincerity. The Principle sees Jesus as his own worst enemy, too. From whuppin' moneychangers out of the Temple to his incendiary speeches to Jewish authorities, he made it practically impossible for his enemies to consider a change of heart and his friends to dismiss the danger. Since the Principle asserts he didn't come to die but to spend a long lifetime restoring the Fall, his attitude can only be seen as self-defeating. *At least I'm in good company shooting myself in the foot.*

But I didn't want that. I wanted the church to restore its vitality and relevance to Americans. For my countrymen to understand and appreciate the simplistic beauty of the Principle and its life altering message. The last thing I wanted was for the whole world to join our church. In short order we'd have a global theocracy ruled by Korean thugs through Japanese *yakuza.*

My mountain prayer gave me terrific spiritual energy to confront the difficulties and tribulations I endured with church and campus. School and fundamentalist Christians knew me as The Moonie to ostracize, criticize, mock, and humiliate. Opponents used my precarious church affiliation against me during student elections as well. It was a tribulation I had to surmount with a smile like Rev. Moon, on his way from court to Danbury prison, shaking the government lawyer's hand for his well-played prosecution. What else can a man of God do? Ranting at the stars or in their face doesn't change anyone's discrimination nor alleviate their hate. It would only make me look the lunatic cultist they took me for anyway. I adjusted. I didn't trumpet my Unificationism but never disclaimed it, either. In some psychologically tortured way, I might've enjoyed the notoriety.

Robert and I happily created vexation of our own for our foes. We achieved infamy provoking ethnic group apoplexy over our European Cultural Club. Then I was struck speechless walking into the campus clinic to a bulletin board eyeful right in front of the double glass entry doors. A letter-sized visual explanation for installing a condom replete with four black-and-white hard-knock woodies wrapped in variously unrolled condoms, with instructions and errata, unhinged my jaw.

Besides my Moonie pedigree, I was first and foremost a committed Christian and accordingly opposed to secularists promoting 'responsibly' condomized cocks. I preferred abstinence for stabilizing relationships, avoiding pregnancy, STDs, AIDS, and promiscuity's emotional destruction generally. People only encounter these troubles having sex, so just don't outside a committed relationship. It made no sense condemning promiscuity's destructive aftereffects while encouraging the unchaste with the illusion that 'safe sex' is profligately painless.

I yanked the flier down and flung it in my erstwhile partner's face. Robert was no kind of Christian but sputtered epithets at its stark dick pics. Condoms—campus gays called them 'seal-a-meals'—were just entering the public consciousness and most of us weren't used to clinical erotica. We brainstormed our concern into three sets of 500 open letters: "Condom-Mania" with the cock shots and our witticisms denounced the clinic's public porn. Over some weeks, we salted *The Guardian* in its vending boxes, bulletin boards, campus mailboxes, and so on.

The firestorm blindsided us. So many hollering, threatening, fulminating callers burned up President Ramirez' line that his secretary disconnected it mid-morning. Probably red-faced over distended neck veins, he pilloried our council president on his carpet. "I want to know who on your council did this! Get me their name!"

"But we don't know any—"

"Don't jerk me off, sonny," he growled. "If you want to stay in business, you'd better get to the bottom of this!"

"It's not us! It's not our fault."

Weird. Why would his first suspect be a council member? Was he clairvoyant? Word-chopping, stuttering, spitting readers deluged *The Guardian*'s switchboard. Its editor demanded the campus police investigate. The ruckus sure validated our position. If hard-ons and condoms were no big deal, why the fuss?

I strolled nonchalantly into council chambers early that first-salted afternoon. Inexplicably, hard eyes angled my way. "What?"

"You did it!" someone shouted.

Councilwoman Kim said, "Yeah, we all know you have a . . . shitty reputation."

"Nice job, Chris!"

Gay and Lesbian Alliance folks, who'd cleaned out all our initially salted papers, were sure of it but admitted, "Chris isn't anybody you want mad at you."

'We know you're a sly Moonie fucker! Exactly what you'd do."

"Hey, right on, man!"

"We're voting to put condom machines in the bathrooms. So, fuck you."

Not one of these bigot motherfuckers spewed pain-in-the-ass Robert's name. It was *hella* weird. I set my straightest face and blankest eyes. "So, what's all the commotion? Why are y'all mad at me? What'd I do now?"

Someone roughly shook the flier at me. "This! *This!*"

I feigned shock, indignation, then admiration. "Whoever did this," I crooned, "sure gets my vote. I totally agree with it!"

GALA's president said, "Is that a *man* saying that? Excuse me, you have a penis?"

"Am I talking to you? Ladies don't—"

"I'm no lady!" she shouted. "I'm a *woman*."

"Oh. Sorry I overstated your place in the world."

But now they weren't so sure. Friends and strangers accused or congratulated me for weeks. *The Guardian*'s boiling mad editor wanted the culprit(s) on a spit, claiming their property was vandalized. We didn't think so. It was free; abandoned in uncontrolled vending boxes, whose property was it then? All we did was stick an official campus communication with a few added comments into an official campus newspaper. At worst, it was unpaid advertising for CCSF's clinic. Then he offered me editorial space. But we'd made our point. Most agreed explicit, pornographic images had no public place on campus. Not even the clinic.

"If you can't read the instructions or figure it out in practice," I'd said to Robert, "you're not ready for sex anyhow."

He'd laughed. "I sure wasn't expecting an eyeball-flick fuckin' advertising it."

Unfortunately, Unification Church leaders in the Bay Area never appreciated my efforts to defend and legitimize God, Divine Principle, Rev. Moon's values, and the church on campus. I was effectively a one-man CARP center—Collegiate Association for the Research of Principles that Rev. Moon imported from Korea in 1973—but got no tolerance or respect from them, the church, or students. When CARP later tried establishing a campus presence, I was the lone councilman arguing for their inclusion against a tide of vitriol and discrimination. CARP had no thanks.

IN LATE DECEMBER 1985 a wildfire rumor had Mr. Kamiyama 'discovering' his evil ways bending and corrupting the American church to his personal preferences and bringing ruination to recruitment and retention. Knowing tongues breathlessly wagged he was conducting extemporaneous workshops with any member who cared to sit down with him. Encouraging them to vent their spleens for whatever he'd done personally or through his office. Folks said he was *apologizing!*

Incredible! Unprecedented! I told friends, "I *have* to be in on this!"

Nanami, whom Boss Choi exiled to New York City for falling in Alaska, offered to spring for half the roundtrip. I dropped everything. People Express was $99 coast-to-coast. Affordable (if I deferred rent) even for me. A steward quaintly collected my fare in flight like a train conductor between stations. I arrived December 29.

I was so broke Nanami had to help me with food. She'd completed a truncated repentance period and now toiled a penitent in the Blessed Family Department (BFD) earning a lowercase stipend. She lived rent-free in the wreckage of the New Yorker Hotel—"a dump, spiritually and physically," I wrote, ". . . the floors where people live are so trashy and dirty"—that Rev. Moon had snapped out of a 1970s drug-blighted bargain basement. Members got 50% off. Nearly renovated by 2003 under Ramada, I'm not sure he still honors his pledge (any more than others) that we could *always* stay at a discount. If not him, it's leaders vitiating his promises. Ramada is just one more cross to bear. In 1985 it was a shell of its former gloriously Art Deco self, 43 floors of mold, peeling walls, broken wood, and general ruin.

Rev. Kwak's World Mission Department, the BFD, other groups, and the church headquartered in it along with every member in the city needing a roof. It later renovated two floors into apartments that rented to members with jobs; an exotic, deitic rung on Moonism's climb to heaven back then. Like most, Nanami had her own room. Privacy turned into such a hotbed of bootleg sex that Rev. Moon at last ordered his freeloaders to go mooch elsewhere. Orders are one thing. Obedience another. It was years before most vacated; everybody was church mouse poor working full time for Rev. Scrooge. Giving up cheap if not free rent in the Big Apple was like coming off quality heroin. Visiting members paid $5 a night, $20 if you wanted sheets and blankets. Nanami paid my first night to get me a key, but neither of us could afford more. I occupied my room on the sly for more than a week before the front desk caught on. In those days, the church maintained a 24-hour security desk and metal detector at the door. Every day I ran management's glint-eyed gauntlet.

At the January 1, 1986 God's Day events I met many old friends. I wrote,

> It's awfully hard to be one of the very FEW of the unBlessed members, especially when my *whole* character is designed to operate properly only in conjunction with a good wife; someone I love deeply and vice versa . . . an incredible struggle for me. The burdens on my heart and spirit are *so* heavy, I can hardly operate.

Then for the first time in three years I ran into Shiori,

> the Kobayashi's eternal house-servant. What a surprise! She even talks to me now. She was so eager to visit with me, and she bought me a gift of Korean Holy Songs on tape ($12). No light present. She even invited me in to Kobayashi's house for a drink . . . How nice to see her like a human being . . .

Johnny McGurk turned up a paid employee of the church-owned Manhattan Center. He'd gone back to then got fired from the boats in Kodiak. He said, "Jonathan and Dana got into a big fistfight. Dana got worsted, though."

"Brother! Seems to be a lot of enmity up there."

"And Billy's stupid program of tyranny isn't helping at all!" *News, man.*

Mr. Kamiyama stupendously disappointed. Defensive in the meetings I attended, he quit responding positively to the caustic criticisms and undying grudges mainly Americans hurled with increasing candor. He turned to berating, belittling, and demanding obedience . . . his old, Imperial self reborn. I supposed he made a good try but couldn't bear the withering taste of hell heaped on him like dry kindling. He canceled the meetings. I approached him and Mr. Matsuzaki, who'd worked with Jerome in the old days—CARP's Dr. Seuk beat me off with unquenchable rudeness— about Papasan's violence, his unPrincipled philosophies consuming California, and my imperishable longing to be active in True Parents' mission.

"Yes, Mr. Choi does seem contradictory and confusing," Mr. Kamiyama said over a couple-hour brush-off, "but is very senior. I don't have authority to do anything about him." I blinked. Thoughts collided. *But you absolutely control the church! You're Father's right-hand angel. You are it. The Man.* "You should solve your issues with your local or regional leader. To be Blessed, they must clarify your position."

"Everyone I meet wants him out,"—he showed zero surprise at that—"yet don't want me in anything. I've tried. Can you assign me a mission here? Somewhere?"

More headshaking. "You are part of Bay Area church. I need their permission. You must work things out with them. I am sure they will find something for you." *The hell's he saying? Damn. I bet he talked to Papasan!* "To connect with headquarters, though, talk to Dr. Durst. But, finishing school might be best for you."

"It appears there's two levels of membership now, off the street and big shots."

"It's true. General members are so spiritually low. Father never wanted street witnessing. He wants high-level people. That's his focus now."

I whiffed. "The cart before the horse, we've been riding." His lips pursed.

I recounted my sob story to every top leader I found. Famous lecturer Ken Sudo's delicate, refined features moved with emotion at my travails. He was renowned as the "man of no sleep" for lecturing nonstop till falling asleep mid-sentence.

"Your sincere love for True Parents and your desire to follow the right path is deeply touching. You are a good member. I feel your heart, K'risutohua." If he was, he might be the very first in this church. I explained my destitution. This guy. He cracked his wallet and fingered out every bill he had. "I think it is $28. Will that help you? I'm very sorry it is all I have right now."

"Pshh! You kidding? Are you sure?" I didn't know his salary level. His head quick-bobbed. "This is so kind. Just incredible. I don't know how to thank you."

"We are family. Brothers. This is True Father's way."

Well, double shit. Father's way? He was the kindest, godliest leader I found in New York even if his security blocked me half an hour. His generosity punched hard. To rabble like me, $28 was half a Rockefeller. To his wonder, I paid him back in 1989. Nanami had my return airfare. Now I had food money. Snacks were my peace offering for our on–off squabbling over my negativity and her Blessing.

I talked to Nora running the BFD about my Judah Street spiritual children hanging on by threads. She said, "I know about them. But members expect too much of us. Every story's tragic but I can't make someone accept their husband, wife, or leader. They need to solve their own problems."

"Then I dunno what to do at all!" I struggled to reconcile our HQ's indifference to suffering. The unPrincipled injustice of brutalizing violence. My position as an outcast. Rev. Moon's vision totally enchanted yet, once again, my spiritual beliefs, sense of duty, and practical reality was Vulcan's forge, anvil, and hammer.

After visiting CAUSA's Antonio Betancourt the next day, I whistled up 34 floors to my top flop in dress pants, shirt, and sweater Nanami bought. I turned the knob and gelled: double locked. A note read, *Belongings inside. See front desk.* A dark breath sawed out. Owed rent was all of Mr. Sudo's gift. I'd have to steal back my seabag and briefcase. Scouting around, I found an empty, unlocked room (not uncommon) down the hall. Its window let out onto a somewhat oval-shaped terrace 15 feet by 10 as part of its Art Deco setback façade. A wall rose maybe seven feet around the patio in patterned brick. Scrambling atop where it met the building, I dropped down the other side to a 20-inch ziggurat ledge that partially fronted the 34th floor. I edged along. *Wonder how safe this old thing is . . .*

I trooped along then around 3-foot high, angled wrought iron fences (over 34 floors of air) periodically blocking the ledge for no apparent reason; maybe I wasn't the first idiot out here. Gusty, 40-knot winds tugged and buffeted in the high altitude, sub-zero January weather till I reached my window. These rooms were unrenovated and, except for my $5 special, unoccupied. Through scummy glass I spied my seabag and briefcase set like bait in the middle of the room. The window was unlocked; no foresight on my part. I pushed it up and climbed through, grateful to be inside walls.

There was no way in hell I could open the double-locked door. I tried everything, even prying at the old-fashioned valet panel that allowed the hotel laundry to retrieve a guest's clothes from the compartment between them via the outer panel. Only one opened at a time. If I wanted my stuff without management's ransom, I'd have to lug it out the way I'd come. *Damn. Nothing's ever easy with these people, is it?*

Warmed up, I slung my seabag's double straps over suited shoulders, gripped my briefcase, and climbed out. I thanked all my Rocky Mountain adventuring strolling ledges, scaling cliffs, and curbing my fear of heights. A timeless void hung over the street where miniature ants scurried oblivious to my presence. It brought to mind Rev. Moon a couple years earlier how members must be willing to die for God's providence. A few dimwits took him literally. A Japanese brother swan dived off the New Yorker's 40th floor and plopped a mess on a neighboring building's roof far below, a sensation of blistering headlines. Another leapt off San Francisco's Bay bridge. Funny no Americans did this *kamikaze* shit . . . that I heard about.

New Yorker Hotel in its plenilune, ziggurat glory.

Rev. Moon lost no time clarifying, more or less saying, "Suicide for any reason is not Principle and absolutely against God's will. You must never do it no matter how much you want to sacrifice yourself for indemnity. You must *live* for God!"

Humping my gear to the terrace, I thought about my own potential swan dive. I marveled how I ambled the ledge in confidence as if on a sidewalk. The guts (or folly) of youth, I reckoned. In the warm corridor fretfully checking for management, I banged down the ever-empty stairs to bunk in the free albeit bedless members' dorms. A sleeping bag here or there was all the same to me. I hated being on the lam but I'd been lucky to get one meal a day now for weeks. Overall, Personnel had lost me in their files, my MFT ID card caused conniptions, beloved friends like Young Soon and her toddler son comforted me, Dr. Durst well-nigh said, "Elders are practically perfect; respect and follow them," I'd helped Nanami switch rooms, painted walls, and repaired equipment to be helpful. Yet, I'd solved nothing.

As People Express rolled off the Rotten Apple's runway January 11 for Sour Frisco, my psyche was drained of all but Nanami's friendship, Mr. Sudo's loving heart, and my grinding determination to graduate college and build credibility.

AFTER MONTHS OF saving, I purchased a crapped out 1966 Volkswagen Beetle with a broken, half-open sunroof for $125, talking the owner down from a ridiculous $250. It left the factory white but was now scarred, flaky paint and rusty metal. It had a speedometer, malfunctioning gas gauge, a yawning hole for a radio, no bumpers, and twisty-wire standing in for a hood latch. I rebuilt the sunroof mechanicals but its worn out weatherstripping leaked onto my head so much in heavy rains I was obliged to don my Alaska foul-weather gear. It got so wet inside the car it made more sense to roll down the window to defog the windshield. A raincoated arm on the sill and beloved Sou'wester on my semi-curly locks, I spluttered down the road waving at goggling drivers like a sunny day. In spite of its defects, the car gave me freedom for the first time since I'd sold my Opel and CB750-4 on my way to enlisting in Los Angeles MFT. I was mobile. *What a treat!*

Now I could drive to Holy Ground like the hoity toity. No more dashing after buses. It leaked a quart of oil every week but was reliable rain or shine, winter or summer. I could visit friends and my brother Teddy 25 miles down the peninsula in Milpitas, a small suburb just north of San Jose in the South Bay.

Whenever I choggled up to his homeowner's association-controlled house he'd ask with a big evil grin on his face, "How's your piece of shit running today?"

"I'm here, right?" Always these *gottverdammte* self-esteem issues.

At home Jerome tore down April '86 with, "I told Al I'm moving out when school ends. Now I'm telling you. I'm taking all my deposits."

I coughed a breath. "What for? That'll put the landlord on me for $1,300!"

"People here accusing me of illogical things, like I'm impossible to get along with, or leaving the kitchen a"—air quotes—" 'disaster area.' Betraying me."

"Well, it is! You're a total slob in the kitchen. Ever since Robert. Jill said the same thing after she moved in."

"All of your motivations are evil. You're seeking to destroy my character and excuse your own satanic ways."

"Man, don't judge my motivations. You're not a mind reader."

He tossed something in the sink. "I'm spiritually aware. Connected to God. I can see your heart. Her heart. Everybody's racistly trying to bury me."

"That's just crap, Jerome. You're a hypocrite making excuses. You have this chip on your shoulder that everybody's a racist and only wants your ruination. You've turned into this intolerant, vengeful, vindictive person at war with everybody."

He boomed. "You are racist! Or you'd never say or do half of what you say and do. You don't know me. You, everybody, judges me from their white advantage."

"The hell's that mean?" He ignored me. Shoed crumbs 'neath the counter. My heart racketed apart like a billiards break. "You're forcing us to move out, too."

"Al already promised this place to his brother-in-law. Not my problem, man."

Homeless! I ground rocks stewing over his knife in the back. And Mr. Kamiyama and leaders rejected every plan I'd hatched to reconnect. "Just go to college," Rev. Moon said through Peter Kim. I was an 'S' member: *spurned*. Dejected, despairing, I let myself fall in-like with Roxanne even as the back of my mind bayed, *The Blessing! Be single! Be celibate! Be faithful!* Torpedoes sinking every raft of happiness.

Alone again. I could've cried. I punched phone keys. "I'm on the street, Roxanne. Jerome and I and everything is dead. I want to abandon all these hateful fuckers!"

> I'm beyond words. Between the church, God, my life, school, and the student council, I'm at the peak of frustration. Goodnight! (April 23)

"You'll be okay," she purred. "You can use my apartment while I'm in Europe."

Her fine attributes matched my ideal spouse in beflagged, sworded Columbia over Key's Golden Gate memorial. I moved to 455 29th Street with May. Our life was pleasant and embracing so long as I leashed my demoniacal Moonie guilt and the Blessing's Damoclean sword. Her biological clock was clanging; we talked of marriage. Then friends said, "Dude, your eyes are *yellow*. You look jaundiced."

"What's that mean?"

"You need help."

"Well, I *have* been slowing, feeling a tad unwell." A torment of exhaustion.

"Go see a doctor."

"Pshaw! Like I have money for that. It's just a flu. Nothing unusual."

"Your funeral."

Friday afternoon mid-May I collapsed into Roxanne's bed. Except once to pee, I didn't wake up till Monday morning. My throat was in a strangler's grip, every swallow broken glass, lungs pumping a vacuum. She hustled me to the hospital. I tested positive for strep, tonsillitis, and mononucleosis.

"Never heard of that last one," I told the doctor.

"Didn't stop you getting it. Complications can be fatal if you don't treat it."

"Fatal?" I wheezed. "What's that entail?"

"Death, usually. Ha ha! I mean, rest. And lots of it. No drugs for it."

"Rockin' bedside manner, Doc." I'd never been knocked down like this. I said to Roxanne, "I can't even believe it. How sick can I be? Seems like just a bad flu."

"It's *mono*, Chris. I know all about it. Shut up and get in bed."

It pulverized me. I crumbled in bed two full weeks waking only for the head, medicine, and teaspoons of salty beef broth Roxanne pinched my nose to get down. I dropped from 225 lbs to 160, so feathery she hoisted me in her arms. Relapses from ignoring afternoon naps—"Stop eating ice cream, it's giving you false energy"—had me borderline playing cards with Archangel Azrael two tedious months. Final exams came and went. Professors considerately marked me *incomplete*. Roxanne lovingly saved my life from a scruffy Skid Row statistic. I regained my strength and built a regimen of afternoon naps and early bedtimes. Short nights and hard-charging days were all I knew. But for two years, if I didn't sleep at least ten hours I'd wake to a 2-week relapse. Accepting my limitations was agonizing. With time, I dispensed with naps but not the ten hours. That took four years. Can you spell *bullshit*?

THIS PERIOD CRUSHED me. The Family excommunicated me in all but name. Its implacable rejection was less ecclesiastic and more *la cosa nostra*. I swore by Divine Principle, Rev. Moon the Messiah, the historic value of it all. Yet, his venal leaders sabotaged and crippled me in severing our tether. A potent sense of victimization evolved during these years that undermined every facet of my life and any chance to happily love a woman. Conquering acrimonious rancor for persecutory Japanese and American eunuchs was inconceivable. Blood boiled hearing how this or that leader spat my cursed name in Sunday service or at a regional leaders' meeting or to members, admonishing contamination by my brand of Americanism.

"And what brand is that?" I bitched. "The conscience kind?" Rev. Moon rejects the Imperial drone. To rehash our mind-meltingly dangerous cult leader:

> Don't simply believe the Principle is true because you respect me. You must study Principle yourself. You must pray to God for your own understanding. You must live a lifestyle through which you can discover the truth of the

Principle in your daily activities. The Principle must become your own truth, part of your own bones, just as it is with me. Unless you do that, you can never say that you know Principle, that you know God.

Okay, I'll do that. I'd ruthlessly pored over *Divine Principle*, underlining passages with questions and comments in the margins until filled to bursting. Grilled leaders like Mr. Kobayashi on the tricky and troublesome that cropped up. Contested Rev. Moon's statements to grasp exactly what he meant. It was all too much for vacuous leaders so ignorant of the Principle they couldn't answer my questions anyway. I marveled at the pristine condition of the average member's *Divine Principle*. Did they even use it? *It's so bloody clean, like it's never left the shelf.*

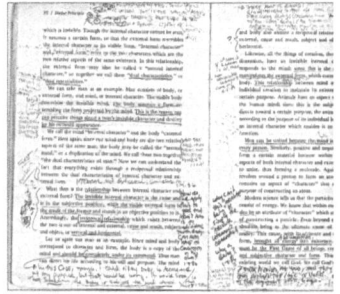

A typical page in my 1973 DP.

Mine was filthy. Dirt begrimed its pages; spine and covers worn and bent. *Am I the only one reading this fucking thing?* It's a fair question. Every person joining the church received his or her own copy. It's our Completed Testament Bible. My soft NIV was just as scribbled up. I'd reglued clumps of pages fallen out from overuse. I'd so used up these texts they were literally falling apart.

This is what Father demands of us! Why then do leaders and members persecute me for being diligent and inquisitive? Isn't religion's task to comprehend its sacred texts? How else does one discover its truth? Naïve, that was me. Religion isn't for seeking knowledge. It's not about questioning authority nor understanding Jesus and True Parents. It's about conformity. Obedience to its Way.

I was learning this simple truth the hard way, a crown of thorns scourging my mind. Great men like Rev. Moon, Jesus, or Buddha easily digest skepticism because their truth is in their bones. The confidence of living it. Disbelief never threatens. Early Christians questioning St. Paul's understanding of Jesus never crucified his personal experience. He had nothing to promote, hide, or remove from the prying eyes of the too clever. His experience was real to him, as was Jesus' knowledge of God and Rev. Moon's commission from Jesus. Dissect and assail him. He's supremely comfortable in his truth. Secure in his faith. Unbreakable.

Followers are second-hand versions of the archetype. The mall cops of religion. Members didn't personally experience Jesus, God, nor the deepest truth flowing through Divine Principle and the Bible. What Moonie ever met Adam and Eve, Lucifer, Moses, Jesus, and Abraham as Rev. Moon claims he has? If true, no criticism can possibly threaten his own experience. He was there. He *knows*. Unlike him, the beliefs and principles of members are easily threatened. Few if any experienced the root of the Fall nor the anguish, guilt, and weeping, groaning sadness of Jesus. They can only *believe* based on their respect for Rev. Moon and a sense his testimony is true. If someone like me challenges it they have no experience to defend it beyond tired arguments marinated in cliché. Their truth crumbles. Infects other truths. The holy *Weltanschauung* dissolves before their very eyes.

At that point they feel compelled to uphold their worldview, religion, and sense of self with force. They take a person like me and trash motives and intelligence.

They deploy *ad hominem* caltrops. If nothing works, they expel me from our shared community. Not because I'm a physical threat, but because my effort to advance to the next level of comprehension leaves them in my dust. They don't have what it takes to rise to higher awareness, understanding, and experience. They've told themselves the truth they *now* know is the *whole* truth, the everlastingly *only* truth. Religion tends to equate temporal authority with spiritual enlightenment. Lowly members spiritually advancing beyond their temporal leaders creates a crisis of credibility, status, power, self-esteem, and *faith*. Ergo, religious authority's intolerant response to out-of-the-box thinking and post-founder spiritual experiences.

Unlike most members, I was in the noodle-press of dire circumstances. Coerced out of the church and its spiritual protection compelled me to confront every aspect of Unificationism to justify it for myself. Most of all, I had to stare Rev. Moon's messianism in the eye and figure out *for sure* if it was real enough for me. It was a tough nut to crack. I hated almost every minute of it. But I was learning the Principle through my own life experience as Rev. Moon wanted. At the bottom of hell I was discovering Real God. And I was finding, too, that in the world of organized religion there were damn few in my shoes.

Yes, I felt victimized. At the same time, I felt special. Empowered. Cut loose, even, to raise my own church . . . except, I didn't want to do that. I've resisted it as long as I've been a Unificationist. In the mid-1980s I couldn't see myself starting a schismatic movement because it seemed tantamount to treachery against God. Rev. Moon hadn't failed in his stated aims spectacularly enough for me to consider a new church necessary nor a benefit to God. All I'd be doing is adding to the confusion and ruining lives. I resist it less in 2003 for different reasons through seeing more value in a new expression of faith in Divine Principle without the arrogant trappings. Unfortunately, I feel neither especially called to it nor particularly capable of it. To start a church one needs a sense of arrogance, meaning a belief in the unalterable truth and justice of your cause which *only you* can lead. Without it, one sinks into the mire of equivocation, doubt, sin, and failure.

In 1985 I made a mild attempt in that direction by 'nailing' *a la* Martin Luther my *General Discourse on the Symbolic Relationship of Cain and Abel* to the front doors of the Bay Area church centers. I didn't have 95 points, just one: the church had conflated the Principle's Subject–Object (best described as that between proton and electron) with its Cain–Abel Restoration relationship. This refers to entities in any mutual give-and-take. A professor, for instance, is Subject and a student Object. It applies examples from the natural world to human experience. But this is a primary relationship of *nature*. Insofar as it applies to humans, it describes the dynamic between individuals or groups but not the relationship itself. I believed the

My Cain and Abel thesis 'nailed' to Bay Area church doors, 7pp.

church consummately confused this distinction and, within it, found a convenient rationale for totalitarianism (and, in Papasan Choi's case, violence).

Cain and Abel, on the other hand, describes the dynamic between humans from the point of view of God's plan for Restoration. In an effort to fix the corruption spawned in the human heart through the Fall, God wanted the person (or group) representing the unPrincipled (more Satanic) portion of the Fall to voluntarily, heartistically submit to the unconditional love of the person (or group) representing the more Principled (less Satanic) aspect of the Fall. That's Rev. Moon's approach to Satan and the absolute core of his ministry. As the second son and symbolic fruit of Adam and Eve's sexual relationship (originally planned by God but acted on before spiritual maturity), Abel represents this good side. Cain, symbolically the fruit of the first portion of the Fall (Eve and Lucifer's relationship in stark opposition to God's original intent), represents the evil side.

I argued the church messed this up in equating Abel with Subject and Cain with Object. An electron as Object is always and forever within the scope and power of its atom as Subject, and the church came to see Cain as always and forever within the scope and power of Abel. This stripped unconditional love from it. Cain–Abel morphed into one of controlling authority above and beyond any system of ethics and morality, a vehicle for spiritual growth and development, and providential Restoration. Why? Because, in the institutional church view, that's simply how the universe is and God's Restoration works; all else is subservient.

The church drumbeat against individual liberty and conscience sounded loud and clear in its immutable insistence on absolute obedience to an individual's local leader, his *Abel*. Leaders paid lip service to Rev. Moon as the ultimate Abel, himself obedient to Divine Principle as God's truth. In practice, local leaders enforced it for local leaders answering to local leaders. Abel segued from God's way to authority. They made obedience *itself* the ultimate Abel, which is the very essence of *Bushido*. This remade the American Family into a shadow Imperial Army, its emperor not Rev. Moon, Divine Principle, nor even God but The Way of Obedience. As Americans vaguely figured it out they said, "Get lost!" Rev. Moon confronted this trend:

> Japanese leaders aren't you teaching a principle that I do not teach, when you say, "I am Abel because I am a church leader. You are Cain. Cain obeys Abel. This is the Principle. So obey." There is no such principle. The person who does not fulfill his mission and become the embodiment of love is not Abel. (*A Day When We Welcome the Blessing* 1978)

> Abel's role is not one of commanding or directing people to do this or that. Abel is the one who should sacrifice the most. I don't know where this kind of strange thought that Abel is the central figure and in the position to command came from. I don't know how that idea crept into our movement here in America. Many young members have left the church because of their leaders. Abel does not kick someone out of the church. Abel is the one who will bring people in and embrace them. (*Today's World* December 1983, 9)

> Some of you may feel that you are Abel, and somebody else is Cain . . . But Abel must always suffer himself. You must serve others . . . Father does not like to see anyone, leaders especially, thinking that he is Abel and trying to command other members. Father will never allow that. The typical Abel is Jesus, who lived to serve Cain . . . Jesus spent his whole life serving, even until his death. (*Father Speaks to the Crusade*, London 1978)

But he did allow it. His obvious contradictions in paying a studiously blind eye to malefactory Papasan Choi aside, I concluded that,

> absolute authority of "Abel" over "Cain" is erroneous and is simply an excuse to . . . promulgate careers for a limited number of "leaders," while consigning the vast majority of members to a nondescript life of toil and hardship.

My paper caused a minor uproar, but no one knew who'd authored it. I envisioned it as the "first in a series to delve into the contradictions and inconsistencies of the Unification Church, and to stimulate the search and application of a solution." I never did get around to nailing additional theses to doors. But I felt kith and kin with Martin Luther. I'd struck my blow, by God. Done my part. Ideally, an interested member would've taken down and read my paper, then passed it around under their leader's nose. I was pretty sure it flew into the local center director's hands to disappear down a rathole under members' noses. Then three years later at Bush Street center I met a burned-out, 7-year MFT veteran who'd taken it down and still carried it for inspirational reading.

"Everything you wrote in that is totally true," he said with a heavy yet appreciative air outside a Sunday service. "It changed my life. Revived me! You saved my faith." At that moment, I believed I could've had my own church if I'd wanted it.

The struggle with obedience to leaders over Principle, love, and conscience is the stake in the heart of Rev. Moon's dream to Restore the world to its Edenic state. The internecine war between Cains and Abels spills into every campaign the church attempts and ruins them one after the other. At times, he's literally slapped senior leaders upside the head for it. But it never sinks into their Cain–Abelized brains . . . partly because he *appears* to advocate it.

Beginning not long after the 1982 Blessings, members by the thousands had enough of the conflict between their own conscience and the suspended conscience of the church. Thus began the long decline which in 2003 marks the Unification Church of America almost a failure, hanging by a broken fingernail or two.

~

Well. Back to the moment.

Nanami called end of May with her frustrations over her as-yet unconsummated Blessing. "If I was your wife, I could take such good care of you, K'risu."

"Are you proposing?" Shit. Despite Roxanne's recent interaction with my visiting parents turning me off, my heart was tangled up in care for her. But I *loved* Nanami almost to distraction. The only reason we weren't married was this goddamned Divine Principle of a despising church chewing through our happiness.

"I'm just thinking things." She was quiet. "I might to come visit. If you want."

Do I? Interrupting her Blessing felt satanic. So many pitfalls just to experience love. "I'm not sure. It could . . . get complicated. Let's think about it."

I was feeling dismembered. The next day a letter postmarked Nicosia, Cyprus arrived from Floyd, my spiritual mother Ginny's Blessed husband. I'd believed them a marital has-been with her news he'd left the church until, a long while later, she'd gleefully announced he'd faked it all for safety in a communist country.

In paraphrase he said, "I'm editor-in-chief for *The Middle East Times*. How about you come work on our staff?"

"Hmmm..." I neck-nodded the notion, trying it on for size.

"The American church has unreasonably pushed you into a corner. You need to get out of meatball-land awhile, and away from all its neuroses."

"They sure as hell have!"

"It's a crime for anyone to deny members the Blessing. Ginny thinks you'll have a better chance at it from here."

"Hell, yes!" I thundered, waving his letter. "When can I start?"

"Call and let us know. We'll explain the deal and send you a ticket."

Roxanne was profoundly sad, convinced I'd never return. She was understanding I had none of the feelings for her I'd had for Diane, which told me I didn't love her enough for marriage. Honestly, I didn't know. She was a wonderful, beautiful woman who'd succored me through my lowest ebb. Confusion reigned.

I'd recovered half my strength by July 2, salvaged my finals, packed up, stored my POS Beetle in a narrow concrete slot in her condo's basement, and taken wing. When things are a mess in my life, a road trip always hits the spot.

Act IX

In the Middle East
Journalism and Censorship

It was one ass-necrotizing flight to Cyprus. Seven hours from San Francisco to New York, then swap flights for another eight to Brussels where I parked three bustling nights in Sleep Well youth hostel for BF250. And—cue the music—*loooved* it.

I hiked the not-megalopolis from its tourist attractions to canals and through antique neighborhoods the Romans might've recalled over a warmed flagon. I spied out the city's daily life, screaming drivers in traffic jams, young lovers on park benches. My rusty, clumsy French got a workout as I strove to fit in as a local. I disliked coming off a tourist. Somehow it made me feel the wrong end of peeping. Whenever traveling the USA or abroad I went for the local tongue if I could, dressed accordingly, and above all avoided strutting the quintessential noisy American tourist *a la* Jackie Gleason's oaf in 1969's *Don't Drink the Water*. When I couldn't catch all the French I played the quiet, aloof, artsy-fartsy, left-bank Bohemian.

Brussels is the first place I saw blacks outside their American context. Darlene and Jerome were the only blacks I'd met in the Unification Church up to this point although I knew there were others, like that suave US Navy commander at Judah Street. Prior to the church, my only experience of blacks was an elementary schooler in just-desegregated Maryland flapping about in unholy size twelves, then not till my Coast Guard hitch, which wasn't too flattering for them. Many bottom-end enlisted aboard ships and Group New Orleans were, to me, variously poor in spirit, ignorant, obnoxiously loud, and some version of felonious. Blacks scaled our base fence to mug our sentries, including the front gate guard. That eye-blinked me.

Isn't this a military *base?* How were civilians scaling our soldier-grade fence and taking out boot-camped personnel? It was nonsensical. We begged permission to arm up but our base commander denied us, probably wise to our shoot-first mood. Seeing our friends' busted up faces, bruised bodies, and cracked ribs had us royally tense and graveyarded any sense of legal restraint to which we otherwise subscribed. Command finally authorized night sticks. We sniggered. Hardly comparable in the knife- and gunfights our extreme sportster nemeses could deliver. I guess it was par for the handjobs-for-criminals late 1970s. Plus, Vietnam was the military's spoiled meat at America's barbecue still fresh on every comedian's tongue.

I mostly grew up in the Nordic Rockies. Urban race wars flaming and sputtering around the nation were only in my peripheral vision. I didn't know the first thing about it. No opinion on blacks either way. My sophisticated, world-traveling parents reared me rigorously away from skin bias. I assessed individuals through character, behavior, and weight on the shitsack scale. Many blacks I met in the American South and USCG seemed badly educated but I hardly considered it an excuse for badly behaved. Posted summer of '79 aboard *Acushnet* homeported on a banana pier in Gulfport, Mississippi, a Cajun–black petty officer third class occasionally swaggered into our morning galley with his hard, bony pony in hand.

"Where de women at?" he sniggered.

Invariably somebody said, "Put that ugly motherfucker in your pocket."

"What for? Chuck wagon's here."

Most took it for goofs in our male locker room and brooked his pornanigans so long as he didn't bump too close in the chow line. Not knowing anything, I figured it for his demographic benchmark and that he *wasn't* kidding. As a practicing Christian and no doubt a prude let alone urban rube, he fired my bile. His was the most vulgarly inferior deportment I met in the service, but only the *most*.

The Coast Guard was my first adult swim through the South. Visits with East Texas relatives mostly occurred before twelve. Racism sailed over my head. Perhaps children not awash in it naturally don't notice. It's a fact the races play happily till adults crab it up, and mine never did. But in the '60s South, I had no relatives who didn't live in apparently whites-only neighborhoods. I didn't know what that was, only that no blacks entered my memory. My older brother Teddy drank from *Colored Only* water fountains and pissed in *Colored Only* toilets to impotently disavow Maryland's Jim Crow nicking his soul at the gates of Freedom's capital city.

"Say, don't you know that's the colored restroom, boy?" baleful Whitey said, self-righteous choler splashed through his face in burnt Indian red.

"Is it?" Teddy smirked with a daring eye.

"Now you mind your manners, boy, else . . ."

Fortunately, Dad was usually around and anyhow even uppity whites rarely got the Mason-Dixon treatment blacks did for bucking the system although it happened, some even murdered and sometimes lynched. Teddy might not have fully considered he was risking the Klan treatment. I bet Dad did, and jumpy over its side effects besides. Segregation seemed to phase out while I was too young to notice or challenge fuming white folks the way Teddy, ten years my senior, did.

Belgian blacks may or may not have been the same low class I got used to seeing in ghettoed America. But the strut, brassily abrasive language, and thuggish looks in knurled brows and ferocious eyes maybe contemplating crime against or punishment by The Man wasn't there. In Brussels I saw African, not American, blacks. There seemed a striking difference. I encountered them mostly lounging in public places, neatly dressed and speaking French. Possibly I'm the ultimate boor, but up till this point never saw a black anybody speak anything but English and that often not well. These Belgian blacks . . . well, dang, I was entranced.

"Wow, they're so normal. So educated. And they're speaking *French!*"

I suppose I dimly realized it was simply the local dialect, but never mind. At that time in my life anybody spouting *la langue diplomatique* was surely educated, therefore worthy of respect. So, they got it. Don't get ahead of yourself, here. Well-educated blacks by Euro-American standards date back to the 17th century and beyond in both continents and probably a majority of their populations today. But black Americans take silent majorityism in a strident minorityism to the ends of the earth even in 2003. Almost invisible to me, educated blacks with whom whites easily harmonize aren't casually found. Anyway, it's how I observed it then.

My first foray past an American beachhead saw me mouth agape and eyes wide that the parliamentarian barbarians across the pond kinda sorta looked pretty high cotton after all. Touring Brussels on foot I ate myself sick on Belgian waffles, something we could use more of in the good ol' USA. Three days was too short to absorb even a tidbit of Brussels' charisma, but my plane was revving on the fourth. I batwinged five hours south over Europe sloshing heavily sugared blood.

CYPRUS IS A tiny, if aspiringly mountainous, island. Hard to believe the Greeks and Turks fought a war over it in 1974 after Greece ousted President Archbishop Makarios to achieve *enosis*, unity with Greece. The porkchop-shaped dual nation splits along the Green Line. Agriculture seemed to dominate the flatlands but, overall, its bone dry and blazing 100°F air spoke barren American Southwest to me. It suckered my breath stepping out of air conditioning into that furnace. Air defines a place, which is why driving through a neighborhood with the windows sealed and AC pumping will never tell you what five seconds of local breathing does.

The Middle East Times (MET) headquartered itself in a nondescript, not-too-tall office building near downtown Nicosia, the island's severed capital. Its boundary zigzagged through Old Town demarcated by 6–12-foot stone, barrel, chainlink, even potted-plant ramparts topped with sandbags, razor wire, and sometimes Turkish soldiers thrown across oft-narrow and now dead-end streets. Nearby buildings lay abandoned and pockmarked from bullets and shrapnel and maybe bone. Travel to the Turkish side was troublesome and virtually impossible for the foreign journalist I now was. Ginny's husband Floyd, MET's editor-in-chief, made it over for a tour but Turkey, a NATO ally, required he travel camera-free with an East Berlinesque security officer. He had to pay all expenses plus a stiff gratuity. Grateful, I'm sure.

Floyd seemed affable, a veteran correspondent for *The News World*-cum-*New York City Tribune*, the defunct predecessor of *The Washington Times* (TWT). He put me off third-world touring with horror stories of North Africa, the Sudan, and mad locales where petty, small-minded bureaucrats used and abused the traveler. Now he ran church-brother Thomas Cromwell's weekly English language conservative brainchild aimed primarily at the Arab world. I ran the news and business sections, wrote and edited stories, helped Floyd as necessary, and learned journalism. At first, I incessantly wrangled over him butcher-knifing my work.

"Why'd you change that? It's a perfectly—"

"Just shut up and let me edit. These aren't meatball college papers, ya know. Your newspaper writing isn't very impressive."

I dropped in my desk chair. "I'm just gonna sit over here and stew."

"Best thing you could do."

Chris of Arabia c. 1987. Jordanian red over Palestinian black on principle.

Once over my butthurt, he realized I only wanted a good rationale for his slicing and dicing. I improved. He quit babysitting. I made sure to pick up every publishing doodad I could: copy writing, editing, headlining, layout and paste-up, production, pre-plate camera work, the Linotype machine . . . the whole Bill Clinton. Professional skills in all parts of news printing was my thing. Who knew? Might start one someday.

MET had a tough row to hoe. Its masthead called Thomas the publisher but the Unification Church owned and subsidized it via Newsworld Communications. Colonel Pak, our *Truth is My Sword* warrior-sage, held its purse strings through Newsworld's Robert Morton while I was there. MET's editorial slant rankled them and haunted us. Aimed at the Arab world, it could hardly harp TWT's pro-Israeli stance. The colonel had Morton squeeze us.

Erwin, a Luxembourger and long-time church member with MET from its 1983 founding, averred Morton the previous November said something like, "Newsworld owns your paper. Bottom line, I expect editorial control from your next issue."

"What does that mean?" said Thomas.

"We'll adjust and approve your news and editorials before you publish so they reflect Rev. Moon's vision in line with Mr. Pak's responsibility."

Thomas choked. "We'll have to fax you everything, wait on your changes, and still publish on time the next day."

"It will be fine. You're not the owner, here, Thomas."

"It's logistically impossible! We'll never make our weekly deadline."

"Yes, you will." But it was all pretense. Logistics are immutable physics. Holding up, editing, or nixing work that forced delays was a given if not a weapon.

Thomas groused to Floyd, "It's bald censorship and I'm having none of it."

"Father's the only person who can overrule these meatballs." He contemplated realities. "But I don't think he'll help until Old Hockey Puck interferes."

To Morton, Thomas later added, "Our readers will abandon the paper wholesale if there's even a hint we're taking a pro-Israeli stand."

Old Colonel Hockey Puck might've in truth wanted that, but it's hard to assess through the hocus-pocus politics of our church. Morton said, "Well, I'm sure that's not the case, Thomas. But it's not your concern."

"What's the point of risking it?"

"Editorial consistency in line with Newsworld and Israel's role in the world." Stolid. Brassbound. "It's Mr. Pak's responsibility."

"Our audience is Arab, not Israeli or Western. They won't stand for any pro—. Look, those countries will ban our distribution outright."

"I suggest you let him worry about that."

Thomas had to reach deep. "No . . . *I'm* responsible to Father. He set it up under me and I'm not relinquishing editorial control to the *Times* unless he says so."

He made good on that with our next issue. Our wise iron eagle promptly cut off MET's annual $200,000 and it shut down. In the couple months it took Thomas to get in front of Rev. Moon, then Rev. Kwak, the paper lost credibility, readership, and distribution channels it took years to regain. The good news was he negotiated a deal for our subsidy to route automatically from the church to MET without passing through Colonel Pak's *fingerus interruptus*. Yet when I arrived, and despite Rev. Moon's fits, MET was again waiting on Pak-delayed funds. It proved to me he didn't control his church and even less its money. Minions ruled his roost.

We weren't anti-Israel per se—I sure wasn't—but tended toward the Palestinian viewpoint. As I familiarized myself with the facts on the ground, not sympathizing with them only got harder. The Israelis seemed so brutal and vindictive that I couldn't help comparing them with their Nazi bane. The Palestinian *intifadah* of the late '90s permanently altered my sympathies back to Israel. Even so, I felt it had only itself to blame for its Arab travails. You kick a dog in the balls long enough you should expect it'll bite your foot. Both had to learn to embrace the other since, biblically speaking, they're Abraham's descendants; family, however dysfunctional.

Predicated firmly in Cain–Abelism, MET dedicated itself to educating and serving Cain, the Palestinians. Unification Church businesses, concentrated as they are on money and avoiding independent thought, rarely have an appreciative eye for Divine Principle beyond the parts convenient for control and corruption. MET's general antipathy for Israel grated TWT's nerves. Newsworld and TWT seemed saddle sore riding a rag promoting an opposite editorial slant. But they were forgetting it's only good business to own the competition.

I SHARED A small, thickly walled, whitewashed stone house with Floyd and Ginny atop a hill walking distance to our office. I hiked it when I could take the heat or noxious diesel fumes and discovered a sour appreciation for California's draconian pollution laws. It really hit home nearly passing out alongside bumper-to-bumper traffic belching thick black diesel and a massive overdose of carbon monoxide. I fish-gulped till stumbling into a cleansing breeze. *No wonder Cypriots aren't walking rush-hour sidewalks!* It was a revelation.

My new, mostly gregarious best mate Erwin was a borderline or high-functioning alcoholic, often enough drunk-sleeping at his desk. A majority of teeth were in greener pastures and dark, broad gaps punctuated his easy smile. He was hugely interested in Pakistan and Afghanistan, making several trips to the latter to shoot us videos of firefights he witnessed of unlucky Soviets versus adroit *mujahideen*, our friends during that war and terrorist enemies after. These were my first visceral taste of modern warfare. Jumpy color with an I-am-there ambience dramatically differed from World War II's black-and-white combat shots on TV.

One showed *mujahideen* ambushing a Soviet truck column on a high mountain road. It reminded me of a scene in 1984's *Red Dawn*. But this wasn't Hollywood, no sir. As the battle unfolded, *mujahideen* speedily overwhelmed the Soviets who fell riddled struggling to escape armored vehicles, tanks, and trucks. A Russian rolled out of his BMP and collapsed, wounded. *Mujahideen* scrambled down the rocky versant swarming the road, firing off hip and shoulder. The soldier scooted down an embankment and Erwin's camera followed him from 30 yards away, looking up the road's incline. A *mujahideen* spied the unfortunate bastard and ran for him, crossing Erwin's frame left to right. Comrade *soldat* put up an arm, palm out, and shouted something in Russian which I took for quarter. A short burst of automatic AK-47 point blank into his torso said *no, thanks.* He jerked. Collapsed in a heap. Presumably died. He sure looked it.

Goddamn! This was real combat and real men gunned down and burned up. A heavy pall fell over me. It was war, and I definitely supported *mujahideen* over Soviets, but the spectacle of merciless killing of living people jabbed me with the stark reality of life in this world. I wondered why those *mujahideen* couldn't tend the enemy wounded, capture them like civilized soldiers. Even Nazis did that. I figured ideology, else their war was too personal: homeland invaded, families murdered. *Red Dawn* brought up this same question in 1984 and responded the same way.

Planning to execute a Soviet soldier and their traitorous high school friend, Matt (Charlie Sheen) says, "Tell me, what's the difference between us and them?"

"Because we live here!" Jed (Patrick Swayze) screams. And . . . *bangity-bang!* The brutal calculus of war. So very sad and, historically, pointless.

Boozed or dry, I liked Erwin. But when I eventually announced my return to America to finish college, he seemed somewhat bitter and accusatory. "In six months you won't remember anything of your time here." *Of me,* he meant.

"Why wouldn't I?"

He shrugged, turned back to work maybe swigging a draught in his mind.

I didn't forget. I supposed his bottle anesthetized his loneliness like Roxanne tried to mine. Church-owned overseas businesses often cut western Unificationists a lot of slack because their skills were needed more than righteousness. No one really judged Erwin though we felt his degradation. Alcohol was *verboten* in the church except for senior leaders, including Rev. Moon. But they weren't drunks that I ever saw. Erwin wasn't staggering, you just nosed in the permanent hooch and sometimes he seemed woozy. His drinking was a coping skill perhaps in despair at being a square peg in a round hole. Not unlike me. I tried many times but couldn't enjoy alcohol of any stripe. If I had, coping with all my tribulations hunting me through life in the church might've left me a fall-down souse.

After I returned to America, Erwin and his Japanese bride got permission to start their family. Off they went to set up house in Peshawar, Pakistan where he worked as a stringer for our newspaper. I never saw him again.

A MONTH INTO my tenure Thomas' wife Catherine said, "Chris, do you want to fill out a Blessing application?"

"Yes!" I jumped for it but tripped hard over breaking Roxanne's heart and her chance for children. I twisted myself into fid-worthy knots without finding a solution. No Blessing hove across my bow, so I didn't have to decide. This and my moral and emotional conundrums with church services, Pledge, and God had Ginny then

Floyd crossing swords with me. I was inspired and considered myself a full member. Yet, my internal feelings for it were dead. I felt wedged. They felt I was "really off." To be sure, I'd burst her bubble after she'd bragged I was a "holy roller."

A professors' International Seminar on the Unification Movement got Floyd's attention. He packed me off to Athens for Divine Principle from Islam's perspective. *Sol Phyrne's* 3-day sail called at fabulous Aegean islands. Landing during some Greek Orthodox thing, I was startled by maybe a hundred mainly old women crying prayers on bloodied hands and knees up the steep street to an imposing church at the island's crest overlooking the bay. Hundreds relaxed over food and drink in the roadside cafes talking, laughing, drinking, and kissing while these devotees wore themselves raw

A bonny couple & 'normal' Moonies. Athens, Christmas 1986.

along their torturously slow pilgrimage. An incongruous melding of the sacred and profane. My yokel eyes mutely soaked it up.

The taxi driver robbed me in a roundabout cruise from Athen's port that I'm certain carried us at least twice past a few landmarks. But you always expect that when arriving in a foreign city unfamiliar with the going rates, local currency, and roads. If they rob you twice, you're an idiot. The city was beautiful. As customary, I roamed its glittering canyons and shadowed byways exhausting myself—tempting another of my eventual six mono relapses in Cyprus—and all but crippling my feet. I lounged hours on the angular boulders lining the beautiful bay at Piraeus, imagining ancient navies duking it out in vicious battles thousands of years ago right where I was sitting. America lacks this historicity. I practiced Greek with folks I met on the streets and in shops where I bought gallons of ice cream on sticks and cones.

My thieving driver dropped me at a Japanese church couple's modest yet spacious top-floor apartment where I spent two mind-mending weeks. The wife had recently delivered her first baby. She idled many a listless hour under the slow-turning fan over their four-poster, her infant sleeping soundly on her quiescent breast. A slim breeze threw life into lengthy white muslin dressing the balcony's several French doors. Shouts and horns off the street ten flights below faintly wafted up. Memories harbor that scene of peace and tranquility as a happy home in love. I acutely hungered for its ambience in my life. Desire pricked an abyss in my heart.

Thomas carted bricks persuading Rev. Kwak to move our newspaper to Athens for a happier operating environment. Part of our less happier Cypriot one arose in our running a story from one of our stringers in Lebanon that referred to Greece's then-prime minister, Andreas Papandreou, as "a one-man stand-up comedy act." It seemed perfectly fitting because although (or perhaps because) he was Harvard trained, tongues wagged he'd succeeded through his socialist delusion to bankrupt his up-and-coming nation, accomplishing the impossible when he sent the country's now state-owned cement industry so far into the red it nearly went belly up. People build almost exclusively with cement in the Middle East. It's difficult to bleed such a sure thing dry in that market through any means than malicious or negligent—dare

I say, *socialist?*—mismanagement. The European Union laughingly trolled Greece in those times as the "sick man of Europe," its corrupt stupidity hopelessly excluding it from any future EU table scraps.

Our story incensed pompous Papandreou. He hotly phoned his colleague in Nicosia demanding our newspaper's immediate expulsion. Tightening screws, he forced compliance. They ordered we close up and get the fuck out in a week and don't let the door . . . you know. The local newspapers were happy to see us go. They abhorred our locally headquartered competition and already had their government pals ban our shadowy, foreign-financed publication from soiling their sales.

We could live with it. The Arab market was bigger anyway. But kicking us out over a story unrelated to Cyprus was an outrage. One thing I'd discovered in Athens was that, while Cypriots seemed to believe their mainland cousins loved them so much they'd happily bleed to save their storied isle from the nasty Turk, Greeks held them in contempt. Perhaps it was their inability to defend their own home against the invasion they'd provoked with their coup and Greek soldiers had to die for it. Perhaps they see them no better than basement cousins the family prefers not to acknowledge. Who knows? It's an enigma.

My first front page byline (below the fold). Nov. 1–15, 1986.

It seemed ironic Cyprus jackbooted us with Papandreou's condescending demand. It ignored every argument Thomas made against its ruling. *Democracy, what's that? Free enterprise? Not here. Rule of law? Fuhgeddaboudit! Free Speech? What, you think this is capitalist America with rights?*

They weren't wrong. Cyprus was practically lawless in a corporate sense. For example, with no legal statutes backing them up, police enforced the customary habit of shops closing by 6 PM, willing or not. A friend of mine owned a video store and tried staying open one evening till 8 PM to generate more sales. A competitor complained. Police dropped by with inestimable haste as we chatted and ordered his prompt closing or else arrest and confiscation of his shop. He complied with a grumpy smile and no hope of redress. Meanwhile few if any of his thousands of videos were even genuine Hollywood. Nearly every tape was an illegal copy sporting hand-scrawled labels in black marker. This was the norm despite the country's signature on the Universal Copyright Convention. Same deal with audio tapes. When I ambled into any department store or music shop for my favorite artists' latest hits, I couldn't pluck it off the shelf for purchase like home.

"Pay up front and it'll be ready in four hours. Come back then."

I said, "I have to wait for it? It's right there on your shelf."

"That one's not for sale."

I chatted up a friendship. On my return, the owner led me up narrow stairs to his duplicating den housing 20-plus machines churning out copies with hastily printed labels—handwritten, if he was behind on production.

"Here's your tape," he said, plucking it off a pile. "How we do it here."

"Does it sound like the real thing?" I'd seen enough smeary videos to wonder. "Sure. No problem."

I gave him shifty eyes but it was what it was. There was scarcely a legal piece of recorded entertainment to be found on the island and exorbitantly priced if you did. Overtaxed, is why. Socialism is an expensive business.

One thing we did a lot of in Cyprus was watch TV and illegally rented home videos. There were only two channels: Greek and Turkish. The latter was far more cosmopolitan and sophisticated, broadcasting top American shows and movies than what the Greeks put on. We got a kick out of *Knight Rider*, chuckling all the way through David Hasselhoff and his American starlets' guttural, dubbed Turkish that so mismatched their vibe. The Greeks had movie night on Fridays. Their American commercials outshone and got our full attention. Halfway through the movie a somber, dour-faced official in a drab office read a lengthy propaganda tirade against the Turks in a 30-minute intermission. Like many Cypriots, we abandoned the TV for drinks, snacks, and conversation until his clock ran out.

Greek TV indulged in communist films from Warsaw Pact countries. These served up virulent antireligion that was sometimes horribly, gut-wrenchingly, mind-numbingly gory and brutal. I shuddered through one movie highlighting—possibly exaggerating, but maybe not—medieval Catholic perfidy backstabbing its most ardent supporters for minor transgressions, such as a nobleman the defenders of the faith impaled on a 10-foot pike slowly screwed up his ass and out the top of his back in excruciating, full-color detail. When his friend found him hanging off the upright pole, he put him out of his misery like a lame horse. Pitiless. I learned a lot about the filmmakers' godless mindset from suffering through their satanic vision for the sake of learning what I'd need in my future Unificationist missions . . . if I ever got any. With entertainment like that, I imagined Soviet-controlled countries as dark, despairing hellscapes.

There was little else to do. The government—ever slavish to the Greek Orthodox church—forbade any witnessing whatsoever. Speaking even casually about Divine Principle could land us in jail and maybe worse. Some of our missionaries were brutally murdered by other governments. You didn't know who you could trust. A person who was your friend might feel threatened, vengeful, or obligated to report your casual, friendly spiritual talk. Already some Greek Cypriot church members had been arrested after miscalculating interest. A ruthless care to not mix religion—even in our personal life—with our business visas was a must.

Floyd was somber and careful when I'd first arrived. "While you're here, you have to forget you're a church member in public. Our services are strictly private."

"Erwin must've taken that to heart," I later chuckled with Ginny.

She drilled me. "You just leave him alone, Chris. You don't know his life."

"I'm sorry. Yeah. I was only . . . " *Yeah.*

"Don't let anything slip," Floyd scolded. "Lives could depend on it. For sure the *Times* situation is always precarious with these meatballs."

"Sounds crazy, Floyd. And a quasi-American ally, too."

We had missionaries here. I knew some of them. Their names were supposed to be top secret, never uttered aloud. None of us let it slip because it could mean jail or deportation. It meant summary death elsewhere. Especially overseas, we keenly felt each Moonie's murder. Still, our missionaries recruited about 20 Cypriots who formed a mousy corner of the global Unification Church. They even put on a low-key Blessing ceremony for a Cypriot couple while I was there since it wasn't possible to attend the main event. Ostensibly, Cyprus was a democracy. An elected government with laws. But, in many respects, it functioned autocratically. Extragovernmental bodies accomplished purposes best left quiet. Police had no legal authority to enforce, say, a business curfew. But those I spoke with were afraid to challenge them under a theoretically (not necessarily in practice) independent judiciary.

I said to my video friend, "You're gonna take them enforcing their own shit?"

"Repercussions are problematic. Leave it and prosper." His kettle boiled. "Tea?"

Plus, Archbishop Makarios and his role in government along with the attitude of Greece toward Cypriot politics still roiled the island. It was a difficult and unstable albeit not impossible environment for our independent, one-Cypriot-obligatory-board-member newspaper to function and thrive. These attitudes on the island's Greek side came into play when *Herr* Papandreou awoke to the offense of our Lebanon man's story. We saved ourselves from expulsion through a last-minute appeal to the American embassy.

"What are we getting," Thomas more or less excoriated the ambassador, "for the millions of taxpayer dollars the American government is pumping into Cyprus? We just bought them a new telephone exchange!"

"I understand. Freedom of the press is key at home and abroad."

"Is it? Why are they importing our exchanges but exporting *us*?"

"I'm calling Washington and the locals to see what I can do. I'll let you know."

Thomas stalked out. "Fingers crossed, then."

At the time, it took five years to get a new phone line installed. That was a helluva lot better than the ten our people in Egypt and Turkey said it was taking them. The new American exchanges shaved our waiting time to a lickity-split two. Floyd was still waiting at our house when, in America, he'd be roasting Ma Bell after three *days*. The reason it took so long, of course, is socialism. Instead of investing profits into its infrastructure to better serve its customers and earn more money, the government funneled the department's earnings into the general treasury for other uses and budgeted scant maintenance. These mismanaging and embezzling countries then begged America to buy them equipment to meet the "totally unexpected rising demand" for such a basic service as though too unforesightedly poor from capitalist exploitation to buy (much less build) their own. What a scam.

Thomas' arguments made an impression on the ambassador who wiled his way to the Cypriot top, wondering in a suited-up, gangsterish sort of way, "Just what kind of a democracy is your prime minister running? Look at all the money we're giving you, and this is how you repay us? Kicking out a legitimate American newspaper for wisecracking at the prime minister of *another* country?"

"Yes, yes, I understand."

"I've talked to Washington about this,"—not sure he did but, diplomacy—"and the United States may be rethinking its very generous taxpayer aid."

"I'll bring it up right away, Ambassador. I'm sure it's just a misunderstanding."

The government sulked but stayed our execution, warning we'd better watch our press. Relocating MET to Papandreou's backyard might seem at first blush skinny-dipping in the fire instead of the pan, yet Greece had *working* legal protections and customary practices regarding the press that Cyprus lacked. Thomas concluded there was less Papandreou could do about us there than here. By 2003, MET had abandoned the actual Middle East to publish about it from Britain. Hilarious.

My return trip from Athens was less enjoyable. At every port Israeli security loomed like Super Mario's Goombas. Apparently, they were necessary because my ship called at Haifa and other rat-infested wharves that buggered Israel. Its agents were obnoxious cocks of the walk. I don't jell with bossyboots anyway. Mountain men can't stand checks on their person. The Israelis fired off a billion questions, most of them ten times each, until I fumed. Inexperienced with interrogation methods, I didn't realize they were parsing the dubious from the dross.

For the nth time, this soldier-uniformed bastard said, "What's in your luggage?" He scoped my gym bag like dirty locker socks and didn't touch.

"Just clothes and a book."

"Did anyone pack it for you?"

"Why would anybody do that?"

"Did they?" His beady eyes slugged me.

"No, dammit. Why would—?"

"Did anyone ask you to carry anything for them?"

My eyes rolled around. "Like what?"

"Like, anything."

"But, like what?" I didn't even clue in to where he was going. "Why don't you just look in my bag if you're so worried?"

Brows scrunched over a squint. "Just answer the question."

"What. You don't want to look in it? If you're so curious, why not just open it?" I reached out. "I'll just unzip it and you'll—"

"Don't touch it! Now, did anyone—?"

"No, dammit. Nobody gave me anything. Nobody packed my bag. Nobody . . ." I harangued holy hell out of the guy to take a peek if he didn't believe my regurgitated story but only got his chundered *nope*.

Not a good omen, this trip.

Floyd said, "He was trying to fluster you enough to betray a tell. Really, how'd you not figure that out?"

"Because I'm an American with—?"

He burped a snigger. "Not out here you're not. Get used to it."

I horsed my lips. "If I drank I'd need a drink right now."

Our last day at sea, I relaxed several hours over my book on a deck chair atop a shaded deck. Unbeknownst to me, the flat-calm Aegean reflected its ferocious sun's ultraviolet onto the white-painted steel overhead. It rained into my bare shoulders, upper back, and neck. I scampered below after noticing hot, tender skin. By evening it was bubbled up and sloughing off to make George Romero proud. I'd never seen the like, not even my whole-body burn in 1969 or '70 from a catnap on an inner tube in an eddy of the *Rio Frio* near my aunt's house in Texas. I could barely move for a week. She'd slathered it with butter; '60s technology. Home in Nicosia, the slightest twitch terrorized the fried nerves in my extra-crispy hide. My torment was so bloody harsh I couldn't lift my arms. Ginny dressed my torso the next three weeks till I shed my inflexible husk. I should've known sun-blasted water works like glaring snow on eyeballs. Always relearning what I already knew.

~

MANY OF THE news stories I handled were depressingly sad. Pakistan suffered major riots. Men yanked up children by the ankles to spin headfirst into rocks or cast shrieking into a flaming pyre a moment ago their happy home. Police disappeared daytimes so rioters could rampage, then deluged nighttimes for curfew. Order and civility was a fairytale. It seemed so futile. I couldn't imagine invading whole towns to kill and maim for being a different tribe, sect, or whatever.

Wire stories rattled into our office from the AP, UPI, and Reuters cataloging the savagery in vivid photos of dead children, gutted women, mashed infants, burnt towns, rocky debris strewn about like meteor strikes, police beating whoever . . . one unpublishably gruesome, Maoesque still-shot after another. In the midst of it Iraq industriously prosecuted its surprise attack on Iran but, to our laughter, was having their ass handed to them. But the combat brutality was nothing to jape over. Trench warfare wasn't as bad as immolated children, but not by much.

At the heart of it I'm peaceful. I'll fight when pressed but prefer wordage to knucklage. Peace over war, order over chaos, law over edict. That's me. The Middle East was a cauldron of everything *not* me. If Islam really taught its noble virtues, the faithful universally ignored it like medieval Catholics the gospels. By December, my underwater psyche was down by the bow. I pined for America's predictably tolerant if not necessarily harmonious habitat more than ever. I was homesick.

~

SEVEN MONTHS IN-country burned through my last vestige of spirituality, care, idealism, God, even the Blessing. Floyd's aloofness with MET's business fueled it along with Ginny confusedly interpreting my searing torment on the heels of Mr. Kamiyama's supreme-court dismissal of my travails as *my* 'problem memberism.' Meantime, the region's disheartening inhumanity gratingly blared in the background. My life was circling. I itched for my elusive college diploma. A life on *my* terms.

"You're totally leaving us in the lurch," Ginny said.

"With five weeks' notice? Come on. Erwin says he's fine picking it up. Thomas is giving his employees here only four weeks' before moving to Athens."

"Erwin's lying. You promised a year. Floyd hoped for two."

"I thought this was a real business, but it lives and breathes Rev. Kwak. Floyd cuts me out of everything. He made me a drone. I feel like a glorified typist."

"You're being unfair."

"Well, I'll never fit in. You hate me skipping Sunday service and Pledge. You're a dedicated member and I'm . . . not sure what I've become."

"You know, Thomas told us Father just said that if a person falls then their membership terminates. It's Day One from the next day. So . . ."

"There you go, then. We all know where I'm at. I'm sorry to Floyd. Maybe I'm not as fair as I think"—her face was, *yep!*—"but he's kept me on a stiff arm."

Members' eyes read betrayal. I was dead to them. On c£240 ($463) a month, I'd paid my airfare and other MET debts after child support and food, and Floyd agreed to a half-airfare loan. I'd paid Monica myself since Papasan Choi. I now wrote her the well was dry at least a few months. February 2, I flew Larnaca to Jordan.

The airport bus to downtown Amman bulged. Riders squeezed into uncloseable doors to hang by a hand in the wind. Nonsmokers were invisible. Asphyxiation seemed certain in our sweatily putrid sardine can. I almost asked the nearest ones to abstain, then remembered where I was. Another reason to appreciate in dry irony the rise of absurd, control-freak laws in America. If I wasn't careful, I'd be voting Jimmy Carter dressed up as Michael Dukakis.

Waiting on my connecting flight, I passed a close day with my MET friend Sharif (deported from Cyprus) hiking Amman's streets, its warren of bazaars, and shoveling down its tasty cuisine. I exercised my 98-lb Arabic skills I'd worked up in Cyprus but didn't impress. I knew some words and could read some signs, but if I got lost I'd stay lost. Soldiers roamed everywhere. I was nervous as hell. These paramilitaries marched past gripping shoulder-strapped submachine guns at belt level aimed at *my* belt level, usually with a possibly itchy finger on the trigger. I imagined one tripping on a crack to burp half a mag through a crowd of mothers' backs. Maybe they took precautions, but I didn't catch their safeties.

My next leg was ready February 4. Customs, not so much. They scoured passport and itinerary with a fervor and scorn worthy of Israel's Piraeus Port Goombas.

"So, you've never traveled to Israel?"

"That's right." I admired his clean Saddam 'stache.

"You're a journalist and an American, so you must have."

"Just check my passport."

"I'm asking you, not your passport."

"That's where my visas are. I thought you want—"

"*Feh!* You Americans. I think you have been to Israel . . . maybe overland?"

"What? Hardly. I'm not—drive there?"

"Unhh . . ." He fingered over some lingering uniform. Abruptly, I was negotiating a 3-inch ledge a mile over jail. "Do you not have a second passport?"

"I've never—a second? Who has—? How would I even—?" Was he looking for a tell? Intentions are murky with officialdom. I met Uniform's doubting eyes. He knowingly flipped my passport pages. *Puh.* "I've *never* been there."

'Stache studied me. Took back my passport. "Don't you people check?"

"When I got—Wait. Who 'people'?"

He was shaking his head. "Jordan allows no entry for travelers to Israel."

I sucked air. "So . . . if I had an Israeli stamp in my—?"

"You would be in jail now. Do you see how this works?"

I groaned but checked an eyeroll. Now I recalled Floyd skirting the rule with two passports, one for Muslim states only. Amusing that our federal government supplied multiple passports when so largely unconcerned with its domestic constitutional duties. A hefty fee, I wagered. The business of America is business after all.

"Nobody asked me about it when I landed. The guy just flipped through—"

"Yes." He clammed up, impassive as a *moai* on Easter Island. He flicked Uniform away with a chinned eye. "Well! It seems you are lucky today." I kept my mouth shut. He half-smiled, stamped my passport. "You may go. Enjoy your flight."

You're goddamn right I will. I would've snatched it from his fingers but this was Jordan, not La Guardia. I felt them laughing at my back. *These fuckin' people.*

Jordan's last official act was reaming me through three metal detectors and three physical searches before qualifying me to board their majestic Alia Royal Jordanian. On the tarmac atop the airstairs at the door into the fuselage two grim guards were rectal-exam thorough, flipping through my books for hollowed-out pages with the ubiquitous, "Did anyone put anything into your carry-on?"

I might've slapped my forehead. "Oh. My. God. No!"

They traded cocked eyes. Drama school had to figure in their training. "Welcome aboard. Please enter. Next, please."

I scooted inside to a refreshingly pulse-quickening stewardess who rolled me along. At last in my plusher-than-average seat, a drawn-out lungful of tension sighed forth. If there's one thing government the world over excels at it's boiling up anxiety. I considered the century of soldiers ringing my plane, guns fixed outward. Nothing for granted in this place. *What a way to live.* It didn't make me feel all that safe. They could swivel on me in an instant. Still and all, I felt reasonably certain a hijacking was improbable and wasn't that the point? If one did, I thought through faking my quality Irish accent to, God willing, avoid an American fate.

At cruising altitude stewardesses beamed alluring smiles and sharply tailored uniforms under model-perfect features and snappy caps evoking the fashionable sixties. Dinner came on china with stout silverware you could stab a pilot with. First airline I'd seen do that since hijacking got popular. The food was pure tongue orgasm. A culinary treasure more sumptuous for the shiny metalware by which I'd now forever judgily look down my nose on all plastic-utensiled airlines.

A few hours' layover in Amsterdam then a mind-tearing overnight when Nanami unexpectedly met me at JFK and shared my Viscount room. We talked everything for hours. I didn't want to start any fires and along midnight made a floor pallet.

"I love you, K'risu." She stripped and smiled our happy future.

My heart boomed her love right back. I resisted like France in 1940. We got as close to the real mamma-jamma while not, but kicked off a year of tormented, disconsolate vultures circling the Blessing. Rev. Moon's fluky offer to reBless broken-Blessing members was as yet unknown and still a crucifixion we avoided. I walked her to the bus stop the next day around 12:30 PM aching for my ring on her finger. Our eyes were wet. A few days later she wrote she wanted my baby and was ready to fly to me but then Sam persuaded her to stay and . . . she loved him, too.

My fourth leg landed me in San Francisco on the scarce end of February 5 exhaustedly half-crippled by the no-room legroom but raring to sprint for college.

Act X

University of California, Berkeley
Conflict, Love, and Duty in a Blender

Returning to California and evolving a reconciliation with the Bay Area church leadership swelled up in my mind. It dominated my daily life over the several years I worked my way through City College (CCSF) and into the history department at University of California at Berkeley (UCB). Stepping across the airport's threshold into San Francisco's coolly moist, late night winter air I wondered how it would all play out. I sensed my final showdown with California's Unification Church grinding into gear.

I'd trudged the freeway under my seabag two hours when the highway patrol kicked me off. A pay phone on El Camino Real got me Roxanne's ear near 1 AM.

"This is unexpected," she said. "It's okay, I was still up. But, I didn't expect you back . . . well, I wasn't sure *if*."

"Had to come for my car, didn't I?" *Chuckle, chuckle.*

"About that."

"What? Did it—ahhh, you were driving it?" I felt her nod. "No worries. Glad it runs. Thanks for taking care of it. Really appreciated."

She plucked me off the chilly roadside. All my worries and stress melted and love reblossomed in her lovely, smiling eyes. Yet, the next morning I wrote,

> All of my best sense tells me to stay with the U.C., but I cannot. That dilemma is the basis of my stress. It ruins my sleep and waking hours. I'm so mixed up . . . How I wish none of these bad things had happened so I could be a happy Moonie . . . Why are so many members seemingly so easily living their lives, while I am rent and shaken by these conflicts? . . . Do they just suppress their real feelings of difficulty? or do they actually exist in such a "blissful" way? If I could [I'd be] a monk . . . [S]uffering between God and love is too painful.

In days we'd accepted that, however attracted, our relationship had no legs. I slept on her living room floor and she hunted a roommate. I rented a room but, a week before my March 1 move-in, she persuaded me to leave my briefcase unlocked "for trust." Breaking into my diary, she gagged over my tortured struggle between her, God, and Nanami—"I feel totally used!"—and threw me out at 10 pm.

I snuck inside my friendly, elderly Chinese landlord's 9×10-foot room he was still fixing and painting on the second floor of his group house at 225 Harold Avenue, mere steps round the corner from my pre-mono Ocean Avenue flat. He went the extra mile, later letting my $220 rent ride for seven months until I got the pathetic proceeds of the 'new' VEAP GI Bill, the sorry excuse for an educational benefit that Congress didn't wait for Vietnam's dead to cool before enacting as a cheaper, 2-for-1 contributory alternative that maxed out at $8,100. But it paid my back rent, some living expenses, and most of my dirt-cheap $50 full-load tuition. I made the Dean's List six out of the eight semesters I spent rectifying my disgraceful 2.1 GPA at Western State in 1977–78. Amazing what 10 years of growing up does for a fellow.

I got some cashflow when Daniel Solomon and Associates off the waterfront hired me part-time at $390 then $921 a month to office manage. Dan's primary test of my abilities after verifying my 130-WPM, zero-error high school typing skill was to see me decipher his handwriting that shamed physicians. He was an impressive man, though I can't say I had much affinity for his taste in architecture; too modernist. A tenured professor at UCB, he was an avid bicyclist doing 100 miles every weekend. Fifty years old, in tip-top shape from hard abs to a springy step, I'd estimated him mid- to late-30s. I admired that. In no small part it inspires me as I strive to keep my body in some semblance of vigor and tone. I learned a lot about management and administration while running his 12-architect operation.

We hired Victoria, a minikin young woman from India maybe 80 pounds wet. Her long, silky midnight black hair, attractive features, and oddly sexy figure riveted me. In her presence is when I discovered sex appeal. Whatever it really is, she had it in spades. Or she spritzed pheromones for perfume. I felt inexplicably drawn to her and constantly low-level flirted while ever conscious not to mess with a married woman and upset our holy applecarts. I doted on her strictly hands off despite my uncontrollably inquiring eye. I liked her a lot and we got along famously. Dan told me to fire her for incompetence, though. I objected and took her for a 2-hour lunch to inspire a renaissance in whatever was lacking.

His chief architect Kathryn—her kiss and flowers for secretaries day blushed me—said, "Whatever you said over lunch, she's like a totally different person!"

"Just the right kind of TLC, I reckon."

She eyed me. "Well, we definitely need her. So, I'd say you rock!"

Victoria's top-chef husband hired into a five-star hotel in Cartageña down the line and she sailed out of my life.

My relationship with the church jalopied over tottery ground. To fit myself back in, I visited its grand Hearst Avenue mansion, originally built circa 1915 for the Phi Delta Theta chapter, at 2717 Hearst Avenue next to UCB. It wasn't easy. I was a pariah with a capital P. I just couldn't ignore my staunch belief in Divine Principle. It's not easy doddering off a going worldview. Not only a personal interest but a public duty dragged me by the ear to push for church reformation as if God Himself depended on me. After my one nailed thesis, I was a rolled up Martin Luther and his rebels fomenting their medieval uprising against Catholicism, Inc. Like him, I took my faith's core values as holy orders, including its founding Messiah. I could no more reject him on account of the mendacious slavery his institutional minions farmed than Luther could Jesus over the pope pushing phony salvation schemes to ballast his bank vault. There's a logical separation 'tween faith and founder.

It seemed that Moonies turned *ex-* in rejecting a crass leadership and structure never appreciated the distinction. They blamed Rev. Moon for its SNAFU, recasting him a false prophet counterfeiting God. But the Principle stands or falls on its own merit regardless its use or abuse by him or his cronies. Do Christians reject Jesus or his core gospel over his followers' corruption? No, and why should they? Rev. Moon needs castigating for his faults, aye. That

Hearst Ave. sans grassy lawn.

includes how he organizes and operates his church. But the Principle, like Jesus' core teaching, needn't be a collateral casualty. It transcends him and I daresay even he doesn't appear to get that, judging by his visible fruits. This developing mindset had my reconciling with the church front and center.

NANAMI CALLED MARCH 25. "There's a Matching on Friday. Please come!"

Lungs deflated. "In just two days?" *And it won't be with you! She'd already said,* 'I want marry you,' but now . . . ? "I don't even qualify. Uh, what are they?"

"A 7-day fast. A 21-day workshop. Tithe ten percent and special days. Be 3-year active member age 24 up. Negative AIDS test. Plus three spiritual children."

"That's all?!" A hard breath was her *yes.* "I can tithe but all my spiritual children were pushed away by those Judah Street loons. And I don't meet the celibacy." That last admission built into a flame-broiled argument. I almost hung up.

"Many members are coming who don't qualify, K'risu. Is your decision. I won't take responsibility for that."

"God, I feel so humiliated and beggared, here." I imagined the scene. "I'll be thrown out once they know I wasn't celibate . . . it seems such a mockery for me to ever get Matched along with those who've denied themselves . . ."

"You sound *baka.* You say is what you want. Maybe just try. Father has very big heart. He might see other thing besides your situation."

Yeah, that's true. I used my rent to buy a $188 terrifying roundtrip. *What weirdo will I get? What do I deserve?* Thoughts shuddered through me. *And I'm head over heels for Nanami. Fuck! Has to be a wild goose chase.*

Sheri now ran the Blessed Family Department (BFD). She said, "Call Nick at Bush Street about your situation."

Nick said, "You have to talk to Rev. [Zin Moon] Kim or maybe Ricky, first. After this Matching is over."

"After?"

"Well, yeah, it starts tomorrow. Tell him the situation and take it from there. The minimum requirement is two years celibacy."

"Now it's two? Or is it three?"

"I heard two. But, things change." My $188 was swirling down my sewer pipe.

Nanami said, "I won't tell you what do. Father could extend Matching, but also maybe not. Come in case. Father likes surprises, neh? And also, members with no qualifications are coming, same reason. We never know with Father."

I was ripping to shreds in a vortex. "Okay. I've already bought my ticket."

I launched a 3-day fast. Now-ex-member-broken-Blessing Julian dropped me at the airport with a grin and a prayer. I arrived at the New Yorker at 7:30 PM. It was sardined under a 100 miles of spiritual pressure. Its vibe reinflated my spirit. For a moment I was a light beam ricochetting through mirrored possibilities.

Nanami's BFD position let her do a lot of groundwork but she'd struck out. "We call Cyprus, but they say you leave. That ended it." *Thanks, Floyd. So much for your 'Nobody should be denied the Blessing.' If I'd stayed even two more months...* "I can do everything to get you into Matching, but I cannot give you recommendation. If I could!" She sent me after a leader who might get me in. I lost him in the throng.

"Just push in, Chris," friends echoed her.

But my sin, my degradation, my untimely incelibacy now wracked my heart. "If I bulldoze into the Matching to play on Father's heart, it'll be wrong and make a mockery of the other members attending. At least they've been faithful!"

"You can't think like that. Just *try* to get Matched. You can work the details—"

"I don't want Father taking responsibility for me in my condition and cause him even more headaches. I want to relieve him!" *And, goddamn me all to hell, but I love Nanami!* Just seeing her on the main floor with Sam was a gut punch.

"This is warfare, Chris! Satan is doing everything to block your Blessing through every person and means possible. You have to push through!"

"Okay! But, I feel like that dirty homeless bum at Father's fancy soirée."

My humiliation, ignominy, my *unrecommended* status scourged and flayed me all night in the surging, bubbly crowd of *couples*. No one with authority was willing to walk me onto the Matching floor. Nanami couldn't. I tried to lie and dissemble but, in this august moment, I couldn't get the words out, couldn't blank my face, couldn't bluff through. I abandoned the main deck to avoid Nanami.

I slaked a parched thirst in a hideaway 40th-floor bathroom. On the roof I tried beseeching God but it seemed impossible to express my heart. My delirious mind ran to Papasan. If he hadn't roughly shoved me into a moral corner I couldn't weasel out of, none of this would be my lot. I'd be functional. A reasonably happy Moonie. Kyung Mi, Bernie, Roxanne, and especially Nanami never would've entered my life. No impossible heart-wrenchers. I'd be here *recommended*. Matched. Looking at a happy marital future... well, some managed it, anyhow. I wrote March 27,

> It seems, at times, that I'm very religious—my beliefs and all—but I can't seem to do the things normally associated with religion, like prayer, and rituals and ceremony... I expect some tension to exist between Nanami and me after this failed attempt. It's hard for her if she really loves me, to help make arrangements for and watch me get Matched. She's such an incredible friend sometimes. I don't deserve her in the least.

I visited Mrs. Kobayashi and an unhappily Matched Shiori and chatted up Judah Streeters Shinichi, Hiro, and Kayoko, all Matched to Japanese. Maria, my friend from Boulder church, and her Match ran into me in the stairwell. She seemed almost in tears seeing me. "You're extremely special, Chris, especially to me. I almost didn't attend because I didn't want Father to suffer more."

"I'm not the only one, then."

"I've thought of you so much over the last year. You're such a great person."

"Well . . ." *Wow.* I forced a half-chuckle. "You're in a very small elite." Who else might've thought I was the catch of a lifetime? I felt my closed hand thrice tap my Catholic heart: *'I have sinned through my fault, through my most grievous fault.'*

> I think that if I believed I should be Matched, I could have wormed my way in. But I couldn't believe in myself. How can I burden Father with just the sight of me, all evil and yukky?!?

No room at the inn for the un-missioned. I slept two fitful hours on the stairwell landing at the roof door, then found space for more as MFT vacated. Nanami wanted out of Sam and the church, but her feelings anguished her also. Many years later I discovered she was waiting for me to make a firm commitment, to take her by the hand into *our* life. I couldn't. I loved her *and* Principle. I believed leaving as a broken-Blessing couple meant our Blessed future was forever lost. I'd be Satan's heel doing that to her when I knew (yet didn't know) how conflicted she was.

She met me over water in the pizza place across 8th Avenue. "I was so worry I could not find you. I think you must be sleep on street or at airport . . . maybe you were leaving right away to avoid me."

Tears choked me. "I couldn't be Matched with my past the last couple years. And then being in love with you, too. I can't use Father's compassion for that."

"I care about you so much, K'risu. I want see you get Blessing because is so important to you." Her own eyes overflowed.

"I promise, if you want to start your family with Sam, I'll disappear. I want you to be happy more than anything." I wanted *her* to choose so I could be sure.

Her eyes dodged through the restaurant. "I don't know . . . if he is not change, I am maybe quit church." *I could only hope.*

The New Yorker throbbed all night. Around 3 AM I visited for a goodbye. She crumpled, weeping. "Please to leave my room, K'risu. Is too much difficult! I am so frustrate. Maybe must to cut off friendship." We fell into each other's arms anyway but faith pulled me loose. Horsekicks crushed me leaving. Here we were, so intimate. Married, without marriage. *God, I love her so!* My plane sailed home on tears.

WHILE FLOYDIANLY FORGETTING I was a church member in Cyprus, Papasan Choi—perhaps after a sit-down with Rev. Moon clutching my letters—pushed me over with a feather declaring in a Sunday sermon that he'd made a mistake how he'd handled Jerome and me and now regretted how things had turned out.

'Ha!' says Amphialus in *Zelmane, 'hold my Brain; be still my beating Heart.'*

Papasan never said anything to me directly and I wasn't surprised, but I like to believe he knew I'd hear his mea culpa. It couldn't have been easy to admit his failure behind his Sunday lectern of power and glory. That he'd said anything . . . must've been drunk or inspired by God, or maybe threatened by Rev. Moon tired of my posted complaints. He deserved worse for the damage he'd wrought on the church. He got some of it, too. I soon heard he'd been retired, stripped of Japan and the West Coast, and now operated independently from his California home he called "Alamo." His sun was obviously setting and I'm a practical man, so I left him to God.

Shortly afterward Hiro, my friend and Divine Principle student turned persecutor after Matsumoto's 'bad man' beating and taking over Mr. Uchiyama's position, cozied up to me following a Sunday service at Hearst Street.

"*Saaa*... sometimes, this life is so difficult to live. Things so often different."

I dropped eyes into him. "Are you saying I was right all along?" He didn't give a straight answer, but his sense of regret was palpable and I felt his attitude softening. I took it for the only apology he had in him. I wrote April 6,

> look at Choi and Julian—the once supreme dignitaries both out of the church—
> you can see that he must be wondering how to view me. I don't know if he
> knows how Julian has decided to quit everything and get married... two
> "greats" have quit, and here's Chris, still plugging away... food for thought.

I Julian-clapped him on the shoulder with the gracious nod he was looking for. We parted ways for the last time. *But here's an opening.* An admitted chink in the armor of these insufferably arrogant, infallibly inscrutable Oriental leaders. My tormentors publicly admitting they'd transgressed my righteousness went down in smooth satisfaction. I felt vindicated even if my reputation didn't.

~

RICKY WAS NORTHERN California's new state leader and wanted to reach out and touch some of us 'B' members. In the 1980s the Unification Church sorted adherents into four houses, all but one it considered worthless. 'A' members were full-timers, godly front line troops devoting their 24–7 lives to the Providence and True Parents by living in church centers. 'B' members, later known as 'home' members, lived outside the centers. Most were Blessed and supposed to be implementing Rev. Moon's Home Church ministry. Sometimes they were just ex-members, 'negos' (negative attitude), or fed up with 'A' membership. The bulk of 'A' members, especially leaders, felt they alone were sacrificing to build the kingdom on Earth. They usually took 'B' members who'd once 'A'-listed for traitors, apostates, and noncommittal scum too selfishly fallen to live for God and Principle.

Moonies give you a pass if you've never heard Divine Principle but, if you have, they mercilessly toll your service. Great tension therefore existed between the groups, at least in Northern California and New York City. 'B' members agitated for more respect and greater (just short of 'A'-list) participation in church affairs because, now raising children, they were seeing it more a Sunday affair like Christians.

'C' members accepted Divine Principle if not necessarily Rev. Moon as the Messiah but were unwilling to leave their own churches. They helped our activities in various ways. 'D' members were willing to support and encourage Rev. Moon's ministry from the fence. Typically, 'C' and 'D' members enjoyed some level of social credibility, hence leaders showered them with a respect and recognition they'd never stoop to dousing on 'A' and especially 'B' members. The enemy's minions always seem preferable to the religious—the thrill of future conquests?—than their own trod-upon brethren, ironically writ worse by virtue of low rank or assumed apostasy which, for many leaders, is any kind of critical thinking or disobedience.

Church leaders now generously classified me a 'B' member. They wanted me at Sunday service preferably long enough to tithe my 10% to qualify as a warm body they could report to Rev. Moon. They neither asked nor desired more of me. In that milieu I more often visited Bush Street in San Francisco and developed a friendly relationship with Ricky, who doubled as its center director. After some horse-trading, he agreed I could fundraise on Saturdays and donate all my result.

That's real white of you, Ricky, I chose not to say.

Saturdays I arrived early at Bush Street to load into my 1966 half-shoebox Beetle— junkyard bumpers wired on to satisfy the State Police who'd ticketed me while unconvincingly extolling their crash-safety value—several 3×4-foot red-on-white, hand-painted plywood signs advertising roses and four 5-gallon buckets of water holding dozens of roses each. A card table, folding metal chair, and a beach umbrella rounded out my tools. I set up on street corners and even forested dirt roads that Bush Street designated and handed over 100% of my result. I paid my own gas and food. Even so, rank and file scorned my 'B'-ness and chastised me for not quitting school to rejoin their 'A'-ness. That Ricky might take me aboard was itself a heartstopper. In reality, my reputation with Papasan preceded me due in no small part to his ever-clanging gong regardless his apparently regretted contrition.

Eventually he said, "Frankly, I don't want you in Bush Street despite what I said."

Leaders could be confusing when tap dancing around the Principle. "Well, then, what do you want, Ricky? I'll do whatever. I kinda need an answer."

"Just fundraise on Saturdays. Okay? That'll be enough."

Then out of nowhere he invited Bay Area home members to Hearst Street to discuss integrating us more fully into church life and his 'B'-community's growing desire to purchase their own building. Perhaps he was sniffing denominationalism like I was and wanted to nip it in the bud. More likely he was responding to Rev. Moon's recent assertion that the vast hemorrhaging of American members the last five years was due not to rejecting the Principle but leaders' unconscionable devilry. He charged them with bringing back these wayward souls by loving and appreciating them like good and proper Abels, allowing them to contribute as they could while not judging them by their level of commitment.

This was precisely the point, wasn't it? Most of us were gone from the church mainstream because we'd been kicked, forced, or walked out over irreconcilable differences. It was funny Rev. Moon admitting such an indictment of his hand-picked leadership cadre after seeming to give me no justice at all vis-à-vis Papasan and then telling me, through Peter Kim, to forget about the church to graduate from college. So far, no leader was willing to accept or tolerate my direction from on high as anything but my own Satan-invaded fallen selfishness. It was all flat-out contradictory. I took it as I found it and joined Ricky's meeting.

Some 30 of us chaired up in a circle in the first floor main room. Ricky presided. From my point of view, he failed miserably to reach out and touch us with less than a slap when he said, "I hear what you're saying. But the fact is that center members are the only ones sacrificing *full time* for the providence. We alone are accepting the heavy responsibility of Restoration and *following* Father's directions through his appointed leaders. Because *that's* where the providence is."

"That . . . is the most absurd thing I've heard you say out loud, I'm here to tell you," somebody gasped, igniting our teapot in tempest. Ricky stuck to his selfish-lives–unselfish-mission guns with signing hands belaboring his pious visage.

"The way I see it," I said as the tirade waned, "the major issue for home members is our sense of being persecuted, belittled, and ostracized for our non-center lifestyles and opinions by the center members. Led by you, Ricky."

"That's ridiculous. Home members are Blessed families. Integral to the church."

"We don't feel very integral," said a brother.

Ricky checked his watch. "What about this buying a building idea? Who wants to talk about that?"

I supposed he was playing up to Rev. Moon's desire to win us back despite his enmity showing like party lines at a political convention, because by now I thought he was going along with their foolish plan to create their own church.

"With respect," I said, "I think what home members are actually wanting from you is permission to set up a separate denomination and I can't disagree *more*." Dark eyes sunk darts in me.

"That's not it at all!" someone said.

Ricky said, "It doesn't seem to me that's their intent."

"Nobody here is trying to set up a different church, Chris," an older sister said. "That's preposterous! Home members just want a church environment targeted to our needs. That works for *us*."

"Exactly," a brother said. "Hearst Street, Bush Street, all of them are aimed at center members, not us. But we're the future. Father said so."

With my characteristic lack of filter I said, "That's the practical reality, but it stems from all of us feeling disenfranchised by leaders like you, Ricky. I mean, you just told us so." *Don't you get it? Estrangement begets denominationalism.*

"That's not here nor there, right now."

I had to smirk. He'd opened the can then pretended there were no worms. "Well, they want a place where they feel at home and in control. Free to pursue their own personal and public objectives."

"And what's wrong with that? Nothing! It's Blessed families' mission."

"They have that here," Ricky said.

A different brother took to his feet. "If that was true, we wouldn't raise the issue."

"Chris isn't entirely wrong, Ricky. We aren't being served by the church as it is, but it's hardly a new denomination. That's totally wrong."

"Nooo . . . that's exactly what it is. The proof is home members disparaged as not just *different* but *less than* center members who reject our validity *as* members. It's a useless, elitist distinction and why they get no spiritual nourishment here."

"Center members don't reject anybody's validity," Ricky said.

"Home Church doesn't recruit center members or fundraise for the national church. Its mission is entirely different. Its needs are different. But we're still the one-and-same church! If they go off—"

"Totally wrong. We're not—"

"The point is, setting up their own church for home members means preaching a different message that's focused on *their* way of life and *their* truth. Not full-time members' mission at all. Regardless Principle or Father. Isn't that the very definition of denominationalism? Home members separated from center members all across the country will spawn endless competition and even conflict, just like Christianity. That's the logical outcome besides the practical and financial . . ."

Ricky was shaking his head through most of it. "You're not even Matched, Chris. You don't speak for home members. Your uninformed opinions aren't needed."

I ground my teeth. "You're the one who said I'm a home member, and therefore don't belong in Bush or Hearst Street. You forget that?"

He was looking flush. "It's not something I can approve or deny anyhow."

"They're not asking you to approve it." I almost laughed. "It's *permission* they want, which isn't the same thing. And it's a big mistake."

"Ricky's right, Chris," the older sister said. "Butt out!"

The room erupted in dissension and calls for a new venue. Already struggling to handle an independent thinker like me and now surrounded by even more senior versions of it, Ricky blew up. He jumped to his feet, yelling and berating me. I unflinchingly defended my point of view, then realized he wasn't listening. I wrote him a much less emotional letter.

> Needless to say, I did not exactly express my thoughts cogently the other night at Hearst Street, and it was all too evident that you became rather hot under the collar, and I would like to redress that . . . The history of the early Christian church . . . should serve as a warning that . . . splits for various and sundry reasons [are] a real and abiding malignancy in God's providence.

Did we want the ragtag fragmentation in the Unification Movement the Catholics got through Protestantism? By rights I should've been long gone from this dysfunctional Family, wrapped up as it was with ego, power, authority, and feudalism over God's sorrow, spiritual growth, unselfish love, and public duty.

Why am I not gone? I roasted myself in these years. Praying over Twin Peaks I cried out to God for answers to my dilemma. I loved Rev. Moon. His vision of a Restored world aroused me yet, implacably, I despised the institution he founded because it rejected all sense of justice, duty, honor, and law. Then and now it's a preserve of party hacks and impractical idealists locked in a death roll, the visionless fixed on ruling diametrically opposed to the emasculated disregarding the practical realities of human nature. Church bloodbaths over one thing or another mired this era and felt like counterrevolutionary pogroms and cultural revolutions without the death but all the (spiritual) terror, as with Nanami. There was no room for those willing to live for the greater good of the church thus God's providence of Restoration. It marginalized them, extolling their virtues for a quick dismissal. That's why virtually all thinking Americans got the fuck out of the Moonies.

Perfectly aware of this, Rev. Moon often reminded us he founded the Unification Church to sacrifice itself for the will of God. "In business to go out of business," he said. If it turned from its duty, God would abandon it to raise up another from the dust. The problem wasn't so much its unwillingness to sacrifice on suffering's altar to embrace Cain's world like a good Abel, but leaders' willingness to exile members to the vanguard like penal conscripts while ensconcing themselves in the rear to slit throats and backstab church credibility, finances, and spiritual reserve for personal aggrandizement, abandoning members to a "nondescript life of toil and hardship." Members wore to nubs as leaders rose to greater promotion despite ever greater failure, the religious mirror of corrupt, derelict, incompetent Sovietism.

"Reform!" we cried out.

But the members gathered this evening in Hearst Street weren't asking for reform but *separation*. A student of history, I was appalled our church might blithely embark on Christianity's fragmented path and Ricky bit my head off for it.

> There is a strong undercurrent of reproach and elitism between many "center" and "home" members. To say that "center" members are the only ones who are willing to . . . follow leaders' directions with a "Yes sir!" to anything . . . [implies] that only "center" members are willing, and are in fact doing, God's Will, while "home" members are nothing more than hangers-on and spiritual misfits who are trying to grab from the Church what they can't earn in real life. "Home" members want to work with "leaders," but reject the dictatorship . . .

That was the crux of the wound in the heart of the church through which sluiced its lifeblood of do-or-die membership.

Home members were, for the most part, *Blessed* members who, according to Rev. Moon, were the only true embodiment of the Unification Church . . . his own very embodiment. Whatever they did was God's will so long as it was Principled. Ricky and most center members were challenging his view like they'd challenged my college mission, insisting that home members, in distancing themselves from the official chain of command, *weren't* members.

Friendly fire mode: enabled.

The church saw upholding its *central figure* system crucial. Members come to God only by his or her central figure. His will works through them from Rev. Moon down. It seemed biblically sensible but was a rebirth of medieval Catholicism and its cult of the priesthood. Gone was the Protestant view of individual inspiration, independence before God, and our 5% providential responsibility. I reviled it.

What's a central figure anyway? Rev. Moon says he or she is whom God works through in any moment. We need obey them to stay in His Restorational grace. Rev. Moon is *the* central figure and anoints others to represent his, thus God's, will. To accept each leader as *central* warranting absolute obedience on par with that given to Rev. Moon means subscribing to the view that God works *exclusively* through them, rendering them *co*-central figures that eliminates 'central' from the term. Tentacles of the central brain. No regular member is therefore privy to God's grace or calling, only central figures. Strictly speaking any central figure's activity, regardless how heinous, unPrincipled, or inhuman is God's will that *necessarily* mandates obedience. This is the institution's core belief. Salvation predicates on absolute obedience to an *immediate* central figure *consistent or not with Principle or a higher central figure, such as Rev. Moon.* Chain of command is all.

Obedience to an immediate superior justifies the American soldier when an order is lawful and consonant with the institution of the Uniform Code of Military Justice. Obedience *as* the institution of the church justifies a Unificationist. One's central figure's consonance with the Principle or Rev. Moon isn't of concern nor interferes with one's Principled standing before God. This is how Mr. Kamiyama caused subordinates to falsify ledgers to the IRS and (Mary Ann at Hearst Street told me) how Bush Street ran secret books to backdoor money to our backstabbing church president until the IW's ended it. Rev. Moon publicly propounds we can't hide wrongdoing behind obedience. Privately, he ends up teaching absolute obedience is how God's will is done and one's faith and loyalty are ascertained and rewarded.

It's a conundrum. Members like me pondering these issues saw only one solution: adhere to Divine Principle as our ultimate guide, trust in our conscience to interpret its workaday relevance, and largely tune out leaders. In the mid-'90s Rev. Moon formally advocated individual conscience as the cornerstone through which God communicates with fallen humanity and therefore needs be respected, pursued, and upheld. In the Imperial '80s, though, 'conscience' was a dirty word proclaiming you an individualistic Westerner, a traitor to True Parents, and Satan's dupe for imagining that *individual* conscience was a better guidepost than obedience to central figures as *collective* conscience. For me, you just couldn't get more Japanese that that. Nor more Korean, if you recall Papasan 'fist-banger' Choi.

My analysis pissed off Ricky. By suggesting the alienation home members were trying to escape in raising their own church center—inevitably, a denomination— was a result of impacting an unyielding (Imperially Confucianist) institutional habit betraying the fundamental (Christian) values of Divine Principle as they understood it, Ricky viewed me, not them, putting a saw to the very trunk of the Unification Church. I wasn't attacking Divine Principle, which was easy enough to discount, but the *institutional principles of church governance*. That was so dangerous that,

> I've even had church leaders refuse me admittance... because they didn't want their "center" members exposed to the heresies of a [philosophy] student.

"Ricky has the wrong impression of me," I said to friends. "That's why he's so hot under the collar with me disagreeing with a separate home-member church."
"He doesn't know you, Chris." *Well, I think he needs a refresher.*

> Despite the fact that I was excommunicated for upholding Father's teaching over Mr. Choi's, I nevertheless involved myself every day in public activities relating to God's Providence, to wit: I ran the student government at CCSF as an avowed Moonie... spent numerous hours in exposition on the nature of God and True Father and Divine Principle in public, Jerome and I were the associate producers of a Channel 25 TV talk-show aimed at the black community... [and] working with Rev. Dr. Welbon, we set up under permission from John Didsbury a pioneer church/CARP center at our previous Ocean Avenue address, and numerous other activities... so... that I finally collapsed in the beginning of May 1986 from exhaustion and malnutrition, compounded by mononucleosis, strep throat and tonsillitis... and I was denied every moral and spiritual comfort and support due one brother to another.

He was giving me my first real chance since 1984 to reinvolve myself with the religious side of the church. Lord knows I was tired of the business side. I certainly appreciated his outstretched hand and said so. But he was slyly lumping me into his evil home-member category without actually saying so, and *that* I didn't like.

You should lighten up . . . Be ready for a discussion if I disagree, but if you can prove your point, I am easily humbled. If you expect me to "Yes, Sir" my way around . . . the perpetuation of that attitude, even despite evidence that it's a false methodology, is one of the primary reasons for the collapse of the American movement—this notion of monarchical hierarchy and absolute obedience to individuals at the expense of the Truth.

The church may be an institution needing organized authority to accomplish its collective goal but it's not the military nor at war. It's a church, which traditionally accomplishes its militarily rigid imperatives in dramatically different fashion. Why must ours be any different? Why must authority and rank supersede brotherhood, the very core of Christ? Isn't that what we're fighting for in the first place? Most Bush and Hearst Street members saw me through Ricky's eyes. And why not? They were the obedient ones, the center members, the heavenly 'A' list, the haven't-left-yet. But I was discouraged that, regardless my efforts,

> no one yet thinks I am willing to participate in special fasting or prayer conditions . . . I have my name on every phone list . . . hardly one phone call!

"What's it take to get through to him?" I wondered aloud, then wrote about my 3-tiered 'formula course' of "fasting, prayer, and, active missionary work."

> I fast each Sunday for one day; I fast the first 3 days of every month; and I fast for the first 7 days every third month . . . and just completed a 4-day fast, as well as all the Sundays in between . . . to rectify . . . my own ill-preparation for the Blessing; and . . . indemnify the failure of Americans to respond to Father's message and of the American movement to properly elucidate that message . . . it is the best I know how to do.

> [Whatever benefit] prayer has . . . it helps to draw me closer to God and distance me from satanic influences . . . I rise at 0430 every day and travel to Holy Ground where I say pledge and then pray for usually 30–45 minutes or more. The weather plays no part in this, and the only times I miss going is when I am so tired that I fail to hear my alarm clock ring . . . I average probably 4–5 hours of sleep per night, in direct contravention to my doctor's recommendations. But, what can I do? . . . the Blessing is more important than anything else in life, including life! . . . if I should sleep more, then I sleep less; if I should eat more, then I eat less . . . I fell as low as 180 pounds . . . I have significant problems with my knees and general health . . . but [I can't] possibly "qualify" for the Blessing without such a serious commitment.

> I am hoping that this week or next I will actually be able to begin meeting with ministers with the view of inviting them to the Korean banquets.

> Though I haven't given money to the movement since I was excommunicated, I have always used my money for public purposes . . . The only significant thing I spent my money on in the last 4 years was the computer I am writing this letter on, and I bought a car (for a whopping $125) last year for the specific reason of being able to go to Holy Ground each morning . . .

> I don't think that by working I've been living a life much different from that of any other member . . . I've done my share of bookkeeping in the Church, and have seen how money is embezzled—and that's the only word for it . . . Bush St. has amended its prior practice of bankrolling certain people, buying fancy

sports cars, fancy oriental food, fancy china plates, fancy et cetera (*ad nauseam*) for "leaders" and their minions, so I am willing to tithe money now . . . you guys eat immensely better than I do. My first year of excommunication I lived almost exclusively on beans, tortillas, rice and ramen for want of money . . . Jerome . . . was forced to live on the street and go to soup kitchens.

Well, he was getting a dose of me. I didn't get opened arms, but he did soften his attitude and I felt more accord. But he genuinely hated me being in school. Even CARP, an organization ostensibly devoted to education and students, vigorously encouraged new recruits to quit school for full-time church work. I wanted to join as a UCB student because the church wouldn't have me. The "very disciplined" Mr. Aoki of CARP MFT and less-fanatical but obedient Mata, CARP's local leader, demanded a *mano a mano* to gauge my appreciation for obedience. Guess what?

"You're not a good candidate for CARP," Mr. Aoki said on our chairs and sofa in Ashby Avenue's closed-door front room.

"But I'm a UCB student! What more qualification does CARP need?"

"You'll be happier if you try some other group."

Would I. Their 'don't call us, we'll call you' send-off was my last official word. Leaders like Ricky and these CARPster frauds could, with some prodding, understand home members feeding and clothing themselves but not the rank selfishness of a secular education over attending the Messiah even though Rev. Moon was now floating to us he'd only be calling PH.D.s to lead his movement.

Yet, Ricky struggled accepting me living on my own attending school while claiming I wanted to be a church member. "Quit school if you want to return to the church. If you don't, well, then I'll know your real heart for True Parents."

"Father's the one who *ordered* me to school over the church! Can't I do both?"

"You say."

Arrgghh! After leaving Papasan's gulag, I wrote him, I was "starving on the streets, [with] no place to live and a sudden . . . dearth of church-friends." Papasan's vicious phone calls made finding welcome at church centers impossible, so graduating was the only logical thing to do if

> I was ever to amount to anything in life . . . I tried on several occasions with John Didsbury and Hiro . . . of Judah Street to convince them to allow me to live in the center as a student, and participate in the center life . . . they didn't want a student (and particularly me, in the case of Hiro) living in the house who could "lead regular members astray" . . . who wasn't under their direct thumb . . . Hiro, in particular, made that point explicitly clear.

More to the point, I'd dreamed of Unification Theological Seminary (UTS) since discovering it back in 1982 when it was only a 5-year-old institution. And our own graduate school required a secular undergraduate degree to matriculate.

"Ricky, are you telling me to forget attending UTS?" That would be the equivalent of the servant burying his talent in the ground.

"Not if Father directly sends you. Otherwise, your ambition is just arrogance taking you from True Parents."

Sigh. Our running argument rooted in the foibles of leadership abounding in the church plus the widespread belief that everyone's life course should match their leader's. Rev. Moon, of course, publicly says we're responsible for our own choices and have our unique course to follow in life. This is in line with the Principle that says each of us have different spiritual histories, sins to indemnify, problems to overcome. The church won't take this seriously as a practical matter because it means ceding vast amounts of self-governance and personal authority to the individual, which undermines the hierarchical authority that most appeals to him and his corps of Japanese and Korean motivators.

Despite his Christian values, Rev. Moon is fundamentally Confucianist. He lives and breathes its family and societal values. It's not Christianity nor Unificationism driving his belief in a world government built around his True Parent self, his True Family, and his functionaries as a ruling dynasty above criticism. Unificationism denounces collectivism and monarchy. It cedes all responsibility to the person in its simple declaration that he or she is the direct expression of God, an "individual truth body." Modern Protestantism tends to view obedience in terms of our adherence to Jesus' core teachings and church governance a pox. Rev. Moon is almost a throwback to medieval Catholicism positing his infallibility and centrality over Divine Principle. The dilemma for Unificationists is: to what am I loyal? the Principle or Rev. Moon? This is a pickle for Unificationists today as much as for politicians treed by loyalty to party and ideology over Constitution and public weal. Even UTS students struggle fervently twixt the highest morality as ultimate obedience to Rev. Moon and True Family regardless their transgressions, and the Principle as God's highest expression where Rev. Moon is merely its messianic advocate.

Ricky couldn't see me as a man loyal to church and Principle, the former an expression of the latter and Rev. Moon its expositor. Loyalty to the church needs be loyalty to the Principle else the symbiosis dissolves. That's precisely the problem: the American Unification Church broke the holy bond by putting its members in the untenable position of upholding the institution over the principles that founded it. This promptly collapsed its foundation as members slipped away.

Unforeseeing church leaders reeled gobsmacked. "How could it happen? Why are they leaving? Because they're weak, satanic, disobedient, disloyal, unPrincipled, dirty low-down rotten American Western whores!" Their same confident contempt till American torpedo aviators, hopelessly pouring down on the Imperial Japanese Navy without fighter cover, bitch-slapped their 'decadent, *Bushido*-deprived individualistic American' stereotype into some version of real Japanese *samurai*.

UTS President Shimmyo's 1995 take was that, "Americans don't deserve to know the Principle," because we're arrogantly ungrateful scum. School wasn't making me any easier to deal with, either. I was getting educated and more easily lassoing the church with its own words. I wrote to Ricky that

> I don't expect to be treated like some miscreant [for trying] . . . to ensure God's success . . . persecuted on the one hand for being a moonie, and on the other hand by church members for being an "apostate" . . . denied all spiritual, moral and emotional support . . . forced to live in a world where either I looked to myself, or died . . . No one can expect me, now, to reduce myself back to a quivering, inexperienced, ignorant and intimidated new member . . . I am well-enough educated in Principle and good sense to know right from wrong.

In the end, Ricky put up with me. I attended services and activities as well as fundraised Saturdays, turning over all my result. Still, he never respected me as a real member nor included me in prayer and fasting conditions... in anything. It was my initiative or nothing. While the church suffered its greatest loss of membership, leaders like Ricky resolutely pushed me out and kept me out for no reason than my independent thinking and commitment to the Principle over institutionalism. But I'm hardly unique. Even St. Paul battled the orthodoxy of institutionalism to save individual churches from themselves and his own place in them. That said, Ricky was a teddy bear next to the pompous jackass who was about to take his place as Northern California state leader and Bush Street's chief dick.

I'D FOUNDED A business with school chum Robert in March 1988 at CCSF. His idea was selling the beautifully decorated restaurant matchboxes given free to customers. He named our company for himself and dragged me to Macy's for a presentable sports jacket on my dime. We set up a manufacturing operation in South Bay contracting the mentally retarded at a discount.

We hit up restaurants with our proposal and walked off with free cases of product. One Fisherman's Wharf owner saw grim resolve over my fancy linen jacket and took me for cops on a raid. Our business plan was simple: seven matchboxes in a stylish, colorful, shrink-wrapped flatpack called *CityMatch*, the obverse a blurb for each eatery. We wholesaled for $2 each on spin racks; shops retailed at $4. Our cost per unit was maybe 10 cents. A brilliant idea and made money. Just not enough.

Top: Product front; bottom: obverse.

I'd put up $2,000 and raised $3,500 from friends. Work was intensive and earning profits, so I quit Daniel Solomon. Then I found Robert abusive and unscrupulous. We ran afoul. An ulcer chewed up my guts. My stomach exploded vegetating on my loveseat in my second-floor room at 225 Harold. I called my old friend Julian who'd married an outside woman when the church, Blessing, and Papasan at last rammed his conscience at the waterline. Evil eats its own, eh.

I was in tears. "My stomach's on *fire!* What can I do?"

"Drink Maalox, and plenty of it," his physician wife said.

"That's all?"

"Well, see a gastroenterologist, obviously."

"Right." Dr. Pillbox prescribed a new drug and in a few months I'd healed. In the meantime I finished up CCSF with a caustic, clapperclawing belly.

I sold Robert 40% for $25,000, kept 10% silent, and said *adios*. So blackhearted over his blackguarded mind—e.g., too lazy to add oil to my sham-white, diarrheic cow of a Beetle I'd sold him for $1, he'd abandoned it with a seized motor; ruined my '74 Super Beetle; racked up hundreds in unpaid tickets; left me bankrupt, credit dead, in debt, bench-warranted then in court, destitute, and homeless—I'd lost all moral qualms about leveling my Ruger .44 and, as Clint Eastwood advertised, taking his "head clean off." This motherfucker had it coming, so help me. Only the cold, hard reality of the law checked my trigger finger. Something to say for near dead-certain capture and punishment deterring crime . . . for the rational. Damn sure, risking prison wasn't for me. But I saw up close and personal why some do.

Much as I hated my ongoing enrollment in the School of Hard Knocks, I was grateful to God for the education. The sale of my stake to Robert was mere paper. No money would change hands for a few years under certain circumstances. You won't be surprised I never saw a dime, will you?

∼

I GRADUATED CCSF with a 3.98 GPA in June of 1988 and transitioned to UCB. My Western State 'D'-student days were well in the bin. I'd discounted UCB because of its commie rep. Useful ideological idiots dragging the unwilling to a Leftist doom chapped my ass raw. The last thing I wanted in school was perpetual aggravation. I opted for San Francisco State instead. Jerome was now on his graduate degree and we'd more easily pursue our revived vision together on one campus.

Even so, I wasn't content. A friend on staff advised me CCSF was UCB's history department's top feeder school. "It's not a crowded field," she said. "They'll probably accept you automatically with your high GPA. It's not communist now, either."

I puckered and drinking-bird nodded. Comparing SFSU and UCB, my choice came down to a no-name diploma mill over a globally admired, nationwide top-ten separated only by $300 per semester. "You're right. The heck am I thinking?"

Now late summer and unexpectedly CityMatch-broke, tuition was a no-go come September. Normally, a person applies for financial aid in the spring to be assured of an autumn award. I applied, fingers crossed, days *after* school opened and received a grant–work–loan combo. Verifying my paperwork with baby sister's down-payment, UCB's financiers agreed to late tuition *sans* late fees till the money arrived.

"We're making an exception," the clerk assured me, "only because you're a nice guy. You may continue in class."

"Can't argue with that. You are *such* a godsend!" Manners got me far there.

Finances and my church relationship made school nightmarishly toilsome. My unflaked-blue '74 Beetle was a bloody sight snazzier and a hairsbreadth more leggy despite Robert's ruination that left

My '74 rod-thrown corpse at 225 Harold.

me with a bad clutch. I dropped the engine and replaced the plate and seal four times but it never helped. I missed my reliable if thirsty old clunker. The engine threw a rod on my way to my brother Teddy's house in Milpitas. It was a better car for me fitting a junkyard short block in my driveway with no demon-possessed seals.

UCB was fabulous, though my first semester nosedived when a Chinese student suicided over headlined claims of staff racism and neglect.

"That's some stupid solution for that," I scoffed. Blacks leveled the accusation, but the reality was affirmative action forced the school to admit students with weak academic chops. My top GPA didn't make my first two semesters any easier. I needed a 3.3 GPA or I was out and didn't think I'd make it. Confident from CCSF, I'd signed up for 21 credit hours. Seven courses; five history requiring 500 pages a week. I was flunking in three. I dropped several and managed 1,500 pages with speed-reading skills. Regardless, I head-banged knots earning nothing higher than a 'B+.'

I approached my Japanese history professor, Dr. Mary Berry, after class. "What's it take to get an 'A' around here?"

She regarded my 'B+' paper. "How long did you spend on this?"

"I suppose six or eight hours."

"Pfft! Hand it over. I'm marking it down." Awkward pause. Big laugh. "Okay, if that's what you can do in six hours, then . . . write something I've never seen before if you want an 'A'."

"Really," I drawled. "Just as a hint, what *haven't* you seen in your twenty years' experience in this field?"

She slugged off a coy smile. "You're a smart young man, Chris. I dare you to figure it out."

"Well, okay!" She didn't know I'd studied Divine Principle with its unique theory of history. It armed me with an understanding of human behavior these intellectuals *had* never seen before. I argued concepts and historical interpretations that surprised and interested them. I made no 'A's till my third semester, but found my teachers challenging and staff helpful, willing to bend over backward to help and genuinely concerned with my learning. It wasn't because I was white, since the race was turning second class. It was because I was friendly, polite, considerate, and humble. I saw other whites prattling arrogantly, angrily, obnoxiously and, accordingly, stonewalled by ticked-off teachers and aggravated administrators. Good old manners got UCB's faculty and staff on my side. And brains. Not sure they easily suffered fools.

Teachers posted grades on office doors my first two semesters, social security numbers instead of names as a convenience for anxious students. The university sank it over privacy, but it was fantastic finding my grades without waiting months for the mail. Eyes pooled at the 'F's each class racked up, some as many as half. It was the same across all disciplines; I checked the doors. Folks opined it was mainly students failing to withdraw from a class they'd quit attending. There's my earlier point: you're at a top-10 school yet too stupid or lazy to follow a simple withdrawal process? Then you get an 'F' and bellyache its unfair or racist? Spare me.

IN EARLY AUTUMN Ergela Arsch replaced Ricky. A conceited, dour-faced American with a penchant for megalomania and twisting knives in backs under ribs, he rebuffed my residing in Bush Street as a student-member. He'd seemed a welcome replacement with his air of humility and open-mindedness; gregarious to a fault with an infectious grin taking the edge off his otherwise austere face. I'm still not certain if that was initially sincere, a false front, or a maddening psychosis. At a time when only 12–15 members populated cavernous, 4-storey Bush Street, he *asked our permission* to use public funds to fly to New York City to conjugate with his Blessed wife, as they were struggling to conceive a baby.

Wow! "Sure!" we said all circled up on the floor. "And good luck!"

What kind of leader solicits advice much less *permission* from members? It stunned and won us over despite our ingrained reservations. We were most of us skittish, walloped dogs. Dare we . . . trust?

Then inchmeal he transmogrified into a Mr. Hyde fraught with inexplicable outbursts of violent spite and Queegish witch hunts. Maybe he was shooting blanks into his Blessed future and the stress of failed salvation was grinding him down. Maybe our Korean hooligan was busting his dodgy balls. Possibly, he was just a moderately adept sociopath who frequently overloaded. It was hard to really tell these things with all the providential bits and bobs swirling in our heads. I listened to him bawling lungfuls at senior, decade-plus veterans, castigating their efforts and running them into the ground, demanding they shape up or get out. Bush Street was down to seven in months. These losses were reflected nationwide.

Without a job or CityMatch and rejected by landlords including Bush Street's, I threw straw in my Beetle. Parked wherever I could. But Berkeley hamstrung cars lacking a residential permit with a 2-hour limit and Ergela wouldn't let me claim Hearst Street to get one. Then I discovered I could park on its broad front lawn; hell, everybody did. Sundays, a blade of green couldn't catch a ray. One had to bump over the curbed sidewalk, but it was the center's only parking and didn't even kill the grass like . . . well, a miracle. I parked all day for class and stole back only after the libraries closed at midnight. The less that Ergela, or Katerina half-running the center, might accidently spot me with my car was probably best.

I had a simple routine: up and out of the car by 6 AM, shower in UCB's locker room—had to buy a pass for that—attend class and study all day, periodically visit the center to talk with friends, fundraise and donate my result (less food and gas) Saturdays, which Ergela didn't object to, find quiet campus sites to pray when the main library shuttered up, plop into my car circa 1 AM to study the Principle and Bible by red-lensed army flashlight, then sleep through an earthquake. This went on for months. You can only do this shit in your twenties.

It seems strange I continued fundraising after Ergela blocked me, but my goal was keeping the moral high ground over his determination to show me up as a Quisling slacker. Still awaiting UCB's financial aid, I had next to no food. I usually scrounged one bagel a day (with peanut butter, when I could get it). I drank water because I couldn't get anything else. Sundays I made sure to cycle through Hearst Street, campus events, and friends for free *hors d'oeuvres*.

A quiet glade near a thin babbling brook cutting through campus was the perfect spot to pray and ponder my life away from bustling students and prying eyes. Cross-legged in leaves one midnight, I was my usual spent self and nodded off. Crunching footsteps zapped eyelids up, cranked a stiff spine and neck upright. Two shadowy figures hove into view. I tensed. Flashlights cast light on hands atop pistol butts.

"What are you doing back here?" forbidding campus-cop rumbled with authority as they formed a two-man flanking maneuver.

Options making the least-threatening sense to cops raced through my mind. I went with improbable truth. "I was praying. I guess I fell asleep. Y'all startled me."

Body language behind the glare registered genuine surprise not to mention indecision. I wasn't one of Berkeley's ubiquitous hippie bums skulking in the dark trees shooting up heroin or some creepoid jerking off. They stared some seconds. Graveled eyes flexed fearsome force quizzing the other.

"Are you a student here?" said Forbidding, inflection looming on friendly.

"Yes sir. I transferred from City College in San Francisco."

He pondered that a moment. Grunted. Clicked off his flashlight. "Okay. Well . . . goodnight. Be careful back here."

"Yessir." I might be the first 'pray-er' they'd ever flushed from UCB's secular, materialistic, post-communist but still atheistically socialist grounds. Probably the butt of their morning reports. I breathed relief as they filtered into the dark wood. Some minutes later I made my way to my Beetle on Ergela's power lawn.

My suffering life was one more indemnity condition I felt called to endure to qualify in God's eyes to reform our movement for a positive difference. My heart beat fire over Ergela's harassment. He didn't *have* to be the way he was. He didn't *have* to persecute me. But I wasn't cross. This was the front line in the war against Satan. The adventurous consequence of adhering to a moral line, an inviolable standard. I may have been wrong in my perceptions and beliefs, but I was consistently dedicated to them. When you jump off a cliff, you can only plummet with dignity.

I LOVED MY classes. I was discovering ancient Rome, the middle ages, Chinese and Japanese history . . . it was hog heaven. Yet, I was slowly starving to death, too. I didn't know anything about the social safety net. Welfare was so far removed from my consciousness that I never even thought of it. I simply endured my gnawing pit. Wasn't that what people in my situation did? Looking back on it all, I'm glad because I experienced something every idealist should. A large part of the world is hungry every day. Idealists wanting to help haven't the slightest idea what it's like and consequently do stupid, unhelpful shit. My stomach *burned* from an emptiness that felt like it was swallowing me, like I'd gulped hot coals. Sometimes, so devoid even of the energy to wail and rail, I could only weep in silent pain.

UCB's East Asiatic Library in Durant Hall miraculously hired me to clerk via college-work-study in late September. I reshelved books. Naturally, the titles were in Asiatic characters not roman letters. The clubby, cute, smallish square stone building in the classical style rose two very high-ceilinged storeys with an equally spacious basement. I was down there on the can when the 1989 Loma Prieta earthquake shattered the elevated freeways and bridge linking Oakland to San Francisco. It shook my library and me like dice in a cup that felt thrice or more as long as its reported 20 seconds. Racing outside before the old stone pile buried me, I caught the news in a jockeying crowd around somebody's hand-lofted radio, then galloped to the collapsed Nimitz Freeway and its pancaked cars to help with rescue.

Our library was my tiny community, a social anchor on campus where nobody judged my spirituality or loyalty. I didn't have a home, so I spent all the time there I could. I met some beautiful women I could have fallen for. Some, like stunning, round-faced Simyoung, fell for me. But I was bound and determined to make it to the next Blessing pure, spiritually whole, and morally intact. No more screw ups. I was chaste, prayerful, and active with the church to the extent Ergela permitted. What else could a body do?

Despite my idyllic library home, I was so hungry that sitting through class and working my job was falling beyond my power. A wet pile on the floor shelving books along the bottom row or bored deskbound in class, I often dropped unconscious from blood sugar sucking air. I'd jerk awake seconds or minutes later, eyes darting especially round the library to see if I'd been spotted and wiping away the inevitable drool. Karl, my boss, wasn't fooled because in October he took me outside to fire me in private, a kindness all its own.

"I'm dismayed to see you turn out such a bad hire. It's an easy job. I don't see why you're such a slacker." I opened my mouth but nothing came out. "You look intelligent and you got into Berkeley, so what's your problem?" I probably wobbled. A hungry fire roasted my belly and now hot fear burned through my chest, neck, and scalp. "Unless you've got a good reason why your work ethic is this bad, I have no choice but to fire you right now. You're just not working out and there's plenty of other students who need your work-study slot."

Fuck. What could I say? "I'm sorry, Karl. It's not like me. What happened is . . ." and with great difficulty and blistering embarrassment fusing fear and hunger and pooling tears, I tumbled out a jumbled story. "It took weeks to get this job, but I haven't received an actual dime. Financial aid said I probably won't till Novemberish." He took in my woe with a passive face, so I couldn't tell how I was faring. "I lost my apartment, so I'm living in my car. My stomach's burning with hunger 'cause I'm lucky to afford a bagel a day"—rivulets now wet my face and neck, my voice cracked and choked—"and my emotions are so strung out . . . I—"

The dam burst. I slapped hands over my face convulsing in tears at my utter ridiculousness and grinding pain in front of this man on the grass alongside the busy sidewalk in front of the library. He settled on his heels, visibly moved. The story of stories at rich and pampered UCB. The best he'd heard. He believed me and pressed a twenty into my hand like Ken Sudo back at the turn of 1986.

"Go get yourself something to eat right now. And if you stop falling asleep and at least keep trying, I won't fire you." Wiping my tears, I felt like a little boy in front of my dad. In the back of my mind I was cursing myself and every leader son of a bitch in the Unification Church who'd one way or another led me into my dysfunctional predicament. "I expect it's hard what you're going through, so I won't judge your performance by normal standards until your money comes in and you're eating again. After that, we'll see how you do."

My gratitude soared. Work-study was required. Most of my aid would disappear without it. Painful days. I sobbed tears to fill the stream along which banks I prayed fervently to God day and night to guide me with strength to bear my cross without falling, like Rev. Moon who'd borne worse. At the peak of my hunger, I had midterm exams. I knew I was in trouble when I finished my Ancient China test, worth more than 50% of my grade, with many unanswered questions.

"I'm pretty sure I flunked this test, Professor Keightley," I said all sheepish, one of the last if not the last to hand in my work. I wasn't his best student but I'd maintained a 'B' average and he liked my limericks. He had us compose one every week along with topical papers he demanded be "no more and no less than exactly two pages in length, active voice, and no fluff or adjectives or it's an automatic 'F'!"

He ran poker eyes over my effort and placed it on the pile. "Don't worry, you probably did a lot better than you think. Let me decide what your grade is."

He did. An 'F' on the test and a 'D' in the class. *Damn.* I was too famished and weary to productively study. His was my toughest because he required heavy memorization, such as the physical and political geography of a blank pre-dynastic map. I couldn't even remember the rivers. His 'D' was my worst at Berkeley—my CCSF Dean's List roiled in its alumnus grave—and it murdered my coveted dream of a stellar 4.0 GPA. Mid-November I told my journal,

> Life's been tough. Hungry, hungry. It sure was cold Thursday night. I could hardly sleep.

Regardless, I was set on maintaining my spiritual life. I felt alive and meaningful in it; God guiding me into reforming the Unification Church for the sake of the world. Yes, I was suffering from douchebags like Ergela, but I was experiencing the misery of the human condition and, in the errors of zealotry, what *not* to do as a leader. Through my abuse and suffering I practiced humility and forgiveness, finding my road to success in being pummeled along the church's road to failure. It was the same road Rev. Moon walked in Korea. I keenly identified with his suffering as I understood it and felt it as my own. God was preparing me for a greater mission. Long-suffering faith and obedience to the Principle was all I needed. Mr. Kamiyama's casual prophecy in Judah Street haunted me: "Someday, you will be president."

One of my Hearst Street friends discovered me living in my car on the front lawn. Incensed that Ergela would leave a brother on the streets, he confronted him over denying me space in the center. Ergela hadn't put me and the blue Beetle together despite our Bush Street experience and paid no attention to one more car on the front lawn. After my friend's intervention, he promptly ordered me off.

"The members find it inconvenient. Anyway, it's for real church members, and you don't tithe. If you park here again, I'll have to tow you."

"Come on, Ergela. There's nowhere to park in this dumb town. I'm not taking anybody's space and, besides, I am a real church member. I'm here all the time for services, fundraising, house maintenance, giving DP lectures—"

"Not the point. Nobody's supposed to park here anyhow. What I said, stands."

He turned and steamrolled away on some other persecutorial task. I knew him well enough to know my car would be towed in an hour, so I crankily reversed in a possibly turf-ripping half-circle and bounced over the curb into the street to play musical cars with the City of Berkeley for an empty 2-hour space. *Goddamn.* One more headache to manage on a half-torn shoestring.

Days later I lucked onto the only street of all the streets in town, nestled right up against the hills at the back of the city—the very last roadway before countryside took over—where the ubiquitous 2-hour signs were absent. What an oversight. What providence! I parked days and days at a time, afraid to move lest I lose my precious port. Near the end of my homelessness the city discovered its error and up went bird-spikes-on-ledges signage I saw through a pigeon's cold eyes.

The Berkeley campus and surrounding town is a big place. I spent considerable time between classes loping to my car and moving it in time to jog back for my next class before the city fined me for my vile crime. Quite often I simply scooted out of the space enough to spin the meter reader's chalk mark on my tire to a different position, then reversed right back in and without a ticket. Theoretically, that is. I never tried wiping the chalk off because those fine-ferreting meter readers could tell. It had to look like you'd driven round the block and fortuitously found the same spot still empty. It was a legal duplicity if you weren't caught in the act.

Up from that last street at the back of town was a path winding into a dark, tree-shrouded gulch with a thin brook struggling through it. The pitch darkness under the foliage sometimes hid homeless criminals till it was too late. I took to shoving my Ruger .44 through my belt under my army coat just to be on the safe side. Only once did I have to part my jacket for its shine to scare off a homeless mugger—one rarely ever need shoot—stealthily sneaking up in the gloom. I laughed at the incongruity of climbing a mountain to pray to the God of Love packing Dirty Harry's "most powerful handgun in the world." But it beat having my throat slit or guts split by some enterprising bum's knife seeking a warmer coat, better shoes, or shiny baubles. Many of these 'disadvantaged' were bastards deserving not one iota of sympathy, vicious thugs pouncing in darkness on unsuspecting prey. The ravine was the only way from the road to the mountain and friends had kindly forewarned me, so I was forearmed—literally. What I'd legally do if I'd had to shoot somebody didn't get as much forethought. Surviving the encounter was my chief concern.

The path out of this dry-gulching venue led up a steeply rising hill to the top of one of the mountains overlooking Berkeley. Upon its tall-grassed, windswept slope I found a place where I could pray nighttimes. It was especially beautiful and magical under a clear, black starry sky. I imagined myself in Rev. Moon's worn shoes overlooking Pusan from the Rock of Tears in the early 1950s. I tried to reach into his mind and heart, wandering through his possible thoughts and feelings gazing out upon his own Jerusalem and longing to save his own people. He now and again spoke about those experiences. I never really appreciated how he must have felt till planted in waving long-grass, drifting across twinkling lights to the blackened bay and San Francisco and the Golden Gate beyond. I wondered how on earth it would ever be possible to teach the whole world (let alone that one single city) Divine Principle. It seemed impossible, a lunatic's quixotic dream. I wracked my brains questing for answers, grilling God and beseeching Jesus for guidance.

At some point I realized it *was* impossible to expect the planet to join the Unification Church. At the time, that's what it really meant to accept the Principle; how could one not? But it couldn't happen. Maybe it was never even Rev. Moon's plan although the church careens along with that goal firmly in its sights. It expects humanity to acclaim True Parents. Abandon its Redundant Testament imagination for Completed Testament truth. Get Matched or Blessed. Obey central figures. Looking on the hundreds of religions and denominations, I had to admit it was bloody unlikely. About as unlikely as the world sharing Rev. Moon's pet rock that— assuming the Jews and Romans accepting Jesus meant Aramaic or Hebrew would've supplanted Latin—Korean necessarily is the new lingua franca. It seems doubtful. Latin letters are ready-made for computers. And it will dramatically distort anyway absorbing hundreds of cultures and languages into its lexicon.

In November 1988 I participated in the International Conference on the Unity of the Sciences (ICUS) at a prestigious Los Angeles hotel. It spooked Ergela finding me on Rev. Moon's personal security staff. He and our regional leader, Rev. Zin Moon Kim, tried ejecting me but his security chief was my staunch friend. I provided close personal security to the Big Man and Missus for the week.

I'll never forget her ambivalently, blankly asking me while gliding *Mars Attacks!* fashion into her *en suite* bedroom, "Have you eaten?" without slowing a beat nor glancing for my reply. I take my victories where I find them and overlooked these small-time idiosyncrasies. Then, wandering their evening floor, I found every door open and folks milling in the most familial air I'd ever breathed. After all my trials, it was a sucker punch. I hung out till 2 AM chatting with Rev. Moon in his room.

Dazzled by my influence with True Parents as to get right inside their private quarters all buddy-buddy with their chief of security, Ergela politically invited me out of ten weeks in my car to "Come on! Move right in!"

"You don't want to move in here," a brother counseled. "Ergela keeps this center tense as piano wire."

"Does he? I've seen him treat members weird but . . . better than my car."

"That's not the half of it. Don't forget Rev. Kim. Find a Blessed family."

"If I could do—" I cupped my chin. "You know, I remember everybody warning me off our 'evil' skipper on my second Coast Guard cutter, but we got along fine. I should probably wait and see. Give him a chance."

"Uh-huh. Don't say you weren't warned."

"Then why don't *you* leave? I mean, nobody's holding you here."

He guffawed over his departing shoulder. "You're kidding, right? You know Principle. Why is *anybody* here?"

Yeah. I got that. A mere three weeks later I wrote, "This house is a spiritual disaster. What it needs is strong doses of love and truth." In for a penny . . .

My deal—Ricky might've confided my gullibility in the handover—was that I follow Bush Street's life, fundraise, donate my result, and Ergela would accept me as a 'real member' worth my living expenses. He liked my '74 Beetle, as it carried a goodly flower load plus a fundraiser or two I could drop. I was employed but he declined rent. He didn't have to say that would imply I was independent thus outside his power and control. Rent-free on his good will presumed a secure master-servant bond in satisfying Abel–Cain manacles, the disciple to his master.

I agreed to his devilish bargain because my chief goal was developing my religious career into UTS to work directly with my mentor, Rev. Moon. I believed

L–R: Moons, Bo Hi Pak, Rev. Kwak, Pres. Neil Salonen.

God wanted me living an exemplary life to infuse reformative energy into our pale movement propping up Rev. Moon's expiring ministry. Supremely conscious of my spiritual and moral fishbowl, I reMoonied with abandon.

From the day I moved in, I tried in every way to set an exemplary standard: services most every day, hardy prayer, fundraising enthusiasm runneth over, the works. Though doing my best, Ergela rejected my efforts like Cain's failed offering, admonishing me for real or perceived failures and low result even when hitting top-seller. He promised to write up our deal then broke it to mandate a $200 rent. Falling out was progressive. He was impossible to please though more than once I stung him that ranting at members was going overboard. He especially resented me pointing out the severe drop in members since he took over.

"You're the bad influence, Chris. Always talking to the other members and telling them 'things.' "

"Like what 'things,' exactly?"

"You should know. Your fundraising is not up to par, either. Raise it to our dedicated members' standard or move out."

Hmmph on both counts. "I made $943 Christmas weekend! Are you saying you prefer I quit school? Fundraise full time?"

"Nooo . . . that's not necessary." A real head scratcher. "But you only did $10 yesterday. Do better or pay rent. Or move out. The minimum's $400 a month."

"There's a minimum now? So, if I make $399, are you going to kick me out?"

"Yes."

I blew air. "That's brutal and ruthless, Ergela."

"No, full-time members do more. I'm giving you a break because you're a student. You'll have to sell weeknights to make it up. You're just a part-time member, Chris. A home member. I'm already bending guidelines by letting you stay here. Rev. Kim doesn't want you here but, anyway, I'm letting you stay."

"If Rev. Kim—"

"I'm the state leader! Not him. The centers are my authority."

"Well, I am a full-time member. Home members don't live in the center."

"If you're full-time, you'll go on the fundraising team I'm making for next week." He frowned at my question marks. "I'm state leader. I can make full-time fundraising teams if I want!"

"You know I have school and obviously can't disappear for a week."

An oily grin squirmed up his face. "So, that means you're a part-time member."

"No, it doesn't. Other members like Satomi—" Eyes flicked away over his adversarial bookkeeper who'd later flee to Seattle. "That's right. They have full-time duties besides fundraising, witnessing, or whatever. I do that and building maintenance here, at Hearst, and up at Aetna Springs, prayer meetings, clean, teach DP, plus Sunday service. What's so different about me? At school and not your beck-and-call?" His face was stone. All his unctuousness dripped away. "You're saying that

Borrowed suit for Rev. & Mrs. Moon's security at ICUS LA. Nov., 1988.

280

UTS students are only part-time home members! I don't think Father sees it that way." He stalked off, as I never flinched an inch with his indefensible stupidity.

My friend 'Big' Mike said, "He's a complete shithead, Chris. Totally Satan's representative. You know he told Evelyn"—a rare black sister—"the same thing? Make more or move out? He doesn't like her despite her top result. She'll never make enough to please him. Freeman's the only one here who even *likes* him."

I motorboated lips with a heavy, inconsolable sigh. *These fuckin' people.*

A day later, I knocked on his office door. "Hi, Ergela. I just need to pick up my *Speaking Korean* book you borr—"

"Don't come in here with your shoes on!"

I backed up, palms out. Not skinning off cowboy boots for a 2-second pickup. "I'll just wait at the door then. You can hand it to me if you wouldn't mind."

"You come barging in here and I'm trying to study?"

"Barging? I knocked—"

"Yeah, you knocked and barged in."

"You said, 'Come in'!"

"I don't want to argue about it. If you keep this attitude, I'll just throw it at you."

"What attitude?" I put my spine to the doorframe. "You have my book, you didn't return it like you said, I have to prepare for class, you're making all sorts of baseless claims against me . . ." *Damn.* I sounded like Jerome in 1984.

"Here!" The door slammed loud in my face, almost punching my nose.

We apologized a few days on. He followed it up with, "You need to fundraise Valentine's Day if you want to stay in the center."

"Can't you just ask me these things without all the threats?"

"That's all you respond to."

"How would you even know?" His apologies were only ever ceasefires to prep his next round over school, fundraising, authority, and disobedience.

To counteract the hot blood and simmering grudges now uncontrollably welling up in his members—the same long-suffering boil-over in the national church that was now *Titanic*'s lookout shouting, "Iceberg, right ahead!"—Ergela had soundproofing installed in Bush Street's basement prayer room for a supposedly Wesleyan-style 'therapy room' he anyhow called "the psycho room." He crazy-house padded it and added mattresses, pillows, punching bags, and a carpeted cylinder for stick beating. In went the frazzled member who'd throw the half-inch bolt on the 8-inch-thick padded door. He or she prayed God's forgiveness of their inability to control their fallen, Cainish resentment, then beat unholy hell out of their effigy of choice.

"I hate you, Ergela!" they screamed. "I *hate* you!"

"*Fuck you*, Kamiyama!"

"Go to hell, Ricky!"

"You're a bastard, Rev. Kim! I hope dogs eat your balls off!"

"*I hate this fucking church!*"

"Take this, you fuckin' motherfuckerin' bastard fu . . . take that!"

Wham! Bam! Up yours, you goddammed Man! A hell of a sight. Passersby in the poorly lit corridor heard a muffled version of the whirlwind within. Like a number of desperate solutions to the collapse of our church in the late 1980s, this one came from the 'new age' movement that Blessed members living outside church centers were embracing to save their marriages, children, faith, and sanity.

I said, "Jeez, Ergela, this scream box of yours is outrageous."

"No, it's not. It's perfect. It helps members release their negative energy"—on pillows instead of, potentially, his face—"which then becomes positive energy." My headshake was *no fuckin' way*. "You worry too much." His tone was a scold.

"It's a wet bandaid on a cut artery. You're just fooling yourself."

"This is a Principled way for members to release unPrincipled feelings Satan uses to invade them. Like, that Blessed brother never would've shot his landlord."

"Principled?" I was stupefied. "Members are imagining *you* and others in those pillows. Some of them are taking photos and drawings along so they don't lose track. They're directing all their hatred and anger not on pillows but the target of their vexation! Which is mostly *you*. It's practically voodoo without the stick dolls. You don't see a problem with that?"

"No, why should I?" He was always so smoothly confident in everything. Nothing he did ever went wrong that somebody else hadn't fucked it up. He suffered no evident self-doubt whatsoever. Looking back, he reminds me of schmoozy, self-assured Bill Clinton redefining 'is.' An apt comparison, too, considering we heard he was later caught in New York City with his wiener in the wrong bun. Like most leaders and Catholic priests, he'd get a transfer and a slap on the wrist.

"It's not Christian, Ergela. Think about it. The Principle doesn't support venting resentment against effigies. It demands we 'digest' troubles and difficulties through *indemnity* conditions, not act them out in a rubber room like Cain visualizing for Abel the rock in his heart." Our hallway convo drew some queer eyes.

"You're being melodramatic. I'm their leader and I know what I'm doing."

"This isn't helping members, though. It's just venting negative emotion. When they come out, they're sucked right back into their problem that didn't change. *They* don't change and their *problem* doesn't change. What's the point?"

"The point is," he took his time, thinking it through, "I'm not going to change anything about how I lead this church center. I'm not the problem, the members are. They expect too much. They demand this . . . that. Till they mature and learn to relate with their leaders, they're going to struggle. It's on them. The room stays."

He meant it. Every time I heard the muffled, screeching tears I felt our center descending deeper into a darkly negative spirit world, bringing upon itself unseen influence from malevolent forces it would rather not know. Medieval Christianity recognized some value in self-flagellation insofar as it overcame weakness, sin, and Divine wrath. The Unification Church adopts this tradition in its prayer, fasting, cold shower, work, and other indemnity conditions. But never did I hear Rev. Moon support give-and-take with festering hate and for good reason. The Principle is all about Restoration of the self from the post-Fall to the pre-Fall condition. Besides selfishness, the number one obstacle on this path is resentment, which led Cain to murder Abel. Even God, he said, couldn't untangle our convoluted resentments.

Ergela's asylum wasn't where members pushed themselves harder to overcome their base emotions to accept the world as it is in the best tradition of Jesus or his flagellant monks. It was a place to vent into the world all the malice and loathing they could pour out of their suffering souls to swirl around the target of their animus like Pigpen's stink in *Charlie Brown* with all the rest of us in the bargain like an evil wraith. It was a pipeline for negative *chi*. The room smelled like animals now, too unholy for prayer. Beating a faceless punching bag, long walks, or bicycling to physically work out negative energy is healthy stress relief. Beating a pillow with someone's face in mind or pinned to it with the sense you're beating (if not directly transferring your venom to) him or her is *not* healthy but malignant.

"When members beat their enemies to death in effigy, I wonder if they aren't really Gatling their psyches. Like murder in absentia." Rev. Moon warned us that negative, hurtful words and thoughts are spiritual bullets.

"Dumbest thing you've ever said, Chris." Ergela was unswayable.

I laughed. "That's Father talking, not me. You should read up more."

"I know what I need to know. You should know what you need to know."

I scratched along my nape. He zipped into his office. Members evince so much difficulty absorbing Rev. Moon's explications of the Principle. What they do grasp without hindrance are teachings about power, authority, hierarchy, and control. Rarely do especially leaders get the subtler points regarding sacrifice, service, equality, personal responsibility . . . all cornerstones that he's sermonized A to Z.

Enabling Bush Street's shriekers was a sign of desperation. The Church by the late '80's was a shadow of its former self, reduced to the quivering mass of a few thousand souls across our vast nation, maybe a majority imported Japanese. As American Blessed marriages broke down and the Blessed Family Department (BFD) and local leaders proved inept or unwilling to productively counsel these couples, members turned to their own devices. A popular 'new age' husband–wife guru based on Vashon Island in Washington State's Puget Sound offered Blessed members 'hospital ward' counseling and active therapy. Questionable therapeutic activities, including alleged unPrincipled sex, scandalmongered coast-to-coast. Rev. Moon denounced this new trend of finding solutions outside the movement, and on Vashon Island in particular, as a disruption of central figurism.

Yet, he never implemented any therapeutic role in the church. BFD was overtaxed, untrained; *Blessing Quarterly* shut down; real healers, MIA; Korea's Cheongpyeong Lake out of reach. Members suffered faithfully through dysfunctional marriages, divorced, cheated, left the church, killed themselves, or secretly took outside therapy. In this respect, he dreadfully failed those he'd trained, Matched, and Blessed. I felt he (or BFD) had a responsibility to counsel couples. Who else could?

I'D DISCOVERED VIA outside sources that Rev. Moon held a 6,500-couple Blessing October 30, 1988 in Seoul for Koreans and Japanese. Now one was coming up in January 1989. At last, another chance! I strolled on Mercury's wings into Ergela's office. He read my face.

"So, you're going to go to Korea on your own, right?"

"I'm part of Bush Street. Shouldn't I be part of the members going?"

"There's a few points you need to be in agreement with first." He leaned back, crossed his legs. Fingers interlaced over a thin stomach. "The three most important are that if you go, you're being mobilized for four years in the *Segye Ilbo* providence."

Rev. Moon's latest newspaper launch. "Second, there's no rejection of Father's choice. You accept it or no Blessing." I felt the alchemy in my stomach turning my golden mood into lead. "And you have to pay the $4,500 cost. But I'm not sure I can even sign your application yet, anyway."

"Come on, Ergela. I'm practically a full-time member here. I deserve—"

"No, you don't. And you aren't."

"Will you discuss it with Rev. Kim? Isn't he the one who—"

"It's my responsibility as state leader, not Rev. Kim's. Just because you've lived here a month or so doesn't make you eligible for the Blessing."

"My eight years' membership and fulfilling all of Father's qualifications for this Blessing makes me eligible! And I've met yours and Rev. Kim's too. He said if I quit school for full-time mission work he'd sign my application right away."

"But you're still in school."

"There was no Blessing. I'll quit for this one if that's what . . . You're shaking—"

"Father wants Americans to finish school. If you want to attend the seminary, you have to graduate. No, I don't recommend you quit school."

I chuffed at that. "Then . . . what? I've helped since Ricky to build up the $100,000 that Bush Street's socked away for the Blessing." I was realizing I might have to sell my car and everything to choke up $4,500. "What if Rev. Kim says—?"

"Well, he doesn't tell me how to run my state or this center. Just keep doing what you're supposed to and we'll talk again. I'm sure it'll work out."

BFD's representative to Northern California interviewed prospective candidates. I met with Reiko (Blessed to my friend 'Academic' Mike who was just finishing up his UCB PH.D.) in a room at Hearst Street to explain my past. One of Rev. Moon's qualifications for this Blessing was sexual chastity for at least two years. I met that but, instead of keeping my mouth shut like a lot of (if not most) Moonies, confessed my brief affair with Bernie and Roxanne at CCSF three years before.

Hearing this along with my overall thinking about God, True Parents, the church, and Ergela she said with solemn assurance, "I see that you love God very, very much. Don't worry. You meet all True Father's qualifications. You will go to Blessing."

Incomprehensibly, Ergela used his position to violate BFD's strict sanctity by pressuring her to reveal our interview. These were as confidential as the Catholic confessional and you can guess why. Her only authority was a yea or nay. But she wouldn't commit and threw him my details to decide. Maybe her Japanese civility could only lie to me and spill my tea to him to avoid a confrontation.

He sashayed up on a campus sidewalk after meeting Rev. Kim in LA. Some cheery, grinning pleasantries then he smoothly let rip, "By the way, Chris, I'm not recommending you for the Blessing."

"What?!" I gasped at his sledgehammer to the solar plexus. "Why not?"

He threw even BFD under the bus to lighten his load. "Reiko told me what you said, and your life just doesn't fit the pattern of the kind of people True Parents want to Bless. She told me about your girlfriends at City College."

Her betrayal stoked a raging furnace. She knew what he was. I'd told her! Trying to snag a barrel already over the falls, I swallowed the hard edge in my voice to puke up a more congenial tone. "That's not right, Ergela. I meet all of Father's qualifications.

I've been pure for three years and worked hard for the Blessing. I have a right to go. For Father himself to tell me I don't deserve it, not you."

"It's not just me. Rev. Kim said he's willing to sign your application, but now he knows you have a son . . . you really should've told me about that, Chris." *Goddamn you, Reiko!* "I'm sure you know Father is excluding married or divorced."

"I've never been either! He never said anything about children."

"That's how Rev. Kim is taking it." *But is he, though?* Ergela had already proved himself a manipulator and a liar. "Anyway, isn't a bastard child worse?"

I thought I tasted bits of teeth. "It's not up to him or you. True Father decides!"

"That's not how I see it. I'm responsible for weeding out candidates before Father has to deal with them. You don't meet the qualifications. That's the way it is."

Slimy pride slathered his face like avocado on toast. He had a smirk I was dying to beat off right there in front of passersby. "I've been in the church eight years. How much longer will I have to wait to get Blessed? I'll be thirty in May!" It was a long time to wait when all your friends were busy raising Blessed families.

"As long as I'm your central figure, you'll never go to the Blessing. The way you carry on, thinking you're all that, I don't see you ever deserving it. That's my job."

"How can you say that?" I flushed red hot. "The Blessing is our salvation! It takes us out of the fallen world. You're telling me I *never deserve* to be Restored?"

"Not for me to say. I just wanted to tell you not to get your hopes up, because I'm not recommending you. Sorry. I really am. But I have responsibilities, too."

I restored some inner civility. "I'm willing to quit school and move to Korea and work with the newspaper." Rev. Moon wanted all Americans who could to go, though Mary Ann at Hearst put the lie to Ergela's claimed 4-year deployment as a condition of the Blessing. "I'll leave right away."

"Do what you want." He'd barely contemplated it. "But you should stay right here and finish your degree. Father needs educated members." He saw I'd run out of words and stepped around me to march into oblivion. "Have a nice day!"

I saw him a hungry virus sharpening knives. I could've ignored him, but traveling centers without permission was impossible. Arriving *overseas* to shove my way into the 'newspaper providence' and hopefully the Blessing was playing Russian Roulette with a high risk of *bang!* Anyway, *my* Blessing money was in Bush Street's bank. All I could do (per Jim Carrey) was "piss and moan like an impotent jerk and then bend over and take it up the tailpipe!" *If only Mr. Kobayashi had let me go in 1982!*

I phoned Rev. Kim. The simp wouldn't countermand Ergela. Calls and letters to Sheri at BFD and other leaders fell on deaf ears. These motherfuckers were stabbing my spiritual life to death with a Cheshire piety. Watching brokenheartedly from afar, resentment simmered. I spent weeks minding Aetna Springs with the Brundretts and Rev. An (up teaching a 40-day, he called me "six-six") doing maintenance, riding and caring for Cyrano and Lad oft-ridden unshod on pavement, shooting guns, and incinerating a hand on hot iron. Six weeks of professional care, that.

The Blessing is how one reacquires Adam and Eve's pre-Fall state to achieve God's three great blessings. You're hardly a Moonie without it. It's import is analogous to Christian baptism, a forgiveness from Jesus no right-thinking Christian withholds. Ergela's permanent denial erased it from my life. He was technically right about weeding out members disqualified by Rev. Moon's published qualifications, but wrong to exceed his mandate by cheating the Messiah out of deciding on the qualified. He'd performed all four of Divine Principle's fallen natures: failing to take God's viewpoint, leaving one's proper position, reversing dominion, and multiplying the criminal act. Congruent with institutional tradition, he claimed absolute authority over me. The last straw was using it to expunge me from the Blessing. He saw me as he did many others: Satan's excrement, unfit for inclusion. A state leader was a position of power in the 1980s. Between him and Rev. Moon stood only the Korean regional leader and continental director. Papasan Choi proved how easily a leader can blacklist a member in America. I was certain Ergela wasn't bluffing.

His threat was a grim milepost. I took it for my spiritual death warrant. Rev. Moon doesn't accept the unBlessed as real members because that alone engrafts the wild olive shoots to the true olive tree, a biblical symbolism he relishes. This filters through Korean leaders to the membership. Indeed, despite opening the Blessing to nonmembers in 1992, many Blessed members, especially in the 1980s, looked down their noses at the unBlessed with a barely disguised contemptuous pity. To protect myself, I quit answering one of the three questions members have when first meeting: "Are you Blessed?" For those breaking their Blessing in extramarital sex or leaving the church to (re)marry, no indemnity is too great. Rev. Moon said these traitors wouldn't be forgiven till after Satan. Fair game for induced indemnity.

I had to cogitate awhile on what Ergela was really saying. He dangled the Blessing ever just out of reach to coerce my obedience to *him* not Rev. Moon, certainly not Divine Principle. Like any psycho, he felt justified. My reliance on the Principle and Rev. Moon's published guidance was an affront to his vision of morality as with Papasan Choi. Now he'd bared his longest fang. I'd never accepted Mr. Kobayashi holding me back from *the* central event in a church member's life and I didn't Ergela, either. This was my fourth denied Matching/Blessing, my fifth being a small, ironic Blessing for previously married and Matched members on April 7, 1989.

The Principle was the root of my soul, the core of my spiritual life. My options? Abandon conscience and Principle for blind obedience, die a priest, marry outside the church, or abandon it altogether. They all sucked. Like every Moonie, my dream was Rev. Moon Matching and Blessing me. If he's the Messiah then my ancestors dream it, too. I had obligations. Was it okay to condemn my lineage to satisfy Ergela's ego? He was Cain murdering Abel and I felt killed. My mind blanked. I could only bleed. *I lost Nanami for this?* I spent my day in a spiritual frenzy, all concentration shot to shit. Life lost its color and greyed out.

PERHAPS PART OF my problem with Ergela was that I considered him a colleague, not a master. He was very much a control freak and when it slipped from his fingers he was frantic. In May 1989 he handed out a gag order against me: I must follow his way or I couldn't be a Unification Church member, converse with members, and certainly never live in a church center. Like any good tyrant, he saw enemies everywhere. That's one reason he was so harsh with the old-timers, those directly responsible for our stunning success in the later '80s getting thousands of (mainly black) Christian ministers over to Japan and Korea to see Moonism close up.

Most of these ministers had positive, profound spiritual experiences. Especially moving them to tears were visits to the prayer ground and Rock of Tears where Rev. Moon spent much of his early ministry on bleeding knees. Some had visions of Jesus, Rev. Moon, angels, and saints. The church unfortunately embraced paternalism on their return, treating them like new Moonies than the seasoned, senior pastors they were. Frustrated and peeved, most of them in due course told the Unification Church, "Get behind me!" And Ergela was slicing off the heads of the very members who could've turned this shitshow around with some good old-fashioned Principled American leadership. Instead, it would be another ten years before Rev. Moon built steam to reach out to them for another go-to-Korea program.

In any event, Ergela was invested in reducing the Northern California church to confetti. Anything I said to the contrary only made me his greater enemy. Money was his sharpest and longest knife in my ribs.

I headed over to Hearst after classes mid-March. "Hi, Ergela!" I was practicing being friendly and respectful now he'd returned from a leaders' meeting in New York City. "Welcome back from the Big Sin, ha ha! Hope you had a good time."

"Yeah, thanks. It was fine."

"By the way, you ever pay that fundraising ticket? I got a bench warrant."

"Check with Satomi."

"I gave it to her a month ago. She said you have to approve paying it. Respectfully, I've asked you about ten times now to give her the word. The cops are—"

"Didn't I tell you to see Big Mike about it? I told him to deal with it."

"Yeah, but he'd already left for LA and was gone for two weeks. And yesterday at Sunday Service he said he didn't know a thing about it." He'd then confided all of Ergala's rigamarole was a ploy, that he had no intention of paying the fine.

"Go to Bush Street and straighten it out with Satomi."

"Just call her. One minute. Easy-peasy. She won't do it, otherwise."

He took in my demeanor a minute. "Were you fundraising while I was gone?"

"Nooo . . . I couldn't get ahold of anybody at Hearst to find out the schedule. They were either all still up at Aetna Springs or nobody ho—why are you shaking your head? I went by every day between classes and could never catch anybody for product. And this weekend, too. I figured they must be busy elsewhere."

"If you don't want to fundraise, how can you consider yourself a member? How can you stay at Bush Street if you don't? I'll have to ask you to leave."

Whaaat? I wasn't making excuses, but now I hardened. "Well, you can ask but it won't make any difference."

"You're no Unification Church member unless you fundraise, but for sure you're not unless you change that attitude! Are you fundraising? Or paying rent?"

"I fundraise all the time and you bloody well know it! You've arbitrarily changed our agreement more than ten times, then made me an official renter at our last house meeting because I couldn't fundraise Valentine's Day. Your word's not worth saltwater to a dying man in a desert, Ergela."

"I know I don't like *that* tone."

"Let's recap. We agreed to a lockable basement room to protect my computer and for a quiet study, then you sent me upstairs to the brother's room and my school gear to a public room, else 'Lock it in a closet,' you said." These were desktop, CRT, and cable days. "That I'd fundraise Saturdays, maybe Fridays. Then you said, 'How're you going to earn your keep? Fundraise through Christmas.' Then through January. You demanded me only in prayer meetings then witnessing, fundraising, building maintenance . . . all of it. That's five things we had agreements on that you changed unilaterally." I was Jacob doing time at Uncle Laban's.

"I'm trying to help you be the full-time member you say you want to be."

"No, it's all calculated to benefit *you*. I paid you $1,200 in February for six months advance rent. Now you're pretending it's just February's result."

"If you're only bargaining to stay in the church, you're not a member and should just get out. Why are you even here?"

You son of a bitch! I was hot and tingling and breathing shallow. *God, I hate conflict!* "*You* arbitrarily changed *everything* and made me a *renter*! What bargaining am I doing? I've only tried holding you to your word. Now you want to change it again so you can milk me of more time and money? I have tuition!" He needed a punch in the nose worse than anybody I knew. Well, except Robert. *Maybe.*

"If you don't fundraise or have a better attitude toward me, you'll never qualify for the next Blessing, and I won't send you. Place yourself in the Cain–Abel relationship and be humble to me and have the right attitude. That's the standard."

"Isn't it Father's job to decide who's qualified?" This motherfucker was still using my salvation to coerce me into swallowing any splooged unrighteousness he could whack out. Where'd he establish any right to *be* Abel? How's he arrogate to himself the power to decide who's qualified? I might've landed five knuckles but for my importunity with the Blessing: he had to sign off on my candidacy. *Goddamn!*

"Look, Chris, I've supported you and stood up for you in the past for the Blessing, but I can't let you go if you keep this attitude."

"You totally denied it forever in January! What are you talking about?"

"I did nothing of—"

"You absolutely refused me throwing away school for the mobilization and Blessing in Korea. Not to mention making me the only member paying the fee out of my own pocket after fundraising into the house fund. You wouldn't even talk with Rev. Kim. I had to call him to verify your story. And it was all a lie!"

"You're misunderstanding the entire situation."

"If you don't pay that ticket *today*, I'll have the cops drag me out of Bush Street in handcuffs for the TV. Everybody will see how Moonies welsh on their fines and let members go to prison for it! I bet Rev. Kim will *love* the publicity when I tell the news how you stonewalled Big Mike and Satomi to avoid paying it!"

He paid it. We settled nothing else. He called the office phone from Hearst on April Fools. "I'm evicting you. Our original agreement required you fundraise and participate in Bush Street's spiritual life, and you're not doing that."

"Ergela, you broke all those agreements yourself, heedless of my protests, and you made me a renter. I paid you $1,200 rent in February, and that's—"

"I'm not counting anything you gave me in February because now it's April. But, if you pay rent now, today, you can stay one more month."

"I paid your rent plus my fundraising result. I'm not going anywhere."

"If you don't move out on your own, I'll *move* you out."

"Ha!" My voice lilted in laughter. "You gonna send over a goon squad?"

"Yes."

He didn't waste half a second on that response. Must've already thought our convo through. I was taken aback and considered my options. When in doubt, go with bluster. "Who are you going to find who's big enough to throw me out?"

"You'll see."

No one except Big Mike had the sand to give me serious trouble. He'd recently absconded to New York City after rejecting his Korea Match and wouldn't have helped anyway. But I was feeling shades of Matsumoto and 'Small' Mike in 1984.

At Julian's urging, I hustled over to Judah Street for a long, same-day talk with Rev. Do Wan Kim, a 49-year old stocky, round-faced 24-year Korean leader who considered many of the seminarians and leaders, particularly Ergela, "incompetent. Just a little bit more love, and so many problems would be solved." He leaned back in his chair. "Already, three members have brought this to me. If I tell Father about Ergela, he'll get angry and remove him. Right away, yes. But . . . I don't interfere because of Rev. [Zin Moon] Kim."

"Why? What's he—?"

"You know Rev. Kim just wants to say what he wants to say, and that's it." Fingers clenched knees. "He doesn't like contradiction. We listen to him at leaders' meetings without interruptions so we can quickly wrap up and leave." *Well . . . shit.* "You'll be thirty next month, right?" He exhaled heavily. "*Saaaahh.* The ninth year is always difficult, especially 29. That is just before Jesus started his mission. I think things will get better for you in June or July, probably."

"But what about now? What should I do about Ergela evicting me?"

He shrugged. "If Ergela is fired, can you take over as state leader?"

"Me?" A tornado whipped my thoughts under his gaze. "I could, yes . . ."

"If he succeeds in kicking you out of Bush Street, you can always live at Washington Street. Some indemnity course must be going on between you two . . ."

"Yes! Totally! I've worked out how it's almost exactly like what happened to Jerome in 1984 right here in Judah Street. But all the members support me over Ergela, the exact opposite of that situation."

"That was Rev. Choi. I don't know much about it." *Perhaps.* "All is not lost."

"Thank you, Rev. Kim. I feel some hope for unity from your words."

After Zin Moon Kim's "convoluted and spastic Sunday Service," Freeman and Evelyn said the next day at Hearst Street, "After Ergela talked to you on the phone, he came downstairs and said to a bunch of us, 'I have a problem . . .you guys know Chris McKuen? Well, he's lied to me, broken his word, won't pay rent at Bush Street, and *threatened* me, saying, Who's gonna move me out?' And literally, Chris, we all said, 'No, thanks!' " *Checkmate.*

I laughed. Clapped hands. "Don't get yourselves kicked out on my account."

"It won't be for that," she said, surveilling Freeman now migrating Ergela's way. "By the way, I'm leaving at the end of the month for Ricky's center in New Mexico. Otherwise, Alabama, I guess."

"Gah—what?" My gut clenched.

"Freeman, too. I don't know where, exactly. Maybe a workshop."

I might've hyperventilated. So many staunch supporters.

Ergela dismissed Freeman and wandered over. "I want to mention Bush Street. I don't recognize any money you fundraised in February because now it's April. But I want to be your brother, Chris, and have a good relationship."

"What are you saying, Ergela? Exactly."

"Just that Bush Street isn't for you. Unless you can establish a good relationship of trust and live like a proper member under *my leadership*, you need to move out." I wondered if he'd heard something from Do Wan Kim.

"I want that, Ergela. But I don't see how it's possible when it's you constantly breaking your word over rent, fundraising, what's required . . ."

Hands found pockets under his suit jacket. "Yeah, I'm sorry. I'll change—"

What the hell? "I appreciate that, but saying you're sorry isn't good enough. You backtrack so many times yet nothing changes. You keep breaking your word."

"If you can't forgive, how can you have any place in the church?"

Ah, short blade in the gut. "It's got nothing to do with forgiveness. You—"

"I treat you perfectly nicely. I do want to see you Blessed . . ." despite his promise to cut me off from it so long as he had the power to do so. This guy.

"Look, Ergela, I appreciate the good and kind aspects of your personality. I like you for it. I think you're a good person at heart. But then you threaten me with the Blessing like a political tool to . . . bend me to your will. Until you operate from a righteous standpoint, I can't accept any of your kind words. It's just heartache."

"You're making a mistake there, Chris. None of that's—"

"Well, my position's unchanged. I won't under any circumstances leave Bush Street until I'm ready because I'm fully paid up through—"

"In that case, then, I'll call the police and have you forcibly evicted. I'd rather not have to do that, though."

"Go ahead. Call the police. In fact, let me call them for you." I got a quizzical eye. "Have them come around three or four. I'll be there. But you'll find out they can't evict me." This Cain and Abel shit was exhausting.

"We'll see about that. I have another meeting now. I think you should go."

I hauled air to my belly and wished I could puff my douchey dragon out to sea. Mid-April, he announced Bush Street was now the seat of a new tech company called World Research Institute for Science and Technology (WRIST). Out of it came Wacom, inventor of the pressure-sensitive pen-based ArtPad and ArtZ line of art tablets used in computer graphics. Rev. Moon funded them but not a place to work. Nearly deserted, gargantuan Bush Street was a sensible choice.

"We have to be out by May. I'd like to see you solve your situation by then."

"Not even two weeks?"

"It is what it is. You have to deal."

My eyes narrowed. He was too chipper. "You know, I see you in a providential role with the church, Ergela. You have a terrific personality for it centered on truth."

"Okay. I appreciate you saying that."

"We've had our differences, but to me it's providential, not personal. That's how we need to approach our situation, what with our movement on the knife edge."

He was thoughtful, if crossed arms. "I'm . . . really inspired to hear you think that way. I hope . . . well . . . I agree with what you've been saying these last few months. It's a good attitude that can be used by God. I always thought you could do great things for the providence if . . . you know . . ."

I was blindly obedient. Like all good members. We debated our Cain–Abel role restoring church vitality. He waxed and waned excited, supportive, discerning, but ultimately hostile and muzzling because he was its epitome.

He shifted his flag to Hearst Street as Northern California's headquarters the last week before finals. I couldn't move in the midst of it. Wishy-washy to a fault, he used that to lock me out citing disloyalty, independent thinking, disobedience, and troublesomeness. I begged and pleaded. *Unfit*, he claimed. Ever the Unsuited Moonie. I didn't give up on him or Hearst Street and caught him on a Saturday.

He said, "Everybody thinks you need to make an acceptable condition, like construction work on the house." My eyes were flat. "Rev. Kim also expressed his reservations. You need to show some commitment to the church."

"Who's everybody? They really don't want me moving in?" Breath left me.

"It's—ehmm—well—everybody . . . I mean, I make the final decision no matter what. Everyone just thinks you need to establish trust."

"I thought we had established a trust between us."

"And we have. I trust you."

"Then I don't understand why I need to make some other condition to build trust. What did I do that I suddenly have to make a condition to repent for?"

"You need to establish a spiritual commitment to the church, in a practical way."

"I'm not committed to the church? You know why I'm wanting to move in here. I explained all that. There's no other reason than God told me to be *here*."

"I do think we have a relationship between us, Chris. I feel some unity . . ."

"Really?" Eyes quested over the high, paneled ceiling. Maybe I'd find it there.

"Yes, and I've seen some commitment. Nobody disagrees with your ideas about unity but, still, there's an issue of trust . . ." Someone was calling him away. "You needed to be out of Bush Street a week ago. When—?"

"Finals have me tied down a few weeks. Do you want me to flub my exams?"

"No . . . but you have to get out. Sooner than later. I'll put your moving in here to a majority vote. If the members want you here, I won't interfere."

Leading up to it Ergela's disagreeable Belgian muscle Marie-Pierre said, "So, you are moving in . . . *pour la commodité*? For ze . . . convenience?"

We loitered in Hearst Street's kitchen. "No, because God told me to."

She sniggered. "Katerina and I support Ergela *absolument*. Zat is what must be done. Ze younger members are a terrible example. Attitudes are rotten."

"Maybe that's because they see rotten things."

That sent her on a 5-minute jeremiad. "Yes, yes, I see zat you zhink I am very arrogant." A genuine Gallic shrug matched my eyebrows. "I suppose I am."

"Naaahh, psshh, not at all." *At least she admits it.*

"Zis Christophe is far too uppity," she told Ergela and anyone (but me) who'd listen. "Always talking back to leaders as zhough he knows better zan zey do. Always behaving as zhough he is just as good as his central figures."

Katerina quizzed me, too. These headstrong sisters had usurped Ergela's authority at Hearst (Rev. Kim later made Katerina's official). "If you go to the seminary and they make you a state leader, how are you going to work under a Korean leader?"

"Why wouldn't I?"

"It doesn't seem like you can work under any leader."

"If they're Principled, it's no problem."

"What if they're not?"

"Like Ergela?" *What are you up to? Surely you know me better than that.*

"It's just a general question."

"Uh-huh. Okay. I follow Principle, regardless. I can't help it if . . ."

Using Marie-Pierre's lone negative vote Ergela said, "It's too bad, Chris. I tried. I gave you the opportunity. But the members voted you down."

"That's . . . hard to believe." He shrugged. My supporters exposed his foul play for all the good it did. I was on my ass kicked out of Bush by geeks, barred from Hearst by goons. Washington Street was out after all and I wrote "[I'm not] going to set myself up for another [Papasan] disaster with Do Wan Kim." My paltry possibles went back into my '74 Beetle. What didn't fit, like my gun case, I stored with Julian. My only space was the driver's seat. I dozed sitting straight up.

Ergela and I were obviously playing at Cain and Abel. In my providentially dystopian thoughts, we *had* to succeed. I couldn't let him victimize me and our church too as Cain did Abel. Jacob's victory with Esau was vital. I tried everything, from personally apologizing for my arrogance and accidentally turning members against him—his claim—when advising them to reconcile and not quit the church, to ceasing questioning and disagreeing with his decisions. I could accept these conditions because I knew I was right. It wasn't necessary to force-feed him. God could break our logjam only in my humility. As a last measure, I offered him my 'Isaac' (a sacrifice of something as beloved as Isaac to Abraham): my top-of-the-line Fender guitar. I loved it as my comfort and companion these past 10 years.

"Whatever I have is at your disposal for God and Principle, Ergela."

"Thanks a lot." It seemed anticlimactic. "But I have no personal need for it."

It killed me putting 'Giselda' into strangers' hands. "We disagree on a lot, but this symbolizes our unity under God and True Parents. As brothers."

"Okay, I appreciate your motivation. I'll use it for the church."

Perhaps feeling considerate, he stuck Giselda in his closet. I got it back untouched when CARP and the Bay Area church denounced him to Rev. Kim, threatening to separate members and money if he didn't end Ergela's tyranny.

Before leaving Big Mike said, "Freeman told me Rev. Kim wanted you as state leader, except you aren't a seminarian." *Huh.* As if UTS improved Ergela one whit.

～

AS MY ADVENTURES with Ergela unfolded in early March 1989, the brand-new president of the Unification Church of America blew into town on the winds of an old-timey revival. Jim Baughman was gentle, decent, honest—a far cry from his two-faced, machinating predecessor. We'd met at November's ICUS. Heeding members' demands for democracy in leadership, Rev. Moon had state leaders shortlist their preferences for Dr. Durst's replacement, selected his own from this pool, appointed him president, and called him elected.

I said, "Jim, your quasi-democratic installation into the presidency gives me more reason than ever to give you all the support and service I can."

"We all do what we can. But, thanks."

He was a reforming man. Amongst many shared attributes was our desire to see 'real' Divine Principle reform the institution. My notion entailed jettisoning our Confucian hierarchy and the Cain–Abel master–slave dynamic controlling our every relationship. It would be a tough row to hoe and we both knew it.

His Korean elders resented him as intensely as old-timey whites did "uppity niggers." My favorite image of Korean Unification Church leaders interacting with American leaders who'd kept their balls was the scene in the 1967 movie *In the Heat of the Night*. Black Philadelphia homicide detective Sidney Poitier—accompanied by the white sheriff—confronts the white Mississippi industrialist controlling the town of Sparta. He slaps this "uppity nigger" across the face who then shockingly, instantaneously backslaps him to a passive sheriff. As Poitier leaves, Whitey turns his back to weep in frustrated rage, shame, and humiliation. That exactly portrays Korean leaders' contempt for Americans represented by uppity Jim. Past presidents knew their place. Remember, he came to power at the insistence of Americans dirt tired with appointed losers. But the Koreans weren't letting him grab any Poitier counterslap, no sir. When Jim stood up the manly American, they deballed him.

Their story was that he'd bought himself a modest house (highfalutin for a member) with church money and had his vp's do likewise. The halcyon days of $100,000 salaries and secret books were AWOL for Jim's big tent days. I recall him saying, "The president of the Messiah's church warrants a decent, upscale home rather than my crummy, undersized apartment. The church pays so little my wife has to work." He said his in-laws downpaid on the property. Either way, he'd riled big dogs apathetic of the facts. Echoing Jesus (Luke 14:7–11) Rev. Moon said,

> The [leadership] principle is simple: you sleep in a humbler place, you eat poorer things, and you wear poorer clothing. Leaders will have many opportunities to appear in public scenes, so your members will . . . have you put on good clothing and look nice, and that is what your members should do for you, not you for yourself. (*How To Be A Leader* 1973)
>
> A high priest needs to eat the kind of food that beggars eat, and climb up from there . . . wearing the humblest clothes . . . If he wants the nation and the people to become one with him, he has to start at the bottom before he can go up . . . experience the misery of the people . . . in this light, I am often thankful for the persecution I get. (*Cham Bumo Gyeong* (1976) 2015, [21] 998)

Sit in a coveted spot right off the bat, you get humiliated by bigger wigs. Jesus was right and so is Rev. Moon. The point of humility isn't phylacteric godliness but to avoid the arrogance of overreaching. Jim outmaneuvered himself.

A better tactic would've been moving from his crummy apartment to a crummier one, making sure to invite top American and Korean leaders along with ministers and politicians for frequent dinner engagements. I imagine this would've sat well with Rev. Moon, as he'd done similar relationship-wise with Hak Ja Han to get the spiteful Korean shrews reviling his marriage to transfer their revulsion off her to his heartless treatment and thereby befriend her. Korean leaders weren't really heartless shrews and even more pragmatic. Important community figures would've wondered aloud why their president was living in a shithole when they and Rev. Moon weren't. They might or might not have hated it, but funding better digs would've happened one way or another with Jim as above reproach as Rev. Moon ensured his very young wife eventually was of those spurned elder sisters. In a church as viciously political as ours, that was only good business.

Instead, he bought the house without laying the political groundwork. Korean leaders demanded they return their houses and get the money back. Jim refused, citing his just need for decent housing that wouldn't embarrass the church at political mixers. Powerful enemies who never met a slight they wouldn't stew didn't see it that way and made him miserable, outfoxing and blocking his every initiative. Korean leaders care little for the welfare of the church or God's providence. Their prime concern is maintaining institutional structures propping up their authority. To be fair, they tended to view it as complementary if not integral with God's providence— Korea *was* Abel. Yet, Oliver Cromwell held a similar view and check his success. Some were surely motivated by Judas' concern over wasting money on ointments but forgetting their Lord's admonishment—as, perhaps, Jim did not—that money advancing the greater providence, however unlikely to the blind, is well spent. It's a top-end business maxim.

Thereafter, Jim was a hamstrung man (how some American Indians ensured no slave had the moxie to escape twice). He rightly knew he'd have to pick a fight with the Koreans if the American presidency was to ever gain their respect and its independence. They're contemptuous of American members because, for the most part, we've been a passive, slavish people sifting our powerful Christian heritage into the winds for the golden shackles of inimical power. Rev. Moon and Divine Principle rest on two millennia of Christian tradition. They don't exist separately but entwine Jesus. Yet, the vast majority of pre-Moonie Japanese and fewer Koreans weren't Christian. In recognizing Rev. Moon as an Imperial and cultural Messiah, they threw Jesus like salt over their shoulder and his great, enlightening Christian tradition with it. They leapt from Confucianism, Buddhism, animism, agnosticism, and atheism across 20 centuries of spiritual agriculture, martyrdom, personal transformation, and our human reinvention from primitive brute to modern liberal. Then they brought the former as a contagion to appalled Americans who struggled then deserted in droves of conscience.

Yes, he needed a fight. But he picked the wrong one and lost. My first semester at UTS he periodically joined us around our cafeteria table and (maybe rhetorically?) asked, "Am I right? Should I just knuckle under and do what they want? Or should I still stand up for what's right?"

"In my experience, you just have to follow Principle. It'll focus your conscience. But, it's a hard road." And I should know.

He perfectly represented the generalized American member: in love with the Principle, driven by duty to God and humanity, yet consumed by inner conflict with obedience to temporality over conscience. Probably why I glommed onto him like a personal flotation device. After seven years of impotence and failure, Rev. Moon dismissed him for a man who was everything Koreans (though for many, none of what Americans) wanted in an American president. Castration decapitated Jim's big plans to restore the American church to its vital root and revivify American Christianity. That's why he'd sallied forth in March of '89 with his traveling revival. He planned to crisscross the country through every major church center to preach reformation. His first and last stop was Hearst Street in Berkeley.

The great hall was packed with hundreds of members camped on the floor or standing and swaying in song. We were wild with excitement. Speakers orated their undying love for God and True Parents. We hadn't seen anything like this since the 1970s and early 1980s. Jim was a good speaker and preached up a storm. Plenty of music and testimonies. Even Rev. Zin Moon Kim got up and cried crocodile tears down his broad, well-fed Korean cheeks.

Jim solemnly boomed, "Our movement is in crisis! How we respond to this crisis, and what we do from today will determine whether we live or die as champions of God and as a movement!"

"Oh, yes!" we shouted in accord.

"We're behind you!"

He said, " 'Home members:' I don't even like that term. *I* live in a home. *I'm* a home member!"

"Right on!"

"Preach it, Jim!"

I wonderingly laughed if, behind inscrutable eyes, Ergela was rethinking his "You're just a student, Chris. That makes you only a home member. How do you think you can live in the center?" He sermonized and lectured DP while treating us like dogshit. Ignorance in knowledge. A flammable contradiction.

Yet, all the piety somehow forgets humanity: *Yes, I love God and True Parents but don't expect me to live for others, that's God and True Parents' job.* And there you have the reason why normal, intelligent people enslave themselves to religious leaders. It's not their great sales pitch, it's the undeniable need to be more important than, and waited upon by, one's fellows. If Unificationists spent more time bringing love and happiness to their brothers and sisters, the Unification Church today would be a thriving faith throbbing with the vigorous heartbeat of millions of Americans. But that's not fallen nature and members did little to confront it. Instead, Moonies spent inordinate time scheming to get closer to Rev. Moon and his cat wranglers, revel in the glory of their own self-importance, and persecute those upsetting the political precariousness that came with it.

In our 'big tent,' Jim and others encouraged us to stand before the crowd to confess our sins. There were few takers because, in the Unification Church of the late '80s, a person's confession on any topic was often weaponized against them and collateral bystanders. Only a fool uttered their personal failings aloud in our Maoist environment. More than once I'd seen myself and others regret mentioning a personal problem in our search for counsel. Leaders harangued us to confess our sins to our central figure because an important precept of our faith was that only Rev. Moon could 'forgive' our sin in the sense of paying a globalized indemnity in which it was bound up. This was the Completed Testament Age. Jesus' sin-forgiving days ended with its advent. Since Rev. Moon can't hear everyone's confession directly, central figures fulfilled that role as priestly proxies.

This theology was fine if you believed it. Its stake in the heart was leaders and even the BFD abusing the confessional for a panoply of heinous purposes. This was a problem in the Catholic Church, too, which is why it instituted secret confessions and rigorous confidentiality. Unificationists explained it away (as with most problems) by noting our faith and institution were young and less organized than the mainstream. True, but that hardly exculpates treachery. Jim sagely suggested we write our sins on paper, read it silently to God, then throw it into the room's great fireplace now snapping hot sparks to symbolize our commitment to parch our fallen nature. This was a big hit because it relieved our anxiety that we were bound for hell on account of our sin without the downside of having it come back to haunt us at an inconvenient time... say, just before a Blessing.

After wrapping up the emotional portions of the program Jim set up Divine Principle workshops to reeducate members and guests. Part of his rationale for the revival crusade was his opinion that members didn't understand the Principle. That's why they'd led our movement into its deathly despair. I couldn't agree more. But his idea of a DP workshop was regurgitating the same old boring, shallow drivel with calls to take initiative and better follow our leaders—a gross contradiction— that members had already turned their backs on. What we needed was a dynamic seminar to dissect, analyze, question, probe, challenge, and investigate the Principle. Our questions and concerns should be gauntlets at our instructor's feet. *Inspire us with truth! Excite us with knowledge! Challenge us to think and discover the Principle through interaction with each other!* That was too radical even for Jim, suspecting maybe just how thin his ice was. His workshops durably put audiences to sleep several days more, leaving us with an unexpected collective gasp of relief when he turned off the lights.

Critically, his revival didn't challenge our fundamental problem of abuse by and between leaders and members, our seminal misunderstanding of Cain–Abel and central figures, nor inculcate a stronger pursuit of truth and understanding although it did challenge us in general to change the small things we were doing and thinking. What it did most, however, was tip off Korean leaders that Jim was a gathering storm preparing to roil their placid waters. They reacted swiftly and decisively, banning him from conducting any more revivals in America on the grounds they were unPrincipled and anyway unnecessary.

Thus came to a scurrilous end the one and only effort to reform the Unification Church of America. With their heads firmly planted in sand, Korean leaders were adamant their oldfangled religion was good enough for us. Jim's slyer efforts didn't stop and possibly accelerated even more members balloting by foot. He spent off his presidential power and glory a frustrated and impotent token of an American church wholly owned spiritually, financially, politically, culturally, and institutionally by Koreans on a Japanese spit. An incredulous retrogression. Americans were the token Western face on a placard tightly nailed to an Asian stick, a modernized Korean version of Japan's 1930s co-prosperity fraud. Tojo was dead-eyes green.

TRUDGING 1.5 MILES to UCB from Ashby Avenue's CARP house—I'd hauled my desktop here to type a finals paper since parking was too precious to lightly give up—I felt the heavy blow of Jim's failure to crusade past Berkeley. For a second, I thought our church had a chance. That we Americans might not just say we were taking responsibility for the spiritual future of our country, but do so. The greater blow was my grinding despair at Ergela rejecting *two* Blessing candidacies. It finally penetrated that I'd only ever founder conforming to Unificationism's institutional *modus operandi* as a nobody trench-jockey. I'd probably never win permission to a Blessing. I'd lose out on a wife and family. Suffer the priestly life I'd always rejected but without the perks. Eat dust. The former distressed me more than the latter, as it wasn't mere earthly happiness I wanted but Restoration from the human Fall.

Chattering along like a street bum to his liquor spirits I griped, "Chris, what are you doing? Where are you? You're living on the streets, practically begging for food, unable to pay any of your bills, tormented by leaders and members . . . Why is it that way with me? Am I too independent? What? Everyone is feverishly studying for finals except me. My mind is at least 99% occupied with the providence. I can think of practically nothing else." *I. Am. Exhausted.* I wrote,

> I am following the right path. The *only* question is, "Will I *continue* to follow the right path? And will I be successful at it?" . . . Oh, I am sorrowful unto death; overwhelmed with grief. I am desperate to do the will of God, but cannot discern it. I am flat busted and living on the streets: oh, Mama! How you would lament for your son! but that you knew. I am considered a madman.

Katerina said, "I wonder if you're not following selfish desires instead of noble ideals. You're not following your central figure. You reject him. It's unPrincipled."

"Katerina, this house has devastated me. I don't know if I can go on."

"Maybe you shouldn't, then. Consider leaving."

"Like Evelyn, when Ergela chased her out of the house with all her things in a screaming match and then sent you to fetch her back?" Her *fuck you* eyes cored me. "Is it really so hard to encourage than disparage?" But she'd walked out.

Between semester's end and July my psyche fell apart. Ergela broke me and I gave up. In my negative frame, I never imagined Rev. Moon opening the Matching and Blessing to nonmembers in 1992. That was a faith too far.

⁓

I REPAID MY parent's January visit with my own in early June to their home over a dam-flooded canyon along Los Escondidos Street outside Marble Falls, Texas. I phoned Shiori, that enigmatic silent sister from Judah Street now a part of Houston's church. We'd recently carried on a light correspondence in tortured Japanese after she wrote me seeming to agitate for some kind of relationship. It wasn't clear.

I stayed a night in the Houston house her church-owned Japanese restaurant used. Surprising me, she spoke functional English. Her co-workers treated me with dirty looks, incivility, and ostracized me from all conversation. We weren't Blessed. I got it. I switched to a hotel the next day. Shiori popped by after work. She declined to depart like a church lady as I was conking out around 11 PM.

"I can sleep right here," she said.

"The chair? Are you crazy?"

"Is soft and fine. I have much room."

Tired, I let it go but forced her to switch places. You won't be surprised to hear we ended up atop the covers, softly breathing hard. My feelings about her were inexplicable. I couldn't make sense of it. She was virtually dysfunctional, yet I'd felt drawn since our first meeting. Tonight, in the unchaperoned confines of a hotel room, our attractive energy was increasingly sexualizing. We spent the night fitfully sleeping in our clothes. Although I felt myself barely a church member on account of Ergela's abuse, the Principle's story of the human Fall was in the front of my mind. The last thing I wanted was to repeat it. But I was realizing Shiori had been in love with me for years. I hadn't noticed. Now it viscerally slammed me a couple feet from her body. Tortured, shallow breathing rang my ears. Her galvanic tenseness zapped as we now and again brushed. Intense loneliness haunted me. My response to her confused holy hell out of me.

Her strange alienness once again subsumed into her apparent humanity. She revealed herself a film fanatic and expert swindler in buying the $1 multiplex matinee then sneaking theater to theater for several other films until the evening crowds sobered up management. We spent our second and third days talking, walking, and watching movies. When I on-ramped to I-10 for Marble Falls, I didn't know what to think. Might she be 'the one?' By late May–early June, I'd accepted the reality the Blessing couldn't be less likely. I was now 30 and unexpectedly pining to settle down with a wife. Nanami was long lost to Sam by my inability to leave the church.

Could I marry her? Was she truly interested? Was I ready to break my church-rejected purity and faith to wed outside it? Could they more viciously ostracize me than now? I'd spent over three years preparing myself physically, emotionally, and spiritually to qualify for the Blessing only for Ergela to unceremoniously jerk it from my hands not once but twice. What was the point of trying further when even my Korean regional leader rejected my best effort to be a good Moonie?

I wrapped up Mom and Dad then car repairs in Denver and motored to the Bay Area. John, my only non-Chinese Harold Street roomie, got into UCB for a teaching certificate. His rental worthiness got us a third-floor 2-bedroom in Oakland. I'd jerked up hard at the end of my rope after months living in my Beetle while telling all and sundry I was fine and dandy. How delicious to have a floor to stretch out on and a kitchen to cook food in. My new sense of security was draining my tension. I found myself studying Shiori every day and contemplating dating. She called me in July and brought up Matchings and Blessings.

"I didn't say it before, but Ergela blocked me from all future Blessings and kicked me out of the church for insubordination. I'm fed up. I think I've quit."

"What?" She rattled off some tetchy Japanese. "He is no good. Contemptible."

I laughed. "Contemptible? That's some pretty good English." She pushed me on my church plans. "I'm not sure anymore the Blessing is in my future, Shiori."

"They are send me to restaurant in Florida because I am stay overnight with you." She paused, breathy. "Do you still like me, K'risu?"

"Err . . ." I struggled to assess the consequences of not saying maybe. "Yes . . . I like you fine." Her 'like' was qualitatively different than mine, but it didn't register.

A few collect pay phone calls later she said, "I am think maybe to visit next Thursday. Is okay? Maybe I stay your apartment? Only short time."

My heart jerked in thrilling trepidation. *Yes, I want to see you, but* . . . "Okay. Why not? I have a big room with lots of floor space. No problem."

Imagine my shock to find her at Oakland International trucking a 7-piece like I was the Queen Mary. I huffed her portly gear into my sagging Beetle.

I squinched an eye. "Are you here to stay? You're not here to stay are you?"

"I don't know." Her stock response to whatever she didn't want to answer.

"But look at all your luggage! It must be everything you own."

"Yes, is all my things." She was demure at the curb, eyeing my stevedoring and radiating her Japanese alienism in a scrunched up smile beneath Mrs.-Moon-celebrity sunglasses. She might've wondered if I was going to bolt and desert her and the seven Samsonite dwarves. I was too much of a gentleman not to take her home with me now and sort out her inconvenient details later. She could be using me to escape her circumstances, sure, but why not head for Japan? Probably liked America better, as Nanami did. I bullied her luggage into my choking Beetle and, the wisp of a feather, she wedged nicely into the jammed-forward passenger seat.

Anyway, a part of me was hoping she liked me enough to stay even in a platonic relationship. That's how lonely I was feeling. I'd gone and blown $300 on a 10-inch California King futon exclusively for Shiori that now flattened my bedroom carpet. I might've bought the largest available not only for my long legs but somehow suspecting—hoping?—I'd end up sleeping there, too. While I had every intention of remaining chaste, a part of me was definitely falling in love and secretly wanted to consummate my feelings. But I wouldn't let myself think it. It stayed an unspoken, near unthought part of my motivation for welcoming her.

That night her spiritual mother rang up. Yoko, you may recall, was Blessed to Mr. Kobayashi, my favorite leader from Judah Street who'd nevertheless started this epidemic of leaders rejecting my Blessing. She was practically apoplectic.

"Is Shiori there?" Her tone was rough.

"Yes, she's right here. She came out for a visit," I lamely offered.

"She's not visiting you," she sternly informed me like I was mentally retarded. "She's moved in with you!" Cold fingers squeezed my struggling heart.

"What do you mean?" Suspicious eyes fell on Shiori pretending I wasn't there.

"She took all her things, everything, and left her center in Houston. Her central figure called today. He said she'd told him she was leaving to visit her mother!"

"To visit her mother?" I repeated in stupefied disbelief. *Well . . . fuck me.* Mrs. Kobayashi's wrath vibrated through the phone. She wasn't exactly yelling at me but was so hard a-boil as to crack her Japanese reserve. I could tell she was thinking I'd orchestrated the whole deal. I drilled harder into Shiori sitting politely Japanese style on the futon, eyes cast down to avoid my darkening own.

"Yes, you idiot. She lied to her central figure to come out to be with you! She's left the church. I *trusted* you . . ."

"Left? Well . . ." I couldn't think of a practical response. What had I got myself into? Did I care? I'd called the Kobayashis pleading and cajoling them to intervene with Ergela or Rev. Kim so I could go to the Blessing and they'd gone autistic.

"Ergela is your central figure," he'd said. "You must respect his decision."
She'd been more blunt. "Neither of us can interfere. It's his area."

Yet, they were high totems. Rev. Moon had earlier put him in charge of the books for all church-owned businesses in North America. She was working with Mrs. Moon, Mr. Kamiyama, and other senior leaders. They were obviously political animals and well understood the downside of coming to my rescue even though Ergela was an American leader with a dodgy reputation. Rev. Kim had seconded his denial and maybe the Kobayashis didn't see themselves top-tier enough to challenge a 36-Blessed couple, the most sanctified cadre next to Rev. Moon. But they could've organized my transfer to a leader who *would* give permission, *such as themselves.* No, they'd left me hoist on Ergela's petard. At the moment, I didn't have a lot of sympathy for her feelings after hosing me for politics.

"Well, what?" she snapped. I'd never seen her angry. She sounded scary.

"Um . . . well, Shiori says she's unhappy in the church. No one treats her well. She wants to stay here, away from its oppression, to think things over." I was defending her but damn sore she'd lied to me. What was I going to do about that?

"What are you doing, K'risu? Shiori is a Blessed sister!"

"No, she's not. She was only Matched. She never went to the Blessing. Anyway, there hasn't even been one since January or April and she didn't go."

"Yes, she is. Father had a small, private ceremony recently and Shiori went. She's a Blessed woman. She has a Blessed husband!"

Goddamn it. That changed a lot of things. These fucking leaders and their special privileges and secret goings on. A *private* Blessing? What the fuck was that? I glared daggers at Shiori. Why didn't she tell me any of this in Texas? How was I going to get rid of her? Instinctively, I knew she'd never just pack up and go of her own volition like, "Sorry, Chris, I don't want to ruin your life, I'll go to make things easier for you." Like *Nanami.* It was fucking laughable. I was in real trouble.

"What's your plan, K'risu? Do you know, Mr. Kamiyama is very upset with you."

Oh, terrific. I pick a woman tethered to the top. The last person I needed for an enemy was that guy. I'd have only done worse if she was Rev. Moon's own daughter— one of whom, close to my age, I'd befriended on campus.

But I was still a fuck-you *American*, dammit. "Well, I can't help that. Shiori's got a right to do what she wants. She said she didn't want her Match, anyway."

"Are you going to marry her? Take responsibility for her eternal life?"

Screeching tires. I stammered, "I—I don't know. I haven't really had a chance to th–think about that. I want to go to the Blessing."

"Father recently said to some members who left the church to marry each other that if they stayed together for seven years, he would Bless them. Is that what you're thinking?" *Fuuuck!* as Nanami banshee'd through my heart.

"I didn't hear that. But I haven't done anything with Shiori. We didn't fall or anything. She's just visiting. I have no intention to break her Blessing." That much was certainly true never mind all my wishful thinking.

"K'risu, she's 37 years. Almost a 40-years woman! How old are you? Thirty?"

"Yes," I said glumly. Another lie from Shiori. She hadn't explicitly said so, but she'd implied she was only a couple years older. I'd figured 32 or 33. But, 37?

"Maybe if you marry her, you can get Blessed in seven years. I don't know."

"You don't know? Didn't he say it? How can I take—?"

"It is Father! His decision. But, you must tell her to leave. Right now. Tell her to go back to Texas, or she can come to New York. She must not stay with you."

"How," I stormed impotently at the phone now clutched a foot from my face, "can I do that? I'm not her central figure! I can't just order her to do something! How'd it work for him? She already said she's not going anywhere. You know how stubborn she is. You talk to her! You tell her to leave."

"Let me talk to her, then!"

Shiori's sweetly high-pitched but growly-growing monotonic Japanese filled the room while I stood around like a dodo bird looking at its future.

The phone call was a ramrod. "Why the hell did you lie to me about moving out here? Why'd you lie about lying to your central figure?" She was quiet. "You even lied about the Blessing . . . about everything!"

"I am sorry, K'risu. It was only way."

"*Ichh!* Was it? You've got me into more trouble than even I ever did!"

Her guts tumbled out. "I am very unhappy there. I not like church. They treat me not nice. Always push me around with most dirty work. They say I am very s'tu-rain-gee"—*Ha ha! What a*—"I am fed up! Like you are say." She was old-line samurai, she'd said. Her family guarded Japan's emperor, her father a chamberlain in Tokyo's palace even now. Her family had all but disowned her when she'd joined the church and it had got her nowhere. She didn't say she loved me but, "I do want to be with you. That is what I want."

I had a soft heart and the sweets for her, besides. We tired of arguing. She slumped on the futon. Calming down, I laid out my sleeping bag.

"What you doing? You not sleep there."

"Yes, I certainly am sleeping here. The futon's for you."

"No," she gently said, lightly patting the futon. "You sleep here, with me."

Was this really the same bashful lassie from Judah Street? "No, I don't think so. I always sleep on the floor. Been doing it eight years. Nice, soft carpet."

"You don't need sleep on floor. Sleep here, on bed." *Pat, pat, pat.*

"Look, Shiori, we're not married or Blessed or anything. It's better if we—"

"Is stupid! You are silly. This futon big enough for both. We not need do anything. But, I not want you sleep on floor."

We went round and round half an hour till, half asleep, I capitulated like I'm certain she knew I would. Some fuck-you American. She wrangled in bed over sex a week till I wondered, *What in hell am I doing? There's a beautiful woman next to me angling for a shag and I'm saying no? These bastards won't let me get Blessed now or ever and are forcing me to find my own wife. Why not Shiori?* At least I knew and liked her, which was more than I could say for many of the Matchings I'd seen. *This is the eighties. What's wrong with sex if you love a person?* A great rationalization. *But, do I love her?* We at last settled down to a married-but-not-married life.

John said, "She's moving in? You're throwing me over here, Chris."

"I'm sorry, man. I didn't know this was her plan till she got here, and then it was too late to kick her out. She has a situation. Can you give it a chance?"

Shiori smoothed it over cooking him restaurant quality meals. Life settled into a routine. Mrs. Kobayashi called back once, then gave up on us. Amazing that her indignation never once paused to wonder how our actions came to be. I would've never got involved with Shiori if I hadn't been five times denied the Blessing—six, if you count the friends-only—and freighted by Ergela's threat backed up by Rev. Kim, other leaders, then the Kobayashis. That's the blindness of Unification Church members. Like a tyrant condemning rebellion, they censure your actions never acknowledging nor taking responsibility for their culpability.

A MONTH LATER, hands quivered at the end of a tremulous heartbeat tearing open a letter from UTS arriving like a sniper shot before its report from across the valley. I hadn't expected my reputation to make the cut but, "Welcome to UTS . . . " lashed my brain. Besides genuine feelings for Shiori, overwhelming hopelessness is the reason I let my guard down. I was heartsick scanning what I'd taken for rejection. My seminary dream shattered on the floor and it wasn't Ergela's black hand or the Korean mafia but my own poxed member. I revered Malcolm X's chaste mind.

What's my problem? Too concerned with my feelings? I'd wanted marriage since I was ten. It was practically my only life goal. I felt unloved by my family, definitely the church, and believed I'd find happy acceptance in a wife and children even if I had to scrounge it up on my own. Was that my true cause, like Katerina intimated? *No! I'm sincerely dedicated to Restoring humanity through Father's unconditional love, the indemnity course, Restoring myself . . . eliminating my vector of sin.*

Yet, for all that, I wanted a spouse plain and simple and the Unification Church had squandered eight prime years denying me as all my friends got theirs. I felt cheated by the duplicitous tyranny of leaders weaponizing the sacred Blessing—the fount of all salvation—to force obedience to their unPrincipled personal wills. Love aside, I fell in with Shiori perhaps because she was there when I most needed her warm, reassuring if not exactly unconditional, embrace.

My weakness had now cost me my second principle goal in the church. Ergela defeated number 1: my Blessing. Now I'd defeated myself with UTS. With it went number 3: working directly with Rev. Moon. Volcanic frustration, impotent rage, and self-reproach lit every capillary afire. I blamed Shiori for it even though I knew it was my fault. Who controlled my libido better than me? I could've ignored her. Dragged her in my car to her Houston house. Slept on the floor; though, without doubt, she'd have only squirmed in next to me. Crassly told her to cross her ankles and made it stick. Forced her on a Kobayashi-bound plane. Persuaded the cops to drag her out on a housejacking charge. I didn't do any of it or was half-hearted. I took it lying down because I wanted her—*somebody*—in my life. I was lonesome. Abused. A mangy dog in a frigid gutter yearning for a dry heat.

I felt unmitigatedly victimized by the end of 1989. Ergela shafted me in the cockiest, most galling way. Regardless my physical and spiritual sacrifices—fasting, praying, witnessing, fundraising, DP lecturing, poring over Principle, humbling myself to his egomania, living in my car, starving, so much more—he'd poured all of it and my trust with it onto the ground as so much poison. It bitterly vexed me. I resented him to his white-whaled marrow but I'd left his fate to God. I had live my own life. If I let him rule my future then I'd be more my own victim. I wanted to be a victor. To succeed. I'd accepted my grating reality but would work for my goals even if the church was oh-so-plainly showing me the door. Rev. Moon and Divine Principle is what mattered.

Discovering I'd had girlfriends and a son sent Shiori's emotions hopscotching A-to-z through friend-zoned cold shoulders, turned backs, and silent treatments. She came up for air now and then but I supposed it was a hard blow for a 37-year old virgin. I coped. She loathed the church with a startlingly caustic bite.

"After you visit me, choice must to leave Houston or church and break Blessing. Of course, I choose you. Ha ha, I am kick-out person, too!"

" 'Ha ha' wouldn't be my first choice of words, Shiori."

She whole-body shrugged *I don't care.* "I hate no freedom in church."

"I was surprised Mrs. K. said she'd string me up if I'm only playing with you, but a sexual relationship is just fine and dandy as long as I'm serious."

"Because we already fell, silly. She had to give up lecturing and forcing me." As bankrupt as communism. "Stop talking Blessing. I no want hear."

That cratered me every time. "If you want to be my wife, you have to take the good with the difficult. It's important to me. Jerome says—"

"I hate him! Jerome, Jerome, Jerome! Don't go UTS! We can stay here. Sail with your friends. Roller skate. Have a *life.* You can write your stupid book."

Pitfalls of Heaven: The Decline of the American Moonie. "Too strong, Chris," Jerome had said, still committed. "Way too strong." But, inspiration was tardy.

Shiori surprised me a practical-minded girl aboard a sailboat. Every week she busted one stereotype only to reinforce another. Rollerblades saved my fitness and gas money to UCB. She dumped her ass a few times on quads in Golden Gate Park but could *skate.* What a far cry from Judah Street she was. Even Julian noticed.

"I'm not dumping you for a Matching." Her cold eyes iced mine. "I'd never. We're for better or worse, now."

"But if you go UTS, I think we should separate. Because you only think of *your* future, not *ours.*"

"You're being unreasonable. You want me to spend my life in retail? I'm a teacher. An ordained *minister.* You may as well ask me to be short, like you." Tears. *Goddamn her crazy emotions.* "I think you love me less than you need me."

"No! I love you. Yes, church made me so lonely, but . . . I only want *nothing* to do with church!"

"Jeez. Okay. I get it. But I don't want to be unequally yoked, either. Think about it. Because graduation's coming and I'm going to New York." My stomach hurt. A maddening flame right under my breastbone. A new ulcer was knocking.

"You have so much experience with relationship. I am scared—"

"I love you, Shiori. I've no interest in anybody. Just you and the Blessing."

"*Bakateri!*" Rattling Japanese shot holes in our room.

Sigh. "There's always the Kobayashis if—" She threw something that broke on the wall near me. *Flame on!* I fired something back. Felt myself losing control.

"I wait twenty years and Kobayashis not Bless me until I reach 36 and I hate him! Hate *her!* Hate church! Don't go UTS! Stay with me!" She rampaged through my books and papers then piled into our strewn carpet a wailing shambles. "I am sorry. You so *baka*. You make me *baka*, too."

"Maybe. Not today." Her pendular emotions were causing me to question my feelings and compare her to the ghosts of love past. *Shit.*

At last, Christmas 1989 closed out UCB's Far East Asian history and language bachelor's and my Bay Area providence. *College edumacated!* With my UTS acceptance letter in hand like Willy Wonka's golden ticket, I cranked the starter on our chic Hyundai Sonata her disapproving dad donated $1,500 for to roadtrip to the Big Apple and see if I could matriculate despite . . . you know. I loved her but off and on lusted for a separation so UTS wouldn't find out and rescind its offer.

"You should've kept your job here"—she'd turned out a crackerjack saleslady for Yokohama Okadaya in San Francisco—"till I got set up."

The fam honored me at my UCB commencement. Dec., 1989.

"You must too crazy. No, we go together. That is best way. Is *our* life now."

Pfft! These supposedly docile Asian women were turning out decidedly bossier than advertised. But it wasn't possible much less in my character to disappear into the night. We'd disposed of our extraneous belongings, packed the rest into the Sonata—hauling stuff down three flights, she'd revealed a monstrous physical strength—bid John a fond *adieu*, then it was rubber-to-road. I wholly misread the repercussions and tribulations the searing conflict between my private love for Shiori and public love for God was soon to create.

Act XI

Off to the Big Apple
Leaping Into the Tiger's Maw—Not!

We cruised to New York by way of Los Angeles, the snowy Rockies, Denver, New Mexico, Dallas, Houston, New Orleans, Key West, Disney World, Lexington, Cincinnati, Lansdale, and Washington, DC visiting family, relatives, and friends along the way. After years in school, weighing anchor for the open road was stepping through dungeon doors into eye-watering sun. I wanted to visit everyone. Family wasn't too thrilled with our unpremeditated advents. My parents found Shiori bizarre. She was already clinically introverted, rigidly old-school Japanese, and reticent but even more so around them. Dad battled the Imperial Navy in the Big One but I never asked if she'd rung his bells.

Mom point blank pulled me aside. "Are you sleeping with her, Christopher?"

It took a few seconds to loosen up my wrung throat. "Come on, I never talk about that part of my life with anybody. Take it to the bank." Judging by her expression, I reckoned she'd thought I'd said, "And how!" but thankfully let it go with a *You dumbass* kind of look.

After a month on the road, even my wagon train bravado was punctured. I wanted a roof, a

Shiori and Hyundai at the folks'.

bed, a life. We ground over the Verrazano Narrows onto the elevated Brooklyn–Queens Expressway and sifted through New York's afternoon rush hour.

"What a dump!" I gulped at the gritty cityscape and wildly weaving cars.

This was the biggest, sprawlingest, grimiest city I'd seen yet. Los Angeles—even fading, stockyard-stinking cowtown Denver—felt more bounded, clean, and open-armed. Knife-fighting traffic spurning menacing pedestrian eyes like baseball bats fondly recalling swingier days along mysterious, dottering surface streets froze my blood. Heinlein's *A Stranger in a Strange Land* popped into my head. Bleak as death in mid-January 1990 under ice, snow, lifeless grey skies, and dirty traffic, the city's jaunty 'Big Apple' moniker witheringly deceived in the cold shadow of crumbly brownstones and wall-to-wall, bumper-to-bumper parked cars. With my rumpled Rand McNally gripped against the wheel, I navigated to Jerome's 53-4th Avenue apartment in Brooklyn without a fender-bender or xenophobic mobs dragging us out of our hateful California-tagged seats. But that very night some bastard burglarized our Sonata with a screwdriver punched through the door lock. I presumed he turned it just like my owner's key to swipe the radio and all my cassette tapes.

Relaxing post-graduation with Mom.

Jerome said, "Ruining only your door's lock instead of a hammer through the window tells you it was a considerate thief."

"*Hmmphh.* Some favor." Two weeks later I skipped a jaunty tune outside to haggle my mint chariot over to the insurance adjusters. I full stopped. Stared at the New York tag using my spot. "The hell's my car?"

Somebody said, "Your Cali plates were a 'For Theft' sign. Shoulda changed 'em."

I gawked. "The fuck town is this?" Shiori's face was my echo.

"The happeningest town ever," said the over-achieving cop who unhelpfully found it trashed weeks later days shy the waiting period for an insurance write off. Instead of a double-digit payout now it was clear how pointless cars were in this subwayed city, I had a $200 tow for my undriveable Sonata to a distant Hyundai shop. Meanwhile, car payments.

Going on four months' radio silence they indifferently explained over the phone, "We're waitin' on parts from Koh-rea. We'll call ya." *Click.*

"Yeah, right. Thanks, dial tone." New York City hadn't started well.

Jerome lived with his bodybuilder brother Ronald in a mildly run down 4-storey brick walk-up near Flatbush and Atlantic. It sat on the dividing line between upscale Park Slope bordering Prospect Park and our crapped-out semi-ghetto. A giant Art Deco clock tower atop 41 stone floors dominating west Brooklyn was the landmark I needed to figure my way home. When Jerome and I were at 225 Harold in 1987 his aged, drug-dealing West Indian mother died and he'd tearfully packed up for New York City to handle her affairs. After serious run-ins with his drug-dealing other brother usurping the family home in St. Albans, Queens he'd moved to Brooklyn for safety. He offered us space in their first-floor 1-bedroom's living room, which we partitioned with a blanket. We scoured the ads for work.

I supposed he was surprised I was canoodling Shiori, but he understood our situation. His own relationship with the church was rocky because, like me, he was an ethically minded intellectual prone to voicing opinions while poisoning his personal life. He'd broken his Blessing with Carol then shacked up with an English twit named Sharon who "can't get enough of my black cock to save her life." I'd stood up for him in those days. Helped him explain his impression of Carol's abuse. Despite my costly loyalty, he'd been frazzled enough to split on unfriendly terms when I'd interrupted his big plans for us in the church to fly off to Cyprus.

High school business class and a boring, off-the-rack suit made me an administrative assistant for three video producers and a suave corporate trainer. Jack Morton Productions (JMP), a midtown corporate communications and talent agency at 641-6th Avenue, paid me a well-heeled $28,000 a year. Our pixied, cat-lady-lonely Brazilian office manager admitted my Berkeley pedigree was a deciding factor over my qualified competition.

With Shiori at Mom and Dad's.

"Sooo . . . a school's rep means something after all! My brother was right that Berkeley was the successful play."

"Smart brother," she said. "Good choice on your part. Nice suit, too."

Though my lowly position didn't require more than jeans and a clean shirt, a business suit dramatically enhanced attitudes. 'Assumed competency,' I called it. Casual, I had to prove myself. Suited up implied smart material going places. Even worked on street cops. I was a quick conversion from a whistle and flute cynic.

A few months later CEO Bill Morton put me wholly at genteel John Jones' disposal, JMP's one-man Learning Group. The multimedia learning revolution was getting underway and he wanted to sell more interactive CD training programs to our Fortune 500 clients. John gave me the option of coding them or farming it out, a stentorian opportunity knock even I heard. JMP bought the software, training materials, and consulting tutor as needed. I leapt into a new engineering career that supported me for years to come. As I produced the product, managed our vendors, and did the paperwork, John sold the projects and operated our 2-man department. We made a great team, sextupling our revenue over two fiscal years. At one point, we carried our $70 million dollar firm over the rocks of bad decisions and 20% layoffs haunting it through the economic downturn from Gulf War the First.

John routinely called me "sir" in his gentlemanly Southern way. For the first time since the Coast Guard I began feeling 'sir' less a derogatory statement of personal submission and more a social lubricant. His manners, fairness, and professionalism largely transformed me from bitter Moonie and rebellious ex-serviceman to happy employee enjoying the work life. I often worked long hours and sometimes full overnights meeting deadlines. He ensured JMP paid me comp time and sent private limousines with wireless phones whenever I had to be somewhere outside business hours. Too, he'd creep up on my cubicle 10–15 minutes to closing with, "Yeah . . . if you could stay after five, that would be greaaat," like that shitface Bill Lumbergh in 1999's *Office Space*. I didn't mind. Mastering programming was making me valuable even if my salary hadn't caught up. He took care of us with sumptuous sushi platters and other 4-star bribes plus limos home to avoid late-night subway thrells. I felt *big*. He *made* me feel big. Where was his kind in the Unification Church?

Increasingly, I felt uncomfortable with Shiori. *I have to separate*, I near daily berated myself. *I'm destined for True Parents. God doesn't approve of our unPrincipled, unBlessed relationship. My personal feelings are corrupting my public duty.* My soul-sucking anxiety and yearning to end our love affair for my higher mind popped *Titanic* rivets along her hard, sharp insistence we stay a going concern.

"You no love me. This is why you always talk about leaving."

"Oh, my God. I'm just torn up inside over the church."

"Psshh! Stupid UTS."

I felt trapped, consumed by love and duty. Her despairing tears broke my heart. "I swear, I won't abandon you," I went back and forth. A fucking pendulum. There was no middle ground for her. No, "I understand, let's just be friends for now." In many ways it was the relationship from hell despite, or because of, my passionate yet incomprehensible feelings for her and God.

I drove two hours upstate with Jerome in late January to visit UTS. Shiori refused to stay behind yet waxed only more reclusive. I parked in the front circle. She hid in the passenger seat, a bandana over her face presumedly to avert recognition.

Jerome glanced back. "She's just too weird, Chris. She'll wreck your plans."

"I'm not saying you're wrong." I pulled the heavy oak entrance door. "But I don't have a solution, yet. Somehow, I have to make it all work out."

He made a sound that felt a harsh klaxon. In our Sunday best, we conversed with Bill Peat of CAUSA Ministerial Alliance and Cathy Capelli in admissions. Jerome turned in his application and she confirmed my accepted status. A heavy weight fell out of my soul for Shiori's heavier quicksilver. *Just shoot yourself. Get it over with.*

We strolled the halls. "Everybody's glad to see you, Chris. They obviously see your capabilities and future greatness. You'll make a great name here."

"Flattery will get you everywhere. But you're the one with the track record."

Besides quick chats with Dr. Ang and Dr. Shimmyo, newly PH.D.'d Mike Mickler said, "Well, I'm surprised to see you out of Berkeley so quick."

"Four semesters. Not that quick. I did all my lower division at CCSF."

"He determined it and did it," Jerome all but gloated. Mike squint-eyed.

"Yeah . . . You're applying here, eh? Huh. Well, good luck, I guess."

Jerome splayed that big ass grin of his. "I don't need luck, Professor Mickler."

"Maybe not."

I said, "How come your student government isn't elected? I heard the school president just appoints it. What's even the point of—?"

"This isn't a democracy, Chris. You . . . don't have ideas about that, do you?"

"Nah, 'course not. Just wondering." It hit my bucket list all the same, along with founding a student academic journal. He shook my hand with a wary eye.

When we exited to Shiori's grotesquerie, I wondered how no one had knocked on the window and said, "Hey, why are you sitting here with a bandana over your head?" No one in the church ever thought your business wasn't theirs, so it puzzled me. Maybe they did and the mannequin didn't respond or they assumed she was sleeping. I shrugged it off and counted my lucky stars as we sped past the guard shack.

I phoned Mr. Kobayashi with the news. "That is surprising. I didn't think you'd try." Considering what came later, I wondered if he hadn't fired a flare.

Shiori's emotions battled raging tears or quiet understanding all over the map. "If you start seminary, I maybe move back church."

"You must be joking."

Her head wagged. "Mrs. Kobayashi will help. Do you want pray together?"

Eyebrows fired. *Her vigorous nod.* "I . . . we can only trust God and try."

She was a beautiful woman with B-movie good looks despite her seven senior years. We couldn't resist each other. Whenever together, we spent hours lovemaking. Quarreling, fighting, crying—once through it, we melted in the other's eyes. I hated myself every time I said I wanted out and the church for even existing and fomenting this inner push to split up. My unshakable sense of duty to God demanding I save our backfiring church through institutional reform reviving its Principled, Family spirit was a barbed thorn in my paw. It's familial camaraderie (when it existed) and opportunity to serve was all I really liked about the institution. The Blessing was my duty to forebears and descendants, not merely a personal happiness. The Principle, though: that, I truly embraced however poorly.

Getting to New York City and hooking up with Jerome, our creativity growing by leaps and bounds, spoke to God pushing us to succeed where we'd failed in 1984 at Judah Street and me at Bush–Hearst Street. This would be our third and final try as the Principle reckoned things. We founded Family Home Church Association and published our monthly *Family Times* with that desperately in mind.

And Shiori was getting in the way. More than once she physically prevented me going to Manhattan's church center in 4 West 43rd Street's headquarters building or some evening event. Or later, from getting out the door for Army National Guard drill. Her arms boa-snaked a leg and I stumped for the door, dragging her along the floor pleading that I stay, maybe afraid that once out gone forever. I'd have to practically beat her off but wasn't really up to being so drastic. I couldn't blame her, but in her pique she castigated my devotion to the Principle and censured the very idea of a church revival. She accused me of not loving her while punishing me with aversion and indifference, turning a mute back in or out of bed for days.

Jerome now criticized me boffing her. "She's corrupting you," he said, full-on judgy. "She's corrupting our mission. Get rid of her, throw her off. She's trash!"

"Easier said than done, and you ought to know." His words stung. She'd never leave my side regardless her rage for me or mine for her. This was my first truly dysfunctional love relationship. I was clueless what it was, what it meant, what it was doing to my psyche . . . a silent-but-deadly in a sealed pressure suit.

JEROME AND I invested our time at 43rd Street. This 7-storey classical arts building showboated marble floors and gorgeously curved marble stairs with wrought iron railings in both foyer wings. They'd converted the top floor to bunkbedded dorms now so badly fouled by moldy air that only portable HEPA purifiers averted lung infections. The ground floor accommodated shops with American and Unification Church flags putting on The Ritz on poles over the heavy oak, main double door. Wren Meyer was its middle-aged American center director. Rev. Moon directed him to get his PH.D., but then like Jerome and me offered no financial aid. In addition to full-time leadership, he worked outside the church to earn tuition. *Is he a part-*

timer, Ergela? He wore the harried face and stooped bearing of an eternally harassed bellhop ever attired in cheap, rumpled suits on the lam from the dry cleaners.

4 West 43rd St., NYC.

He loved Jerome and me because, at the time, his Japanese and American members mostly disrespected him. The Japanese tended to follow their own leaders (often those from before America, but any Japanese who grifted them off a hapless American) even though Wren was their official central figure. Such was the Japanese disdain for Americans that anything an American leader said pertaining to Japanese could be nullified by the flick of a Japanese leader's tongue regardless his position or authority in America. Wren heaped up stress unable to command resources and get things done. Jerome and I arrived like a working fuse and energized 43rd Street's Americans by taking responsibility for anything we could get our hands on while shouting Wren's praises to their cynical rafters.

Jerome's philosophy was to make his leader look good and push him into success. "That's the teaching of Cain and Abel in the Principle, Chris. Father says Cain isn't Abel's slave but called by God to make sure Abel succeeds in his mission no matter how incompetent, like Wren. If he fails, Cain fails. It's win-win or lose-lose."

"I tried that with Ergela and it blew up in my face."

"Doesn't matter. The relationship itself holds the value, not the players. Cain's best interest is ensuring Abel's success but, even more important, vice-versa. There's no middle ground in the Principle. It's all or nothing."

"I totally agree!" Jerome was my 'leader,' yet he never stinted on praising me.

He wholeheartedly applied his philosophy with Wren and I unreservedly joined him. We pulled his incompetent bacon out of Rev. Moon's fire and ire more than once. But ours was a minority view. In practice the church (especially Japanese and, less so, Koreans) valued Abel over Cain and discounted mutuality and in particular their intrinsic equality. Abel and Cain didn't *symbolically represent* but *literally were* good and evil, Adam and Archangel, God and Satan. A deathblow.

I came to New York City full of ideas for a Home Church campaign, Rev. Moon's latest witnessing fad. His must be the only church that needs press and cajole its members to proselytize. He was ever inventing new means to drag his troops from their barracks. Those assigned to Home Church—Blessed couples who'd started their families but more often single members (usually Japanese with little English)—were supposed to witness to potential members in their homes the way Jerry Falwell built his church out of the ground, developing long-term relationships that blossomed into membership and tithes. One more sound plan, on paper. But our member-starved church forever shifted these troops to other fronts. Their work withered on the vine or suffered under a replacement's ignorance. Like most campaigns, it failed to stem the membership drain, diverted our energies, and depressed morale. Where it achieved anything near to Rev. Moon's vision it was Americans ignoring leadership, putting down roots like ex-members, and planting their own vineyards.

Jerome and I built our newsletter, a witnessing team, and devoted most of our spare time to supporting Wren's campaigns. He needed it. The Manhattan church was busted glass, each group devoted to itself at the expense of others. During the '80s heyday of church feudalism, Korean regional leaders oft-prevaricated with Rev. Moon's calls for warm bodies to work campaigns, as they knew that once sent off a local feudal lord might contrive ownership, undermining their status and economy. Serf poor and broke isn't much of a lord. It left Rev. Moon a lemon.

For example, Wren wanted Jerome and me to run a 3-evening Day of Hope festival in New York University's (NYU) Student Union. We contended with a multi-layered bureaucracy ad hoc parceling out bits and pieces of responsibility for the infinitesimal to the averse. Whether they had the time, inclination, competency, or were even serious wasn't a factor. Control hogs missed or ignored planned meetings with members and nonmember helpers, then rejected decisions they hadn't approved. CARP was supposed to organize the first night's event but its local leader, Mr. Kuneda, turned out a moronic asshat. In 1990 NYU CARP was in the ballpark of 98% Japanese and apparently hadn't bothered to advertise the event. I noted in my diary that "[Kuneda] strutted around like a fat cock-of-the-walk, like a total imbecile," paying attention to no one, taking no responsibility or leadership, allowing the event to spin with no axis. CARP's one function was witnessing and running events *on campus* yet forgot the Student Union was students-only after 6 PM.

I said, "Half our staff just spent 40 minutes locked out in the cold!"

"The meeting is seven. Of course, everyone should be here by six-thirty. If not, they do not come anyway." Kuneda shrugged. "Anyway, no problem."

I scrutinized this alien clod. Then Wren murdered our three guests and 28 church–CARPsters with a disjointed speech on the Principle of Creation. "There aren't any registration forms, Wren. How about sending someone back for them?"

"This is CARP's meeting. Let them register their own guests."

"They didn't bring 'em, either. They figured it's your event."

His Kuneda shrug meant no follow-up for potentials beyond who invited them. Then I spent an hour salvaging a Chinese guest when his CARP host mysteriously vanished. I journaled, "[Kuneda] and his two Japanese cronies came dressed in these raggedy clothes like they were construction workers or something . . . no music, no entertainment: nothing." It was embarrassing associating with them. Such was the lazy departmentalism crippling the Unification Church.

To his credit, Wren was embarrassed. He insisted we fully manage his future events. So we'd painstakingly plan, invite guests and speakers, and advertise only for some kahuna to unceremoniously cancel us, sometimes the day-of, when a fatter kahuna's priority changed or Rev. Moon made some off-the-cuff remark. Guests felt insulted or betrayed and loathe to commit twice.

"Well, it's Father's church," I said to Jerome, "and he can do what he wants with it. But it sure makes us out like a couple of duds to avoid."

"You can't think like that, Chris. You have to be Abel even when you're Cain. That's why Father says Abel's job sucks while Cain is on a pleasure cruise."

"I wouldn't say blind obedience is a—"

"Basic Restoration through indemnity. Abel as Cain does what he has to."

Hummph. Following a particularly grueling campaign where Jerome and I played crucial leadership roles, Wren unexpectedly pulled the two of us to the head of 43rd Street's massive, second-floor banquet room for some fulsome praise in front of members and Japanese and Korean leaders.

"These are my two best members in the New York City church. I totally rely on their amazing talents and devotion to God and True Parents." He looked us over. "I predict great things for them both." *Applause, back pats, handshakes.*

"That was really gratifying, Wren. I appreciate that." But I knew he hadn't yet talked to Papasan Choi or Ergela Arsch. That was on the cusp of changing.

In the spring of 1990 Rev. Moon or a Korean sacked Ergela after tormented Northern California's unrelenting campaign. He landed in New York City's dumping grounds at a fluff job for a salary. He was a grinning shark bearing down on a bleeding skin diver running into us in the Manhattan Center's second-floor Garden Room on West 34th next door to the New Yorker.

He couldn't contain his surprise. "You're out here going to school now?"

"Yes, I'm attending the seminary in the fall." I spoke with relish, savoring it.

"Our . . . seminary? . . . UTS? . . . Oh . . . good deal . . . uh, okay, see you around." With that, he went off to quietly dig a shallow grave for my New York reputation.

In the midst of the activities and campaigns Jerome and I had involved ourselves, an Indian from Pakistan named Stanley popped into 43rd Street for one of our Wednesday night Bible studies that we ran for Wren so he could study. His heavy accent seized our meeting for half an hour.

"Jesus told me to work hard and give my money away. I travel and work wherever he sends me. Yes, some 35 countries since 1973."

"He's pretty whacked, man."

Jerome's face lit up, his large white eyes falling on me. "Don't you feel it? I think Jesus *is* speaking through him. Maybe directly."

"What, how he's talking? His weirdly prescient inside-info about the church?" My hair stood on end to say it. He preached eye-to-eye to each of us in the room, umbrage with our church rattling through his voice.

"Jesus wants to come here!" he shouted. "He *wants* to come here! But he can't, he won't, until the church members clean up their lives! You are living selfishly, in great sin." He iterated on his fingers. "Jesus says illicit sex, drugs, drinking, stealing, no love, abusing each other . . . so many problems here."

"How's he so spot-on?" I whispered. "Sex, I'm sure. Drinking . . . but, *drugs?*"

"The minister"—referring to Jerome's earlier preaching—"speaks one hundred percent and yet the church is only a quarter full. Your culture and lifestyle . . . all is satanic and devoid of God. You are all sinful!"

"He's definitely channeling Jesus about the church," Jerome said.

I couldn't agree more even if I wasn't secretly shtupping Shiori and Jerome whatever it might be he wasn't sharing. If it *was* Jesus, then he was talking to *me!* He lit off a renewed call to unhook myself from Shiori's "possessive . . . destructive . . . not constructive" love. She wanted to control my life just like the Moonies. The only people who *didn't* want to control me were the satanic bastards ruining the outside world. *Arrggh! Why are* they *so much more congenial than church members?*

"It's because you're one of them," Ergela had sneeringly said in his California domain. "Satan doesn't attack his own, only those aligned with God's will."

A universal truism in the church, that. And because I fared well at work with 'outside members,' many church brethren explained it away as my participation in their satanic lifestyle. On the face of it, Shiori had left the church. But, like me, she couldn't really do more than push herself to the fringe. More and more I recognized her love's semi-violent, church-flavored dictatorialism. I frequently stormed out of the house after fighting over my spiritual viewpoints and inner turmoil and conflict with our relationship. Might be a typical Blessing in all but name.

~

THINGS HAD BEEN going too well. Unaware that Ergela was industriously spreading vile rumors and innuendo to all who'd listen, the good reputation I'd tirelessly built up in New York City's church was inexplicably turning sour.

Then for no reason I could fathom Jerome said around April 2, "I'm no longer dealing with Wren. My prime concern right now is Ronald."

For months, we'd been unstoppable church go-getters. Partners and brothers. We took responsibility for anything and everything to lift up Wren a stunning example of leadership. Our idea was to spark a spirit of revival amongst Americans that spread across the country, our only reason to work so hard in the chaos we called a church. Like Pope Innocent III, members liked our Franciscan ideals so long as it didn't mean challenging the status quo. Jerome shortly instigated a landlord fight over maintenance and suspended rent. In seven legal days we were on the street. Ronald and he moved into their dead mother's house in St. Albans.

"You should move in with us. Shiori can come if she wants."

"Thanks, Jerome. That's really kind"—I was feeling a premonition and bad spirit vibes—"but I think it's better if she's not in your face."

"You should've got rid of her like I said."

"Whatever. I'm pushing her to find her own place now." A golden opportunity to get out of our once embracing now tempestuous relationship. Hobbling to the door like Pegleg Pete was a sign. I had high hopes.

She settled on a Japanese group house and desperately wanted me with her. But I couldn't. Not only did I want to purify my standing with God to pursue the Principle with a clear conscience, but her new flat was too dysfunctional even for me. Among the menagerie was a 20-something Brazilian buttonholing a Japanese. They shared no language. How they'd hooked up was beyond me. They fought like wild pigs, screaming their own tongues off body language—crying, clawing, and slapping till exhaustedly tumbling into bed to fuck it all away as the next go-round built steam. With so many American–Japanese church couples, I now regarded Shiori's own soap opera from the corner of my eye with some alarm.

I called up my old buddy. "Say, Wren, we lost our apartment and I'm currently without a roof. Can I temporarily stay at 43rd Street while I find a place?"

The line was quiet. "Nooo . . . I think that would upset our tax status."

"How? I'm a church member and it's only temporary. A week or three." No response. "Well, could I use a shower so I can go to work clean?"

"That wouldn't work, Chris." His voice was cold and distant.

"What about sleeping just midnight to six? Nobody can claim I'm actually living there in that case, and it won't affect the tax status," *which has to be bullshit.*

"No, that's not something I'm allowed to permit. I'm sorry."

"Well, who is?" Nothing. I was getting weird vibes but couldn't make sense of it. I thought he'd be easy. "What about the New Yorker? It's full of rooms and dorms for members. I stayed there before."

He called back later. "They said no. I don't have any suggestions."

Something's wrong here. I'm in good standing with Wren and now he's stonewalling me. Why won't he help in my time of need after all Jerome and I've done? Does he know about Shiori? Nah, the only people who knew were Jerome, the Kobayashis, and Julian. None of them would betray me. They all knew I was wrestling with my conscience and anyhow never gave me a deadline or consequences. I trusted them all, and they'd been kind enough and mostly understanding even if opposed. In any case, the church didn't even see me as a real member. I lived and worked on my own. I was 'B'-member trash it tolerated and used, Wren's praise notwithstanding. *There's no way he knows about Shiori, and if he did he'd have said something.*

Whatever her dysfunction, I was just so bloody in love. Yet, I believed God truly desired we separate. I wrote April 8, "Anything is okay if it separates me from Shiori and brings me closer to the movement." I tried to convey my humility to Wren, but he probably saw me as desperate. He shot down every idea to temporarily stay in any church building. I couldn't understand his harshness when he'd only just praised me as a model member. Too underpaid for a hotel, I slept on the street.

I was blissfully unaware of Ergela's dirty pool and what Jerome, my trusted brother whose life I'd saved at the hands of Small Mike and Papasan Choi, was spilling to Wren. Rejecting his St. Albans' house had balefully peeved him. Out of spite (he later said) he'd spilled to Brooklyn's center director Barry Geller my sordid Shiori story along with unsubstantiated innuendo and outright fabrications—sex at Judah Street—to ensure he'd hammered the stake home. As Jerome expected, Barry ran it past Wren who took it to his leader, colleagues, friends, acquaintances . . . the *New York Times* if he could've. I'd never confronted actual treachery. My trust in Jerome was absolute. I loved him. Would take a bullet. Even as events unfolded, I couldn't accept that he'd lit my coming immolation to reap revenge over a minor hiccup in our activities. I called Monday a week after our eviction but he literally couldn't speak. His sentences were jumbled, disconnected, erratic. *He doesn't do drugs for sure so, what the hell?* The call lasted under a minute.

Wren phoned Tuesday. "Can you meet me at 43rd street Thursday at six?"

"Sure," I said. "Any special reason?"

"Um, well, to discuss your situation. It's better in person."

He's found a place for me. Must be it. I trusted him. "Ok, Wren, see you then."

With my own job and apartment, I'd kept my personal and church lives distinct. The church despised 'B' members but for tithing and event stuffing. I'd pushed past that disability taking on so many duties and pumping up Wren to his bosses and underlings. A core tenet for Rev. Moon is taking responsibility; that God can't condemn a sinful man who's fighting for His providence. I operated from that premise. I was often at 43rd Street weekends and after work to contribute to projects and campaigns, help with Bible study; a myriad of things. My home and public life was as distinct in my mind as for any Catholic or Baptist.

Wren rejected that perspective and, really, so did Rev. Moon. Private lives one can't safely expose to public scrutiny are the Devil's breeding ground where satanic invasion decimates God's will. Rev. Moon extends this precept to all members, not just leaders. Unlike Christians forgiving sinful televangelists' sex and money scandals in the '80s, Wren now saw me not as a man struggling with my conscience over poor choices I could rectify through God's grace or even indemnity, but a treacherous fang in his godly yard needing quick disposal.

Still developing his response between Monday and Thursday, he found me Wednesday speaking in Japanese with a sister in the second-floor main room where he'd earlier sung my praises. By 1990 I was conversational along with Korean, which I often used as a language of prayer to feel more kinship with Rev. Moon. This was in keeping with his direction and set me apart from 99.99% of Western members. Yet, it only got me as far as skepticalville with leaders and members. Sitting at a six-foot diameter hotel convention table surrounded by tens of members at my and other such tables, he cop-carred up behind me.

Casually, "What are you talking about?"

I twisted in my chair and looked up. "Just stuff. Faith, life, that sort of thing."

In fact, we were discussing the nature of the Japanese church, the problems with the American church, and her view that Wren was a shit leader. I could complain with the best but nursed an interest in the Japanese and Korean church and conversed with their members to understand their heart. Of course, I'd never tell Wren we were talking church issues. It would only stoke his imagination, as it had Mr. Uchiyama's at Judah Street, that I was spreading negativity to defenseless, pure Japanese.

"Maybe you're tempting this sister," he blurted.

"What?" My antenna shot high. Hot blood flashed through me. *What's going on? Who's saying what to him? Ah! He must've finally heard from Papasan or Ergela.* The real spiders in the woodpile. "What do you mean saying such a thing?"

"Well," he backpedaled, airily chuckling, "I just guessed that must be what you were talking about . . . you know, life and stuff." I screwed my face up at that. More ominous: "I don't want you sitting around here talking to the sisters, okay?"

My heart fluttered in a vacuum. Skin heated. My convivial sister was now visibly uncomfortable. She spoke little English, precisely why I was using Japanese. But she sure as fuck could read tone and body language.

"How can you tell me not to talk to her, Wren? It's a free country, and we're just having a simple, *public* conversation."

"Not in here, it's not. You should probably go home now." His attitude wasn't mean but not friendly, either. "I have some work for her to do, anyway."

He whistled up a Japanese brother to help him round her up and I was left at the altar as the room magically emptied. I sat steaming. Wherever in this fatuous church I tried to fit in and support my leaders, even rescuing their ineptitude and impotence to bestow the glory of victories I made, I was blacklisted and ostracized. Not even basic intellectual conversation was safe. Because I'd briefly had a girlfriend or two during my exile from the Bay Area church—dirt spread far and wide courtesy of Reiko—people like Wren saw me a sister-raper, Lucifer in a Shepherd's guise. After awhile I ambled into a depressing Manhattan night.

I had a strong sense of foreboding. *What part might Jerome be playing in this strange turn of events?* We'd already had a falling out in our Ocean Avenue flat and hadn't talked almost a year. Not till he'd knocked on 225 Harold to apologize did I dismiss our past and embrace him. He'd fallen into vagrancy struggling through graduate school and lived in his crapped out, 4-door American sedan, his relationship with his second wife Sharon having gone to shit. She'd kicked him out of the house after a violent quarrel over another black man knocking her up.

"If you can't give me children, I'll get them from any man who can!"

"She's a vicious bitch, Chris. Stay away from her." I offered to share my 9×10-foot floor or my 4-foot sofa. "No, man . . . thanks. But could I use your shower?"

When he had work, I recommended the landlord rent him the vacant room next to mine and he'd moved in. I'd vigorously defended him to his denouncers during his breakup with his Blessed wife Carol with incalculable spiritual and emotional support when her church-member, martial-arts brother was credibly threatening to kill him for desecrating his sister. Now I faced potential treachery from the same son of a bitch. Was it really pointless to forgive people seventy-times-seven times? How does a person reconcile the Christian command to forgive and forget with the practical need to keep treachery at arms' length? I blithely assumed 'forgive and forget' meant precisely that. I often forgave *and* forgot his excesses. Now my Christian naïveté and misplaced trust were shades of ravenous piranhas.

Thursday arrived. I set off from work at West 20th for 43rd Street. Everyone knew me. I entered the vestibule and waved to the security guard behind his bar-height counter where he quizzed the nobodies. Rumply Wren shifted feet in the foyer.

"Wait here," he commanded with unexpected rudeness. "I'll be back in a minute."

"Sure thing." I strolled to the members' rear dining area close to the basement kitchen for a cool sip from the fountain. Jerome and I once bought and cooked a West Indian dinner here as a gift to the center.

Wren anxiously found me sauntering back. "I said wait up front."

"I was just getting water." I was feeling affable despite his odd-sock behavior.

"I don't want you back here in the members' area."

"Now, why on—"

"Go on, I'll be there in just a minute."

I met his eyes, trying to size up what was on his mind. "Okay, all right." I sighed. *Boy, is he acting weird. I wander all over this place for months and months, respected as Rev. McKeon, and suddenly he doesn't want me in a members' area?*

I planted myself atop three marble steps to the landing at the left wing of the building-width foyer. Behind me, marble stairs and wrought-iron rails gracefully curved up. An ancient, smelly, coffin-sized cold-molasses elevator opened in the marbled space beneath. Wren shortly appeared towing two hulking brothers I'd never met. He heavily pulled up, wingtips to cowboy. Like a guilty puppy watching its home-alone pleasures spin across the mind's eye I took in their harsh, judgment-rent faces. It wasn't looking good. Still, no clue my neck was in his guillotine.

316

"I heard some very disturbing news about you," he said. "You've been living with a Blessed Japanese sister named Shiori Takashi for the last year or eight months."

I could only gawk speechless, flabbergasted. My mouth opened. Nothing.

"Don't bother denying it," he droned on. "I've already checked it out with three or four people, including Mrs. Kobayashi. She told me everything about you. She said you led her on to believe there was nothing, no sexual relationship, between you and this Shiori." *Led her on? Ha! What effrontery.* I'd spoken only truth to her. Her attitude meant Shiori had since lied through her teeth. "She said she's shocked at who you are"—in a Soviet kangaroo court, but probably not in reality—"and by your past life. She said she doesn't even know you anymore."

That hurt. "Wren, you don't know what the situation—"

"I know she came out here with you. You brought her from San Francisco."

"Well . . . it wasn't my idea. She insisted. I've been trying like hell to break it off, to get back to a Principled life." Watching his face, I could tell he wasn't in the least moved by my contrition. "Who told you all this?"

"That doesn't matter," he snapped, waving his hand dismissively.

"Yes, it does matter. Who is this mystery tattletale?"

"Somebody called me with this information. That's all you need to know." He paused for effect. "You betrayed me, Chris. You *deceived* me. You really hurt me!"

What arrogance! My voice upped an octave. "How'd I do any of that?"

"You came here under false pretenses. You're carrying on an unPrincipled relationship with a Blessed Japanese sister while you're over here pretending to be a dedicated church member!" His contempt seethed a rank cauldron.

"First of all," I all but snarled; he needed a reality check, "I'm a part-time member. I live in my own house. I have my own job. I come over here out of my commitment to God and True Parents as a *volunteer* to help *you*. My personal life is none of your business! It's between me and God . . . and besides, it's not germane to my helping you make signs, organize events, greet guests, or run Bible studies." You might think I'd been caught molesting boys in the sacristy. "And second, Mrs. Kobayashi counseled me specifically to keep my situation with Shiori to myself. We've been working it out together following *her* guidance." I thought that might defuse him a bit, to realize I'd been working with a senior leader close to True Parents—who'd just denounced me, goddamn it—to find a way out of my mess.

He was nonplussed by that news but shrugged it off. "Give me your ID card, right now." Boy, was he in his imperial element. His hand thrust out, expectant.

I glared. Humiliation and rage tornadoed through me. My face was probably beet red. It felt hot enough. Fire and ice enveloped me couched on the steps. Wren perched over me not two feet away on the rail-high marble wall separating the landing from the main floor three steps below. Twenty-some members milling in the foyer cast furtive glances my way, hushed conversation shooting between them, but mercifully kept their distance. Without even thinking to tell him I'd left my ID card at home since I hadn't produced it for the security guard in quite some time, I reached inside my $700 suit jacket and pulled it out. It had taken a long time to get it with my California reputation. I'd felt pride knowing it defeated many of Ergela's prophetic threats against me. In these days, a cardless member couldn't attend Sunday service at Rev. Moon's East Garden estate in Irvington, any function he attended, or many other church functions and properties, like 43rd Street. Now I was losing it.

Happier id'd times visiting Rev. Moon at East Garden.

I can't explain why I handed the ID over except I was so trained in obedience that, although the most rebellious not-ex-member in the American church, I complied out of custom. *Sonuvabitch!* I loathed myself handing it over and more so not thinking up a speedier fib. Perhaps an odd, delusional brain cell thought we'd work it out.

He tattled my situation as Joo Chon Choi had Nanami's to every ear in New York state having any authority. Unwilling to make his own decision despite being Manhattan's pastor, he'd gone to heartless Old Testament samurai Mr. Matsuzaki. No discretion at all. He could've confronted me privately. Remembered my positive attributes. All the good things I'd done for him personally and for the church. Asked me, "Why did you enmesh yourself in this contradictory, unPrincipled situation? Do you want to repent and do an indemnity course?" as Boss Choi and the BFD had offered Nanami in Alaska. All without forgetting the broken-Blessing couples whom Rev. Moon promised to reBless if they were together in seven years. Why not me? us as a couple? I *did* want to indemnify my situation. I *was* desperate to get out from under Shiori's ersatz love and the Principle's condemnation rending my heart. Wren showed no interest. I wasn't Japanese. I wasn't some top dog's favorite. If I'd been his, I wasn't now. He felt wronged. Panted for revenge.

He didn't have the stones to slay me. He wanted his Japanese master to order it so he could spiritually murder me with a mafia hitman's clean hands. A pastor and brother, why wasn't he concerned with my spiritual life? my salvation? I could've explained everything as I was now trying to do. He could've properly handled it. Mrs. Kobayashi could've insisted on some perspective. Maybe persuaded Mr. Kamiyama to positively weigh in. *He* already knew. Did Wren know that? *Damn!* I'd forgot that potential ace up my sleeve. Regardless, she'd washed her Pontiune hands with his confrontation. Wriggled out of a possible political hot seat. Threw me to the wolves from which she resolutely protected Shiori. *These fuckin' people.*

With Mr. Kamiyama pissed over Shiori and Wren spreading our business all over the church, the seminary had to permanently bar me. *My God!* My life was crumbling before my eyes because I'd despaired at Ergela proscribing the Blessing and hands-off leaders forcing me outside the church for a wife. I'd found solace in Shiori. It was my fault. They were my decisions. She'd pressured and seduced me but hadn't physically forced me between her legs. Satan never compels us into sin. We do it because our selfish (if tormented) mind wants to. How else can the Bible show him accusing us for our sins? You can't indict a person coerced into evil, only one willingly ignoring his or her conscience. As I had. I knew the Principle, the Fall of Man, Adam and Eve's mistake . . . well, I had an intellectual understanding of it, certainly no deep, emotive cognizance. That, unfortunately, comes with vicarious or firsthand experience. We're all of us looking for something in life and take action to get it. I wanted to be loved, valued, and appreciated. Shiori alone offered, however impolitic or contrived. I took it despite my smarter nature's warning.

I detested Wren for his vicious, unPrincipled treatment when he well knew my mistake was his to make, just as self-righteous Ergela was later caught in the cookie jar. My diary boils with raging pain. But it didn't Restore me. Or justify me, either, dammitall. I couldn't let myself sink into the quicksand of victimology. Why should I? I'd become an old hand at suffering abuse. It should be easy by now. Wren was a product of a Unification Church demanding obedience to law and authority over and above love, forgiveness, compassion—the hallmarks of Divine Principle and the very thing inspiring him and me to join in the first place. Yet, like most members, he'd morphed into a firm belief that if you're not a sinner *right now* then, regardless your past or future, you're better than those who are. For a religion to root its core philosophy in the instant present bespeaks a deep failure of gnosis. In this respect, the Unification Church is steroidally Old Testament. Wren was enforcing a Levitican eye-for-an-eye devoid of Jesus' New Testament compassion. I thought I'd seen the worst leadership the church had to offer in Ergela. Now I saw its hell went still deeper. Despair washed through me. Tears welled in my breast. *Mommy!*

Wren said, "Mr. Matsuzaki's decision is that you are banned from the church, banned from the 43rd Street building, from Sunday service, and everything else. You are excommunicated." He was right. Without my ID card, I was a nonperson.

"Come on, Wren! Don't you think that's a little extreme?"

"It's not my decision," explained the good mafia soldier to the man on his knees how it's nothing personal, just business. "It's Mr. Matsuzaki's. I didn't ask him—"

"I'm not living in the church. I'm not dragging sisters into closets. How can you make such a distinction between me and all the other sexually sinful guests and ministers you fawn over, the ones on Sunday with multiple sex partners? You don't kick them out. They're not even contributing to the church. They're only hanging out for what they might get from it. At least I'm trying to serve True Parents!"

"They don't know the Principle. They haven't joined the church."

"Well, lucky for them. Won't they be surprised by the inquisition waiting for their inevitable mistakes." As, like Ergela, Wren himself later would.

"The bottom line is you seduced a Blessed sister away from her husband."

There it was. The indignant, self-righteous accusation that was hot, greasy pig fat daubing his lips. I could see him licking his chops, savoring the bouquet. He was painting me now, and soon to all and sundry who hadn't already caught the scent, the vilest criminal a Moonie knows: Satan, knavish world wrecker through Eve's sacred garden of good and (apparently for Shiori, never) evil.

That wasn't how it went down! I contemplated throwing her under the bus in a terminal bid to repaint myself. She'd said she was only Matched to get me to take her in. Ergela had kicked my celibate self from Hearst Street with a promise to forever block my Blessing. Couldn't Wren—anyone—understand its devastating effect? Shiori offered me love and family when I thought I'd never have it. It was a mistake. I accepted that. I'd spent much time hashing it out with Mrs. Kobayashi,

Julian, and close friends. I'd been moving—slowly, *yeah*—out of her orbit, bit by bit extricating myself as best I could. There was a whole chain of events that Wren, Matsuzaki, Kamiyama, and the rest of those hyenas ignored.

I said, "Shiori left the church on her own accord because she never wanted to be Blessed in the first place. They never lived together or started their family. She showed up in San Francisco all on her own. I didn't ask her to leave the church. I didn't encourage her. I didn't suggest it. She's a grown woman making her own decisions." I wanted to shout and rail at him, but the fear of greater humiliation conspired to strangle my voice to a hoarse whisper.

"It doesn't matter what she did. She's a Blessed sister and you victimized her."

I practically bleated. "How can you talk to me like I'm Satan, stealing the virtue from pure Japanese sisters?"

"You *are* Satan. You're the archangel in the Garden tempting Eve to fall."

"Well, you're wrong." I almost said it was Shiori who took the initiative, who seduced *me*, but a sense of loyalty and desire not to get her into deeper trouble than I was already in checked me. *Should I fall on my sword for her?* His face said he wasn't listening and wouldn't believe it anyway, that he was interpreting my defense as all four of the Fall's fallen natures: not taking God's viewpoint, leaving my proper position, reversing dominion, and multiplying my criminal act with Shiori. In a split second I gave her an out, yet she never told Mrs. Kobayashi how she acquired me, how she was more like Eve seducing Adam than seduced by Lucifer. "I've been trying to separate from Shiori almost since we got together, because I believe in the Principle and the Blessing. It was a mistake, one I've been struggling to rectify without wrecking her life in the process. But she won't let me go."

"Sure, right." Not a glimmer of belief or empathy in his cruel voice.

"Why do you think I was pleading with you last week to move into the center? It was to have a place totally separated from her. But you wouldn't let me."

"You don't deserve to stay here, that's why." *Ha!* Like he'd kno—had he?

"Isn't there something I can do?" Pleading rankled. "How can you just throw me out into the street like this? I've been a member for ten years! It's not like I'm trying to destroy True Parents or anything. Sincerity must count for something!"

Nope. Not a fucking thing. "Mr. Matsuzaki's decision is that if you want to come back to the church, you must prove you've permanently separated from her."

"And I do that by . . . ?"

"First, she has to go back to her previous mission and her Blessing."

"I can't make her do that! She does what she wants. Do you think I'm her master or something? Why do you think—?"

"Then she has to leave New York City. She can't live here in this city at all if you want to come back to the church."

"I'm supposed to order her out of town like the cops? She has a job and an apartment here. You expect *she'll* pack up and go so the church will take *me* back?"

"You convinced her to follow you here from San Francisco."

"I didn't convince her of anything! She came on her own." If only he knew the pressure she'd put on me not to abandon her, the seduction she'd practiced to get me in her arms. Yes, I was eventually willing. At least I'd resisted a minute.

"You convinced her to come here, just like you convinced her to fall with you. I'm sure you can convince her to leave New York the same way."

There was no getting through. I finally caught a glimmer that Shiori had been thoroughly dishonest with Mrs. Kobayashi, never admitting it was she who'd seduced me, not the other way around. Everyone was so adamant that I was Satan seducing Eve in the Garden without ever stopping to consider that perhaps I was Adam seduced by Eve. Rev. Moon certainly never appeared to consider Eve might've come on to Lucifer and fomented the whole mess. I wasn't looking to excuse my lapse, but on the other hand I damn sure didn't deserve Wren's lynching.

"Mr. Matsuzaki also said you have to tithe and attend a 40-day workshop. This is Principle." He was Yul Brynner in *Moses*: '*So it is said, so let it be done.*' Evidently, it was also Principle to craft a set of demands so impossible it was inconceivable I could ever meet them to their satisfaction.

"I *do* repent, Wren, and I will make the indemnity conditions. But I can't make her leave New York. I can't make her do anything. You have no idea."

"That's Mr. Matsuzaki's decision. You do whatever you want." He clenched lips a hot minute. Sized up his two meatsacks flanking me. Malevolent, to my eyes. Shafted angels dying to pounce. Not an ounce of sympathy in their dead eyes.

Mrs. Kobayashi later said, "He brought them because he was afraid of you."

"Like I was gonna beat him up? Come on."

"Jerome told him you own a gun. That you might bring it. Is that true?"

I sprained eyeballs I rolled 'em so goddamned hard. "Blame it on Joo Chon Choi." Maybe Wren figured two beefcakes would soak up my raging bullets before they could blast his dumb ass to perdition. What a shit.

It was just so typical, wasn't it? Members preach love and Restoration but always raise law over love, authority over relationship, form over content. Wren wasn't interested in my emotional or psychic desolation, how I struggled to overcome my past grief and abuse to live a righteous life. Why in hell was I bothering with the New York City church after my experience with Ergela if it wasn't on account of my sincere commitment to God, True Parents, and the Principle? That was insignificant to him. He cared only that I'd violated the Principle, broken a law. Punishment, not forgiveness or even Restoration, was his only recipe for success.

Well, if there's one thing I've noticed, all those who persecuted and abused me—not because I was evil needing opposing but simply a man with foibles—ended up in the dregs themselves. Over the years the self-inflicted hard luck stories from Uchiyama, Papasan Choi, Small Mike, Hiro, Ergela, Wren, and many others were sublime concertos. Each of these pious pharisees fell from grace to a similar destruction through their own bouts of illicit sex, adultery, embezzlement, theft, homosexuality, abuse of authority, violence against members, *ad nauseam*. It may only be a small comfort, but it *was* comfort.

My ID card safely tucked away, Wren posed in his ever disheveled suit in what he considered an imposing posture. "Get up and get out," he coarsely ordered. "Don't look back, and don't come back."

He supervised his muscle march me quickstep to the broad, heavy wooden double front door. Members dead in their tracks ogled the queer sight. His Goombas stood fast just inside the entry. The heavy oaken door resisted as if not wanting me to go. I lurched weak-kneed into the night air in shock and disbelief. My world lay in a wreck at my feet, my very soul prostrate. I thought I might kill myself. Jump in front of a bus. The subway. A car. Maybe pounce on a cop to get shot dead. I wasn't sure I could live anymore with no spiritual future.

"Heavenly Father!" I cried whispers staggering down 5th Avenue's vacant sidewalk for the grand Greco-Roman public library's grubby subway entrance. Humiliation drizzled off me a soaking rain. I hated myself. Cursed my every bone tramping forward, the very image of defeated Germany stumbling home to the devastation it had wrought. Wren stripped me of every dignity till I only saw disgust. Hindsight couldn't torture me enough. My conscience wished it was blind.

Over the next days and weeks, he refused my calls. Eventually, I set up a meeting with his wife Estrella at a local café. She canceled twice before making it then refused to listen to attack, judge, and condemn.

"We're a family," she said across our booth. "You should've told us everything."

"You say that, but look how you're taking it. Anyway, I did. Mrs. Kobayashi *and* Mr. Kamiyama knew everything and advised me to keep it quiet." But they weren't Wren or Estrella or even Mr. Matsuzaki, so it didn't count and she didn't care.

For two years, I'd withheld news of my son with Monica from my parents, yet they'd supported and loved me even while giving me no break on my stupidity and responsibility. Scathing thoughts underlining my despair went into my journal:

> Wren's version of family is to murder those who violate it's laws . . . Moonies demonstrate the lowest form of "love" on the planet. Except for the Blessing, I'd have nothing to do with them . . . what a contradiction!

Besides the Principle, the Blessing was truly the hook that Rev. Moon had snagged deep in my soul, no doubt about it. I despised the church institution and the people running it. Most were totalitarian parasites living off members' life force, bending them to their will by building an addiction to the collective guilt of their providential failures. Yet, they were only responding to Rev. Moon. His speeches ached with guilt trips and the dire consequences of our failure to obey, to achieve, to witness, to (most ironic of all) love unconditionally, to be good Abels to suffering Cains. I believed in the Blessing's efficacy only because I accepted Divine Principle's veracity. I longed to transcend my selfish desires to marry a woman chosen by unselfish God, a marriage through which we indemnified the sin of our ancestors and opened the door for them to pass to a higher and happier spiritual realm. This was my duty, my honor, my devotion. I could hate the church all I wanted but I couldn't hate the Principle, it was too sensible; neither Rev. Moon, its devoted architect for all his quare faults; nor the Blessing, the core of a Principled life—Adam and Eve's before they blew it in their Fall. One of my three life goals. I *had* to achieve it.

If I wasn't before, I was now in the most official way Unificationism's *bête noire*. Its curtain wizards barred me from all services, church events, anything the Great Swami attended, and especially church buildings housing sisters. I called Barry Geller at the Brooklyn center. He mumbled, "It's above my paygrade," and hung up. I tried digging to the bottom of my betrayal.

Mrs. I-don't-want-to-be-involved Kobayashi said, "I don't know who it is, but someone is spreading very negative information about your past." She sighed heavy judgment. "I'm so shocked. You are like a stranger to me now."

Yeah, cry me a river. "Tell me so I can tell you if it's even true or not!"

"I can't even speak it."

"The heck are you on about?" I pestered her my every chance. No joy. That she believed all of it came through loud and clear. Moonies childishly believe the vilest canard without discernment while plugging their ears against knowing. I couldn't begin to imagine the rumors. But they were plainly a foul stench wafting through our shuttered church staining delicate noses. Hounded and hated, I didn't know who my accusers were nor of what they'd accused six-times-denied me beyond child-luring unwillingly Blessed, church-loathing Shiori into rape. I was living the Middle Ages . . . though, absent its dulled beheading axe, at least on my feet.

My experience in the church has perhaps been more extreme than most, if not all, but it's emblematic of its core problem and why it's failed over the decades to achieve any of its temporal goals beyond money and property. Indeed, the church drives out nearly all those whose full-time devotion it labors to inspire. Others left for less extreme reasons than mine. I was only more dogged bending the church to accept me and thereby amassed worse.

Mom said, "Your church life there is more like *The Ransom of Red Chief.*"

"Ha! They're too cheap. But that O. Henry sounds like Dante's prophet."

Julian and Shiori punctuated my positive attributes to Wren, Mrs. Kobayashi, and Mr. Kamiyama to no avail. I was radioactive. Then a few days after my kickout I discovered Mrs. Kobayashi and Wren weren't even on speaking terms.

She said over the phone, "Mr. Kobayashi and I recently ran into Wren Meyer on the street. I brought up your situation and he started screaming at me! Later, he called me and screamed over the phone, too."

"That's too weird. But his master, Mr. Matsuzaki, is even worse."

She sniggered. "He is just a little barking dog: *bark! bark!* All day long, *bark!* You should ignore him like I do."

"Ha ha! But I can't do that as easy as you." I had to pick up my jaw. She was a revealing insight into the interpersonal politics at the top of the ever-tricky Moonie food chain. Surprising fissures rent our monolithic Japanese.

Following these dramatic events I collapsed in despair. I was coming up empty in my frantic search for a room and reduced to sleeping on the streets in one of only two delicate work suits. I stayed awake as long as I could, wandering briefcase-in-hand into coffee shops and diners till huddling somewhere in the frigid weather to fitfully sleep with one eye open. I washcloth bathed in JMP's restroom in the deserted mornings. Stayed two nights with my friend Bentley, a JMP game designer. Then he cited landlord issues and let me fend for myself.

It occurred to me I still had my apartment key. *Holy shit!* I scurried over the bridge to Brooklyn and slyly scoped out our ex-digs. The lights were off. I peered through a black front window, a careful eye out for cops or concerned neighbors but sure my suit would cut me an awful lot of slack. Inside was the long, wooden floor dissolving into heavy darkness beyond. *Empty!* Jerome's slumlord hadn't found a new tenant. Too good to be true but there it was. I pushed through the vestibule door like I lived there. Surreptitiously turned the key in our old lock (some New Yorker, he hadn't even changed it). Edged open the door a thief in the night.

Chilled blood toe-tipped icy cheeks. I unkinked my spine on the hard planked floor, now in jeans for a spry getaway. My rolled coat was a pillow. Electricity but no heat, yet fabulously warm compared to outdoors. I made sure to wake by 5 AM, showered in a nail-biting rush lest early-bird painters arrive to catch the worm, threw on a clean shirt under my suit, and dashed the hell out of there to work. I breathed a frosted sigh of relief and congratulated myself . . . then wondered how long I might keep my purloined place. Five days, it turned out, because then I lucked into a 1-bedroom's ex-walk-in closet at 94-26 50th in Astoria for $300, bodies on the street from a bodega heist as I moved in. Beggars can't be choosers. For two ticks I was probably the highest-earning, best-dressed homeless man in New York City.

MY DIARY ENTRIES are saturated with infinite versions of "I have to leave Shiori." I ran away from her many times, one evening in the Times Square subway cursing myself, the church, and God for forcing me to abandon her for the sake of duty.

"I hope it's worth it," I viciously berated God while tearfully power-walking through the station, losing myself in the crowd till she'd fallen behind.

She had a knack for tracking me down from place to place. Sometimes I trepidly visited for talk and to ease her heart. Without fail we'd wind up in each other's arms, comforting our sorrows and hopelessness. I harbored some real hostility for her not publicly defending my honor and confessing the truth about us to Mrs. Kobayashi. Though exasperated, I let it slide. I figured she was afraid of getting the treatment I'd got and didn't have my guts for it. No matter how hard I tried, I just couldn't leave. I loved her so much it hurt. Or maybe I was used to her. I wasn't sure I could tell the difference anymore—if I ever could—between love and habit.

After Wren's kickout, she often read *Divine Principle* to me, face glowing with a spiritual energy I'd never seen. Gazing on her countenance, I fell ever more deeply in love. Yet, I was also realizing she was too old for me. It didn't seem she could have children. She'd deceived me so much and yet transfixed me to my cross.

Gah! I'm so hopelessly in . . . we separated, came back, split up, returned, on and on, month after month. At one point we rented a 2-bedroom. I entertained a fantasy she'd sleep in hers and I'd sleep in mine and we'd reorganize our church lives, but of course we didn't. For a few months we lived rather happily married. Typical of New York City, it cost four months' rent to move in: first, last, security deposit, and the realty agency's fee, the only sure way to find an apartment in that godforsaken town. Pulling it all together was herculean.

Seeming at ease, I dreamed one night of Satan chasing me as a fish through the seas to murder me. I instinctively knew if he but touched my furiously kicking tail I'd die right there and never wake up. It was that kind of a dream. I thrashed shrieking from sleep into stark, raving terror. Shiori alarmed awake. I'd never had such a dream nor felt such a primal dread. She comforted me as best she could, but I took it as one more sign that God was not smiling on our relationship no matter how ardently we dysfunctionally loved each other.

Then our double-dealing realty agency said they'd made a mistake in the rent, that it was actually a few hundred dollars more per month. Outraged, we refused to pay because we couldn't. We demanded they honor the lease they'd signed. They denied all responsibility and forced us out. Unable to gin up a shared ransom for a second go, we separated once more into affordable rooms and visited on weekends here and evenings there while I struggled with my feelings, earned a living, and came to grips with my own personal hell.

I worked at rebuilding my life *sans* church, but it was tortuous cut off from the spiritual sustenance I relied on. In the meantime I involved myself serving others, taking my inspiration from Rev. Moon's early days of suffering. It was this motivation that led me into the fabled 69th 'Fighting Irish' Infantry Regiment, part of the New York Army National Guard's 42nd Infantry Division, to run around weekend woods shooting guns, playing soldier, deploying for storms, breaking a finger. Then the first Gulf War kicked off. They were all set for my signature on orders sending me to helicopter school and a commission when I walked in with the glasses I only occasionally wore. In those days, corrected vision was *verboten*. I turned down Officers Candidate School (OCS) because at 31 I'd have to do the full six-week school instead of two 2-week stints during my summer duty. I was afraid JMP wouldn't hold my job regardless the law. That my nascent engineering career would sputter and die. It was a decision I'd kick myself over as much as any in the church.

I must've been hiding a lot of anger. In the 14th Street armory's elevator coming up from the gun lockers, one of the senior West Indian sergeants affably said, "Why is almost every other word out of your mouth an expletive, Specialist?"

I froze, eyes glassed. Probably my mouth fell open. "What the fuck are you talking about, Sarge? I hardly ever cuss a goddamn word any fuckin' day."

He chuckled, looking over the other knowing, nodding black and mixed faces fixed on me. "You see? Practically every other word. Should work on that."

I hadn't heard myself using foul language more than anyone else in my unit, but the elevator crowd was enthusiastic endorsing his observation.

"Well . . . shit." I realized a witch's cauldron of pent-up wrath was stewing over the church that now eked out through bad language. It was later I began understanding the truth behind a remark directed at some criminal I'd heard on TV: "You must be a very angry man." I didn't get it then or even when I wanted to plug Robert, my evil CityMatch partner. How could anger make a person a street thug? Well, I got it now. My biggest wake-up call happened on an empty, 12-foot sidewalk in Astoria, Queens. Two guys were heading my way along the same patch of concrete. Neither of us slipped aside even a foot. We bumped biceps and bad attitudes.

Fists balled and muscles tensed. Looking a foot up into my flashing eyes the guy's friend said, "Ain't worth it, bro. Let's go."

He thought it over. "Yeah. Sure. *Motherfucker.*" We turned to go.

My conscience bit down hard. *Why are you suddenly so obnoxious you couldn't drift over a foot? What difference did it make?* My angel beat my devil a moment. I turned back. "Hey!" They swiveled round, maybe expecting a fight after all. "Sorry I bumped into you, man."

Same guy furled a brow. Tipped his chin. "Yeah, man, same here."

Now swanning along to my forgotten destination I mumbled, "I've been in this city too long. I gotta get out."

I blamed the Big Apple's famously aggressive, osmosing personality but had to accept it was really because I was so flaming pissed off. The church, life, Shiori, money, my suddenly clouded future . . . I was morphing from easygoing, happy-go-lucky mountain boy to case-hardened, sonofabitchingly callous New Yorker. Like Robert. I had to arrest that personality before it entrenched itself. I made a point to hash words with the city's abundant homeless population with whom I now felt a kinship. Whenever they panhandled me, I asked after their situation and, as a motivator, mentioned I'd been homeless a few times myself.

Sometimes I'd monish, "God is giving you this money through me, so you better use it for food and not drugs or liquor."

"Yeah, man," they often slurred, "don't you worry about that!" *Right.*

I met a young black woman in Manhattan on my way to work who pushed a stroller with a toddler on a hip. "Got a few dollars, mister?"

"You're panhandling with kids?" I felt mildly shocked even in this town.

She backed off, defensive. "So what if I am? My landlord kicked us out this mornin' for not payin' rent." She read my face. "My man lef' an' I got no job. I jus' got approved for benefits, but my letter an' first check ain't comin' for weeks."

"Didn't you tell your landlord?"

Guffaw. "He don't believe me. I gotta pay all my back rent to get in."

I considered handing her $20 but pitied her children. I caught a pay phone a few steps away. Dialed up her landlord. Presumedly.

"I already told her the deal. She's in arrears four months. I look like a charity?" We hashed it out. "Okay, she mentioned welfare. So, if she pays at least a month's overdue, she can stay that long. And it better pay up. No more seconds."

She looked skeptical till I pulled 300 fat ones out of my ATM. Almost all I had. "I get a paycheck in ten days, so I'll manage. But this ain't charity, it's a *loan*."

"Okay, mister. Whatever you say. You got my address." She signed the agreement I penned on a paper bag. I didn't really expect her to repay and wasn't disappointed. The motions were for both our sakes.

"Maybe you're scamming me, but it's these kids I'm helping." Part of me bet she was, but . . . maybe her performance deserved it. No, I was walking in Rev. Moon's footsteps and this was part of the deal. "You'll pay the karma if you are."

I had to accept my sergeant's observation and promised myself I'd stop the profanity. I mostly did. It surprised me, an elevator full of blacks chiding me for dirty language. I had a stereotype gleaned off the media and the Coast Guard, and they were a cussy lot. Maybe these soldiers didn't fit the cliché because they were older, Christian, or married West Indians whereas my image was of younger, single Americans. I'd learn quite a personality difference separated them but, for now, had no idea. Besides useful feedback on how folks perceived me, I discovered how often previous experience colored my own observations. After all, a stereotype is nothing more than opinion plus expectation formed by observation in personal encounters or via friends and media. Despite my infuriation with Wren Meyer and the church in general, I resolved to temper my mood with some greater objectivity.

One constancy in my travails with the church has been my faith I was traveling a course of growth and development in preparation for some yet-to-be revealed mission from God. When I first joined the church, I resolved to achieve the spiritual equivalent of a 10-year member in just two years, meaning I'd develop in that time the kind of spiritual awareness, sensitivity, understanding of the Principle, and accomplishment that saw Julian promoted to the Family's officer class in mere weeks and months. This wasn't unlike my grim determination to make petty officer first-class or OCS by the end of my first tour.

Instead, I ran afoul of church leaders and their authority structure. Evidently, I had no business expecting a bright future in a Confucian hierarchy; the military's was challenge enough but at least had rules. Even so, I felt grateful for the lessons forced on me. It helped me grow into a more sensitive, loving, conscientious, empathetic man than I ever might've managed in an easier environment. That's the one great thing the Unification Church inadvertently bequeathed me in its abuse.

While I stormed a fury with specific church members, I appreciated that I was learning and changing. Most importantly, I was rising to a better man than the assholes iron-booting me around, because I now felt certain I'd never treat them as they'd treated me. That's why it came as a surprise in the armory to realize I was expressing my savagely wounded heart through words and actions more than I ever imagined. Doing things without awareness is how Hannah Arendt's everyday banal turn themselves into murderous, totalitarian psychopaths. Could I blame Wren, therefore, in a moral sense? Probably not. He was a church beast conditioned in its untended zoo and nothing unusual. But, Jerome. Different story there, mate.

I MET UP with Professor Shimmyo at UTS in early summer regarding my autumn matriculation. "The seminary will never admit you after all that business with Rev. Meyer." *Reverend. Pish!* "You should go find another life. UTS is not for you, it's for true members who are pure and want to serve God and True Parents."

"That's exactly what I *want* to do."

"Regardless."

"Surely there's some indemnity condition I could do." His craggy visage was unmoved and immovable. An ice creature. Not even a querent brow.

I supposed he was pleasantly unaware of, or used his multi-degreed theological superpowers to rationalize, Rev. Moon's unmarried sex and illegitimate children. Or Hyo Jin Moon's whispered embezzlements and publicized sex orgies, drunkenness, illegal drug abuse, and violent assaults on members he didn't like. Or his siblings' psychoses, addictions, and manias. Or the not unknown sexual shenanigans of some of our hallowed 36-Blessed couples and sanctimonious senior Japanese, Korean, and American leaders—some of whom, like Ergela, were even UTS graduates.

If I thought I was blacklisted in California, Wren put me on the express to the basement. The experience rang through my life a Unification Church rendition of the House un-American Activities Committee. As for any blacklisted Hollywood star, my meeting with institutional Dr. Shimmyo was dwarfishly short. When he bid me a good riddance, he was confident he'd never see UTS darkened by my Luciferian presence ever again. I couldn't find a single reason to disagree.

On November 2 I tried again, arriving in a rental. His 6-months' rounder edges said, "To attend UTS you must separate from this sister one-hundred percent. As if she does not exist. Totally forget about her. Can you do that?" He pressed hard.

"I'll have to do it before I'll know." His face clouded. *Why lie when I don't know if I can abandon her so? or hang up the phone? or walk away like I don't know her?* "It's hard! Nobody gets my situation and how stubbornly she holds on."

"*Maybe* you can get into UTS for the January term if you totally cut off from her. But, the school might want you to wait for the next year to see how you do."

"That's awfully cruel! Like kicking somebody into a pit of wild dogs with the admonition, 'Don't get eaten,' and watching what happens." I needed an *escape* from this dangerous satanic world to build my character to defeat it. *Strange Moonies!*

"There is no middle ground with the fall, Chris. I talked to Wren Meyer about you after our last meeting. He believes you have what amounts to a personality disorder." I must've scowled. "Meaning, one person then suddenly another."

He did, did he? Moron. "He knew me all of four months or so and was so fit to judge my character that way? Pfft!" Dr. Shimmyo eyed me beetle-like. "He's harping on what happened when I was kicked out of the church and leaders stole all my hope for the Blessing." *At least I'm not out popping men up the ass, like some ex-Moonies. And I always pursued permanent sex relationships, not playboy fun.*

"I am not saying you can't or shouldn't come to UTS. It may take time for things to calm down. Nevertheless, you must do your duty and so must Shiori." He seemed much less opposed than before. Any jetsam in a raging sea. I wrote November 5,

> I talked to Shiori . . . [she] is willing to endure anything to keep [our] relationship . . . She will be deeply hurt . . . and I feel so responsible and guilty . . . [I hope] I can have the foundation to ask Father to Bless us. That means we'll never have our own children, but at least [she] could be happy at last, she loves me so much. . . . I'm trying to work, but I am flooded with thoughts of [her] . . . I feel like I'm in a great black pit with no air. I can hardly work. I am so crazy in my heart. I can hardly breathe . . . Oh, God, thou art the Great Sufferer! How I longeth to cut my bonds and restore thy light to the world, that the world's light might then shineth upon thee . . . My stomach wrenching and turning and filled with butterflies over this whole thing. I wish I could articulate the emptiness and remorse and other feelings . . . Earlier I was feeling "sorrowful unto death," and I suddenly realised a little bit about how Jesus felt when he realised he had to depart this world with a failed mission. What incredible sorrow and remorse and anger and difficulty and broken heart.
>
> I talked to Jerome [now the big UTS student] . . . he acts like he never did anything to me at all, even though I know he is the one who denounced me so thoroughly to Wren Meyer . . . But, he wants me to come . . . [He] introduced me all over the place, telling people how great I am (brother!), etc. I was embarrassed.

When I began my journey to New York City, I'd believed I could put California and its rotten tomatoes behind me. Resolve my feelings for Shiori in some considerate way all around. Make it to the seminary, the Asian tiger's maw and the beating heart of Rev. Moon and his Unification Church in the Western world. Now, it seemed, that finicky cat couldn't stomach the taste.

Act XII

A West Indies Life
Sex and Marriage in the Missionary Position

Call me crackers—okay, then: stupid—but Jerome and I reconciled a year after he orchestrated my opprobrious departure from the New York church. I did it because he was going through his own deportation and explained the circumstances of his treachery à la Wren Meyer. *He apologized.* We'd been best friends ten years and I'd regretted our break up, whatever the reason. Still, it was a harbinger of shoddier happenings.

In the meantime life after Wren was an unqualified train wreck. A wandering-in-the-desert period. Jerome ceased all communication with me, followed by Mrs. Kobayashi and the rest of my so-called brothers and sisters in the—*hahaha!*—Family, as the church occasionally recalled itself. Excommunicated almost in a Lutheran sense. A plague upon my house. By now, a commonsensical chap would've packed spiritual bags, kicked Unificationist dust from sandals, and pounded bricks. Indeed, tens if not hundreds of thousands of Americans who'd joined in fits of ebullience since the sixties had done just that over the decades with far less provocation.

Not me. I was symbiotically attached through Divine Principle. For a whole year my diary is awash in grief and mourning and my unquenchable thirst to work directly with its author teaching it across the nation toward a meaningful contribution to humanity. I couldn't imagine life not fulfilling my heavenly duty and obligation to the past and future as he gave me light to see it.

It's easy to look back at Nazis for how hapless Germans stupidly let their sense of societal and national duty—really nothing more than obeisance before authority—railroad them into barbarism. But it didn't seem so clear cut to me wallowing in self-pity and aghast at the sanctimonious perfidy of my fellow travelers. In spite of it and Wren's wildly excessive reaction to Shiori, the church was my home, society, career... nation, even. I think all of us have a tendency to over-identify with the groupings to which we attach where loosed on earth means loosed in heaven.

I was certainly as hardcore as a Moonie could get. Routinely kicked out of the church with prejudice, I determined to overcome my ugly duckling syndrome to prevail, to feel my detractors' congratulatorily repentful backslaps. Julian quoting Rev. Moon in my DP endpage that "the way of the righteous is a life of overcoming" now seemed a subtle prophesy. Perhaps he'd glimpsed in me a life continually striving to overcome (often self-made) obstacles. Life certainly seemed exactly that. While others with less talent and worse behaviors easily skated by, I crashed and burned over the smallest details. I wouldn't be the first to lament the stunning success of the evilly mediocre over the curious failure of the righteously excellent. Thousands of years after the ancients first put history's stylus to clay and bone it remains a stubborn problem. I was a talented, gifted individual in a corrupt, viciously minded organization fruitlessly striving to make peace with the devil.

With family in Texas circa Feb., 1991.

Well, Germans got hooked by Hitler's skillfully woven purls of plausibility embroidering 'good' into his bulk shite. So, too, Unificationists. Our plausibility is Divine Principle, our bulk shite the institution—rules, dogma, liturgy, institutional behavior—rooted in Abel's righteous rape and pillage of Cain. It's scary to think how I might have made a pretty good Nazi in seeing this distinction. Like Germans rationalizing evil in appearing to serve a higher good, I rationalized our fundamentally abusive church personality. Collecting films for Judah Street's video center in the lower end 1980s, I came upon a copy of *Triumph des Willens* (*Triumph of the Will*), the blockbuster 1935 documentary of the sixth Nazi Party congress in Nuremberg. Fifty years after it debuted in shiny black and white it swept me up in the superlative energy of Nazi self-sacrifice for the sake of the world.

I watched it with the cold appraisal of an American well understanding the true nature of Nazism as I do any totalitarian ideology, yet still felt its spell shimmer through me. Hitler hadn't hired director Leni Riefenstahl for nothing. I think it happened in part because I was a do-or-die member of a ruthlessly hierarchical and authoritarian organization worshipping a God as apparently punitive as the Nazi State. Even then, the Unification Church exhibited many of the positive traits the film majestically showcased: faith in God, True Parents, the Principle, his sagely appointed leaders, and determination to sacrifice himself (and us) for the sake of the world to establish the Kingdom of Heaven . . . so what if we then squashed recalcitrant, counterrevolutionary satanic miscreants and Cain-type nonconformists in the process. Wouldn't they be eventually Restored in spirit world by the grace of God and True Parents' indemnity conditions in their name? As he said about American Indians: so long as America lives up to its providential responsibility, they could forgive Europe's colonial invasion; if not, those chickens would end up vile clouds of roosting locusts. As German youth pledged their blood to Hitler's grand *Deutschland über alles*, we young Moonies pledged ours to Rev. Moon's Divine Principle Universal. And we mostly didn't think twice about it. Till we did.

"Many are called, but few are chosen," is how Matthew puts it. "Many are chosen, but few are left" was more apropos because the church was a warfarin-snacking hemophiliac in a thorn bush. It saw those of us staying the course the true martyrs. The Chosen Men dedicated to unwavering righteousness. Rev. Moon certainly made such remarks. As more members departed the greater its sense of martyrdom. This formed a part of the larger matrix of guilt I found myself increasingly caught up in. I was go-for-broke yet constantly kicked out over one thing or another. What was I when living on my own apart from the church and its traditions? Not satanic, that's for damn sure. I wouldn't allow myself to slide into that world—except falling in love—and worked hard to maintain my strongly indoctrinated traditions: 5 AM Pledge, individual Sunday service when barred from church centers, reading the Principle daily, and relentlessly pressing on with my sense of duty. The Mission was all. It didn't matter (*yeah, it did*) what befell me at the hands of brethren.

Loosely, The Mission is the foundation of the kingdom of heaven on earth, Rev. Moon's ultimate *raison d'être*. Whatever I organized myself to do, it had that for its ultimate goal. Forcibly deprived of spiritual nourishment and justification through the church, I set to work recasting myself into a mission I could do on my own outside church boundaries and control that would propel me onward to my goal, the church's goal, Rev. Moon's goal, God Almighty's goal.

Regardless its misbehavior and violent, Stalinesque intolerance and Rev. Moon's own, if indirect, culpability in my undeserved suffering, the Principle ever beckoned in pure righteousness despite the pall the church and sometimes he cast over it. Duty and obligation to the Principle, God, The Mission sang as sirens to Odysseus lashed to his mast as I'd bound myself with a sense of righteousness, godliness, and global citizenness. To ignore that for even the Messiah's totality was tantamount to suicide or betraying God as for Odysseus betraying his crew. Unthinkable.

Thus, when Jerome approached me a year later with a humble apology and a plan I did not, like Odysseus' crew, row past his siren call with plugged ears. I steered straight in because my duty was to follow the opportunities God placed before me. And, too, I didn't yet appreciate the danger presented by his fundamental character flaw: high intelligence running through gutter ethics. Looking back on my third go-round's judgment, I feel like *The Simpsons'* Ned Flanders blinded by "hi diddly ho" intentions and unhealthy "kettle korn" understanding.

I never dragged it out of him, but sensed a connection between his outing me to Wren in April and acceptance into UTS on its heels . . . an unholy looking quid pro quo regardless his January application. I was surprisingly thunderstruck he was a seminarian while I, acceptance letter in ashes, scrabbled through a human desert vainly seeking manna from an invisibly reasonable and sympathetic God.

Jerome now proposed a Second Coming to his island birthplace of St. Vincent and the Grenadines in the West Indies. I was far less surprised when he disclosed his recent UTS disgrace slam-banging a sexy wet Japanese turned dry informant when he'd jilted her over deflowered marriage. He'd more furiously backpedaled cresting the falls than I had with Shiori. Summarily thrown off campus then arrested and charged with trespassing by the school's buzz cut, Lavrentiy Beria chief of security when he snuck aboard for his personal possessions, he was now as *persona non grata* as he'd made me. Well, it brought me no small sense of satisfaction to hear the news. His comeuppance exceeded Wren's on his best day. As he explained the affair's beginnings, I sighed to hear his oft-repeated story. Drowning in embarrassment and humiliation, I imagine, he finally responded to my demands to explain how he'd betrayed Shiori and me to Wren Meyer. I guess a year made a difference, because I didn't have the emotional energy anymore to bust his chops. I just wanted closure and nodded along with empathy and understanding, resolving to never again trust him with personal information.

Sex is right up there as the most frequent sin human beings commit right after our self-centered thinking giving rise to it. As sundry illegit children attest, even Rev. Moon isn't immune and, like any good cheat, he's replete with fabulously plausible deniability rooted in his messianic position—"It's good to be the king," Mel Brooks reminds me. Nor, sadly, are Rev. Moon's children immune to the booty call. Jerome and I were just two more idiots in a long, regretful line. The bigger problem was the hypocritical church response. While it judiciously tempered its handling of 'Chapter Two' problems—the sexual nature of the Fall is found in that chapter of *Divine Principle*—amongst leaders and notably charitable of Rev. Moon's, it was anything but in its handling of my case let alone Jerome's vis-à-vis *graduated* seminarian Ergela. One of its worst features is a tendency to excommunicate its (unconnected) most able members for their imperfections while promoting its (connected) least able in spite of theirs. I keenly felt this injustice and was even then in the midst of reversing my misfortune by any means.

We devised a plan to relocate to his home island for a 3-year stretch. We'd build the country's first Unification Church and send candidates to the next Blessing event. On the foundation of our spiritual and practical success, we thought we could invite Rev. Moon to attend a nationwide revival and Blessing during which we'd bequeath our island church to him and, impressed, he'd reinstate us in the American one. At the time, St. Vincent was theoretically serviced by a circuit missionary couple out of Barbados. We'd spied a vacant market but it was stupid to build a church only for its official leaders to show up to shred our credibility and steal our results. I phoned. Too beggared for St. Vincent, I got their buy-in.

There was a method to our madness. For years, he'd secretly attempted a kinder and gentler *coup d'état* in a country (preferably without effective laws or government) to give himself a tangible, exemplar Nation of God from which to diplomatically reach out to the community of nations with his messianism. He feels it's imperative he find a nation to publicly venerate his mission. Jesus failed with Israel. Stymied in Korea and America, he's fixed on avoiding that fate. The mid-'90s news that he'd tried seizing a small African state by infiltrating local rebels astounded us. They were apparently nearly successful. But the members pulling it off got corrupted—who saw that coming?—by their rebel power. That'll happen when you figure bullets for ballots comes with a silver lining. To be fair, he'd hoped for a peaceful, persuasible revolution however illogical his expectation could only ever be. He right smartly pulled the plug. I never ferreted out the country. Mr. Kamiyama, Rev. Pak, and other top bananas zipper lipped the upper echelon's gossip in chagrin, fear of the press, and some healthy terror of The Hague.

The church, all but incapable of recruiting year over year, was headed for the coroner. We jeered Rev. Pak preening over the "fabulous victory" in 1991 of *three* new members over the previous month in the entire United States. Our collective brilliance, unhindered by headquarters meddlers, could surely spiritually conquer St. Vincent to draw in hundreds if not thousands of new members, thoroughly shaming our detractors. The best revenge is success and I, for one, wanted both.

I had my qualms. Aye, serious concerns. On the other hand, an environment that discounted and even resisted friendship and trust meant Jerome offered the only real, if exasperatingly imperfect, friendship I'd known since best-friend-forever Lance blew me off after high school for joining my cult. Jerome occasionally stood by me and believed in my intelligence and intrinsic value when others never did or devalued me, accepting me warts and all when he wasn't rejecting me. That counted for something in the trenches. I felt an unspoken point of honor. For all our spats, his treachery, and my declining trust I figured "better the enemy you know than the friend you don't." Who else would take a chance on me? I was anathema to the church. A prat cast as evil Lucifer, seducer and defiler of the Rising Sun's purity. If I truly felt a duty and obligation toward advancing humanity's understanding of the principles of peace and unity then I had to accept seemingly unreasonable measures to get around my reputational disability. It rationalized out quite well.

Besides, our plan seemed pretty good. Rev. Moon values results. Perform, and he overlooks most anything. Hell, he'd yoke his own child to Satan if Restoration got marked paid. We wouldn't get very far preaching the Principle in America without sanction. It was a saturated market and we weren't denominationalists. Our movement's top leaders were gunning for us and we'd only be in their caustic sights for poaching into Satan's tucker bag. No, drastic circumstances required drastic action. A beachhead in St. Vincent more and more looked to be the only way we could expect to transcend our reputations and prove our value to The Mission.

～

BEING 50% RESPONSIBLE for revenues jumping from $700,000 to over $4 million in two years, I wanted a raise. Making $28,000, I considered $35,000 (0.875% of our department) very reasonable. Jack Morton laughed all the way to the want-ads when I quit for a new-hire raise from my next job, which is how my replacement got $32,000 and JMP suffered his training cost and the blip in John's production. A greedy company and also stupid. Instead, I joined Jerome in August of '91 for bigger dreams in St. Vincent. To prepare, I read James Michener's *Caribbean*, idly chuckling to myself, "Wouldn't it be just oh so interesting (if ever so unlikely) to meet my bride there like that one character of his did?" After all, I was off and on seeing Shiori while religious duty slowly beat our—at least, my—personal feelings to death. Running away to St. Vincent was also looking like the perfect solution to my chaotic love life, the fiendish saboteur of all my yearning aspirations.

"Please!" she implored. "I promise I am not in your way. I can manage Jerome." She hated him, so that was wishful thinking if not a calculated lie.

"No, no, no." I conjured every thinkable rationale against it. "Just hold the fort till we get back." The last thing my craving for space needed was a dysfunctionally possessive woman cocking hammers on a shotgun wedding.

Jerome said, "We don't need her antagonizing the locals and especially my family with her whacko Oriental aloofness, Chris. Keep her far away from me."

"I not think it will be what you think," she said, perhaps having glanced at Michener. "You want Blessing down there? Is that why you no want me?"

Stumbling out of her bed into a West Indian's wasn't in my calculus at all. Not even a fantasy. "Why would I jump from the frying pan into the fire, Shiori?" when I imagined Rev. Moon Blessing me to a divine Korean? "I *don't want* an 'outside' wife!" In 1991, that still couldn't be more *extrem verboten*.

With Jerome at Shiori's. Jul., 1991.

Our St. Vincent mission was rehabilitative baby steps, one which Jerome helped me take in July after he did some cross-country fence-mending. I was fighting a cruel cold at Shiori's apartment typing *Divine Principle* into my computer. The city's 100°F cooker had her doors thrown open. He strolled in, plopped on a dinette chair.

"You'll appreciate this, Chris. I visited Dr. Thibodeoux in San Francisco, a real insider for church info. Taught at UTS. He said Rev. Kwak pressured Wren Meyer to kick Ergela Arsch out of the church for screwing some Filipino, or maybe it was a Thai, bitch."

I blew iced tea up my nose. "Wren did? You believe it? I mean . . . this fuckin' church!"

"I trust him. He told me she was plowing through the church 'servicing' members."

"That's weird." He shrugged. "And Ergela jumped into that? Well! I knew he'd fall afoul someday. Seems to be a pattern with everybody who violates me. Wren's next."

"You prophesied it in California. You must feel satisfied he got his."

I thought about it. "Not really. But maybe now he'll understand how we felt."

"Heh. He's Blessed to a sister close to True Parents. He's in the shit."

"Wow, Wren has some balls! But . . . Ergela's connected. Slap on the wrist."

Like a single raindrop augers the deluge yet in and of itself doesn't predict it, my decision to uproot my newly built New York City life (when I hadn't done it for the Army) led me into a future I couldn't predict wouldn't upend it. Was this how a person progressed from naïve childhood to cynical, burned-out old age? No one starts off life dreaming of fucking it up to die a stinking, snarling failure. Each decision, every action is geared to fulfilling one's desire. My problem was that however astute I thought my analyses of potential consequences, reality often turned out a bent spike in the brainpan. Road signs ever point to disaster yet innocuous and devoid of any presaging, suspensefully menacing score to all but the bitterly ruined. Only tearful hindsight seems to flush hints like red-flagged quail.

Why didn't I see this? Why not that? Because I wasn't looking. There seemed no need to view friends as enemies. Pursuing my dream was my agent of destruction. But fool me once, shame on you. Fool me twice, shame on me. Lingering confusion around Jerome's treachery with Wren and his own post-UTS importunity perhaps allowed me to over-exercise my Flandersian nature.

MID-AUGUST 1991 we touched down heavily in Kingstown, St. Vincent on airfare I'd paid for. Beautifully green and ruggedly mountainous, it was a far cry from Barbados, a fluffed up pancake I thought at first glance any barely motivated tsunami could smoothly wash away. Customs as usual in small, wannabe countries was oppressive, obnoxious, and inane. Uniformed agents made a bold effort of treating me like a returning citizen to tax my 'portable' Macintosh computer hundreds of East Caribbean (EC) dollars until I persuaded them I was a visiting writer and the computer my tool, merely a modern typewriter. They were skeptical. Came off as rustics having never seen such a rare bird in their mazy Xanadu. Bajan seaworthiness was certainly questionable but not its dispassionate professionalism processing us through customs for our LIAT propjob to St. Vincent, which aggressively lacked it (a product of its dearth of unfuckable tourism, perhaps).

Irked as always with officialdumb, we all but fell out of the McDonald's-sized, 1-storey blockwork terminal into thick, leafy-green air, precipitous hills, and the arms of waiting taximen. Of course they plundered us on the fare. That's a rite of passage the first time in-country without a local escort and it mirrored Cyprus, Greece, and Jordan. I chalked it up as a truism. An intense greenery saturated marveling eyes an order of magnitude stronger than even

Kingstown; above Cane Garden & Town Hill. Old British fort-cum-prison on the far point.

summertime Kodiak, perhaps even my cherished Emerald Isle.

"Man, what a gorgeous island! I could definitely live here."

Jerome peacocked. "I told you that you'd love it here. Wait'll you see it all."

Fast-roving eyes soaked up the sun-drenched valley and towering mountains rising off the sea behind us lapping the runway's rocky end. Third-world shacks and barefoot pedestrians along the road winding through steep-sided hills and plunging valleys toward town wafted away the stink the airport's petty officials had put up my nostrils. Our thieving taximan chattered up a novel of the Vincy life. Living in Cyprus made me keenly aware of an island's dry-land limitations and I hadn't liked it. I'm a big-horizon man used to land rolling on forever, certainly farther than a tidal wave might swamp in its perkiest apocalypse. On Cyprus I'd felt trapped, imprisoned, its distant mountains no comfort. St. Vincent had no such fetters. Perhaps because Cyprus was my first island or St. Vincent's mountains were so up close and personal they hid its ever-present 'islandicity.' Whatever the reason, it was the first of many reasons I fell in love with this lovely, mismanaged paradise.

At Jerome's insistence, his cousin Vinla Bramble in New York City had signed a power of attorney giving him control of the land and houses his sprawling clan owned in St. Vincent, most of which was gone to seed or conquered by squatters. His extended family owned some of the best land in town and a few parcels overlooked beautiful Kingstown Bay. I'd shortly get the nickel tour, but for the moment our taxi negotiated the roads to Vinla's house in Town Hill. Theoretically, it was a bit upscale though compared to the digs in Cane Garden—where most of the local and foreign white folk lived—our neck of the woods was a shantytown. Still, "Bramble House" as we called it was a unique, 2-storey semi-Tudor style affair. St. Vincent had two basic house forms in 1991: the wretched poor lived in a 'wood house' and the middle class and well-to-do in a (concrete block) 'stone house.' If you're in stone, you're good to go in Vincentian society. Fortunately, Vinla's crib tacked a middle class flag's credibility to our leerily unusual appearance on the local scene.

Mesopotamia ('Mespo') Valley. We visited unelectrified, candlelit homes for church.

Bramble House rose imposingly from a plunge in the left- and right-climbing road where a third rose up to meet it from downtown below. An honest stone-block retaining wall varied between a few and more than ten feet above the road grade that gave the house its foundation. Cheap paneling sheathed flimsy interior walls; 2×2s on gaping centers. A measly two outlets electrified the upstairs. We dumped our nigh-taxed bags.

My room butted up on a heavily treed hillside in the rear with the neighbor's wood house maybe ten feet upslope. A single six-paned, metal double casement crank window opened onto free-ranging roosters towing their clucking harems. They ear-screechingly squawked all hours in some West Indian lingo, else that 5 AM-cum-dawn *cock-a-doodle-doo* bullshit's for city slickers. The rooster path cleaved Vinla's from the upslope house. It wound front-to-rear to the French-style, double main entry opening onto our second floor. Daylight flooded the spacious central living room through the French entry and two front and rear same-style casement windows. To the door's right, Jerome's bedroom. To its left a rickety, wood-railed staircase down then two bedrooms (one mine) flanked a dark-paneled hallway to the only bathroom at the other end.

Downstairs, an aboveground basement opened into a kitchen beneath the bath and two bedrooms. Besides the single, six-paned casement window next to a door set perpendicular into a jog in the stone wall we had a metal sink–counter–cabinet unit, 2-burner propane stove, and dinette table with a padded-metal 4-chair set. The door opened onto a small, stone-paved courtyard area atop the retaining wall with steep steps down to the street. No refrigerator. No phone. No lights. It would be a chore to remedy these mundane deficiencies.

I felt frightened surveying this strange new land and contemplating my purpose. I wasn't here on holiday but to upset a nation's apple cart injecting a few heady drops of controversial thinking into it. Did I really want to do that? Did I want to become a spiritual enemy of this people when I'd only just arrived? My first missionary journey and I was feeling the need to revisit the airport. On the other hand, adventure beckoned. The island pulsed in a way Cyprus never did. I wanted to explore it physically, intellectually, and spiritually. We'd drug our bags from the taxi and I'd thrust out my hand to curious neighbors wondering why long-shuttered Bramble House was coming to life. *Who you be? Wha' mek you here?* But they'd put aside suspicious curiosity and welcomed us, and we handily broke the ice.

We sauntered down the easy incline from Bramble House and then up the long, lazy rise folks called Long Wall. It wound up from the city center a hundred feet below, snaking toward the bay's southern point and into Cane Garden. We traversed past eclectic stone and wood houses and literal shacks stilted on steep slopes above and below, some less than 100 feet square.

"My family lives up there." Jerome pointed along the cliff's edge looming some 75 feet over a small, stone building at its very base atop a thick green rise swelling some 15 feet up from the narrow road to the cliff's rocky foundation.

"Lovely." I squinted in the bright sunlight. Shaded my eyes like a salute to nature while side-stepping along. As a Colorado mountain man I could only approve the fine terrain Kingstown nestled into. "Maybe we can find something up top there where there's a breeze." Bramble House was over and above the sweltering town but not enough for me. Sweat by now trickled past my ears into my open shirt collar. Beads glistened hotly across Jerome's forehead and dampened his dully white, necktied collar.

Small stones bounced and clattered around us in a light drizzle, thrown from what looked in the blindingly bright distance high above to be a couple of wildly gesticulating children at the cliff's edge. I chuckled.

Middle Street up the hill to Bramble House in Town Hill and Long Wall.

"Must be having fun with the strangers."

Jerome scooted unhelpfully to the road's edge. "Before we get brained, man."

We arrived at a sharp bend near the top. Straight ahead to the south and the headland were expensive, multi-storey stone houses of mostly whites. Hairpinning back to the north as well as east up and over the point's mountain sat stone and wood houses of blacks. Jerome beckoned me north through his memories from before emigrating to New York City at age eleven. We found his relatives close to the road bend, perched atop the cliffs overlooking Kingstown and the bay on a large tract they'd subdivided over the years for children and extended family.

Nathalie and Hugh's home was stone. A simple colonnaded veranda along the seaward side of the upper, main floor overlooked a spectacular Mediterranean view of the city and bay going on 275 feet below. Introducing ourselves to Jerome's extended family on the veranda, I found myself five yards from scrawny, excruciatingly shy 16-years Tamela and 15-years Seranie. For months I'd mispronounce her name on account of her broguish West Indian and my reluctance to say "I didn't get that" more than three times. She hovered beside their family's van in the shade of the carport ell-ed off the concrete-floored veranda. Sneak peeks slyly flashed off eyes firmly tethered to the deck. *What a blushful, spindly little girl*. I gave her no more thought. She confessed they'd stoned us on the road.

"Wha' de Mor-monn," she'd squealed, spying our white shirts and Jerome's tie.

Seranie had grabbled up a handful of small stones. "Le'we ha' some fun!"

I sure didn't expect Jerome to then fling himself so completely into the arms of Vincentian womanhood . . . according to some folks its manhood, too. He met attractive Gem, a policewoman, inside a week and proposed over a lunch date. She cut a handsome, robust slavic figure in her white constabulary uniform and flashed a broad, sparkling smile from her dark face. The very idea was so farfetched I convulsed with laughter while ironing out a stern, straightlaced puss for Jerome.

She gazed on him with a smirk under coy eyes. "I will give what you said very serious thought."

Down the road he said, "I knew when I met her we were destined to be together. She's perfect and she's Vincentian!"

"She'd be your third wife and you barely know her. Forgive my doubts."

"Don't get in my way, man." My lips thinned hard.

She came back with, "I'm sorry, Jeh-rome. I like 'de single life for 'de time."

He pouted a minute then shook it off seemingly without regret and moved on to the next in line. And it seemed many women were lining up to service him. But it was his country. Out of the loop, I minded my business.

As time passed he grew agitated and upbraiding. "You walk around without a Bible. The way you talk . . . you don't look or act like a real minister. And I don't like how you're taking so much initiative. We agreed this was my mission."

"It is. I'm not trying to take over. I'm—I'll shut up. But I am what I am."

"Chris, you're totally ignorant how Vincies perceive you. Here we are, a white man and a black man working in a black country. You don't think for a minute they aren't automatically seeing you as my 'master' every time you act in charge?"

"That's insane. I agreed to be the junior partner here, but not some mindless Japanese drone. It's my mission, too. We're a partnership."

"We're Cain and Abel. I'm in a messianic position to my family and St. Vincent. They don't need another white savior. They need *me*. One of their own. I should've had a foundation in America to stand on for this."

"Yeah, I know. Local boy made good."

"Don't mess with me. This is my life! My providential mission! I can't build my foundation here on my home soil if people have even a drab of the idea that I'm some white man's lackey."

"I know that. But . . . dang. Okay, I promise I'll defer to you more obviously—in the interest of our greater mission."

Of course, my deference to him was rooted in my understanding of the Principle's Cain–Abel symbolism. Members constantly divide each other into these opposing camps. Ordinarily, it wouldn't be problematic if a majority correctly understood it. Sadly, the church thoroughly braids Cain–Abel with the Principle's Subject–Object relationship. Cain's role is tantamount to the Object-partner in any Subject–Object interaction. One is thereby always Object: passive, following, responding, controlled. People naturally rebel. No doubt there was a semblance of it in my attitude toward Jerome on occasion. When I decided to accompany him to St. Vincent, it was clearly his initiative, his mission, that he expected my deference. I accepted that. Yet, even though I made sure to play second fiddle on arrival, he nevertheless felt threatened by the positive and friendly response folks showered on me. They seemed to instinctively defer to me as the white American assumptively leading our expedition, and him Mr. Nobody Vincy. Jerome wasn't wrong picking up on that.

Despite insisting on role-modeling me "until you develop into a real minister and missionary," he was increasingly not around. I was the naggy wife. "Where've you been all day [half the night]?"

"Out teaching the Principle [street witnessing; visiting family]" with ever-strengthening annoyance. "You think I'm some black monkey out screwing every coconut falling into my hands?"

Several spiritual children hailed from Mespo.

"What? No. I don't know where you are. Nobody does. And we're a team. I'm not twiddling fingers if I can't find you."

"Don't worry about it. I'm doing my mission."

I found out that meant getting laid by sundry women, but for months hadn't a glimmer. I trusted his ministerial mores. This wasn't UTS. *It's a mission.* Yet, he was sowing the literal seeds of our failure.

In a few days we were preaching in the local churches. We began amongst the Spiritual Baptists squatting on his land in the old stone building along Long Wall's cliff, practically a straight plummet from Nathalie's veranda. Mother Francis ran it, a charismatic and strong-willed woman in her sixties with a baseball-sized goiter bulging from one side of her neck. Her husband, the former pastor, had run off to America to marry another woman without stopping for a divorce and she believed he might one day return to her. She'd assumed his post to maintain his congregation. Like most Spiritual Baptist preaching, hers was interminable. One-line songs went on for twenty minutes, the 90% female congregation falling into a dancing trance amongst the wood benches, rhythmically waving over their heads colorful flags fixed to thin wire rods. Her services lasted 2–6 hours.

Jerome said, "Don't look surprised. It's a holdover from slavery days. Church was their only time of entertainment and freedom to be how they wanted."

"Well, it's woefully inadequate for the spiritual needs of a free people today. In my view, it exacerbates the island's already disastrous problem with divorce, drunkenness, infidelity, incest, premarital and extramarital sex, teenage pregnancy . . . the whole shebang." Many seemed enmeshed in it to a flagrant degree I'd never seen in America or Cyprus. Mother Francis scolded them in sermons.

He said, "You, the white man who helped create it, are in no position to judge. We have to work with what they are."

"I'm not. And white—well, Christianity should be curing it, not enabling it."

"Let me deal with that. I understand what's going on here."

Mother Francis accepted us the minute she grasped Jerome's lineage and installed him as her assistant. She said to the congregation, "Rev. Trumpet is our new pastor and I follow him," in recognition of his land underlying her rent-free church.

That suited us fine. We could use a tangible base of operations from which to credibly operate, and preached there Sunday morning and Wednesday evening. She introduced us to the brothers Free, identical twins and co-pastors of a ten times larger Spiritual Baptist church on the backside of Sion Hill not too far from Cane Garden and Bramble House. We had a hell of a time telling them apart, as apparently did the local women. They operated a Sunday radio show live from church that motivated the political establishment to pander their electoral influence. With her endorsement, they embraced us as brother preachers and routinely invited us to preach and pray. We taught them Divine Principle in a roundabout, unthreatening fashion through the Bible, like Rev. Moon in his early Korea days.

My biggest hurdle was that Spiritual Baptist services—a big, if poor, force—were so heavy on emotion. The Principle is an intellectual message, a logical exposition of God and humanity. Rev. Moon isn't a melodramatic preacher building up a feel-good performance to an emotional orgasm. He's analytical and carefully explicates the Bible and his message. We were naturally his kind of minister, rejecting a rock-n-roll service for one shedding real light on the human condition with clear guidance and education. That happened precious little in this denomination however ardently it felt superior to the dry, sleep-inducing, impotent white man's religion in downtown's Anglican, Seventh-Day Adventist, Mormon, and other churches.

The brothers Free preached a more intellectual game than Mother Francis, but still whipped up a theatrical whirlpool to pump up the entertaining energy to bring folks back with their heathen friends for more next Sunday. I might've bored my agreeable listeners more than anything else. But they genuinely laughed at my jokes and congratulated me on my "interesting," "affecting," and "unusual" sermons. Still, they expected preaching not teaching and preferred the former.

Jerome and I debated the difference twixt white and black churches. We agreed whites tended toward boring dryness and intellectualism that disconnected the real joy and emotion through God and Jesus' sacrifice. Blacks tended toward showboating emotionalism and anti-intellectualism that disconnected the life-changing awareness of a Christian way of life and the reality of our human experience from God's point of view. I'm stereotyping, but it fit most of our experience back then.

I thought the black *or* white churches that seemed to do the best struck the right balance between heart and mind for their particular congregation. I love singing, and within limits the more the better. When the Unification Church invested a lot of service time in Holy Songs, I felt energized and closer to God and open to hearing the Principle castigate our human reality. But I also love an educational sermon that teaches me and especially helps me solve life's problems even without music, and even if it's more a seminar than church. An emotional charge makes you feel good but does nothing to help you navigate the ethical and moral perils of the real world that motivate crises of conscience and turn life upside down. You cope but don't solve. Over time, we felt our mission needed to include inspiring a general change in the ubiquitous Spiritual Baptist churches, from forging a reunification between its two alienated branches to drawing the church as a body to the next level of spiritual and temporal development. But as Jerome metamorphosed into a vengeful phantasm of triangle trades past, self-sabotage entered our mission.

We steered clear of the mainstream denominations who might've responded with a government crackdown. Meanwhile our preaching achieved success in Kingstown's Spiritual Baptist churches and we invested more time directly teaching the Principle one-on-one to potential converts. "Inspired by the principles of Unification Thought taught by the Rev. Sun Myung Moon," we'd founded our Family Home Church Association (FHCA) in January 1990 out of our 53-4th Avenue apartment "as a means to bring families together in free association in order to mutually investigate and understand the nature and purpose of the Family and to apply that understanding in their respective communities." It published our *Family Times* monthly newsletter. We invited Vincentians to Bramble House under its auspices for lectures and, hopefully, to join our gladsomely unAsianized version of Rev. Moon's '90s global goatfuck.

Jerome was more gregarious and skilled in challenging people's religious comfort levels and directly asserting the Principle's primacy. I never liked witnessing and shunned it like a scarlet letter. Jerome often said "a man convinced against his will is of the same mind still," quoting who I thought must've been his sage Plato but paraphrased from Part III of Samuel Butler's seventeenth-century *Hudibras*. I felt ever reluctant to force-feed my faith down anybody's presumably unwilling throat. Jerome took the proselytizing point while I struck up casual conversation in the rear to naturally introduce the Principle without seeming to recruit.

My most successful effort was Charles, a young lad who waitered downtown. A strong, even borderline fanatical, Christian he was nonetheless deeply interested in following spiritual inspiration and searched out new truth. Refreshingly, he hadn't hardened his belief system like most Christians who, frankly, eschew improvement. These are the narrow-minded, brain-locked believers who traditionally go after Moonies with pitchforks and depositions. Let's be fair: the Principle improves over traditional expositions of biblical truth by reducing blind faith in answering more questions than it raises, which is a good benchmark. In a religion mired in theological conundrums, contradictions, controversies, and cruelly murdered dissidents, I saw it a solid step ahead. Charles appreciated that and visited our Town Hill house for my lectures. In a month he'd signed our FHCA membership form to become our very first member. *Wow!* We were pastors of our own church and successful proprietors of a cult branch.

Another successful witnessing method, which developed accidentally out of my natural inclination to chat with any willing body, was casual yet pointed street conversation. It might surprise you but the best, most open, interesting, intelligent, and articulate religious conversationalists were the Rastafarians. I regularly hiked up the hill into the Rastized neighborhood atop Sion Hill where they'd built a corrugated tin bungalow about 30 × 20 feet or so. In it, they'd stacked cool-dirt floor to oven-hot ceiling and wall-to-wall with steel drums hand-hammered out of 55-gallon oil barrels they manually tuned on the spot as necessary with ball-peens. Their bands practiced there every day. I happily hung out on splintery wood bleachers along a wall soaking in their fabulous music pounding the thick air and echoing through the tinned atmosphere. Many Rastas cornered me for sit-downs on stone walls, logs, rocks, or the sandy ground to pepper me with tough questions about God, the Bible—they were certainly textual experts—Rev. Moon, and Divine Principle. Many of their eyes were yellowed if not bloodshot from prodigiously smoking *ganja* (marijuana), some more heavily than others which, without fail, they offered me as the gracious hosts they were. But even stoned as Long Wall, they were remarkably rational, intellectual, academic debaters.

It was a happy surprise that Rastas (St. Vincent's, anyhow) weren't anything like Steven Seagal's bloodthirsty Screwface in spirituality-hating Hollywood's 1990 *Marked for Death*. I considered them typically hard-working, honest intellectuals, not that they didn't have a petty criminal element on the island. But cutlass-wielding Rastas coming up on me never sparked the fight-or-flight I'd have felt in America. Their *ganja* use didn't thrill me. I thought it was problematic and their *Predator*ish eyes only reinforced it. It's a mind-altering drug after all with negative physiological not to mention psychological repercussions regardless some scientists giving it a clean bill of health. Vincentian Rastas seemed to scour their Bibles with PH.D. levels of analysis, time, and interest (even by ministerial standards) and were never unprepared for a knowledgeably stimulating discussion on biblical topics. I loved it and could've spent all day enjoying that Rasta life. I didn't buy their philosophy one iota and we had spirited debates over 'I'-based philosophy and language. These issues were insignificant and I overlooked them.

Generally, Rastas respected me as a missionary, intellectual, and person. I never encountered a Rasta who berated black–white history, my whiteness, American imperialism, or anything except me not carrying my Bible one day while casually promenading through downtown. Jerome nailed me for it. They were some of the friendliest people I'd ever met, which is how I recognized Seagal's unfair treatment— I can't speak for Jamaican Rastas—to an audience mostly ignorant of Rastafari. Virtually all black Vincies I met treated me with respect and even brotherhood. A far cry from Moonies and Christianity. They showed me a truer black culture.

While American blacks often strut about nursing hyperbolized chips on their shoulders, West Indians seemed very comfortable in their skins and society. I'm sure the fact it's 98% non-white contributes mightily to their attitude. Even so, a tiny minority of Vincy whites (during our time there) controlled critical businesses like food and national politics. Prime Minister James Mitchell is white yet, except for suspicious chuckles he didn't really like blacks—derived from allegedly divorcing his wife after finding her under a black man—I never heard any blacks disliking him on account of it. As Jerome spiraled out of control, it was me our black neighbors rallied round to protect from his brash malice when a dedicated anti-racist racist might expect them to grab their golden opportunity to get Whitey.

Until I went to St. Vincent, my experience with blacks was mostly negative. Sure, I'd met 'normal' middle class blacks but always lurking in the wings were the resentments and aggravations rooted in the unresolved racial issues you might think the Civil War and Reconstruction should've fixed but didn't on account of majority-vote, government-sponsored segregation. Blacks feel hurt, victimized, and resentful and whites annoyed, accused and, in varying degrees from nil to suicidal, guilty. My parents raised me to look through skin color, so I couldn't have cared less. But living in a race-obsessed culture ideologizing politics for a cudgel colored my comparative thinking on a subconscious level. The point of it, I'd supposed. There hasn't been any solution yet presented that seems capable of resolving this historical chasm that doesn't rely on force and reverse oppression.

"Except Divine Principle," I told folks. "Let me tell you about its vision."

In Rev. Moon's understanding of God and humanity—he claimed Martin Luther King his favorite American—lies a simple solution to the enmity. Americans need take him seriously before it can be applied but, as we know, they decidedly aren't. Vincentian blacks walked and talked in a way I considered normal (the oreo life, maybe) as opposed to strutting, Ebonics, and a red grievance machine. Except for culture and language differences, I felt at home around Vincy blacks in a way I never did American (and only tasted with Belgian) blacks. In that comfort, I grew a new viewpoint. Not merely different but emotive.

American blacks shit on whites who empathize—for good reason, considering the cynicism generated twisting it to political and financial advantage—as though whites have no right to work at resolving their half of the black–white dysfunction, as if it's the purview of (liberal, democrat, civil rights but definitely not conservative, republican) blacks alone. Jerome and I had long talked of writing a book to apply lessons from the Principle to the black–white conflict. Yet, in private conversation he now often shouted me down as having no right to say this or that because only blacks had that right. Our reverse racial conflict germinated my idea for a book spiritually analyzing American race hate head-on through Divine Principle.

My brother Teddy had openly dared Maryland's segregationists by sidling up to colored-only water fountains and into bathrooms just to piss them off. I was too young to notice the point and it never blipped the radar in my all-Nordic corner of the Rockies. Few blacks seemed to appreciate Teddy's white-child rebellion in these last gasps of government racism. But surely his slap in its face removed that much more of its defense and helped adult whites turn against it. Only after I joined the church and ironically experienced firsthand virulent Japanese and Korean racism and xenophobia did I develop a recognition and appreciation of, and empathy for, black suffering in America's overwhelmingly—and according to region, hostile—white society. In spite of St. Vincent's many cultural and social dysfunctions, Jerome and I decided the West Indies presented a good model for healing black American resentment and social pathologies.

It turned out American blacks had little love for their West Indian cousins whose superior, non-hostile attitudes made them the darling of employers. Malcolm X tartly remarked a fake accent and a towel round his head would get him through the front door of any whites-only establishment in New York City but, if it slipped, he'd get chucked out the back for being American. I was no expert but, from the colossal bitching and moaning I was overhearing, it seemed to me that a West Indian accent in the Green Apple was an entrée to a job an American black might well be excluded from on the assumption he or she'd be a vexatious hire.

A Rasta cleaning out a drainage ditch said to me traipsing down a blazing street in Town Hill not far from our house, "Aye, mon. Hold up if you be havin' 'de time." Propping his shovel against his wheelbarrow full of dirt clods and grass, he posed a biblical question he'd mulled over the years. "If Adam and Eve were 'de first and only people in 'de world, who 'dem chil'ren marry as 'de Bible tell us?"

"Well, uh . . . in my Divine Principle view"—I'm paraphrasing here—"there were already many humans living in the world then, but God chose Adam and Eve as prototypes of the new, spiritually oriented human race to come. It was always His plan their children would marry these other humans, who'd then be naturally incorporated into God's new human paradigm through education and works of the Spirit. That's why the biblical writers even mentioned their existence."

He stood agape. His animated finger jabbed. "Irie, mon, 'dat 'de best ans-uhh I ev-uhh get. You know, mon, all 'dem uddah missionary come roun' here gimme ready-made buuulll-shit, nev-uhh mek no sense. Ignorin' 'de plain writin' o' 'de book. Else 'dem be tell me, 'Don't question 'de Laahd' or, 'Don't confound 'de Holy Word.' " He grinned. "You know 'dem be say 'dat."

"Ha! Do I ever! It's because they've got nothing to go on beyond faith in doctrine." I wasn't sure if I was defending them or just punctuating his point.

We chatted some more till he said, "Jah, mon, you be fine for 'de time," and went back to work. He spread my word around Sion Hill and then it was easy (and a booming) business discussing the Principle with that community even if they weren't likely to abandon Rastafari. It didn't matter. All was good for God.

Jerome and I now fenced over teaching the Principle. "We need to preach in the churches five days a week. We can teach Principle two days and be fine."

"That's crazy, Jerome. Our mission here is teaching Principle not preaching up churches. We should do lectures here or wherever twenty-four-seven."

"Preaching is how we'll get these people to come over for lectures."

"I see what you're saying, but that makes us *Christian* preachers, not *Moonie* missionaries. The uproar breaking convention to preach Principle meaningfully, like Father did, means preaching Christianity more than Unificationism."

"Right, but even Father had to walk a fine line there, you know that. He had to do his real teaching privately, away from those pastors who'd shut him down."

"Exactly. So . . . maybe you preach the churches and I'll lecture DP here."

His head shook hard. "I don't like that division of labor. We shouldn't be seen separated like that. That's Cain–Abel disunity." I flippered lips.

We had his cousin Beverly's Mormon group over for a Divine Principle lecture. Even more unusual than salt-and-pepper Moonies, they blew in on a $20 million church raised on a hill visible all over town. It sported a fancy, deep baptismal pool and pro-level classrooms we borrowed for abstinence programs and a somewhat deMoonized Divine Principle they wouldn't lock us out over. Few Vincies saw them more than wolves in sheep's clothing; hobnobbing Utah racists pragmatically building membership outside their white enclaves. Thus, Tamela and Seranie raining stones our first day. Vincies were quite aware Mormons excluded blacks right up till its grand poo-bah's convenient revelation from God years after the US Congress passed its Civil Rights Act already explicit in its flouted Constitution.

Beverly's group might've reported our big medicine. Two youthy Americans now visited daily, hoping they were Elijah to Baal's toadies. Theology such as God and his wife living on their own planet and the afterlife faithful getting their own to rule rang preposterous. We rained down a million questions. Jerome took great delight reproducing his hero Socrates' dialogues. So logical were we that our unwitting proselytizers—perhaps their two best to make short work of meddling Moonie amateurs—ultimately questioned their own faith. The visits abruptly stopped. There was no percentage converting Mormons in a small town dominated by a large congregation in its priciest church. We'd only listened with innocent, if pointed and somewhat barbed, queries. I discovered the Socratic really was an effective means of drawing knowledge out of folks who'd never learned it. *Respect, Socrates.*

～

In early September Jerome's younger, muscled cousin Seranie revealed in a giggly phone call that her spindly older sister Tamela was in love with me. Speech. Less. I'd never heard such a come-on.

"Is she serious?" I junked the heavy old phone in its cradle on the small table near our second-floor, street-side window. "Heck, isn't she that skinny sixteen year old throwing stones? How can a kid like that even mean it?"

Bedeviled, he contemplated it awhile. "It's a heaven-sent opportunity, Chris. How can you marry Shiori"—he all but spat her name—"and expect to do anything for God and True Parents, like Restore slavery and racism?"

"Well . . . ."

"She doesn't understand a damn thing about blacks and doesn't like us, either." He swaggered over to wedge himself onto the opposite-end casement windowsill, all but hanging out over our streetside courtyard. He hammered me with reasons why marrying Shiori was my spiritual death knell. "I'm telling you, she'll create nothing but trouble for you and wreck our mission, whether it's here or in America. When a man marries the wrong woman, he's as good as dead."

Don't you know it! I was imagining breaking the news to Shiori and not liking my prospects. "I don't know, Jerome. How about the Matching? The very idea—"

"Marry Tamela." Stridence mushroomed. "She's the obvious choice. She's my cousin, part of one of the most important spiritual families on this island. And she's young. You can easily train her to follow you in your mission so she won't be the pain in the ass American women are. Or Shiori. And," he stabbed a hard 'B' at me, "she's *black*. When we're back in America, she'll be the perfect wife for a Unification Church leader. Father's big on Restoring blacks and whites and he'll definitely look on your marriage and lick his chops! Isn't that what you want?"

"Father's approval would be a nice touch, I have to admit." I'd be golden and not just for the Blessing. But, still. "I'm doing okay as a single minister. I don't need to get married to a local girl to make our mission work."

He laughed in that you're-so-adorable-when-you're-stupid way. "Nobody trusts single missionaries. In fact," I could see the wheels behind his eyes grinding into motion with their few busted gear teeth, "we should *both* get married."

"You?!" I practically shouted in surprise. "Who would you get married to?"

345

He grinned but I didn't catch his knowing secret. "Man, the women on this island are throwing themselves at me. I can have anybody I want!"

"Pshaw! You didn't get Gem."

"She threw away God's gift, that's all. Girls like her are a dime a dozen around here. Anyway, we can have a double wedding! Think about it, Chris. It'll be the biggest thing this island's ever seen . . . ever! A white American and black Vincy from America marrying into the island family. It'll open all the doors for us." As the idea phalanxed itself in his head to ward off my trepidation, he got more and more adamant that God was now directing us in this direction. "Even Father had to get married. Otherwise, everybody's lurid imagination would've had him willy-nilly banging all the women in his church. Tamela is a Vincentian True Mother."

"Hmm." I was warming to his persuasive argument. Still and all, I was hardly amenable to marrying to pick up a mission asset. What if it changed? what then? No, it was ridiculous . . . on the other hand, I felt some cockeyed attraction to her. Not a physical one because she was only a twiggy kid, not a woman. Some vibe, maybe. Something undefinable like . . . God's call?

"Besides," Jerome continued, "Shiori barely speaks English. Nobody understands half a damned thing out of her mouth, least of all Vincies. Tamela speaks the lingo and everybody knows her through me and my family. And, she's likable."

"Point taken, but I'm lucky to get forty percent of anything she says." Her speech hardly seemed English. I did more "What? what?" with her than with Shiori by far. But she was taller, younger and, critically, more likely fertile. These last few years I'd been pining hard for a family. For whatever reason and despite no precautions whatsoever, Shiori hadn't so much as mused a missed menses.

"I see what you're thinking. You'll have great kids. The most beautiful mixed-race babies out there. What's Shiori gonna give you? She's barren, man, you have to see that by now. I know you've been screwing that silly bitch bareback."

"For God's sake, Jerome! Watch your bloody mouth!"

"Aren't you, though? You ever knock her up? And how long you been at it?"

"Whatever. I don't want to marry outside the church anyhow. I want Father to Match me! I want to be Blessed!"

I dreamed of a Korean bride although the exotic, romantic mystery had faded under Kyung Mi's cultural realities. It now rooted shamelessly in church politics. But the more Jerome silver tongued me, the more I was seeing the hopelessness of ever persuading a church leader to recommend me to the Blessing much less Father Matching me to sacred Korean womanhood and the increasingly qualitative value of a union with Tamela. We'd committed to at least a 3-year stay in St. Vincent. We now had business plans that might keep us here longer, maybe years more.

Jerome had a point about Shiori, dammit. She'd never accept living in St. Vincent. She'd nag me endlessly to go back home to America and we'd end up fighting about it so much—she was already vexatiously badgering me over the phone to come home—that nobody would fail to notice the minister's bad marriage. It would be a black mark against everything I wanted to accomplish. *Shit!* And what use was a childless marriage? As much as I loved her—I damn sure did—a childless couple in Divine Principle's view, where fruitfully multiplying is a key component, was destined for true Restoration's dung heap. This is why the church encourages fertile Blessed couples to donate babies to second-rate infertile ones.

I was ready for marriage. I'd tired of bacheloring. All my church friends were Blessed with children on their knees. I felt left out, family and salvation always just beyond my fingertips. Would I end up waiting into my forties, my sixties or, God forbid, till never? Not me, no sir. I wanted a family and the church was cheating me out of it. I had to break with church doctrine and the Principle howsoever much I abhorred the very idea of marrying in the fallen world—at last, the mindset Nanami had yearned for in '87—and trust Rev. Moon someday opening the Blessing past the previously married to ex-members who'd *chosen* to marry an 'outside Eve' from Satan's side. After Ergela and Wren, what was realistically left to me? My Principled future looked bleak and tragic and nothing else.

TAMELA AND I spent time at Sion Hill beach in the company of her family and cousins falling in love. I felt even more drawn to her when we raced each other over the sand and she beat me by a leg. I'd had to dig deep at the last moment to lose by only that much. *Wow! A woman who can outrun me!* It was endearing. I felt her a woman of strength, endurance, power. In weeks, we broached marriage. My walls were falling like Jericho's at the sound of her many intriguing horns.

I was scared to announce my possible intentions, as she was so young. A 32-years American marrying a soon-to-be 17-years Vincy would be staggering news, the subject of all manner of leery gossip. Conventions oddly seemed to prefer white men screw Vincy women for fun than take them out of the culture as *bona fide* brides. I'd balked and she pressured me to broach it with Nathalie. We talked on their veranda: damn near my Waterloo. If Hugh were there he might've

Sion Hill Bay. We raced its beach.

thrown me over the railing. Facial contortions howled her thoroughly scandalized distrust. Friends and family opined I was marrying to drop Tamela in a shallow American grave for the life insurance I'd be sure to take out if I hadn't already. In Texas, even Tamela briefly construed this ruse in my innocuous words.

The reality was that I'd genuinely fallen for her innocence, humor, kindness, compassion, and a vernal *joie de vivre* as yet undiseased by the cynicism wearying my own. One of the things that impressed me (and made a good argument God was smiling) was that, in the staggeringly sexualized milieu in which she was raised, Tamela managed to remain a virgin. Seranie and their close friends were sexually active or amateur prostitutes extolling the unbanked riches languishing between their legs. Having met me, she ached to cast her overaged purity to the winds.

"We is made for each oth-uhh and now be 'de time. I been wait long enough." Her friends described its flaming, orgasmic sensations and flashed their booty cash to prove their credibility. "I wan' know it for me-self!" Painfully shy in almost every respect, she could jabber on about sex like lunch till my face colored sunset.

Unfortunately for all her lobbying—a red flag I didn't pick up—I begged off kicking tires. After Shiori, I was more determined than ever to honor celibacy. Nathalie was slowly coming round to the idea that I might soon be her son-in-law. Yet, strong opposition deluged her with terrifyingly plausible scenarios. She gave then revoked permission, recanted under pressure from me, then refused, recanted, refused, and recanted even more till promising to hold fast. Still, she didn't believe I was serious and made no effort to plan ahead until, in America with Jerome raising funds, I sent US$200 to pay for a dress. This was more than enough EC dollars and she took my honest intentions to the bank.

Although I'd decided, I wanted a 40-day spiritual condition to feel certain I was making a wise decision. To feel God's comforting hand on my shoulder. Jerome's off-the-cuff remark that if "a man marries the wrong woman, he's as good as dead" still loudly belled in my head because he was the expert. I paraphrased it to Tamela in my interviews as, "The wrong woman will destroy a man's life," which she waved away like flies. If I only knew then what I was talking about.

IN THE MIDST of this, Jerome and I sailed home a week into September from a day trip to Bequia Island, south of St. Vincent, on board the 5 PM state-run ferry. We approached Prime Minister James Mitchell, whom I'd spied clambering aboard as the crew threw its lines for departure. Being an American used to fanatical security around my president, I was too chicken to try. Jerome saw no security detail and casually strode right up to him in the wheelhouse. I videotaped their meeting but a minute into my turn he called, "Sorry, dead battery." He left the private cabin to where we'd repaired to fetch batteries and to puke up the kicking seas.

Mitchell said, "You two'd never have been able to meet me like this under other circumstances without specific government business." I took it as providential we'd missed the 2 PM boat my bored self had tried for. "How long are you staying?"

"As long as our visa, to start." I cycled through some of our plans. "Besides that, I'd like to start some businesses to help St. Vincent."

He grunted, gazed over the cabin rail into the sea as Bequia fell astern. "It'll be difficult. You'd need to do something new . . . that a Vincentian can't or won't."

"I don't know. I see many possibilities. I'd like to start a newspaper, though."

He perked up. "That's a good idea. It would be good for those . . . publications to have some competition."

The politicized rag called *The Vincentian* and the semi-politicized opposition paper *The News* hammered him every week with no friendly outlet of his own to report his point of view. "I'd definitely run it apolitically; you know, American style. News is news and editorial is editorial. It wouldn't be just another tabloid devoted to whoever's in or out of power."

"That's actually just what St. Vincent needs. What's your experience?"

"Besides writing and some journalism in school—I graduated from University of California at Berkeley—and running my own business in San Francisco, I was news editor and assistant editor-in-chief of *The Middle East Times* in Cyprus."

"That'll do."

"So you know . . . my editorials will trash government players if deserved."

"I have no problem with that. Welcome it, in fact."

"Even you. Policy-wise, not personal attacks, I mean. You'll have an unbiased opportunity to air your side, too. No bad attitudes."

His expression turned thoughtful. "If you move forward, the government would be willing to give you duty-free concessions without any customs interference to bring in whatever equipment you need—computers, presses, just give me a list."

"I'd appreciate that! Had trouble getting my Macintosh out of the airport."

He didn't even blush. "I know you can find all the investors you need right here in St. Vincent, and I can connect you with all of them."

"Well . . . that's quite . . . enticing."

"They'd be more than willing to invest in a good newspaper. We can set up some government printing contracts and advertising to help get you started. I could help you with those things, no problem."

I reeled and not from the corkscrewing sea. "That's absolutely terrific. We will totally take you up on that."

"You have a name for it?"

"*The St. Vincent Times*, 'The heartbeat of St. Vincent and the Grenadines.' "

"I love it!" We shook hands. "You can talk to me anytime about the paper. Just call my office. I'll set it up."

This was easier than I could've imagined. Too good to be true, yet it was. Mitchell was tired of the constant drumbeat of political enemies and longed for a news outlet that would at least report the facts without a counterclockwise spin.

Coming into Kingstown's harbor, he described his plans for a cruise ship terminal. "It'll be right there." His eyes followed his pointing arm over the lapping sea.

"That's right under Jerome's family land. We were thinking of expanding that small church at the bottom of the cliff . . . or putting up a small, local university."

He braced me. "A school? Hmm. Maybe."

True to his word, he set up a meeting with Sir Karl T. Hudson-Phillips, one of the wealthiest lawyers in the Caribbean basin with homes on multiple islands. Recently knighted by the Queen of England, he carried *mucho* weight. Bringing him on as an investor plus a board member would be a real coup.

"I am very enthused with your newspaper idea as the Prime Minister explained it. To do it, I will set you up with a printer in Trinidad and a line of credit."

"Isn't it easier and cheaper to print here?"

He breathed a smile. "There isn't one for a proper newspaper. But Trinidad prints and ships in one day."

"Oh. Okay, then. I should think we'll bring in our own at some point."

An early mock-up.

"I will bring you up with the business community in Kingstown for advertising commitments. However, we must keep this all very hush-hush. If *The News* finds out what we're up to, they'll move heaven and earth to thwart our plans."

"Could they shut us down?"

"They'd try. And it wouldn't look good for the Prime Minister. But don't worry about *The Vincentian*, he's almost out of business anyway."

After meeting with Hudson-Phillips, Jerome and I thought it was a good idea to buy *The Vincentian* outright and knock off our weakest competitor from the get-go. Its owner was a political malcontent but locally connected in the business and political communities. We'd heard through other sources that he was interested in selling because his paper was unprofitable in its current form.

He showed off his large offset press one afternoon with me in the same linen sports jacket Robert had forced me to buy to bag our restaurants in San Francisco. "My local and foreign vendors will supply everything you need. No problem. A straight hand off. You can go over my records with an agreement in principle."

We deemed it a simple matter changing *The Vincention*'s mast to *The St. Vincent Times* without losing much if any of his anemic readership. We'd expand it. Some days later we did a repeat with the chief editor and an owner of *The News*.

In 1991 both newspapers sold weekly editions Fridays along the sidewalks and at certain shops in Kingstown and a few major towns. If a person wanted a paper, they had to get to one of these distribution points. I calculated circulation was far below the number of literate Vincentians and figured to boost circulation with those potential readers through home delivery, a method as yet unutilized. I designed a route system, distribution, delivery procedures, price, and pay. If it worked as hoped, it would make us local heroes for creating new jobs. Not great jobs, maybe, but paid work nonetheless. To entice workers to sign up, I chose to pay 40% of the cover price to our delivery people, which was 10–15% over what the other papers were paying their street sellers. In short order, they'd have to meet our pay plan or fall in our dust. Either way left us economic icons. That was Plan One.

Plan Two was using high school students interested in gaining experience in writing and journalism as stringers around the island to ferret out news stories, photos, and interviews. This helped our bottom line and effectively incubated future media professionals to jumpstart their careers and improve our business prospects. We'd pay EC$10 per photo and a sliding scale for stories. Without a professional, adult staff to pay besides Jerome part-time, a secretary, a senior reporter–editor, and me, we could operate well under *The News*' bottom line. It would help us over initial losses developing home delivery, a stringer network, and the certain short-term dearth of early adopter advertising *The News* would certainly instigate.

We were still short two crucial items. We needed several computers and printers, and eventually our own press in St. Vincent. We could generate offset press revenue as well as print our paper for less than cost-plus-shipping from Trinidad. *The News* was often held up by printing or shipping problems (such as weather) that delayed issues from a half to several days. Disastrous for the new baby on the block.

"I can help you purchase a press," Hudson-Phillips said, "but later."

"It's worth it because I imagine we can build a profitable joint venture to locally print *The News* like some US papers do."

He'd nodded throughout. "When you have proved the paper. Don't worry."

Jerome witnessed and we kept up our heavy preaching schedule with churches in Kingstown and the oft-unelectrified hinterlands. Meanwhile I developed software on my Macintosh to automate the project from classifieds to stories. I printed a full-sized mockup of our 24-page publication showcasing its sections. We carried a television listing the other papers didn't or else abridged for paid space, a regular interview, local news by town and parish, East Caribbean and general Caribbean news, American news pertinent to Vincies or their families in America, England, and Canada plus select international news. I designed a comprehensive business section unknown to the other papers. The PM's and Hudson-Phillips' connections would bridge relationships to top business leaders here and on neighboring islands, further helping me produce useful, discriminating business news. I gratefully appreciated Floyd for my journalistic street cred both men had bought into.

One of the financial problems I wanted to confront head-on from the start was the local retail industry's refusal to provide credit. Everything required cash on the barrelhead. Near Christmas, businesses offered credit to a select few but the poor-waged public was usually excluded. I felt St. Vincent's economic picture would brighten considerably if everyone with a job could obtain store credit with weekly or monthly payments. More refrigerators, stoves, chairs, and other appliances could be sold, better liquefying St. Vincent's molassic velocity of money. Ironically, though, we justified their tepid attitude when nearly a year later our own credit-purchased refrigerator was repossessed by a squealing pickup truck of men when my cash-starved bank and credit cards couldn't meet the payments. Well, they got their like-new fridge back for resale anyway.

I planned to make *The St. Vincent Times* the premier option for the few tourists passing through and ensuring it sold alongside *The News* in New York City, Toronto, Montreal, and London where Vincy immigrants congregated. It was a stepping stone to my bigger dream of creating the West Indies' first regional news magazine, the *Time* magazine of the Caribbean. With a successful newspaper supporting my pocket and reputation, I knew it would be relatively easy to secure the necessary investment and collaboration to pull it off. I thought I could accomplish this dream within 3–5 years. Once accepted in the market, I planned to sell my majority stake and move back to America to pursue working directly with Rev. Moon. This feat seemed achievable on the back of my Caribbean success story. As I've said before, he loves a winner and the church a man with a chubby checkbook. My mission outlook underwent a subtle shift as my plans for the newspaper unfolded.

While I still intended to witness in St. Vincent and build up our local Family Home Church Association entity, it morphed into more of a philanthropic effort than a missionary activity. Business and especially self-support was taking center stage due in no small part to Rev. Moon now routinely insisting we were responsible for our own support and should become billionaires like him. I didn't think I was abrogating any agreement I might've made with God owing to my partnership with Jerome and the church's closed-fisted pocketbook. Jerome was more interested in developing our internal, spiritual mission of church-building anyhow. I gravitated toward developing our external, physical mission of support. I was St. Stephen to his St. Paul. It was a good arrangement. The prime minister, Attorney General Parnell 'Pointer' Campbell, Hudson-Phillips, and others supported us. It would've worked if Jerome hadn't self-destructed in the process.

IT ACCELERATED IN earnest after returning to America in October for a cross-country fundraising trip to finance our FHCA mission, double wedding, formal establishment of our newspaper, and airfare back. My Shiori situation didn't help. Jerome could be puritanical regardless his lasciviousness. Notwithstanding he and his brothers not wanting me in their St. Alban's house, he castigated me for sharing her rented room for the week it took to get his old Ford on the road. She was ecstatic having me back in the flesh, anxious to renew our bond whilst I to break it apart. I hadn't yet mentioned I was engaged to Tamela. I still wildly loved her and this macabre situation I'd put myself into was conflicting me on a cellular level.

What should I do? whose heart do I break? It had to be Shiori's. Not only was she probably too old for children or anyhow infertile—I just couldn't overlook that—but I'd spent the last two years at war with God *and* Satan over her. I was convinced God didn't approve our entanglement. Every minute I clung to her like a lifebuoy in the Sea of Alone I was wrecking both our lives and heavenly standing.

Tamela's send off at the airport.

Love is tearing me apart! Isn't it supposed to do the opposite? I resonated to the old lyric, "If loving you is wrong, I don't want to be right." Yet, I *wanted* to be right. I wanted—*had*—to do my duty to God, not shirk it. Weighing up my future, I realized it boiled down to this: my love for Tamela was public and my love for Shiori personal. If there's one rubric in Rev. Moon's life, it's that public duty outranks personal desire. The former served me but the latter God and His providence to Restore humanity out of suffering into happiness. It was impossible to sacrifice humanity on the altar of personal feelings. I knew I had to leave Shiori and marry Tamela for exactly that reason.

How do I tell her? how to take a life to save a life? That's what it was: slay her heart for humanity's. I couldn't bear her tears nor the image of her fractured life. So, I did what every good coward does. I procrastinated by motoring west with Jerome selling metal foil prints, an MFT favorite, in every moneyed town and city in our path. He had thousands all matted and ready for sale jammed in his car's trunk—where he'd got them, I'd no idea—and we marched house-to-house and shop-to-shop earning our food, gas, and mission bread. It was a grim three glacial months slogging ice that carried us across the forests, plains, mountains, and deserts to California and back, sacked out in the car or with family. And much to my chagrin and frank surprise, my family recoiled the moment they met and lambasted me for the temerity of bringing him over. They later said they found him arrogant, selfish, strange . . . not much different from their experience with Shiori in 1990.

Well, shit. I was batting 3-0 with my family if you include Rev. Moon in the standings, and I hadn't even broached my impending marriage *to his cousin*. Worse, my parents and siblings flashbanged me with their belief the two of us were gay lovers. I practically keeled over in convulsive electric shock. My face drained dry from white to dead. If for a second I'd imagined them picturing me over, under, or in between Jerome—not sure how they saw *that* role—when we retired to our guest room for the night, I'd have bedded down with the bugs or snow.

Mother! Fucker!

They made sure to clap their backs with their Liberal nonjudgmental tolerance—"I mean, it's perfectly fine if you are, there's nothing wrong with it"—but their facepalming disgust was only too plain. Nor can you backpeddle out of the accusation because then they say, "Well, the lady doth protest too much, methinks."

This was the second time people just meeting Jerome would say he was giving off queer vibes. In St. Vincent following our American roadtrip, Nathalie's son Errol said (through Tamela), "When I been see 'dem two 'de first day, I know 'dem be queer and Jeh-rome 'de 'wo-maahn.' "

"You be so?" Tamela said. "You do so?"

"Ohmigod, no. How could—you see how it spreads? *No!*"

"I jus' been ax a queh-stion."

Glaring. "No, you weren't." I couldn't feel more devastated and disgraced by all these wrong assumptions by those who mattered to me. It tarred me from my hetero balls up through my ministerial career to my Blessed-life fantasy.

"All 'dem time you an' Jeh-rome wen' 'de beach"—planning and strategy sessions in the warm, paradisaical waters like real entrepreneurs—"ev'rybody been watch on 'de way say, ' 'Der go 'dem mission-arry to have at each oth-uhh in 'de bush.' "

"*Oh. My. God.* You must be kidding!" Her tick-tock chin said, *no fuckin' way.* My ribs dropped into a hollow cavern. I all but wept on my ministerial cross.

Deeply religious and Unificationist to boot, I'm staunchly heterosexual. The Principle views homosexuality as a perversion of right-ordered relationships twixt husband and wife conceiving children in the Principle's Four Position Foundation, the root of everything animate and inanimate in the universe. Rev. Moon spewed a vitriol on it I'd never seen from him during his 80th birthday party at the Washington Hilton. He'd stamped his feet. Lugied the carpet with a visceral contemner exceeding even his antipathy for Communism. The liberal and probably half-gay Washington elites sucking their wine were certainly disquieted, though no one stormed out. Maybe the $1,000 spaghetti came after the speech, I forget. Drowning in loneliness brought on by ruinous heterosexuality—let alone church leaders—there were times I thought I could try a little homosexuality for some no-strings-attached comfort. These swirling thoughts prompted a comprehension how same-sex behavior (versus same-sex love) develops in some heterosexuals.

In the church we tend to believe emotion and sinful spirit people expressing through living persons are primary motivators for aberrant behavior whether sexual or criminal. Behavioral genetics is a red herring. It's all about like-minded people finding common ground. The Principle teaches that if we endure and overcome then the sinful, influencing spirit person(s) is liberated from their sin, too, and free to grow and develop to a Principled, godly state. Unificationists view it as a public duty to resist sinful, especially sexual and in particular homosexual, temptations. The church kicking me out twelve times and denying me eight (known) Blessings wore on my sense of personal duty to public morality. Sin's temptation gained strength.

Thankfully for my own peace of mind I never gave in to it, although saying so is about as effective as *I never did that!* to, "Say, Bob, still beating your wife?"

I felt a distinction between homosexual *activities* and homosexuality as a *lifestyle*. I could see a person wanting to experiment or, deprived of the opposite sex, fulfilling needs with the same sex because, as Rev. Moon said in another context, a hole is a hole is a hole. And, too, lips are lips and skin is skin. *Midnight Express* eloquently expressed it through a squalid Turkish prison shower scene in 1978. I comprehended physical needs crying out for satisfaction and dropped my previous moral judgments beyond the basics of sexual fidelity. I never got the lifestyle elevating it to love, female mimicry, strident 'buffing,' and living together whether committed and monogamous or not. Homosexuality's perversion didn't necessarily come from going downtown for sexual pleasure as from corrupting God's original blueprint for ordered, happy, family-centric love relationships between birth moms and dads.

The monotheisms don't forget that humans are the very image of God. The Principle clarifies it by claiming God divided his unified nature into two parts. His masculine nature represents the majority of a man's nature and His feminine the majority of a woman's. Men observationally have a feminine self and women a masculine self. It's these minority selves that allow us to cognize and harmonize the opposite sex. Like all balancing acts, these characteristics can lose equilibrium in a sinful, fallen world especially under the influence of unseen spirit persons.

Thus, religion typically sees homosexuality's perversion in the acts themselves. Not me. I saw it in the abandonment of family oriented relationships regardless a minority adopting children. Homosexuality was self-oriented toward one's partner and the present, and heterosexuality other-oriented toward children and the future. Fertilizing eggs in a Petri dish didn't change that. Homosexuality was a threat to social health when an aggressive homosexual minority coerced the heterosexual majority to accept and tolerate its ideologism to discount its intrinsic familial deficit. It was in unsanctioned public expression that the perversion of relationship norms most effectively spreads. The dichotomy follows mindset and is thus irreconcilable in the context of today's spiritual and secular worldviews.

There will always be closet homosexuals and sanctimonious hypocrites. If it's in the closet, or as publicly modest as heterosexuals are expected to be in the public square, who cares? It's their business and between them and God. No one has any right to stop consenting behavior. But force fed as propaganda it's no longer consenting but coerced and people have a right to resist compelled behavior in themselves and their children. Go your consenting way and do what you want, I say, but don't shove it in my mouth and tell me to swallow.

My family's belief I was gay bit deep. But friends and family presuming Jerome gay drew blood. *Is he?* No spiritual aura or behavior ever tipped me off. I'd caught no vibe or sly cat eyes. Frankly, I disbelieved it. *I've known him ten years!* To miss something so profound about a person for that long unsettled me. But, I'd let that sleeping dog lie. Part of my reasoning was that, after returning to St. Vincent in late January 1992, I'd discovered he was anything but chaste.

Tamela would say, "Chris, *ev'rybody* say him homosexual. 'Dem see he go for hours inside maahn house."

"Probably witnessing or something. These people are such gossip mongers."

"People 'dem say 'de maahn 'dem be homosexual. I believe 'dem."

"Everybody I meet says he's between any woman's legs . . . stop shaking your head, darn it. Hardly the queer's moniker, that. And he's marrying—"

"Maahn can do both. You willfully be close your eyes. He is a baahd maahn."

Jeez. I couldn't catch a break. His intemperate outbursts with family escalated his libertine rep and was scaring off investors and advertisers. He was a Salem witch trial millstone taking our ministerial credibility to the innocent bottom.

FUNDRAISED OUT, JEROME and I reappeared January 6 in Hellhole, USA. We stayed at my former (not CCSF) roommate Robert's at 34-38 42nd Street in Queens. I'd called Shiori from St. Vincent about my mission but she'd ordered me home. I wrote her of my impending marriage from California. She'd closed our joint savings account then pretended she didn't know my intentions. I collected my belongings.

Then called two days later. "My passport and computer disks are missing."

"Why should I know where it all is? Ha ha ha."

I grated teeth then showed up with Jerome as a human shield around 10 PM. She let me hunt through her apartment half an hour before revealing the disks in a secret compartment. "You hiding my passport, too, just to get me over here to see you?"

"No! I not want you." At last she pulled it from one of her make-up purses.

I snapped it up. "Are you trying to force me to love you like this?"

"Do not be stupid. Am I child like you?"

"Shiori, I asked you to marry me under the condition of following my mission, and you said no."

"I not say no. Are you crazy?"

"You sure did say no. I asked you very specifically to support my God-given mission a hundred percent without argument. Instead, you tried talking me out of my commitment. To get me to live a private life. That's a big fat no in my book."

"You not know what you talking." Her voice pouted.

"You disobeyed me at every turn. Spent our money on two new apartments when I said not to move. You refused to consider Jerome, my *brother*, and turned him out in the cold when we returned from St. Vincent. You cursed him and blacks over and over." She was silent. "Your September phone call was an hour of crying to force me home, to abandon my faith and mission. My heart broke!" Tears burnt hot and heavy. My antagonistic desires were contesting armies hacking through my ribs. "My feelings . . . I don't know, changed somehow from all that."

"What you mean?" My heart was in my throat. "Stupid. You no love me."

"You don't love *me*! You just need me. Hiding my passport was childish and unloving." She traipsed around her apartment. "You rejected *me*. I love you so much but I can't shut out God! We're Moonies! What do you expect of me?"

"You think this person in St. Vincent will follow your so-called mission?" Her laughing punched my ears. "She is fooling you. Using you."

"No worse than you! She didn't reject my mission when I explained myself. She was honestly unsure, yeah, but willing to try."

"Pfff! I read your letter to Mrs. Kobayashi. She is very angry you separating."

"That's rich. She's been harassing me all this time to do just that!"

"She say you only follow your own desire, not Principled way."

"So what? She hates me now. Nothing's changing that." More tears flooded. My thoughts battered. *I love you so much, dammitall to hell! I don't want to leave you!*

"I can go to St. Vincent with you. I want to do."

"Now you say that?" *Sonuva. Bitch!* "I want you to be happy, but I have to follow God as I understand it." I wanted her and a private life but felt a greater duty to God and His public life. *Fuck me to death for ever devastating her, for selfishly letting her love me!* The pressure was crushing. It seemed my heart had to burst. *I'm rejecting the woman I truly love to marry one I don't even know for God's providence.* I wrote, "I barely got out of Shiori's house. I was in tears. I didn't want to abandon her." My Matching was agony.

Jerome and Avril at our left.

THE CHURCH OF Canon Carlisle Free in Sion Hill was a void when Jerome and I scooted inside February 8 for our 3 PM double wedding. We'd met his next wife Avril (an off-and-on prostitute, he said; sable features were my German great grandmother's doppelgänger) our second day at the door to her aged, ramshackle wood house she platonically shared with a Trumpet cripple halfway up Sion Hill edging Rasta country. Perfectly aligned ivories dazzled from a sunny smile. I was immediately delighted.

"Some smile! What a handsome woman."

He'd belched a guffaw. "So, you want to sleep with her then."

"Don't be absurd. It was a simple observation, not a come-on."

"If you say so." But now look how things were.

Within an hour, the Free twins' church benches were shoulder to shoulder and included a few top ministers from the government. We'd invited Prime Minister Mitchell and AG Campbell, but they'd begged off at the last minute; probably politics. I invited my whole family, too. Disappointment hung heavy that not only did none of them turn up—to be fair, it was short notice and an expensive haul—they didn't call or write congratulations. My parents mirrored Nathalie when I'd announced my engagement during our road trip visit but kept their disparaging shock resolutely close. I hadn't noticed beyond taking for mere surprise their dour expressions and wary eye shots. I'd anticipated a certain level of disagreement. To stave off needless argument, I'd advanced Tamela's age to a respectable eighteen.

Mom said, "Our only"—verbalized—"concern is whether you'll be happy with a woman whose educational level is so far below yours."

"Pssh! That's only now. She'll do college, no sweat." And . . . right outta mind.

Younger sister Blair said as we opened car doors on her cold driveway, "Remember, Chris, we're a Catholic family that doesn't believe in divorce. Be sure it's right."

I was 32 not 12. "She definitely doesn't approve," I told Jerome off the driveway. But within ten years only Blair and my folks . . . well, their stories to tell.

He shrugged it off. "Forget 'em. They don't know God's will."

A bit tardy, Tamela's car nosed aside a throng of some 300 lookie-loos blocking our packed-to-capacity church's road on three sides. Our double wedding was sensational. Add in a white American marrying an underaged local . . . a spectacle for the ages. She warily climbed stone steps from the road through hushed admirers and glided through the cinder-blocked front entrance, pausing a moment to survey the whitewashed, rectangular high-ceilinged room. The intensity of the day backlit the lustrous, classical bone white wedding gown that arrayed her form. Only now I saw what my money had bought. The crowd flocked round the building. Shifting faces pressed to glass to catch her parading up the central aisle to my waiting side and the coming show. Her hazy face and burning, darting bright eyes lay under Catholic lace. Lifting her veil showcased Nathalie's cosmetic arts. Beauty sucked my lungs dry.

In true Spiritual Baptist fashion, the brothers Free rattled over an hour through a regular service before

Marrying Tamela Feb. 8, 1992.

getting to the elephant in the room. Finally, Jerome and Avril stood themselves to Tamela's and my left at the raised concrete dais. We repeated our vows. Signed the marriage documents laid out in the altar's corner. Headed into brilliant sunshine and a cheering, gaping crowd. I wore Shiori's beautiful white custom linen, double-breasted suit she'd made me two years ago in New York City. My gall wasn't lost on me, but it was my only appropriate suit on the shoestring funding our operation. Jerome, financially defunct as always, borrowed a dark suit, tie, and shoes.

Our driver gingerly pressed us through the crowd. Outstretched hands from cheering well-wishers brought me leaning out the front passenger window with my elastic grin a plastered-up billboard. I shook hands and slapped palms till we cleared the crush for the open, one-lane road. I felt like a movie star. *This is how it'll be someday*, I cheerily told myself. *When my newspaper and magazine are successful, people will know me, appreciate me, want to be seen with me. How unlike my treatment by the Unification Church and its maleficent leaders!* The press snapping photos of our celebrity affair seemed the first savory taste of more to come.

It almost didn't even happen. Not ten days before, in the excited wake of our return and Tamela's new certainty her wedding would happen, she'd visited Bramble House. "Chris, I ha' to tell you a sec-ret. If you don't wan' marry to me, I'll go and nev-uuh both-uhh you again. Ma say I mus' tell you. She understan' if you change your mind." Tears wet her eyes. She struggled with her voice. "I—I can'a read."

My stupefied mouth fell open in a wordless scream. How could a person *not* be literate in this day and age? Uniformed schoolchildren littered the streets morning and afternoon. Did she grow up feral on Mt. Soufrière's jungled, volcanic slopes? "*Pshaw*, come on, quit pulling my leg. Anybody can read."

"No, really, me a' lyin'. I was top-marks when my skull got broke open at fifteen. I lose me talkin'. I write notes for Ma in hospi-taahl. When I could talk again, doctor 'dem say keep me out o' school a year." She shrugged. "Then I forget."

"How's a person forget—?" Stupefied understated it. "How'd your skull break?"

"I fell." She clammed up with that. Days later under quite a bit of pressure from me she said, "I did some t'ing and Ma hus-baahnd chase me aahll ov-uhh 'de house before him catch me arm. He beat me head wi' Errol police stick."

"He—? A truncheon? The hell you didn't tell the police? Errol's a—!"

Tears wallowed down her cheeks. "Ma insis' I lie to protec' 'de family. She say him be go jail if people 'dem know." Beatings were hardly uncommon in St. Vincent. I'd witnessed plenty in homes and streets myself. But not nightsticks over a child's head. *Shit!* "You mus'n'a say anyt'ing, Chris! Not even to Ma. I not s'ppose tell you. Ma warn me. Please! Don't tell no-body! Especially Jeh-rome!"

I slapped my forehead and not metaphorically. It took awhile to absorb her preposterous truth. The crossroads it put me in set me afire. It smacked of Shiori. I desperately wanted to prosecute the bastard then and there if not hunt him down in the night like a mangy cur, but she'd have none of it.

"That's crazy," I seethed. "No! He ruined your life! He robbed me of my wife!"

"I serious, Chris. Don't mek Ma even suspec' you know!"

Fuck! I was in a conspiracy. She'd seemed so reasonably normal to me. Mentally active. Inquisitive. Even without an educated vocabulary and knowledge base, she came off articulate. She'd dreamed of becoming a lawyer but her family, recognizing reality, pissed her fire out. Contemplating how she skillfully and quickly cored out contradictions and fallacies to shut arguers up, I thought (even after this bombshell) she'd make a great trial lawyer once she re-learned reading and I'd put her through school. On that basis, I felt compelled to marry her, that God was giving me an opportunity to symbolically 'raise her up' till my equal in every sense of the word. *I know*, goddammit. The White Man's disease. But in my defense it was rampant then and in my Unificationist mind didn't seem haughty or scornful at all, just our basic Restoration through indemnity work for God.

Jerome forcefully said, "Chris, your marriage carries a powerful undercurrent of racial reconciliation with black and white Americans still race rioting. It's a no-brainer anyway. Aren't you a Unificationist? Forget about her situation."

"Father's Way of the Servant? Resolving resentment and historical wrongs through a life of indemnity?"

"Exactly. It's your cross. Your special opportunity to contribute in a meaningful way to world reconciliation. It isn't just your marriage but the world's. Symbolic Restoration of the relationship between hateful whites and vengeful blacks."

"Yeah, it's true I'm seeing it that way . . ." *Because. I Am. A Moonie.*

When I married Tamela, I was powerfully enamored but not sure I personally loved her the way I desperately loved Shiori, Nanami under the surface, and far-back Diane. But I loved God. In Tamela I saw God and His mission and love for me. God never asks a person to do something they hate or can't do. Rather, as Rev. Moon taught us, there's always some element of a mission that a person is capable of loving more than him- or herself. God was asking me to marry a woman for a greater cause than my own happiness while at the same time finding me someone *I could genuinely love in happiness*. I did and still do, even though . . . well, that's later.

"I expec' you be call off our weddin'," she said after tying our knot. "I was sure you would . . . I a' wan' tell you. My blasted conscience wouldn'a shut up."

"You only gave me a week or so. Cut it pretty close."

"I put it off. I sorry!"

"Why not just—?"

"Becau' I mus' go back to Seven Days . . . 'dem people shame and humiliate me wi' out mercy, becau' 'dem hate you. 'Dem kick me out for marry to you."

"Because I'm not Adventist?"

"An' white. 'Dem people nev-uhh be ha' you nor us togeth-uhh in 'dem church."

"Pish!" Yet, little different from what I'd soon encounter with the Moonies. We had that in common, at least. I'd never run into illiteracy. It seemed so easy . . . unthinkable she couldn't re-learn unless brain damaged, and I didn't see that. With confidence in my own perspicuity I'd stuck with her, happy to pay for school. I had complete confidence in her story and educability. Who would lie about that? What could go wrong?

Concluding our lengthy photo session— extended family, children, cousins, God knows who else—at the hemisphere's oldest Botanical Gardens on 20 acres, we set off for a rented hall on a forested slope for our

Botanical Gardens with Rev. Free.

evening double reception. Nathalie and Hugh funded most of our two-cake-two-meal guest list. Avril's beggared share banned music, dancing, and alcohol.

"We're ministers," Jerome pontificated. "We can't give in to their satanic rituals."

"Now you're a Puritan? Don't be surprised if they bring their own."

"I'll kick them out!"

I chortled. "More likely they'll put you on a rail. Better watch out."

Our caterers brought the tools. Crashers amped up the sin. Guests stalked into Jerome's grim determination at our long, white-clothed table at the head of the room to vociferously complain. " 'Dis be 'de absolutely boringest reception ev-uhh to disgrace our is-laahnd. And you, who should know bett-uhh!"

He impotently relented as music, dancing, and spirits flowed past him. Tamela's family slit a goat's throat that morning with a cutlass. Jerome videotaped its awful bleating. Our cooks now served it up deliciously spiced on plates with rice. My first goatmeat was savory. I forced its staggering, arterial-jetting image out of mind so I could fork it in with a gracious smile. Americans aren't used to seeing dinner depart the barnyard on wings of angels.

Our evening reception drunkenly wound down with only one fistfight, whom the mostly sober crowd arm-twisted out the door. Jerome and Avril waved away in a rented car. Apparently cruising a victory lap, a grinning Jerome idled past us hoofing along the darkened road to Town Hill in my linen suit and Tamela her expensive gown clutched above her ankles. Avril laughingly lorded Rich Man wheels over Poor Man shoe leather. It brought to mind lugging Tamela's leaden suitcases on foot from Cane Garden to Town Hill in the dead of night because Nathalie refused me a ride as an insult. Then they ran our own wedding-night victory lap off road.

No sooner stumbling in on sore, cowboy-booted and bare feet (Tamela's medium heels weren't roadworthy) Jerome said, "I misplaced my mic and wire. It's mission critical. I need your help before one of these t'iefs find it. Please, man?"

"You must be kidding." By midnight, energy spent, I found Tamela crashed.

Auntie Nathalie and Tamela.

Jerome had carted home the wedding gifts in his opulent rental. The next morning we opened them in our second-floor living room. Tamela plopped into my newly married lap. He snapped at her to get off. We refused, gayly. Sullen, he turned to unwrapping and excitedly discovered all but one of the 25-plus gifts were addressed to them and proudly opened them in front of us like hens clucking over eggs.

"I'm sooo sorry, Tamela," Avril laughed all day long, "that nobody t'ink to give you two anyt'ing. It's because you're so young."

"It seems awfully weird, Jerome, that—"

"Are you accusing me or my wife of taking Tamela's wedding presents? This is St. Vincent honoring its own. You're the stranger here."

"Well, Tamela isn't!" We hadn't checked the pile, though. *Was* she just young and friend-poor? her family tapped out? Then she fielded dismaying inquiries from friends and family about their gifts.

"You couldn't at leas' phone a t'ank you? Your white hus-baahnd be stop you?"

"Wha' mek you say so? We get nothin' from you. From no-body!"

As each described their gift, she soddenly realized Jerome and Avril had received not a one. During the night, and possibly as soon as Tamela went into bed while I was out helping Jerome find his unfindable video thingy, Avril had (with or without his connivance I never knew, but he never apologized for her outrageous dupery, either) readdressed all but one of our gifts to herself. I don't know how on God's green earth they imagined there'd be no blowback from such a fraud. Tamela blew up in a tabletop demonstration of Mt. Soufrière's pluming days, which launched a scandal that pyroclasted through every ear in town with all the heat and fury of the real thing. The damage between them was done. It was a catfight, now. Some of her friends replaced their gifts, but most couldn't.

That scurrilous morning heralded a new reality between Jerome and me, too. No longer were we intimate friends good naturedly discussing our mission and conflicting points of view via the rules of philosophical discourse. Our conversation was cantankerous. It hammered home after asking AG Campbell to help cut through my work visa's red tape as Jerome pried our finally-arriving barrels of belongings out of customs without being overtaxed per the usual.

"It's unPrincipled and unethical to use Campbell for that. Forget it."

"You just bribed the customs inspector and Avril's brother in the warehouse $230 EC to look the other way and pass our stuff through." Which I guessed was a bargain. The government mandated annual licenses of EC$100 for a TV and EC$250 for a VCR, stupidly forcing people into poverty or pre-industrialism. Satanic.

"That's not the same at all. The attorney general—"

"What's the difference? I'm not asking him to break any laws, just his help. You paying bribes to avoid taxes *is* illegal!"

"It's how things are done here. It's normal. You need to learn that."

"But not with Campbell? That's the same hypocrisy as you telling me, 'There's no excuse under the sun for beating children' when Yoland was beating Monique right in front of the church. But now it's okay for Avril to ruthlessly beat her kids here in our own house because, 'That's a mother's love'?"

"No white man has any right to interfere in how a black man deals with his family! You're twisting things to humiliate me. The white man takes power—"

"The hell are you talking about? What power? I'm not after controlling anybody! I don't like hearing her whacking her wailing kids, that's all."

"It's not your place. You have no say in it."

"Don't I live here?" Round and round for hours till I threw my hands up. Thus began my slow dawning that something serious was happening inside Jerome. It seemed like any other disagreement. But his hostile reaction to my observation and making a simple, *legal* request to the AG *for our mission*, and the complete absence of his usual deference to philosophical and rational standards of discussion sparked a worry I'd never felt with him. It was only the beginning.

A week into our marriage Tamela burst into our room where I hunkered before my computer god, music blasting through earphones while I furiously programmed my automated newspaper system.

"Jeh-rome jus' *hit* me! Wha' you g'wan do about it! You need to defen' me!"

My mouth fell open. I hadn't heard a thing through my headset. When I entered the living room with Tamela nipping my heels, Jerome was wearing a clouded, dark expression. Black eyes seized me. "Tamela says you hit her."

He was Papasan smooth. "Never happened. She's a lying, corrupt woman!"

I ignored his posturing and the 50–50 probability. "I can't do anything, Tamela. I didn't see it. You expect me to punch him out on your word? I can't do that."

"You care more for 'dis rot-tehn maahn than me!" Her tone edged violent. "Wait till Ma hears you le' some maahn jus' beat 'pon your wife!"

Ice gripped my gut. I was caught between my best friend of ten years and my wife of not even ten days. A paralyzing he-said-she-said. I followed my training. "Why didn't you call me out? I can't jump on anybody without seeing it or knowing—"

"You a' hear him bad mout' me becau' your stupid music and stupid newspa-pah!" She burst into tears. "You ain' love me! You love he!"

It was after our double wedding that Jerome began dangerously delaminating. My biggest mistake was thinking I could live in the same house with Avril, or that Tamela and Avril could get along after Avril stole all Tamela's wedding presents and heartlessly mocked her for having none. Half the trouble arose in Avril's control freakishness. She insisted on doing all the housework and cooking herself while refusing to teach Tamela, whose cooking skills were exactly zilch.

"Nathalie really dropped the ball with you there," I said with sympathy.

"Don't talk bad 'bout Ma. Jus' show me an' I can cook anyt'ing."

Then Avril complained to Jerome, "Your white man frien' be turning me into a slave. You let him bring back slavery to me? Wha' man are you?"

In this milieu Jerome revealed everything I'd said in confidence regarding Tamela and disengaging from Shiori (periodically calling our house, inciting Tamela to fits of jealousy). She gleefully shit every word into Tamela's ears who, in turn, violently confronted me with my own private feelings. I overheard Jerome's antagonistic bent in the kitchen through the floorboards responding to Avril's complaints.

"That's his strategy," he said. "White racism creates problems between you and me. Your response was just what he wanted. You fell right into his trap. I thought you were smart, but you did exactly what he wanted you to do." News to me.

"And wha' you g'wan do about it, eh? Is here your house or not?"

This, mere days after our wedding as they blamed me for their knock-down drag-out quarrels in their bedroom at the other end of the house that often barged into the living room. Time and again, he accused me of his own behavior. I should've moved out the instant this level of crazy popped up, but I couldn't. I didn't have a farthing. Our trip across America had only paid our expenses, airfare, shipping, wedding costs, and marginal pocket cash. Back in St. Vincent I was having to draw down my personal savings and credit cards to fund our entire household as well as our mission because Jerome didn't work and had no money.

Avril's control and martyr issues had her hating me and despising Tamela as "a stupid gyul." She cooked the food bought with my money, fed it to Jerome and her two small children on Tamela's gifted kitchenwares, threw away the remainder or cooled it in the refrigerator that I was paying for monthly, or after eating their fill sometimes called Tamela and me to come for their cold and soggy scraps, our only dinner. I guessed all that was her giant slapback for somebody else's slavery days of yore she'd never lived and I hadn't one goddamned thing to do with.

I was finally moved to say, "Don't bother cooking enough for us, because it's clear you salt it with the poisonous hate in your heart. We won't touch it."

"Whuh?! Hear 'de white maahn, Jeh-rome? Well, I don't cook *for you*, no how."

When Tamela tried to cook, Avril ran her out of the kitchen. Chasing her clumping up the rickety stairs Jerome hollered, "Stay outta here or I'll whup you!"

"The fuck you will, Jerome," I said clumping down. "You lay a hand—"

"You let this corrupt cunt get between us? I thought you more Principled."

"Which is why you'd better not touch her. Now go wash your mouth out!"

"Tell your bitch she has no business in this kitchen if Avril wants it."

"Tamela can use it anytime she wants. Why are *you* putting Avril between *us*?"

"This is my family's home! No white man can ever tell—"

"I'm paying for every bloody thing here. Nobody's running us out!"

My *force majeure* secured our rights to the kitchen but it didn't matter. Deferring to Jerome to mollify his anger resulted in his greater fury and rancor. His warring with Avril didn't help. Theirs was a match made in Bizarro heaven.

Two days off our wedding Avril demanded a divorce. Jerome hollered a week later, "Chris! Drop your newspaper and come out here to witness this. I'm divorcing this bitch." He thundered through the windows into the street, "I divorce you, woman!" She strutted into the bedroom. Her thin door slammed to rattle glass.

He took to physically beating her as their quarreling escalated. She was no small potato like Tamela but built like a Slav scything grain for a living and hoisting the Red Banner over defeated ramparts in her spare wartime. She shrieked and wailed under his brawling hands when I thought she could've mopped the floor with him. She did whack him in the face with her shoe, leaving a sizeable red mark and a black eye he only explained away to the brothers Free with some difficulty and a lot of lying. Tamela and I cowered in our room like paleoliths crowding a dying fire as the beasts running their world racketed the darkness beyond. I often taped their violence in case we needed evidence. Who knew what might happen?

As their marriage deteriorated, Jerome ever more maniacally kept appearances. It hardly mattered. The neighbors easily heard every shout, scream, wail, whack, slap, and shattering dish on our stone kitchen walls. One night Avril ran him out the kitchen door in a hail of Tamela's crockery we had to sweep up, glancing sour eyed at the shelves bared like an exhausted powder magazine. Their mêlées were wildfires exploding through dry tinder till they made up in drunken sex binges—Jerome bought his liquor with our grocery money—as 2-years Nikisha howled blubbering and pounding their bolted door. Tamela took her into our room for comfort, food, and care while we waited for their husky groaning to crescendo and breathlessly die away. Avril then snatched Nikisha from us like foiled kidnappers.

Other times I'd be unnervingly startled to hear the *thwack! thwack! thwack!* of a leather belt or shoe across Avril's 8-years son's back and butt above his riotous, shrieking sobs. She once beat him so loudly, all the while hoarsely and not a little windedly shouting the Psalms and for God's patience, that I broke into her now separate room across the hall from Tamela and me.

"I swear to God, Avril, I will beat you just like that if you don't stop this instant!"

"You t'ink you can beat me?"

I snatched the belt out of her hands. "I know I will. Then I'll send you to jail!"

Another day I plucked her descending arm from her son in the living room near the telephone window snarling, "Don't beat your son in front of my own eyes!"

This time she let go a high-pitched, banshee wail that shook the open window glass and rang my ears. "Help! *Helllp meee!* 'De white maahn beatin' me! 'De white maahn *beatin' me!* Come save me!"

Jesus Christ! I let go and stumbled back entirely confused how to handle this god-awful mess and diabolical woman. Damn certain I didn't want her screaming bloody murder from my white man's window into the black man's town.

"Don't you worry so," Tamela later said. "No-body get into no-body business, least of all Jeh-rome and Av-ril own! Ain' no-body like 'dem. Even Rev. Free."

"Oh, my God, Tamela. I've lost all control of our home inside this . . . madhouse to a demented psycho and her lunatic husband. And nothing I can do about it." Bramble House was rent free and no way could I take on even one EC dollar more in expenses. "I feel well and truly stuck in amber." She pulled me in tight.

Jerome soon picked up beating Avril's son about the shoulders, butt, and especially head reminiscent of the way he'd said his own mother had permanently deafened him in one ear. He went after Nikisha's back and butt . . . thankfully, not her toddler's noggin. So, some restraint was left in the snake pit of his heart. Any real or imagined infraction merited their molten rage. While I relaxed on our living room couch, he hit the boy so hard he flew into my legs and somersaulted over me.

I leapt up. "Jerome! What the holy fuck? Stop it! Stop beating these kids!"

"Mind your own business! Avril and her sinful, devilish children have it coming. They're bastards from her satanic relationships and deserve what they get."

"Why'd you marry her then? What? She pull 'em out *after* the wedding?"

"Shut up! It's none of your concern."

Tamela and I knocked on Avril's door one evening and opened it to wee Nikisha straddling Jerome's fully clothed lap on the floor mattress, gyrating 20-year-old lap dancer hips she'd no doubt observed in her mother. Tamela's hand flew to her mouth to cut off a gasp. He drilled a shit-eating grin right into her gaping eyes.

She wound up to verbally flay him but I pushed her back and closed the door with a guttural, "What the hell, Jerome!"

"Wha' mek you close 'dem door?" she demanded in a rage-thickened accent.

We retreated into our room instead of leaving the house in case Nikisha started screaming. "Tamela," I said quietly, "you know we'll only get hours of fighting and Nikisha will only be in the crossfire."

She sat hard on our bed and stared out the window. We wondered what actual sexual abuse might be happening. In 1992, St. Vincent's laws about that were a paper tiger which nobody, even the police, had any intention of invoking.

"You can tell story 'dem and show pick-chuhh," she said, "and no-body will even slap 'dem han'. People don't mess in people 'dem business. Mudd-uhh Francis or Rev. Free might say somethin', but 'dem will nev-uhh *do* anyt'ing." She shared our horrors with Nathalie and anybody who'd listen, but no police ever came a-knocking. It was obvious that domestic violence and child–sexual abuse was too commonplace to bother with. "Anyway," she added, "people ha' 'de cust-ohm to beat 'dem people. No-body will suff-uhh no law ov-uhh it."

"So, it's just okay to beat kids half to death? Like with you?" She shrugged.

Several times the Free brothers made a special trip to our house as senior pastors to dress Jerome down for fighting with Avril and especially his relatives—his war with his sister (my friend) Paula was legendary—and sometimes me for squabbling with Tamela. The tension in our house certainly energized it. Sometimes, I wondered if I'd fall down the same ravening maw gobbling up Jerome and Avril.

Drawn by Jerome's harsh voice, I leaned out the second floor living room window and watched him get into a verbal spat with the woman living next door who'd come to his crippled brother Adolphus' aid, whom Jerome was verbally abusing outside the house. As a crowd gathered—an increasingly common occurrence—to watch the spectacle like a walk-up vaudeville, Jerome tried shaming her into leaving with words like, "You know, you have a big fat mouth and a fat butt. You just want me to touch your big fat butt. You're just a dog, barking at me."

The crowd forced his apology. Lively dog ears wilted looking down from on high, ashamed to be seen with him. He had regular foul-mouthed arguments with everyone in his family in the streets or their homes from which they booted him and sent me roundabout reports. Taking me to a packed Middle Street lunch spot, ostensibly to complain about Tamela disrespectfully bickering with him, he worked himself up to boisterously calling her a "bitch," "slut," "asshole," "criminal," and worse. I tried to quiet him. Protest his verbal abuse. Patrons glued themselves to a sight seldom seen: a black man tongue-lashing a white man in public. Even in 98% nonwhite St. Vincent, that focused people. The talk of the town in two hours. I scooted back my chair and bailed. Eyes lasered holes in my back.

As he descended further into his well of madness, our racial divide yawned ever wider. He daily accused me of attempting to split him up with Avril or treating them both as slaves. I guess voluntarily living on my white man's dole at his auntie's house in a society where his citizenship and skin color boosted him over me and nothing but attitude held him back was indistinguishable from slavery.

In the midst of it all, Tamela and I took a peaceful, hand-in-hand stroll up the street in Sion Hill's direction (opposite Cane Garden) and visited some of our acquaintances. The evening turned dusky and we headed down Kingstown Hill for home and dinner. Rounding the last bend in the road, a surging crowd of 30-some onlookers outside our house brought us up short. We warily approached.

Several quick-stepped over. "You need to get out o' 'dat house, mon."

"Protec' yourself and move someplace else."

To Tamela, "Your white maahn a fine sort, gyul. It's 'de black one crazy."

Crashing ceramic and a scream cut the darkening air. Eyes shot to Jerome and Avril wrestling like grizzlies in a second-floor window, elbowing yet another pane of glass from the open casement that tinkled over our stone courtyard. The crowd swelled in a rush to a hundred, which must've been everybody in Town Hill. Tamela and I heavily climbed the steps for the kitchen door and crunched over broken crockery—this is when Avril had emptied the pantry shelves for missiles—littering the stone like shrapnel. Inside was disaster. Nearly all the crockery, including all of Tamela's personal wares from her friends, lay in fragments across the kitchen and basement, hardly a clear spot to set our feet. Tamela visibly quavered while savagely eyed. The hue of her red-brown face was the blackest volcanic pall.

"Wait here," I advised and hustled upstairs. They'd demolished our wood stairwell railings, now scattered in pieces. The furniture lay wrecked, windows smashed, Jerome and Avril locked in mortal combat. Maybe I broke his concentration because she broke loose and chased him out the French doors with a slashing cutlass, the West Indian version of a machete. I smartly backed out. He footled in the street shouting up obscenities. Avril hung out the second-floor window wearing a mostly ripped-off shirt. Pendulous breasts all but spilled out of her exposed black bra. She taunted him. Rhythmically slapped her cutlass against the stone side of the house. Raucously threatened him with death to match his gaudy insults.

Nothing we could do but shut our mouths and join the crowd taking in the spectacle, a West Indian street version of Othello in the Bard's old Globe. What a show! A hardshell Toyota police jeep blatted down the road we'd only just ambled along and pumped to a halt. Four tropical-uniformed constables disgorged. The crowd pointed. Two pushed Jerome into the back while two called down Avril, still hanging out the window brandishing her cutlass. Heading up to arrest her, they stupidly let her round up her children. She evaporated into falling darkness. The cops shrugged and hauled Jerome off. Tamela and I couldn't bear the devastation inside our house. We headed up Long Wall to Nathalie's and a debriefing.

Jerome's radical behavior went viral in the midst of my relationship-building with Hudson-Phillips and his contacts for operational funding. Only hinting at the reason, they now brushed off the opportunity. St. Vincent's business community is a staid, conservative lot. His public outbursts, wife and child beating, and vulgar arguments spooked them into a collective Pontius Pilate. Burning through US$20,000 in cash and credit on our year-long Vincentian gamble to change our American Unification Church fortunes flatlined my missionizing, entrepreneuring, and solvency.

Work interviews went: "We always hire Vincentians over foreigners. Even if we dispense with the . . . custom, you're obviously overqualified. I'm sorry." Imagine getting away with such honesty in America. But I knew where I stood. Money and food ran out. Jerome found small jobs to feed himself and Avril. Tamela mooched off Nathalie. I starved weeks on crackers and fruit until she persuaded her to send me a daily ration. She'd refused on the grounds I was dumb enough to share it with Jerome. The chicken in her pelau was welcome but decidedly rat sized.

"She'd nev-uhh, Chris," Tamela said, offended. "It be chick-enn!" *Okay.*

I lost 40 pounds till I landed hard at an emaciated, mono-redolent 160.

IT WASN'T ALL Jerome. Tamela's undiagnosed cognitive and emotional disorders often got her into life-sucking combat with him and Avril she'd then project onto me. It was now I encountered her blockading exits and grappling to stop me leaving to force a dispute's continuation long past its prudent bedtime—Shiori only snaked a leg. Once, so enraged feeling trapped as a wild cat, I pounded fists into the lightly paneled closet door just behind her head—ever unwilling to strike her—until there was nothing but holes. I panicked her so badly that pee coursed down her bare legs. Struck by shame, I resolved never again.

Then she bloomed hysterical in the kitchen at my departure with Jerome to preach in church. I suppose she was sensing, which I wasn't, our impending doom as insanity metastasized in him. *Surely a slap will calm her just like the movies. Not!* She belted a barely dodged slapback and bayed hellhounds in a praiseworthy reprise of Avril till the neighbors began ritually gathering. I hulked outside perplexed. Passed humiliated through the crowd. Tamela had a strange fear of these churches. She refused to accompany me because, a Seventh Day Adventist, she disliked the Spiritual Baptists . . . yet, felt compelled to prevent me attending. When she physically boxed me into our second-floor bedroom, I leapt out the side window into the delicious green orange tree we picked for snacks, shinnied down its trunk growing three feet from the house, and sprinted off.

She called out our 6-foot picture window, "Come back! Pleeease!"

"Later!" Not till America would she chase me.

Her assaults left me steamed and pressed. I'd fallen so deeply in love that I was certain she'd grow out of it in a calmer environment. Her fear and skeptical belief I was worming into the bushes for trysts with Jerome motivated some of her irrational behavior. It was impossible my denials could ever defend me and I silently endured her malicious stares and mute contempt. Other times she thought I'd leave and never return. Herds of irrational fears and suppositions suffused her perceptions of the world around her and filtered through the tangled skein of unrecognized cognitive chaos. I chalked her mental instability up to cultural variance, educational deficiency, unworldliness, and Jerome and Avril. It seemed impossible that education and experience wouldn't eliminate the problem. I held out hope.

Divorce—she and Nathalie talked annulment as our hostilities escalated—was unthinkable. I may have married outside Rev. Moon's Blessing, but a repugnance for divorce in my Catholic roots and Moonie training was a vital tenet of my personal culture. For good or ill, I was married and had to overcome our difficulties to make it work, especially as Jerome's marriage embodied only quarrels, beatings, and unrestrained make-up orgies that ever signaled the completion of one cycle of violence and the start of another. And I resolved to succeed lest I endure his endless taunts. Already, he was predicting our divorce before his and Avril's, his "I divorce you, woman!" thunderation now conveniently exorcised. I didn't comprehend that I'd ensnarled myself in a trio of batterers.

I tolerated my absurdities six months, struggling in vain to reconcile my religious mission with Jerome's behavior. At long last I picked up on the sheer number of women he'd been nailing. Some (I heard) as young as fifteen.

During one of his many quarrels with Tamela and dripping with accusation he said, "You have a very corrupt mind, woman."

"If I ha' a corrup' mind," her response rocketed from her mouth before he'd hardly closed his, "I would ha' gi' you sex aahll 'de time you pest-uhh me for it."

I rocked, sucker punched, on my heels. Jerome and Avril said nothing beyond swapping leery expressions, eyeballs shooting round the room like a Sergio Leone spaghetti western. Total silence for once reigned in our house. It was the last straw for Tamela. She packed her bag in a storm and hied home to Nathalie. My psyche was all our stolen crockery in bits on the kitchen floor.

At last, I accepted our mission was dead. So completely wrapped in the Cain–Abel indemnity cloak, I'd given it a 120-day condition before abandoning all Dantean hope. Then another two months sick, starving, feverish, weak, and broke hoping against hope my newspaper might get an 11th-hour funding reprieve.

According to Divine Principle, Restoration of sin and resentment occurs when people or groups represent the original Cain and Abel relationship that mirrors the dichotomy raging within Adam and Lucifer by and through the Fall. The Unification Church teaches two things about it: Cain needs voluntarily 'enslave' himself to Abel through total obedience and Abel needs 'serve,' meaning living for Cain's sake. The idea is for Cain, the first son, to voluntarily place himself in the second son position so that Abel, the second son representing God's side, can claim the first son position that Lucifer stole. This is because, in the process of the Fall, Lucifer's sexual relationship with Eve came before Eve seduced Adam. Lucifer's relationship was wholly unPrincipled. But God destined Adam to be Eve's husband. His relationship with Eve, unPrincipled by timing and motivation, was nevertheless closer to God's intent than Lucifer's with Eve, which God never intended.

In the Bible, Cain represents Eve's first relationship with Lucifer and Abel her second with Adam. That, in a nutshell, is the reason Cain represents Satan's side and Abel, God's. His intention with Cain and Abel was to reclaim what was stolen by Satan through the Fall. Since almost everything in the Bible symbolically represents real spiritual transformations of reality, Cain's proper response would have the effect of once again subordinating Lucifer to God and reversing the effects of the Fall from which Cain and Abel, thus Eve and Adam, could successfully reverse their fallen nature inherited through the process and motivation of the Fall. The whole point is to reverse the Fall and Restore Adam and Eve, thereby all human persons, to their original pre-Fall condition; the end of original sin and the fallen world.

In working with Jerome, I'd accepted our relationship as Restorative of the general black–white relationship in some local way. I'd voluntarily placed myself into Cain's position accompanying him to St. Vincent. I allowed him to dominate our mission, call the shots, be Abel . . . not too unlike how we played Cain to Wren Meyer's Abel or me vis-à-vis Ergela Arsch. His Principled duty as Abel was to love, care, and live for my sake. Our double wedding somehow turned him into Cain hefting a rock.

Tamela said, "It been trigg-uhh a spite always 'der an' it devour him, Chris."

"That sounds like what happened in the church after the '82 Blessings."

"Somethin' mus' be wrong wi' your church, then." I shifted and stared.

Recuperating mind, body, & car with Mom & Dad in Marble Falls, TX; late 1992.

Despite my voluntary submission, he sought to spiritually waste me with verbal, social, and psychological abuse. Stress drained my immune system. A sunrise swim cultivated a viral malady's charbroiling fever. Deathbed months of malaria-like sweats that Tamela vainly sopped my head in cold showers to break was enough. I gripped her hand.

Weakly, "I'm going home to Texas."

Her face collapsed in lament. "Nooo . . . wha' 'bout me? Don't leeeave me!"

"I'll be dead if I don't. You want that? I promise, I'll send for you with a visa."

"You ain' g'wan leave me on 'de sly? Like Mudd-uhh Francis hus-baahnd?"

"I promise. Trust me." To Jerome I said, "My parents are sending me a ticket home before I die. I've reached my end."

"It's the best thing for you now." But to Avril (who told Tamela, thus me): "Forget him. He's just a traitor abandoning me."

Beyond a core loyalty to Divine Principle's process of Restoration was my loyalty to Jerome. Not feeling particularly accepted growing up, I'd sought it through others.

Jerome was the first church member to accept me as I was and stand up for me when no one would. On that foundation, his treachery with Wren Meyer seemed aberrant, inexplicable. The strength of a decade's friendship through the minefield that's the Unification Movement wasn't easily broken. My need for acceptance manifested in loyalty even when forgiveness wasn't warranted and led me into danger. That was a truth I'd now bitterly learned. Forgiving him had traded me a crumbly cliff for a breaking branch. I was $30,000 poorer, drowned in debt, psychologically and physically broken. My mind ran on Papasan Choi . . . a shrewder judge of character than I'd taken him for, eh. Jerome was the danger of relationships that don't honor and uplift. Good memories of our friendship and my need for at least one ally led me a few years later to meet up with him in New York City. Our animus was obvious and this time I split for good.

The airlines refused my boarding in Barbados because American Express stupidly scheduled the connection closer than international flight rules allowed. Nothing can express the hair-pulling tempest hopelessly welling in me watching my airplane to safety close its door and roar homeward past whipping palms.

I choked to Mom over collect-call tears at a payphone, "It's so unfair!"

Sick. Stranded. Penniless. Licked. Inconsolably prostrate. I sobbed for 15 long minutes struggling to form words. We found a flight hauling out in six hours. Two hard-flying days later I put down on Austin's runway a wrung-out rag. Solid American doctoring healed my persistent bronchitis in a couple weeks. Several months of recuperation

I kept sane rebuilding my car from the ground up.

and weight gain readied me for a job. In the meantime I initiated Tamela's 6-month green card process. Five months into it she destroyed me in a strained phone call with her story of rape by a childhood friend.

Fingers near to breaking whitened round the receiver. "He's in jail?"

"I a' tell no po-lice."

"The hell not?"

She chuffed, shaky. "Ma say po-lice an' news would be bad."

Clenched teeth ached. "I swear to God I'll fly down and beat that motherfucker senseless! Then your cops can have him. If I don't hand him over a cliff first!"

"No, Chris! Promise me you won't do nothin'. Leave it!"

"Why not? He's a bastard! Didn't your family do *anything*?"

"Just leave it. Please. For Ma."

I was powerless grounded 3,000 miles away. My wrath was seething worms. Feeling untethered in the midst of it—don't judge me—I sent Shiori a guilty postcard. She paid a surprise visit. We met in Austin so I could explain marrying Tamela over her. To once again apologize for stomping her heart. She was unmollified.

"Satan ruin my future with you. Ruin *our* future. Because you are too stupid person. She is Satan's tool to drag you out of church. *Satan!*"

Chopping wood was restorative.

"That's exactly what *our* relationship did, Shiori. You hate it anyway."

"No. Mrs. Kobayashi would help us."

"Not a chance in—. How many times—?" But there could never be a meeting of our minds. What did meet was flesh. She came on strong. I had only what my unBlessed wedding band represented to resist my feelings. I said leaving, "Now I've ruined my marriage for you, too! I'll never speak to you again, Shiori. I just can't."

Rape and guilt gridlocked my emotions. I turned rude and cross. My sister and aunt's visit burst me like a storm-drenched dam. I sobbed a wet baby's anguish.

"We'll pay your way back," Dad offered," and rent you a house until her visa comes through."

"I can't work there, but I'll pay it back later."

His head shake said, *Forget it.*

Then INS announced it was ready to screen her in Barbados anyhow. Down I went to collect her, knocking on wood.

AWAITING OUR AIRPLANE outside Kingstown's terminal I spilled my Shiori beans. It seemed the right and manly thing to confess my sin, but I'd later realize it served no purpose except to shatter Tamela's heart and ruin her trust in me.

Much later even Shiori said, "You are so idiot for that. Just too *baka*."

"I couldn't help it. Father's teaching on spirit world had me scared," especially how our sins are clearly observable there, that if we don't solve it here it'll be a thousand times harder there. I didn't want that. It terrified me how Tamela might torment me forever like the characters in *A Wanderer in the Spirit Lands*, the compelling life-after-death story of Italian reprobate Francezzo transcribed by British spirit channeler A. Farnese in 1895. In one account, he comes across a couple who'd murdered the woman's husband to live together. They'd hanged together instead and now spent every moment fighting and accusing the other. It made a frightening impression. A strong motivator to confess and apologize so *we* didn't become *them*. "It just seemed better to get it out and resolved."

Eyes full of memories Shiori said, "Stupid. You not understand anything."

"Yeah, I didn't get how destructive a confession can be . . . or how witless." After a lifetime of joy and love, would Tamela really have turned werewolf in our sunset days or in spirit world because of a one-day fling while separated under extreme emotional duress in our first year of marriage?

No, was a peal of awareness. It was more an act of contrition to placate myself. I'd only ravaged her heart with a husband's worst crime. Her response perched on the stone wall came off muted even if a bit dark. I thought the worst was past, that I'd got off lucky. My infidelity simply hadn't sunk in. She was lost in a denial that wouldn't break till we'd set up house in Hawaii. Hell hath no fury as a woman scorned, they say. I'd given her just cause to querulously battle me over a past I couldn't change nor apologize for enough from that day unto eternity. I'd built my own Francezzo woes. Shiori was right. I was moronic beyond measure.

Her rapist flew the coop to Canada when I arrived January 2, 1993. No doubt to avoid my revenge. I didn't want to slay that fucker for real, but did feel a masculine need to hammer his rapist's tool to pulp. *Damn . . .* probably for the best, though. I got over it and moved on. I spent no time interrogating her over maybe provoking it—she'd adamantly protected him from the cops *after confessing it to me*—that she'd spend tearing me apart over Shiori. But, so it goes with life's cheap shots.

"Jerome's back in town now," his brother Ronald said a year off. "It's all I can do to keep the family from killing him over his extremist statements. He says he was 'victorious despite the traitor Chris.' But, welcome to the family.

Bound for St. Vincent and Tamela.

Maybe you can save our dysfunctional clan before the coming race war."

"Thanks," but *nope*. I happily distributed Christmas gifts for everyone and their kids, including a pound of chocolates for a shocked Avril. Days later at the American embassy in Barbados—our honeymoon, at last—Tamela clammed up over probing sexual questions. Our pessimistic embassy interviewer gave me my pestered chance. I read weary skepticism in his mousy government features and struck out.

"We have our wedding photos," I said hopefully. "Would those satisfy you?"

"Wha' mek you a' t'ink our marriage be real? We're honest people."

Flat eyes flicked over. "It couldn't hurt, at this point." His tone had dismissed us. Tamela handed over our album. He pointed, eyes wide. "A church event? Your minister? This your family?" All of us in our best clothes like the real thing.

"Yes. At Botanical Gardens before our recep-shuhn."

"Well, it's a lot of people. A church, too. Never seen anybody go to this kind of trouble for a phony marriage and I've seen at all. Okay, I'll approve your visa."

We made Texas January 7, 1993. Days later we drove Mom's Audi to San Diego where Tamela met my whole family. I was moved, grateful, and surprised my siblings felt meeting her was important enough to fly in when they'd never bothered with congratulations. I treasured it, even so. *Just when I think my family hates me, they do something like this. Who can understand them?*

Tamela was a fish out of water. Traffic lights were exotic. Big eyes swiveled round a deserted 6-lane Austin intersection. "Wha' mek you stop in 'de middle o' 'de empty road?" And, "Are all"—leafless, winter—"tree 'dem in Ameree-cah stick tree?" Then, "Chris! Wha' 'de white men push wheelbar-row! 'Dem do hard lab-uhh here?" Ditto Dallas International's automatic doors, sinks, toilets, the cinema, doctor, dentist, optometrist, and so forth. We visited Austin's Moonies.

"It's a faahlse church, Chris. You should leave it or I g'wan back St. Vincent!"

371

We bickered all the way home. Dad said, "There are many roads to God, Tamela, and all religions are following some part of God's truth." That mollified her. But it wouldn't stick as she got to *know* the church.

I'd arranged to stay in Honolulu with my Alaska shipmate Johnny McGurk and his wife Takako and their two small children. It was enough like St. Vincent that I thought Tamela would feel at home while acclimatizing to American society. It was the only home open to us for me to get back on my feet. Perhaps I could've stayed with my parents or sister in San Diego, but I don't recall them offering and anyhow I probably didn't want to be anyone's ward. Maybe I just wasn't comfortable around them. I've always felt unaccepted and unloved by my family, feeling forced to strive for their affection and respect without ever seeming to attain it. I wondered if we lived in the same town if we'd be our childhood family again. Yet, my attachment to Rev. Moon, Divine Principle, his global mission, and my church career seemed to call me to wherever they weren't.

After my debacle in St. Vincent, I longed to reconnect with the church. For sure it couldn't happen in New York because of Wren Meyer and the rest of the circus. Plus, Shiori was there. I hadn't fully quelled my heart and was determined to find a galaxy far, far away. Deep down I knew if I was in touching distance our need for intimacy would pull me in like an electromagnet. For obvious reasons I wanted Tamela far from

Honolulu bound via Cali. Jan., 1993.

her, too. I loved her and hungered for a happy marriage. What's farther than Honolulu (but not Guam) and still America? On January 15, it was *aloha* Hawaii.

Act XIII

Aloha Hawaii
Seeking Love, Getting Hate

I'd reconciled with Jerome naïvely persuaded his degeneracy and ethical dereliction was an anomaly. Time plus experience cleared my cobwebs. Now I'd put a 5,000-mile barrier between us. I felt safe. I knew I'd rightly divorced him out of my life when, lounging on our Bajan honeymoon before Tamela's green card interview, she'd shared his cupidity.

After I'd fled to Texas she set up in a 6×14-foot unelectrified wood shack on stilts—two glassless windows, wood shutters, 1-burner propane cooker, wayside hand water pump—on the steep hillside topping Long Wall on the way to Cane Garden. He'd tried tiptoeing into her pants and she brutally rebuffed him. In revenge, he oozed through a puss-boil of loathing how, though engaged, I'd flopped into bed with Shiori the second we hit bricks for our trip across America.

Mona's with family. San Diego. Jan., 1993.

"That's who he *really* cares about, Tamela. You should forget him like he's already forgotten you . . . and me. I mean, who's here? Him? Or me?"

"You t'ink you can break my heart for spite to ge' me into your bed?" She seized up her local-made, 2-inch thick tree-branch-handled broom and came at him blazing like Avril with her cutlass. "G'wan! Get out! *Get out!*"

Now here we were casting our lot with another Moonie friend and fingers crossed he'd play us straight. Johnny McGurk's baby 2-bedroom fronted a metal-railed balcony atop a 3-storey cinderblock perched on optimistic pylons over a parking area at 1471 Thurston Avenue. Punchbowl crater, home to the National Memorial Cemetery of the Pacific and some 53,000 Pacific War dead, rose above our short, straight street. Superstitious, Tamela wasn't keen living under a big-box graveyard, though she relished our grassy picnics 'neath its billowy shade trees.

A second negative was that Native Hawaiians detest Honolulu-born Lorrin Thurston for his prominent role overthrowing Queen Liliʻuokalani in 1893 with US Marines acting without orders. The US flip-flopped on disavowing his theft of American force for annexation when the Spanish American War altered Hawaii's strategic value. We got some flack now and then when native islanders heard we lived on a street stolen from a real Hawaiian. This introduced us to the unexpected native-mainlander tensions rife in the archipelago sabotaging our fitting in.

I'd met Johnny at Judah Street sometime after the '82 Blessing. The minute the two of us were alone in the brothers' room, he'd unwrapped a shoebox full of pistols rolled up in tinfoil. A man after my own heart. We'd bonded like brothers.

I'd said, "That doesn't seem very credible. Don't x-rays see through tinfoil?"

He shrugged. "They're here, aren't they? I wrapped 'em thick."

"I guess. Canada woulda thrown away your key, otherwise."

"You better believe it, brother. Them people don't mess around with guns."

"Fuckin' douchebags."

He'd hitchhiked some portion of the 1,387-mile Alcan Highway till catching a plane to San Francisco. He regaled me with avoiding gun-hating Canadian cops who'd melt his big-ticket self-defense into slag. Like England, Canada has the fanciful delusion that disarming the honest somehow makes the violently dishonest less so and even less likely to inflict harm. Another faux-free government depriving its nonviolent populace their chance to beat death for an obsessive safety-first.

He said, "Canada's where you go when you want your life and property to count for nothin' if it means the government can't coddle murderers for votes."

"Damn right. Just like the Canadian states of California, New York, the seat of freedom in DC, and all the rest. I'd stay the hell out of Canada if I was you."

"No shit, Sherlock. Alaska's the place. You should try it someday."

Despite hailing from New Jersey with the accent to match, he was really a country boy like me. Neither of us understood why anybody wanted to take away guns from the law-abiding absent nefarious motives. They bought our liberty in the first place and guarantee it home alone, old and frail, on dark streets, and overseas.

"You imagine us kicking out the Brits disarmed, or nightsticking bobbies"—I choked on laughter—"putting down Hezbollah? We'd be bowin' to 'em all."

"Speakin' German, more like. Government loves guns. Just not yours."

"Pretty damned foolish letting them toss ours and not theirs, too." Practically everybody I knew in Colorado owned firearms, more often than not a rifle or three in their pickup's back window rack and a pistol (illegally) cached under the seat for emergencies. Regardless, in 50 years my hometown Evergreen never had a single homicide except a woman many years earlier murdered in Denver then shoved over the cliff in her car behind the gas station at the east end of town. "Makes you wonder. Maybe I'm a bumpkin, but it's suspiciously counterintuitive."

"No, it don't."

Johnny was there to meet his Blessing wife. She was a medium-tall Japanese with a strong, solid build when I met her. Muscular, even a little thick. Gregarious to a fault described her well. She spoke precious little English. They'd hilariously gabbed and tittered through a translator in the first floor dining room and, yet, bonded. Johnny saw her as his savior, the one decent and valuable thing he'd ever possessed in life. He never knew his father and a raft of bitter feelings floated him into car theft and armed robbery before meeting the Unification Church. He'd transformed from social parasite to self-sacrificing missionary and wasn't alone in the church, either. Oddly enough, these crusty types mostly congregated in the Alaska church . . . probably offered them all the thrill with none of the prison calories. Johnny loved Alaska and felt at home in our Kodiak seafood company. But, like me, he was always running afoul of authority. Especially our boat captain, Jonathan. With permission to start his family, they'd set up in Honolulu.

By 1993 he'd made chief of maintenance for Tensuke, a church-owned fish company at 2696 Waiwai Loop in the industrial section near the airport. He'd previously wooed the church to pay for diesel training. His mechanical skillset had him as financially set as any breadline member could want. They showered about $50,000 a year on him—not far above cheap-at-half-the-price Hawaii's poverty level but a king's ransom to me—

Tensuke fish & Honolulu church.

which he supplemented with side jobs fixing cars. Looking back, it's ironic my old friend Julian from Boulder and Judah Street earned the same right out of law school while Johnny took in his on nothing but experience and a high school diploma. But, as Dad once said, Johnny's 50 grand would mostly be his top end while Julian's would grow to six figures or beyond. That was a lesson I'd vicariously learned but determined not to ignore. I wanted education with a 7-figure potential, not some quick high-pay ceiling. I'd put myself through Berkeley Hell for just that reason with every intention it somehow got me readmitted to UTS. I'd show those rats who thought I was only a hairy wart on the church's ass that I could and would make a valuable contribution . . . and out-earn them, besides.

Johnny had a good thing going at Tensuke and was careful not to screw it up. That meant he kissed Japanese ass when called upon. In return, they mostly left him alone. His technical prowess made him a necessary evil for Japanese leaders. Somebody had to maintain all their complex refrigeration equipment and the truck fleet, and Japan never airmailed us skilled members. Each tread carefully within this symbiotic relationship. The payoff for Johnny was fake respect from the church but real respect from nonmembers, a great salary as church jobs go, a decent standard of living, and an ability to invest in mutual funds which he assiduously tracked. And, boy, did I envy him. Green, I was. He was doing what I only dreamed of: Matched *and* Blessed, working at what he loved for a livable wage, and contributing however minusculely to Rev. Moon's mission. Living *my* dream!

Tensuke was one of the few viable church-owned concerns. Our operations often endured depressed earnings or self-destructed because of the propensity to run them like church centers, which included misappropriation. Despite Tensuke's slavishness to church events, activities, and orders from far away New York headquarters, it professionally managed itself. For the most part its leaders were Japanese who knew their fish and how to run a trade. In the midst of church businesses crashing and burning worldwide, Tensuke grew its revenues regardless economic downturns. With few exceptions, Johnny claimed a handsome Christmas bonus each year. In spite of my adventitious aversion for Japanese Moonies, I was impressed with these managers' sensibility and respected their work. They knew their limitations, too, because James, an American, headed up their US sales.

Flying San Diego to Honolulu.

It was this tropical teapot into which Tamela and I disembarked on a fine, sunny day. Johnny met us at baggage claim. Two scruffy-haired children even blonder than Johnny shyly crowded behind his legs. It gave me a start knowing Takako's was Japanese black. He gave us the kids' room. Tamela and Takako warily eyed each other to size up any potential threats to their husbands' fidelity. Even so, they got along famously before Tamela's quirks, unrecognized cognitive disability, and propensity for battery manifested. She tended toward notably polite and deferential manners for strangers, the character trait I mistook for her essential demeanor. As her relationships got close and familiar, she gave her irrationality and temper a longer leash until slipping it entirely.

Johnny and Takako got their first double-take during an argument in our room. Tamela was livid over Shiori in New York City and Texas, though she never gave Jerome the satisfaction of seeing it. It's not that she wasn't right to be angry; I was furious with her rape. Her attitude had me wondering how forcible it really was. How a man even came to be inside her tiny shack . . . literally a bedroom partitioned off a sitting room with no separate space to cook or pee. But I'd let it go as history she couldn't undo. My problem was her unwillingness to move on from mine as if it was ongoing. Wrangling heatedly in hushed tones—doesn't work in real life—she got carried away and punched me in the jaw. My vision went white. A hand shot a slap across her bow. That hadn't worked in St. Vincent and it sure didn't work now. Enraged, she launched at me with solid blows to the chest and a heaving big shove. I fell noisily backward into the wood partitioning wall. Takako's knickknacks clumped to the carpeted floor.

Johnny may have been used to physical disagreements but Takako wasn't. It scared and angered her. We were giving Satan the means to invade her home and attack her children. From that moment on, though I didn't know it, she pressured Johnny to show us the door. I can't blame her. I wouldn't tolerate our behavior in my house around my wee bambinas, either.

This was the beginning of Tamela's descent into a rage that eerily mirrored Jerome's. It was another warning sign she was unstable. My feelings of guilt over Shiori told me she was right to be hurt and angry, but it clashed head-on with my conviction she was completely out of line failing to control her behavior as well as to carry an angry red torch for what I couldn't undo. I hadn't yet figured out what a complete moron I'd been for confessing in the first place—"Fixin' your damn guilt at my expense!" she'd later echo Shiori, though Jerome had sowed the seeds—but I was getting a picture of marriage behind a scarlet letter I wanted no part of. Fights like this were happily back-burnered by our need for cash flow.

I applied for advertised jobs but one employer bluntly said, "Don't quote me, but it's unlikely you'll ever find a job in Honolulu because you have three strikes against you. First, you're a *haolie*. That means white. Second, you're a mainlander. Third, your résumé shows you in different cities the last several years. That looks suspicious, like you can't hold a job or you get into trouble."

I gawked like I hadn't in Kingstown. "Isn't that illegal, though?"

"It is what it is." He had Johnny's aplomb. "Try temp work as an entrée."

A fourth strike he only hinted at was that jobs were unofficially reserved for the Hawaiian-born albeit not actual Native Hawaiians who bitterly complained of their marginalized, disadvantaged, and landless home-turf status. Minus the racial undertones, Hawaii was St. Vincent all over again. I found that hilariously ironic. In cliquish, small-town minded Honolulu, my travels made me a dodgy hire.

Hungry for cash, I felt led into brand-new Equinox International. Down-on-his-luck ex-millionaire Bill Gouldd built this multilevel marketing scheme to tout water filters and like products. Several got-rich acolytes were a neon signboard for wannabes. Hawaii-born Kalé, whose father bought the island's first McDonald's franchise when other (luckless) investors balked at such a loser deal, reaped $30,000 *per month* with downline residuals and $5,000 'manager' startup kits. *Impressed. Absolutely.* Native Hawaiian Paul and Hawaii-born Japanese-American Gregg pulled in $5,000–7,500 a month each. Our mainlander *haolie* Andrew out-earned his $10,000 TV ad sales job working Equinox part time. Gobs of

$1,500 Equinox training in San Diego.

dough rolled through their hands. *No doubt about it*, said covetous eyes.

Regardless their bling, they could be lying and I was cynical. Crossed arms and probably a scowl on my face, Kalé verbally whipped me one evening in front of the mixed crowd of old hands and enthusiastic new recruits—exactly how Moonies stacked their events—like a passing bum snacking off his sidewalk table to "blast away your negative energy" constipating his excited, once-in-a-lifetime-opportunity performance. That embarrassment almost sent me scurrying foul-mouthed for the door. But the lure of $5,000 a month humbly held me to my seat the way Restoration through the Blessing less humbly nailed me to my Unificationist cross.

Bill Gouldd said you can abuse a person in any way to any degree, but embarrass or humiliate them and they'll turn on you. Kalé wasn't subscribing to that pithy business philosophy that night, and it broke down over greed anyway. The Federal

Trade Commission sued Gouldd for financial mismanagement and defrauding his distributors out of $300 million in a pyramid scheme and forced him to shutter up in 1999. We sold real merchandise—excellent water filters, nutritional products, breath fresheners, skin care products—that worked as promised. I never felt defrauded just because I couldn't build a downline, so I don't know about all that. I was and still am just no kind of salesman for God or bank.

Lacking the family and friends most Equinoxeers built their downlines on, I resorted to stopping shoppers in posh, unroofed Ala Moana shopping mall with a senseless survey. Afterward, I invited them to an evening presentation that would change their financial lives. Of the hundreds I tried this on, one showed up but didn't buy. Depressed, I strove to maintain my dignity and good spirits. One way was laughing at the top of my lungs clattering down the H–1 on my balls-numbing, ratty '80s Suzuki GS450—affording even the crappiest car in usurious Hawaii was out of the question—to the Equinox center for inspiration. Andrew and later even Kalé were impressed with my effort though not my results. I'd bought their $5,000 starter kit on credit and rapidly discovered it was a manager's rathole.

The products were great. I loved them all. I just couldn't sell. At the core of my being I loathe sales. Browbeating people into buying was anathema to me, and that's the essence of the luxury goods business. A person obviously doesn't *need* it and you have to convince them they can't live without it. I hated that part and couldn't put my heart into it: you can't escape lying through your inviting smile. I didn't love money that much. In the end, no sale. A car dealer accepted my application with a 2-month stipend that shifted to commission only, but I didn't see myself making the rent with the requisite rhythmic clockwork. I needed tried and true wage slavery and this racist island wouldn't let me have it!

Fortunately, a temp agency on the 20th floor of a downtown, shiny glass high-rise sent me to work a few weeks at a one-man show called Mannix Media. Lem Cane, its *haolie* owner–operator, claimed he'd quit Hollywood soap opera stardom's $250,000 a year after taking all the spunk he could swallow from the low-brow Hollywood homosexuals who'd taken over the industry and ruined it. In a huff, he'd dumped a catered bowl of pasta over his gay producer's head and that was that. Priceless, but I felt his pain only too well having suffered numerous run-ins with the one-track-agenda gays at CCSF. He bragged about dating the famous bare-breasted native Hawaiian model on the cover of Kim Taylor Reece's *Hula Kahiko* book when I commented on her sexy postered figure in his office.

"A real babe," he said, "and she's absolutely gorgeous. In the sack, too."

I nodded with admiration for him. "Why'd you break up then?"

"Ehh . . . I didn't think she had the brains to be the mother of my children." *Ha!* My own goals had narrowed to just not crazy. "I broke up for a really brainy mainlander"—a *haolie*, apparently with none of the island temperament nor frank sexiness of his Hawaiian—"who gave me a son. But . . . we're divorced."

"Sorry to hear that, man."

"Oh, well. It's life. But, tell you what. You're the best temp they've ever sent me. Fuck the clique running this island. I'll hire you full time for the same $1,400 I'm paying the agency. What do you say?"

"I say, *great!*" Then realized that still meant poverty in Hawaii. Not even lower middle class affluence. After taxes it paid the cheapest $750 rent on our fifth-floor studio at 824 Kinau Street a few blocks from Johnny and Takako. Yet, we struggled to meet my Vincy debt and the overpriced gas and groceries, like milk going for $4.10 a gallon versus $1.29 on the mainland. I sweated bullets to insolvency.

We'd had to vacate Johnny's apartment after too many run-ins between Takako and Tamela. Discounting the usual kitchen conflicts and our quarrels, Tamela got between Takako and her pet project Kumi, an underage colleen near Tamela's age. Daughter to a fabulously wealthy Japanese divorcée whom she hated, Kumi guzzled alcohol. She resented Takako interfering in her activities but took an instant shine to Tamela. Coming from a dysfunctional and abusive family herself, Tamela intuitively grasped her situation and mentality, and reached out in a naturally productive way. They were on their way to a movie to cement their friendship when she unwisely blabbed to Takako, who scotched it. She forbade her having anything to do with Kumi. That peeved Tamela, not least because she and Kumi genuinely liked each other as equals. Despite her faults, Tamela is quite incorruptible. Her notion was that Kumi would respond to her pure sisterhood out of affection and abandon her liquored-up life. It was Takako's breaking point, though. We remained friends, which I took for a win, but had to scoot.

It wasn't long after moving into our new place that I died in a frightening dream. I told Tamela all about it the second I cracked eyes. We didn't know what to make of it and dismissed the implications. But I dreamed it that night, too.

She said, "Wha' happ'n if you be dream it t'ree time?"

"I don't know. Maybe it's only a dream."

That afternoon she kick-started a brawl over Shiori on our motorcycle and carried her invective on for too long, as usual. I flipped. Hollered fire. In my squabbling confusion I lost track, imagining I was a mile farther back up the road than I actually was. The intersection went unnoticed.

My head corkscrewed to the right so she'd more effectively hear me bellowing, "Will you just shut the fuck up?!" I barely registered the crossroads and missed the traffic light glaring redly down at me.

I motored right into it with her scathing voice blaring, "You shut down! Don't you dare taahlk your foul mout' 'pon me! Wha' mek—"

From the corner of my left eye a white, industrial-sized tow truck loomed large on a collision course. I slammed on the brakes. Her hot weight slammed forward hard. My front wheel scraped unmolested along the truck's front bumper. The left handlebar stopped cold against the fender and snapped back. The bike jackknifed. I flew forward into immovable metal at whatever speed I'd been going. Tamela bounced off my body sideways into the truck's heavy-duty side mirror. The next I knew, my vision and hearing were filtering back from total blackout. I struggled to pull my leaden head off coarse pavement. A bulbous gut roared round the hood.

"What kinda goddamned moron runs a goddamned red light! You stu . . ."

"Is that what happened?" My mouth was groggy.

Tamela came to on her side seconds later and bolted upright, eyes wide and maybe unseeing. Blood thick as a pencil hosed from her left temple.

Eyes froze. I found air and hollered at the cursing driver, "Call an ambulance! My wife's hurt!" Soaking tears burst out realizing she was probably dying right in front of me. That *I'd* killed her. I pressed the heel of my hand over her gushing wound to staunch the jet. "I'm sorry! I'm sorry! I'm sorry!" Tears flooded my cheeks.

I believed my dream foretold the accident. That (in keeping with Unificationist thinking) Satan had struck us to stop me pursuing the church in Hawaii. Why Satan and not God? Because, the church believes the left side of anything represents Satan's side and the right God's. It's clear that left-side suffering, illness, accidents, and the like are all or partially our or our ancestors' faults. If it's right-side then God's giving us the chance to pay indemnity to forestall accusations from Satan in preparation for some providential blessing. Many of us withered under verbal abuse from members convinced, with nothing more than left-side evidence, that we'd brought our suffering on ourselves through our sin and therefore deserved it. Such an incident might get a zealous leader inquiring into your life and activities with the KGB's enthusiasm for your loyalty. Some members saw a brother or sister's suffering as a green light to inflict even more sorrow and pain to help them grow. God bless 'em, the bastards.

The truck approached from the left, the left side of my motorcycle took the impact, the mirror gouged Tamela's left temple, and my injuries were greater on my left. Though we hit the truck's right side, we struck it and fell to the ground to our left. Therefore, Satan obviously struck the blow as a result of our sin and it wasn't hard to guess which. This was our opportunity to pay indemnity and repent for it, then move past it closer to God. Miraculously, a fire station with an EMS crew inhabited the corner lot to our left. In half a minute, more than a dozen firemen and paramedics swarmed the crash site, crushing my eyeglasses underfoot just as I reached for them, thanks very much. A wailing ambulance whisked us away.

Assessing her trauma the paramedic said, "What's your telephone number?"

"72569. It's 72569." The medics traded eyes. *Brain damage?*

"That's her home number in St. Vincent," I yelled over the siren.

"Am I g'wan be die? Am I dyin'? Will I die?"

"You'll be fine. You're okay." Maybe lying, EMT lady whipped out her scissors and with alacrity stripped Tamela to her panties.

"Don't cut that!" I shouted, but she'd snipped through Mom's exorbitant, gifted bra. "Shit! I can't replace that." Ms. Snippit damn sure wouldn't. Roughly checking Tamela for broken bones and internal injuries, she pointed her scissors at me. She got a long snip through the elastic cuff of Johnny's heavy leather motorcycle jacket before I racketed, "Don't you dare cut it! I can take it off myself."

"That's not procedure, sir. You could have internal injuries you don't—"

"I don't have anything! Am I so gravely wounded I'm gonna throw away my friend's $400 jacket? No way. I'm together enough to get out of it and any other clothes you plan on throwing away for me. Help me sit up, if you don't mind."

"Sir, I suggest you lie calmly and let..."

"You need my shirt and pants off, too?"

I was okay and relieved Tamela was, too. Tears and dramatic stress faded weary and spent. The Queen's Medical Center had the gall to bill me 10,000 motherfucking

American dollars for nothing more than x-rays, emergency room, a couple hours of observation, and an overnight for Tamela she didn't need but too easy for QMC to pass up. In its lengthy line items was probably the envelope, paper, ink, and postage stamp times 100. An impossible sum. I fumed over its greed—bald larceny is why people scream for free healthcare without shrinking from government's regulatory thievery creating the inequity—and Tamela causing the distracting ruckus in the first place. Native Hawaiians love Queen Lili'uokalani, but her namesake hospital is Lorrin Thurston reprising his regicidal life through medicine.

I could barely move with all my torn, bruised muscles. Johnny was very solicitous. Between his building's hopeful parking columns, he helped fix my bent-up bike. He added a few improvements, too, such as a basket for groceries and gave me his cuff-cut leather jacket to keep. A real first-rate mate, he was. I bought a used helmet from a junkyard but couldn't afford a second one. Probably not a good place to obtain a safety helmet; it had a circular series of cracks from a previous crash. Tamela refused to wear one anyway lest it muss her hair. A month later came the same dream. I bought hers that very day.

"I a' put 'dat old t'ing on me head. You can jus'—"

"You can wear it or you can walk." I held it out.

She stared. "Ugh! 'Dis will ruin me hair. An' it look stupid."

"Not as stupid as blood hosing out of your head." She squinted a dagger.

Day three after dream two we put-putted through our underground parking garage for the exit when the motorcycle inexplicably surged forward on its own. I released the throttle and applied minor braking but the wheels slipped out from under on the slippery smooth, polished cement. Down to the left we went.

Bang! bounced our heads off the cement with near neck-snapping force.

It would've cracked our noggins for sure but we hardly felt a thing in our rickety helmets. We slid along with the bike till it scraped to a stop, said a prayer of thanks, levered its four-hundred pounds upright, and went on our way. No more dreams or accidents, either, thank God. Or Satan.

ERNIE WAS HAWAII'S state leader and pastor of Honolulu's church. Hawaii-born, he was the epitome of the laid back island surfer boy in flip-flop sandals and I rather liked him. Short and rotund with cropped black hair and dark eyes set in an expansive, jovial face, he was out of step with a lot of things. The Honolulu church, like the Unification Church everywhere, was a dying institution in 1993. Their only membership success during my year there was a *haolie* techie who joined part time. Unlike the Unification Church of old, it was now more provident that he keep his job and tithe than quit and donate his cash on hand to become yet another mouth to feed. Leasing instead of buying.

We met Ernie at Sunday service on Tensuke's second floor behind its wall-to-wall front windows. It lacked all the trappings of a church environment except a large photo of True Parents, a couple of potted palms, rows of hotel conference chairs, and some atmospheric odds and ends. The Japanese held their own service so they could avoid English and Americans, and we rarely encountered that side of our local Family on the Sabbath. It was the only time of the week we non-Japanese got together. They came from Honolulu, Pearl Harbor, and Kaneohe and it was fun to feel even this tepid Moonie crowd. I sorely missed the vitality of earlier days.

Our Korean regional leader, Rev. Sun Sang Lee, lived on the mainland. He never found a reason to like me . . . it's possible he'd heard my reputation. We gathered one Sunday for his big sermon. After some pleasantries and pious comments, he brutally condemned Ernie's lackluster, even failing, job performance. While he ranted and raved and reviled Ernie through occasional spittle, his target was stone in his chair just in front of mine and Tamela's. He cursed and sputtered under his breath every dirty word I could think of and some I couldn't. My mouth fell open. I'd heard a lot of stupid shit out of leaders' mouths over the years but never the truculent, disparaging, vulgar, denunciatory, raging vituperation spewing, however mumblingly, out of Ernie. He was quiet and restrained as befitted a state leader but manically incensed under the skin. He was incompetent in truth so that Rev. Lee wasn't even lying. But he'd called Ernie on the carpet in the most churlish way: before his own family and congregation instead of privately, a common failing of arrogant Korean leaders who generally prefer to work members over than up.

Part of Rev. Lee's ire came from his fear of Rev. Moon. Mrs. Moon was soon to speak in Hawaii as part of True Parents' historic tour of American cities officially declaring themselves Christ's Second Coming. Headquarters was mandating that every state produce a record turnout and Hawaii was at the bottom of their tally. Rev. Lee was merely passing on a verbal, and possibly his fear of a physical, whupping he might receive from Rev. Moon if Mrs. Moon's speech ended up a nondescript affair with low turnout and no swanning press coverage. He'd made a special trip to Honolulu on this Sunday for the express purpose of putting the screws to Ernie and inspiring the rest of us with his pointed example and whipped up tears to "Get out there and witness for God and True Parents' victory!"

It's ironic the ears upon which his words fell with greatest effect were Tamela's, probably the most Unification Church-loathing person in the room.

"Ernie is a los-uhh," she boldly said, "and he a' lead 'dis church to grow or bring any-body to God. Don't follow him, Chris."

"Don't be kind on my account."

"He ser-monn be hog-wash, and you know it. Pitiful tries to inspire memb-uhh wi' nice word bu' him be stuck in 'de mud."

"Spiritual lard."

"Ha ha, whatev-uhh you like. Rev. Free bett-uhh. But 'dis Rev. Lee whooped it!"

I laughed in disgust. "You must be nuts. That sanctimonious—"

"No, Chris. I saw he commitment for God first above all, to live and breathe—"

"God, God, God. I get it. Okay. That's awesome. Honestly, I'm so happy you finally got inspired in my 'false' church."

"Shut it. I wan' follow wha' 'de maahn say."

"Man, I've never seen you like this. It's like you're enraptured."

She looked thoughtful. "Mos' 'dem doltish memb-uhh sour an' racist. I can'a stan' 'dem. But Rev. Lee moved me. You a' understan' 'dat?"

"So, from the lips of that arrogant, greedy, ruthless, ass-kissing toadie you gained your greatest inspiration in the church. There must be a God!"

"Wha' kin' o' memb-uhh you be, then? Don't blas-pheme."

So, out we went witnessing for True Mother's speech. Not me. The Royal We. I was too busy scrabbling after money to meet our bills and debts. I did do a little witnessing to Christian pastors when I wasn't helping the church sell roses chairside Saturdays at roadside stands or in front of Safeway where I strove to improve reading and writing Japanese. As usual, I was throwing myself into being as helpful as possible in hopes it would rub off on their attitude and shine up my reputation. Ernie paired Tamela with Julie for what they called the rose providence.

Julie was a 30-something, Hawaii-born Filipina living with her folks in the aged wooden shacks on the old pineapple plantation workers' tracts that were surprisingly capacious and airy, and now well-furnished. She and Tamela hit it off. They often fundraised together on weekends and holidays as much for the friendship and conversation as to help the church raise money. Julie was a kind, low five-footer with curly black hair, deep brown skin, and a joyful smile. She was Blessed to a Japanese she didn't know very well and was industriously pushing the powers for permission to start her family before menopause.

"He isn't interested in leaving Japan, and I'm *not* moving there," she said.

Eventually, the impasse resolved when her husband's leader ordered him to join his wife in Hawaii. Julie was a laid back Hawaiian modeled off Ernie and not particularly interested in witnessing for Mrs. Moon's speech.

I said to Tamela, "How's your Mother-witnessing going with Julie?"

"Fine for 'de time. She res' on a bench at Ala Moana an' I do it me own self."

"Sometimes it goes like that. This is the first initiative I've ever seen from you."

"So? It be a prob-lemm?"

"Can't you take a compliment? I'm just impressed by your guts and determination to wander a strange land preaching an unwelcome message."

She laughed. "You a' 'de only one!" She took a beat to take stock. " 'Dem Rev. Lee himself be witnessin' at Ala Moana . . ."

Now I laughed. "An example of leadership in action aimed at Ernie."

"We done run into each oth-uhh. Chris, he tek one look at me like he nev-uhh see no black wo-maahn before in he life! Him didn'a even remem-buhh was me right in front o' him eye at Sunday service."

"He was too potty for Ernie. And some of these leaders look right through the members they have no use for. He blow you off?" *Because, Korean bigshot.*

"No, no. Him say, 'I is very surprise to meet another church memb-uhh here! Wha' be your name? Ha' we met? How many did you invite?' I explain who you be. I t'ink tha' tek he by surprise, too." And maybe that he'd caught any of her lingo.

I slapped my forehead at the impossibility of lying doggo. Tamela flabbergasted him enough that he spread the news hoping to shame the Honolulu members into making a worthier effort. It must've worked. Mrs. Moon spoke to a full ballroom at the local Swank Hotel. A few offenderati walked out at her pronouncement that she and the Mister were the Second Coming of the Lord, the True Parents of all mankind, but most stayed through her untranslated closing prayer. Rev. Lee was overjoyed he'd get a slap on the back instead of maybe upside the head, though not enough to keep Tamela—"that black sister"—in his selective memory.

I believed my mission in Hawaii (as anywhere) was to restore the Unification Church to its former greatness. But I had no base. The members openly scorned me for marrying outside the Blessing and Tamela besides, despite Rev. Lee's copious if short-lived praise. She wasn't a *bona fide* member who'd been witnessed, attended workshop, and joined the traditional way before abandoning the church to wed outside it like the real McCoy. And she was black. Even in brown Hawaii, being *pōpolo* was onerous. No one would help me do anything church related.

"And especially," Ernie warned me, "we don't need you speaking to Christian ministers. So, please don't."

"Why not? I'm an ordained minister." His head waggled Indian style at that. "They're more likely to give me a hearing when they'd reject a regular member."

"Regardless. I don't want them confused about our real members *here*."

"I'm not a real Hawaii member?" He shrugged to flip-flop off.

I tried reinventing the old Family Home Church Association that Jerome and I founded in New York City and used as our witnessing tool in St. Vincent, but it was a rocky road. At my own expense, I sent out several mailings to about 500 churches on Oahu, one reminding them about Mother's speech and another asking permission to speak in their churches. Most never replied. A few wrote back telling me to never write them again. One called my home to emphasize his don't-call-us-we'll-call-you message. Whatever Ernie was doing wasn't winning friends.

I visited several churches anyway and was welcomed as a fellow minister when they found out I was ordained and not just another untutored Moonie. As usual, the black churches were the most open, even more so when they discovered it was the black National Baptist Convention that ordained me and not the old slave-owning Southern Baptists and their ilk. But I could never reach white majority ministers, whom we all believed were key to representing America as a nation accepting True Parents. That was very discouraging but, by now in my church life, hardly unexpected. White churches tended to be the most arrogant, unwelcoming, and abusive. Black churches tended to be the most humble, welcoming, and embracing. It's ironic the intellectually oriented Unification Church makes no headway in the intellectually-oriented white churches but goes far in the emotionally-oriented black ones. It's they who've once more become the key to Rev. Moon's interfaith outreach.

THE FINANCIAL AND spiritual pressures of life in Hawaii were wearing me to the nub. I was earning (pre-tax) $23,000 a year as Lem Cane's office manager. Rent and utilities took up half. My student loan, credit card (including $7,500 I'd racked up with Equinox), gasoline, and motorcycle insurance were increasingly unpayable in full. Food was a burden in a land where milk and honey were three times the mainland. Sam's Club and Super-к's lawsuit that broke Safeway's blockade and forced the grocery cartel down to only twice the mainland was scarcely chimeric.

Members scorned us. A Japanese attending our English service said, "No Blessing. Not real member. You do not belong in here." We quit showing up. You'd expect any pastor wallowing in a 15-member congregation to call the lost sheep missing in action three months. No one asked why I wasn't at service, fundraising, or socializing. Was I sick? dying? fallen on hard times? *Never mind. Not our worry.*

Johnny and Takako knew our reasons, but he's a close-mouthed chap and wouldn't stick out anyhow. I think he only attended for his kids and to please Takako. That's what mattered, not me. Kind of like our halibut long-lining days.

Working on my own, I visited a new group called the Church of Christ. Not the familiar, mainline version but a newer, youth-oriented iteration. The pastor was Mr. Smiles. Singing or preaching, his high-wattage face and stupendous physical energy never dimmed. The congregation was energized, singing with a gusto that carried me back to the early Moonies. A dynamic, healthily growing church jam-packed with some 200 souls. We soaked up Sunday service and midweek studies in our group leader's home, all friendly and familial and centered on biblical lessons and their circled-up members. It resonated an educational, spiritual, and social event all at once. Tamela witnessed with them once a week at Ala Moana.

"I think we've found a new church, Tamela. It feels like God here. To hell with witnessing them Principle. Luring them onto Ernie's deflated rubber ducky for Rev. Lee's roughshod motivational harangues feels practically criminal."

"Good! Whoev-uhh your Rev. Moon be, God done wi' all 'dem doltish people."

"Well, out with the old and in with the new!"

"Wha' 'bout so-caahll Divine Principle? I t'ought you love it like your god."

"Funny. Right now, they feel like sorely missed family. I'll figure it out later."

She attended reading classes and visited a tutor but was still functionally illiterate and couldn't read at Bible study. "I don't wan' go," she said at last. "I terrified 'dem mek me read an' ev'rybody fin' out me secret."

"If it mortifies you, why don't you study more? How hard can it be? I mean, it's a paradox, isn't it? You say you want to read but you hardly put any effort in it."

"Don't push me 'bout it."

"But it makes no sense! You need—hell, Frederick Douglass did it on his own! What happens when we have kids?"

"Who him be?" I opened my mouth but let it pass. "Wha' mek it matter to you, anyhow? Becau' Shiori read? You don't love—" And . . . off to the races.

"You're just being lazy and it's infuriating! I didn't marry an ignorant illiterate. You promised you'd learn and I'm paying for it. That was the condition to go ahead with our marriage when you gave me, like, a week's notice. So, what gives?" She shrugged, lips tight. "Well, you need to up your game, sister."

"Don't you sist-uhh me! Me a' Shiori. Me a' no church memb-uhh. Tha' be wha' you want? 'Dem who you really be wan' marry? Wha' mek you be tek me from me country to 'dis strange place if aahll you—" and . . . second lap by a nose. Only years later did I learn it was partly her cognitive disability and emotional instability.

All this heavily on my mind, our new friends suddenly recoiled from us like diametrically opposed Moonies and Christians at CCSF both skewering me as an apostate. It happened in casual conversation in their downtown high-rise church.

We'd circled up in study groups. "So, what church did you attend before?"

"I'm Seven Days. Me hus-baahnd is Unification Church." *Was. Was!*

My heart viscerally sank deep and hard in my gut. I'd played that a close hand but forgot to forewarn Tamela. *Damn.* Steely, barbed eyes swung onto me.

"Well, that's not exactly . . . I mean, I was but . . ."

It was impossible to clarify myself in the hubbub. Our pastor sirened up moments later. "Since you're from that group, you're not welcome here."

"But we're not—"

"You need to leave."

"We're here to *join* your church, not—"

No high-wattage smile but a darkened grimace. "Right now, please."

His arm pointing out the elevator was a heart-thumping replay of Wren Meyer in West 43rd Street's foyer. *I'm not witnessing!* They were giving *me* spiritual sustenance after my own church elbowed me out. But, no ears to hear. Haters hate. Down the drain of Tamela's innocence went the only inspiring church we'd found on Oahu.

The elevator thrummed. "I'm not gonna blow up, Tamela, because I know you didn't know they'd do that. But . . . *damn!* Couldn't you say something else?"

"I sorry! I didn't mean to . . . it be your own fault joinin' your faahlse church."

Yeah. Sigh. Ten floors down, I lurched into raw sunshine.

ONE DAY OUT of the blue Tamela said, "Why don't you write Shiori? She mus' be sufferin' a lot since you done leave her."

I stared dumbstruck. "Are you crazy?"

"What ev-uhh. It was jus' a sugges-shtion."

A week later her comment came to mind while she napped. *Why not?* I can't fathom it. Maybe zombified feelings drawn to the sound of her name. I sent a short note, careful to leave out all tracking data. The phone rang anyhow.

Her Japanesed "Herro, K'risutohua" sent such a withering voltage though me I hung up, panicked. "Wrong number," I tremulously said to Tamela's inquiring eyes. Undeterred, she called another day. We exchanged dooming words. "It's Shiori," I told flashing dark eyes. "I sent her a note with no return info, like you suggested."

"How she fin' you, then?"

I mouth shrugged. "Maybe the postmark? Directory assistance? I tried."

"You is a stupid maahn, Chris."

"Me?" I liked Shiori as a friend. But she called off and on like St. Vincent which I'm sure, but hadn't considered, Tamela was recalling with ever greater clarity. Our short conversations were about church and life, benign 5,000 miles away.

Tamela, whose inane overture triggered it, said, " 'Dis wo-maahn set on an interference," her West Indian for an extramarital affair.

Instead of saying, "You're right, dear, I'll get an unlisted number right away," I said something like, "I can talk to anybody I want. She's the other side of the world, and it was your suggestion in the first place."

She cussed me all the more. I don't know if taking her calls was residual feelings or my obstinance when ordered around. Likely both. We quarreled vehemently over Shiori and my past infidelity. It was unwinnable. I dashed away to calm down. No kind of quitter, she lit after me. She once cornered me in the open-air stairs and locked us out of our unit. Neighbors called the manager to shut us up.

"If there's a repeat," he said darkly, "you'll be served an eviction notice."

At the same time, she proved what a cad I'd been. Her McDonald's manager demanded sex for a 40-hour week, a promotion, and extra pay. She proudly took the 16 hours he gave her in revenge for the "Go fuck yourself!" that boiled out of her mouth in a long string of probably indecipherable oaths.

Our brawling increased in frequency as she harped on what happened with Shiori in New York and Texas. I couldn't apologize enough and, boy, I tried. It was endless. Jerome could bask in his revenge. Tamela posed the same questions over and over and over, each worded a hairsbreadth differently which, in her mind, meant different questions. If I didn't give the answer she wanted to hear, she considered it a lie and grilled me all the harder. If I said what she wanted to hear, she considered it outrageous proof of her suspicions and my deception. She then launched into a new argument without letting go the original. A scathingly violent rendition of Monty Python's side-splitting 'argument clinic' skit.

St. Vincent was my unawares orientation to domestic violence. I did my 101 class in Hawaii. I'd never heard of it and certainly had no idea it marked the reality of my marriage. Her increasingly querulous personality, vituperative interrogations, and inability to cognize my responses or empathize led to brutal, knockdown altercations. Sometimes a porcelain cup flew past my head and I hotly returned fire. She sucked me into rows even after I'd realized there was no resolving her hurt or whatever demons drove her so madly to cuss me instead of love me.

When I realized it was time to let go a clash, I wanted space between us till our passions cooled. Yet, she physically barred me escaping our fifth-floor apartment. When I was too fast, or muscled through the door, it was a dead heat down the stairs ahead of her hot pursuit . . . remember our race across Sion Hill beach? Then down the sidewalk at full throttle till panic outdistanced her. Safely alone, I slowed to breathlessly, sweatily storm along furiously cursing under my breath like Ernie in his goddamned chair, so ragingly vexed I could've beat my head on every passing palm tree. I usually found myself wandering Waikiki. If nighttime, I climbed atop a picnic table under a sun shade to lay down and sleep. Then midnight–2 AM I trudged home tired, aching, and freezing in the damp air to eat some humble pie and crawl into bed with a now calm and apologetic Tamela.

"Why do you chase me like that? I just need space to calm down."

"I don't mean to. I afraid you be run off and nev-uhh come back."

"And go where? It's an island! You're making me *want* to never come back."

She squeezed me. "Well, you is back now. Don't run away again."

"Don't cuss me like that again. Let it go, move past it."

"I know . . . but, wha' mek you ha' to—"

This was our cycle of violence. She couldn't accept my repentance, give me space to grow out of Shiori (I finally did), recognize my feelings for her, and not act out her own. I hadn't yet divined my marital future was an alt-reality Vanna White.

Yet, our second year of marriage was rocky and happy all at once. In between crazed quarrelling we joyfully sexed all over our apartment and private *lanai* (a balcony; porch). We buzzed our Suzuki through early morning rambles before work. Arms tightly wrapped me. Jolly banter lit my ear. We tooled round the south end of Oahu, north through Waimānalo, Kailua, Kaneohe and the Polynesian Culture Center. Afternoon jaunts took us up Tantalus Drive's cool slopes and its Honolulu overlook to play in the Pali's mad-thrusting winds and make love under palm fronds on the slopes above. Shared hardships carting groceries from Sam's Club on our diminutive motorbike in knifepoint rain and so many peaceful, loving experiences conveyed a sense of real family. I treasured what should've formed the core of our marriage. Instead, the immutable past defined it in violent altercation. To add gasoline to her roaring passions, she wasn't yet pregnant.

"I wan' a baby! You mus' be dry as dust."

"My son with Monica says no way. Sperms are maybe backpedaling from your raucous neighborhood, possibly preferring death to dishonor."

She slapped my shoulder. "Go see a doc-tuhh. I should be pregnant by now."

Near the end of our Hawaiian delight one of the buggers took a flyer. A picture of enchantment, she was. We had Kaiser for the birth but I was terrified in my near-bankrupted state of the financial burden the lying media ginned up with 'studies' proving it took a million bucks to raise a child. Tamela interpreted my joy lack club a rejection of her baby, therefore her, and simmered herself another bitter stew.

BETWEEN MONEY, THE church, and Tamela's despotic violence, I was a beaten man at the end of a year in Hawaii. I'd come to terms with bankruptcy and suspended payments on certain debts after explaining my situation. They canceled my accounts and threw me to collections wolves. *Bye-bye, rebuilt credit.* I was near suicidal for months coming to terms with my financial picture. I couldn't pay all my bills. Some now need be sacrificed that others might live; a damning weight left my shoulders. I felt liberated. My debt wasn't gone, but I'd seized control. It didn't enslave me. I chose what to pay. I accepted the consequences and reordered my financial priorities based on what I, not my creditors, needed. They had cashflow. I didn't.

It's a simple action yet fraught with crushing psychological obstacles rooted in a false desire to please others. It seems unscalable. But creditors have an obligation to recognize the financial hiccups in everybody's life in the system we inhabit. It's inevitable. To not do so is a mental illness, a detachment from reality, a psychosis. Any person owed money has a duty to respect the solvency and family obligations of honest debtors. Creditors' merciless indifference and slavish devotion to policy infuses hate, resentment, and revolution in the hearts of debtors who, for the most part, took on debt planning to repay it.

I'm sure creditors were appalled when America outlawed debtors' prison. Yet, it was a net positive for both. Creditors rejecting my need to reduce or suspend payments was a slap to the face. They're all smiles when you're borrowing and paying, but a difficulty creeps in and you're a cheat meriting the virtual debtors' prison they construct around you built out of whatever collections, credit scores, and shaming corncob they can shove up your ass. Being caught inside this loop is what destroys the minds and hearts of debtors. It's said that debt destroys marriages and families but in truth it's misplaced priorities. Debtors feel they need sacrifice if not destroy their personal lives, loved ones, and families to maintain social–credit worthiness. For me, it was a matter of personal honor. Still and all, the staggering burden was more than I could manage as creditors bleated *pay, pay, pay.* Sure, if they're a friend, relative, or suffer financial hardship at your failure to repay then it needs be a priority. But for corporations having millions of borrowers, you're a minority red mark on their majority black balance sheet. It was a painful, Greek island crawl to comprehend this dynamic.

I opted out of their reality and into mine. I made sure to pay myself 10% of my earnings first, deal with utilities, then consumer bills. My new mindset relieved me. Naturally, I had to figure out how to earn a better living and ultimately pay what I owed if I didn't want bankruptcy court's own kind of corncob. But, at my pace.

As part of this plan, we chose to abandon exorbitant Hawaii for less-extortionate New York City. Former colleagues seemed my best chance for employment and that's where they lived. We had friends and Tamela family. That Shiori lived there was a fact we pretended wasn't. Tipping over broke and $30,000 in debt, I tried funding our move *sans* surviving credit cards by selling off unsold Equinox product. I printed a product–price flyer, blurbed it we were moving and, if possible, please buy what you can to defray the expense. It went to my family with news of Tamela's pregnancy. I got only a silence for the damned.

I felt kneecapped. I wasn't begging loans but selling tangibles. Maybe they saw me a multilevel version of the street corner windshield washerman or peeved at us throwing away their help getting us to Hawaii. I'd have preferred a "Thanks, but no thanks" to dead air. It wasn't the first but maybe the most noticeable in a long line of painful slights that, over the years, gelled into a realization that not-seen-nor-heard was how they preferred my troublesome self. My own Moonies.

Tantalus. Last day in exorbitant paradise.

I sold a few items to friends in Hawaii—*thank you!*—and put the rest of my $4,000-plus of nicely packaged products in temporary storage at Tensuke (I couldn't pay the shipping from New York to beat the pilfering so, *poof!*). We moved on a shoestring. Days before slinking off, I called Ernie with the news.

"You're leaving?"

"Yeah. We couldn't survive here spiritually or economically."

"Gee, I thought I hadn't seen you for awhile. Uh . . . have a nice flight." *Click.*

We almost didn't. So caught up in cleaning our apartment to rescue our security deposit, we'd missed it. A $100 penalty got us out the next day. We said goodbye to our pineapple paradise from Tantalus Drive with a nervous eye on the time.

I came to Hawaii seeking love and acceptance as far from New York as possible to start a new marriage amongst fresh possibilities. We left under a bankrupt, abhorring fog of scorn because, besides the Church of Christ, I'd married outside the Blessing with a reputation which for Moonies (and Tamela) never dies. The longer I associated with the church the squarer I transformed in its round hole. Bit by bit, I was being squeezed out like a constipated turd—unwelcome to the end, yet somehow full of hope. And what other place to pursue it than once more unto the breach of Moonie hell itself to cry God for Sun Myung, Unificationism, and Holy Indemnity.

So, *aloha* Hawaii. Thanks for the memories.

Act XIV

Return to New York
Discovering My True Worth

It's not that I wasn't happy with Moonism—despite exclusion—it's that I was perennially poor devoting my life as full time as I could to the holy pulpit while expected to look after myself yet foreswearing wealth building activities. That was a bit much. As the years rolled by and the hair thinned, contradictions like that wore heavily on my ever bushier brow.

I hadn't traipsed all the way to Hawaii for the view. My name was mud in New York and California, probably Texas, and all points coast to coast integrating the one or the other. Hawaii was so way the hell out there it functioned practically as an independent satrapy when Rev. Lee wasn't paying the rare visit. The Hawaii members didn't appear to judge me by my mainland reputation even if it lurked in the background as a handy club if I stepped on the wrong shoes. But—and this was the kicker—they were preposterously insular and cliquish if not racist for a supposedly universal church. Tamela and I were irreparable outsiders.

Superseding their xenophobia, my real black spot was marrying a nonmember outside the Blessing although a semi-ex-'B' member. Rev. Moon legitimized our despised status the previous year, rendering fatuous their mighty righteousness, but such was their stubborn rationale. They went as far as having Julie cease fundraising with Tamela to avoid her nonPrincipled contamination and crushed her feelings. My reputation for out-of-the-box thinking and aversion to blind obedience made me their poster child for fallen humanity and Tamela my acolyte, all the while the very sort Rev. Moon formed his ministry to save and the *raison d'être* for his church. It preferred its lily-white hands well washed of our kind, regardless. In a church having salvation and Restoration through the Blessing its core faith, its overt denial and ostracization indelibly impacted my soul.

Going to Hawaii wasn't only for Tamela. My refusal to give up on the church and find an outlet to contribute no matter how arduous they made it for me was a mighty motive. Now I'd lost some of that grit. Exasperated with the church and my stubborn poverty, money entirely motivated our move to the Big Apple for my professional, high-tech connections. My colleague Bentley was thrilled to see me again. He offered his apartment as a 1–2 day a week starter pack. I took acceptance where I could get it, but it meant part-time digs. So, before leaving Honolulu, we'd cast around long-distance for alternative roomies.

If you heard the Moonies were an inescapable cult with Kool-Aid tendencies, you were had. By now I'd been kicked, pushed, nudged, or impolitely asked any number of ways to get the fuck out of the Unification Church 11 times in 11 years. It has to be a record and possibly one of the greatest forms of stupidity and self-hate to say nothing of the very definition of insanity. Still, I believed one need give faith the upper hand negotiating with clashing practice. Here's a recap:

1. 1982 High St. Center—kick out (physical health from church work)
2. 1984 Judah St. Center—kick out (rejected violence; questioned authority)
3. 1984 777 Broadway Center—kick out (Judah Street reputation)
4. 1985 Hearst St. Center—get lost, not a request (revivalist; troublesome)
5. 1986 Bush St. Center—get lost, not a request (reputation)
6. 1988 Berkeley CARP—get lost, not a request (reputation; insubordinate)
7. 1988 Hearst St. Center—kick out (revivalist; questioned authority)
8. 1991 4 West 43rd St. Center—kick out (Shiori; me, the very image of Satan)
9. 1991 Belvedere/East Garden—get lost, please (too much of a hot potato)
10. 1991 UTS—get lost, not a request (Shiori; reputation)
11. 1993 Honolulu—get lost, please (unBlessed marriage; rep; too enthusiastic)

I'm not perfect. I was a thorn in the side of some leaders but only because I had an opinion. I did my work, followed orders (except to shut up, usually), and tried lifting my leaders above their incompetence. I contributed to and participated in church activities as requested or required. I never committed a crime or sexually tripped up a sister, including Shiori who ran her come-on like a raven-eyed Eve on a Saturday night when I was officially a kicked-out, teeth-gnashing nonmember promised eternal damnation outside the Blessing. That I was beguiled Adam not despoiling Lucifer should've counted for something but didn't.

My UCB friend Academic Mike later said, "I don't know, Chris, so many incidents bespeaks a pattern. It seems more likely you're the one being unPrincipled and forcing your leaders to act." He had my confessions stockpiled in long-tongued Reiko to draw upon, so I couldn't just poo-poo his conclusion as uninformed.

"Mike, nearly every leader who ever tormented me or booted me out have, themselves, been thrown out, quit, got ostracized, or demoted from big cheese to servility because they were abusing members just like they did me or got caught doing the same 'crimes' they accused me of. You don't think there's some karma going on there? Some indication how they acted wasn't me but them?"

He looked unconvinced but his face registered a subtle surprise that my nemeses weren't the righteous vestal virgins he'd instinctively presumed. "Well, sure, I've heard a few things, but—"

"You remember the Uchiyamas? Used to run Judah Street and helped Papasan Choi kick me out in '84 because I was supposedly disobedient, thus unPrincipled? Why, I ran into them at the New Yorker Hotel and guess what? They went from respectable center directors under Rev. Bigshot to working as a cook and waitress in the Japanese restaurant there—*Soko Bana* or something, the one in the corner space." That made him think . . . and maybe that it wasn't *my* pattern doing the speaking. "You know that losing your position in our church is textbook indemnity."

NEW YORK WAS still as frightening as in 1990. We landed over the Hudson River at Newark International at the end of October 1993 under grey, leaden skies. Rain dribbled and misted in a pall redolent of old Norseland's Niflheim now sporting skyscrapers and yellow cabs. Cold. Wet. If you've been to Gotham in late fall, you know how miserably washed out it rubs on you when nature feels dark, damp, and dead. It's a hundred times more depressing to an island girl raised in sunshine never cooler than the mid-70s. Tamela stopped dead in the blast of baggage claim's double sliding doors when its stark reality shot through her body.

In all seriousness she said, "Can't we jus' go back Hawaii?"

"Are you kidding? Baby, we're *here*!"

I had no illusions about the reception I'd get from the church and didn't bother. We drove my credit-card rental straight to Shiori's swindling trade at Yokohama Okadaya's Japanese tourist trap inside the Hilton Hotel at West 51st and 6th Avenue. She was the only one who'd offered solid accommodations till finding our own.

Twisting common sense again Tamela had said, "Ask Shiori. She'll agree."

My head instinctively wagged. "Nooo . . . that's a disaster waiting to happen. *Titanic* on turbochargers."

"I promise I won' cuss. I'll get along. I mean, no-body offerin'. Besides, I wan' meet 'dis glorious wo-maahn wha' t'ink she can tek me maahn."

"Uggghh. I don't want her! You just remember you insisted and I refused. Maybe Bentley will give us more days till we rent a place."

"Bentley don' wan' us in he apaaht-men'. You a' feel it?"

"Whatever your real ulterior motive is, Tamela, you better not forget I love *you*, not her, and not start anything."

"I promise." She smiled invitingly but I only saw cheshires. "It be fine."

Meh. I looked forward to their meeting like a convict the hangman, but didn't have a choice. We were insolvent with no prospects in racist Hawaii. Down to my last nickel of credit and my family's silence following my Equinox flyer nixing any possibility of relocating to their cities instead, we'd had to follow the money. Unsurprisingly, these two drama queens straight-off clicked as frenemies, each courteously drawing thin blood with daggers for eyes. The whole thing looked to be an elaborate death dance. What were polygamous Mormons even thinking?

Shiori's boss called her back from slitting eyes with Tamela to pushing overpriced tchotchkes on extravagant Japanese tourists confused about exchange rates. She was a virtuoso, making them high five figures for low 4-figure pay. We buggered off to Bentley's Court Street apartment in Brooklyn's Mafiosi Carroll Gardens. He'd schooled me about it on our first 1990 outing.

"Do not *ever* say 'mafia' out here on the sidewalk, Chris. I mean, *never.*"

"The heck you saying? It some mafia garage? Made men on the lam?" I laughed.

He gave me a look. Pointed with dark eyes. "See the old guys playing chess?"

"What, all those senior citizens we've been passing?"

His head bobbed. "Mafia," he practically whispered, mouth stretching for my tall ear. "See those young dudes sitting on that stoop?"

"Yeah . . ."

"Mafia. Those guys talking at the corner? Mafia. It's like that."

"Come on." It was kind of farfetched but a little scary, too. "What if I slip up? Somebody gonna chop me up or gun me—"

"Just don't talk about it," he coolly said. "*Capisce?*"

"Man . . ." He was creepily antsy. Reminded me of my dad warning youthful me after some flippant quip in an early '70s airport, "Just shut up! Don't utter a *word* about hijacking or terrorism." *Okay, okay, both o' youse. I get it.*

Bentley lived in a fourth-floor walkup unit of a 'shotgun' apartment building built in 1900. It smelled a century of cooking, stairs were shoulder narrow, floors creaked and sagged. Pure architectural vintage. He pointed through his window to the 140-year-old St. Mary Star of the Sea across the street where a courageous priest married Al Capone to his sweetie in 1918, funnily enough in a white linen double-breasted suit just like mine in St. Vincent *sans* cowboy boots.

He designed and sold board games, too. I met him on a Jack Morton (JMP) project developing the instructional design I built into learning software for Fortune 500 clients. Months afterward, he published his first book to rave reviews. Longing to be an author myself, I admired his achievement and tried reviving my commitment to write, especially the book on racism Jerome and I had toyed with.

A week of combat arms twixt Tamela and Shiori after the honeymoon wore off an hour into our stay and I begged Bentley to take us in. His wife Adelaide was open, gregarious, and welcoming. We laughed watching his wee lapdog slurp hardy beer out of a kitchen bowl and stagger away to sleep it off. Bentley previously had an indiscretion with a black woman that resulted in a child, and Adelaide more and more suspected his attraction to slenderly curvy Tamela. I airily tried dismissing the issue when Tamela unwisely raised it, but Adelaide wasn't placated. Eventually, Bentley cited landlord concerns and renewed our two nights a week. So, it was back to Shiori's dark basement flat for most of the week and Bentley's the remainder. I felt like a fly in a sticky trap furiously beating wings yet flapping them out by the roots for the effort. It was impossible to make peace between them. Shiori saw Tamela as an interloping homewrecker who'd stolen *her* man. Tamela saw Shiori as a threat who'd already interfered more than once with her *marriage.*

Shiori inanely said squabbling, "If I get chance, I take back K'risu!" Tamela flexed like Spielberg's venom-spitting Dilophosaurus set to chow down on the fat guy.

I said indignantly, "I'm not some piece of furniture to be yanked back and forth till one of you loses your grip! You two can shut up!" *The guilty ignored.*

Tamela was a snapping turtle that never let go. Shiori showed a predilection for confrontation I'd never suspected in her silent treatments. She was so frothing while profaning Tamela one night that she lapsed into Japanese mid-sentence.

"Wha' happ'n?" Tamela smugly jeered in her breezy and oft-incomprehensible West Indian. "You forget how to taahlk Eng-lish?"

Fuming in machinegun Japanese, Shiori snap-kicked at Tamela from six feet away. Her shoe flew across the room on the wings of Tamela's derisive laughter. These two went hammer and tongs for hours at a time then seemed best friends forever. Shiori cooked us all delicious food and Tamela cleaned the kitchen, the house, did laundry, or some other helpful thing. *Très putain de bizarre.*

My experience taught me that love is more violent and unpredictable than Russian roulette with most chambers loaded. Everything Rev. Moon ever said about fallen love bared its funnel-web fangs in twisted suspicion, jealousy, hatred, anger, resentment, and selfishness. Shiori rejected my reason for marrying Tamela was valid; who refused to believe I loved her and wanted a happy marriage *sans* Shiori; who saw me as a dupe needing rescue from an unscrupulous, nonmember barbarian; who saw Shiori a godless hussy she'd protect me from daggers drawn till I'd blame her for my cussy, sometimes jaw-punched, plight with Tamela.

Years later Tamela said, "The reason I cuss you aahll 'dem years over Shiori was to save me marriage."

"You couldn't see that all you were doing was stabbing it to death?"

"I was afraid!" she cried, eyes drooling. "An' too young."

Shit. Can you say, 'oxymoron'?

After a month of trench warfare—who says women are naturally more peaceful leaders than men?—we scrounged up a 1-bedroom in Astoria not far from the East River and the 30th Avenue N train. Our 23-34 28th Avenue fourth-floor Apple walkup at $640 a month was a bedroom or two cheaper than the Pineapple after all. Regardless, I sweated bullets over next month's rent.

In the meantime I discovered all my JMP colleagues had moved uptown to its arch rival, Caribiner Communications. Conveniently, they landed a big project with Digital Cable Radio and hired me as the production manager for a king's ransom of $30 an hour. *Woohoo!* But with a baby on the way, I needed salaried security over mo' money's feast-and-famine consulting and peeled eyes for a full-time gig.

Caribiner's job wound up. A small company based out of Connecticut hired me for their contract rewriting the Prodigy Internet portal client from DOS to Windows. I was the only applicant who met their test of writing an if-then-else statement in Visual Basic . . . who'd even apply without that skill? I pushed my salary to $50,000 plus three months travel expenses, making me the highest paid employee in their stable. It shook out to $5.50 an hour less than DCR but full time with benefits. It felt good. I was a nervous horse my first day, wondering if I could really code well enough to build a Windows product. My bosses and colleagues gave my work great reviews and I eased into middle-class industrial software development.

In six months or so a Deloitte *&* Touche unit providing database development and maintenance services to Fortune 100 clients lured me away with a 27% pay rise. *Honolulu, eat your spiteful, cliquish heart out!* My own stuttering ticker jittered negotiating this fortune on a top floor of their Wall Street high-rise. I'd never earned anything more than $28,000 a year before the Prodigy job. I tried playing it cool and danced around annual sum queries like all the advice.

"I do need a number," my interviewer pressed me. "Just shoot."

With burning reservations and a faux calm, "I would need $70,000."

She flashed shined pearls of negotiating prowess across her *Vogue* features. "Well, that's a bit high . . . would $68,500 be acceptable?"

I reckoned saving $1,500 over a year was her professional high ground. *Acceptable? I struggled to hold a poker face as good as hers. You bet it is! Yes! Yes! Give it to me, ba—!* I gravely nodded after some feigned mentation like I was running numbers on a pro forma. "Yes, that's acceptable. I look forward to starting ASAP."

"As do we. You're a heckuva catch." I wasn't sure but starting to believe her.

Long Island Sound on our African friend's boat with his smoking hot bikinied Japanese.

It wasn't the elevator I rode down from her office but Cloud 9. I was a leaf on air to the hellish, humid subway. This *is how it feels to be valued! They want me. Value me. Paying me virtually top dollar.* Subpar wages? *Pfft!* Nevermore. *I'm worth $68,500. Hell, man, I'm worth $70,000, even $100,000!*

No more penny-ante $12-an-hour shite for the hard work and grungy forevers of take-responsibility-for-my-business-like-it's-yours bastards who'd keep the payoff then dump you over the side in lifeboat times. Thoughts ran on the church. *Look how the working world values me,* I told those parsimonious leaders. *Even fallen people have more sense of fair play than you pious Moonies.*

The church demanded full-time work for next to nothing while scorning my American humanity, devaluing my contribution, and discounting my effort because they saw me as disobedient, a revivalist, results oriented, or satanic for falling with a disgruntled sister *after* ostracizing me out of their august company. The workaday world cared about my professional competence. Who I bonked was my business. *What's it to the church how messy my head is when it comes to employing me in any capacity* as a home member *to meet its goals? Why discriminate when I'm capable, qualified, and willing to do what's needed when so many 'A'-members they brag are oh so Principled, holy, and competent aren't any of it?* Religion's self-righteousness is the prime reason it gleefully murders people for the greater glory of God.

These thoughts chewed through my mind on the rumbling subway home, my reflection studying me through the tunnel-darkened window. I desperately wanted the church to accept me, to value and appreciate my hard work and dedication to God and True Parents. I didn't care about its money or a fancy lordship but affirmation of my human value. The business world shows it accepts and appreciates you through salary, benefits, and upward mobility. My church wasn't into profit-making but soul-saving. Though mine needed copious salvage, what difference did it make to the job of keeping Rev. Moon's financial boilers lit or helping him reach humanity through compassionate Divine Principle or comforting God?

Look at Rev. Moon denouncing sin and backsliding followers while praising Martin Luther King, Jr. as the greatest American of the twentieth century, a man not unknown for extramarital affairs. Yet, few—least of all, he—reject King's greater faith and singular contribution to desegregating America in order to punish his immaterial moral failings. While Rev. Moon hears St. Paul's admonition that "all have sinned and fall short of the glory of God," including himself, his sanctimonious, phylacteried leaders can't let go of Jesus' Old Testament hyperbole to cut off your sinful body parts as a metaphor to fumigate their institution of its vermin. A dying church shouldn't censure me over nonfelonious stumbles when examining my donation to Rev. Moon's vision. That's bad business it can't afford.

I suppose I need to respect the pesky fact that belief Satan invades God's providence through its sinful providential actors plays a big role in this problem. Rev. Moon said Satan was able to kill King because he made bad spiritual conditions through his sexual (maybe other?) indiscretions. God couldn't protect him, as Satan would demand equal treatment.

Sailing a hot second through the good life. Jun., 1994.

There's no doubt that backsliding, sinful members and his own family have cost Rev. Moon dearly in the world of public opinion and the courts. It isn't a problem that'll go away soon. It'll probably get worse. Indeed, the top tier of leadership appears to me so suffused with greed, avarice, sexual infidelity, and abusiveness as to make the general membership's transgressions seem innocent. The difference between them and me is position and connections. Unlike many of his leaders, Rev. Moon doesn't ever, to my knowledge over 21 years, destroy his worst enemies much less those having even the most tenuous relationship. He unconditionally loves and promotes the penitent—the impenitent usually quit—even knowing he or she doesn't deserve it, because he's shooting for a loftier goal. His leaders lose the plot to oft-rely instead on psychic floggings in best British naval tradition.

Assessing the remains of the day and savoring my win–win with Deloitte & Touche, I felt a pang of resentment for the church constantly demeaning, abusing, and deprecating me when the fallen business world was only too willing to embrace my *work*. It was just galling, that's all. And blocking my sense of mission.

Having accepted the new job, I was now faced with the unsavory task of resigning from my current one. I was too embarrassed, and conflict averse besides, to tell my company after just half a year that I was leaving for another employer.

Instead I said, "My grandmother's very ill. My family wants me home for it."

"Are you sure you're not just changing jobs?" my cynical boss inquired, his knurly brows incriminating me. He was probably asking from experience.

"Oh, no, no," I smoothly assured him with *what're-you-gonna-do?* taking center stage on my face, my acting chops happy and sad. "It's an unexpected family disaster." I comforted myself it wasn't a total falsehood. She indeed was ill. Just her 1992 death from it was preventing recovery. I hoped I wasn't spawning unwelcome karma.

"We don't want to lose you. How about you telecommute from Texas?"

If I wasn't prevaricating I'd have jumped at it. "Well, gee, that's an incredible offer . . . but I can't mix my obligations to the job with her and then miss deadlines and . . ." I scotched it with great difficulty. I didn't want to seem ungrateful for their good salary nor jeopardize my new job. I stuck fast to fibbing.

My effort was wasted. Four months later the client Deloitte & Touche hired me to service hired their own in-house talent and fired them amidst rousing praise for my superb work. *Uh-huh.* Deloitte laid me off with two weeks' severance amidst heavy blame. A real karmic thrust up the tailpipe after all. Lesson learned.

∼

IN MAY '94 I was strung out over rent consulting *pro tempore* for JMP, my friend Louis Berman, and Caribiner for $30–50 an hour, depending.

Tamela clutched her vast belly at 7:30 PM. "Me baby comin'! Le' we go!"

I was engrossed in the exciting, climactic episode of Stephen King's hugely popular TV miniseries *The Stand*. I looked her up and down from the sofa. "Just don't let that baby come till this is over. I have to see it!"

"Chris, you—! I wan' go now!" She let fly a stream of accusation.

"Your water didn't break. It's a false alarm." I called the hospital during ads.

"The contractions are five to ten minutes apart?" Our nurse listened attentively. "Sounds like she's dilated less than five centimeters. We'd definitely send her home were she here. You were right to call." *Damn straight.* Pharisaic eyes lit her up.

Friday noon, May 13 she entered The Zone. I called a cab to truck her an hour north. Afraid the driver would dump a near-birthing mother, I warned her to zip her lip. Not a peep. Tough lady! I was fine with the birth, probably from ignorance of what I was getting into. I kept up a steady stream of one-liners for distraction on the way, then for the nurses and midwife.

In the midst of Tamela's unmoderated pain and cussing I said, "Hey! I'm standing in a puddle of something here."

Our nurse looked down. "Shit! That's the spinal. No wonder she's hollering."

"Kaiser ain't gonna like me standing in their money," I said. *Botchy doctor.*

Who then strode in. "It's too late to reinsert now. Just grit your teeth."

"*Arrrgghhh!*" Altogether, her labor took 24 hours. She writhed in pain the whole time, struggling through each contraction with sweat boiling down her contorted face under a black beret cockeyed on her head. *I hope our son appreciates this.*

"Why are you wearing a hat?" the nurse said with a chuckle.

"Becau', " slow voice strewn with tears and agony, "I didn'a comb me haiiirrr!"

That was a laugh even an embarrassed Tamela grinned over. Then out popped our son—literally. He squirted right over the midwife's eager hands and splayed with a plop right at the edge of the padded table. Fibrillating, I thought he'd slide right off the wet plastic to the linoleum-tiled concrete and jumped for the grounder, but he teetered long enough that she got a firm grip on his slimy ankle.

She said, "That's some white skin! Wow! Didn't see that coming." The nurses clucked surprise. "Tamela! Look down here and see what you've done!"

I jolted, staring into Dad's age-wrinkled face. Over the next week it morphed substantially (and over months, browned), but those first few hours he was a dead ringer. I didn't really mind, but wasn't thrilled, either. I suppose I didn't think Dad's a handsomely aged face, or else it reminded me too much of all my suppressed resentment of which I'd only recently begun feeling dimly aware.

Our baby was a wizened, crinkly little fellow crying softly as the nurses batted him about. Then he was in my arms and all my fear of babies evaporated. He lay effortlessly in my hands. Somehow I knew that however I moved him about I'd never hurt him. Babies, it turns out, are not so fragile as they appear. They're more like the "rubber cutty" my best friend Lance called his cat. Their bones and joints are soft and malleable and, within reason, flop around. I'd feared snapping bones, broken necks, and screaming pain but got none of it. My coronary subsided with his birth but the coming financial hit loomed anxious. Thank God she delivered him on Kaiser from her jackknifed Hawaiian McDonald's stint.

She was too tired to hold the baby, but eventually took him in her arms. He wouldn't breast feed more than dribs and drabs for a week. We called in Kaiser's home nurse to sort it. Tamela was an emotional wreck, wailing at the top of her lungs along with our starving baby. What a din. Our home nurse straightened everybody out and he happily slurped down gallons of milk. Tamela was entirely worn out.

I called Mom. "Can you fly out on my dime to help us a few weeks?"

"Oh, my gosh. Well, let me talk it over with your father."

It was a difficult call to make. While my retired parents extensively helped my sisters with their babies apparently without being asked, they hadn't extended a similar hand to us. I was hurt and chagrined and not sure I wanted their help at all. My family's universal excuse was, "You live too far away." Yet, I saw them travel farther distances for my siblings. In 1994, I had yet to form any conscious sense of grievance with my folks, but it was coming as, more and more, I was seeing what I took for clear disparities. By 2003, it was dominating a major part of my persona. Right now, I swallowed hard and reached out.

"Okay, we'll come," she said. "But we can only stay a week." *Yeah.*

Tamela reluctantly agreed with my choice for a name. A good if trivial Moonie, I decided on a Korean name, but not up front. Too many were doing that and it was boring. Many members considered it the greatest honor for a Korean leader—the higher the better—to virtue signal their child's messianic moniker.

"Rev. Pak named my son," they said.

"Rev. Oh gave my daughter her name."

"Oh, that's nice. Father's most trusted disciple, Peter Kim, decided my boy's."

"Ad fucking nauseam," I squawked at Tamela; a hare fleeing hellhounds. My child was a past, present and future global citizen . . . if Rev. Moon was right that history had passed from Jesus to him, anyway. A Hebrew, Christian, and Korean name would represent the Old, New, and Completed ages.

I consulted my dentist. "I always liked Kal-el, Superman's real name."

"Did you know it's Hebrew for Voice of God?"

"No kidding! You made up my mind!" I slapped it on the birth certificate. He'd earned it, flying from his mom's womb like that. My Catholic confirmation name was his middle. The man I most admired and my role model served as third.

Someone later said, "That's wrong! Father forbids it. You need to change it."

"I never heard him say that."

"He's the *Messiah*, Chris. Come on."

"So is Jesus." Maybe they worried, if Korea followed Spain's example, the future would be populated with scruffy, ironically named ne'er-do-wells. "It's done recorded and anyway I'll name my child how I like. Naysayers can suck it."

"Like me? That's always been your problem."

"Is it? He'll change it later if he wants." I was satisfied. Hoped my son was.

It was then I decided all my children would be named something-el. Names have power but have become blasé. Meaningless autonyms. Pleasing sounds. I recalled Young Soon's parents changing her name to Joo Hwa at Judah Street to improve her fortune and future. We technologically marvelous Americans shouldn't be so quick to forget millennia of close attention to names . . . Argentina's tyranny knows it and promotes a list of approved names else no birth certificate. I wanted my children to have strong, image-defining names that might guide and influence their futures without the trauma of my boy named Sue. A parent's duty is to prepare the soil in which a child grows to adulthood. I can't control life's circumstances, but perhaps a uniquely potent name will draw some spiritual mojo to help them cope.

~

JOB SECURITY IN 1994 seemed merely a pipe dream consulting or salaried. Soon after Kal-el's birth I was thrown into unemployment. Caribiner pitched consulting work and kept me afloat the next four years despite its feast-or-famine lifestyle. Careful planning weathered the January–June drought seemingly as inevitable as broken air conditioners on the Big Apple's rackety trains.

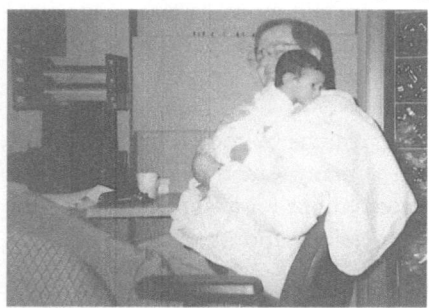

With Kal-el at Caribiner. Jun., 1994.

I contacted UTS on a lark in December, noting my 1989 acceptance. I didn't have high hopes but Hong Yu Kovic, the new admissions director, didn't know me and was enthusiastic. Her American husband Jim landed fame and notoriety punching out Hyo Jin Moon over his verbal abuse. Meeting Hyo Jin myself, I aspired to Jim's stellar rep. I sent in my application with recommendations from Dr. Mary Berry, my professor of Japanese history at UC Berkeley, and a sympathetic church leader. Hong Yu wrote, "The seminary is very excited to have you. I'm rushing your paperwork."

She called in late December. "Congratulations, Chris! You can start UTS as soon as January's winter quarter."

My heart skipped a few beats. My three life goals—Blessed, UTS degree, working with Rev. Moon—were hell-freezing lulus forever squelched by faulty choices and satanic leaders. These last 14 years had my psyche a rip-roaring tornado. Now I could begin accomplishing the one that might lead to the others.

I vibrated with excitement. Tamela was dour. "Wha' mek you need more school? You already have all any-body could need."

"A college degree these days is just yesterday's high school diploma." Half her face shrugged up with an Indian head bobble. "I'm not getting anywhere in business and for sure nowhere in this church without at least a Master's degree. If you want your white picket fence, this is what I gotta do."

But her unrecognized cognitive disability stood in the way of her understanding. I had to press on with her acquiescence instead of support. She was happy so long as money rolled in because that meant stability and safety. She'd fast got used to $5,000–$20,000 paychecks and didn't want them disappearing. For a Vincy girl, I was neck deep in Scrooge McDuck's money bin.

"You mus' put work ahead of school," her voice firm, "for Kal-el sake."

"School is for his sake." In one ear, out the other without stopping for coffee.

As 1994 wound down, I reflected on its tumult. Jerome and Tamela had been the left and right thieves to my cross. Believing 1995 would turn out better than 1992–94 was a comfort. I never figured it was slated for worse.

I'd met Mr. Bramble's son Alfonso in St. Vincent. In December '93 he'd said in New York, "Jeh-rome physically figh-tin' up me fadduh, Ro-naahld who banish him to 'de base-ment, an' his drug brudduh who been follow you roun' since you got here an' know you work at Jack Mort-ohhn." He gave it a second to sink in. "He be tellin' aahll 'de people you were queer in St. Vincent, screwin' in church cent-uhh . . . just all kin'a shit. Go 'de house an' deal wi' him. He be killin' you, mon."

Ronald said the same thing, then had Stoff turn us away at their St. Albans' door in February. I punched a pay phone. "Why are you at the corner? Jerome's not here. I only see people with appointments. I made it clear I wouldn't see you today."

"You said this morning to come by this afternoon when you were back from church. You said you can't wait to meet Tamela, and she's right here."

"I never did. I operate by appointment."

"The train was two hours!" *Hiss.* "Well . . . you saying we misunderstood you?"

"You sure did. Bye, now." *Click.*

Tamela toe-tapping in the cold was hot with indignation. "Him become jus' like Jeh-rome, now. Wash your hands aahll 'dem, Chris. 'De whole family pois-ohhn."

My spiritual mother Ginny had run into Jerome for an earlier earful. When I talked to her over the Christmas holidays, she referenced my "sexual exploits."

"What did he tell you? From what I'm hearing, it's what *he's* been doing."

She lowered the boom Mrs. Kobayashi style. "I don't know about that, and I'm not repeating it. I don't know anybody as stupid as you! Who even are you?"

"You're condemning me on his hearsay? I can't even—?"

"My advice to you is don't try connecting with the church for several years. It doesn't want you. To be honest, I don't think I want to talk to you, either." *Click.*

I realized Jerome's slander was national when I called Hemi working Seattle's Ocean Church in January 1995. "Is he the guy going around the church telling everyone you're a homosexual? I was surprised you swing that way."

"Goddammit! None of that's true. You oughta bloody well know better."

"Okay, man, if you say so. Then . . . you should fuck that nigger up." *Click.*

Eyes popped. "*Ehh?* What did he just say?"

My right-side thief was jacking up her hornet-maddened rhetoric to a shrill roar. She'd lashed me to rail tracks under a locomotive whipsaw and no Dudley Do-Right in sight. On occasion she whomped up such a melee over my engagement dalliance with Shiori in 1991 while perhaps no Sarah Straitlace herself in her wee Vincy sugar shack, plus taking her calls at home—spite; else her voice was a longed-for peaceful memory—that more than once but for a tether I leapt out our fourth-storey window to the concreted courtyard to escape. It took all my common sense and fear of hell to stay my stamping feet as it acceleratingly seemed a portal to blessed peace.

I was beginning my unwitting 'death plunge' into domestic battery not unlike a sinking ship reaching its irreversible descent beneath the waves. The stress and strain were telling in my daily habits, shortened temper, irascible mood swings, and a growing inability to concentrate on the task of earning a living. I turned passive in the face of life, fatalistically allowing economic difficulties and office politics to strike home as if inevitable, well-deserved natural disasters.

There was no doubt I'd truly and cruelly wounded Tamela. She was innocent, naïve, and gullible in part because her cognitive disability limited her understanding of adult life. She was only 20 by now anyway. Just a kid. Still, the complete lack of distinction between thought and deed in her mind was disturbing. I suppose it should've clued me in that something was horribly wrong with her information processing system, but I was trapped like a rat by my own conscience and her inability to move on. I knew I was wrong to ever fall with Shiori and consumed with guilt for that as well as for leaving her out of the blue (from her perspective) for Tamela. Two incompatibly reconcilable guilt complexes.

Despite my confidence that God willed my marriage, I just couldn't surmount my guilt for dumping Shiori and disrupting her life. It chained me. Left me vulnerable to her own kind of battery. She'd started our relationship by vigorously seducing me and was now anything but standoffish. She wanted me back in her life and was more than willing to open her legs in the hope it would do the trick. Regardless, I was death-locked to my marriage. I may have screwed it up worse, but I wasn't walking away. In my confused way I loved Tamela, cherished my belief that God wanted it, and desired our coupled eternity as Divine Principle taught. Unlike the Blessing, marriage is a New Testament convention based on fallen love. Because of Jesus' mission-interruptus, God can't sanction it; death dissolves it. I wanted to grow old with Tamela then spend all eternity in love with her.

Her blood naturally boiled at me disrespecting our Christian marriage. I got it. All my high-minded, self-righteous—when you don't live by it—morality flew out the window every time I beheld Shiori as if enthralled like a beast of Circe. Realizing I was behaving like the low class dregs I despised heavily dosed me with self-loathing, which I suppose is guilt's necessary corollary: how can you feel guilt without hating the behavior and its chooser? Catholicism taught me to hate the sin but love the sinner. Yet, it was a struggle (as it seems for most folks) to maintain that fine distinction regarding my own. I hated myself not only for violating Christian morality long pounded into me by priests, parents, and society but also because, through my awareness of Divine Principle, I *knew* the root of the Fall and failed relationships. Even so, my fallen emotion enslaved me to repeat Adam's fall.

I'd somehow built a distinction in my mind between conventional marriage and the Blessing. The Unification Church had so indoctrinated me that conventional marriage was beyond God's purview, unsanctioned and temporary, that all the moral rules designed to uphold the sacrament's sanctity dissolved. I knew it was wrong, stupid, and bad to cheat on Tamela if for no other reason than the harm it inflicted in my name. My heart simply recognized no moral restraint. Rev. Moon let alone Unificationists would be judgily appalled by my admission because he teaches (though evidently himself forgot) that a committed relationship of any kind should be monogamous until the Blessing sanctions it. Once Tamela alienated me through incessant quarreling and Shiori opened her heart and arms to comfort me in my domestic crisis, my moral compass lost all bearing. Emotions ablaze steered my course. Though instinctively I held a notion of my moral true north's location, I ignored it and settled for self-loathing to ease my insoluble pain.

There's a word for this: imbecilic. This isn't a justification but an explanation of my internal dynamics. I wouldn't recommend infidelity to my worst enemy.

In any case, my *gottverdammte* emotions were killing me, pushing me this way and that like flotsam, inciting behavior I found repugnant and alarming. And it all centered round this little, itsy-bitsy feeling called guilt. My sense of it for leaving Shiori to marry Tamela absolutely forbade me telling her to fuck off out of my life. I was lost in her pain and willing to do damn near anything to alleviate it however temporarily. Sex is an all-purpose pain reliever albeit, like alcohol, has its own vicious hangover. But all it did was dig me a darker grave as I wounded her ever more deeply by not abandoning Tamela, aggravated my sense of guilt and self-loathing, and further frayed the bonds of a marriage increasingly needing jumper cables.

Guilt consumed me in my relationship with Tamela, too. Our cycle of pain and violence just wouldn't be complete without it. Unlike Shiori's smooth mothering and affectionate understanding of my misery and torment under Tamela's bitter lash that only prolonged my desire for her, my sense of guilt reacted to Tamela's cussy warfare like water on hot grease. She'd start calmly enough, digging with a hooked barb till poking a sore spot. Then my guilty, remorseful, why-the-hell-did-I-ever-tell-her-and-why-can't-she-just-let-it-go feelings kicked in and I responded in kind. She then stormed, inciting guilt and humiliated acrimony until our cycle double-clutched third gear. We screamed. Threw dangerous objects. I contemplated my leap through our high window to thwart her blocking me at the door.

I tried escaping when no apologizing, temporizing, nor reasoning stopped her thrashing binge. Single-mindedly caning my engagement and Texas transgressions, she was no-quits till spent. My response degraded into fight or flight, classic Animal Planet. Fighting my ship was foolish and hopeless, though I gave it the good old college try like I'd never learn. When her machinery showed signs of perpetual motion, I felt trapped and helpless as in Hawaii. Like a wild-eyed roach, I scuttled for any egress. If I hadn't slyly worked my way close enough, Tamela usually beat me to the door and physically barred me. We scuffled as I tried forcing my way past, but—don't laugh, now—a sturdy roustabout, she was. It wasn't my nature to smack her though sometimes she knuckled me. I could only shove her off to yank the door and squeeze through the rampaging mass whanging it shut.

403

Three months before our son hit air, I made it to the door first and flung it open. Tearing round the corner and down four flights, she was in hot pursuit.

"I sorry! I sorry!" she cried. "Come back! I'll behave!" But it resurrected a dark image fleeing down sunny Ward Street in Honolulu.

"Forget it!" I gasped, not loudly. I was in flight mode, blind and deaf to the world. She gave up partway because she didn't want to risk the baby, but I didn't know that. Six-six, I take two steps at a time. Now I was doing three. On the last landing I miscalculated, thinking myself two steps up instead of three. I stepped on air. Toppled forward. My left ankle crumpled like tinfoil on the floor with a stupefying *pop!* followed by a rush of eye-watering pain. Feeling her breath, I sucked up the agony and rushed the first floor. Hands supported my weight on the banisters. I hobbled one-legged into the street. In tears I limped to an emergency room two merciful blocks away. I'd torn damn near everything in my left ankle. A 6-week cast to my knee. Many hours later I banged through the building's heavy entry on crutches. Tamela was just arriving all coated-up to track me down.

Shocked yet indifferent she cagily asked, "So, wha' happ'n to you?"

No motherly affection, no rush to comfort, no sorrow that I was crippled. But, really, what did I expect? I'd been feeling tenderhearted all exhausted and late at night, but now a stifled exasperation snapped on. My voice was even albeit, to be honest, sheepish biting off what I really wanted to scream. "I destroyed my ankle escaping your stupid, endless cussing."

In bed she said, "I sorry for cussin' and mek you run off to ge' hurt."

"Thanks, but I'm not feeling it."

I needed months of physical therapy when the orthopedist found my freed ankle a welded angle iron. His hands of Samson forcibly remade it flexible, coolly stretching the ligaments and tendons now hard as rawhide. Through agonized tears and choked screams I silently cursed Tamela for triggering my headlong frenzy.

This was the general state of our 3-year marriage on the eve of my entry into the venerated halls of UTS, which required the most rigorous spiritual discipline in our efforts and the love of Christ—Jesus or True Parents, take your pick—in our hearts. I felt like a fraud because of Shiori *and* Tamela, but no way was I opening my mouth to anybody. The church had proved time and again it was no friend to the sinner or the penitent. With a heavy heart, I kept my follies and foibles between me and God while I worked them out. Meanwhile I had to exorcise Shiori from my life as expeditiously yet tenderly as possible, heal Tamela's wounded heart, and eradicate the painful battery that was now my norm. Then UTS turned out a stepping stone to something else altogether.

Act XV

At the Seminary
Blessed Dreams at the Gates of Despotism

*T*o me, the Unification Theological Seminary was Moonworld's fabled Shangri-la. The moment I discovered its august existence I determined UTS would sit like destiny on my résumé. From my earliest days in the Unification Church I'd felt set apart from the sheeple, called by God to a special mission serving Rev. Moon as he'd never been served before.

Like many Moonies, I was appalled and disgusted by Neil Salonen's resignation from the presidency of the American church over his implacable differences with the Koreans and Japanese. I saw no integrity nor moral strength in his replacement, Dr. Mose Durst, which so indignantly played out with Papasan Choi at Judah Street. Even worse was Michael Warder's treacherous court testimony against Rev. Moon out of resentment and malice largely instigated, again, by our Asian elders. Every which way he turned it seemed to me Rev. Moon was being cheated, tricked, and betrayed by Americans and it angered me. Embarrassed and humiliated me.

Every day I endured the thousand-and-one slights and jeers of the Japanese. Their low energy racism twisted my guts till I was tempted to grab Mr. Uchiyama, our arrogant, American-hating five-five Japanese pooh-bah at Judah Street, by his collar and belt buckle and fire him like a torpedo through the front window. *You small, puny bastard.* I blithely sized him up like the US Marine Corps before the Imperial Army proved to be its toughest nut ever. *I'm so big and strong . . . don't you have any sense I could literally stomp you out of existence?* Apparently he didn't, and would've justifyingly seen me proving my satanism for thinking it.

What American members needed was a president as tough and Principled as the Koreans and Japanese (wrongly) took themselves for. *That person is me.* I was incorruptible. Unbuyable. Principled and (excluding my fallen ways) sufficiently moral. On fire with Rev. Moon's mission. My love for God. His physical kingdom of heaven on earth. Sure, I was a little rough around the edges, missing a few chips here and there. Maybe my elevator didn't always reach the top floor. Nothing a little education and experience couldn't smooth out. All I needed was the chance.

All around me American members weren't living up to Rev. Moon's expectations, from our mealymouthed presidents down to the foot soldier. It irked me and irritated hell out of him. He overflowed with opprobrious criticisms and complaints about Americans, starting with those he'd bequeathed the highest positions and most comfortable lifestyles. He especially complained about the lavish prominence he'd showered on backstabbers like Michael Warder who turned on him as if a through-and-through charlatan. For all his many faults, he certainly isn't that.

He often spoke of the loneliness of his position. That he'd never been able to find a friend. That only the fatuous and *idiots savants* congregated around him. Three people like him, he pined, and he could Restore the world.

> Rather than one thousand followers, we need one person who can lead. (*The Way of the Spiritual Leader*, Witnessing 1998)

Well, I knew I could be that leader. At least one of those three. Unlike the Asians and milquetoast Americans, I didn't mince words with leaders, nor would I with Rev. Moon. They lied to him like unbuttoned hookers leaning in a car window about their victories, how many attended events, or the bookkeeping. I was disgusted and dismayed by the falsehoods and cheating saturating leadership's every word and deed. They were only succeeding at wrecking the movement, sabotaging his vision, wasting my life. My confidence in achieving the goals set before me while truthfully reporting my ups and downs was unshakable. A real American president and not a Japanese puppet on Korean strings was what we all needed.

Yes, indeed I was the man for the job. I was young, confident, energetic. All I needed was Rev. Moon's recognition that I was the savior of his American church and my opportunity to shine. If I failed, I'd be no worse off than the rest of the losers he perennially plunged into authority. So, why not me? Over my three years at UTS even its backbiting president would proclaim my destiny to lead the American movement. Too, there was Mr. Kamiyama's 1983 ladder prophecy: "Someday, you will be president." It was hard *not* to imagine I was a fated Moonie. And the seminary was the last venue in the church where I'd ever get a real chance.

～

THE EARLY CHURCH was lost in cobwebs. Gone forever were the days you could join the movement and two weeks later command an MFT crew, then rise to center director and in a year or less one of 50 state leaders. Of course, all positions beyond that were strictly off limits to non-Asians except the token American presidency, certain administrative jobs in New York City's national headquarters, and eventually a nominal American regional leader position. Still, I was confident I could break down those barriers and earn trust, respect, and authority from the Koreans and Japanese even against their better judgment. I just needed to prove it.

After those heady, woolly days of the American Family in the late '60s and early '70s—before it turned into a feudal, theocratic empire—Rev. Moon decided he needed a viable leadership training facility if he was ever going to reach deep into Christianity to rip out its false notions and skepticism of his messiahship by the roots. He settled on a Christian Brothers monastery called St. Joseph's Normal Institute in upstate New York and took it off their hands in 1974 for something like $1.5 million. Rechristened Unification Theological Seminary, he solemnly declared that only its graduates could be Unification Church leaders or work directly with him. When I heard about it in 1981, it soared to my bucket list's top spot.

Bucolic popped into my head when I'd sussed its 260-acre campus in 1990. Situated on a wooded estate next to Rhinebeck, the school instantly stroked a sense of peace and wellbeing in me. Largely cut off from the church by 1995 when I matriculated, it was a place unto itself although previously very much a local church center writ large.

God's eye view of UTS; Massena House in front.

Until maybe 1991 students paid for UTS by fundraising, the time-honored Moonie route to quick cash. Their result supported the school as it would've a church center. Summer or winter, blistering sun or crotch-tall snow, they hit the streets portering buckets of flowers and heavy, whitewashed plywood signs proclaiming roses or whatever product *du jour* for sale. Some students, of course, were Hebrews in Egypt's desert bitterly soured on the never-ending regimen. The more compliant accepted it as the price of unaccredited educational empowerment and church advancement and ready to hawk wares till the holy cows came home. Me, I was sour. But, as in 1990, I'd pay the piper.

The curvy entrance drive I remembered from my abortive foray here before St. Vincent was only recently replaced when I arrived in the depths of January 1995. A sad, straight shot now paved past a guard shack crewed by disinterested or sleeping students (often unaware you were there, if you stopped at all, until you blew your horn) if not inopportunely manned by the administration's Lavrentiy Beria chief of security who'd had Jerome arrested. On one side of the central circle drive was the old bishop's home, a beautiful though rundown 3-storey Victorian mansion called Massena House. Now a group home for Blessed students with children, it was in the early stages of renovation and even more a mess than usual.

On the circle's right, the main building housed administration, classrooms, dorms, cafeteria, library, and whatnot. A cavernous, H-shaped building constructed of heavy stone blocks and brick, one of the few Christian statues the Brothers failed to uproot and take with them topped its imposing, arched main entry. Evidently, many felt selling out to Rev. Moon was a spiritual disgrace and unwilling to desert anything remotely sentimental. That included most of their statues and the entire graveyard that once reposed behind a now burned-down apartment building farther down the dirt main road. It was creepy walking through those field-stripped consecrated grounds. I wondered if they'd forgot anyone who might now be mischievously wandering the property in frustrated pique.

The school's first president was Sang Chul 'David' Kim, a satanically-arch-browed Korean who'd served up 19 years when Rev. Moon unceremoniously fired him for neglecting to implement too many of his traditions, such as teaching Divine Principle.

President Kim was of the opinion that UTS should be like any Christian seminary if it was to garner their respect. This, of course, defeated Rev. Moon's intent.

He founded UTS with a $3 (I'd heard $10) million endowment. "Only its interest earnings are legally spendable," my UCB now UTS friend Academic Mike said.

"Huh," said I. "The buzzy word is that President Kim raided the account to fund business ventures selling luxury items and buying land." He might've heard some of Bill Gouldd's inspiring Equinox speeches.

"Well . . . "

"The older students say they weren't surprised these failed. They *were* surprised all that legally protected cash went with them."

"There was an issue. We've had some financial situations as a result. "

"I heard a lot of mandatory maintenance was deferred."

"That's been rectified as part of the ongoing accreditation process."

"Well, no disrespect, but I hope this Cratchited seminary stays in business long enough for me to get my degree."

"You're lucky you were admitted, Chris. You should settle down about it."

Palms out. "Okay, Mike. Sorry. I'm just exploring my new home."

"Just explore your classes. You'll get along better." *Yeah.*

President Kim instituted some nifty annual events such as a forensics competition and an annual open house and picnic to dispel local fears the school might go after their children. But he'd let his charge run into the mud to beg its salvation. Revival began in 1991 on a student ballot implementing a regularized tuition (overclocking fundraising) and administrators' salaries over

Here, we greeted and waved goodbye to Rev. Moon.

stipends. I paid $142 per credit in January 1995. That made my planned 3-year divinity degree worth about $16,000, a Rockefelleran fortune for the typically impoverished but anti-revenuing Moonie to cough up. Still, I was paying for *opportunity* not education per se, and I swallowed the bitter pill and wrote the checks. Rev. Moon fired President Kim along with his academic dean and chief administrator in May 1994.

"No, it was mostly a gentle but firm push," Mike said.

"That wasn't my impression from the scuttlebutt." Plus, I knew a euphemism when I heard it.

"You going to believe me or the rumor mill?" More like rudely admonished for his failures then dispatched to shuffleboard with Papasan Choi. His threadbare chair went to a Japanese associate professor I liked but viewed as surly and troubled.

Dr. Theodore Shimmyo—unexpectedly holding a nuclear engineering degree from Tokyo University—was maybe a 20-year US resident. He came off wholly hostile to our culture, nature, personality, and society, his back teeth aching from anything American that book-checked his high-brow, Messiah-approved Japanese culture.

Rev. Moon unhelpfully buttressed his view every time he opined on America's corrupt nature. Anti-Americanism spilled into his view of Unificationists, particularly UTS students whom he viewed with a mixture of malice and disgust.

"Learning Divine Principle"—the agent of our salvation, mind you—"was the worst thing that ever happened to most UTS students." He leaned righteously forward in his big president's chair in the old Abbot's ornate if rug-worn office so I'd hear every word perfectly. "They learned the Principle and it made them arrogant and complacent. It would have been better for them if they'd never heard Principle at all." He seemed to hold all but toadies at UTS in contempt.

Our gun-toting security chief and Hyo Jin Moon ran a shooting gallery in the basement, behind which Heung Jin's smashed-up '84 death car sat forlorn.

I said, "That seems hard to square with all of Father's speeches poured into our heads of our sacred duty to teach the Principle to all humanity so nobody could complain they didn't hear about the Messiah."

"Nevertheless." Vintage Dr. Shimmyo. And I *liked* the guy.

I **DIDN'T REALLY** know what to expect my first day at UTS. A $50 an hour consulting software engineer for Caribiner Communications in New York City, I was pulling $104,000 a year full-time. I felt strangely embarrassed unfolding my Apple laptop in class or the library because no one had one. My cell phone, too, made me feel unusual and prosperous thus important. A silk necktie above fellow Moonies.

You see? I've thrived in spite of your persecution.

Then laptops seemed to flow in on the next big Japanese wave that overtook the school when Rev. Moon, concerned by the diminishing student body, ordered the Japanese church in 1996 to send UTS 150 more, pushing the Asian count up over maybe 80%. Disgusted with the low quality arrivals, he lashed out during a campus gathering—I beamed stars to see him—bitterly complaining how, in spite of his call for their best and brightest, Japanese leaders sent their worst and dumbest. He then rebuked the faculty for failing to turn UTS into a respectable school that educated students into first-class Unificationists. It seemed a bad year for him and us.

Dr. Shimmyo and Hong Yu miscommunicated, too, because he didn't know it was *me* he'd approved to matriculate. I encountered him in the empty, dimmed cafeteria on my way home shortly after the quarter began. He flagged me down.

Eyeing a predator, I lifted a kabuki mask. "Nice to see you, Dr. Shimmyo."

He edged toward a 6-foot round cafeteria table, his open hand extended toward a commercial plastic chair. "Can we talk? Do you have time?"

Like it was optional. "Okay, sure, no problem," injecting some levity into that total lie. Nothing good ever comes of *can we talk?*

He smiled disarmingly. Crossed his legs. Dr. Earnest. "I did not realize it was you when I saw your name come across my desk." Now I appreciated the danger. My nape tingled. "If I had known the name went with you, I would have opposed your admission to the seminary."

At least he was straight. "Look," I blurted, already riled, "if you want to kick me out, don't wait till I've invested my time and money and heart. Just do it now."

He seemed jolted. But he could've just remembered his bathtub was running. "No, no, I wasn't planning to do that. I don't necessarily want you to leave UTS."

Necessarily? "Then, what's the problem?"

"No problem. I just want to be sure you're committed to the UTS way of life."

Ah. *That you won't be diddling any of our innocent Japanese sisters* is what he was saying. The church was like one big mouthpiece for Tamela's eternal complaint and Jerome's dirty pool. "Well, I am serious. That's how I made City College Dean's List six times in a row and graduated UC Berkeley with just under a 4.0 GPA."

"I saw that. But to be here, one must be morally as well as academically suited."

Ohhh. I was annoyed if sheepish I had to share my private life, but I was certain that's what he was after. "I'm married now. Three years ago. Outside the church. We had a baby last May."

"Ah, yes, I heard about it." What a faker. It was obvious our commessey church had wildfired the news through every interested channel. And did I ever have a mean reputation. "That's the main reason I think you're stable and responsible enough to stay in UTS. If you were single, I would not give my permission."

"Well, then!" Good thing the commasse hadn't caught up with my post-nuptial chaos. And Tamela was a good luck charm after all. I'd have crashed and burned my first week without her. Too bad she was so unenthused. Yet, in that moment, I felt it was indeed God who'd arranged our marriage. That even though leaders denied Rev. Moon the opportunity to Match me six times, God Himself had. And now I saw the payoff, the brilliance of my decision to end-run the regional leaders and Blessing Committee to find my own wife. Yeah, she endlessly quarreled over Shiori and rejected my every apology and demonstrated loyalty to move on, but so what? With time, things would smooth over. I was more than a little myopic. By 1995 we'd been wrangling three years over Shiori with no letup in sight and I still didn't have a clue to the mental–emotional disability underwriting it.

"We'll have an orientation meeting soon," he said, "and you'll have to sign the student code of conduct and pledge to stay here."

"Sure, no problem. I'm still a student, then?"

"Yes. You can stay here and study, but I'll be watching to make sure you're a good student. Don't disappoint me."

"I'll do my best, absolutely." He could always be so maliciously helpful. But I knew what he meant by "good student." *Obedient.* Not rocking his boat. Compliant in all things. If I shined academically like I might give disbelieving Christians a run for their money . . . well, that was a bonus, my feather in his cap.

"Goodnight, then. Good luck in your classes." He ghosted up the stairs I'd just come down to the student wing. Maybe a surprise inspection on the Japanese.

"So, that's that," I breathed. Relief rained across my psyche's parched savannah. My dreaded confrontation with The Man and he'd backed down from what I knew he really wanted to do: renounce my admission and have his jackboot security chief drag me off campus by the ear. And he could. UTS was an absolute dictatorship. In hindsight I realized he wouldn't have, that he thought it would make him seem petty, venal, unforgiving, even unPrincipled if not financially imprudent, and maybe he really didn't want to be those things. Whatever his faults, he was still a Moonie in some kind of service to a God of theoretical love. But, as America's UN ambassador Jane Kirkpatrick dryly noted in her *Dictatorships and Double Standards*, tyrants seldom do what's in their actual best interests. He'd prove he was no exception.

Now earning good cash, I could afford the 220-mile round trip from Long Island City to UTS. But it was tough on the '88 Taurus I'd had to buy for a job.

"We're moving upstate to Kingston, Tamela. It's over the river from UTS."

Her face screwed up. "In February? Wha' mek? It's too cold and here is fine."

"I have three years ahead of me. Plus, Caribiner pays all of my expenses." At 34 cents a mile, that was car maintenance. "It's a win-win for our bank account."

Earning tuition at our Pierpont house.

Moving out of Queens was a Stephen King movie. We spent 24 nonstop hours hauling our life out of the fourth-floor walkup we'd lived in over a year to the rental truck. I hadn't imagined we'd half that much. Tamela, bless her heart, helped grunt down our leaden sofa bed and what I couldn't handle on my own. Strong and tough. I very much admired it when she wasn't muscling exits and jaws. I was glad to leave to the next tenant all our knock-down drag-outs and ruined ankle memories, let alone the glass maw ever seducing me to a one-way concrete flump to an infernal peace.

It was a unifying exercise. Then midnight I collapsed weeping on the carpet. Maybe what finally slayed my emotional bearing was exhaustion plus the stress of my marriage, raising my first child, and my uncertainties with the church and job market. I was inconsolable for an hour like I'd just got heaven's memo via grinning leaders I was booked for hell. It was one of the few times Tamela ever comforted me. I loved her even more for it. At last, we rumbled our worldly goods north to a furnished, single-family house at 46 West Pierpont and our new life at UTS.

IT WAS A fortunate, if unfortunate, time to swing into the seminary with George of the Jungle's cockiness. Fortunate in that the worst of the church-center-style regimen departed with tuition. In retrospect, I'd have chafed even more heatedly on David Kim's bit despite his avowed love of mavericks than ol' Theodore's. Maybe it's a tribute the latter was more responsive to reason—someone must've mentioned it was dangerous (illegal?) to sheep graze their endowment—which seemed more a Japanese than Korean trait anyway. It was unfortunate in that I arrived right after the switcheroo from a pushy, gangsterish Korean raiding the school's financial lifeblood to a self-righteous, dictatorial Japanese raiding its collegiate lifeblood.

It was also when the administration was perceiving just how much water had filled its leaky hull over the last 19 years and struggling to grasp its magnitude. Like Islam's ninth-century sages, Dr. Shimmyo seemed convinced the real problem was spiritual deviance and anomalous—*gasp!* independent—thinking. He was prepared to spare no rod rectifying our moral (unPrincipled) depravity. But he was about to meet his match. Not me, who was only an aggravating burr under his saddle, but the semi-Unificationist African students who outclassed me in their unwavering dedication to keeping other people's shit from raining on them.

Our dining room and social center, though tables tended toward national or ethnic ghettos.

I considered the seminary the pinnacle of Divine Principle life, whatever that was; our divine foundation of glory in Unificationism's God. There was a Holy Rock out back, the Rock of Decision, where Rev. Moon earnestly prayed over his 17 pre-purchase visits to receive the spiritual assurance this was *the* place to buy. The beautiful albeit spartan chapel, perhaps the length and half the width of *Titanic*'s first-class saloon, dominated UTS with beautiful stained glass images.

The school had swapped the murdered Jesus statue behind the altar for a hanging ring simulating the ever-present *yin* and *yang*, or give and take, infusing all aspects of Divine Principle. The seminary felt sacred even with Dr. Shimmyo's desperately escalating fundamentalism. I wandered its grounds in prayer (or prayerful rage) seeking answers and solace to my problems. Any building is just walls and roof. The people inhabiting it creates one's sense of joy or dread. The seminary was both.

My first quarter in a nearly accredited graduate school went by with a pitter-patter in my heart. I was learning Christian church history, spirituality, and theology. Contrary to what you might assume, we weren't indoctrinated into Unificationism. Ninety percent of our academics were Christian themes and history. Maybe a David Kim holdover. I preferred more Principle, but UTS wasn't ready to truly study it.

One of my favorite, if at times most irascible, professors in this regard was Dr. Constantine Tsirpanlis, a rough hewn, Turk-hating Greek from the old school whose English was a kinder Count Dracula's. I quickly became his favorite.

We were chatting affably in his office. "Young man, after looking over your vork, I say you are the smartest student to come through this seminary in ten years."

Praise, I could use. "But my friend Nanami's husband—Sam—graduated top honors. I'm not sure I can match that."

"Vell, smart is all kinds. Vhen I was young man in seminary like you, the Turks rampaged against us Greeks in Constantinople. They invaded our school. Only I hid in some equipment on the roof. They killed whoever they found."

"Holy cow!" His grinding wrath spilled over his desk between us. I felt a chill looking in his eyes glazing in sorrowful reminiscence. "That was smart."

"You see?"

I found his teaching difficult. He refused to stop his presentation for questions like American professors, but happily talked for hours and answered anything outside of class. The spiritual connection he had with the early church fathers permeated our classroom. He lovingly recounted their lives and spiritual journeys. In my bones, their presence filled the room. Raised our emotional energy to a point that electrified and deeply moved me. It seemed almost possible we'd glimpse them gathered all around him, nodding approval and beaming their love for Jesus Christ into our hearts. Irascibility aside, his connection to our Christian past is the greatest gift he brought us seminary students. I treasured it. And him.

Dr. Shimmyo and the board of directors didn't. He reputedly scooped up $60,000 on a couple classes per quarter, their highest paid instructor. Like many of them, he wasn't a Moonie. The school had to pay competitively (more so him, even), which it never enjoyed, to draw professors to our much-maligned institution. The administration didn't think he was pulling his weight and was dissatisfied with his teaching style. Maybe other things.

Soccer was our sports passion, tennis a close second. We played weekly.

I complained to Dr. Shimmyo. "It's totally unfair to fire him after 20 years. He's maybe the best professor at UTS. The kind of guy Father wants."

"Hmm. It's ironic you say that. It seems the Japanese students like him best."

I burbled a laugh. "That's hard to believe. Half of them can barely speak enough English for a pot to—er, even we native speakers . . . well, his spiritual presence is powerful. That's what we students really need to experience here."

"The consensus is that he's not right for UTS."

"But he's been here since the beginning, right? I mean, there's so few Westerners here now. How'd their complaints motivate the board to reconsider his position?"

"Yes, that is interesting. I'm sure the board knows what it's doing."

It was more certainly the school's shaky finances; he'd never admit that to a mere student. I argued his case to newly Academic Dean Mickler, several members of the board, and some of the other professors no avail. UTS fired him in his sixties with no pension or meaningful severance that I ever heard the administration crow about to repudiate his complaints he'd received nothing.

"I'm utterly disgusted, Mike. I'm gonna really miss him."

"It's not my bailiwick. It's the board's decision. I suggest you let it go."

I cocked my head. "Whatever his problems, and they're less in my opinion than his value to us students, he deserved better after all his service to Father's mission right from the seminary's beginning."

"I don't know what you want me to say."

"But wasn't he just used? Dr. Tsirpanlis sure thinks so." In no uncertain terms he'd let me know how bitterly steamed he was with Dr. Shimmyo and the board.

"No, that's an incorrect assessment. He was employed, like at any school."

"Something to bear in mind." His mingy remark was writing on my future wall: look to my own devices, not loyalty and service, for retirement.

Dr. Tsirpanlis (along with Dr. Arthur and a few others) was instrumental in catapulting me into the divinity program. Ordinarily, a student can't apply for the 3-year degree until they complete one academic year. I didn't know that when I went soliciting my application form and letters of recommendation from administrators and instructors who didn't find that detail worth mentioning.

Mike later scoffed at my presumptuousness. "Since you've already gone to all that effort, go ahead and submit your application. They'll turn you down just because you've only been here one quarter, but it can't hurt to hear their advice."

"Okay, thanks. I appreciate that."

"It'll help you when you're ready to apply according to the rules."

"Harrumph."

Mike thought I skirted rules to bend UTS to my will for special treatment. In truth, I was just ignorant or thought a rule didn't apply to my circumstance. Isn't that how the courts apply laws? Otherwise, we're lemmings blindly conforming to cookie-cutter rules that may or may not be relevant, which is how communists run their national prison camps. People like Mike thought my rule-breaking was motivated by a selfish belief I was above them. I am, stupid rules. And who better to decide stupid in my case than me? I'm who's affected. If I thought a rule did apply or it was only fair to conform, then I did even if I hated it. *Question authority*. Right? Revolutionaries love that phrase till folks are questioning *them*.

On Sunday, April 16 Rev. Moon Blessed his children Kwon Jin and Sun Jin in the New Yorker. I represented UTS as an usher and the only American. Only 25–30% of our students agreed to participate. *This is your spiritual leader, the Messiah! You don't want to be here? And I'm the wrong-way Moonie?* The ceremony was wonderful. He was full of good humor and jokes, though his kids were ill-humored and somber. Kwon Jin's Match had only days prior withdrawn over some physical defect.

A day earlier Dr. Shimmyo said, "True Mother was crying tears when Father announced the situation Friday morning."

"She must've been very heartbroken to withdraw." I prayed for her.

"Yes. But Father could quickly reMatch Kwon Jin Nim. So, it worked out."

Did it, though? They sure didn't show it. Mr. Kobayashi ignored me when I ignored him—shame plus aggravation he'd thrown me to Wren Meyer's dogs was gargantuan—but later on we shared insipid words. Mrs. Kobayashi daggered eyes while conversing with somebody before pelting away. Besides Julian, I logged,

> They're the only people in the UC I ever loved; I even think of them as my spiritual parents; but they don't seem to want me around them now. So. I'm thinking of asking Dr. Shimmyo to be my spiritual father, as I like him a lot.

I ran into Ergela Arsch in the New Yorker's elevator. He tried for cordial as if never hatcheting my Blessing tree. Twice. I fidgeted a 3-year old waiting on the doors to open. I ran into Wren Meyer on the sidewalk. *Seriously, God?*

"Oh, you're back in New York now?"

Flat eyes. "Visiting the boss upstairs."

His flexed. "You're up at the seminary now, I heard."

"Well, chop me in half and call me shorty!"

"Umm, Congratulations. You finally made it."

Fingers clenched. "Wren, as I live and breathe . . . ," *you shameless SOB!* I wasn't sure he caught my tone but his face plainly registered my sharpening knives. He beat feet. Later, I tried getting into the Blessing's follow-on Korean ceremony.

Dr. Shimmyo said, "No, you're responsible to get your team back to UTS."

"*My* team? Just because I drove them here? Can't somebody else do it?"

"They're your responsibility. Please, do."

I pestered them. "You guys, the Messiah is here in the same building with you! Don't you want to be around him every chance you get?"

"Just get us back, Chris. This isn't our place." *Well, it's mine, dammit!*

SIX WEEKS LATER Dean Mickler called me to his office. "The divinity admissions committee approved your application, Chris. I'm pretty surprised."

My feet floated. "Wow. I can't believe—. What happens now?"

"It goes to Father. He decides the divinity candidates." Because he draws his top leaders from it, exactly why I wanted in the program. The 2-year Religious Education (MRE) degree was for members lacking ambition to lead our movement, to make things happen. If I couldn't enter the divinity program, why waste two years on a disrespected let alone a hollow degree? Achieving Father's M.DIV. standard was absolute. I couldn't wait even a single quarter to court it. "Don't get your hopes up. Father's who made the one-year rule."

To everyone's shock and awe, he approved me in early July. The news came in the cafeteria as Dr. Shimmyo and Mike Mickler showed off the 5×8 cards showing our photo and info under Rev. Moon's darkly inked thumbs-up spiral mark.

"Well, big man," Mike said, "you're the first student in UTS history admitted to the divinity program before completing your first year, let alone only two quarters. It's an honor. Others were turned down. You should be happy."

"I am!" I giddily babbled.

"Don't let us down," Dr. Shimmyo darkly said with a beaming smile.

My thoughts waved him away. *Wow, do I feel special. Is Father foreseeing a great future for me? My special qualities and utility to his cause? That my rough edges can be smoothed under his unstinting hand?* Maybe I'd never know.

At the same time and strongly, affectionately patting my shoulder Dr. Shimmyo warmly praised me to Tyler Hendricks, our new American church president replacing Jim Baughman, and other leaders hanging out at UTS. He wondered, with maybe a sarcastic grin, "How soon until you become a big church leader, Chris?"

"Ha ha! I don't know, but it'll shock a lot of people." Most of all me, considering the turmoil in my life. I brooded over him catching a Wren Meyer glimmer.

Even as Dr. Shimmyo praised me, it was evident just how far apart on the critical issues the two of us really were. At an impromptu roundtable discussion that summer in the school cafeteria on the collapse of the American Unification Church, UTS staff Katie Zahedi, Jennifer Tanabe, Dr. Shimmyo, and one of the re-translators of the under-construction new edition of *Divine Principle* argued the church needed stronger central figures and a proper theocratic structure to recover its zest.

I said, "I think what we need is nobler internal Abels. Love-oriented leaders. An internal, heartistic-oriented system, not a hierarchical structure." They listened, but I wasn't sure how receptively. "I think we're suffering a classic conflict between spirit and law that's rent our American church much as it did Jesus and the Jewish leaders. I'm on Jesus' side, if you're wondering, ha ha." Coolly unwelcomed was my notion originally propounded to Jerome's brother Ronald in January 1994 that, the 36-Blessed couples are the reason the UC in America failed. They did not inherit Father's nature or Heart or understanding of the Principle. They passed on to members a false view of the Principle and of TPs, and they misled everyone. They failed to deal with the problems of the Church correctly. Any alienation and problems that came up in members were not addressed by them, and they basically forced people out of the movement.

Dr. Shimmyo's roundabout response was that I was a seriously maladjusted Moonie with such silly ideas painting my head red.

"And . . . that's the classic conflict between American and Japanese members," I said, "with the Koreans oddly caught in the middle."

"Not hardly, Chris," Jennifer or Katie or maybe everybody said.

GOOD AND BAD moved fast. The *bad* was that, in the spring quarter before all the good news, two canceled contracts kicked me out of middle class to beggar. Ruined. I couldn't support Tamela and our year-old son. They'd visit Nathalie in St. Vincent till I got back on my feet. We broke our lease. Our white-lipped landlord waxed apoplectic at Kal-el's long scratch in his family's antique dining table—$250 on the spot to avoid the law. I moved into the summertime dorms. UTS wanted $150. The finance office never asked. I didn't offer. Full-time night watchman for an Adventist nursing home run by a military martinet didn't pay my expenses. From $50 to $5.75 an hour—the fall of Rhodes' Colossus. Two half meals a day to save dough for my family, and St. Vincent's mail service kiped some. A transcription correspondence course was sunk money. UTS advertised an administrative job. I begged.

"No, we don't want you to drop classes for it. We're hiring someone else."

"*Pshaw!* I'll have to do that anyway if I don't find some money."

American Express rang up. I explained my straits. This motherfucker said, "If you can't pay, return what you bought, sell your stuff, or borrow to pay us."

"I'm not stiffing you. Suspend my account and defer payment till I recover."

"Where's your money going?"

"Besides basic expenses to live, I send $150 to my wife and son."

"They're at their family's, so that's a misuse of funds. Pay down your debt with it. Why did you use our card if you couldn't pay? We don't tolerate fraud."

"I was making ninety a year then, you son of a bitch. Now I'm making nine!"

"If you won't agree to a payment right now, I'm sending this to collections and legal. You'll be in court for theft and fraud. Are you prepared for jail?"

"Fuck you!" *Slam!* I cut up my AMEX and defaulted on my student loan, debt, taxes, and outstanding tuition. My bankruptcy lawyer was back on speed dial.

In my economic nadir, overstressed and incensed by Tamela's endless quarreling (now by phone) and even as her absence sharply cleated through my mind, I visited Shiori's pillow in June to cry on. We carried on for weeks amidst growing tears, honesty, and then a hard-fought chastity.

She said, "I am now realize it was mistake to fall. I should have made spiritual relationship first before thinking of physical."

I let go a heavy, breathy *yeah*. "I suppose I was too focused on it, too. My love . . . well, kind of selfish. Not thinking about your situation in a fair way."

"Yes." Her voice rang bitter. "Is very difficult, but I not want physical anymore. You ruin our situation. I want start over with right attitude."

"Nooo . . . It seems like—I hate her cussing to death, she makes me so fucking hostile! but . . . —in my heart I know that's where I'm supposed to be no matter how I feel about you." I wanted to commit to Tamela but—*please, God*—without her violent wrangling over the quotidian host interrupting her dream life. Shiori was crying. I pulled her close, my own face wet with regret, self-loathing, and loss. "I remember your first letters were always about True Parents, God, faith, duty . . . you were always comforting me in my travails with the church."

"Because: my friend. My motivation to love you was protect you from Satan and stop you falling away from Principle because of *baka* leaders."

"You always sent me money, food, advice, a shoulder to cry on. Everything. Like my best friend ever. I think I must've fell in love with that."

"My feelings were so strong. I was very lonely and unhappy with Kobayashis and church. I mistake my feeling for you."

"Damn. I did the same thing. I thought you were in love with me."

"I do love you, K'risu. Like sister. Like wife. I not know. Too much confusion." Tears wracked her petite frame; wet face and warm breath trembled through me.

"I didn't leave because I didn't love you. I never stopped loving you. Even Tamela sees that!" I kissed her forehead. "Just . . . God was telling me our relationship wasn't right and Tamela's was. For Principle." I wiped my eyes. "I feel your anguish to the bottom of my soul, Shiori. *God!* If I could ever undo it! Mrs. Kobayashi was right, goddamn her to hell. I should've protected your Blessing." *Like I did Nanami's.*

"I'm sorry I push you. I not want lose you, K'risu. But I want follow Principle again. I want Blessing."

My heart shattered while my thoughts applauded. *Fuck.* She's my unPrincipled lover and I'm mourning her like my Principled wife! *Stab yourself and just die!* "I was wrong to let you break your Blessing, Shiori. I can hardly live with myself feeling your tears. I should've protected it. I could've if I wasn't so fucked up!"

"Yes, my life is very broken. I feel much bitter heart. I mean, sorrow. I—" She clutched my tears-wetted shirt near to ripping. "Is my responsibility, too."

My passion for her was near to overwhelming. Yet, I felt Tamela filling my soul. Was I crazy? a split personality? "I don't get it, though. My love for you feels like it's been growing more brotherly than husbandly. But I want you so bad."

"I am same way. We are cursed, neh?"

"By Mrs. Kobayashi, for sure. She hates my best guts." *I'm sooo sorry, Heavenly Father! Please show me the way to Restore this mess.*

"Yes, very much." She kissed me.

It's impossible to stay romantically and lovingly attached to a person nonstop fencing a poisoned tip. Shiori was so much kinder, gentler, quieter, and comforting in these days of grief regardless whatever was boiling inside her. She never abused me over Tamela once I'd clarified my loyalties. She took it on the chin like a rain she couldn't avoid but did expect to end. It acted a kind of magnet between us, a truth Tamela never appreciated. Having told her about Shiori, I felt I'd corrupted our relationship. The fact she'd feuded over Jerome and our St. Vincent mission before

I'd ever wounded her heart got lost in the Shiori shuffle consuming me with guilt. I was convinced our strife peeled directly off *my affair* and not *her reaction* to it. But three years over a dead desire? And yet . . . here I was on rinse and repeat.

Such was the bad. The *good* was Dr. Shimmyo unexpectedly sashaying up mid-May. "I've decided to recommend your and Tamela's application to the Blessing."

"In Seoul? I mean, *in* Seoul?" It was slated for August 25, 1995.

"Yes. There is some issue whether or not you can participate in Korea or here via satellite." I screwed my face up. "Because you're a previously married couple. Father hasn't decided on that, yet."

So much discrimination in this motherfucking church! "I don't know what to say. Thank you! I really appreciate you believing in me."

He thoughtfully looked me over. "Why do you have so much trouble?"

My voice caught. "I don't know. I try my best."

"Hm. Maybe you have a future in the church." Yet . . . even *that* felt changed. Rev. Moon seemed detached. He dealt with ever shrinking circles. We were now supposed to 'attend' him *and* his fucked-up gumbo. It vexed me. "In any case, your application is automatic with my signature. You can pay the $4,000 Blessing fee?"

"You betcha! No prob—" *Shit.* I needed a plan. No, a miracle. At least I wasn't in Japan. I'd heard they had to rummage up $29,000 per couple.

He squeezed my bicep. "Okay, then. More information will come soon."

In fear I'd only told Shiori in early August. I saw her inner collapse despite our late June epiphanies. Though cool under fire, she'd believed I'd leave Tamela and she could wait it out. She had no more respect for unBlessed marriage than I did. But there was no way. If she'd only accepted this reality after I'd rudely dumped her and told *me* to fuck off—like I should've her—adultery never would've entered the picture because I wasn't looking for it. I just had a foot trapped in her gooey resin. My marriage might've been happier despite Tamela's mental bearing.

"That's your wishful thinking, Chris," friends said without a sugarcoat.

"You never know, though, do you?"

"She is what she is, man. Deal."

I said to Shiori, "I may be confused, but I'm married to Tamela *and* a baby. My life is *there*. I'll never leave for hypothetically greener grass." Saying it was heart-stopping and terrifying. I'd shunned it like leprosy. But Dr. Shimmyo was offering me the Blessing for the first time in 14 years.

Her whole body flamed. "You betray me! You have two mind . . . I not think you are serious about Blessing anyway."

"Yes! I have two minds. I love you to death and can't hardly control myself with you. I love Tamela . . . and I have a baby! There's no other option now."

"You not care . . ."

"I can't set aside my feelings for letting you break your Blessing. I didn't rape you! I never tricked you. But, yeah, I feel responsible. I'm the man in this. I want you to be happy more than anything, but I can't manage our situation anymore!"

She went from livid to full dead zone with Mrs. Kobayashi's shattering news. "She tell me no brother my age, so not possible get re-Match. I need marry outside church and go to future Blessing."

"In the whole church?" I plopped hard on my ass. At 42, she'd lost everything because I'd been weak. "It never should've got—I thought she'd help *you*."

"Because she resent you so much, that is why she would never help you."

"How appropriate for a leader close to Father. Like Mark changing his mind to help me move in May because 'it's not a good time for me,' while Tamela's *outside* friend took time off from work for it. Members bitch about no true friendships in the church when it's never convenient for *them* to be a friend."

"It take her time to overcome her feeling, K'risu." *But not me for you, right?* She was on her knees, Japanese style. "Will you wait for next Blessing and we can all go together? You and Tamela, me and my future husband?"

My head flopped back with a heavy sigh. A hammer anviled my heart. "I'm afraid to wait, Shiori. I might never make the next one." She didn't know the day-to-day with Tamela on the warpath. "Leaders are fickle as hell. Besides, I have a mission to do and the Blessing is a requirement."

She turned her face away. Her voice thickened. Hardened. English slipped. "My future so lonely. I not want talk you again."

She warmed up later, but by then I was Blessed. For all my faults and lack of fidelity to conventional marriage the Blessing was precious, holy, my future, and I'd legit met the quals (as I'd usually done). Breaking it for her was unthinkable. And I didn't. Not ever. I was faithful to Tamela and our Blessing in thought, word, and deed. I expected to stay with her for all eternity, the Blessing's expiration date. Not that she appreciated my heartistic growth and development. She wouldn't retire her near-daily contemner over Shiori for another three years yet.

Dr. Shimmyo's change of heart front-ended me like a truck. Stopped my heart. But members know the church suspends all logic, morals, Principle, and personal enmities when it comes to quotas. Rev. Moon demanded 360,000 couples for 1995's Holy Blessing Ceremony for World Peace Through Ideal Families and the church scraped the bottom of anybody's barrel to find them. This even meant Matching longtime, full-time dedicated members *to nonmembers*, those with little or no fidelity to Divine Principle. They agreed, sincere or not, because they got a spouse.

One of my UTS friends went through a whole series of nonmember Matchings: a Korean, Brazilian, another Korean, then a woman professing her willingness for him just to *stay in* the church. His cruel experience soured me on Rev. Moon's Matching qualifications. My dearest desire since I'd joined was him Matching me. But to a nonmember? *Pshaw!* It was idiotic. A recipe for marital disaster on par with adultery and I should know on both counts. I was appalled and disgusted by how low he was stooping to meet his (maybe self-imposed?) quotas and the damage he wrought in the lives and fortunes of his trustingly faithful followers. I couldn't help but feel more than glad I'd found my own wife and married outside the church regardless the self-brewed hemlock Tamela had me quaffing like chasers.

On top of treating me as an outcast since 1984, the church had viciously scorned my nonmember marriage. In our Blessing interview, Dr. Shimmyo now bathed me in a parental compassion I'd never experienced. Possibly from Rev. Moon so unhingingly accepting sinful, unPrincipled me in less than half a year into the *current* divinity class from which he exclusively drew his top leaders; the pressure to get with the Lord's program, perhaps. Even so I was softening, seeing him as a spiritual father now my real spiritual parents had abandoned me over my rebel rep and Jerome's mudslinging. His outreach was gratifying. Did it signal my new, happier future in the church? *God* couldn't foretell that. I welcomed it, regardless.

I had no money, however. With airfare, lodging, fee, and incidentals I figured on $6,000 all told. *Where am I going to get it?* I was despairing. *First leaders, now money!* My $5.75 an hour was no opportunity in sight. I tried flower selling with other students but couldn't reel in that kind of lucre; didn't earn much over cost from the local Moonie reseller working out of the half-buried barn on campus. Then God answered my distraught prayers.

John Jones rang out of the blue in mid-July. "I've got a project paying $6,000 for three weeks' work. Mileage, too," for desperate repairs. Ten times my watchman's wage. "We have work forever now, Chris. I'll keep you as busy as you want."

"Well, lay it on, amigo!" I danced to unheard music. Dove in like a jello wrestler. For weeks I held onto my $5.75 in fear and labored 18–20-hour days. After one too many 2-hour sleeps in 36, I quit the martinet for John full time.

My project manager fancied himself a bit of a programmer to save money. John had me in to fix it. My earnings climbed to $21,000. I felt God blessing me with prosperity through my Blessing. "Amen, brother!" echoed a festive IRS. I swelled in life-altering gratitude for Tamela, our bedlam notwithstanding.

My Korean holy robes.

She returned for Dr. Shimmyo's interview shortly before our August 18 departure. My heart twisted a wrung-out rag when Kal-el, now 13 months, recoiled from my outstretched arms at the airport. Uncertainty and fear lit his eyes. At that moment, I knew deep in my heart how Rev. Moon felt when he saw his own children who, for most of their early lives, rarely spent time with him owing to his ministry. It took Kal-el a month to trust me as his dad. I never wanted that look again.

KOREAN AIR HAD us canned up 14 hours. We knee-banged hours on a chartered bus to one of the many mountain resorts the church had contracted and began the long process of the Blessing. Workshops taught us the meaning of the Holy Blessing of Marriage, its roots in the Fall of Man, and Rev. Moon's work reversing it. We did the Holy Wine ceremony. Our leaders said it contained a portion of Rev. Moon's own blood—semen, some alleged; heavily diluted, we hoped—that we swallowed as a purifier and commitment to the Blessing. Three years later he said,

The holy wine contains all the essential elements of things which are without Satan's accusation . . . but if a person who received the Blessing makes a mistake ["a position more fearful than Satan's"], he commits the sin of treason against God's substance in the perfection level . . . [that] person will not be forgiven through eternity . . . The holy wine, which is made of 21 [novel] ingredients representing all things and levels . . . contains in it the life force of the Father . . . for original restoration, one has to set a condition of having gone through Jesus' body . . . [it] is given to the wife first . . . [to] establish the restored woman in a position to find the man . . . [who] receives the wine . . . through the wife . . . and makes the indemnity condition for the separation from Satan . . . this wine has a meaning equivalent to Jesus' saying that one who drinks the water of life will have eternal life . . . [it] represents the original core of life. After this ceremony, there should not be any falsehood. You should not ask about the past . . .[live] to fulfill the Blessing. (*Blessing and Ideal Family (Part 1)*, Holy Wine 1998)

The organizers conducted it in Seoul's massive Olympic stadium with great fanfare and grim seriousness. Korean members dressed in robes of white passed out the Holy Wine to each couple and attended our individual vows.

The next event was a long-held state secret few members spoke of even to members: the Indemnity Stick Ceremony. We'd heard of it but Blessed members must've signed an NDA because mum's the word. My inquiries over the years met a wall of silence or dissembling. Nobody in Korea made us sign one, so I concluded their silence was faith in True Father's admonitions it would scare folks off. For bloody good reason, too. Boy, was the truth a kick in the pants.

The indemnity stick—*symbolic, certainly!*— was in fact a solid motherfucking oak baseball bat. The ceremony's point was for a husband and wife to pay indemnity for the Fall of Adam and Eve and one's fallen nature and sexual impurity. They took symbolic responsibility (punishment) for their sexual sin to indemnify the abuse men and women have doled out to the other ever since. With Rev. Moon Blessing nonmembers, many of whom didn't give two shits on a fig for Divine Principle, this cat was now out of the bag.

Tamela's Korean wedding dress at our mountain resort outside Seoul.

We foot-shuffled in a blockbuster cineplex line outside a window-blinded guest space in our resort. Hands wrung wondering what was happening inside, persuading ourselves that indemnity sticks were—*had to be!*—metaphorical. A Korean leader popped out, grimly motioned a clutch of us through the door. The previous group exited through a far-side door where we, who had yet to go through this mill, couldn't see them stagger out duckwalking tears.

Tamela was first up. Sisters started us off because it was Eve who'd initiated the Fall. I describe my experience on the receiving end as if brothers were first up. You can infer hers from that. We were in a lobby-sized room, about ten couples.

The ceremony leader said, "You brothers spread your feet shoulder wide. Bend over, grab your ankles, and grit your teeth." I gawked at Tamela. She eyed her stick. "Sisters, do not hold back. If you don't strike your husband square on the buttock with necessary force, you must do it over until it is indemnifiable." Strident chattering buzzed the room. "But be careful," he solemnly cautioned them. "Be sure you strike square across the pelvis, not at any angle"—he demonstrated what he meant on a brother—"so you don't break bones or hit something you shouldn't."

Well . . . *goddamn*. My blood gelled. Heat and goosebumps prickled my body. That there'd be physical blows was obvious even before his morbid warning. But I thought—even as his helpers pulled robust, samurai sword-looking skullcrackers out of a duffel bag—they'd say the hits were symbolic taps, not for real pain.

Nope. Who'd I think had been giving me the indemnity stick life for 14 years? We were *supposed* to feel all the agony possible short of shattered hips and busted balls. The Japanese sisters looked the most rattled and frankly incapable. But when it finally came to winding up for the score, they lost all reservation. Maybe their long-suffering history in Japan's patriarchy was spiritually newsreeling across their mind's eye. They followed through like mighty Casey at the bat and whacked their man's ass out of the ballpark. Some of them collapsed, tearfully bellowing loud as a cow pushing out a breeched calf. The ceremony crew helped them up for the next one. I sneered in respect knowing the Uchiyamas and others had got theirs.

The ceremony leader was careful to snoop around observing, loudly reminding us, "You must hit squarely on the butt. Don't miss and hit the coccyx—that means the tail bone." He translated the anatomy for the Japanese. "Especially, avoid the family jewels, ha ha,"—this, to men and women who barely knew each other and still couldn't imagine sharing a bed—"if you want Blessed children, ha ha."

Why didn't they issue us steel cups, then? I was nervous as a hen, hoping my jewels weren't in the wrong place at the wrong time and Tamela's aim was true. She'd never swung a bat in her life. A man's never so vulnerable than when he's bent over gripping his ankles. My mind raced. Was I wearing tighty-whities?

Embracing self-preservation, I encouraged Tamela to lay it on so we wouldn't have to do more than our required three blows. She surely imagined Shiori's face plastered across my back end. Her first one blasted air from suddenly flat lungs. My body resonated with shock. Numbness shot through my back and legs as if my nerves were shorting out. She whaled her duty unbridled till I fell down paralyzed, waiting for my central nervous system to reboot. *If this doesn't square my infidelity then nothing ever will and she doesn't deserve me, warts or not.*

Seoul's Olympic stadium. Aug. 25, 1995.

How many spouses in this cheating, backstabbing world would *love* a chance to thrice swing an oaken homerun on their cheating partner? I hadn't verbally repented for my second infidelity only this summer—she'd cured me of its stupidity plus I met the quals—but she didn't need to know. It was enough I'd stopped with no intention of resuming and repented to God. She was literally beating my ass for it anyway. I supposed it cleansed my sin. I'd have felt better verbally repenting to her or anybody, but my lips were sealed. I was only too aware of her reaction, and the church was predictably savage toward anyone (not connected or rich) caught *in flagrante delicto*. I'd paid my dues through her biblical rod. I *was* forgiven, dammitall. Full stop.

The day of the Blessing ceremony dawned grey and wet. Seoul was inundated with rain, the same storm at that very moment creating a flood crisis in North Korea. The Han River overflowed its banks in Seoul. By early afternoon our riverside bus parking, from where we'd hiked to the stadium, was under ten feet of water.

Tamela said, "Vin-cehn-shun see rain as a Blessing. It's great! God be smilin'."

"I'm a sunshine man, myself," shucking into the chintzy, see-through plastic raincoat that was part of our kit. Mine was characteristically too small.

We trooped to the big stadium floor and found a first-row position in front of the stage where Rev. and Mrs. Moon would invocate. We rooted lensed by the satellite camera beaming the Blessing worldwide to every participant and interested news outlet. *Unification News* had us plastered on its spread. A ferocious Korean grandmother hustled up to our catbird seat.

September 1995 Unification News.

"You are previously married couple," she said. "Let Matching couple stand here. You go farther back."

I gave Tamela a quizzical frown. She cut hard eyes through granny. "Wha' mek you say so? Wha' 'dat ha' to do wi' our Blessing, eh?"

"You don't deserve to be here"—she gesticulated—"in front of True Parents."

In her lilting accent Tamela said, "I not movin' one inch, an' you a' mek me. We come aahll 'de way from Ameree-cah, an' we fin' 'dis spot fairly." With some menace and all but dismissing her she added, "Go trouble some-body else."

Some suit zipped up. "They are an international couple. It is okay to be here." Granny sputtered indignation in retreat, cursing us disobedient and unPrincipled previously married American posers barely under kimchee'd breath.

"It tek me breath away, Chris." Tamela beamed, eyes roving the curving stadium roof. "I feel like I'm standing in a palace!" I squeezed her hand.

When Rev. and Mrs. Moon stepped onstage, the rain literally stopped as if God stoppered the tap. It was amazing. We all talked about it. The press mentioned it. He gave a long prayer in Korean. Threw holy water right, center, and left. Exited as if a waiting flambé was crisping. Pent up rain promptly poured on the rest of us. You have to admit, that's impressive. Not just anybody gets the weather's respect.

Joy and happiness surged electric attaining a goal that months ago seemed beyond impossible. I didn't want the Blessing only for myself. The church developed in me a strong awareness of and responsibility for my ancestors. The Blessing is an important step in liberating them from sin and suffering. Once you come to feel that, it's hard going back. Like sex, you never unhave it, forget it, or stop wanting it. Awareness of the Fall of Adam and Eve, of my ancestors and their need for liberation, of God's tears and suffering as a result of the Fall and humanity's evil lifestyle . . . this is the real grip Rev. Moon has on his followers, not some faux cultish mind control. There's no Jim Jones loyalty even if there is a sense of guilt in letting him down, as it bottlenecks God's will. But, now . . . I'd cleared all that from my plate.

Rev. Moon's ministry, reputation, and goals eventually experience failure because of his own, not his members,' stupidity. If you measure success by the dedication, sacrifice, and loyalty of his followers and his overall business acumen, he's the world's greatest rags-to-riches story. But measured by achieving his messianic goals he seems a failure reduced to claiming this or that victory in the spirit world. That he's accomplished anything at all becomes a matter of faith, not empirical reality. For me, that faith would stretch taffy thin during my tenancy at UTS.

Achieving the Blessing was a great victory even if my self-Matching made it only half an accomplishment and it felt marred by my third go-round with Shiori. During the ceremony I'd wondered if I truly *was* squared with God, if my Blessing *wasn't* built on Shiori's brokenhearted tears. Still and all, I felt a better heart and reformed behavior could make my Blessing what Rev. Moon hoped for.

Friends at Jamsil Olympic Stadium.

Tamela wasn't so optimistic. She'd grilled me on a patch her sharp eyes spied on the pants I was wearing waiting on Korean Air at JFK.

The idiot said, "Shiori fixed it awhile back."

"You be visit Shiori while I gone?"

"Uh . . ." Now in Korea *after* my ass-beating and our palatial Blessing, after climactic times when feet settle back to Earth, she remembered that patch and cross-examined me. She laid on accusations and demands as we semi-happily sightsaw Seoul. I crumbled. "Yes. You were in St. Vincent. I was dying of stress, guilt, loneliness, starvation . . . but I finally ended it."

Eyes flashed over stone. "You t'ink you can jus' say 'dat?"

"Yes! I couldn't before but now it's over. Forever! Out of your life!"

"You carry me here under such a faahlse pre-tense!" She went wild with Wren Meyer's rage and tore our Korean experience to shreds.

Fuck! I got three new years of verbal and sometimes physical abuse piled on the last three that drained all our love and affection and ran our marriage onto the sharpest rocks. No tearful apology nor demonstrable troth placated her. I battened hatches to ride out her maybe endless storm. I'll never know if she'd have dropped Shiori as the Blessing demanded. I did know her trust was deader than ever.

What is it with insisting one's mates are property? I'd wounded her heart yet was a free man who'd chosen *her*. If she hated me, take my child support home to Nathalie. Why dump toxic emotions into me that only ruined the marriage and family she ostensibly wanted? Fallen love's worst presumption is a lover is to be controlled, to bark and mewl on command. It's a recipe for warfare. Not surprising. It's slavery not love, the rank selfishness Rev. Moon chastises in railing over Adam and Eve's betrayal of God's Ideal. I was getting a bellyful and hating it. Life was a cauldron of simmering rage and heartfelt enmity. I'd solved my worst quandary only to seed a greater one. So *baka!* Stuck fast in Tamela's Shiori-cum-cognitive-disability, our Blessing went from heaven to hell inside 72 hours.

The 1995-96 academic year was a busy one. We moved into Harvest House, an old 2-storey chicken coop and almost farthest campus outbuilding. I took in $40,000 July–December. Feeling flush, we road-tripped through a month and $3,000. First stop: Disney World's legendary A-framed, monorailed Contemporary Resort.

I barked tires at the front entrance. "Wait here, Tamela. I'll get our room." Strolling up to the front desk like Bill Gates, I slapped my now-functioning credit card on the marbletop counter. "You have an available room? I'd like to book a few days."

The clerk narrowed her eyes. Eyed my card. "Yes, sir! I believe we can find something."

A grand, right there. Then a whirlwind multi-week through my Southern relatives before visiting the folks in Colorado. Tamela got pregnant with our second somewhere along the way. Back at UTS, I launched America's first Unificationist theological journal in a hail of controversy and expectations in winter 1996 that hella riled Dr. Shimmyo.

The seminary then was a mud pit of indifferent ignorance. Many Japanese washed through like

Our Disney Ritz. Dec., 1995.

flotsam, plagiarizing because their English wasn't good enough to write their own or else, hating every minute of their forced academics, too lazy, stupid, resentful, or disinterested; the seminary's greatest disgrace. The administration only haphazardly countered it. Some professors, like Mike, bluntly threatened an automatic course 'F' if caught even once. Others were less cross so long as something got turned in to justify a paycheck. Occasionally, even the laziest professor came across a paper plagiarizing his or her own work or one they recognized and, especially in the former case, lowered a delicate boom.

These students could choose from whole catalogs of papers written over the years as well as long passages from published works. Usually, they started their paper with a paragraph or three in their own broken English that magically transitioned to native prose. They used previously written, already-graded UTS papers from earlier years hopefully forgotten in the minds of professors, or lifted page after page from published works and shamelessly put their name to it.

To see for myself, I checked Dr. Tsirpanlis' in-box crammed with term papers. I pulled out twelve and examined them. Nearly all were from Japanese. All but one followed the broken-to-fluent English formula. Papers fully in broken English were probably, though not for certain, original works. Since none of the students in my class flunked, I knew he'd accepted all their papers, perhaps with an air of resignation for the inevitable. Could be that's why the board fired him, though he was hardly academic integrity's only lackadaisical lover at UTS.

Starting an intellectual publication amongst these philistines was no cakewalk. I trudged uphill finding interested partners. Early on, I understood I needed not only allies, but to set conditions to ensure an abundance of positive, Godly energy around my endeavor. The Principle is adamant that spiritual conditions—actions and

425

attitudes that reverse some satanic human nature—be employed to ensure success. The most problematic human nature prevalent in the American Unification Church besides widespread sexual infidelity was the race and culture war between Americans, Japanese, and Koreans. This problem has evilly worked its wiles since the 1970s if not earlier to strangle Rev. Moon's American ministry. I believed most ministerial failures sprang not just from his oft-erratic helmsmanship but the perpetual warfare between East and West, with gloryhound Koreans seizing the upper hand in all things; that sin was dooming UTS even as its Japanese head refused to heed the warning signs from its Western body. Well, I wanted to be different and prove East and West could indeed meet, work in harmony, and execute a common vision.

The hat's mine. Denver. Dec., 1995.

At last I recruited Jesús as my base. A heartistic and smoothly diplomatic Venezuelan, he was Blessed to sweet Chieko. I liked and respected him—and crucial to my venture. Sadly, at UTS only a Westerner could get enthused about starting up a print publication. Even so, we managed headway in Divinity student Istvan from Hungary who joined next. Over several weeks we reeled in four more: In Hoi Lee from Korea, Adza from Ghana, Joaquin from the Philippines, and Hiroyuki from Japan. A world-oriented undertaking of seven, our Principled number for success.

Jesús and I worked on Dr. Shimmyo who adamantly opposed any publication not under his direct censor. He flatly refused to permit it until I convinced him he was powerless to stop it. Then he tried rallying the students to oppose it, but they couldn't be bothered. The Student Council, a semi-elected body appointed by Dr. Shimmyo much like our church president, informed us through their Academic Affairs Committee that *our* journal would be *their* thing.

Its chairman said, "If you're not going to follow the Council's guidance, then your journal just won't happen. It's that simple."

"I understand, Alan. Shall I laugh now, or you prefer I wait till I'm outside?"

"This isn't a joke, Chris. The seminary—"

"—is a nearly accredited *graduate school*, not a center or somebody's MFT van."

Nothing like a gauntlet at my feet to wash my competitive spirit in life-giving testosterone. Our attempt at a professional, independent theological journal flustered Dr. Shimmyo. He couldn't help but equivocate, sometimes daily.

"Your journal needs to be an official UTS publication if I'm to allow it."

"Does that mean you're paying all the equipment, operational, printing, and shipping costs? Do we get a secretary?"

"No." Some days later he said, "UTS won't have anything to do with it."

"We understand. You prefer us being independent." I got a double take.

Later he said, "I'm really shocked you changed the name from UTS *Student Review* to *The World Unificationist Student Review*. I'm not sure I—"

426

"Because you objected to us implying a connection between *our* journal and *your* school." I chuckled. "We were only obliging you."

Then, "I can't let you use our 10 Dock Road address. That would imply an official UTS position. You need to find somewhere else."

I shrugged. "Okay. We'll figure it out." *Small potatoes.*

He reversed himself in the morning then pressured students to block us. One afternoon I met five scowls in our cavernous, 2-storey cafeteria. Tough-as-nails Englishwoman Rachel—her black American, *taqiyah*-wearing '82 Blessing husband working our midget bookstore hated me just on anti-white principles till brotherly friendship won him over— tried impressing on me the godliness of censorship for orthodoxy.

Ghosts of chickens past at Harvest House.

"If you have no intention of publishing unPrincipled"—*disobedient*—"material, why should you oppose it? You have nothing to hide, right?"

"Come on, Rachel. That's the old rubric Nazis and Communists love. 'If you're innocent, why fear spilling the beans?' You know that's only dangerous."

A brother said, "England's censorship laws don't hurt its free press."

That merited a peal of laughter. "Every day at the *Middle East Times* wire articles had caps across the top saying, 'Not for publication or distribution in the UK.'"

"That's not the same thing," a sister said. "This is a church, Chris."

"But it's the very definition of an unfree press, isn't it?" I eyeballed her. "Why do you think that, unless we're controlled by Dr. Shimmyo, or maybe you, that our tiny publication must be a threat to him or the church?"

"Because Satan invades through that kind of thing."

"It's just a printed version of somebody talking. You gonna shut up anybody you hear saying what you don't like? Take a look around." I waved an arm across the cafeteria. "You want to police all these tables for unPrincipled speech?"

"Don't get ahead of yourself," said Yoshizumi. His *yakuza*-mind was overtones of Hidetoshi at Judah Street. He'd cycled out of classes into Dean of Student Affairs after Dr. Shimmyo unceremoniously vacated it for too much independent thinking. "We're only talking about your proposed journal. Nothing else."

"I think you are. The Brits keep people in the dark about what the rest of the planet's reading. Americans believe in real freedom of speech and this here"—I stomped a foot on the floor—"is America, not England."

"It serves a good purpose," Rachel said. "I don't see why you think opposing—"

"Everybody keeps saying UTS is a church. Is it not getting through it's a college awarding Master's degrees? Soon, accredited ones?"

"Catholic universities exercise this kind of oversight," a second sister said.

"*Psshh!* While letting its phony liberation theology decimate the world."

"And then stopped it through oversight."

"It ran its course. Like ignoring pedophilia."

"Maybe, like them," Yoshizumi snarked, "you want to use it to fight Dr. Shimmyo and church leaders. Your own liberation theology for you own purpose."

My head was shaking. "It's a theological journal exploring Divine Principle, not church inequities. And its articles are written by *other* students. Even you."

"You're the editor, aren't you?" I peered through brows at him.

Rachel said, "That doesn't mean they won't be used to attack the church, to push unPrincipled ideas that undermine central figures . . ."

"Freedom of speech is rooted in freedom of conscience. You're arguing we have to police our conscience, our own mind, lest we stray from doctrine—which is whatever some leader says it is any time of the day—and blab it out."

"Yes," Second Sister said.

"We British are quite happy with how our press operates, by the way."

I glared. "Well, Americans absolutely loathe censorship and Gestapo tactics."

She bridled, face flushed. "We are *not* using any sort—"

"Aren't y'all Americans?" I looked over their faces. "Why you want censorship?"

First Sister said, "Stop twisting things! It isn't censorship. It's just oversight and there's a difference!"

I wanted to laugh but was feeling as bridled as Rachel. "Father advocates freedom of conscience, as Divine Principle does. Therefore, so do I."

The chapel altar. Sept., 1995.

It was hotly contentious and went on awhile. It came down to censorship ('oversight') and my visceral hatred of it and love for liberty. My journal underscored the depth of fear the Unification Church has of media. It's great if it's church-governed and spouting the party line, but evil and satanic in members' hands; well, non-leaders—anyone doing their own thinking without right guidance from above. My fight with Dr. Shimmyo over WUSR was really about his fear we'd be printing diatribes against him firstly, and secondly against the church that would net him trouble with his Korean lords. Theoretically, if not practically, the seminary was where our future leaders learned to grapple with institutional issues and the Principle as truth to do better. *Duh.* He didn't see my integrity, either.

Rachel said, "Will you agree to Dr. Shimmyo pre-approving your articles?"

"*Pfft!*" A corner of my mouth turned up. "No."

"How about handing it off 24 hours in advance, just as a courtesy."

"No. I feel like Thomas Cromwell arguing with Colonel Pak." Question marks in their eyes. "Never mind. But, really, you don't wonder why the spoken or printed word so frightens church leaders that they need"—air quotes—" 'oversight'?"

"We're trying to find common ground, Chris," Yoshizumi said.

"It's because they're tyrants, not spiritualists."

"Now you're being unfair," First Sister said. "We're every bit as Principled as you think you are, which doesn't seem like much from where I'm sitting."

"I said 'spiritualist,' though. You're focused on law. I'm focused on heart." That furled her brow. "Well, look, y'all. I'm not agreeing to anything that removes our complete and total control over our own publication published by us at our own expense. Unless you want to pay for it. Then *you'd* be the publisher and I'd quit. You could always start your own Shimmyo version, see which one gets read."

Rachel crossed arms. "We're obviously not going to solve this here."

"It's a peer-reviewed *theological* journal, Rach, not some revolutionary rag calling on the Moonie masses to rise up and hang leaders. It'll be fine. Nothing to solve."

And that's where things stood as we put together our first issue. For that, we secured Dean Mickler's interview.

Dr. Shimmyo said, "I see that your editorial board is very international, Chris. It's commendable. But, without a Korean, I can't approve the interview."

"You have a suggestion?" Because, of course he did.

But his unprequalified spy wasn't interested and naïvely referred us to an independently-minded In Hoi Lee. He represented Korea's up-and-coming

I endlessly prayed in our cavernous chapel (not that eagle-eyed Dr. Shimmyo ever noticed) wondering how to best serve God and Rev. Moon.

younger leaders and was, if not at first enthusiastic, genuinely interested. He and Hiroyuki individually met with Dr. Shimmyo in his tower of power to explain our sincerity as well as our academic rights. I think he was finally swayed by a respected, even if younger, Korean leader—the brand is always a tie-breaker—agreeing to join us who also backed my censorship position. We got Mike's interview.

I've long had an anti-Japanese, anti-Korean, anti-leader, and generally anti-social reputation in the church. It isn't deserved, but in an organization where discontent is viewed as Satan's invasion and a potential threat to hierarchy it was impossible to avoid. It turned out I was sufficiently good at inspiring others with my vision to win them over to my point of view. Hiroyuki flatlined Dr. Shimmyo, disdaining his opposition by openly allying with me. In Hoi Lee served up the *coup de grace*, communicating a warm and respectful appreciation of me and an enthusiasm for our journal that was, in the end, infectious.

Dr. Shimmyo formally capitulated with, "You have my permission," the day before our first issue was due to hit the stands. It seemed so incongruous he'd so adamantly oppose our journal (and suspect me of nefarious motives) when, in the midst of this controversy, he admiringly praised me to students and leaders alike. In early April 1996 I preached the mandatory 6 AM morning service in our gloriously titanic chapel. I exhorted my fellow Moonies to remember we need love Jesus more than Christians do just as Abel needs love Cain more than God if we expect to win them over to the Principle. Unlike with other students, he spun my sermons to counter any pathogenic agents.

This time he unexpectedly said, "That was an excellent sermon. I was very inspired! I can see that Chris really loves Jesus. I believe there are thousands of Christians spiritually with him, waiting for him to revive American Christianity." *American Unificationism, you mean.* "He seems to be the man with the mission from God to Restore America and unite it with True Father." Members swiveled heads in my direction with expressions of admiration or an expectation (or hope) I'd stepped into a bear trap. I could only smile my acknowledgement and wonder if his praise was the stand-by-your-man kind. He continued his effluent praise the next day during dinner in the cafeteria. "I think Chris will be a great preacher."

Yet, he vehemently opposed every activity that prepared me to do just that. Such arbitrariness really irked me. With Dr. Shimmyo it was a symptom of the wider malaise eating out the church's heart. UTS, the spiritual core of the American movement, was circling the toilet. It furiously vexed me the Asians were wrecking our movement with American collusion. My feelings were definitely syncing up with Rev. Moon's own harsh, thumping attitude especially with UTS. It seemed in some (if not his best) respects, I was thinking like him.

Regardless, we frantically worked to get the first issue typeset and print-ready on my computer. We prayed as a group to infuse our undertaking with spiritual meaning. God was definitely with us. I instinctively felt it. What we were doing through our journal was beginning the process of reformation for which our church so desperately yearned. And through our small journal, we were being trained in the tasks and interactions necessary to accomplish far bigger objectives. It was a heady affair. I loved it. And, to proud eyes, so did my crew.

First copy off the press and our first dollar earned.

We all chipped in for a laser printer, and a student's color inkjet did our cover. A self-imposed deadline was for midnight March 1, 1996. After innumerable printer problems, breakdowns, computer crashes, and a gamut of probably Satan-made disasters we stapled the first copy's 16 pages minutes to twelve. I flew out of my first-floor Harvest House office to my Taurus. Raced to the seminary building in a squeal. Barked a halt in the circle right out in front. Jumped out, door open, bell dinging, engine purring. Tore full speed down the far-flung hall beneath the chapel to the cafeteria. A few witching-hour students chittered. Palavering taboo, no doubt.

"Hey!" I breathlessly called out. "Got a dollar?"

A brother fished in his pocket. The second-hand swept through the wall clock's last ticks to our sworn deadline. It was vital to us—*me*—that our first issue sold by then. It was a spiritual condition. A promise to God that we'd come through on our word. It was a miracle in my eyes that Dr. Shimmyo had so abruptly surrendered to us—to me, really. In the process, I'd morphed into an arch enemy. A nemesis representing everything he hated about America. I'm sure it galled him that he couldn't find any leverage to keep me in my place. Selling our first issue on time was an act of faith that God was behind us, counting on us, helping us, cheering us on . . . that Dr. Shimmyo was wrong.

At length the student said, "Yeah, I got a dollar." I gratefully snatched it.

"Here," I said, triumphantly thrusting the journal into his hands one second to midnight, "you just bought the very first, the collector's edition, of *The World Unificationist Student Review*. Your dollar just made Unification Church history!"

"Whoa." They gathered in to admire the issue and read the articles. *Success!* I celebrated with an ice cream sandwich out of the flattop freezer behind me.

The next day we stacked over a hundred copies at a newsstand we'd built in the cafeteria and sold more than half that first day. We sold subscriptions to readers from every continent and turned a profit. Running it as a business, complete with a treasurer and a bookkeeper, we rigorously tracked everything on the up and up to avoid any charges of corruption by Dr. Shimmyo. The journal was an international undertaking. A magnificent achievement in our deeply divided church. My dream was it become a permanent UTS fixture, owned and operated by the divinity class that, year over year, published insightfully better quality theology to a worldwide audience. And why not? There was nothing like it!

It was a great victory for me. Not just getting out a publication, which I loved doing, but proving to myself, Dr. Shimmyo, and all my detractors that I was capable of marshaling the support and alliance of members from countries all over the world. I sensed the journal was a test, a dry run by God to see what I could do, if I could handle the pressure and stress of such an undertaking. I believed with all my heart that, upon graduation, I'd be tasked with such challenges to win the hearts and minds of critics inside and out of the church.

Jesús was the real diplomat. I owed him a great debt for his wise counsel that helped me accomplish my vision. I'm a doer, a challenger, an out-of-the-box thinker but tend to fizzle when diplomacy is needed. That's why I aggressively courted him in the first place. I knew him as a judicious man whom Dr. Shimmyo liked and respected. I usually do very well in these types of ventures when I can properly align myself with such a statesman. Whatever I did in future, I'd need my team.

With the journal published monthly (later, bimonthly) rather than annually as Dr. Shimmyo insisted in a final bid to render it a nonentity, I brought in articles from all over the school and church. We peddled subscriptions to church leaders in America, including Rev. Moon's adopted son Peter Kim, making sure to send Rev. Moon a complimentary copy. It's notoriously difficult to get his feedback on anything, so I still don't know if he ever read it or had any opinion on it.

I'd run into Peter at UTS just before my Disney trip. "I'm the guy Father had you call back in '84 for writing him every day at Danbury about Papasan Choi."

He looked me over like a prime cut. "That was you? Well." He smiled a chuckle. "Yes, I remember your situation."

I rattled on about Rev. Moon. "I feel God wants me working directly with him. When I graduate, I hope he gives me a chance to show what I can do."

He might've rolled his spiritual eyes. "Father should be coming back to America in the spring. I'll try to introduce you to him at that time."

"Wow, thank you! I look forward to that!" He and Mrs. Moon were probably the only Moonies Tamela truly liked. After all my abusement, I longed to get on his personal radar. In the end Peter forgot, blew me off, or Rev. Moon said *no dice*.

I sold eight premier copies at West 43rd Street and a subscription to Rev. Chen Fong, a jovial Chinese-American now its big dong. We warmly shook hands. "I heard about Wren Meyer kicking you out over that Japanese sister."

"Don't remind me."

"And there you are in the seminary publishing a magazine. Well, he got himself into some trouble, too, and is now selling Magic Pens at some highway rest stop."

I snorted. "With a PH.D.? What'd he do?"

"He hasn't got it, yet. As for . . . I just heard it was 'an unPrincipled thing.'"

I chin-wagged the very idea. "The ups and downs of Unification Church leaders is so Wagnerian, Chen. Better watch out for the Stalin chop."

He chuckled. "Happily Blessed, my friend. I look forward to reading this."

Appreciating Wren's heart in his (well-deserved) sticks, I felt vindicated and somewhat satisfied withal. I made sure to update judgy Dean Mickler.

Dr. Shimmyo was profoundly embarrassed I'd beaten the school—*him*—to the punch. UTS had talked about publishing an academic journal for years while doing nothing. Now the administration announced plans to publish its own magazine starting in 1997. Dr. Andrew Wilson, our resident Judaism expert, would edit *The Journal of Unification Studies*. It was a direct result of the slap in the face I'd delivered publishing ours on our own dime to a worldwide audience. Having that kind of clout was one of my most satisfying accomplishments at UTS. I set up a talk radio station but stumbled over FCC licensing and didn't want to Wolfman-Jack it.

Two months later Jesús screeched, "Wow, Father just told Dr. Shimmyo he's decided to quit funding the seminary!"

My blood curdled. "I can guess why. What's it mean for us, you think?"

"He expects him to make UTS successful." He crossed arms. Looked down.

"Huh." I thought back to Boss Choi and ISA. "He can be like that. Unfortunately, I don't think Shimmyo has the mettle for this new twist. He's just an academic thrust into administrating. For all I know, he doesn't understand or even like it."

"You think he'll do what he has to for high-quality students to enroll?"

I grumbled out a laugh. "Nope. He's a fanatic and unwilling to let go his anti-American Japaneseness or his attachment to autocracy and quelling independence. Who'll pay second-tier UTS for that? Certainly not Americans."

His chuckle was mirthless, too. "Even the Japanese long for home. If *they* . . ."

"You got it. Let's just hope we graduate first." The school suffered a reputation as the place Divine Principle went to die, producing anti-Moonies and misery, and earning the moniker Unification Theological Cemetery. I could read the wall.

∼

TAMELA'S PERSONALITY AND instability chafed our Harvest House roommate. Chaz was a bald, fortyish, heavyset Westerner with a fondness for verbal abuse and physical violence. Mike mentioned that he'd once threatened his talky wife Reiko with a fist over some cafeteria kitchen dispute. I'd no idea the kind of person I was moving in with but lived peaceably. Tamela frayed his nerves. Her Tea Party to his Stamp Act was him getting touchy flirty on several occasions.

At last he said, "Chris always abandons you. I can keep you company."

Her tone was derisive laughter. "You? 'Dat nev-uhh gonna happ'n! Wha' mek I go wi' you and not me hus-baahnd?"

"He spends all his time away and you're pregnant. He's no good to you." A few heartbeats. He softened his voice. "I've never been with a black woman."

Her volume spun up. "Well, it surely won't be 'dis black one here!" Maybe casting back to St. Vincent she added, "You bes' gimme no reason to tell Chris. He might be kill you." Chaz blew off. He thought he was untouchable.

Their Lexington and Concord kicked off when he clumped in from managing the UTS kitchen. He plopped into his faux Barcalounger, which he'd aimed at his TV on a rickety, tubular-metal stand. He snatched the remote off the sofa arm where Tamela was curled up and changed the station in, for her, contemptible silence.

Never letting an insult escape unmolested she said, "Wha' mek you do so? I was watchin' me show. This boring Jeopardy is for old people."

He eyed her like spoiled meat. "You need to apologize for opening your mouth about *my* TV and challenging my rights as the man of this house."

"You 'de maahn roun' here? You t'ink we a' pay rent?"

"Shut up and—"

"Shut down! You—"

"—apologize, or get out of here. This is my spot."

"—don't tell me nothin'! We pay for 'de place here same as you."

By the time I ground up our dirt road from work in New York City and climbed the dark, narrow stairs to our side of this 2-unit old coop, they were at each other's throats. She met me on the stairs, tears streaming off her chin. Instead of relaxing, I spent my evening defusing the time bombs ticking in both their edgy heads.

Soon enough they were spoiled milk. Part of his hatred for her was that he

Tamela escaping Chaz outdoors with Kal-el.

couldn't intimidate her after losing an argument. If he was anything, it was a loud-mouthed strong-arm. My mind was scattered bowling pins seeing her shut him up. I didn't think he'd ever been so challenged by a woman. Despite her cognitive disability and lack of education, she debated like Cicero condemning Catiline. It only reinforced my sense she *could* be a trial lawyer if she'd only try.

"Him a dast-aardly maahn," she said in our bedroom, her accent heavy on the adjective, "an' disgus' me. 'De way he treat Mitsuki and Rimi"—his Japanese wife and under-two daughter—"show he ha' no God in he life. How him be at UTS?"

"He just works here. I have no idea about his spiritual life."

"I do! Wha' mek he carry on wi' 'de wo-maahn an' her pickney so?"

"Trixie?"

"Who else wo-maahn? He marry to her? No! He has Mitsuki. He's you and—"

"Don't start, Tamela. We're Blessed now."

She sucked teeth. "If 'dem not havin' interference, Chris, I a' know nothin'!"

"I don't know. Maybe. He said he's faithful to Mitsuki."

"Wha' mek he carry on so, then? And she treat Kal-el *bad*!"

"You should keep whatever it is to yourself because we don't *know*."

"You wan' turn a blind eye. Your church be a whole bed-room of unchristian corrup-shun. I wan' no part o' it. I wish you nev-uhh carry me here!"

Rimi was a sweetie. Yet, he and Mitsuki oft-showed real disinterest in her and only haphazardly changed her diapers. She couldn't urinate without bawling through the habitual rash. Her vagina was so raw and scabbed that Tamela felt compelled to heal her skin at our expense. Rimi found refuge in our room playing with us and Kal-el through the day. Her laughter wafting back to Chaz and Mitsuki in their room chewed through his attitude like fire ants.

He yanked her from our floor mattress. "I don't want her playing in here."

"Why not? She's lonely and having fun wi—"

He lasered Tamela. "I don't want her in your low-spirit atmosphere."

"We'll play wi' her in 'de livin' room," Tamela said. "It's wha' she need."

"You won't play with her at all. Don't let me catch you." He whooshed her out.

"He is a baad maahn, Chris." I neck nodded, lips pursed.

He sometimes locked Rimi out of their room as punishment for not properly praying with them and other misdemeanors. She screamed and wailed, banging on the living room side of their door and tearfully begging entrance or else running into our room begging we open it for her. Tamela was beside herself.

Kal-el and Rimi.

" 'Dem be Jeh-rome and Av-ril wi' little Nikisha aahll over again. I could cry! *Do* somethin'!"

"Like what? She's his kid." She knew it. Eyes burned black. I didn't worry about Kal-el praying. That's a mental illness I didn't need. He was a month older than Rimi and they often bathed together. It saved water, electricity, the kids loved it, and Tamela and Mitsuki enjoyed the company without their men around, I think Mitsuki the most. Kal-el one day playfully reached up and grabbed Mitsuki's rear end as she listened to Chaz in the doorway. He exploded.

"Get your satanic, sexual pervert out of my daughter's tub!"

Tamela gyred liquid nitrogen. Waxed taller than her five-seven. "Don't you call my chile no sexu-aall per-vert when you be aahll up in Trixie face day an' night."

Mitsuki's eyes landed on the ground. Chaz said, "Shut your mouth. You don't know anything. Keep your pervert away from Rimi or else."

"Else wha'?" She didn't take to ultimatums. "You g'wan beat me like Rimi?"

"Get her out of here, Mitsuki." He dirked Tamela cut-eyes and tromped out.

TIME PASSED. TAMELA more and more perceived not only Chaz but Trixie abusing Kal-el emotionally, verbally, and sometimes physically. Her response had no restraint. Chaz spit feathers for the tornado he couldn't ride.

Tamela's African friend Marra said to us, "He mistakenly thought she was a humble African, like the ones he abuses in the kitchen. But what happened?"

434

Tamela laughed. "I turn out a tiger by 'de tail! 'Dat no-count maahn will regret 'de day he ev-uhh mess wi' a Vin-cehn-shuuhn!" *Yep. Don't I know it.*

When I stopped hassling Tamela's behavior to please him he said, "You're not as smart as I thought you were. Learn how to control your wife."

"You mean, you thought I'd bow down to you and abuse my own wife for your pleasure. Sorry to disappoint ya! She's right. *You're* the one out of line."

Chaz and Trixie segregated Kal-el. Tamela's voice reeked with denunciation. "How you treat little chilleren so? 'Dem deserve to play togeth-uhh an' be happy, not how you lock little Rimi out o' your room and love Trixie daugh-tuhh more than yours own!" She'd only meant to stab Chaz but I saw Mitsuki bleeding.

He said to me, "You need to make more children with that wife of yours so your unBlessed pervert has someone his kind to play with."

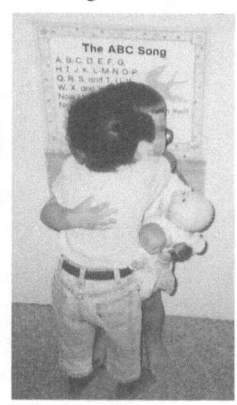

And there we were, back to my marriage to a nonmember outside the church. *Goddamn.* "Fuck you, Chaz. You're just a racist who hates your own mixed family."

"Pfff!" Yet, he physically gravitated farther from tanned Mitsuki in my eyes and closer to whitewashed Trixie.

Tamela's calls to discipline her child from abusing Kal-el fell on deaf ears that rebuked vigilante hand slaps, once from Chaz in Japan. Moonie racism was nothing new.

"Get me 'de *hell* out o' here!" she harried me ever louder. 'Dirty words' scarcely barged off her tongue, so I knew her shortening rope was unraveling, too.

Best friends.

"And go where? With what money? We have bills and debts. Plus tuition."

"You a' need 'dis stupid school! Jus' ge' a good job."

"Why do you think I'm . . ." And then *we'd* fight. *Shit.*

I couldn't blame her. Life in the same house with an unbalanced lunatic like Chaz was getting impossibly unbearable for an unstable hothead like Tamela. I was so stressed I sometimes sat in the cafeteria and gobbled down ten ice cream sandwiches in a sitting. I bulged fatter and detested myself all the more. In the meantime Trixie lived her strange relationship with Chaz. We couldn't tell for sure it was sexual but the flavor reeked and hiked not only our eyebrows.

She often squatted like a vagrant. Tamela said, "You a' ha' no home?"

"I have every right here, Tamela. It's not your concern."

"Oh, you pay rent here?"—*stiupp*—"Like you could treat me as a guest."

Mitsuki cooked and served. Chaz and Trixie laughed, played, touched, tickled, and talked around the dining room table as if married, their toddlers flinging food off their highchairs like barbarians. Mitsuki dutifully mopped up, the live-in servant. Her nerves were blistered—Tamela steamed up our room over it—but she rarely complained in front of us. Their hot war in some approximation of hushed tones behind closed doors sometimes broke free as she scathingly condemned him and Trixie's presence in her home. Tamela and I traded sorry eyes.

Tamela said, "Mitsuki say Chaz and Trixie 'dem been lovers before 'de church. Now 'dem can'a stay away no matt-uhh 'dem so-caahll Blessin' to diff'rent people."

"Damn. I guess I can't be so judgy with him over it, then."

She hit me with a knowing eye but was cooking better fish. "Before you ge' home, Trixie hus-baahnd come ov-uhh to collec' her becau' she a' go home. You know, she actually refuse to go and tell he to leave our apaaht-men'?'"

"Told Dude? That's—I heard they were having marital problems."

"Like everybody in your faahlse church."

"Well . . ." It was hard to disagree. "There's lots of happy Blessings."

Rimi visited as often as she could. We loved her.

"*Hummph.* He try take she arm, drag she out. 'Dat wort'less maahn ge' all up between 'dem, all big chested to frighten he off. Like Trixie he own wife!"

"What did Dude do?"

"Him a smaahll maahn, Chris. Chaz force he to leave Trixie an' 'dem gyul in he han.'" Pooled eyes gazed into mine. "I never see such a soap opp'a even in St. Vincent. A man do so 'der, he be dead from some-body cut-lass."

"Ha! Reminds me of Avril hanging out the window."

"Ugh. I tellin' you, me own mout' fall op'n." Her thoughts might've run to Shiori and how I'd never stooped so low, but she never thanked me for being a better man than I was. "You mus' do somethin', Chris. You can'a le' 'dem suff-uhh so."

"Dammit, Tamela. Shimmyo already told me to stay out of her business." She looked at me disbelieving. "If I carry it around then I'll be like all the shitheads who rampaged through my life. Fight him to his face if you want. But it's Mitsuki's Blessing. She has to choose to keep it, not me."

"You crazy. I tell 'dem people me-self."

"They'll hate you for it, I promise you. Not a soul will thank you."

She slumped against the wall with a heavy pout. "Your church ha' no God. If it ev-uhh did, He done wash i' t'off."

Ahh . . . jeez. I considered how to get a restraining order against Trixie. As Chaz and Tamela's conflict amplified, she more openly vented her disgust with what she took for an interference. To get her under his thumb, he attempted to put Trixie in control of our apartment.

"She'll decide what goes on here in my name."

Tamela was scathing. "She done try 'dat already. But, do she pay rent here, which I do? She ha' no business here or sleeping over, neither. She a' be your wife. Mitsuki be! Tend to your wife and leave Trixie to her own hus-baahnd." She eye-pointed at Mitsuki. "Look, she cry becau' wha' you do her!"

I sometimes wondered if Chaz was correctly decoding her fuming West Indian. He might've punched her out for that impertinence but wasn't the sort to cross that line when psychological torture was his stock in trade. Too, he might've sensed I was no kind of Dude though, so far, I'd only spatted in mild language.

He attempted a soapbox chastising. "This is the Unification Church and women know their place. You shouldn't be arguing with me. It's unPrincipled."

"When ev'rybody in 'de house here learn to love 'dey *own* spouse 'dem, then 'dis will be a Unification house. Chris, 'de maahn 'de spit-tin' image o' Jeh-rome!" He clammed up red faced and stormed off. I minded my own business.

I loved Tamela. But her struggle with his drama, her bad blood for the church, the seminary, my life, undying resentment of Shiori, refusal to forgive, and her indissoluble riots were a wrecking ball to our marriage and my internal nature, my personality, my very psyche. I couldn't pray, say Sunday Pledge, nothing. I was lucky to get through my classes and manage work. Existence was a nuclear wasteland. Hounded by guilt regardless God's will or Tamela's professionally wielded indemnity stick, I often felt I deserved all her spite, her wounded, judging soul crying out to me like Ahab his dooming whale:

> Towards thee I roll, thou all-destroying but unconquering whale; to the last I grapple with thee; from hell's heart I stab at thee; for hate's sake I spit my last breath at thee . . . since neither can [thou] be mine, let me then tow to pieces, while still chasing thee, though tied to thee, thou damned whale!

It was all of it destroying my ability to serve God, live a religious life, be a minister. I tried to meditate but couldn't transcend our state of war. I desperately wanted to graduate UTS but she was implacably opposed to my efforts and loathed to her last breath being on campus. She tried forcing me back to New York City which would, in practice, sever me from my M.DIV. future. With our collective frustrations and fighting, I didn't know day-to-day if I'd even survive a seminarian.

Yet, I was determined to save UTS just like I was the church from the ruin it was driving headstrong into. *WUSR* was one iron. I was dying to throw in others:

1. I designed cheap, modular married student housing and lobbied to build them on an empty field north of the main building. (*denied*)
2. UTS grads sent to foreign countries had difficulty supporting their families, so I developed a program to house them on campus and create a UTS Missionary Fund to support them. If our now-3,000 nationwide members donated only $3–4 per month, we could generate $9,000–12,000 monthly to support these missionary families for 36 months. (*not interested*)
3. I proposed a 3-person team to recruit new students nationwide. (*denied*)
4. I tried persuading UTS and local/UTS-Blessed couples to buy gas station–convenience stores as a family–school revenue stream. We could purchase 100 stores over 5–7 years to pull in a $2.5 million annual net profit, some percentage shared out to UTS. Unlike President Kim's doomed-to-fails, these generate revenue rain or economic shine. (*no thanks*) I made a go myself but financial due diligence was as far as I got on dodgy credit.
5. Since UTS was a mess in every way, I developed a plan to revolutionize the school's four main axes: 1) student quality; 2) faculty–staff quality and compensation; 3) curriculum; and 4) economic foundation. (*no thanks*)

The powers that be weren't merely disinterested in my ideas but downright hostile. It made my every muscle bind. At least I was creatively seeking solutions. Sadly, the Unification Church doesn't particularly care about its members nor, if it's honest, its own survival if it impairs the power and graft of its individual leaders.

Even with all these functional ideas, the mental and emotional energy sucked into Tamela's furnace made shifting sands of my follow-through. My biggest failure over my UTS years was my inability to transcend her preference for warfare over compromise. And the slowly cooking volcano that was her relationship with Chaz was a poison coursing through the veins of daily life and familial love.

Happy moments. Tamela and Kal-el. 1996.

Escaping our house every minute she could, Tamela accidently spent off all our money. Dr. Shimmyo very kindly loaned me $900 but it wasn't enough to relocate. His promises to broker a Chaz War ceasefire evaporated past his lips. In tears, she dragged me out of Dean Mickler's office. Her story sent me to Business Manager Tony Formby: "It's your problem, you need to solve it." Dean Tanabe: "I'm aware of Chaz and Trixie, but a conflict even in a school residence isn't my bailiwick, it's Gareth Davies', " supposedly in charge of student housing. "I can't help you, Chris. Dr. Shimmyo is who you need to see." But he'd reliably been a two-faced Janus: "It is Dean Tanabe's responsibility." And . . . hit restart on the nihilism. Divinity leader Dr. Carlson chose hands off. Former student body president Ken Shafto living in the unit across from us said, "We can hear everything. Thank God I don't live with him!"

Interviewing Dr. Shimmyo for June's *WUSR* he said, "Can you manage this even despite your problem with Chaz Jerman?" *Uhh, can you manage to do* your *job?*

Jesús said, "He was just trying to get out of the interview, Chris. He doesn't care about Chaz or your situation."

In tears again a week later Tamela pulled me out of class. "We ha' a big fight and Chaz t'row me down, Chris!"

I went straight to Dr. Shimmyo. "He's a menace! I don't want to embarrass the seminary, but if something isn't done I'm calling the police this very night and have him arrested for assaulting my 6-months pregnant wife."

He took a minute to process. "You can move into Massena House. I will have Mr. Formby write Chaz a letter to move by August. Will that resolve it?"

"Thank you." *Wait*. Why have him move if I am? And Massena was full.

WE REACHED CRITICAL mass mid-September. Trixie dumped a dirty floor cloth onto Tamela's dishes in the sink. "You couldn'a move 'dem out 'de way?"

"They shouldn't even be there." They tussled shoving shoulders through the narrow doorway to the dining room. "This girl's attitude is satanic! Chaz!"

"Don't worry about it. She's just a bitch."

I burped out of the kitchen. "Man, don't call my wife a bitch."

He leapt to his feet, wildly gesticulating his famously violent body language to intimidate. "I'll call her a bitch anytime I want because that's what she is. She's a bitch." We went round and round. He moved to the kitchen while I steamed.

Tamela was inside. "You is some despicable maahn, you know 'dat?"

He roughly shoved her to the floor. "Shut up, you stupid bitch!"

She caught herself on the counter with a heavy grunt. I caught the noise and Tamela pulling herself up. "Chris! Him try t'row me down again!"

"The fuck are you doing, Chaz? She's eight months—"

"You must've seen it. She fell down on her own."

"How?" I wanted to rip his lying throat out by the roots. My religious training straitjacketed me more effectively than iron manacles. Tamela might've smashed teeth on the spot but for her wallowing belly and instinctive sense of danger from a not-unthinkable sucker punch to the womb. Pros and cons stormtroopered through me. I hesitated. The moment passed. Pulling her from the kitchen, I spent the night in our seething room stewing, chagrined, and uncertain.

"You jus' g'wan let 'de maahn t'row me to 'de floor, and me wi' a baby inside? How can you le' he caahll me a bitch? What kin' o' man—?"

"Tamela, it isn't appropriate to fight over a woman."

She glared Ahab at his hated whale. "You mus' be mad. Your own wife!"

"Dammitall, it's unPrincipled! Unchristian. I'm ordained. It's a seminary, for God's sake! What are you goading me into?"

"Defendin' your wife? 'Dat be wrong? You t'ink Rev. Moon wouldn'a rise up against somebody t'rowin' he eight months pregnant wife onto 'de groun'?"

"That's . . . fuck! a question I can't actually answer." My insides blazed. Yet, how could I let his actual assault rest? How *should* I respond? My mind was a Celtic knot. The whole affair stunk. An unfathomable situation.

I went for genial the next day at the kitchen door. A good foot to ease the tension. "Morning, Chaz . . . listen, I get Tamela can be trying, but I need to ask you to stop calling her a bitch when you're pissed. Especially getting physical with her."

He was frying breakfast and launched into cursing her, this time intimidating me into backing off by wildly waving the 18-inch, two-tined kitchen fork he was using on the bacon. He stabbed at the air a foot from my face.

"Your wife's a fucking bitch, so why don't you train your bitch? This is *my* house. Don't think you can come into *my* kitchen to argue with me."

He could've been Jerome in the wreckage of Bramble House. "It's *our* house and stop calling my wife a bitch!" I wasn't yelling but getting there. "Who do you think you are, talking about her that way in front of me?"

"Your wife *is* a bitch. Everything's her fault because she's running her mouth off in *my* house. She's an evil bitch when you're gone." The kitchen fork punctuated the air with every 'bitch' ripping from his mouth. "If she's a bitch, I'll call her a bitch, because that's exactly what she is, a BITCH!"

"Get that fork out of my face!" Our noise drew Tamela and Mitsuki from their bedrooms. They stood rooted. Mouths hung. Eyes bulk carriers of horror.

"Shove it up my ass if you can!" His voice was surly, daring, mocking. Lips curled in scorn poking his fork at me. I yanked it from his hand. It clattered across the dining room. He snatched up a sharp-edged metal spatula. Thrust it at my chest. "You gonna knock this out of my hand, too?"

Yep. It went flying. He was screaming. Tamela said something. His eyes fired over my shoulder. "She's a fucking bitch! Tell your fucking bitch to shut up!"

My hand seized his throat. Flung him Darth Vader style into the cabinets. Shock and disbelief lit his face. I stood my ground, so he turned contemptuous.

"Now you did it." He was unexpectedly calm, satisfaction a stage curtain from bald pate to chin. "Mitsuki, get me the phone. I'm calling the police. Shimmyo will kick you right out of the school for this and the cops'll put you in jail."

Shit. I'd forget all about Dr. Shimmyo and his overarching antagonism over WUSR and a whole host of my hated Americanisms. "It's your word against mine."

"Who do you think he'll believe? I've got a good track record and been here a long time. I know all about you and Jerome. You two were nothing but trouble."

Damn. He's probably right. But his sneering tone uncorked all my choler and Tamela's Ahabian spite that I'd spent months repressing since their first altercation. I jumped on him a hungry lion. Pounded him twice two steps back. He wouldn't even defend himself, the coward, just covered his body from my blows. He tripped, slapped hard backfirst into embezzled 50-lb rice bags stacked on the floor, ass sunk deep like a beanbag chair. He met then avoided my lightning eyes looming over him, fists balled and body jumpy with adrenaline, wondering if I'd kick a man when he's down. When I didn't, he struggled his overweight frame to his feet.

I was a whirlwind out of the kitchen into the dining room where he and Trixie spent so many nights lording their strange perversion over Mitsuki, who took it. My feet jammed into my cowboy boots in the pile of shoes. If I stayed, I might beat him up more and I didn't want that, not really. I'm not a fighter by nature. I was already despising myself for stooping to his level and trembling at losing my characteristic discipline and self-control with anybody who wasn't Tamela. This was a serious affair. Indeed, the bastard was right. Dr. Shimmyo would snatch this chance to eject me from his sacrosanct UTS. I needed to get away. Think over next steps.

He strutted from the kitchen and grabbed the cordless phone. "I'm calling the cops. Ha ha, you're going to jail . . . and your wife's still a bitch."

My heart was thumping and veins bursting in fight mode. I stood stock still. Took in the spurning hate outlining his sour puss. A need for retribution overpowered me. He was lying to the police dispatcher and I landed a shattering left fist right on top of the phone against his ear. He fell against the wall. The phone bounced across the floor and spilled its guts. He struggled up. I rained more blows till I got hold of myself. Stepped back. Patrolled his movements. He was bent kneed, quivering, eyes cast down, unable or unwilling to fight me. His cockiness was gone. His arrogance dissolved. His rotten mouth shut. In their stead was humble submission, the beaten ex-alpha submitting to its new master. I realized he was a bully. A false shell of a man. A loser, a liar, a poltroon. What an asshole.

Our wives gaped at the overturned dining table and general wreckage. I slugged hunted eyes at Tamela then spun and stomped down the stairs. I pushed my Taurus at high speed down the dirt road. Flew past the gatehouse into Redhook like the very Devil was firing my heels. Chaz called the cops from Ken Shafto's.

Well, I was nervous. What was an assault-and-battery charge like? Hell, he'd threatened me with a stabby fork and then a sharp spatula. I was well within my rights to defend myself. I called the sheriff's office from a pay phone in Redhook, explained what happened, and waited for the cops and handcuffs.

When one arrived he said, "I've already been out to the seminary and heard his story. What's yours?" I explained the whole situation. "Did you strike him with a fist or an open palm?" He demonstrated.

"You mean it makes a difference?" He gravely nodded. "Well, my fist."

"The fist makes it a much more serious case. But, your stories match up. And"—he consulted his notepad—"he declined to press charges. So, there's no legal issue."

That loudmouthed chickenshit. I bet the cop told him his fork and spatula canceled his case, and maybe Tamela threatened to rat him out for throwing her down.

Regardless, there was a *huge* church issue at UTS. News I'd pummeled Chaz was a tsunami rolling through the grounds by my return. Dr. Shimmyo was spitting rivets hearing the police had galumphed over holy school grounds because of a *fight* involving a *seminarian*. He demanded summary judgment even though I'd pestered and begged the administration the previous four months to arbitrate or authorize our move to different campus housing. Even now he was refusing.

I said to Mike, "It makes me wonder if Chaz doesn't have some J. Edgar Hoover dirt on all these administrators bending over backward to *not* interfere."

"Not on me. You should know they're considering expelling you, though it's mostly to cover up their total lack of concern. Chaz is saying they tried to bring harmony but you and especially Tamela Cained out instead."

"What a crock of—! Chaz is unhinged. He needs a leash."

"Well, Dr. Shimmyo wants a written explanation."

I marched into Dr. Shimmyo's office. "You have no business expelling me after all I've gone through seeking help. Tamela and I are clearly the victims here."

He was unmoved. "It's not up to me." This was a perfect opportunity to kill two birds with one stone. He didn't like Chaz any more than Reiko did.

"You're the president of the school. How's it *not* up to you?"

"It is for the cabinet to decide." He wasted no time convening it.

I prepared for my twelfth kickout. Formby and (Aetna Springs) grounds manager Jonathan Brundrett argued expulsion. The cabinet dutifully . . . except for Mike. He cited our seeking help and a panoply of experience with Chaz. His threats against Mike's wife. That expelling me championed unPrincipled behavior. He valiantly argued that UTS was to blame for turning a deaf ear to my pleas. His stirring defense bowled me over. I was always thrown to the curb, no mitigation permitted and none offered. The first time in 15 years somebody defended me and it was Chatty Kathy's husband. A stunning reversal of fortune. I had to believe God was working. That I'd truly paid the indemnity that freed me of my burden. Dean Pocahontas saved me from Dr. Powhatan's freshly honed axe. *Amazing grace.*

Shamed, the cabinet expelled Chaz from campus and his job and me from housing. I'd hurriedly moved us to nearby Saugerties more than a week earlier, so we were unaffected—more importantly, not given the gate à la Wren Meyer.

But later: "Regardless, you crossed the line physically striking Chaz."

"Come on, Mike. There's little if any difference at all between the psychological and emotional violence he perpetrated against us and my physical self defense. Condemning only physical violence implicitly justifies psychological violence, which is literally torture. That's just hypocrisy."

"No, any physical violence is worse."

"How? Bones and bruises heal pretty quick, but hearts and minds which people like Chaz torture with verbal and emotional abuse heal much slower, if they ever heal at all. You know people carry that for years. Whole lifetimes."

"Well..." He had nothing and changed the subject. "Your wife has some real issues, if you haven't noticed. Talking to her is something else altogether."

"What do you mean?" Yeah, what *was* he talking about?

"Her behavior's odd, that's all. The way she reacts to things just doesn't square up. Like she's not otherwise there."

What the—? His words haunted me as I struggled with Tamela living my same reality yet experiencing a different one. Not culturally, but "otherwise."

It was no real surprise UTS authorities missed my point. Students didn't. I was a hero kicking Chaz's hitherto terrifying ass. A few groused I was the same old loose cannon who couldn't be trusted to remember Divine Principle when the chips were down. In hindsight... maybe. Sane soldiers prefer peace but there *is* a time for war. That's why Christianity developed its 'just war' theology. I appreciated, admired, and respected Mike rising to my occasion against Dr. Shimmyo who could've fired him for it on a pretext. I thanked him profusely regardless our disagreements. A new era might be lobbing my way. I wanted to catch, not fumble, it.

Dr. Shimmyo said, "I still need your written version. It's no big deal." I didn't know which Janus face was talking and saw only a future noose in that.

FOR MOST OF Tamela's militarized second pregnancy at Harvest House we brawled tooth and nail over Shiori, money, the church, UTS, or her battle with Chaz. Their struggle blew back on me "dragging" her into the church.

"T'rough Chaz," she vociferously complained, "I don't wan' anyt'ing to do wi' your church nor its memb-uhh!"

"You're throwing out the baby *and* bathwater. Plenty of wonderful members."

"Not in New York! Not in Hawaii, neither. Or Colorado. Or Texas. An' I a' forget 'de sour granny in Korea. There some magic place you ain' carry me, yet?"

"Yeah, I can't say you're wrong. But still, not everyb—"

"Your whole church be like Bramble House run by Jeh-rome and Av-ril!"

During our worst arguments she violently shoved me around or blocked my escape. This only instilled a deeper sense of hysteria the longer it dragged on and led to vicious pushing matches to get out the door to the Land of Nod. She gawked when occasionally I beat my sternum with my own fists in frustrated rage or grabbled a pen, mechanical pencil, sometimes even a knife and stabbed at myself.

I screamed till my voice broke, "I'd sooner die than live a minute longer in your never-ending cussing!"

"G'wan, then! Who be stoppin' you? Me?"

"*Gahhh!*"

It brought her no rethink. In a panic when I couldn't force my way through the door, I whipped round and plunged head first through our open albeit screened second-floor window. I hit the grassy dirt 12 feet down in a shoulder roll, popped to my feet, and sprinted across the grassy meadow sloping to the Hudson River.

Tamela flashed out the front door on wings screaming and crying, "Come back! I'll behave!" like the stairs in Queens.

Pushed to this point, I stampeded. I roamed the rail-tracks shadowing the river until exhausted. As cussing years went by, it took longer and longer to calm down. Once, I made it to the car and dropped locks on her hands beating on the glass. I boiled off in a gravel-shooting frenzy that carried me to Montreal where I rambled two days before laggardly drifting home after a suspicious border search due to my empty child seat. She invariably launched her disputes over Shiori. Even minus my own Trixie, we were hotter than Chaz and Mitsuki.

She'd rhetorically demand, "Tell me 'de *real* reason you marry to me and carry me up here to 'dis terrible country an' your worse church."

Already feeling guilty as hell regardless how many times I thought I'd transcended Shiori through indemnity and now fidelity, instant aggravation flooded me. "Please, Tamela! Just drop it. I can't change the past. Let's build a happier future."

"Ain' no happy fut-uhh in your paahst."

Damn. She could be quoting Nietzsche. Or Hobbes. Our words were only ever at cross purposes. Wound up, she could only run down to stop. She believed I deserved merciless punishment. Accomplishing it meant venting her perpetual rage and resentment like a furious sea beating overconfidently stout rocks to sand.

I didn't know her behavior was classic domestic violence although I'd started mouthing, "I'm an abused husband, Tamela."

"Pah! You ain' be no such t'ing."

Still, I never made the connection between my sense of abuse and *domestic violence* in the newspapers. And I breathlessly loved her. Although once or twice at UTS I wished we'd never met, deeper down I didn't really regret marrying her. There was just something drawing me to her that I didn't want to let go or lose. Her sense of humor, playfulness, compassionate heart, intelligence hidden in her debatement, intuitive understanding of others . . . except me, that is. I thought her a good judge of character—she'd never misread Jerome or Chaz. But, by God, she couldn't control her temper nor kill the fire 'neath her stewing wrongedness. Unforgiven, I was a time-looping dartboard for her rage, interrogation, and brutalization.

"This baby must surely end up a basket case from all the combat," I said.

She gulped a breath. "I t'ink so, too."

"Why don't you quit cussing me, then? Just let go the past so we can . . ."

"I' tryin'! It be jus'—me a' know." Heavy pout.

"You should figure it out."

"I know! I sorry." Dark air sighed forth. "We need counselin', Chris."

"*You do.* I'm not touching those money-sucking charlatans." Not till winter 1998 did I say, "I guess therapists and psychologists are different. One of my professors is certified and will take us free. I made us an appointment."

Despite heated argument she said, "I will nev-uhh stoop to 'dem people."

"He's not a church member. He just teaches here."

Shaking head. Crossed arms. Cocked hip. "Same t'ing. Fin' a real t'erapis'."

"I can't afford it!"

"Then waahk haahd-uhh! Stop wastin' time at 'dis no kin' o' semee-narry."

Post-grad, post-Korea. Jane Street. Aug., '98.

Kir-el arrived in October '96 in nearby Rhinebeck seemingly all bubbly after all. It took weeks for my Grinchy heart to grow new space. She was soon my darling. I was sure to inundate Kal-el with extra love and attention. He reeked jealousy at her arrival. There were times he gloomed positively threatening. Within weeks my lovebombing taught him I treasured him now more than ever. He shifted to helping hold, rock, feed, and change her diapers. He'd march from the bedroom of our 2 Jane Street refugee rental lofting a pillow for a platter when Tamela was putting Kir-el to her breast. *How good and how pleasant it is for brethren to dwell together in unity.* Pure joys in the midst of a dirty war.

Our hastily got flat was a third the chicken coop's size but a welcome respite from mad roommates. We battled less off campus and my blood pressure might've normalized. With mind-ripping terror I'd taught Tamela to drive a stick-shift along campus dirt roads in a rusty but solid, reliably-built '81 4-door Corolla that Trixie sold me for $100. A few snowbank crashes, spinouts, near misses, and life-flashing oddities almost did me in. Defying her disorders, she built a confidence to excel and passed her verbal—who knew?—licensing exam. She has yet to have a car accident. My pride in her ballooned over it. I bought her three more and better cars over several years. In some ways, we achieved a kind of normalcy. I clung to hope.

～

As *WUSR* GARNERED critical success even amongst some of its worst detractors, Rev. Moon ordered up his next splendid affair wrapped in the cloak of his third World Cultural and Sports Festival: Blessing '97. He was going for his biggest fish yet, a 3.6- + 36-*million couple* lollapalooza and the church was sifting through the last dregs of willing humanity. Leaders struggled to mobilize as many members as possible but it was an arduous cat rodeo with so many living outside centers, working jobs, and raising children they couldn't—wouldn't—abandon for one more Big Victory. All the same, hundreds flooded Washington, DC to mobilize attendance. Dr. Shimmyo ordered us into service like Colonel Pak's academy class in 1950 facing down North Korean tanks. We dutifully geared up.

Several months earlier our latest American church president, Tyler Hendricks, had tapped me to production manage his new quarterly gazette, *True Family Times.* Boarding buses smokily idling nose-to-tail in our UTS circle drive, I impetuously ran inside to haul several boxes of overprints to Washington where they might be usefully distributed to clergy. I tiredly plopped 70 pounds of boxes on the foyer's floor in the main church center at Columbia Road and 16th Street NW. Purchased from the Mormons in 1977, we'd heard part of its roof cranked open so the faithful didn't get stuck in the rafters during the Rapture.

Some bucko playing security guard said, "Hey! Carry those to the basement."

I stared, hands on hips. "Can't somebody else do it? I'm with UTS and—"

"You brought 'em. Come on, they're blocking traffic."

Scheisse. "This was stupid," I muttered. "Shoulda known I'd only heap extra work on myself." I reluctantly heaved them up and cantankerously lugged them down. To eye-popping astonishment, Godwin D'Silva barreled up with open arms.

Visiting Honolulu on church business, we'd hosted him for dinner at our single-serving dining table in our overpriced fifth-floor studio. He took to me right away despite the local members poisoning him against me for a time. Now he was Rev. Diplomacy like Jesús and Southern California State Leader (SoCal). He'd amassed influence and prestige doing the impossible for Mrs. Moon while deflecting his jurisdiction from death's door. A feat for the ages, I'd thought. Wished I'd had him up in Ergela's north. I pumped his hand with a grin.

"The senior cheese drafted me two weeks ago to replace Phillip Schanker. Rev. Pak"—our continental director—"says he 'disastrously dropped the ball.'"

"You mean the Blessing's gonna flop?" I was almost shocked.

"Not if I can help it. You're here with the UTS crowd?" I nodded. "You're wasted there. I'm running the whole show and need a deputy director." My jaw broke the floor. "If you're willing."

"*Khuh!* Is that a serious question?" I bowed. "Your devoted servant, Master."

"Funny. You report only to me. Nobody outranks me except Rev. Pak and Father, so you're golden." Eyes went over my shoulder. "I'll square it with Dr. Shimmyo."

Who was stupefyingly appalled. His news floored the milling UTS gaggle awaiting orders upstairs to head out to the streets as cannon fodder. *Those leaden boxes...*

"Look, Chris, I'm a smart guy"—and corporately diplomatic to a fault—"but Rev. Pak expects a miracle and I'm not entirely sure I can deliver."

"We'll make it happen, don't you worry. Tell me what you need."

"I know you're an organizational expert and your UTS journal really impressed me. I'm gonna rely on you to tighten all the loose screws around here. We'll sort out the overall strategy and get the right things in motion for you."

"And inspire us all with your can-do presence."

"That, too." He grinned. "That means you basically run the whole show. Hope you're ready for the big time."

I heaved a loaded breath. "Been ready, amigo. Let's knock their socks off!"

Working with him was a pleasure. I treated him as my friend, colleague, and equal despite following his strategic directions. Unlike most, I never kowtowed to his (much less anyone's) position... Rev. Moon was kind of scary, though, so I employed some healthy circumspection around him. With Godwin, I strongly argued my ideas and insights like we were still around my Honolulu dinner table. We spent 25 hours a day planning a solution to Rev. Pak's "Phillip mess."

Several days went to riding around with Asian leaders who couldn't or wouldn't accept my authority without Godwin's stern reminders, visiting every metro church center, and getting a feel for the operation as a whole. Then I sat myself in front of a computer and wrote up a strategy and operations package which I distributed to the senior and mid-level leaders through a hands-on training seminar. They bossed some 500 members doing all the grunt work, so running a train-the-trainer was essential. We organized a charter network of 300-plus buses from 10-plus states and Canada. My transportation hat also meant designing and executing organized pickups, arrivals, parking, and departures without losing passengers.

Godwin and I had exactly zero conflicts and confrontations. We respected and appreciated the other's skills and abilities, complimented each other handily, and got along as friends and brothers. He wasn't the swaggering martinet as were many Koreans and American lapdogs whose collective chestnuts they'd ordered us to save from Rev. Moon's spleen. Godwin was kind, considerate, respectful, encouraging, nurturing—in all ways, he felt like family. I loved him. Our friendship wasn't then or now perfect, but it's one of the truest I've had in the church.

Rev. Pak, Rev. Yang, Tyler Hendricks, and others invited clergy, inspired members to bring in the sheaves, and organized specific events then passed the logistics off to us. A sixtyish Korean sister known as General Kim—this Blessing spawned a plethora of military titles and mannerisms amongst leaders—airplaned in to make the necessary spiritual conditions for victory and prepare RFK stadium to receive True Parents. She circled it several nights on foot praying aloud and sprinkling Rev. Moon's blood (so she said) on the earth to purify the grounds and drive away evil spirits hell-bent on disrupting God's historic, providential moment. She ordered a 40-day, 120 Korean bowing (*kyum bae*) condition to purify us.

Each late night those of us who wanted—more a command performance at our senior level—reverently gathered in the maybe 20×30-foot first floor public room of the Upshur Street house in ordered rows. General Kim began the night's torture with military precision. I started pretty cocky. How hard could it be kneeling down and standing up? By the fortieth *kyum bae*, many members' leg muscles were melting into the night. I was hearing more and more heavy, carpet-muffled thumps as Darwinian rejects thudded to the floor. My legs were on fire, heart pounding ribs oversexed on Viagra. Sweat drained from my pores. Soaked my shirt. Removed all the slack in my poorly considered, heavy cotton Levi's. Salt stung my eyes. Sweat dribbled a leaky faucet off my nose. *Jeez. This is frickin' hell!*

And there was General old-lady Kim in her singular row at the head of the room. "Ready . . . *kyum bae!* . . . Rise." She robotically hit the deck with metronomic control, counted the number, then floated to her feet. The very image of Nietzsche's *Übermensch*. By one hundred, she was already going down for the next bow while I still struggled to quaky feet. Breath heaved in hoarse rasps then exploded from my lungs as knees collapsed halfway through the next bow and my palms-out forehead slammed into the foresightedly plush pile.

Well, I wasn't the only boob dying a slow death here. I needn't worry for my manhood or spiritual fitness. Even the Koreans, presumedly frequent partakers, were a mass of sweat and shuddering musculature. By the time we reached 120 bows I was swaying like a broken reed in the wind, straining to focus on her sonorous Korean prayer. Then up shot my bile. I fled the room with what dignity I could muster and raced downstairs for the bathroom where I lost lunch and dinner in one heaving, surging spasm. *Ugh.* Hands planted on the wall above the toilet supported my knee-locked legs shivering like a Moscow winter. Tough guys passing the open door threw in their laughs. That was okay. I did the full one-twenty, by God. That made me not just a genuine Unificationist but a General Kim *Soldat*, plain and simple. But I damned sure wasn't doing this daily for forty days. I had real work to do. Fortunately, no enterprising holier-than-thou leader had thought to officially require it of headquarters staff. We avoided her holy hellhole far more often than we didn't and a cold-sweating Rev. Pak could thank us for it.

My legs were sore enough the next few days that I couldn't lower myself into a chair or car without Godwin's geriatric help. A shadow of my Coast Guard self, but otherwise a great spiritual experience. I felt closer to God. Realized my body and spirit limitations. Evolved a greater appreciation for the nature of the spiritual conditions history's saints and sages did at the risk of their lives.

As extreme as some Unification Church spiritual conditions can get, they did remind us of our *raison d'être*. We were heavenly soldiers bent on defeating the enemy of peace and true love to Restore the world of God's Edenic Ideal, not a pack of cultish losers yipping behind a megalomaniac's vision of financial or theocratic empire. If such debilitating exercises really were just to grind down our self will to render us collectively compliant, there'd be no real spiritual component to them nor would we feel individually empowered. The fact is that even after such an exhausting regimen we finished in tearful, boisterous, heartfelt prayer that America rediscover its Christian roots, become a nation living for the sake of the world instead of pillaging it for self-gain, and that loving, God-centered families spread across the planet via the cleansing of love relationships through the Holy Blessing of Marriage. General Kim's example to me was simple: bow 120 times every day and, before long, I'd be doing it without breaking a sweat.

Beyond such strange displays of religious fervor, most everyone I knew engaged in vigorous prayer several times a day whenever their schedules permitted. The local prayer rooms were always full. Many simply prayed on their knees atop their sleeping bags after 20-hour days. Prayer kept me going, too. Godwin and I followed an exhausting schedule for the four weeks leading up to the November 29th event. We had a year's worth of botched planning to eradicate and a year's worth of planning that hadn't been done to get done. Pulling together 300-plus buses in a few weeks was no easy task, either.

For that, Godwin called in his friend Paul Vetterli from Ohio, a short, tousled black-haired former bus driver for church-bankrupted Sun Tours. He understood the industry and saved our bacon. He also had a friend who worked security in the White House who snagged us one of the special, friends-only West Wing tours the White House permits . . . or did, pre-9/11.

The uniformed Secret Service solemnly warned us in the gate house, "If you have any outstanding warrants, including traffic tickets you skipped on, we'll have to arrest you right here for extradition to wherever." We all bargained nervous eyes. "You sure you want to go ahead with your background check?"

"Heck, yeah," I said, furiously scanning my memory for any oversights.

Nobody got taken down. I stuck my head into the Oval Office for a gander, visited the cabinet room, and saw pretty much everything as Paul's friend led us through several floors. I thought over the irony of righteous UTS students out rummaging through the cold, wintry streets for warm bodies while I, maybe the most reviled seminarian in Dr. Shimmyo's eyes, was enjoying this unique and privileged treat.

A bit under 20,000 showed up for the Blessing—the church claimed we hit the global 39.6 million couple mark—leaving RFK's stands half empty. The newspapers wrongly presumed the count was *couples* so, to everyone not there like the *Washington Post*'s go-getter journalists, it appeared the Moonies had filled the stadium with 40,000 *individuals*. We darn tootin' didn't correct them. I must've hiked 25 miles around the stadium and parking areas overseeing the operation, resolving each inevitable crisis wired into the radio network with a walkie-talkie and cell phone. My top-level clearance badge gave me the run of the opera, even into Rev. Moon's personal rooms. Places Dr. Shimmyo himself was forbidden.

On the stadium floor with Rev. Pak, the upper stands had a forlorn, abandoned air. "K'ristopah, go shift those upper groups so the stadium looks more full."

"I'm not sure it'll create the illusion you're looking for. And most folks won't want to move now they've situated themselves."

"Try anyway. Let Heavenly Parent work."

Few relocated. Abject terror swathed his face, mouth starkly twisted down in a painful grimace anticipating Rev. Moon's fury at his failure to fill RFK to capacity. 'Failure' is a terrible watchword in the church, stitched all through the inability of every central figure from Adam and Abel to church leaders and members to fulfill God's will to reverse the Fall of Man. It's ever the reason cited for Rev. Moon's plans and goals rarely coming off as intended. His evident fear genuinely touched me. Gone was the arrogant swagger, rudeness, and glory-hogging. Only an ordinary man's grim realization of failure and chastisement.

"Don't worry," I encouraged him. "It's a good crowd. Look how everyone is so energetically doing the wave. We don't have all the numbers, but we have the enthusiasm. Father will appreciate that."

He stiffly nodded in gratitude for my effort but seemed inconsolable. Godwin later said, "Father was furious it was only half filled. He expected better."

"Well, it was kinda shitty weather. Everybody did their best."

He gave me a what-church-do-you-think-you're-in? look. "But did you notice? Father stepped out through the doorway hand-in-hand with True Mother onto the stage and tripped." I registered surprise. "He nearly fell flat on his face."

"Dang! I guess I missed it hiking hell and gone all day. What'd he say?"

"It was a sign Satan had infiltrated the Blessing through unPrincipled members." *Typical.* "And yeah, the weather didn't help."

It was cool, blustery, and a bit rainy. Some decorations were torn from their moorings by the wind. "Maybe General Kim was a little slothful, too, then."

"Not a chance," he chuckled. "But, I got the sense he was heartened by how it all calmed the second he stepped out. That sunbeam through the clouds falling on his white robes during his prayer? Pretty spectacular, ya gotta admit."

"Yeah, I saw it. Lit him up like the returning Christ. Ministers been gabbing about it all afternoon." I paused. "We did good, Godwin. You should be running the American church." He gave me side eyes.

Whitney Houston, the coward she was, backed out of her million-dollar gig an hour before her performance at the insistence of her anti-Moon minister, claiming she didn't know it was a Unification Church event. *Sure.*

Phillip Schanker fulminated how viciously the church would sue her perfidy. "Not only will she have to give back the money, but pay us reparations, too!"

"That'll be the day," I chortled. We were outraged, as too the crowd. Truth be told, they mostly came for her and Jon Secada. "But you go, girl!"

Secada did his number although stiff as a board to start. Then the young Japanese, Korean, American, and assorted brides and grooms on the stadium floor, robed in white gowns and dark blue suits, disobeyed orders and rushed in a growing crowd to jump and dance uninhibited at his feet. He loosened up for a great show. I guess once he discovered that Moonies dug his music and danced like normal, unbrainwashed kids in front of a beaming Rev. and Mrs. Moon, he figured we must be human after all and deserved the performance we'd paid for.

After the event, gangly Peter Kim was the first schmuck Rev. Moon happened to lay eyes on. Godwin said, "He knocked him over a table with a solid punch to the head. Dodging his hands, Rev. Kim was like, 'Please, Father, it wasn't my fault! It wasn't my fault! I didn't have anything to do with the planning.'"

"Well, dang," I said. "Father can be such a grouch." Godwin's brows did a flip.

Later on Rev. Moon took it out on those who *were* responsible: Rev. Pak and Rev. Yang (not a scarce Phillip, though, whose spilt year most deserved it), who'd blown so much time and energy jockeying for power and glory they'd dumped most of the operation in our hands. Fortunately, we weren't on the hook for attendance or the weather but only operations. I'd pushed into the Regional Leader's meeting to plead for more authority to avoid just such an outcome. My written documents demonstrated how they were going to fail and face their Lord's dooming wrath if they didn't let me have my way. They were enthusiastic once Rev. Pak divined my infallibility. It was a funny meeting, though. Of twelve regional leaders, the eleven Koreans consistently excluded their token Westerner. Such pious frauds.

The next day I met a real snake in our Unification grass, Nimrod Kriss the Tasmanian. He introduced a new technology called pharlo. "It's a radical new paradigm in chemistry and literally worth billions." A skeptical Paul Vetterli took in his all-knowing eyes. "And we—*you*—are on the ground floor."

Through him I met one of its two patent holders in Florida, Bill Merchant. He so enthused me I excitedly kicked off my third entrepreneurial startup under Tamela's unenthused thumb. It seemed a great opportunity, perhaps too good to be true. I brought in Godwin. He opted for a background role hoping I'd make it work.

In March 1998 I persuaded UTS to accept my Blessing '97 Deputy Director work as my Divinity intensive. By May only my thesis, testing out of Korean class, and finals remained. Then Godwin and I reprised our roles for Rev. Moon's *360 million couple* Blessing June 13. Now he was shooting for the stars and anchored himself to Madison Square Garden (MSG) in New York City. This time, however, the Korean leaders had learned their lesson. For the moment, anyway. As with dementia, their slivers of clarity never lasted long. They handed us total control with only the actual ceremony involving Rev. Moon under their command.

Godwin developed a close relationship with the Garden's general manager and me a similar one with the hostile and pessimistic New York City Police Department. I won them over with a detailed planning document I'd organized into a binder for their special events people. We approached with a request for 400 buses, then raised it to 1,000. The NYPD had fits. Called us crazy. Denied our permit. With some private negotiating, they endorsed my plan. Their reasoning arose in two parts.

"I like that it's professionally prepared and detailed with maps, drawings, and contingencies," said an officer. "Most events are verbal or barely documented."

"And crap," someone said.

"An unusual level of planning for a church event, as well as in our events and emergency operations experience," their top cop said.

Another said, "I commend you for spelling out what a typical beat cop can expect to encounter, and how you anticipate each problem will be handled."

"We'll pass it out. It'll really alleviate their workload the day of."

"How'd you manage to create such a well-crafted plan when the Mormon Church, which is known for its organization, only a few months ago brought in 120 buses to your proposed thousand"—he huffed—"and created chaos?"

An officer said, "Didn't they have, like, hundreds lost plus missing buses?" The other nodded. "Yeah, our guys had no clue what to do with 'em. This"—he finger-stabbed my binder—"will fix that mess."

I said, "Well, besides the logic needed for my engineering work, maybe my organizational and other training from the military helped my planning skills."

"What!?" an officer said. "You were in the service? Which branch?"

"You're an engineer? What kind?"

I said, "Software. E-learning and relational database design."

"Jesus—"

"Hold up a sec. Are you actually a Moon—a Unification Church member?"

"Yes. I'm graduating our seminary in June with my Masters in Divinity."

"You mean as a preacher? Priest? Whatever your church calls it?"

"What about the military? Can we get back to that?"

"Oh. I was Coast Guard followed by Army."

"Doing what?" Narrow-eyed skepticism was locker-room socks.

Running MSG ops June 13 for Blessing '98.

"Well . . . drug interdiction in the Gulf of Mexico, classified vessel traffic safety in New Orleans"—big law enforcement feathers there—"and later, during Desert Storm, in the 69th IR out of the 14th Street armory." Now I was practically one of them. "I did some admin, special plans and operations, and OpSec for frontline mobile comms units."

Some fell back in their seats visibly shocked a goddamned Moonie, whom they saw as no better than airport swindling Hare Krishnas, had done a lick of military service and knew the first fucking thing about . . . well, *anything*, their attitude improved on the spot. They approved it all and agreed to close one lane each on 7th and 8th Avenues for x blocks, but on the day of the event instead closed two lanes on each for more bus parking to give aged attendees an easier walk.

They agreed to my offhand request for a motorcade through the city, too. Nobody asked me to go for it. I'd heard some leaders dreaming of it the way you long for air on Mars and made my play. They met Rev. Moon at the George Washington Bridge with two squad cars holding four dress-uniformed officers each and some motorcycles. His Town Car whisked amidst lights and sirens 150 blocks to MSG. The escort waited it out in the inside VIP parking then escorted him around a long block to the New Yorker Hotel. He excitedly bounced out of his car and, instead of striding victoriously through the revolving door like the king of the world he figured he was, turned to wave at each one individually as they motored off . . . and there they were already waving smiles back at him. A real make up kiss for RFK's boondoggle.

This was his first motorcade in America for which he didn't have to pay. I was very excited to arrange it not only through asking—the NYPD initially refused on policy—but via my professional example helping them avoid gridlock and looking out for their cops on the street. It impressed them so much they wanted to respond somehow. Their kindness and respect in turn impressed me.

The duty lieutenant addressed his event patrolmen at their MSG morning muster. "Listen up, you mugs. For these people, Rev. Moon is the Son of God. So for all of you, today, I don't care what you are: Rev. Moon *is* the Son of God. You got it?"

The NYPD even muted the usual protesters in a small box without a sound permit. They couldn't have been nicer. Hats off to the NYPD!

The event was so successful, we overfilled the venue. The Garden's manager said he'd lock the doors at 16,000 but, on the strength of Godwin's rapport, let in 4,000 more so that all who came had a seat, yet if one more arrived there'd be no room. We spilled into the overflow halls and Rev. Moon didn't trip on his robes.

My appreciation to NYPD.

The lieutenant said, "I had confidence in your bus plan, but to see six-fucking-hundred or whatever actually execute like clockwork . . . well, we're all amazed."

"I really appreciate that. Nice to hear I do good work." Our final count: 523.

He slapped my back. "If there's a next time, you got it."

And no leaders got Moonpie'd. My organizational plan prevented gridlock, lost attendees, and problems in and around the Garden. A flawless event.

In our now-quiet HQ Godwin said, "Man, RFK was around $20 million over a year of mismanagement, but I estimate we did MSG for about five."

"Because we didn't hash it up. You delivered and more, brother."

"We saved the church 15 million bucks."

"Maybe we'll get a medal." He hit me with those side eyes.

Rev. Pak said, "K'ristopah, you are a hero for what you did with mobilization."

I laughed. "That's a word I don't hear very often." He stroked my arm.

Rev. Yang forked over $300 cash on the barrelhead as if handing us our own weight in Spanish doubloons from his private stash. No salary like him and Phillip. No consulting fees like others. I journaled, "My name was . . . shouted from the roof tops!!" The exchange rate was short-lived. No one told Rev. Moon what I'd done. My sources in that neck said the motorcade went to a Korean on the down low. Then he posed us for standing ovations at 43rd Street's teeming leaders' meeting. "It was a picture-perfect operation," he beamed. Wren Meyer glitched in my head . . . who, with Ergela Arsch and other old haters, pumped my hand gabbing praise.

I mean, *holy cow!*

But the Kobayashis, who'd started the ball rolling on my nonBlessing, sat dark and disturbed by the copious Hawaiian-lei praise with steady scowls throughout. They'd judged me Satan incarnate for despoiling Shiori and persisted in their silent treatment. Nine years and counting. *These fuckin' people.*

AFTER THE PERFORMANCE I turned in on the Blessings coupled with everybody short of Rev. Moon's effusive acclaim and Godwin's kick-ass written recommendation, I expected to graduate with academic honors to get pulled into higher echelon work. Pay was of no consequence, though I'd need somebody's if they wanted me full time. With graduation I'd be "free of my burden to the church," I wrote December 3, 1997. "Free to serve God and True Parents without leaders threatening my life." If it took free service to earn it, that was okay by me. I'd achieved my first life goal, was on the cusp of my second, and now my third suddenly looked achievable.

Imagine my surprise leading up to MSG when Dr. Shimmyo summoned me. "I'm not approving you to graduate and I've sent my recommendation to the board."

I stopped breathing his stale office air. "What! I mean, why?"

"Despite all you did on the Blessing and all the good reports I've heard from Rev. Yang, Rev. Pak, Godwin D'Silva, and as you know there were others too, you don't meet UTS expectations for what it means to be a UTS graduate and a good member. You haven't earned, you don't deserve, the very serious responsibility and honor of being a UTS alumnus."

Tamping my temper I said, "I've done everything you've asked of me. Not even the *Student Review* caused any trouble, as promised."

"When you first started here, I said you have to sign the student pledge and live according to the student code of conduct . . ."

"I did that! I signed all that stuff. Except for Chaz, which was not my fault, I haven't violated any rules or codes or anything." Well . . . Shiori. But, bygones.

He lounged back. "You refused to sign the Student Family Pledge." This Maoist tool added maybe fall 1997 saw my family here, absent permission, interfering in my school and church participation. Signing it authorized them so long as I engaged as if single. "It is a fundamental part of the student code of conduct."

Many refused, the Africans en masse. Signing it forced us into hypocrisy, as we knew we couldn't fulfill its requirements without literally abandoning our families. He *knew* that. It was only for a control to condition us future leaders to a blind and fearful obedience. Pavlovian. A violation of Rev. Moon's way. We'd rejected it hands down in a flurry of contentious meetings. Our rebellion infuriated him. He'd quietly held it against us all these months like the Imperial Navy sneaking up on Pearl Harbor until our looming graduation offered him a Sunday bomb run.

I frowned. "And my academics with honors, how do they figure in?"

"Your academic coursework is only one aspect of your student experience at UTS. What's more important is your spiritual life . . . and your responsibility before True Parents." Code for vacuous North Korean servility. "My responsibility is to give the final okay for any student to graduate." *Tuition but no diploma, eh?*

I pursed. "I don't think so. We're a fully accredited school, now. According to *law*, I only need fulfill the curriculum. You liking me is irrelevant."

Still high on my glowing RFK praise from the Mooniest leaders of the American church, I might've been less prudent than usual. Only, he'd spun my ship's wheel for the rocks and I wasn't having it. He was nothing if not obstinate, even more so from bickering though I felt more from pride than Principle as I cogently countered each of his objections to my graduating. But the fix was in. Blessing '98 and my thesis were overwhelming. I complained to keener ears and passed my baton to the Africans.

Then Dean Mickler casually mentioned in the long hallway, "It must be nice to have friends in high places, eh."

Deer in headlights. "What friends are those, Mike? I'd like to meet 'em!" I studied his pure disbelief.

My joy and refuge. Winter, 1998.

"What. You didn't hear?" I was shaking my head. "Rev. Pak, Rev. Yang, *and* Rev. Kwak told Dr. Shimmyo that, 'Chris *will* graduate.' So . . ."

I rocked on my heels. "Well! That's—" *Thunderin' tarnation!* Twice in a lifetime that others went to bat for me after 16 years of abuse. Did I get the full nine?

"Amazing how you manage to cut corners, but at least you'll graduate."

Pfft! "Why do you see it as satanic fruits instead of God's will he's defying?"

"The school has rules and policies created from Father's directions."

"Twisted to torment faithful members who love Father!" He tut-tutted.

My fellow rebels lambasted the board for cheating them out of paid-for diplomas. Did it listen? Not till "lawsuit" hit their sizzling pan. With the seminary smoking up the church, it doused the flame. Dr. Shimmyo approved all our graduations.

The church offered me zilch. Tyler Hendricks had me in for the standard exit interview in one of the south wing's upper floor guest rooms, probing to discern a position I'd prefer that he could report to Rev. Moon. "There's a potential state leadership role in New Mexico if you're interested, but I'm not sure if it's vacant."

"I want to work with Father and I'll do whatever I can, of course. So, yeah."

"Remember, Father assigns UTS graduates a mission. I'm just bringing him recommendations. He hasn't mentioned any plans for your class, yet."

"Well, he says UTS grads should be billionaires. I have a chemical venture cooking down south with Nimrod Kriss having that potential. What about Florida?"

"I'll check, but I don't know any openings there." He paused. "I'm aware of Father's words but chasing money isn't a viable seminarian pursuit."

And yet Rev. Moon told a large gathering of alumni in Alaska, "There's no reason you can't do it. . . . With the right attitude and determination, you can do it. God needs you to be billionaires! Every one of you," reversing his earlier attitude that,

> I do not want you to be billionaires here on earth . . . become men and women who can live life in a God-centered way. (*The Dignity of God and Man* 1977)

I said, "I don't want to chase money. I'd be pursuing my core spiritual mission while having a financial base to support it. Like Father's doing." He'd inspired me. Why not? But how to do it and be Dr. Shimmyo's (and Tyler's) "good member"? It was an oxymoron. 'Rich Moonie' is a diplomatic standoff unless your last name is Moon. The church acclaims the laudable life as absolute obedience to its lofty goals. Honestly, none of us cared all that much. We *believed* in what we thus Rev. Moon were doing. Could rationally defend it. Happily sacrificed for it . . . so long as leaders maybe on a marble-veneered tit didn't set us to cold starvation.

In leadership's mind, money-making members live selfishly not godly. Yet, who's the richest of them all? ritzily lives over and above what "good members" can seek? The only wealthy Moonies besides the Moons and cheats are the mammonized apostates who've traded The Mission. Leaders implacably oppose them because you can't install them in a center or an indemnity course or control them yet, adoring money not the money-maker, fête them for hefty alms over the obedient scraping by. The only spiritually pure way to make money besides the perks of leadership and fundraising is in a church-owned business paying a no-mobility wage.

This dichotomy ground me into hamburger. I wanted to be wealthy so I didn't sweat the rent while serving the Lord of the Second Advent. If unable directly, then through his church with no salary. Billionaire Rev. Moon was my hero, my role model, my yardstick of the possible in his demand that we morph into "little Rev. Moons."

Tyler skeptically dismissed me when I raised starry-eyed Nimrod's opportunity.

One of our busiest classes was ESL.

"What dedicated UTS graduate goes off on a money-making enterprise instead of whatever mission Father gives, Chris? That's not our commitment. He sent last year's class to Brazil." The 'farm' near Jardim needed oodles of migrant labor to get it shipshape on a shoestring as an ideal model of heaven, and UTS grads could field a hoe as well as anybody. Humility by the gross. "Do you expect better? We follow Father's direction, not our own. That's our life of faith." *Says you, with a salary.*

As I prepared to graduate, it was clear 1997's class was used and abused. Red McDafft, a tall, robust Yankee with classic Hollywood good looks, was the first '97 grad to arrive. Rev. Moon quizzically said, "Oh, you are here already?" A few more Westerners straggled in over some months forsaking homes, goods, trades, friends, sometimes families. Still, no mission besides back-breaking labor as he contemplated their institutional future. Responding to Red's pesky requests for a formal mission he said, "I will only announce it when more of your class is here." That stranded the devoted answering his call without a pot to piss in, having to sustain self and family like castaways in one of Brazil's poorest regions where locals couldn't find paying work. Its wolfish Korean leader brusquely kicked Red and others off the farm in Rev. Moon's absence. They were splintered inside but powerless.

A grisly challenge turning one's cheek to keep the faith, else jettison precious worldviews. *Anathema*. What to do? Few Japanese and Korean grads showed and left Westerners standing. Rev. Moon considered them collectively absent and at fault, they told me. Friends and attendant children shed scads of impoverished, malnourished weight. They ricocheted through UTS on fundraising missions to feed hungry Blessed kids staring out of tropical photos, though the airlines gobbled most of it. *Burnt cinders*. This was the most egregious example I'd yet witnessed of Rev. Moon betraying members directly or indirectly via unsupervised and unaccountable mercenary leaders. Then his vaunted Jardim Providence died anyway.

Was I willing to traverse Red's or a similar course after graduation? The very possibility shook me. My faith, already under its severest assault since experiencing the pronounced hypocrisy and disregard for truth, compassion, and mission intrinsic in top UTS and church leadership's detestable lives— judged by their duplicitous results—seemed hot candle wax dribbling down an ever stubbier candlestick. My thoughts lashed me. I'd spent half a lifetime nurturing my faith in Divine Principle and the church as its vehicle. As brick after brick cracked out of my foundation of faith I sometimes felt it more a barrier restraining my prying eyes from leadership's private garden than a shoulder-to-shoulder foundation of substance. Nevertheless, even Rev. Moon finally laid bare the

The Christian Brothers left us few statues.

sins of his church. In 1997 he said it was guilty of three dire corruptions dissolving away its spiritual core like virulent Ebola.

First. Members (notably leaders) abused love. Extramarital and premarital sex was rampant in the worldwide, not just American, church.

Tamela said, "I agree wi' 'dat! And not jus' becau' Chaz." From her second-floor vantage in Harvest House she scoped out (mainly Korean and Japanese) couples creeping into the woods along Father's Trail toward the Hudson River. "I see 'dem come out in some while one at a time like, 'No-body business be happenin' here.' You t'ink I a' know wha' 'dem be doin'?" She stiupped teeth.

"I believe you. Shimmyo and his Korean overseer had to forcibly separate two Korean lovers and fling 'em out of school." *Stiupp*. When leaders like Ergela and sundry Japanese got caught in the cookie jar, often enough a wrist slap made do over us proles' psyche-breaking, leprous guilt trips regardless sincere penance.

Second. Leaders and members misused public monies, widely appropriating fundraising and business result for personal use. It's egregious since, unlike a love affair, partners are unwilling; a financial rape. In early days, stories circulated of the obscenely powerful Japanese *daimyo* buying la-di-da violins and tuition for their pampered children, top-drawer clothes, autos, extravagantly imported ethnic meals on porcelain over members downing cheap feed off paper and plastic, and so on. Leaders avoiding soiling delicate palates or intestinal fortitude with our mingy peasant grub when not obliging us to chopstick down their rustic rations in our own culture with a gratefully enlightened smile fuzed me from my first days.

Third. Leaders abused members in being insensate to their feelings, needs, and spirituality. It's best evidenced by Americans abandoning the church wholesale from the 1980s. Despite Rev. Moon's hortatory for Principled change even to this day, leaders flat out refuse to reach out and work with ex-members who, for the most part (according to him), quit over irreconcilable differences with leaders, not because they found him or Divine Principle suspect. Members longed to work with the mission of the church but many found no compatible place in an organization spurning us as an invasive species to be extirpated with a heavenly prejudice.

UTS best friends; Tamela at my right. May 1996.

Knowledge Rev. Moon identified and condemned these practices, experienced and rejected by us all over our church lives, sparked an intense controversy. Strident calls for reform churned forth. That Dr. Shimmyo posted it at all startled me—numbers one and two seemed to apply to him in this way or that but number three as written. He felt abusive in a passive-aggressive way, denouncing us one day then patting us on the back the next while planning our future destruction he'd spring when least expected. We never knew where we stood with him. One moment his big, toothy smile lavished praise and honor, then a minor slip up could have us begging mercy on our knees. His opinion seemed to be that we students were on a bullet train to hell . . . indeed, a sort-of hell was our next stop.

I loved UTS. Proud to earn my fully accredited M.DIV. But my faith in the church had cracked to its core under the hammers of churlish, counterfeit leaders and Dr. Shimmyo's unqualified faithlessness to real versus faux Divine Principle, Rev. Moon, God, spiritual ideals; his fanaticism, contempt. Yet, I *liked* him, dammit! *Respected* him. Saw him a *good man* for all his faults, like Julian. Perhaps I sensed he channeled Torquemada innocently, without malice—more a systemic derangement. As with many 36-Blessed couples, the facet by which he knew faith and reality was singular and exclusive not one of many possible that, by admitting no other, clouded the wholistic jewel. We were a metaphor and allegory for the American Family.

Comprehending the general depravity of our top dogs was the greater blow. Ugliest (despite viewing him a holy man saddled with foibles) were Rev. Moon's grim defects now quilling sobered eyes. I didn't know when I graduated—the soldier fighting on unaware he's mortally wounded—that my UTS experience hadn't cracked but shattered my institutional faith. Against all odds I'd reached the Blessing and UTS. I eagerly anticipated my destiny working somehow, someway directly with Rev. Moon. How surprising a year on to comprehend my Blessed dreams had broken like spittles of surf on the craggy gates of despotism. But, I'm not there, yet.

Act XVI

To the Fatherland
Angels, Beatings, and Disease Near the DMZ

I anticipated graduation day with all the fluttery excitement of a child willing the first drops of Heinz onto a pile of steaming fries. It was going to taste *damn* good. But, naturally, nothing in my church life was ever what it seemed. Or easy. I'd have to shake out the goodness like a wanker-yanking monkey. Primarily, I had to navigate Dr. Shimmyo's eleventh-hour sabotage and, in the midst of working Blessings '97 and '98 with Godwin, finish my thesis and write my pitch to Rev. Moon to assume the American church presidency—yeah, you read that right. All the same, I was proud I'd completed my Master's at UTS even if the ministerial world utterly despised it, not to mention dogged by a Captain Queeg obsessing over ever more foolproof student controls. In 1996 the Middle States Commission on Higher Education accredited UTS. Now, as intrinsically worthless as my M.DIV. was in the pragmatic world of prejudiced Christians, at least it wasn't the unaccredited Charmin Extra Thin from my first year.

At the same time, our church leadership laid bare at UTS altogether disgusted me. Many knew it, probably. If nothing else, my heart rode my sleeve. I felt Dr. Shimmyo nursed a grudge over the bruising he got from us mutineers refusing to ink his new Student Family Pledge. For us, it reflected the dysfunction we imagined sooting up his own life in its demand we Blessed students send our families packing like he did his. Or, in lieu of that and "just as a formality," he'd consent through our signing it to let them stay on the condition we participated in all UTS and church activities "as though single." In a practical sense all of us understood that, besides an obvious future bludgeon, it mandated abandoning our families and doubling our financial burden for the good of the church defined by willy-nilly leaders. This, in the age of ever increasing and mostly impoverished Blessed families.

Used to the infamy merited by Japanese leaders' constant equivocation, we guessed he expected us lying Westerners to place no value on our signatures he'd intimated consummated a wink-wink-nudge-nudge gentleman's deal. He courted our consent promising to stay aloof from our everyday family commitments.

"It's not something the school, nor I, will concern ourselves with."

"Then why are you wanting us to sign it at all?" an African wondered.

Another said, "It sounds like you have no intention of enforcing it. Correct?"

He smiled his broad, toothy grin. "It's only a gesture of your commitment to the student code and the UTS standard. So the school is confident in future leaders."

"It's a gesture of his power trip," my WUSR mate Istvan said, palm to lips.

Adza (also part of WUSR) said, "Our signature on a document you don't plan to enforce means we're signing a non-document. Like blank paper. Which is the same thing as not signing the pledge. Our signature would be without any meaning at all, binding us to nothing. So . . ."

I gave him a nod. That was the nub. Dr. Shimmyo looked honestly stumped. "I don't understand why you are making what they call a federal case out of signing the pledge. It is not something to fear." He didn't see the issue as broken trust.

"Because we know in advance we can't honor its covenants. It makes us liars."

Prince said, "It's ridiculous. We're not abandoning our Blessed families here or anywhere. That's not even Principled. What about Father's True Family Values?"

"That is not the purpose of the pledge, for you students to abandon your families. It isn't asking that. But anyway members must always be prepared to temporarily set family aside for God's providence. That is True Father's way."

"So, what *is* the purpose?" I said.

Adza said, "We're students in school, though. Not missionaries in the field like the old days in Korea. Why would we even need to set our families aside at UTS? Is something coming up?"

"No, no, no. The pledge just expects you to fully participate, as if no family."

"But that's the same thing," said Istvan.

Adza continued, "Dr. Shimmyo, you assured us we can safely ignore the pledge once we sign it. If we sign it under that condition then we're hypocrites knowingly falsifying our signature. This is a moral question. A moral problem."

"That isn't what you are doing. It isn't like a legal or financial document."

"Yes, it is!" Adza said. "We sign it or get kicked out, yet don't have to follow it. If we don't sign, we don't follow it anyway. In the end, it's the same thing."

"That's right!" echoed voices.

"Precisely my problem with it," I said. "Your pledge asks us to do something we can't as Blessed Unificationists, but you say our signature doesn't matter. You just want us to sign. Like a confession everybody knows is false but convicts anyhow."

He said, "You students do not understand Principle or the UTS tradition of service and sacrifice! The pledge is nonnegotiable. It is part of the student pledge, which you are required to sign and obey to remain in good standing. You agreed to that as a condition of your admittance to UTS."

"Then why are you saying that signing it means we *don't* have to obey it?"

I said, "We didn't agree to this part. I smell a rat."

He didn't appreciate the position into which expedient-minded Asian leaders had put themselves inside the Western mind. Adza—from Ghana therefore a Westerner to Dr. Shimmyo's way of thinking—was the most vocal. He ringingly remonstrated our compulsory deception. Not one to easily give up, Dr. Shimmyo let loose the dogs of war in the form of his new student-cum-Dean-of-Students *Mr.* Yoshizumi and a Canadian named Sèssè.

I never took to Yoshizumi. He was only ever half a step away from the heavenly *yakuza* and seldom disappointed. He made frequent efforts to intimidate me into signing the pledge by using his new superpower to possibly expel me.

"I can do it," he said with a dark tone. "It's my job to look after the school."

I said lightly, "You can only recommend. The cabinet decides. And if they did, I'd be in front of the board of directors asking them why the student *dean* had them expel a student for not signing a pledge the school *president* assured us in open forum he'd never enforce." I let it sink in. "I'd call witnesses."

"You are a bad member, Chris. Very Cain-type."

"Here, I'm a *student* not a member."

"Why did you even come to uts if you hate the church?"

"Go back to your doghouse, Yoshizumi. I think your bell is ringing."

Sèssè, on the other hand, I liked a fair amount and considered a friend. That changed when he approached bearing an obsequious smile and chatty conversation while I was shooting photocopies after hours in the second floor hallway a skip from Yoshizumi's office. Within a minute of his disarming pleasantries, he was pressing me to sign Dr. Shimmyo's pledge. Surprising me, he was more ruthless than Yoshizumi, who at least employed a modicum of good old-fashioned Japanese double-dealing dissembling for good manners' sake.

"Come on, Chris, what's it gonna hurt? You can't stay in school if you don't sign it, you know. And nobody supports your attitude."

"Why are you nagging me on this, Sèssè?"

"I just want to see the right thing done, and clear up this controversy."

"Are you here for Dr. Shimmyo?"

"He did ask me about you . . . if you were going to sign it." His face betrayed something he was still hiding.

"So, you're his muscle now, is that it?" My hackles hackled. The gall of these people taking it on themselves to help compel us to sign an oath maybe academically illegal or legally unenforceable and wound round a moral turpitude.

Sèssè's face screwed up tight. His lips pursed. "I'm not anybody's anything. You won't sign the pledge because of your own arrogance, thinking you're better and smarter than Dr. Shimmyo and everybody else."

"Yeah? How do you figure that?" Sèssè was maybe ten inches shorter than me. I was peering right down on his upturned face thinking how glad I was to grow up a looming six-foot-six.

"Look at you," he offered, "prancing around here doing whatever you like. You don't fundraise, you don't like morning service, you ignore your central figure—"

"Uts isn't a church center, Sèssè. When are you going to get that? It's a friggin' school with friggin' rules that have to obey the law—*American* law, I might add."

He decided to let that one slide by with a dismissive snort. "Well, you know, Dr. Shimmyo is concerned about your spiritual life. He doesn't want to see you keep repeating your past." I bit my tongue to suppress the sarcastic laughter that was roaring through my innards at that. I wondered to which past he was referring; he seemed to be engaging in some insider trading, here.

"Then why don't you tell him to argue with me himself instead of sending flunkies to sandbag me? I've already told him my position on that pledge." My soul seethed at hoodlums roaming the halls of UTS enforcing the administration's conformity. "I'm not signing it. And he's too bleeding chicken to sit down with me and hash it out. The man has no . . ."

"What's your problem, Chris?" His voice was cold, flinty. "You're always creating trouble around UTS, always centering your negative attitude on yourself . . . Why'd you even bother coming here if all you have to offer is negativity?"

"Boy, you're layering it thick." Maybe his own graduation was hanging in the balance. But I was already baked. My so-called friend was now a bullyboy twisting me into an arm lock. "You really are his muscle, huh, Sèssè."

"I said I'm not Dr. Shimmyo's anything!" he snapped, visibly irritated. "You're leading other students to rebel against their central figure! Poisoning the school!"

"Shimmyo's the one creating the trouble around here. Accusing Western students of every crime and sin under the sun. Burdening us under chains of rules, laws, and demands till we can't hardly stand up." Jesus in Matt. 23:15 pricked a thought.

"Then leave! You hate it here, get out." *Man, Mr. Uchiyama's everywhere!*

I leaned back, chin tucked in. "You expect me to sign a formal document he can use against me at the drop of a hat, knowing I can't abide by its demands? It's—"

"You're not wanted here. Only those who want to serve God and True . . ."

"—a damned lie! Am I supposed to"—air quotes—" 'temporarily set aside' my wife and children to slavishly follow his every fanatic demand? Because—"

"Did you come here just to follow your own agenda? You know—"

"—that's what his pledge requires. We're not in early times Korea and—"

"—our lives are centered around central figures."

"—it's not gonna happen. Period." I took a beat to catch up. "Centered around Divine Principle, you mean."

"Following your central figure *is* Principle."

"Following Principle *makes* the central figure."

He blinked. "What?"

"Father says a central figure's role is Abel who serves Cain through unconditional, sacrificial love. *That's* Principle, and the only central figure I'll ever bow down to." *Like Godwin.* "Go tell Shimmyo *that*." Times like these I channeled Jerome.

"You just follow your own way. Disobeying your central figure is how Satan invades and corrupts everything!"

"True Parents sure don't need any more sycophants in their stable, Sèssè. They need reasoning, rational members devoted to Principle. Not to power, glory, or position . . . or misplaced righteousness. That's the whole point of UTS."

And so our conversation went till we'd both entirely aggravated the other. Dr. Shimmyo had brought it to this. My friendship with Sèssè irrevocably sundered. I now saw the simpering lickspittle he was. Like Yoshizumi, he was willing to lean on me maybe to any degree to please his master. People like that are dangerous. Truly scary. They're the ones vesting psychopaths like Hitler, Stalin, Mao, Saddam, and the irs with all their murderously gluttonous power.

In the hallway's soft light I caught his shimmer peacocking in Hollywood Gestapo threads above spit-and-polish jackboots. A red armband sported our red-on-white circular Unification arrow. Righteously indignant posed every bone in his body believing how godly he was to flay me till my lips dripped penitent submission to his little god-Führer Shimmyo. I was right on the money, too. Ensconced at Korea's Cheongpyeong Lake following graduation, his desperation for controlling authority took on a despotic life all its own.

Students like Adza and me ever set snares across Dr. Shimmyo's power-tripping path. Maybe we saved uts from even greater calamity than what eventually befell it under his veneer of righteousness until what seemed a jejune zephyr called Tyler Hendricks blew into Rev. Moon's academic keep. By the grace of God and Godwin, my performance in the '97 and '98 Blessings put our top Korean leaders in my pocket for a New York minute—*sic transit gloria mundi* ever soughing in my ear—that was just enough fleeting glory to put the kibosh on my graduation embargo.

~

The big Sunday arrived June 28, 1998. Family, friends, and vips packed our long, wood-pewed chapel. Rev. Moon didn't show but we expected it. He'd been dissing the seminary—mocked as the cemetery—for several years to convey disgust for its quality of graduates. As the first class to show independence of, yet commitment to, the church—exactly what he called for in his leaders when he wasn't lambasting their disobedience—we thought us worth a sterling second look. Dr. Shimmyo spurned us for it, but we wanted to please Rev. Moon . . . nothing worse for a Simon Legree than being ignored. Yet, our class mission ended up a non-mission. So.

Nathalie with some Vincies and my folks unexpectedly alerted me they'd be showing up. Their view of Moonism was jaundiced but not hysterical enough to shell out for deprogrammers. I was merely a black sheep turning my back on middle class corporatism. Somehow my older sister, many years Elizabeth Claire Prophet's right-hand man in her Church Universal Triumphant, reaped respect and admiration as I garnered contempt and scorn. My personality?

Tassel swap after prying my diploma from Dr. Shimmyo's righteously whitened fingers.

Or the Moonies running a distant second to the plausibility of Prophet's Godhead, twin flames, and new-age non-Christian hocus pocus? Still, here they were. I was gratified and honored to be our family's first post-grad since Dad. Heartening . . . yet disheartening I still didn't feel their natural respect.

Commencement was the perfect occasion to upgrade my path's credibility in their eyes. But if I thought they'd be treated to a classy demonstration of professionalism by our school president, I was misinformed. I wrote July 5,

Shimmyo featured me prominently in his speech, which is now known as "The Hamburger Speech." The day before, he asked me why I was so much taller than my parents, and I said I ate more burgers and fries than they did. He made that answer the point of his speech. Imagine!

For Dad (possibly recalling Japan's Big War fanatics), it was a primer in religious extremism. So much for my game future in a sober church. They saw me acclaimed for achieving *cum laude*, the top 10%; I gnashed teeth missing *magna* by two-tenths of a point. We repaired to the gymnasium for a luncheon prefaced with speeches from students, leaders, and Dr. Shimmyo. Here's where I pulled my own Doolittle Raid. I'd commissioned a polished brass-on-rosewood plaque. It read:

> *The UTS graduate is the person who makes the restoration of the human race their personal responsibility —Rev. Christopher McKeon*

A total ripoff from *Starship Troopers'* Johnny Rico but it perfectly captured the UTS mission. If gifted in private, I doubted he wouldn't mount it beneath the Christian Brothers' abandoned graveyard. Finishing his speech, I hustled onstage.

Impromptu valedictorian and my quilled blitz.

His face fell. "What are you doing?"

I palmed his mic. "Could you wait just a moment, Dr. Shimmyo? I have a graduation gift for you." His eyes were mild surprise and wary wonder. A short speech later—there's more than one way to skin a valedictorian, eh?—I fired my gift-wrapped torpedo into his openmouthed hands. "If you please, would you unwrap it to read the inscription so everybody has a chance to hear it?" Well, he was a good sport for the applause and I appreciated him for it. *Yes, a good man.*

"Thank you, Chris. A wonderful graduation gift. I will hang it in my office."

Very satisfying. I might've purred.

But I'd have to see it to believe it. Perhaps fearing visitors might curiously wonder where it was on his wall, he'd mayhap now less easily toss it in the dumpster (regardless his promise) as the bad memory of an intractable student. I'd originally wanted to attach it as a bronze plaque to the school's exterior at the formal main entry on the circle drive. After his hardy *no*, I suggested an interior wall.

"Father permits no changes to the seminary without his express permission."

"Well, can you ask him? Show him the text of the plaque?"

His head wagged. "I don't think I can. Sorry, no. He is very busy."

Not so busy he can't fish. Forcing it on Dr. Shimmyo before the entire school wasn't much of a substitute, but it was something.

Peter Kim was on hand to deliver Rev. Moon's graduation remarks. I took the opportunity to push into his arms a giftbag containing presents for Rev. Moon: a copy of my book-formatted thesis, *Cain and Abel: A Spiritual Analysis of American Race Hate*, a duplicate of Dr. Shimmyo's plaque, and a 6-page letter describing my view of the spiritual collapse of our church and its bold solution.

HERE'S HOW IT came about. For years, I'd struggled with the fantastic ineptness and cruelty of church leaders. I yearned to lead our church into an age of competence and compassion in line with Divine Principle. I gave considerable time to understanding our institutional dysfunction in a practical and spiritual sense . . . nothing happens to Moonies that isn't somehow influenced by spirit world (Rev. Moon once claimed Korea's church was tiny and himself reviled there owing to America).

"For every one member who joins the American church," he said, "three Koreans will join. As long as Americans aren't coming to the church, the Korean church will continue to suffer and frustrate God's providence."

That was heavy, but these mental gymnastics made it natural to wonder what corrupts our high ideals despite Rev. Moon's censure. In books like *A Wanderer in the Spirit Lands*, spirit people's emotive energy—anger, resentment, hate, revenge, kindness, love, peacefulness, forgiveness—influences us and the natural world. In human relationships, a person's ancestral energy plays a defining role in the nature of their interactions. But we're each in command of our destiny, too. We can unite with or overcome any spiritual and emotive influence. We aren't the creatures of forces beyond our control (so long as we're aware of the reality).

In our ignorance of the dynamics of spirit world we get fooled into thinking a feeling, thought, or desire is uniquely our own. This is not exclusively the case. For the church, the defining human relationship is Cain and Abel. We all function by it, mimicking that original struggle. Ignorant of it, we don't understand its nature or antiquity. We focus on practical causes and ignore the spiritual energies swirling within and without like magnetic fields.

American members wanted the church to democratize in the errant belief it would ameliorate Japanese and Korean abuse to free up Western (*vs.* Christian) ethics, liberty, and equality to restore the Family movement of their memories. I felt Rev. Moon, a spiritual

I think Dr. Shimmyo liked the plaque's sentiment even if not its author.

man, built our church to accomplish a purpose outside that served by American ideals. His organization couldn't be this dysfunctional from not knowing better.

My assumption led me to think our institutional chaos didn't follow from Asian despotism but Christian members abandoning their ideals without insisting Asians absorb them. Externally, this maybe arose in self-hating Leftist saboteurs strenuously knifing Western civilization in the back. Internally, it was the Cain–Abel struggle. Americans were in Cain's position and acted it: troublesome, angry, rebellious. But we were in Abel's position, too. God and Rev. Moon expected us to transmit Christianity's heritage to Asian members lacking it in aggregate.

American missionaries had laid a foundation in Korea since the nineteenth century. Sufficient for Rev. Moon's life, it had no effect on his organization fleshed out by everyday Koreans, statistically over three-fourths non-Christian, unchurched or, even when raised in a Christian setting, culturally Confucianist. They sure as hell didn't Christianize in the Korean Unification Church in the sense of inheriting and internalizing the West's 2,000 year journey with Jesus. Even churched Japanese and Koreans jettisoned most of what they'd imbibed from the Bible once aboard the Moon boat. Just witness the abusive and unchristian (later penitent) behavior of Mr. Kamiyama, whose pastor father presumedly schooled him in the Spirit.

Rev. Moon wasn't teaching salvation but *Restoration*, nor transmitting 2,000 years of Christian tradition and its cultural ideals to his Asian followers. He lauded their rejection of unPrincipled Westernism's sex, drugs, and rock-n-roll rebellion and educated them to attend him as the third Adam and Lord of the Second Advent in Divine Principle's milieu. Christian norms that built a religious tradition of justice and compassion to mitigate avarice and cruelty, which built the West's undeniable success rooted in individual sovereignty and intrinsic rights, took a back seat.

Grateful those I loved showed up for my own biggest Day of Hope yet.

Americans did no better. Democratizing the church would do little beyond emphasizing rampant Cain-type attitudes. Rev. Moon made a small bow with his faux-vote seating Jim Baughman as church president, but that's as far as he'd go. Even in 2003 Koreans (except for a token American) inhabit America's top slots. An ambitious fella could get awfully frustrated in this arena. Ironically, the American situation is akin to the early twentieth century Korean church vis-à-vis its controlling Americans. As abused as I felt and a fierce patriot to boot, I saw in 1989 how the democratic road now so popular with our chattering class would hasten, not avoid, our destruction. *The answer?*

I believed I'd figured out at UTS that what afflicted the American church rooted in the same reality that Rev. Moon observed in the American and Korean membership lists: a dearth of empathy. In his world Koreans were Adamic, the Japanese Eve, and Americans the Archangel. Asians scornfully saw Americans as *fallen* Lucifer. For him, we were *unfallen* Lucifer educating immature Adam and Eve into God's worldview, the original task. It necessarily included our 2,000 year (Principled) Christian tradition. They refused to listen. We refused to teach. Much as in the Garden of Eden. *An impasse.*

This fatally poisoned the American church likely from the get-go. Morbidity arose in our failure to practice our preaching. American Christians abandoned Jesus and his ethics in the church. Japanese and Koreans encouraged it in demanding unfettered obedience to not just Rev. Moon's way but, above all, to themselves as his indispensable interlocutors. It prompted him to sharply wonder in 1984 how the servants of the master exercised greater power than the master himself.

Perfunctorily Christian, Rev. Moon concentrated on his own mission, not doing everyone else's job. Korean and Japanese leaders never appreciated this, presuming instead that his oft-aggressive, even ruthless pursuit of his own suprachristian duty was the norm he had in mind for leaders to emulate. *Not!* The dichotomy between him and his leaders set up a fundamental East–West, Asian–American schism.

The answer? Heal the core rift, its ramifications naturally rippling through the church. Tension and conflict ever existed between president and continental director, escalating to the emasculated American pushed out or quitting in frustration. The destiny of presidents like Neil Salonen, Mose Durst, and Jim Baughman—Tyler Hendricks seemed to walk his tightrope with mild success. His strategy was to be as accommodating and uncomplaining as possible. A true Cain. Even so, neither rebelliousness nor appeasement—the latter ostensibly pleasing albeit dispiriting Rev. Moon—bought anything from Koreans than derision.

I thought unconditional love would short-circuit all that. Not the wishy-washy, blabby-mouthy kind. The practical, realpolitik kind. My idea jettisoned leadership for younger, hipper, less power-mad Koreans and baggage-heavy Americans. They'd never solve our problems . . . you can't pour new wine into old wineskins. Rev. Moon said one of Christianity's greatest failings since Constantine was the pope scrabbling after the affairs of state and the king flexing a tight fist round the church. Hijinks ensued, like the 'Babylonian captivity of the papacy.' Reasonable it was, then, to see our top Korean and American as a contesting pope and king.

Rev. Moon had recently intimated shaking them up. Nothing was *more* needed and nothing more *was* needed. Now was a heaven-sent opportunity to solve our American dilemma. My letter proposed Rev. Moon retire Rev. Pak and appoint my uts friend and fellow wusr traveler In Hoi Lee as continental director. He was around 38 to my 39 and recently appointed regional director out of southern California. He rejected the attitudes and behavior of the aged Korean leadership and wanted to heal America's experience with Rev. Moon and Divine Principle. A new future from a ruined past. This trait attracted me to him for wusr.

He welcomed Tamela and me into his home frequently and freely. His wife cooked for us and treated us like family. This was so unusual in my experience. Groundbreaking. It single-handedly revolutionized my attitude toward Koreans and directly inspired my renewed push to discover why Americans couldn't get along with them. Importantly, he'd said, "I could follow you anywhere, Chris." Some Japanese students said the same thing, two of them predicting I was the man sent by God to restore our church. A stunner, aye. And I was primed.

I needed an American to replace Tyler Hendricks. With my graduation, the timing was perfect. Although I was a nobody, what made me the right replacement was my strong, unprecedented, almost familial relationship with In Hoi. We held a genuinely mutual respect for and acceptance of the other as an equal, a colleague, a friend. There'd be no puppet strings, steamrolling, or power trips by the continental director and no timid kowtowing and petulant, passive-aggressive placation by the president. This very quality generated a strong current of real love to work as real brothers for the same goal. I'd proofed it working with Godwin.

Exposed in public, our dynamic would electrify and harmonize the members from our three providential nations, provoke the same between regional and state leaders, and prove it was all possible, profitable, and Principled. A bonus was my extensive skillset, ordination in the National Baptist Convention dovetailing with Rev. Moon courting the black church, married outside then Blessed inside the church to a West Indian, conversational in Japanese and Korean, and others. I was the best choice for the times. Sure, a better American might exist—Godwin?—but I didn't know. Even if I did, would they have my wherewithal and best attributes? I proceeded on the information I had. The time was *now*, not tomorrow: a new 'pope' and 'king' to restart God's providence in Principled harmony.

Godwin said, "Father had Peter Kim read your letter at the leaders' meeting in front of Rev. Pak, Rev. Yang"—the shoe-in for the continental directorship—"and all the other big dogs."

"Oh, shit! For some reason, I imagined it happening privately."

He laughed. "You know Father's intensely public about everything. He doesn't like secrets." *Well, not most secrets.* "Anyway, my friends in the room said he took your crazy proposal 'very seriously.'"

"Really?" I felt a little woozy.

"It threw Rev. Yang into fibrillations. He wants to be continental director."

My guts clenched. "Ugh. I forgot about all that. God, he must hate me now."

"Well, pretty strong argument rose up against you. 'Chris is proposing *himself!*' And, 'That's completely a Cain-type attitude.'"

I saw my own Swedish *Vasa* heel hard and go down. To Tyler I said, "I'm sorry if I insulted you making my case. I tried to be diplomatic in case he publicized it."

"You didn't. I'm *glad* you want to be president because I want *out.*"

Rev. Yang assumed In Hoi Lee my coconspirator and put blade to whetstone. He called me and not a little put out. "Why is Rev. Yang yelling at me, accusing me of stealing his position? What did you do? What is this letter?"

"I'm sorry I didn't tell you." He wasn't disinterested . . . I thought I detected a keen eye. But he was Korean and didn't gush over the possibilities like me. "I'm not sure why I didn't ring you up. I suppose I didn't want to alarm you before Father gave a thumbs up or down, or no thumb at all. But I badly miscalculated him reading it in public and leaders like Rev. Yang's apoplectic response. I mean, if he'd said no, I figured you'd never hear about it."

"I understand your heart, but you put me in a bad situation."

"Yeah. I shouldn't have forgot all the politics. I'm really sorry for that."

We left it there to wait on Rev. Moon. In the end, he bowed to real-church-politik and appointed Rev. Yang because, "He has a woman's face. The male lions are lazy and do not hunt, but the lionesses hunt. Rev. Yang hunts like a lioness."

A stupendously ridiculous, absurd, moronic rationale. Laughable, really. He figured (or hoped) stodgy old Rev. Yang's losing track record allied to the failed presidential strategy of feminine submission held greater potential for bagging Americans than In Hoi's already successful one allied with my admittedly dubious reputation albeit stellar Blessings performance . . . I'm sure my lack of a PH.D. didn't figure one bit. All in all, a faulty decision now huntingly disproved by history.

He noted there'd so far been eight American church presidents—Kaye Allen, the corporate secretary, says twelve—beginning with Young Oon Kim, Galen Pumphrey, Young Oon Kim again, Gordon Ross, James Fleming, Lowell Martin, Gordon Ross,

Phillip Burley, Farley Jones, Neil Salonen, Dr. Mose Durst, Dr. Jim Baughman, and Dr. Tyler Hendricks. You seeing the academic trend? He said,

> I tested each of the first seven leaders, and each one reached a point of complaining and resentment. But I never changed in my attitude to them. I spoke recently to Farley Jones about how he had harbored bad feeling in his heart over how I treated him when he was the church leader. Farley Jones was amazed that I knew this without his telling me. (*Dedication of uc National hq 1999*)

I wondered how I'd have fared. Rev. Yang no doubt enlightened him as to my contrarianism. But, *potayto potahto*. I only aired my thoughts toward solutions to our institutional deficiencies—Shiori, Jerome, and my nonmember Blessing were liabilities, too. Rev. Moon went with vp Michael Jenkins, a man less an iconoclast with, I supposed, an authentic-member Blessing. He retired Rev. Pak and later sent Tyler to salvage uts. I'd hoped my letter would intrigue him. That I'd get a once over. *Nope.* Left me hanging till his Yang–Jenkins' shotgun wedding boomed.

The crux was the colossal disrespect between Koreans and Americans that led to Divine Principle's wholesale abandonment, the Christian scruples foundationally supporting it, Japanese feudalism, tens or hundreds of thousands of ex-members, ruined plans, a frustrated Rev. Moon, and America turning its back.

Welcome to the real world, motherfuckers.

And here he was, its very kernel. He should have sent a letter, a note, a verbal *fuck off* through Peter Kim as with my Danbury letters via Revs. Pak or Yang or even Godwin, SoCal and confidant to Mrs. Moon.

Crickets.

If I could've sat down with him, my passion and excitement pouring forth, he might've appreciated where I was coming from even if unpersuaded. *That's okay. It's his church.* But it might've swung the deal. Who knew? And that's the point. I got nothing and it vexed me. One more straw on my sagging camel's back. My limit with 17 years of abuse, betrayal, and disregard loomed. I pined for this damnably overclocked church to take me seriously. *I just graduated uts! What's it take to persuade them I'm valuable? worthwhile? The perfect life?* Nobody has that. I didn't join for a job nor to fail. Yet, uncritical obedience was a tolling bell. Everything I do (not sinful) is motivated by my understanding of and love for God and trust in Divine Principle. I wanted—*needed*—to substantively contribute to God's providence and humanity's forward progress. That's how I am. What I am. Who I am.

He takes my rejected letter seriously. Why not me? Blowing me off after a top 10% graduation while pulling off two Blessings his Chosen-Man big shits fucked up on bloated salaries harpooned me. It seemed only fawning ineptitude pleased him.

~

Graduation and trepidation over my big pitch to Rev. Moon now past, our class headed to the *Washington Times* for a 7-day media seminar. Deputy Managing Editor Ted Agres led the workshop at a suburban motel. Journalists, editors, and tv producers like Floyd (now ceo of church-owned cable station Goodlife tv) cycled through with cram courses on modern media. We enjoyed in-depth tours of the *Times'* headquarters and plant along with plentiful buffets.

Rev. Moon contemplated sending us out as correspondents, so we drew straws for our countries. I got Spain. The prospect frightened and excited me. He changed his mind a couple months later, but I wish I'd had the chance to follow that intriguing opportunity. It jived with my talents and vision more than software engineering. Maybe today I'd be a successfully happy church member, writer, and editor.

After the seminar we traipsed off to the airport for a 14-hour cattle car to Korea to do a mandatory 40-day *spiritual liberation* workshop at our dreaded if beloved infectious disease manufacturing facility at Cheongpyeong Lake, not far from South Korea's heavily mined demilitarized zone with the North. We had to scrape together the $1,200 airfare and the $300 fee workshop fee. I didn't know what to expect, but it was certainly worse than my wildest nightmares . . . yet, better, too.

Rev. Moon picked up Cheongpyeong Heaven and Earth Training Center as a spiritual retreat in the late '60s after coming up the Han River in 1965 to fish and pitch a tent. He's used it over the years as a place to commune with God and put his body and mind through torturous spiritual conditions. We prepared as best we could given guidance similar to Rev. Moon's on its website:

> Cheongpyeong, the holy site, is the homeland for the people of the world and for mankind's heart. So it must be the very place that is to be respected by heaven and earth in solving God's sorrowful heart on earth. Until now, I have prayed for Cheongpyeong and prepared for this site as the holy land and as the homeland for the people of the world. Now, I am in infinitely deep emotion when I think we reached a point of time to start with all our powers.
>
> I bought 4 million pyongs of land around the training center. This land is prepared to be the homeland for the believers of the world. As there are bases of our Unification Church community in 185 countries, I prepared for Cheongpyeong to be a historical site to show the historical traditions of these 185 countries. Cheongpyeong, the holy site, is not a place where anybody can visit. You must visit centering on God's will. You must not regard Cheongpyeong as a common Christian revival center. You must purify yourself by bathing for three days and pray to enter Cheongpyeong.
>
> If you do that, then you can take guidance of Cheonan mountain, enter Cheonmoon mountain and be welcomed by Cheonyoung mountain. God will not receive your prayer if you are not welcomed.

Mrs. Kim, who in 1998 ran the retreat as a 'channel' for Mrs. Moon's dead mother Mrs. Hong, frequently referred to Rev. Moon "cutting his bones" to set up spiritual conditions for this or that struggle's victory over Satan. Listening to her describe it, I envisioned him knifing through the flesh of his arm and carving bone grooves. Or something. I'm not sure precisely what she meant and she never elaborated. I guess every Messiah needs ambiguous legends.

The story of Cheongpyeong's workshop involves Mrs. Hong dying. She woke up in spirit world, took stock of her surroundings, and noticed thousands upon thousands of spirit folk inhabiting the spirit bodies of living persons like insect parasites. Mrs. Hong—whom Rev. Moon renamed *Dae Mo Nim* (great mother)—explained to us through her Mrs. Kim 'channel' that these spirit people have varying motivations for infesting our bodies: anger, hatred, resentment instigating revenge, and other needs. Without exception, the type of spirit folk infesting living persons' spirit bodies are very sinful, pushing and influencing us to commit the kind of bad, problematic behavior in which they're most interested.

Mrs. Kim (Dae Mo Nim's alter ego) explained that, to her eyes, they seem like small white insect eggs and that some living persons are so infested one can scantly make out who they are. Thus, it's virtually impossible for living persons to be righteous, to hear and respond to God over sinful desires flowing in our emotional veins. She said, "I was shocked to discover it!" Reality was awful, ugly: dead parents infest and torment their physically alive

Rev. Moon's Chunsung Temple—meeting place, worship hall, residence—that grew from lumps of concrete wrapped in mud during my 40 days.

children if in some way it lessens their own suffering and torment. "Forget about parental love in this situation," she chided. "People like these, when confronted with death, spirit reality, and consequences for their lives of sin will do anything to relieve their spirit world suffering."

You can imagine this information floored us. How could Mom and Dad enter my spirit body after their deaths like parasites to torment me and lead me into sin and personal destruction? It was absurd. Many of us had real difficulty buying her fairy tales. Even so, we Moonies have long experience with craziness from the mouths of leaders that's orders of magnitude above and beyond hallucinatory delusion. We were prepared to grant her the benefit of the doubt, however tenuous. We'd already cover-to-covered *The Victory of Love* purportedly written through a spirit medium by Rev. Moon's long-dead son Heung Jin, killed at 17 in a 1984 upstate New York car crash who showed up in 1987 inhabiting a Zimbabwean brother's body whom the church called Black Heung Jin Nim amidst much controversy over his physical abuse. Most of us found it chockablock with profound insights for our life of faith regardless its dubious authorship. Mrs. Kim's assertions, backed up by Rev. Moon, simply ratcheted up our daily dose of incredulity a few notches.

Mrs. Kim described how Dae Mo Nim spent a long time studying this problem and then approached God Himself for permission to do something about it. He told her she'd first have to secure Satan's agreement who, naturally, was more than neighborly . . . for a pound of flesh. He laid out a strict, designed-to-fail regimen that her 'channel' Mrs. Kim would have to endure before he'd let them set up a spiritual cleansing retreat in the hills of Korea safe from his interference. She was an ordinary housewife in the Korean church with a husband and a couple of children. Spiritually sensitive, she had some connection to Mrs. Hong (Dae Mo Nim). She wasn't thrilled with the offer. Dae Mo Nim persisted, explaining the situation and how it ruined the lives of everyone on Earth including, we presumed, Mrs. Kim's own children. The only way to clear up humanity's spiritual lives, she said, was to weed all these rotten, despicable, soulless bastards out of our spirit bodies so we could think straight and perceive God. In the end, Mrs. Kim agreed.

Satan's requirements were ruthless and stringent. She began with a 40-day fast. Then stayed awake for ten days. She cried and prayed almost the whole time. Dae Mo Nim and assistants helped her keep it together. Then seven days in a bathtub of water iced to just below freezing. He specified the precise thickness of ice that must form and be maintained on its surface. Mrs. Kim's attendants broke a hole wide enough for her body to slip through. She suffered permanent joint damage that left her in daily pain. Her conditions only got tougher and rougher. She endured it all. Dae Mo Nim said her rugged resilience and "the depth of her guts" shocked Satan. I imagine he hates mere mortals handing him his presumptuous ass. She said he honored his word and doesn't interfere. I wondered if theirs wasn't a Barbossan deal where Dae Mo Nim failed to include his devils and demons and our leaders.

OUR AIRPORT BUS bounced and swayed off the narrow two-lane out of small-town Seorak across a dirt track that crossed a small brook. It wheezed into a dusty parking area outside a gated fence. Beyond it reposed a 90-foot single-storey wood and cinderblock building with a covered concrete porch. The Cheongpyeong Heaven and Earth Training Center's administrative offices, telephones, infirmary, storage, and other needs were here. In 1998 the retreat was primitive, anything but the Potemkin Village it turned into. It brooded beside the Han River that forms an expansive, deep blue lake that's a popular recreation area. After a sense of worldly isolation had set in over the course of a week, I watched Korean fun seekers with envy cavorting on water skis, jet skis, and speed boats zooming by the chain link segregating us from a narrow, gravelly beach. The ongoing heavy construction on Rev. Moon's universal palace dulled its peaceful, lapping shores to silence.

How I remember the admin building (minus a covered porchway and some updating since 1971).

The retreat was a small wonder for Japanese nonmembers who'd hit upon intractably disfiguring *atopī* (atopic dermatitis plus psoriasis) spiritually healing. As a consequence, the camp overflowed on weekends with up to 4,000 frantic and flush Japanese of all ages. This weekly influx pressed the administration into shuffling up our sleeping venues. To alleviate the snarl-up, the church was throwing up commodious sleep-cum-presentation hutments with a roughly 30×50-foot heated concrete slab surfaced in linoleum, insulated metal–canvas walls, and a peaked metal roof. By day, they jammed to acolytes. By night, toe-to-head gendered bodies snored damp, pneumonic air in sleeping bags.

The lakeshore camp angled sharply uphill, rising ever up an exhausting 650-foot climb to a mountaintop holy tree. Winding along a rushing stream cascading down the mountain, many small- and medium-sized sleeping bungalows clustered amongst the trees populating the sometimes precipitous hillsides. Some were older, wooden structures and others newer, smaller versions of the brand-new stuff farther up the mountain. A 2-storey steel-framed circus tent easily 70×100 feet surmounted a linoleum-covered slab.

Howsoever many dorms, they couldn't add lavatories. Strict laws forbade more, as their one drained directly or via prostrate cesspits into the lake's formerly pristine recreational waters. One side had Japanese-style hot–cold baths and showers, and opposite it some 30 Asian plus four Western—*thank God!*—commodes. Asian ones are a porcelain urinal-looking thing set flush to the floor. You squat until

Circus tent. Demon beating & ancestor liberation.

your ass snugly plugs against the unit's cantle, at which point you can lean back to rest with an eye on never again reaching your feet. It's not uncomfortable, but definitely expects working knee joints. Mine were on the fritz. Toilets were decks awash. Dependably backed-up Asian crappers lacked a Western-style bowl to absorb a single-flush clog and regurgitated rivers of water, urine, and liquefied feces across the tiles into the also clogged floor drains, livid superintendents withal. *Pee-yew.*

The biggest of many construction projects was the temple, also called the palace, a residence-worship-educational facility being raised to Rev. Moon's specifications. It was still a 1-storey concrete-and-rebar pile of junk tight as a tick in the hillside and swarming with hard hats. It eventually became a 4-storey sun-gleaming, marble-veneered white elephant accommodating a thousand or more. We were advised the first and second floors would be public church use and its third and top decks Rev. Moon's family residence. This was his Eastern White House, the spiritual poop deck from which to understeer his global *Messianica Titanica.*

We divided into teams based on language. Mine was our graduating class plus other English speakers totaling about 40. In true Unificationist fashion, these teams obsessed over Cain–Abel power and control structures. Ex-friend Sèssè made his play when the British group leader cycled out of his 40 days. He rudely shoved his way to the fore and tried establishing his dictatorship. Naturally, I lived at the top of his shit list and not only on account of our uts hallway disputation, but my natural ambivalence for coercive rules and regulations in a spiritual context and the shitsticks who ramrodded them. A week or so and he preposterously found himself in over his head struggling to handle the real-world contentions and emotional needs of 40 human beings unresponsive to his rigid dictatorialism. He had the good sense to step aside for someone having greater empathy and spiritual leadership.

Wasn't that why we were here in the first place? to develop a deeper sense of empathy for God and humanity? go through a process of repentance and spiritual growth and development? One of our movement's deepest self-inflicted wounds is the implacable impulse for rigid hierarchical control. Worse than the Brit he replaced, Sèssè had little concern for our individual struggles and suffering in the midst of a grueling discipline made worse by constant bacterial infections. Order need be kept. Rev. Moon emphasizes each individual pursuing his or her own spiritual course in

471

life since no two persons' ancestry and spiritual baggage is the same. Hence, no two persons can walk the same road to resolve sin. Ironically, the world of religion (all recognizing in some form the individual fundament of the spiritual path) emphasizes doctrinal conformity even when it contradicts and inevitably disturbs one's growth and development toward God, enlightenment, and happiness. If there's one thing religion prides itself on avoiding, it's any joy outside canonical bliss. The Unification Church is hardly unique in its rabid quest for lockstep, but it surely had no place at Cheongpyeong and I lost no time opining so as it roughly encountered me.

Sweaty business, liberation.

My day was a 6 AM wake-up to hike down-mountain to the plaguish bathrooms for a wash and shave. Breakfast was two types of red bean-filled bread rolls and juice. Lunch and dinner gave us white sticky rice, *kimchee* (spicy pickled cabbage), some form of twice-weekly meat, noodles, and drinks. Pretty soon and gruesome murder beckoned for a burger and fries. This was northerly rural South Korea, some 40 miles from the DMZ. Our options were scanty, even in podunk Seorak.

Three times a day we trudged uphill to the circus to plunk onto linoleumed concrete in ordered rows for about an hour crooning Holy Songs to prep. Then we got down to business. Dae Mo Nim discovered that getting these bug-like infestations out of our spirit bodies was surprisingly difficult. Many of them weren't in the least interested in leaving, having developed a wee happy home in us. Some, unaware of where they were, vacated without a fuss. Either way, she found these teeny-weeny boll weevils needed significant jarring before her angel pals could jerk them out by the scruff. For that, she had us strike our head, face, nape, hands, arms, shoulders, chest, stomach, groin—lots of infestation in the ol' fun box—thighs, calves, foot soles, and back with our open hands.

Volunteers on a raised stage beat 4-foot drums to establish a cadence for us to cantillate a Korean ditty for a whacking chanty atmosphere. I loved the song and, musically inclined and not a little as-yet undiagnosed ADHD, happily sang it hours on end. We beat ourselves mercilessly. The deeper the bruises, the prouder we felt and the greater the respect from colleagues and Dae Mo Nim. And, man, were we ever black and blue. Some of us, to the bone. It was plain that our bruises were a vital sign of our belief in and dedication to The Process.

I got into it—not all in, but pretty close—except for our backdoor neighbor beating our backs since we obviously couldn't get at that body part ourselves. Many of the Japanese did Dr. Shimmyo proud. Though they slapped our backs with open palms, between our sweat-drenched shirts and the cup of their hand the physical blow was jarring or stingingly, mind-numbingly painful. Many times fanatics knocked the wind out of me and maybe they figured that meant evil spirits, too. *Chris can't slack off! I'm helping him!* I found myself twisting round demanding my non-English speaking partner hit less achingly hard. Sometimes, the brother took my admonition as an indication he wasn't hitting this weak Westerner hard enough. As with my Los Angeles MFT days, these unhearing brothers compelled threats of bodily harm if they didn't take me seriously. They usually heard that. Yes, we all wanted to go the whole nine yards and cleanse our spirits. Spasming my back, cracking ribs, or dislodging vertebrae wasn't in my program, however.

What were we doing? According to Dae Mo Nim via Mrs. Kim, our bodies taking a beating jarred loose these hellbound swine infesting our bodies so angels could pull them free; some, even they couldn't drag forth. The pulling motions of Mrs. Kim's hands where she'd here and there pause wandering these rows was Dae Mo Nim adding her bits (through her) to evict these mules.

I'm not surprised if this sounds

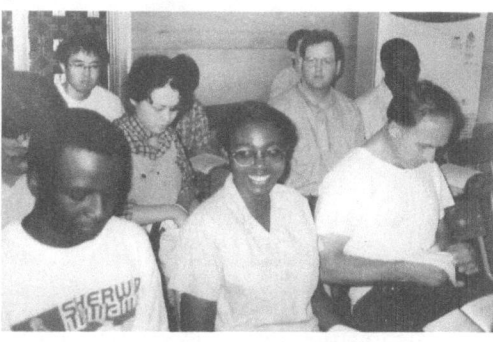

Divine Principle 40 days and nights aloud.

ridiculous. In truth, I saw these angels. Not in a trance or eyes wide shut, but eyes yawning bigly awake. Taking a break against gym mats stacked at the back of the hall, I saw hundreds of burly angels planted in ones or twos at each living person's right side. They rhythmically bent down and muscled spirits out of physical bodies then flung them over their shoulder like yesterday's news to a cadent drum redolent of picking cartoon cotton. My vision was only moments, but long enough to form a clear, indelible, unambiguous picture of the scene in my mind. Crowd hypnosis? Who knows. It was rare hearing others mention it and I'm sure they would've.

Between our flagellations we hunkered in our group's meeting bungalow, each of us reading a page or two aloud from *Divine Principle* for an hour three times a day. I was unenthused because, surprisingly, the seemingly educated often can hardly read a sentence aloud in under five minutes. Why not pick one fluent reader? *Nope.* Everybody needs their chance for . . . spiritual reasons. Finishing the last page, we flipped to page one. These were the times our group leader tried exerting maximum control over us. Finally exasperated with the petty politics and forays into tyranny, I abandoned our reading sessions and retreated to the 15×30-foot sleeping room we were then using. It was empty daytimes when sleeping was *verboten*. It seemed a good place off the beaten path to obtain some inner peace. I strictly followed my group's prescribed regimen even so, praying and reading *Divine Principle* aloud so nobody could accuse me of malingering.

Nevertheless Mr. Lee, the retreat's co-manager maybe ferreting out goldbrickers, found me there one day. He presumed I was shirking my holy duty and lectured me. "The spiritual principle that you must participate is very important."

"I appreciate that. I'm not having a pout. I'm escaping—protesting, if you like— the power politics infiltrating our team like a venereal disease, not slacking."

"Ahh . . . so . . ."

"It's pitting member against member and distracting us. Fomenting anger and resentment. Mine, for sure. And it's spoiling the spiritual value I'm paying for."

"I see." We conversed about an hour. He was dubious . . . but, "I am impressed by your explanation. I see you are taking it very seriously. Okay, for now your private effort is acceptable. Let's meet again tomorrow. See how you feel."

Tree of Blessing 650 feet above the lake.

A few days of his visits and I said, "Fine, I'll try the group activity again. I hope you really did talk to those leaders about control freaking. I'm not playing anybody's puppet on a string. I'm here for serious spiritual reasons, not mind games."

Big smile. "Yes, yes. Don't worry. I'm sure you'll be fine now."

I survived but couldn't see the value he placed on conformity in the quest for spiritual development. It's a satanic invasion our godly church powers refuse to acknowledge. There's value working together for a common purpose, but if process subsumes purpose it's a hindrance that needs abandoning. Those allowing process to rule them lose control of their spiritual development, like victims. Certainly, I felt victimized by Sèssè during his brief Kim Jong Il role-play.

In counterpoint, process is good; it's necessary for a person or group to achieve anything. Writing this book requires a process I have to honor. Still, it's voluntary. The problem with process in the church is that it starts off voluntarily with good intentions then devolves into half-baked ritual and tyrannical conformity that lacks meaning and harms people. The church once had a process of wrapping plastic over the water glass provided at the lectern. Speaking rarely happened without a chalkboard and lots of erasing, so its purpose was chalk-free water.

Friends at Cheongpyeong's corner store.

Julian facetiously said in 1982, "One day, Chris, plastic over a glass could lose all connection to its original purpose. Just a church ritual nobody understands."

Being young and dumb, I laughed. Yet, not long ago I regarded a Japanese sister cart a glass of water to a speaker in a clean, carpeted room with no chalkboard. Tightly rubberbanded over the glass was plastic.

Cheongpyeong designed its process to help rid us of spiritual hangers-on and to liberate our ancestors from whatever hell they'd got themselves into. Every day we climbed the steep mountain up dirt paths till reaching railroad ties stepped in soil.

Up and up we climbed over heavily eroded earth and wood till we managed the top. Along the way we passed holy trees dedicated to love, ancestors, True Parents, and God. Halfway up, folks going higher or lower drank deeply from a holy water spring. Lines stretched especially on free-for-all weekends for the ten or so spigots tippling it into rock troughs. If these highlands were a hard climb for a soft academic in the beginning, it was nightmarishly grueling when a vicious illness struck me down like Sèssè might've dreamed up on his indemnitiest day.

CHEONGPYEONG'S RETREAT IN 1998 was a hotbed of communicable disease. People from all over Korea, Japan, America, Europe, Africa and Mars congregated in enormously congested and unsanitary conditions. Near the lake was a long, covered, common sink with hundreds of public bowls set out from which to drink. People filled a bowl with water, drank their fill, then rinsed it (or not) and plopped it back in the stack. The next person along drank down whatever contagion still clung to their bowl and *presto!* fell sick. Pink Eye was the most common infection. The administrators routinely warned us not to scratch or rub our eyes with our fingers or hands. This sage advice I religiously followed and never contracted it. I caught some sort of lung infection instead. It laid me on my back with a rising fever and a withering, lung-ripping cough. I gave it a week. It thrived. I didn't.

Mrs. Kim said to us, "It is very important you accept the reality that not all illness is caused by sin or spirit infestation. Some are truly regular physical infections."

"With all the shit floating around here," I whispered to fellow UTS-er Prince, "I bet that's not hard for even the hardiest spiritualist to believe."

"*Shhh . . .*"

"Such infections need medical treatments," she maintained. "If you

Drinking, laundry, & oral hygiene at public sinks.

feel sick, you must report to us and see the doctor. Do not wait to get worse."

After they waited a week I got vanned a few days to Seorak's bush-league hospital but got no better. Coming off antsy, its barely English-speaking freshmen doctor ordered up a chest x-ray. He slapped it to the fluorescent board.

"You see much spot?" He pointed. Knowingly nodded. "Is bronchitis. I admit you to hospital." Mr. Lee reported his unwelcome diagnosis to Mrs. Kim.

My three shift-to-shift Korean nurses were drop dead gorgeous. Real specimens of Korean womanhood the country could be proud of. But they must've been Asia's version of dumb blondes. It was routine to plug a saline bag into a vein regardless your medical condition. These fetching-phizzed nurses routinely forgot to change the damn things before they ran dry. They had to yank the needle feed and switch arms. This went on left to right, back and forth till the day I checked myself out three weeks later pincushioned like a heroin addict. Their English was nil and I struggled in my conversational Korean. The chief physician's English was a godsend.

My fever hit 104°F. I stopped sweating. Korean medicine doesn't use pills but injections, so I couldn't verify what I was taking. At last responding to my Korean pleas and fiery brow, my nurse timorously called in young Dr. Kildare.

"Ah! I see now. Your medicine is wrong color. *This* is right color."

"The hell you saying?"

"I am sorry?"

"Never mind. Please continue." He shot me up. The fever dropped. Still, my cough was so demolishing I thought my lungs were hemorrhaging. I tried but couldn't eat. My body craved chicken noodle soup and rejected the honestly tasty Korean the kitchen was sending up. The cook, an elderly, portly grandmother with a charming smile, bobbed fiery eyes at tray after returned, untouched tray. She manifested at my bedside full of castigation.

"I never heard of chicken noodle soup," she said in Korean.

"It's what my body wants," I brokenly said. "It's chicken meat boiled with salt and noodles. Maybe carrots and onions. Garlic. I don't know."

"We don't have noodles here." She whipped up rice with chicken fillets in a broth that lit the fires of my soul.

"Oh, my God! It's perfectly delicious!" Slurping it down, a mushrooming mother-in-law's grin stamped her approval. Nothing had tasted this fantastic since I'd left the land of meat and potatoes. She clucked over me the next several days.

"I'm very happy to see you finally eat my cooking!"

"Believe me, my tongue loved it but my body needed the soup. I'm eternally grateful." Now she smiled like *my* grandma.

Yet, I wasn't getting well; growing weaker and sicker, in fact. And *scared*. Would I be another ex-pat statistic America forgot? It felt like St. Vincent all over again. The fever was stubbornly high. My hacking cough wracked my body night and day. I couldn't sleep more than one or two hours. At some point, I thought I had to be hallucinating. My emotions stretched to the breaking point as exhaustion turned my brain to mush. Mr. Lee made sure to visit once a day, sometimes with a UTS friend or two so I'd feel like he really cared.

"You coming is a real comfort, Mr. Lee. I appreciate not being forgotten."

"Of course. We are worried for you."

"He means it, Chris," UTS Guyanese Simone said as he chatted with my doctor. "Don't be all cynical like usual. He reports on your situation all the time."

"Come on, I never doubted his sincerity." She laughed. Considering how in short supply his kind of care was in my church and marital life, I revered him.

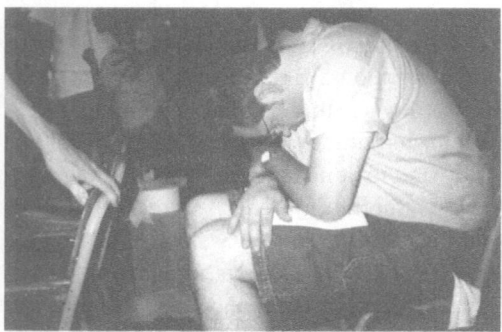

The workshop lost its flavor with fever & cough.

Dr. Kildare misdiagnosed me with a stubborn consistency, injecting a wild cocktail of fluorescent drugs that did apparently nothing. Maybe canceled the other out. Or placebos to cut costs or give the Woodstock Moonies spoiling their quiet town our comeuppance. In just a week their hospital gave me strep, verging pneumonia, gastritis, St. Vincent's resurgent hemorrhoids from that metal wicker, and lower back agony.

Thirty pounds fled home to America. Besides friendly, death looked inevitable. The Asian toilet was an exhausting procedure. Once my ass fell upon the saddle I didn't think I'd make it back to trembling feet. To add insult to injury, the hospital was fine with patients smoking in their beds or stretched out on the broad, opened-window sills. Predictably, my smog-tortured cough gutted my lungs.

Three anti-Hippocratic weeks later I gave up on Korean medicine. "I'm ready to check out, Mr. Lee. I mean, from the hospital." He fetched the good doctor.

The desk nurse said with a big, friendly grin in Korean, "One moment while I print your charges."

Quick eyes to Mr. Lee. "How much, I wonder?" My American hospital mindset could only imagine the Richter scale damage from three weeks of bedrest.

She glanced at the bill and slid it over. "It is one million. Cash, please."

I practically shouted, "A million dollars! I'm not even healed!" *Cough! Cough!*

"Korean *won*," Mr. Lee said. "Much less than American dollars. I think maybe one thousand. Take it easy."

"Oh. Right." My heart downshifted. A thousand wasn't bad. "I pay for this?" He nodded. "Uh, I don't have much money left. Kinda just the change in my pockets." I turned them out for him.

He sighed. "Okay, we will pay. The training center. You can pay us back?"

"Yes, as soon as I get home." And got a job and paid my tardy bills *there* where it really mattered. "I'll mail you a money order."

"Okay, okay, no problem." God bless him. I wondered if he wondered if the Korean church would ever get reimbursed. I was sincere. But the workshop fee should've included an open-cesspit plan with the local healthcare. Right?

I FINISHED OUT my 40-day spiritual retreat with an ever worsening cough and fever. Climbing the mountain was impossible. I limited myself to reaching the holy stream's spigoted headwaters. The headaches and lung pain ate my composure raw. Could I stroke out or hemorrhage a lung from violent coughing? It seemed any moment they damn sure would, whichever moment was the most inopportune. I fervently prayed day and night the 40 days would magically end. That I'd make it home to my incongruously more trustworthy Korean Dr. Park at UTS, who'd save me. At one point, I called across the vast Pacific and fruited plains I wasn't sure I'd ever see again to his office not far from UTS.

"Mail me some life-saving medicine to Cheongpyeong Lake? I'm dyin' here."

"No, of course not. That's illegal. See me when you get back." *Governments.* The day after touchdown I was toe-tapping in his office at the stroke of opening. He said, "Your doctor in Korea was wrong. It's not possible to diagnose bronchitis from spots on x-rays." In 10 minutes with naught but a stethoscope he correctly said, "You have an allergy-based bronchitis. I'm prescribing two drugs via inhaler. Use them both once a day for three months."

"Three months!"

"Yes, because it's persisted so long. Korean medicine is good, but sometimes country doctors don't know so much." Three days later, my indefatigable cough was history. I could've kissed him. Recovery took six months.

Candlelit prayer at the Tree of Love.

However, that was my unrealized future. Mr. Lee, ever breaking my Korean stereotypes built off my American church experience, ordered several daily hours of rest. One of those days on my back atop my sleeping bag hacking, praying, and dying to sleep I opened disappointed eyes. There over me up against the ceiling was the smiling, cherubic face of an angel . . . because, who else would be hovering bodiless? Chubby, rosy cheeks in a masculine face pushed high in a loving, caring smile under eyes sparkling deep blue raptly surveilled me. Gazing into his face, I felt a warmth wash over me. A sense that God was communicating how much He cared about me. That I wasn't forgotten nor abandoned. That I was *loved*. Feeling unloved, unappreciated, and unwanted most of my life, this brief experience was a plow ripping stones from a weedy field. Isn't that what each of us want? To be loved? appreciated? My vision gave me a renewed vigor and desire to not give up. To survive our church.

Besides battling my illness, shedloads of time went to the holy tree uphill of the main circus. It's massive hulk rose 50-some feet over its roots. There are photos professing angels as points of light infesting its branches like Christmas tree lights, but I never saw it in the flesh. Whenever I prayed there, asking God to forgive my sinful life, especially with Shiori as I mindfully apologized to Tamela, I wept heavily and uncontrollably. I never felt so much emotion sweep through me. God felt very real to me then. Close. There. Within me. Around me. Enveloping me.

As with all things in our church, sobbing at this tree was a visible sign of our repentance, our acceptance by God, our spiritual superiority, a signal to all of our heavenly virtue. For some, perhaps many, being seen empathetically communing with our sorrowful, brokenhearted God ranked high. I heard any number wailing what I (perhaps a misanthrope) took for crocodile tears. Oh, well. The Unification Church can be phony like that, each of us a Walt Disney castle little more than rickety timbers supporting a counterfeit veneer. Peer pressure, maybe. The desire to be accepted, respected, and *conformed*. Or, as fucked up as me. To each his own.

I was awfully repentful I'd ever cheated with Shiori. If I did nothing else at Cheongpyeong, I longed to forever wash my soul clean of my foul sin and find a way to heal Tamela's shattered heart. But what more can you do in a love relationship you've abused than sincerely apologize and never do it again? Isn't that what Jesus told the woman at the well? Well, she was me. I'd apologized so many times in agonized tears genuinely wet with repentance and remorse. Yet, she'd refused to forgive. She cussed and wrassled on a near-daily basis, giving me bare moments of peace. I'd screamed and cried I was going all the way insane. She'd partly relinquished damning me over Shiori my last two quarters at UTS but replaced her with money, school, church, and sundry wretchedness. But when her feuding inevitably spun out of control she threw in snide remarks about Shiori or ladled up my motives like a dark nog that only deep fried our combat. By the time I'd bused into Cheongpyeong Lake I'd reached total burnout.

I was desperate for any indemnity that would at least get our marriage past Shiori. On the muddy field in front of the Tree of Love, I recorded a message for her on my miniature recorder. I ended up crying. Apologizing for Shiori. Hating us at loggerheads.

I wept, "Forgive me, Tamela! Let it go. Let's stop quarreling and build a new, peaceful, happy future. I love you with all my heart! Can't you see it?"

Her unceasing warfare boiled my blood, yet deep in my heart I cherished her. How could I revive the best of her and us and deep-six the shit? Doing it alone was a dead letter, though. Saving our marriage required her active, willing participation.

Daily prayer at the Tree of Love.

"Will you come to Cheongpyeong yourself?" I couldn't contain my tears. "I'm sure you need to be here. *We* need to be here! I desperately wish you were here with me right now, healing our Blessing!"

Later in America she scornfully said, "Mon, your stupid tape offen' me!"

"What're you talking about? What's the problem with it?"

"You been cry *too* much! You sound like an eejit."

"Well, shit, Tamela! That's not the . . ." *Fuck!* It was an anvil to the chest.

I'd kept my illness secret from her. I knew she'd worry and panic. But that toad Sèssè wanted to stir my pot and blabbed my situation to someone at UTS whom he knew would tell Tamela. Against the workshop's rules, she rang them crazy.

Each time they said, "He is not available. Too much calling. Do not call again. This is serious workshop!"

"Put Chris on 'de phone right now! Stop be lyin' how he 'unavailable'. I don't gi' no tinker's damn for your dumb rules. I wan' taahk me hus-baahnd!"

On and on till it clicked for Mr. Lee that she was never taking no for an answer. He'd have to break his own rules and pull me out of my activities. "I am making an exception, Chris. Your wife is very insistent."

I laughed then hacked up half a lung. "I'm sorry. She's a force of nature."

Tamela's tinny voice squalled, "I hear 'bout your sick-ness. You mus' come home to Ameree-cah right now! You mus' get well. Come *today*, Chris!"

"I can't. Not till the workshop's done. I can't change my ticket anyway."

"I am very worried, Chris. 'Dem make it sound like you is dyin'. I a' wan' you die! Our chilleren need you!"

I sighed. "I'm fine. And don't tell the kids! I'll be home on schedule." *Cough!*

They were spending time with my family in California. Once home from sickville, she called for a pick up at Kennedy regardless my illness and desperation for real bed rest. No mercy catering to her needs: SOP. I'd got used to (but resented) it. One needs space in a relationship, but also to know they're cared about. Nothing kills one's sense of it more than mad demands rode roughshod over reality.

Cheongpyeong rent my heart and opened my soul. I cried torrents for weeks under its influence, repenting to God and Tamela for every conceivable mistake as if each day was my last, as Rev. Moon advised. Desperation for a different marriage was aboil. My love felt strong . . . enough for a happy family anyhow. Regardless her unending maltreatment, she was my Blessed wife. I wanted to grow old with her. To go to sleep each night and wake up each morning only with her. Tamela's abuse was sending me to baldness. Even after 43 days apart when she thought I might die overseas, her refusal to break the cycle of violence deathly depressed me.

Typical meatless Korean lunch with best friends.

Mindful how my time in Korea had altered my very affect, I pushed her. "I really want you to experience its atmosphere, Tamela. It changed my life! Might revolutionize yours, too. Make you a new person. We could restore our love for each other."

"*Pish!* I will nev-uhh go to such a pat'etic place. 'Dem is not honest people blockin' me taahkin' to you." *Stiupp.* "I hate your church! Aahll 'dem people trash." Within a day of her return from California with our children she was bickering and quarreling all over again. "I wan' leave 'dis place. I hate 'dis little Sauguhh-tees an' aahll 'dem people here. Nobody nice to me. Your so-caahll semee-narry most of aahll!"

"No way in hell am I ever living in New York City again."

"Wha' mek you a' go New Yaahk? Nothin' wrong wi' it."

"I hate its grubbiness. Compared to here, it's stupid expensive. Our rent would probably rise a grand. I don't have the cashola. Do you?"

"Well, I a' wan' stay here. An' I ha' family in New Yaahk."

"If you want to move, my mission from Father is working with the national leaders. They haven't offered or assigned me anything, yet. Not even to test me! Who knows if they ever will. It makes more sense we move to Florida for CFT"—Nimrod Kriss' chemical tech opportunity—"now that I'm the CEO." I'd got the vote of the patent-holding principles Bill and Barry and their board of directors. Kriss would make me David to his King Saul for them giving it to me instead of him.

"I a' trus' none o' 'dem, Chris. Don't work wi' 'dem people. How 'dem pay you?"

"Bill said he's expecting—"

"I a' trust he most of all!"

"—twenty million from our Boston funding group any day now. It's cheaper down there. More like St. Vincent. *Warm.* We can work face to face."

She considered it. Her face softened. "Maybe it would be nice."

She nagged day and night to get out of Saugerties. Like Mr. Lee, I capitulated to her implacability in December 1998. If she'd known Florida was the stake in the heart of her vampiric marriage, would she have given me more time to regroup after UTS and Korea? appreciated my fidelity to our Blessing? embraced a new future?

Nah, probably not.

Act XVII

Trek to Florida
Chemistry, Good and Bad

Chemistry is a bit of a life force, an energy. With it, anything in a give-and-take relationship can positively develop. Otherwise, it fossilizes. My Chemical Fusion (CFT) entrepreneurial startup was all about chemistry. Billions of dollars of it. My relationship with my partners and Tamela was, too—bad chemistry, unfortunately. Of gunpowder, not perfume. The year I'd dwell in Florida would be an explosive alchemy that try as I might I could not, like King Midas, change by my sterling touch from base to gold.

I was crossing a Saugerties street when "I'm an abused husband!" first popped out of my mouth. I didn't even know where the term came from.

Abused?

I had no cognizance of its existence. Sure, I'd heard the term. Who hadn't?

Domestic violence. Part of my curriculum at UTS.

It sits there like a lump in your throat you can't swallow away. Yet, you hardly think of it. You swallow and swallow and swallow, vaguely noticing it while pushing it down a gummy mucus but, really, your mind is coveting other things.

Like peace . . . without conscious awareness of how to get it. How many times had she pull-started her chainsaw-cussing over Shiori? the church? our life? knifing her resentment into me till I was defensively irritated then exasperated with her unwillingness to recognize the argument had reached a logical brick wall?

Stop it. *Stop* it! *Stooo—op it!*

But she couldn't. Not till she'd thrown all her invective at me; a resinous tinder heaped at my feet and built round my body encasing me in a viscous, incendiary cocoon of spite. I tried to disengage, to leave, to flee my coming immolation.

"You can't win it," I told myself. "You can't even hold your own."

No tears, apology, nor fidelity melted the cold, dead anger freezing her heart in a dark and dangerous symbiosis. I had to vamoose. Let her argue with herself.

Getting out the door was never easy. It's the very archetype of collapsing a dug-in defensive line. Tamela blocked me in life-or-death miniature tackle football. I went for the goal. She cut me off. Panic soaked in through feeling trapped, caged, hooked. Prey for the slaughter. She beat me with edged words which I parried in nonstop defensive fury. I struggled all the harder, physically grappling with her, pushing her aside, my hand landing fleetingly on the doorknob before she roughly shoved me off its salvation. She grabbed me, hung on to me, pushed me back, forced my arms from the door. I'd fight harder, all the while restraining slapping hands and flying fists from touching off a nuclear inferno or maybe a legal sinkhole.

Tamela's no couch potato. She's apishly strong, I'm not ashamed to say it. Nor was she the 115-pound slip of a girl I'd married in St. Vincent but a 170-pound she-bear, give or take a loaded sixteen tons. She fought me across the floor, wailing her truculent lamentations while denying me the door.

"Stay here! Don't leave me! Don't *leaaave* me!"

Once fight-or-flight took hold of my brain, I could rarely bat it back into its limbic box. I had to go.

I have to get away! I have to escape!

Rage swirled through me in shrieking, mind-wrecking tornadoes tearing to shreds all compassion for Tamela's sorrows and our children's terror. I felt trapped in fire, surrounded by heat and scorching flame licking right into my life-giving, airless lungs . . . else trapped mere inches underwater, feet mortally entangled in kelp and precious breath exhausted, lungs heaving and burning in suffocation's fire.

I've never panicked at danger. But in the path of Hurricane Tamela, my fear knew no bounds. It was unbridled, rabid-eyed. She wouldn't stop feuding, pricking me with her thousand poisoned barbs. Running me through with her hundred tearing furies year on year on year. Round and round whipped the same words, wrath, rancor, tortured logic, inability or unwillingness to understand—nay, *hear!*—what howled through my heart and wept from my wounds. Pleas for peace fell on deaf ears. If perchance I insulted her—*bitch* was a dumb tactical nuke—then her seething mania shunted onto a side track before hooking back up with the main line.

Now I was drowning and had to—*I had to!*—get out to free, clean, quiet air. Nothing stopped me. Not even our trembling, saucer-eyed children. If at this point she threw something, which wasn't unknown of her, I instinctively, primitively threw something, anything back. I vaguely understood the danger of crossfire and hated her for turning me into a savage psychopath lost to my children's safety.

I have to get out!

Sometimes a little fencing-footsy worked: feint right, go left. Maneuver her off the door, get between the two. Seize enough space to snatch the knob, spin it round and wrench the door all in the wink of an eye before she reacted.

Ofttimes she scorned my panic. "Wha' mek run away instead o' stickin' to fight me like a man? Am I so strong? Am I so scary? Me, jus' a smaahll gyul?"

"Small? You're a hellion!"

"You run away when all I be axin' is a simple queh-stion."

"Ha! There's nothing simple about your umpteenth interrogations over what's *years* in the past. *Yeeeaaars!* You only want war on war!"

"Wha' mek you go wi' Shiori, then?" as if it was her first. "Wha' mek you marry to me? If you knew you were g'wan go cheat 'pon me, wha' mek you ever tek me from me country? Wha' mek you can'a answer such a simple queh-stion?"

"I've answered your loaded, and never simple, questions a million times." Brain nodded lockstep with mind.

Her queries carried the catch-22 of a Salem witch trial: float, you're guilty; sink, you're innocent. My answers proved what she'd always suspected and now had my admission to crucify me with, else wasn't the damning confession she knew was the truth and wanted to hear; I was obviously lying, more scourging needed.

For normal people, a Q&A leads to some understanding and acceptance of the underlying reality. Wrangling it out can close it down. The relationship breaks up or resumes its course. With Tamela, questions didn't lead to acceptable answers and never to understanding or sufferance but only to angrier interrogatives and greater vexation. Comprehension and forbearance of reality could never rear their pacifying heads because she was stuck in the argument groove. It never mattered how completely and honestly I responded to her questions. My answers always led to a greater sense of her being wronged and more fervid quarreling over how I could've done this or said that. An argument with her wasn't a dispute in the classical sense but a dog chasing its barbed tail with an ever harsher sense of betrayal and frustration that it was evading teeth for spite.

I bolted for the door a man in fear for his very life. Even though she was physically abusive maybe 5% of the time, the psychological trauma her maelstrom blew up in me built such a sense of disequilibrium that suicide oft-seemed the better option—indeed, the only sensible course if it was peace I truly wanted.

Is it better to endure the pepper shot, fight back, or simply escape?

I could only shrug. The last six years had taught me fighting back was, at best, a Pyrrhic victory, an outrageous fortune altogether unendurable. Escape seemed best. I more than once girded myself to sail through the splintering window of our fourth-floor Queens walk-up at the speed of gravity to the coroner's slab below.

Would I survive? *Shrug.* Did it matter? *Not so much.*

My only concern amongst petrifying thoughts was to silence her incessantly rattling gunfire. It wasn't my nature to physically harm her. I'd sooner kill myself than violently shut her up. How many times did I wildly fling eyes for a bus to pop in front of? a wall to smash into? a cliff to sail off? yet, never did? Mayhap God saw to it the right circumstance didn't present in these moments.

There were times I prayed, "O, God! Please send me a cop I can beat up so I can be jailed or shot dead and Tamela"—virtually a demonic force in my deranged thoughts—"forever kept away."

I fled her only at top speed. She followed in hot pursuit if she could screaming, "Come baaack! I sorry! I won't do it again. I'll behaaave!"

Over my shoulder I shouted, "I don't believe you anymore! Leave me alone!"

I ran till my brain ached, lungs burst, legs buckled, vision blurred. I cut crazily through town—or woods—so she'd have no hope of tracking me if, by some miracle, she'd dogged my trail. More than once she abandoned our children to fly after me. Then I had to be caught. Bite my tongue. Swallow my fear. Give in to unfair hate.

No way could I permit our babies alone in the house much less the car I'd hastily ditched when she chased me over frozen, snowy fields off the interstate when I didn't yet have it in me to steer directly into a tree at 70 MPH and kill us all. For the sake of our children I came back, convinced myself she'd change, *could* change, that she really was sorry. That if only I checked my temper during her onslaughts she'd calm down. That we'd manage some semblance of a peaceful home.

Yeah. I was fooling myself. Maybe I knew it, maybe I didn't. I loved her and hated her all at once by the time I graduated UTS. She made most days hell. Then we'd sit on the sofa wringing laughter from our eyes over some silly nonsense. I'd think how much fun she was, how much I loved her sense of humor, how much I loved being with her. I didn't know she was developmentally disabled. I thought her problem was attitudinal leftovers from childhood abuse. I railed against her malignant heart oblivious she didn't comprehend my words nor her state. I was attempting to reason with a practical 10-year old. Doomed from the start. The more I applied adult logic the more confused, frustrated, and exasperated she got.

Guilt wracked me following feelings into Shiori. *My fault.* Tamela cussed me and *that* was my fault. I felt indescribably blameworthy. It flooded me every time she brought her up. It damnably incensed me, too. She had no right to torment me over my conscience already consuming me. My infidelity was between me and God, *not* Tamela. I'd repented in my restored fidelity, heartfelt tears, and doting love a million times. How much did she need? how much could I give?

Well, I was done apologizing. Never would it undo what was done. What was the point if she didn't accept I'd chosen her over Shiori? I'd been faithful since our Blessing, dedicated in real love to her and our family. She couldn't make peace with it. I supposed, in her mind, my love was tainted, fouled, unlovable. Maybe it was. I was only human. Cheongpyeong Lake was the last repentance I was prepared to give for falling with Shiori. I'd purified my heart and soul. My house was clean. I felt forgiven by God. I'd almost forgiven myself—not quite, but getting there. I'd suffered near-unendurable physical pain bearing the rigors of the retreat to its last day, my commitment and effort so diamond tough that Mrs. Richardson and Mr. Lee awarded me Cheongpyeong's graduation diploma despite spending three weeks out of six languishing in hospital. I'd earned it, and Tamela absolutely needed to understand and accept it. My penance was real. I deserved her absolution. Our children deserved a peaceful family. If after all that she couldn't see my total commitment to her and our marriage, family, future . . . what power did I have to make it clearer? At some point, she had to step to the plate and swing. Responsibility is a two-way street, forgiveness the bookend to repentance.

Jesus teaches that Christians need forgive even absent repentance. We're duty-bound to find it in our hearts to forgive sincere penance and Tamela certainly counted herself *da kine* of Christ. For some, forgiveness lies only in words, not the heart. One needs work it over time yet not deny the penitent. We can't go before God till our victims forgive us. Jesus commands we leave our gift on the altar to seek our brother's forgiveness and then *together* offer it to God. This principle applies to black and white Americans as much as Tamela and me and the church. It's all domestic violence. And a universal principle. Hence, Jesus taught it.

Regardless, I couldn't transcend my criminality under the onslaught. "It's all my fault," I told myself... as did all and sundry. "If only I never fell with Shiori, Tamela and I would be living a happy life today."

"That's a chimera, Chris," my closest friends said. "As much as Father appointing you president of the American Church."

"But, I feel both truths deep in my bones. All I have to do is please her better. Please the church more." Win Tamela–Moon's heart, respect, and trust."

Heads shaking. "It's just not gonna be your fairytale ending."

My grinding sigh. When Tyler Hendricks interviewed me in his upper room to see what mission I was after I'd said, "I can develop my new business and become independently wealthy and still serve the church, too, you know."

"I don't know, Chris. That sounds pretty external."

"Father wants us to each become billionaires, not eternal hangers-on. I sure can't do that if I don't own a business. Father does both. Why not us members?"

Tyler was skeptical and looked askance at the very idea. "I suggest that you consider taking over the unpaid position of New Mexico state leader if it becomes vacant... maybe it already is, I'm not sure." He scribbled a note in his flip folder.

"Well, if that's what Father wants, that's what I'll do. No problem... though if possible I'd prefer working with the Florida church—maybe around Orlando?—since my business partners are along that area."

Nod, nod. Scribble, scribble.

I knew Rev. Moon liked testing his leaders. To check their mettle with his Mr. Miyagi wax-on-wax-off bullshit. He puts members into impossible situations or asks them to voluntarily jump off a 'roof' to see how they respond. In that respect he's not too unlike Henry Ford, who invited prospective senior-level managers to lunch to see if they salted their meat before or after they tasted it. If before, it indicated to him they'd act on plans without doing their homework.

I was ready for Rev. Moon's test. Frankly, I expected he'd send us to Brazil like last year's unlucky crop because the Jardim Providence still figured big in his plans. I'd brassily told friends at UTS how I *wouldn't* go to Brazil to starve for nothing like the sods of '97. That was before he might've even asked me. And then he didn't. He cut us loose to work with our own national leaders like we didn't deserve a mission. I felt he didn't expect much of us or was giving up on UTS producing worthwhile leaders he could work with. We repatriated to our native lands to do... whatever. My national leaders wanted nothing to do with me, my outstanding work on the '97 and '98 Blessings already forgotten. Tyler never got back to me about New Mexico or any mission plan. The church faded me to black.

"It's all your fault," it said in Tamela's echo chamber. *Yeah. All. My. Fault.*

~

AT $300 A month, our Saugerties apartment was the perfect place to wait out CFT's funding. In the meantime I had software engineering opportunities in New York City even if its church (Chen Fong in Manhattan and my freshly minted UTS diploma notwithstanding) still considered me *persona non grata*. Living in the metro area—Kingston possibly the Apple's farthest-north bedroom community—was probably

485

the best way to troll for investment monies, as the bulk of it resided with Wall Street's displaced *Charging Bull*. Tamela and I were cats and dogs over moving.

My friend Godwin and now partner and CFT executive vice president working very part-time from his Los Angeles state leader's HQ said, "I think Florida's a good idea. It'll change your luck." Hindsight belatedly pointed me to his LA domain.

"Okay, man. I trust your advice." I respected and admired him, not least for his ability to rise like a cork in the murky waters of official churchdom.

"Everybody needs somebody outside their own head, Chris." *Yes, indeed.*

Low on funds, we couldn't bring what outsized our cars and stashed it with a local storage company. Three days later in early December 1998 we washed up like driftwood in Merritt Island, Florida. Our NY tags denounced us to locals for snowbirds fleeing south. Two motel days later we were in a gated apartment for $745 a month, $900 with perks like electricity and internet. I was instantly anxious dividing my bank balance by it. I'd opted for Indian River over cheaper but ghettoey cinder block properties for safety and my immense faith in Bill Merchant.

"Palmer's twenty million is coming in any day now, Chris." Dark haired and circle-bearded, Bill looked a shorter, pudgier version of my brother Teddy. He was the classic sales type: bubbly, cheerful, building situations into more than they were. I helped him negotiate our slow-moving commitment from John Palmer, owner of Boston MoneyHut. "Trust me."

"Okay. And I'm ready as soon as we sign the deal."

Meanwhile, I had bills. I took a newspaper delivery job for the *Orlando Sentinel* because it left my days free for CFT. It paid $1,500 a month, but I fast found it as close to sharecropping as you can get nowadays. Seven days a week. No holidays. No R&R. No inclement weather. If I didn't work, I wasn't paid. Boss Choi maybe took lessons. It was cold water in the face after IT consulting at $70 an hour.

"It's only temporary," I assured Tamela. "Just a month, probably less. Our twenty-mil's in the bag. Don't worry so much. Have a little faith."

Eyes were flinty. "Bill be say 'dis. Palm-uhh be say 'dat. I a' trust 'dem people."

"It's just a matter of finishing their due diligence." Her usual *stiupp*.

This mindset carried into May and June before it was obvious none of our three investors wanted their money where their goddamned mouths were. "We aren't getting Palmer's cash," others then Bill confirmed. "Apparently, he or MoneyHut got involved with the Russian oil mafia and European bank debentures. He bled money like diluted water. The Feds just busted the firm."

"You must be shitting me!" Face shrug. Head nod. "So, what's next then?"

We pursued pockets upbeat about our needful millions. Catering mountains of paperwork Bill said, "We're just not finding the funds we want." We signed an agreement in principle for $50 million, then at closing one of the lawyers decided his cut was too cheap. Our investors wouldn't renegotiate. He sank our deal.

"Dammit, Tamela! I'm on the teetering edge but just can't get over the line."

"Stop pullin' out your hair then and ge' a real job. Your pap-uhh for 'de birds."

"I know, I know. It's not like I haven't been looking around." *Stiupp*.

The *Sentinel* paid me eight cents per newspaper delivered, a few more on Sunday. That averaged over 600 a day if I wanted my $1,500. I stuffed Tamela's imaginatively red, '87 Taurus station wagon rug-to-headliner with the dailies. Super-thick Sunday's mandated a reload halfway through. The midnight to 6–8 AM work was grueling. Without paid mileage, fuel cost 13–20% of my daily take. Mechanical wear and tear was frightful. Eight months of reversing out of driveways tore up Ford's crummy transmission and Florida's ubiquitous sand was a grind on everything.

Newspapers got away with this kind of exploitation because they sell delivery to entrepreneurs like my boss Gary who hire underdogs like me as independent contractors. Similar to IT consulting—a dearth, in tech primitive Florida—it pays for brawn not brains. We got no health insurance. Paid self-employment tax. Full social security. I understood the business rationale, sure. I'd built a similar if a bit fairer set up for my *St. Vincent Times* venture. But I resented my predicament all the same. I thought the *Sentinel's* low-wage system in a high-cost economy a throwback to the Roaring Twenties before the workplace humanized and the Fed killed the dollar's purchasing power. But it kept us eating under a roof with lights.

Tamela and the children sometimes accompanied me. Kal-el especially enjoyed the challenge and fun of throwing a paper log out the window. Kir-el conked out in the back floating on a sea of plastic-sleeved entertainment. Tamela took the seat behind me, folding and stuffing them into plastic bags so I didn't have to. I enjoyed those times. We felt like a family. All in it together. The old generational farm, in a way, with even the tiniest tots pitching in. She was usually too drained by then to fight or argue, so her mere presence never had me overstressed and neurotic as it otherwise did. In some ways, it was the first time she felt like my *wife*—not a live-in maid with benefits or, more usually, a less endearing version of Inspector Clouseau's Kato—since we'd lived in St. Vincent. We were earning our bread *together*, like partners. I cherished her in our shared labors.

But it was hard work and she avoided it. And somebody had to be awake daytimes to supervise our children. Then the local Baymont Hotel off I-95 near Cocoa hired her as a maid for $5.75 an hour. She scampered off to work as soon as I wearily fell through the door. That had me supervising the kids without sleep till she returned around 5 PM. Her ongoing resentment of our lifestyle metastasized. If I laid down before she was ready, in she barged every five minutes to talk or argue till, by 9 PM, I was hollering and crying for her to let me doze off. A few months of this and I was in a state of exhaustion and near-hysteria.

She blamed CFT for the final nail in our marital coffin, thinking my long-suffering crucible had somehow zombified me into a lunatic who could only ever fight and argue. There was some truth to it shortening my temper, aye. I gravely stressed over money thus my business. My mood wasn't exactly stable. Still, I compartmentalized work and home fairly effectively. The real culprit in our final souring was economic stress aggravated by sleep deprivation accelerating my declining patience with her endless capacity for strife and abuse.

THE CONTRACT I developed for CFT carefully excluded Bill and Barry (the patent holders of our technologies) from participating in running the business. Although they could each veto our board—I'd shortsightedly used it to quell their fear of partners—they were obligated to limit their investor interactions to technology and leave business issues to me as CEO. They discounted my role and proceeded to confuse potential investors anyway with information, ideas, and dreams that contradicted the picture I was painting. This alienated investment. Our business wasn't some penny-ante startup. We were running up a revolutionary, multi-billion dollar chemical technology . . . if it ever got out of its sticky gate.

Briefly, CFT held two core patents via Bill and Barry. One was the first patent ever issued to a truly green solvent. The second was a radically new sulfuric acid-based solution crammed with so many positively charged hydrogen atoms that it was safe to swallow as a bactericide and viricide.

Bill named his solvent Orange-a-Peel. He concocted it from three ingredients, one of which was d-Limonene, i.e., orange peel oil. The solution was completely organic and environmentally friendly. It took oil-based products and broke the hydrocarbon chain into micron-sized particulates a microorganism could dine on. One of our favorite demonstrations was taking a bowl of motor oil, adding a small amount of Orange-a-Peel, then water. In seconds we had a milky-white liquid producing that telltale squeaky-clean sound when you rub your fingers together. The bowl of ex-motor oil could now be thrown on the ground as food for microorganisms with absolutely no negative effect on the environment.

Orange-a-Peel was *the* solution to oil spills. Spray it over a slick and the mess disappears into the ocean to power-feed microorganisms. Bill whipped up several different formulations for general purpose degreasers, commercial kitchen cleaners, nail polish remover, and whatnot. We ran successful tests in the seminary's kitchen my friend Rachel was managing after Chaz Jerman's disgrace. Yet, Bill didn't enforce his patent and nixed me doing so till we had a war chest big enough to fatten our lawyers. Nor did he want me developing packaged products to sell in stores or via television. Working with partners and consultants, I developed cash-flow plans in lieu of investment to get us into the game. Bill shot all these down with his deadly veto gun as too risky an exposure of their patents.

Barry called our second technology pHARLO, as in "the pH are low." This chemical blew my mind and is the main reason I jumped on their bandwagon. Concentrated, it had about 1,200 moles of hydrogen and registered below −3 pH. Sulfuric and hydrochloric acid are close to zero, so it was a major breakthrough. Barry built what he called a "molecular plasma reactor" that subjected ordinary sulfuric acid to extremes of heat and pressure and out came highly charged, heavily hydrogenated pHARLO. Many reputable scientists and FDA-approved labs called it a new element on the periodic table. Most didn't believe our stunning claims. One of Bill's clever tricks was pouring concentrated pHARLO over a seashell in the palm of his hand which then exploded, indicating the liquid's highly acidic nature. His pHARLO-wetted skin was completely unharmed, something normally impossible. His stunt usually won over the skeptics.

What was it good for? The solution had the unique ability of rendering metals like copper into micron-sized solution. Drop powdered gold into it and in a moment the liquid was clear. Now dip in a nail and out it comes gold plated. It replaces cyanide in gold and other precious metals extraction methodologies, removes toxic metals from soil, and other fabulous things.

Mixed with copper, PHARLO Blue is a vicious bactericide with a 100% kill rate. A friend of Bill's asked his help saving her chicken ranch from a bacteriological and viral epidemic. Her veterinarians threw up their hands and recommended killing and burning her fowl. Eight drops of PHARLO per gallon of drinking water eliminated the infection within 24 hours. It even killed salmonella in live chickens. We called our first planned product SeaFresh. One gallon of PHARLO Blue in 3,000 gallons of water made a one-part-per-million copper solution that killed all surface bacteria on 30,000 pounds of seafood. Shrimp with melanosis, infected shellfish, and other problematic seafood was a thing of the past with it. This product alone would have earned us hundreds of millions per year and dominated the seafood import–export industry.

Mixed with a crème base, PHARLO Blue is a powerful pharmaceutical. Simply apply it once or twice a day and warts disappear in weeks. I know, because I used it myself. The crème was also a winner as a burn ointment, which I also experienced after scalding my hand on boiling water. It kills the pain and, feeling-wise, returns the skin to its pre-burn condition within minutes. We planned to create PHARLO Silver—chelated silver instead of copper—for this market because silver is a better bactericide. A person whose skin is burned off can be treated by spritzing PHARLO Blue or Silver onto the injury to block pain, kill bacteria, and promote faster healing. And we had tons of reports from FDA-certified labs proving it all.

You bet I jumped on this company!

On the side, I developed a relationship with Hank DeGrasse, a high school dropout, 'B'-member in our church, and self-taught engineer. He looked a poster boy for Appalachian homelessness, illiteracy, and in-breeding. He had a head full of sandy, tousled hair cut short over the ears army style. Several front teeth had gone walkabout. His house was a dumpy, rented affair on a shabby street in a bug-eaten St. Petersburg neighborhood. He had history with the local police, having got them into some legal trouble when they illegally broke into his house. He'd also discovered the oldest fossils in Florida while working as a laborer at a construction site. He ultimately donated them—"worth hundreds of thousands of dollars, according to the experts," he said—to Rev. Moon and his university in Korea. "Got me a private dinner with True Parents," he beamed.

In some ways Hank was like me, kind of an outcast with the church yet devoted to Divine Principle and the physical kingdom of heaven. I took an instant liking to him. He'd developed a revolutionary hydrogen fuel technology and needed money to prove it out. Using a custom-built atomizer, Hank was able to separate hydrogen from water on the fly and built a company around it called CRIPES, Inc. When I helped him get the system running and tested it using a propane/hydrogen fuel source, we averaged 100 miles per gallon and eventually calculated 400 MPG on the 370 CU IN V8 engine in his ratty old pickup truck. Bill and I were ecstatic over his technology because PHARLO—its 1,200 moles of hydrogen compared to water's two—was the perfect fuel source. If it worked, we'd leapfrog past all the complex fuel cell technologies with a simple, off-the-shelf engine retrofit. I had visions of drivers buying PHARLO bottled in propane camping-bottle sizes screwed right into an adapter that 'gassed up' their car on the fly.

For me, his technology worked. But, again, we couldn't find the risky money willing to prove it. All we needed was $25,000 to demonstrate his unit really did pull hydrogen from water on demand sufficient to run an engine. Its only drawback was an engine had to reach operating temperature on gasoline before switching to full hydrogen. We thought it a resolvable defect but, even so, massive gasoline savings were there. It was a no-brainer. I wrote the joint venture contracts and we all met in Tampa to review the technology, verify Hank's understanding of hydrogen, conclude our due diligence, and sign the papers.

CFT was an exhilarating, wealth-creating opportunity almost on the cusp. Right up Rev. Moon's "you must all become billionaires" alley. Might the church reconsider putting my M.DIV. to Moon-level work with business success?

I had a chance to find out the first week in June. In the midst of CFT's chaos I attended Rev. Moon's East Garden (Western White House) top 10% UTS graduates' meeting on Godwin's dime. A happy experience though I chafed at its protocols and bowing. He advised on true love and husband–wife relationships. We did the *Hoon Dok Hae* ('meetings for reading and studying') he'd inaugurated in 1997 and exhausted ourselves June 4–5 reading *True Parents* and Dr. Sang Hun Lee's spirit world books. Nothing mission-wise came of it. But seeing him energized me.

Struggling over CFT, I explained things to Peter Kim. "Would you set up a meeting with Father before the workshop's over to pitch my business?"

"Yes. I'll let you know." Later he said, "I'm sorry, but I couldn't get a minute to ask Father about it. He's too busy with the workshop. Another time, maybe."

I DIDN'T LATCH onto CFT to get rich. My 18-year dream was independent wealth like Rev. Moon so I could focus on his quest for the physical kingdom of heaven on earth. My vision was born of Divine Principle and his example. Before meeting him, I was a confused kid with no purpose or vision beyond a workaday future till joining my ancestors. At Western State, I'd pursued a geology degree with a side of volcanism to inject me into a plum job with the US Geological Survey, working six months in the field and six at a desk writing up my fieldwork. My garden-variety dream went out the window when Diane's Big Dump shattered me, I ran away to sea, got crippled, then discovered Divine Principle and the Lord of the Ages.

How could I do anything in life that wasn't connected to saving the world now that I'd met the Messiah? *Impossible!* I split off from my family's and society's normalcy to camp-follow these biblical ascetics into a wilderness of religious devotees and world-saving dreamers and rebranded as Mr. Bigger Plans Himself.

At UTS I'd been sharply critical of members like Hyo Jin Moon for their self-absorbed, sordid, drug-fueled, bling-bawdy, egotistical lifestyles. In 2003 Rev. Moon chided Mr. Oh, a narcissistic self-styled mini-me messiah teaching Korean at UTS, for unremittingly claiming that Hyo Jin was the only one to succeed his father. *Idiots savants* enabling this coterie have always been epidemic in our evangelical church. He kicked him out of East Garden for it. A year later, he showed up and planted himself prominently in front during Sunday service. Rev. Moon, offended by his shameless pride, rebuked him then and there in a real-life version of "whoever exalts himself will be humbled."

"Yes," he said, "I know what your character is. You like to step on others to get ahead, that's why you come and sit up front." Then, Chief Enabler that he is, he mitigated his own scolding with praise to ease Mr. Oh's embarrassment which only meant, "No worries, fam. You do you."

My criticism included Americans abandoning self and hearthstone to an Imperial Japanese penurious sheepfulness. Their poverty-stricken discipleship stunted Rev. Moon's efforts and their own lofty delusions not with indigence but an impoverished spirit. Members were destitute of ideas, creativity, and especially working together or charitably helping each other toward a shared goal. We had members in virtually every country on the planet. Why weren't they spiritually, personally, and financially networked? UTS grads sped off to the wild unknown with no support whatsoever, least of all financial . . . remember Red McDafft and the Class of '97? It was bad enough UTS grads suffered their own leaders and peers' disrespect and suspicion of dangerous counterrevolutionism that boxed them on a shelf. Poverty only added insult to injury. We needed a global (financial) network that graduates could plug into wherever they were. With millions floating untethered through the church, and notwithstanding chiselers siphoning it off, how wasn't that a thing?

This is where iniquities like Hyo Jin's failure to think past his next coke hit or piece of ass fell into stark relief. Rev. Moon's chief function, in my view, is to spiritually guide the movement through his mission, connect us with God, and nourish the body religic with Divine Principle's inspiring truth. But he seems to prefer being chief cook and bottle washer. His grip on power relaxes only if clubbed senseless. But it's up to members to build the infrastructure and networks that realize his divine vision. It's our responsibility—part and parcel of our own vision for a successful life—to build the necessary tools for our own Moon-inspired vision.

Look at Mormonism's success. From whence does it come? For one thing, they pay attention to the tools necessary to advance their mission. How about Jews? They've nurtured their community and sense of self for millennia by respecting reality juxtaposed with an unshakable worldview and personal faith.

Unificationists? We bill ourselves Christianity's successor, the third Israel led by Christ 2.0. Yet, members are poverty stricken. Our wealthy church is impecunious. Rev. Moon said it's because we haven't resolved our sin, paid indemnity, liberated our ancestors, lived according to God's ideal, conformed to Divine Principle . . . but, really? How does he credibly explain wealthy, nonPrincipled Mormons and Jews living in unindemnified sin? That Satan blesses his own? Come on.

Church and membership are impoverished because we did the one thing we weren't supposed to: lived self-absorbed lives pretending to sacrifice for humanity while throat-stomping our brethren. There's a deep-seated fear of an irresponsible membership. Few Moonie business owners want to hire Moonies because it's widely believed even in the church they're lazy, unreliable embezzlers. You can count on them to think and act in their own interest. In my experience, successful Moonies (home members) often disassociate from Unificationism to self-preservationally cleave to societal norms rooted in the shards of the Christian ethos.

Unificationists aren't poor from undue sin and scanty indemnity. If that were true then non-Moonies would be poorer, because it's the official position of the church that only in serving the Messiah is one in accord with God's will *today*; that Moonies alone live for the sake of humanity and God to resolve historical sin and resentment, liberate our ancestors from historical sin, break down the barriers separating people in spirit world, and set the foundation for the kingdom of heaven on earth. Unificationists aren't financially or psychically held back by evil spirits nor a poor adherence to the Principle or Christian ethics. The church is not practically bankrupt because Satan foils our movement's noble effort to succeed. The problem is 'me over thee.' Of the absolute refusal of Moonies to work with, for, and in trust with each other toward spiritual and financial prosperity. To strive as a family—how we bullishly ran ourselves up in better days—toward our collective goal.

Hyo Jin brags about his money, businesses, how bloody awfully smart he is. Yet, all he has comes by the power of his father who seeds his wealth from our bloodstained hands selling products in brumal nights and searing days with no- or low-wage church jobs. His arrogance and selfishness dumbfounds me. Who better to erect a global financial network linking all our members? has the money, moxie, connections, name recognition, talent, travelability, and the intrinsic trust reposed in his dad? Instead, he swaggers through his loot on drugs, liquor, sex, and violence. His 10,000 songs of love and struggle or whatever is chaff in the wind.

My dream for CFT was to bring this vision of co-prosperity into the church. I formulated a plan to establish the Business Federation for World Peace once CFT delivered investment income. All the money I planned to earn through salary and stock (minus normal living expenses) would fund this organization whose purpose was to own part or all of thousands of small and medium businesses around the world. I hoped UTS grads would arrive in a country, hook up with a local BFWP-owned or operated business, and acquire employment and a means to develop independent, residual income. The goal was to develop the means and process through which UTS grads could develop independent wealth that, at a minimum, covered living expenses. This allowed them to focus on their spiritual mission in the same way Rev. Moon mixes business with his spiritual pleasure.

How'd *he* make it? He built up membership. Put it to work in acquired or boot-strapped businesses. Plowed profits into asset-building ventures that coincidentally advanced his spiritual ones. Members got cracking because they at least had room and board to pursue their own spiritual goals. A team effort. Sacrifice was valued and recognized as indispensable to overall success if you ignored the inevitable bandits and frauds gravitating like blowflies to a corpse. Meanwhile he managed his managers, built more assets, pursued his spiritual crusade. He counsels us to build our own financial foundation, just as he did as part of God's Restoration process. Okay, I can live with that. But working in unison is always more successful than working alone. Bill Gates is rich because others did the work earning his billions and themselves tens, hundreds, or thousands of thousands moving up his ladder. Unificationists need heed this lesson. I wanted to teach it through BFWP.

CFT was a means to an end greater than my own. In my exit interview with Tyler I said, "I want to develop a new breed of leader, people who don't need a church paycheck but fulfill their roles while independently earning their keep."

"That's a laudable goal. I'm not sure it's the church's reality, though."

"Paychecks are just a hindering leash jerking straining leaders into line and promotes corruption. It stymies accomplishment. Don't you ever feel it?"

Poker face. I knew I was right when Dean Mickler said, "I think the growing institutionalism of the church with its leaders converting into middle managers like any big institution is desirable. It protects us and is a logical evolutionary step."

That's how he described the reality of UTS and justified his usual unwillingness to stick his neck out (risking paycheck and family) when I pressed for reform and support in my confrontations with Dr. Shimmyo. Progress fails under such a heavy load. Reform, innovation, and commitment to difficult spiritual truths necessarily fall away. Institutional management, not spiritual fulfillment, becomes (in fact, is) the sought-after norm. Just ask Christendom.

It's true that in 2003's Unification Church there remains a struggle between institutional management and religious inspiration. Yet, the latter triumphs only when it emanates from Rev. Moon, though leaders are careful to filter out his instrinic institutional threat. When God calls an ordinary member to testify truth, the church ignores or outright silences him or her. Bureaucratic institutionalism is the curse of group endeavor, but knowledge of its dynamic can mitigate its effect.

Counting my unhatched chickens I envisaged my thousands of future worldwide businesses forming a critical mass altering the nature of the workplace into more enlightened expectations between workers, managers, and owners. I aspired from such a position of relative wealth to access people smarter than me to inspire and educate humanity toward a global republic that, bit by bit and country by country, put an end to organized conflict spawned in tyrannical deceit between states and groups. To once and for all build democratically legislated global law capable of resolving conflict as legally easily as it does today within a nation's borders. Of upholding the sanctity of individual life, liberty, and conscience. Of establishing an environment where national borders are as superfluous yet Tenth-Amendmently sovereign as between the 50 United States.

For those accepting Rev. Moon's *bona fides*, he's dealing with the internal, spiritual aspect of human Restoration. It's up to us as believers in Divine Principle's veracity to deal with the external, physical aspect and bring the spiritual and physical—the dream and reality—into harmony. Unificationists seem to expect him to lift all boats. In a very real sense that abdicates responsibility. He's a truth teacher, nothing more. He's neither diplomat, soldier, statesman, manager, politician, nor builder. Relying on him to change the world is the sheerest folly because he can't change *you*, only you can. That's the duty and responsibility of those imbibing his vision. A nation's leader charts a course but only the population can sail it, and so it is with Rev. Moon. It takes millions to redirect humanity. Never can one person turn the tiller but only give a heading. Those acting on his or her compass, however minutely, crew and steer the ship whether Hitler's Germany, Stalin's Russia, Mao's China, Rev. Moon's weirdly North Korean Ideal World, or the budding People's Republic of America.

This was the philosophy I adopted for my part in CFT. But it was only stargazing absent capital and has yet to bring me even moderate wealth. Evidently, successful dreams require a sense of money, good judgment, sound decisions, and a reasonably happy home. It seemed I was proving I embodied none of it.

BILL AND BARRY had a long history dealing with weirdos and strange government entities in their quest to bring PHARLO to market. They accordingly had a go-slow policy wrapped around tight security. Because its different iterations made it useful as a pesticide plus a pharmaceutical, it was critical not to confuse fifth columnists in the FDA. It could screw us out of important markets since it was unlikely to approve a pesticide for pharmaceutical let alone food use. In its ignorance and skepticism not to mention industrialized spread-leg corruption, the FDA could simply ban PHARLO outright. But even with these dangers hanging over our corporate heads, Bill and Barry were glacially slow releasing *any* product to market.

"We need sales, Bill. We need to be in the market. We can't wait forever."

"Just wait a little longer, Chris. I promise we'll get there."

Pish! "At some point, somebody's gonna simultaneously invent or legally steal our technology. We have bills. *I* have bills."

"I know, I know. Barry and I are working the issues. It's coming."

I realized I'd deferred too much to Bill. I respected that he and Barry invented this stuff, invested (they said) over a million of their own money into it, and struggled to found their company long before Nimrod Kriss introduced me to it and we'd all founded CFT. I should've enforced my boundaries from the beginning as president and CEO, the business-making king regardless their policy-making veto. They were board co-chairs to be sure, but there's a practical difference between chairman and CEO. The division of labor was important here. I had a fiscal duty to operate the company in good faith, not let it moulder into the ground. I was mistaken to cede my verve to either of them, but it was my first serious CEO job and I was learning the politics. I attempted to enforce our founding charter. In April 1999 I talked with Bill on the phone and shot his fox right off the tree.

"The company needs money. We need to put a product out there. As CEO, that's my responsibility and mine alone to handle. You and Barry's job is to manufacture the product and produce the technical explanations to the investors or customers, whichever. That's what we all agreed to."

"I get what you're saying, Chris, but we don't want you doing any of that till I'm done reeling in Palmer." This was before the feds nailed him.

"That's been going on forever. It could *take* forever."

"He just sent us a contract," he said out of the blue. "We're almost there. You gotta hang on. Have faith."

"Well, that's just one iron in the fire, Bill." I wasn't sure I believed it. Palmer didn't seem a straight shooter. "In the meantime we need a product making money. Think about it: that'll motivate investment better than business plan promises."

"Barry and I are united on this, Chris. We want you to wait."

Well, *shit*. How far could I really push? They had to *make* the deuced products for me to sell. But no Palmer contract materialized. I faxed Barry a complaint that, among other things, Bill wasn't revealing the true state of the game, that *he* was doing things he'd told *me* not to do. He took it like a bola round the neck.

Unbeknownst to me, Barry and Bill had been having partnership problems verging on a falling out. Then Nimrod Kriss gave Barry notice he was moving home to Tasmania. He maxed out a heady stable of credit cards for cash.

"That's a lot of debt you're taking home for a fresh start," I said.

Snigger. "I'm not paying back a cent. And they'll never find me in Tas."

"You're *stealing* it?" *Tomayto tomahto* said the asinine smirk.

My fax only watered Barry's boiling grease fire. Bill said, "It's bad, Chris. He wants to restructure CFT to get rid of you, too. The *other* Moonie. Kriss led him to believe he'd have brought in 200 grand right away if we'd voted him CEO, not director of market development. He said he's in good standing to get Rev. Moon to invest big money without delay. That you can't, no way, because your church hates you." My gut knotted. I hung up and punched Nimrod's number to break a nail.

"That's total horseshit! You could've got Father's money, CEO or not."

"You're the reason we don't have investors, Chris. Nobody likes you."

"Maybe. But I haven't blamed you for no sales. What's your problem?"

Nimrod breathed a shrug. "Calling it like I see it."

"Yeah, all fish-eyed." Barry's Nimrod-built ill will for me heightened his strife with Bill, who still lauded me as the right man for CEO. If he could force me out, my best defense was partnering with Hank. They were anxious to keep him close to milk his potentially huge PHARLO market. I'd gatekeep it. Have Hank's access to PHARLO. It was a darn sight more lucrative than Bill's Orange-a-Peel.

Hank surprised me in late May offering it first. The next day I freewayed across the peninsula to work it out. I met him visibly distressed pacing his sunny St. Pete lawn on the cordless. He clicked off. "It makes me physically sick, Chris."

"That was Bill? What'd he want?"

"Barry and Bill went up to this guy Palmer's office in Boston to find out why they got so close to a twenty-million dollar investment only for him to back out."

"Wha—When was this?"

Shoulders nudged. "Recently. Well, Palmer said his CFO, Jeter Tess, said 'Chris is actively harassing me for donations, to join his church, attend events' . . ."

"*Me?*" Hands fisted. "That could only be Kriss!"

"Bill said Palmer told him and Barry, 'If this is how you're going to do business, then we don't want anything to do with CFT.' "

"Gah!" Eyes roved in thought. "Palmer's kind of a turd in the pool, though. He could've been faking as an excuse to back out for other reasons. I've heard stuff."

"Yeah, well, I don't know. I don't even *want* to know."

"Is that it?"

"You want to hear it? I don't even want to tell it." I nodded hard. "Bill said Barry went purple with rage. Couldn't speak a word. Bill said 'No way!' but Barry believed this Tess guy. He decided on the spot to dissolve CFT and get rid of you."

"*Whaa—?*" Nary a breath coughed up. My stomach heeled in my cowboy boots. Bill vomiting his news into *Hank's* ear, not *mine*, devastated me.

"According to Bill your other partner Donny . . . uhh, whozit, said that *you* said it's your policy to hang pictures of True Parents and Unification Church stuff in your CFT office when you set it up. Like a church business. You really said that?"

"I don't do that in my own fucking house!" I popped screws over our smarmy, white-haired, pockmarked, Janus scalawag of a director of regulatory affairs' calumny. I looked around for something to break, but everything was Hank's.

He tucked his chin. "Well, Bill said Kriss went person to person on your board spreading lies and negativity about everybody else till he'd sowed suspicion and distrust between and against everyone. Your whole board's got knives out now."

"My God! No wonder that motherfucker's running home to Tasmania."

Hank flexed. "He's leaving the country?"

Donny Dicke had stewed over his relationship with Barry. They'd been together for some years and he cleaved to the plumpest, juiciest tit. Nimrod had surreptitiously placed him in the unhappy position of having to choose sides, and so he did. Besides having to deal with Nimrod's jealousy over the CEO job, I had to contend with Donny's self-same jealousy and him secretly trashing me to Barry for the self-same reasons. These people were out and out bastards. Impossible partners.

I'd been bat-blind to it all, naïvely unaware of their sparking, live-wire politics. Tamela and I lived literally around the corner from Donny. Post-brouhaha he quit taking my phone calls, emails, and hid behind his front door when I walked over and knocked—I could hear his weaselly foot shuffle. In the blink of an eye he went from amiable friend and business partner who often had us over for coffee to a wary, stiff-armed stranger twisting a shiv in my kidney.

Days later I burned in fury when Bill crushed me like an underfoot Lilliputian confirming Hank's tale. "I knew Tess was talking about Kriss but Barry doesn't care either way." My heart pancaked. Hardly greater respect or trust did I possess than for Bill. In the weeks leading up to it he'd encouragingly said, "Don't worry, Chris, you're a member of our club forever." Now it looked like so much humbug.

"Well, what do you want to do about our partnership, Hank?"

He was flat-eyed. "You're a church brother and all, but nothing. I'm done."

Is this what you had in mind all along, God? Are my fruits from our business not for the sake of Your greater providence, to aid my ability to serve you and Father?

It *was!* I believed it absolutely. It was only natural for Nimrod Kriss to end up as Judas Turncoat, I belatedly realized. Anytime God works through people to attain a providential purpose, Satan ever waits in the wings for the chance to bollix it up. And now, cometh he forth to destroy it with our own fallen nature.

On Hank's curb that May day in 1999 I felt like the guy catching his wife 'neath a gym rat grunting, "Yes, yes, you! Not fatty!" at the litany of skullduggery, hatred, resentment, and dirty emotion swirling through CFT. My mind wandered to Shiori and Tamela, realizing how these same emotions had washed through her at my infidelity. And once again, repentance and sorrow flash-flooded my heart while I wondered if she'd ever set aside her bitter fruit to build a happy marriage with me. After all, I'd dumped Shiori four years ago and we hadn't even talked. Couldn't she see it was *her* I loved, *her* I wanted? If it wasn't Tamela, it was CFT. If not them, the church. *Fucking hell! Will I find no solace or repose in this life?*

Hank said, "If you want to save CFT and your role in it, you have to adopt Abraham's attitude toward Isaac on the altar. Be willing to sacrifice even CFT in Isaac's symbolic position for God's greater purpose. That's what Principle says."

"I'm not sure I have any sanguine feelings about *that*. Not one bloody bit." But hours of talking it over, and my heavy heart languorously bobbed to the surface of my tempestuous mind. A sense of hope brightened me. A smile cracked my moody, sullen face. "Thanks, Hank. I appreciate your advice."

"What're brothers for?" *Well . . . not bailing on the falsely accused, for one.*

"Exactly. You should be a church leader." He huffed. "Perhaps there's a way out of this. Maybe I can win by dint of righteous truth and convince Barry it was Kriss and not Chris who sabotaged Palmer. I just have no clue how."

"I gotta say, man, I couldn't be more disgusted with the sheer pettiness of it all. Sorry, but I want nothing more with any of you. I just don't have words to say what I'm feeling. See you." He patted my shoulder but didn't look back heading inside.

Sigh. CFT dissolved beneath my feet and Hank's awesome fuel technology sailed out of reach. I fell in my car and drifted three hours back to Cocoa with a heavy, dejected heart once again coming to grips with losing everything.

"Why do people attack me like this?" I shouted over the highway blasting through my four open windows. "What'd I ever do to Kriss? It was the board voted me CEO, not me." I battered the wheel. "It was Bill who marginalized that Tassie fucker for his sheer incompetence, not me. Fuck 'em all!"

I'd deferred to Nimrod's marketing experience and relationship with Bill as a friend. Yet, all the while, that double-dealing ratfuck plotted and schemed like King Saul to murder CFT and me with it for some deluded vengeance. He'd laid his character bare absconding overseas to rob his creditors.

A mere five days after I'd visited Rev. Moon at East Garden Bill said, "Barry never got over your fax. He's closing down CFT."

"He can't. And there's nothing wrong with it. Donny even approved it!"

"Well . . . we own seventy percent. We can do what we want."

"He's being so childish. He's pissed because he still isn't funded after you both sabotaged my pitches with contradictions. Anyhow, votes aren't by equity."

"Okay. Donny has Nimrod's proxy, so we have a board majority." *That snake.*

"It requires a unanimous vote to overturn the 'in perpetuity' clause."

"We'll push it aside. No sales or investment means CFT failed to perform."

"That fails because you vetoed every sales plan I tried to implement."

"Regardless." He paused. "We'll invoke our renewal option."

"That was for the first 90 days, Bill. It's been 14 months. It's expired."

He felt a sieve. "I guess I'll tell you. Me, Barry, and Donny held a board meeting yesterday. We confirmed Barry's decision to kill the company."

"Am I gonna keep finding out new shit the longer this call goes on?" Silence. "Well, a secret meeting violates notice. It's not even legal, Bill. Come on."

"It met the quorum. It's done." *These fuckin' people.*

If he hadn't hung up he might've disclosed he'd already signed dissolution papers. They arrived with eye-bulging horror in my next day's post. It relied on his bogus failure-to-perform claim. I responded with a 13-page give-'em-hell reply, answering their allegations point by point. However things turned out, I had to speak my piece with honesty, sincerity, and integrity. Hadn't it worked so well in the church?

Although I was playing businessman these days, I was primarily pursuing a spiritual track. I couldn't understand these developments in a regular business sense because, for me, human behavior is always traceable to spiritual realities. Satan exists.

God exists. The two fight for our hearts and minds. It's core Unificationism. I viewed myself in the church as a person called by God. Interpreted in spiritual terms major life events. Hank promoted it recommending Abraham's point of view vis-à-vis CFT. Flinging newspapers like Nimrod Kriss' lying smirk out the window, the scales fell from my eyes around 3 AM and I found a sort of clarity.

In a way, Hank was right. As Abraham had conceived Isaac I'd birthed, nurtured, and raised CFT. The tech was Barry and Bill's, but they hadn't known how to move it to market and neither had our marketing genius, Nimrod Kriss. I'd constructed CFT. Wrote the charter. All our founding contracts. Persuaded Barry, Bill, Donny, and the others to trust me and buy into Barry and Bill's offshore manufacturing trust that sold exclusively via CFT. For them to kill *my* business was akin to God killing Isaac. Abraham's course mirrored Jesus' later one. CFT was my mission, my spiritual purpose. Jesus raised his own and refused to accept its forcible dissolution, praying thrice for the cup to pass in order to salvage it till accepting the inevitable.

Why? From the Principle's point of view, the disciples failing their responsibility left Jesus no foundation to continue. They'd made common cause with Satan even if unconsciously. Had he pressed forward he'd be in the external, physical realm like any charismatic leader and doomed to failure. By allowing Satan to unfairly strike him through the crucifixion, he set up the condition to claim ownership over his spiritual mission and his followers' future success. Abraham did the same thing in his willingness to sacrifice Isaac. Both demonstrated they were living in the internal, spiritual realm and rejecting Satan's home turf.

It was incumbent upon me to remember that I was no simple businessman striving to win my riches in a dog-eat-dog world, but a man of God striving to win financial resources to pursue God's bigger picture. I have to admit, this dichotomy in my thinking might've sabotaged my ability to succeed in business. I'd arrived at no sharp conclusion by 2003, but Rev. Moon brought heady success in his financial endeavors. *Why not me? Am I stupider?* Apparently. I told my journal May 27,

> Barry and Bill will lose control over their technology, or something equally calamitous . . . It's the pattern, so it'll happen.

Unificationists see what goes on around us as reflections of biblical events and relationships because of Divine Principle's parallels of human history. A lot of my self-awareness predicated on a robust conviction that God was calling me to some mission in that context. I knew I didn't join the Unification Church to rise to chief toilet officer. I was smart and capable. It was only natural to see myself reflecting events in Jesus' life as I struggled to develop financial and personal power in and out of the church. Everything I applied myself toward was to realize God's will as I understood it at any given moment.

On July 11, 1999 Barry and Bill called a special board and shareholders meeting at a Cocoa attorney's to end run our contract and ignominiously kill CFT. Godwin secured several proxies and tried for Nimrod's but he'd left it with Donny Dicke, serpents to the end. It decided the 1-vote margin to dissolve and liquidate CFT.

"What a fuck job, Bill!"

"Don't take it so hard."

"One and a half years of my life? Thousands of dollars? A move to Florida? My reputation on the line with my contacts . . . ?"

"It's nothing personal," Barry said.

"It feels pretty personal after all your and Nimrod's shenanigans."

"Don't fight us on this, Chris. Behave and let us have our way and there *will* be a place for you in the future. You have my word."

Now that was some bald *caca*. "If I sue for breach? How's 40 million sound?"

Bill snorted. Barry's face was flat. "It's clear you have a lot of potential. Nobody's denying your skill and ability here. I agree with Bill on that."

That's new. "Sounds like a euphemism for the blade."

"Not from me, Chris," Bill said. "Just take it on the chin. It's how it is."

I shifted my gaze. "Why'd you cut me off in May, Don, when evidently all this started? I thought we were friends." His silence was malice percolating viper eyes. "Right. Okay. I see the manure pile you're living in."

CFT's dissolution was an anticlimax. Grinding along to my Cocoa home, a sense of peace and relaxation fell over me. I'd done my best. Prayed my guts out for God's guidance. Made every effort to find solutions to each issue thrown as gauntlets to my feet. Humbled myself to understand what I'd done wrong. Now I was resigned to it. Of course, I grieved. CFT might've been my one and only shot at rising to Rev. Moon's financial level. I was right about future calamity. As of 2003, neither technology has come to market. Barry and Bill shortly had a final falling out and dissolved their partnership. Bill developed a different way to manufacture a superior version of PHARLO not covered by Barry's patent and it ended up in his hands. He went into business with Japanese gazillionaire Mr. Azuma and Mr. Oiwa selling a PHARLO-based breath freshener in Japan. No royalties for Godwin and me introducing them. Donny Dicke deservedly vanished into impoverished obscurity, ignored by Barry's now shriveled tit. Friends averred how Nimrod ruined his second church-arranged marriage and continues on a slimy Tassie con artist. Hank was Hank.

A truism is that evil declines and good prospers. I'd kept my principles over my 18-month CEO tenure and I'm proud of that. I never lied to or cheated anyone. The worst one can say is I was too naïve . . . and maybe not so good at my job.

WITH CFT GONE, I had to hunt up some gainful employment like a Yang lioness. Cash flow, baby. It's life. Meanwhile my marriage was on the skids. Tamela blamed it on CFT's breakup. Sure I was edgy, irritable, and unhappy. January to July we were bearcats over a plump carcass. The real reason was that I'd lost all patience with her abuse, sleep deprivation, and unwillingness to better herself.

I was reasonably happy and relieved after those mooks dissolved CFT. In that respect, I was at peace. But Tamela and I were slashing throats, so clearly it wasn't my entrepreneurial fall motivating me to jump in her face at every opportunity like she claimed. That was only blame-shifting projection. We'd had to move in June from our posh, gated community—exclusivity didn't prevent some slob poaching my tooled Western wallet from my car—to a 2-bedroom condo in a lower-middle class complex across the Indian River in Cocoa. It took $450 a month, a life-saving discount over upscale Merritt Island. I was now slinging 1,000 papers a day for $425 a week because my boss Gary liked me and looked out for opportunities to expand my route. It made my life a greater hell, of course, but you take the good with the bad. It hadn't taken long to develop tendonitis in my left arm. My shoulder agonized whipping these light-yet-weighty tubes of news and entertainment out the window or over the roof to right-side lawns seven nights a week, month after every unfunded, Palmer-lying, Nimrod-scheming, Donny-douching, Barry-hating, Bill-prevaricating month. It ain't kids' stuff on bikes anymore. It's *work*.

Cowboy dress-up in Cocoa.

We brought all our animus into our new home. Tamela was six months pregnant when we moved. Her hardest yet. She was whipped. Jolted sore by ever more pains and kicks from our unusually rambunctious, probably pissed off, third child.

"I wan' me damn tubes tied," she announced.

"The hell you say!"

" 'De social waahk-uhh an' doct-ahh 'dem tell me so." They were self-righteously teaching her childcare, work behaviors, and money management.

"Why? Because of your reading?"

Her face said, *yes*. "No. 'Dat ain' be it."

"They come right into our house pushing their tetchy religion all over us. Now they want you—?"

"Wha' religion? 'Dem be social waahk-uhh! 'Dem say you ha' no business tellin' me I can'a tie me tubes. You don't rule me. 'Dem jus' be tryin' to help us. Chris, we ha' no money!"

"These meddlers have the temerity to trash *me* for disagreeing? As if a *married woman* is an island unto herself? I want more children and *you* demanded this one! Catholic family building doesn't quit just because I joined the Moonies."

"We ha' no money an' I tired! You a' t'ink t'ree is enough?"

"I won't be poor forever. Heck, you're only twenty-five. Isn't that ridiculously young for outsiders to be persuading a married woman to take herself out of making babies against her husband's wishes? These people have no respect."

"Yeah . . . maybe. I a' know. 'Dem say I should jus' do it on me own."

"Without telling me?" A dirty-water dishrag slap.

"Yes. 'Dem ready tek me. But . . . I wouldn'a do it wi'out tellin' you. 'Dem ge' aahll up in me face for it." I appreciated anew her scruples.

"These—" I'd so tensed I could hardly talk. I took a breath. "It's *our* business, not theirs! They can fuck off! You and I can settle it. I mean, if you were over 30 or had some medical issue . . . yeah, fine, I get it. But you're not."

" 'Dem say t'ree is enough, too. An' I should tie me tubes—"

"So no more black babies enter the world. That's what they mean."

"Pssh! Some are black Ameree-caahn. An' anyway our chilleren be mix."

"You know what I mean. Their BS ideology hates blacks. That's why they hate themselves and you know it. Telling you to tie your tubes! They know your white man, whom they hate you for marrying anyhow, wants children and push you to tie your tubes behind my back. Do-gooder busybody motherf—telling you to choose between tied tubes and *me*, your *husband!* Self-loathing, liberal, man-hating . . ." So, we got to tussle over children, too.

What now stood out was her virtual abandonment of family responsibility. She dumped hers on me regardless my midnight–8 AM worknight. She was obviously depressed but I didn't properly notice in the raging depths of my own.

"I wan' stop cussin', Chris. I do!"

"You keep saying it, but every day your fighting ways is all I get. If you wanted to tie your tubes, why'd you even let yourself get pregnant again?"

"I t'ought it would win you back to me and mek peace." She plopped on the bed.

"I didn't go anywhere! There is no 'winning me back.' "

"Well, that you'd love me bett-uhh, then. Tha' we wouldn'a cuss."

"I already love you, like, totally. You gonna tie me down with babies like Gulliver on the beach but never quit cussing me to death at the same time?"

"Who it be, Gullee-vaah?"

"Shiori. Money. Church. Florida. CFT. Always something! *Just. Stop. Cussing!*"

She wasn't sliding out of my heart for want of children but because her abuse had risen to military levels. She'd denied me so much sleep I'd averaged 2–4 hours a night for eight months. I was shattered. Played out. Nigh prostrate.

Then she quit washing dinner dishes after work. "If I cook, you wash."

"If you were working and studying your books four hours a day, that's reasonable. But you're not. I'm earning most of our bread and taking care of the kids while you're over at Baymont all day. You need to run some of the home fires." While she worked, I made breakfast and lunch for the children, cleaned the kitchen, and kept our house in reasonable condition so she didn't come home to wreckage. "I'll happily do half if you spend at least four hours a day on your reading."

"Wha' mek you push me so hard for readin'? You only love a wife wha' read?" My mouth worked but nothing came out. "It be you need help more wi' housework roun' here. An' take bett-uhh care o' me!"

I'd realized in May while scribbling a shredded heart into my journal that I was falling out of love with her. Even though I had a tremendous sentimental connection—as for Shiori after leaving her for Tamela—I was losing all interest in maintaining our massively dysfunctional relationship. I wrote that, in addition to refusing to clean the kitchen after even one meal and stealing my sleep, she was refusing to take the children to the park, brush their teeth, put them to bed, tell them stories, deal with them in the night if I was home (trying to sleep for work), handle the grocery store without me, leave me be at the library studying résumé building, and putting together my portfolio for my post-CFT IT job search. Many nights I was so enraged that peaceful, restful sleep was delusional.

Sex was almost nonexistent. We slept in our bed like strangers on a train. When she felt it she said, "Ge' fat and le' we sex."

"I'm not a toy you wind up. What's wrong . . . ?" We quarreled hours over her implacable demands and my grim refusals. "Where's your romanticism? Where's your love? Where's your heart?" Where was her tender touch and soft lips filled with the electric energy that used to fire up my body and energize my love? "Why you demand sex like you're ordering a meal or a tank of gas? Damn!"

"Wha' maahn turn down he wom-aahn less he done ha'. . . ." And, here we go.

Many times she forced me to satisfy her when all I wanted was to sink into the mattress and disappear. I felt raped. Yeah, if you're a woman reading this you might feel satisfaction with some male comeuppance, but you'd be wrong to cheer a man's mortification for a historical crime that, by the way, cuts both ways. Sex not tenderly advanced nor lovingly given is never lovingly got. Lying in bed with my wife, I felt lonelier than a man freezing to death at the north pole.

Just as the powers-that-be at UTS failed to understand the nature of force and violence if it wasn't physical assault, Tamela couldn't understand how her loveless demands, unremitting psychological pressure, and willingness to badger and quarrel till I capitulated was brutality. It isn't only physical attack inflicting injury but mental and emotional coercion inflicting psychic wounds through words, body language, withheld affection, manipulation, and placing a victim into an untenable position: "If you do *this* for me then I won't do *that* to you." It's slavery's calculus. Life with her was shuddering into my conscious mind as *abusive*. I was imagining our home a POW camp and Tamela my opposite-day Colonel Klink.

"Sometimes I wonder if I even love her anymore, or even want to," I whined in ink. "Yet,"—ever eager to step into another's shoes for the sake of fair play, I'd find reason enough to preserve our manic marriage—"there is some power there that keeps the love alive. It must be God, don't you think?"

Maybe. More likely it was the Tamela that I'd married and loved periodically peeking out from behind the hateful hoodlum that somewhere back in time took her place. It's common to wonder what happened to the person you married. Certainly, she asked it of me. And she was right. I'd changed. I was an angry, resentful, ever stormier man. But she was wrong about its source.

She believed I'd changed because the church had abused me, Rev. Moon hadn't listened to me, CFT was stolen from me, my family didn't love me. Yes, all that affected me, wounded me, left my heart a bitter pail of gall. But it hadn't changed my behavior. They'd maimed me, aye, but hadn't made me a walking time bomb, my fulminant heart just raring to detonate. In some respects, my suffering raised up even greater determination to rise spiritually higher, to develop a truer communion with God and better adhere to the Principle and Jesus' teachings. The slings and arrows shot my way brought more reflection to my failings and a striving prayer to rise to a real Christian—more Moonistic—standard.

The central reason behind my diminishing goodness was my dysfunctional home life rooted in my relationship with Tamela. Day and night we brawled, battled, screamed, hurled objects, put the children in crossfire. There were happy moments in all this, I must say. We laughed, played, visited the beach, saw movies, and enjoyed happy Sunday afternoons with her delicious cooking. Yet, these moments were more and more just falling stars, fleeting aberrations outside the steady norm, the exact inverse it should be. My daily life was conflict and pain. A man struggling through this economic world absolutely needs a peaceful home and a loving wife to balance the keel else he goes mad as if combating the enemy impaled every day on his own comrades' implacable hostility and scorn till willingly throwing himself into pitiless enemy fire before sucking up a second more of their psychic torture. So I felt.

I'd started wondering again, *Is there a way I can be killed? Should I chuck all these newspapers and disappear into the sunrise? into the Banana River?*

Sometimes her abuse left me so black with fury I was back to longing for a cop to attack in exchange for a peaceful cell. Even that seemed a cleansing experience. When your heart and soul are tortured and troubled, abusing your body oft-appears the best medicine, your only drug. The church calls it 'indemnity conditions' albeit with fasting, prayer, cold showers, and the like in mind. In these moments I could only think of beatings and death. Something ruthlessly violent.

Yet, God in His wisdom and mercy kept my flagellant hand at bay. It seemed a cop was never there till my emotions cooled and reason reasserted. If no one loved me, I believed God did even if He couldn't advance any peace and prosperity into my life. He kept me alive, whole, and safe—*aye, Chris, things could be worse.*

Tamela began arguing over something and like a flashover it escalated into full-blown shrieking because she wouldn't stop nor allow me to disengage. The reason our disputes rose to violence at all is that she wouldn't permit me to *not* respond. If I attempted silence or said, "Let's drop the argument, I don't want to talk about it now," she only more apoplectically ranted. I was compelled to say something, anything, in a vain hope of tranquilizing her but only ever maddening her temper. Either what I said confirmed her worst suspicion or it sounded like a dodge. No matter what, I couldn't bring peace nor unlock our horns. At some point I shorted out and we physically battled at the front door, me struggling to get out and Tamela grappling to keep me in . . . all the while furiously damning me.

Occasionally, she broke down and cried—possibly as momentarily overcome by strife as me or just a cynical tactic—begging me to stay and promising to stop cussing. Now and then I did. More often than not I was incineratingly ablaze and mad to get out, get away, get into free, clean air to vent my rancor . . . once so uncontrollably that I punched a stop sign and broke my hand for a second cast. If she successfully caged me in the house, I stalked the rooms a broody captive tiger ready to lash out at anything. Our kids could only hide or proffer some childish comfort. If I made a break for the door, it was a fifty-fifty chance I'd make it first with time enough to wrench it open and flit through before her body crashed against it, slamming it shut. I called 911 on a lark. She batted the phone out of my hand.

"Don't you *dare* call no po-lice 'pon me!"

"Or what?" I thundered back. "You gonna kill me? Go on, then! Do it! *Do it!*" I pounded my chest till my sternum felt bruised and cracked. And then in a potential turning point she left the house. New behavior. "Right on! Get out! Get away from me! Take all your time coming back, too." Later, we talked. "Now, why could I so easily let you go and you can't let me?"

"I jus' afraid you is nev-uhh come back."

Really? "What about our children? Don't I love them?"

"Me a' know!" There was no reasoning with her. She was what she was.

I quit believing she loved me anymore, if she ever did. She loved me in some strange, codependent way. That's not love. It's danger. I was realizing codependency explained our relationship. Her reading skills were kindergarten level or worse. She couldn't work a normal job nor get around town till she'd been taken on routes she could memorize. Dependent, she was. By now, I was thinking she'd only married me to escape her dingy St. Vincent life and loving me was accidental. Though we'd seemed to love the other independent of other motivations for marriage, it was unsustainable. We lacked compatibility and a functional dynamic, the give and take which alone creates the energy of life and love. Our relationship devolved into needs and wants. If they weren't met then resentment festered till war broke out. It's a simple dynamic, even animalistic. And nothing I wanted in my life. I'd rather be single and lonely if not dead than endure such a violent addiction.

After she'd stormed out the front door I'd flitted like a hornet. I couldn't sit nor relax. Most of all I couldn't bear the thought of her coming home with all her negative emotion that would swirl around me all over again like carnivorous midges. Choked with a demented, desperate despair I hurriedly dressed the children and bundled them into the car.

I gently said, "We're going to see grandma."

Kal-el whined, "Isn't mommy coming?" Plattered eyes had attended our fight, terrified as our screaming increased, hard objects got flung, and our door-wrestling edged ever closer to total, unrestricted warfare. I was viscerally infuriated with her for turning me into a psychopath and a bad father. Once or twice Kal-el was even collateral damage. I raged indignant yet helpless. All I wanted was an end to her belligerence. Peace in my time even if a Chamberlainian delusion. Whatever I did, she found some bone to chew. If things went on like this, I reasoned, the children might get seriously hurt. I couldn't endure that. They couldn't stay. Time to fly.

"Your mother's staying here, Kal-el," I finally answered. "You know how she's been fighting with me. It's not right and it's not good. We'll see mommy again soon, don't worry. She'll be all right . . . we'll all be all right."

I was deathly afraid she'd growl up before I got out of the house and parking lot. I buckled the children into my Taurus sedan's rear seat and practically burned rubber. But you know, I just didn't have the heart to leave her like that. *Goddammit! I punched the wheel. I want to!* My mind was shrieking to not look back. *What'll I tell my folks?* They didn't know what was going on, that Tamela was abusing me. How would I even get to Colorado or California? I hardly had any money from my worthless newspaper job. One-fifty a year to this? *Fuck!*

Confusion reigned. Determination melted with my agitation. My white-hot mood cooled. I wondered if I was doing the right thing. Instead of heading for the interstate, I drove the children over the bridge onto Merritt Island and into Cocoa Beach where Major Nelson and his smoking-hot genie yukked it up in the sixties, then north for NASA. In the darkness the booming concussion of rocket engines reverberated through us. Up, up, up into the black sky went a seething trail of bright fire and white smoke. I shimmied to a sandy roadside stop before we missed the show and pulled out the children. Kal-el on the trunk lid 'neath the open sky. Kir-el in my arms. We craned necks for a look at this incredible, ear-splitting machine blasting into outer space. The ground physically trembled up our legs. Humid air vibrated our skin in deep, pulsating waves. A roar filled our ears. We marveled at the power of Man to push that fuckton of a rocket ship to the stars atop a barely controlled explosion.

The awe and wonder of it considerably lightened my demeanor. Driving aimlessly another hour or so, I made abortive forays toward the highway of help. The children snored in their car seats. I shut off the engine in front of our house and lugged them in. Tamela was at the door, eyes drooling suspicion.

"Wha' mek you leave? Where you been go?"

"Just calming down the kids on a drive," I lied.

DURING THIS HORRENDOUS period I recognized the contempt my family had for me. It seemed to me they despised the Unification Church and Rev. Moon. That my decision to join was the stupidest of my life . . . *next to marrying Tamela*, they damn sure didn't have to say. I sent my résumé to my father for advice.

He emailed back that I'd been a loser all my life following Rev. Moon. "It seems to me you're only just now growing up. Your résumé is pretty clever covering up your strange work history." Were it paper, I'd have crumpled and tossed it. For 22 years I'd supported myself; nothing "strange" about my work history at all. I simply omitted jobs having nothing to do with the one I was searching for and emphasized my skills and experience that did. By 1999 my history included IT consulting, full-time coding for the Fortune 500, my startups in St. Vincent and San Francisco, office managing there and in Hawaii . . . all real experience that conveyed high-level skills and the responsibility I was seeking. I omitted when I wasn't working or employed by the church, except my COO accomplishments with Godwin on the '97 and '98 Blessings. I never believed I had to explain to anyone why I joined the church or graduated UTS. What mattered were my skills and relevant work history. My résumé focused on that. I had to work with what I had but never faked it. If pressed in interviews, I explained myself. Dad's scornful intimation I was deceiving the world poisonously nettled me. He wrote, "You live like a wanderer from the 1850s who's just an anachronism now. You aren't serious about work. We're all concerned you'll run off at the next adventure. Your siblings are declining to pass around your résumé for that reason. They don't feel your reliability justifies the risk. We hope you understand."

You're all deluding yourselves. Since 1981 I'd followed a simple career plan: get Blessed, graduate from UTS, work directly with Rev. Moon, and somehow grow wealthy as a business owner or else rise to solid middle class. How'd my unexpectedly bumpy career path differ from joining the priesthood aimed at the Vatican or my family's to marry, graduate in a field, work a meaningful job, and prosper?

I'd achieved two of my four goals. My big worry was financial as I worked to survive. I knew I'd never develop wealth beyond a fat, here-today-gone-tomorrow salary without owning my own cash flow. Hence, I'd founded CityMatch, the *St. Vincent Times*, my consulting firm *Tropical Multimedia*, then CFT. I had sufficient experience and skills to continue as a software and relational database engineer, project manager, and even fill a chief officer slot operating in a small company. I was not some incorrigible *wandersman* who couldn't hold a job.

The other stake in my heart was zero cashflow. I wasn't seeing how I'd make next month's $300 payment on my 1996 green Taurus I'd got for our relocation to Florida after my white '88 dropped stone cold dead (Tamela had driven our floor-to-ceiling, box-jammed red '89 Taurus wagon behind me down I–95's 'iron pipeline' on our move, recovering from a rear tire blowout at 70 MPH that I'd white-eyed through the green car's rearview with a stopped heart; *totally impressed*), but I'd borrowed its $13,000 off my trusting UTS friend Rachel's credit cards. I couldn't default on her. Tamela persuaded me to call my sister Mona, suddenly well off from tech-boom stock options.

"I can't decide on my own," she said, referring to her fiancée. "I need to ask Bob's permission, too." They agreed to a $12,000 loan I'd pay back once reemployed.

My old New York mainstay Caribiner called in September with an emergency project in Atlanta. They paid me $12,500 for three weeks' effort to save two projects threatening lawsuits. I hoped it would segue to full-time consulting or employment, but they had nothing. Then possibilities opened up with Caribiner New York and my other cornerstone, Jack Morton. Things were unexpectedly looking up. We spent most of their money on debts, bills, computer equipment vital for more consulting gigs, and used the rest month-to-month as I hunted full-time work.

On hiatus from newspapering at Caribiner Atlanta I took Tamela's call. "My frien' quit 'de firs' night an' I can'a do your job wi'out she. Gary say you fired."

I snorted hot tea. "How could you frickin' do that?" I steamed at her, careful to avoid swear words that only triggered her quarreling over my language.

The phone shrugged. "She drop 'dem newspap-uhh at Gary feet an' lef'. I can'a do it me-self, can I?"

Our cash flow had come a cropper. "You could've if you'd only—" *Click.*

I rang Gary. "I just found out what happened! What can I do?"

"I knew you gone a few weeks wouldn't work. Had to give away your route."

Back home, he offered me a different, much lower-paying route. I took it but realized my second night training that, if I kept it, I'd forever doom myself to poverty in Florida. I'd already spent four months looking for work from Orlando to Miami as a janitor, secretary, programmer, Disney cruise sailor . . . I got nothing. Employers saw me as too educated and over-qualified for jobs too easy to fill. I stupidized my résumé to get interviews, but the second I opened my mouth employers heard 'educated' fall off my tongue and dropped me like a hot potato. No one wanted me smarter than my work sweeping, answering phones, typing, filing—Disney World, especially. Its cruise ship took one look at my white skin and palmed me right off their brown-crewed boat. Computer work of any kind was alien to central Floridians. The Sunshine State absent CFT's hope was bleak and hopeless on every front.

IN THE MIDST of all our fighting, poverty, and despair Tamela gave birth in nearby Rockledge to our third child, L'or-el (to the light of God). I persuaded her to stay true to our Old-New-Completed Testament convention and she settled for Auntie Nathalie taking middle place. As an act of friendship and because I couldn't think of one myself, In Hoi Lee provided her Korean third name.

There was something special about her, I could feel it. She was born on the 10th day of the 10th month of the 10th year of the 10th decade of the 20th (2×10) century at the 40th minute of the 4th hour of the seventh day (Sabbath). She weighed in at 7 lbs–7 ozs and stretched 21 inches. These were pivotal, weighty, profoundly meaningful providential numbers in Unificationism as well as the Bible.

"What does God have in store for her?" I queried my journal.

She was a beautiful baby and I loved her. Kal-el was a Dad clone at birth. Kir-el shiveringly mimicked Shiori for some years. L'or-el had a look all her own and a sanity-shattering scream from the get-go that was maybe all our cussing now nestled in our arms. Our second Medicaid child, though . . . how could a white, middle-class American came to such a state? Did the church do this to me? Was my faith in Divine Principle destroying my ability to succeed in this world?

My parents arrived for two weeks with us. Shock and dismay colored their faces at our household's condition. Tamela's abuse especially rattled them. She blocked me from finding a job and interfered with building my portfolio. Mom had long talks with her. Got to know her for the first time. Was unhappy with her discoveries. The three of them had some fiery run-ins. Even so, Mom basically liked her though Dad still seemed plenty uncomfortable. From my point of view, he had some historical issues with blacks from his Texas upbringing in the twenties.

MAN, I HAVE to escape Florida!

With great apology, I quit Gary's newspaper job the second night. I said to Tamela, "There's nothing here. I'm going to Washington to find a proper job."

"No, no! Don't go an' leave me here all alone."

"It's just temporary until a job. If we're going to survive, it's the only option."

She processed that. "How will you live in Waahshing-tohn?"

"I have church friends there like In Hoi Lee. You remember him." She uncrossed her arms at his memory. "I called Godwin in California. He's arranging space for me in the DC church that In Hoi runs."

"I'm scared, Chris. Do you really ha' to go?" I leaned back with open palms. I could tell she was petrified. "Okay, then. Hurry and ge' a good job!"

I reversed the green car from its space and puttered out of our sun-drenched parking lot the morning of November 19, 1999 sure I'd never forget Tamela standing at the curb with L'or-el in hand. Her tears waterfalled. My heart physically ached at leaving my blustery family with a sadness I couldn't fathom on the heels of all our combat. I thrilled at the road trip and adventure ahead anyhow—which did *not* make me my father's incorrigible *wandersman.* My own hot tears bleated steering for the interstate. So exhausted from sleep deprivation, I made it 20 miles up I-95 before nodding off at the wheel. I slept away most of the day at a rest stop.

The afternoon sun roused me. I gulped water and pressed the accelerator north. I tried to imagine if, on the other side of the veil through which I only saw darkly, I'd ever go from victim to victor. Because I so desperately wanted salvation from abuse, God laid open a road for me to take as I saw fit. Soaking in blaring rock-n-roll oldies over the hot wind ripping through my hair, I had no idea that within a few short months my life would upend in a way I never could've predicted.

Act XVIII

One Last Effort
Reverend Moon's Call to Washington

I chose Washington, DC because I couldn't stand the thought of another minute in New York City and because Rev. Moon had recently called on American members to pull up stakes for either town. He'd just relocated his world headquarters to America's capital from the New Yorker and West 43rd Street where Wren Meyer had so dastardly run me out in 1990 before he'd segued into fobbing off Magic Pens instead of members. Arriving in late November, HQ resided in a beautiful old colonial home on Upshur Street near 16th Street NW, an upscale neighborhood in the thick of the District sometimes lampooned as Hollywood for Ugly People. One could say Rev. Moon described it to a tee:

> Normally, those who are show-offs in an external way have very ugly internal characters, while those who are proud of their internal character often have ugly exteriors . . . Those who bring great damage to mankind—are they normally very attractive people or very ugly people? . . . those who were proud of their external appearance . . . [O]ften, those who have the features of an Idaho potato are the most loyal members of the Unification Church. (*Our Pride* 1981)

Remember he appointed Rev. Yang continental director "because he has a woman's face"? Maybe it was a backhanded compliment. Just saying.

He was shifting his center of gravity to the seat of the free world because the United States had "symbolically" turned the corner in its relationship with him. At a July dedication ceremony at his Jefferson House estate in McLean, Virginia for his rebranded Family Federation of World Peace and Unification headquarters at 7777 Leesburg Pike in suburban Falls Church he said,

> I consider Washington to be the city with the blessing. If it had not been for President Carter persecuting the Unification Church in the late 1970s, I would have established the Unification Church HQ in Washington DC, but instead I established the HQ in New York. . . . Now elder sonship has been established,

and I plan a glorious future for Washington DC. We have suffered for 40 years and now we are coming back to the original blessed position. (*Dedication* 1999)

For years, he'd condemned Americans for our ever more faithless ways and refusal to heed God's new and improved rod of iron barking from his mouth. He not-so-jokingly chided us that,

Asians appreciate being scolded, but Americans run away. (ibid)

This despite the inalienable fact that when it comes to loyalty to Rev. Moon, Divine Principle, and the need for sacrifice and suffering in the war against evil, American members often stand head and shoulder over the Japanese and Koreans. We require no stern, boot-up-ass orders from leaders to traverse the front lines with integrity. Conscience is all that initiative-minded Americans require. It galled me seeing Asian Unificationists bamboozle us into believing we were inferior and godless. Especially when it was godly America helping the Japanese and Koreans get both free and rich and Rev. Moon to keep his life out of his own people's graveyards.

Ironically, he believes "Americans have trouble uniting, even though they know the one God, and Jesus." Korea—the world—would do very well to appreciate with new awareness our 50 *voluntarily united* sovereign states dwelling in Psalm 133:1's peaceful unity, broken only once (a mere four years) in two centuries.

Frankly, his fact-challenged pronouncements about America, seemingly based on the most shallow observational perspicuity, have done more harm than good to our movement. He emboldens non-Christian Asians to disrespect and oppress American members and elevate their Asian cynicism and pagan institutionalism over Western optimism and its Christian ethos. While he proclaims in word the superiority of Jesus over all world religions, and Christianity the prerequisite to Unificationism, he thoroughly undermines both in deed with his constant drumbeat of Asian racial, social, and historical superiority . . . all cultures which have given little if anything to the progress of humanity much less the will of God.

Can't have it both ways, sport.

I **TOOK UP** residence behind HQ in the church residence on Varnum at 16th NW. A run down, rambling pre-war house the church was trying to infuse some long-needed TLC into on its usual maintenance pittance, it had maybe eight bedrooms on three floors. In Hoi Lee showed me to a small space on the northwest corner of the third floor crowded with junk like our *Ocean Hope 3* head with beer.

"It's okay? Sorry for the mess. It's all we have right now."

"No complaints, brother. I supremely appreciate your gift of a room."

Now to launch my frantic job hunt in a new city I knew virtually nothing about. I cleared a small desk for my computer and enough floorspace to accommodate my long frame in sleeping repose and made myself at home.

Vague memories of our 1964–71 Bowie, Maryland lair bubbled up hauling around town, street map locked hand-to-wheel. I remembered gazing unseatbelted out the tailgate of our station wagon along a shiny new I-495 Beltway, crowbarring cobblestones with Dad out of nineteenth-century downtown streets slated for paving, under the Washington Monument's red eyes oohing-and-aahing Independence Day's fireworks high over smoking grass, and gobbling 5-star pizza in Gusti's at 19th and M Streets NW. The more I traversed this town, the more nostalgic I waxed. Memories of Bowie took me to our old tract house at 3306 Memphis Lane to chat up remaining neighbors, track down my best elementary school friend Eric (a police lieutenant in Annapolis), and visit St. Pious X Roman Catholic Church where I was confirmed and served most of elementary school a black-and-white altar boy.

Civilizationally and geographically, I'm western-states. Thin-aired Rocky Mountains and painted, high-plains deserts ring up my soul, every breeze a whisper of my homeland reminding me of its physical beauty and spiritual solace; my undying yearning to return. However, what future was there for me? What silver or will-o'-God chance existed in cold mountain valleys and harsh desert plains? I needed success before I could return to my unsuburbia

Doing my bit protesting the Washington Post's materialistic, anti-Moon villainy.

of memory—a writer, seminar teacher, business owner . . . independent wealth, not an overboard-at-the-first-sign-of-trouble paycheck. I fixated on securing financial prosperity. How very unlike St. Augustine, who'd tossed off a *rhetor*'s career that he might more devotedly serve God. Well, there's the difference twixt ancient, early Christianity and modern, late Unificationism right there.

The Church of Jesus scorns the world, encouraging believers to keep alive their body as the gift of God and nothing more. The Church of Jesus' Successor embraces this world, encouraging believers to maintain our gifted physicality and billionairize it for the greater glory of God's Providence. Rev. Moon's heady climb from poverty, torture, and public scorn to world famous spiritual teacher and profligate moneybags is our prime example. I couldn't help but carry the burden of this dichotomy between my Christian heritage and Unificationist profession everywhere I went. Like a faithful if hungrily slavering dog you'd probably miss if it jumped ship, it never left my side. CFT was only my latest attempt to secure the blessings of prosperity that alone seem to prove one's true allegiance to God and Rev. Moon, not to mention Christianity and society at large. How he and his coterie of sycophants scorn impoverished members and embrace and praise those rich kinda-nonmembers blowing through our movement like tumbleweeds on a noxious wind!

To my dismay, I'd learned a bitter truth over my last 18 years: Rev. Moon loves and respects wealthy people regardless their low spiritual standard or infidelity to God and Divine Principle. In truth, he uses more than respects or admires them. But I'd be lying to myself if I didn't admit that, in spite of my intellect telling me that using the rich was the more important of the two, deep down I knew without a doubt that he *likes* the rich. They're successful at overcoming obstacles, as he is. Try as we might, all of us in this world seem to be Prosperity Gospelians at heart. The wealthy *are* blessed by God. They've transcended our scourge even if they stole their gold. If might makes right, then money justifies the soul.

Year in and year out I watched him lionize the wealthy while dissing the regular Joes earning his money in the first place as failures, cheaters, and thieves—

> Moonies are good at taking things; if someone brings something . . . you will take it. Moonies will do a little good . . . but then claim to have accomplished it all. You may consider such an attitude ambitious, but it is actually thievery . . . Sometimes you are like a robber or a thief. You are taking things without earning them . . . You American women may want to grab onto Father but if you do Father will kick you away . . . A high nose indicates that you are so proud of yourself. Your large and deep eyes indicate your arrogance. You have the hidden mind of thieves . . . Because your eyes are set deep it means you don't want people to observe you from the side. It is as if you are hiding in a way . . . Father's way of interpretation of the Western features is that your nose represents Satan's spear tip. Your eyes represent Satan's warehouse. Don't you agree that you are greedy? (*I Shall Follow With Gratitude and Obedience* 1987)

—latching onto his coattails for a stolen ride to heaven. Nothing more expresses our church institution adopting this attitude than Rev. Lee romancing multimillionaire Mrs. Iida's checkbook, an idly rich Japanese in Hawaii who couldn't have cared less about our church, Rev. Moon, or Divine Principle. Yet, he disgracefully sacrificed his regular—*poor*—members to win her signature on a seven-figure check. There's a lesson there. I suppose it's not so bad to consider wealth a sign of heaven's thumbs up so long as everyone can equally play. Unfortunately, the church condemns any and all activities that might bring wealth as wholly incompatible with the uncompromising devotion, obedience, and service to Rev. Moon that 'attending the Messiah' means; Tyler Hendricks' stand in 1998. *Make yourselves billionaires*, Rev. Moon says, *but don't let it interfere with your real (free) work*.

We devoted members accept this absurd duality because our eternal spirit life is more important than finite earthly success. But we forget our spirit life follows the earthly one. Even now, Rev. Moon talks about working directly with historical shitbirds like Adolph Hitler and Josef Stalin (allegedly repenting in spirit world only after recognizing him as the Second Coming of Christ) . . . even demonically evil success begets a greater respect than angelically honest failure and penury. Practically speaking, it perchance spews from the reality that even the loathsomely vilest, evilest person commands legions . . . turn the leader and all. Well, I can respect that. But not at the cost of pressing under mud the good and righteous who built his empire testifying to his messianism and selling flowers or building businesses to fund it.

I'd fixed my dream on the American West when 40 hours a week would eventually relinquish my soul. I've been torn decades in our church culture: build wealth or heaven? They'd seemed mutually compatible in Rev. Moon but more and more mutually exclusive in me. Unlike St. Paul and the early fathers, I took no satisfaction from poverty in the Lord. *Useless.* The impoverished wreak only strife in the dupery of their betters gaining power. Christianity required the wealthy then Emperor Constantine to adopt its Lord before transcending the disaffected, neglected rabble. It took Rev. Moon's billions and his followers' magnanimous service to preach his message around the globe so that mainstream religion might take Unificationism seriously enough to consider him a godly colleague however batty.

Washington was one more chance for me to achieve my spiritual and financial dreams: acceptance in the church and freedom from fiscal servitude. Lucien, creator of the best Unificationist website by 2003, pulled in as much as $180,000 a year as a c++ programmer. He donates tens of thousands to the church and they repay him with honors and acceptance because they want his money despite his ungovernability. Without it, to be sure, he'd be just another despised, nondescript 'B' member barely making rent. However many hours of life he donated to the cause he'd ever be a cashless nobody, his efforts unappreciated, unknown, unrewarded. Donate money in lieu of time and see our Koreans drop on bended knee extolling your fidelity to God's will, just as Rev. Lee coveted Rev. Moon's accolades via Mrs. Iida.

Nothing changes. Members rise to financial success only in reserving the church for Sunday mornings and consequential, once-in-a-while events. Just enough to consider themselves Moonies in defiance of the consensus of full-time fanatics believing anything less is flat-out rejecting God and True Parents. *But, oh, shameless me!* I wanted to be like Lucien, like my bookstore-owning friend Andrew, the convenience store-owning Peter. To earn more than mere rent and food; savings for dire times. Donating substantial monies to make God's Restoration providence a reality. *I want respect and acceptance from my peers, goddammit!*

And not even my UTS diploma conveyed it. Tyler, working at DC's HQ, wounded me saying, "What does *that* guy want?" upon hearing I'd tumbleweeded in.

"What do you think?" I later replied in a chance meeting, recalling muted New Mexico. "I want to participate with True Parents building world peace and the kingdom of heaven on earth. I'm not done. I haven't quit. Why not let me?"

I got a whole-body shrug and God's icy shoulder. *Why am I hated so? How do I so offend these Moonies to brush off my every effort forever with a yawn or scornful suspicion?* All around me leaders and members cheat on their spouses, embezzle public monies, viciously abuse and degrade their brethren, or thrust on Rev. Moon legal, financial, and reputational distress. Yet, I alone seem routinely singled out for ostracism no matter how honestly I devote myself to the cause.

And for what? The worst any member can say about me is that I had trouble with love. Yes, in my quest for care and acceptance—denied the Blessing eight times—I fell. Then (*gasp!*) married a nonmember *while kicked out of the church*. But it's a red herring. My real sin in the Unification Church was the effrontery of taking Divine Principle thoughtfully. To critically study it as Rev. Moon demands. To pray over and ponder it. Question it and leaders. Struggle to make it my own as something I *knew*, not just *believed*. In seeking the learner's not the votive junkie's path, I alienated those seeking obedience to their own interpreted Word.

Perhaps it's only now I truly understand the price I paid for taking seriously Rev. Moon's admonishment to build my own relationship with God through my own understanding of the Principle. Leaders abhor, loathe, *despise* being contradicted (Asians in particular) but, regardless pious pronouncements, he reviles it most of all as fire hates water. Thinking for oneself, questioning authority, following one's conscience first and best—uniquely American—is, among Unificationists, the devil's handmaiden. For Moonies, Satan lives amongst those least blindly following. This in spite of Rev. Moon's injunctions in the late '90s that conscience alone guide us.

Indeed, I'd followed mine pursuing CFT post-UTS even while available for any (never forthcoming) church mission in the belief that God was offering me an opportunity to walk in Rev. Moon's actual footsteps.

"You must build your own financial foundation," he told us all. "You must build your own spiritual foundation. You must walk the same path that I have walked in order to bring victory. This is Principle."

What was I to think? Take his words at face value or interpret his 'true' intent via some leader? Thousands of denominations war this way over scriptural and Judeo-Christo-Islamic interpretations of God. What good is it? If Rev. Moon didn't say what he meant or mean what he said, is it incumbent on me to figure out what he *did* mean by subtly reading between the lines? *No*. There's no value in that. When Jesus demanded we turn the other cheek, did he mean it literally, figuratively, just sometimes? How can we know? We can't absent a one-on-one with him, and even then the answer would be useful only to *me*; on what grounds could I possibly enforce it on *you*? As Rev. Moon says, we each of us follow our own unique path of Restoration. What's appropriate for me, now, may not be so for you, ever. This is why religious imposition is problematic and dangerous.

I HADN'T REALIZED how starved I was for spiritual food until visiting the Columbia Road church center (the old Mormon chapel) for Thanksgiving '99. Hunkering in a pew belting out Holy Songs, fingers whitening on the song book, tears leapt down my face as two decades of church life deluged me. I shuddered in the presence of God. I *belonged* here. As much as I hated the church institution, it was my home, my *family*. Long gone were the days members referred to themselves as "the Family" and to each other as "family members." But the ancient nomenclature was still a part of me. It formed my indelible sense of what our movement was and should be. It *was* my family. My *home*. It *was*!

I'd separated from it a whole year in Florida fighting with CFT and Tamela and sinking ever deeper into poverty and despair. Flinging all the news fit to print from my car in the dead of night, I might just as well have been throwing my life, my very soul, into the hellish darkness atom by atom. I felt rejected by my physical family, my spiritual family . . . maybe God. The only place I found respect or acceptance was in the professional world of work. It recognized, appreciated, and put to use my skills and abilities with a smile. Was the difference between work and church merely that between Satan's world and God's as my church friends chided me? If that was true, why would I want anything to do with God's? What kind of world is it where scorn and rejection form one's daily bread? No, of course they were wrong. God has nothing to do with the perverse world the Unification Church created for itself, nor for it steadily declining year over year.

Eyes bled my ruin where I segregated alongside the wall of the big meeting hall opened up behind the chapel. Though they'd finished I continued on, whispering the songs of my youth as the room clamored ever more loudly with laughter and conversation. I sat unnoticed as though cloaked by tears. Perhaps no one had the courage to approach a wet-faced man buried in a song book. After some time my emotions drained out. I put down the book and joined the delightful Thanksgiving meal. For the first time, I met Blessed sisters who were *divorced* and living alone or as single moms. And accepted by church leaders!

Whaaat! Why?

How'd they differ from me? Was it that they hadn't assuaged their loneliness or been caught at it? I wasn't the only member to screw up; many broke their Blessing. Though Jesus admonished us to pluck out our eyeballs if need be to frustrate our lust—what hardcore biblical fundamentalist takes *that* literally?—I knew I somehow had to unearth a route to real spiritual purity. Rev. Moon told us many times that, above all things, God considers it the greatest, most important possession because it was purity we lost in the Garden. When we look at the opposite (non-spousal) sex with all the banality of cold morning pizza then we're on the right road. It wasn't God's plan we live frustrated lives. We were supposed to lust after our spouse while the world's sexuality made little impression. Our innocence disappeared in the Fall when Adam lost his pure mate. In a sense, we're all searching for yet never finding him or her. Rev. Moon tried to address it in the Matching, with mixed results.

I'd wed Tamela with Shiori rioting through my blood; a corrupted union without even realizing it. Married to Tamela I lusted after Shiori because, despite rejecting marriage, I loved her. It naturally generated sexual desire. That's how God created us. Love begets sex which begets love in an endless cycle of give and take. That's why God considers purity our root possession. With it, all holiness is possible. Without it, compromised emotions master even the most conscientious saint—witness St. Paul's struggle with fleshly desire. It took several years and affairs to excise her from my heart to open its grand rooms to Tamela alone. Yet, I couldn't wholly love her either as she spent the majority of our time at war, verbally abusing and physically assaulting me howsoever emotion dictated. My grand rooms filled with shattered furniture and the debris of pulverized dreams. *Bramble House.*

Realizing how far I'd fallen short of God's glory, I resolved to do something about it. Thinking back over the course of Rev. Moon's life, I accepted that the only way to 'meet' him, to 'attend' him, is to be like him: a man of indemnity conditions. We can't meet God in the comfort of our living room. We need visit the wilderness and gain mastery over the physical body that drags our spirit from the seat of God. I set up a 40-day prayer and *kyum bae* bowing condition. In the Unification Church, full Korean bows to the floor are routine. Anytime a church member physically meets Rev. Moon—formally or just in the hallway—they're supposed to bow to the floor. In formal meetings all members bow to the floor, though in less formal situations members bow at the waist, Japanese style. It's a hateful practice to me. I view it as a sign of subservience, even slavery. Western civilization threw it out the window recognizing the intrinsic equality of the person as a child of God. Asians say they accept bowing the way we accept handshaking. *Hmm.* I can't help but view it as a mechanism of disfranchisement.

I mumbled to myself during one of Rev. Moon's visits to UTS, "Father, I bow to you now only for the sake of my ancestors, not for myself." *I reject it.*

Decades, and nothing's changed my mind. Unless he returns my bow with his own, respect is a one-way street violating the Principle's give-and-take action unless interpreting it to mean I give, he takes. To paraphrase Mencius: *that's bullshit.*

A person hasn't exercised till bowing 120 times a day. Sapped, I was. And decrepit. Knees bled out two weeks on my slatted bamboo mat till calluses formed. Legs quivered. Ten days I raced for the can to toss my cookies, though kept it down. Then I mastered it. Exhaustion and nausea passed. I felt pride. Not only accomplishing it, which I thought fantastic, but being on my road back to God. Out of my heavy indemnity condition good things would happen. I was separating Satan out of me, denying evil spirit persons any satisfaction hanging around, or in, me Dae Mo Nim style. I was purifying myself, mastering my body.

Members viewed me a fallen, problem member. In Hoi Lee strangely took me for a typically less-than-committed American despite UTS, WUSR, and my pitch to Rev. Moon. Though he'd welcomed me with a joyful smile and outstretched arms, he implied I wasn't worth his time, our rowing days done. In proportion to his surging aloofness I felt separated from the church I was trying to revive in my heart. Bit by bit it dawned the church never wanted me in its ranks nor would it ever, just as my spiritual mother Ginny had said. If I'd publicly proclaimed my bowing condition, would In Hoi and derisive members respect me, even admire me?

"Wow, he's doing 120 full Korean bows a day for 40 days!"

"I wish I could do that. He's so dedicated to God and True Parents!"

"A true member. I really admire him."

Mere fantasy, alas. I've always observed Jesus' plea we keep our special conditions secret to all but God, that we not be Pharisees and Sadducees shouting rooftop righteousness hither and yon. My bowing was secret and In Hoi never knew my dedication striving to find myself in the church. To rebuild my spiritual life. He never comprehended the ocean of love and commitment in my bosom for God and True Parents. So, he condemned with ease when he felt I'd failed *him*.

In the midst of my struggles with love, acceptance, and spiritual renewal I struggled for survival, too. I'd given up entrepreneurialism. I plainly sucked at it. My plans for wealth were undergoing a metamorphosis. Instead of *starting* a business, I'd now *buy* one. Why build a cash flow from scratch when I could have someone else's? A slap-your-forehead *doh!* moment. While making one more attempt—Earth Environmental Technologies (EET) to license Orange-a-Peel and PHARLO from Bill Merchant; "No, Chris, not doing it"—I hunted up a business to buy.

In the meantime I needed a job. Being 'just over broke' was infinitely preferable to simply broke. The president of an Internet startup hired me as a 6-figure chief technology officer but his outsourced, stock-optioned Russkie tech guru nixed it on the grounds I hadn't *personally* coded a million-hits-a-day Cold Fusion website. My best opportunity to date and I'd flubbed it. I knew I'd been too uptight and failed to convey my wide breadth of programming skills and managerial experience in a context such a hardnosed ex-commie could appreciate.

It didn't matter. I was entering the first stage of a complete nervous breakdown catalyzed by a DC woman who opened before me in stark and cruel relief the anger, unhappiness, and domestic violence permeating my life in Tamela, church, and family. In a moment of levity I unexpectedly discovered a world of peace, prosperity, love, and kindness that after 20 years in the church and eight years of marriage I'd forgot existed. It swamped then sank my world of war, poverty, hate, and violence

I'd unwittingly built and lived these past two decades. I discovered I loathed my world. And, man, I wanted out. Like, *right now*.

In mid-December 1999 I met Linda at a local networking event in DC's Virginia suburbs, the kind of schmooze-fest that might land me a chief officer or engineering opportunity. A slightly heavy, thickly maned, Japanese-black American ex-triathlete standing all of five-five, she was selling stakes in a broadband wireless technology her Hawaiian engineers cooked up. I'd idly picked a seat amongst the milling throng networking the lead-up for tonight's entrepreneurial presentations in the oddly abandoned front row. Advertisements and flyers lay scattered atop every chair. I couldn't tell those reserved from the unclaimed. Scanning the room, I caught this olive-skinned lass pushing in late. Beelining for me.

My thoughts popped. *Kind of attractive . . . in a hard-as-nails bitch kinda way.*

One of those perpetually knurly browed, cut-eyed American blacks. I assumed quite a bit in the seconds it took her to reach my seat. When it was obvious she was aiming to plop into the chair alongside, I snapped up its paper clutter which gave her a look of surprised appreciation.

Later on she said, "I figured you must be new in town . . . no DC man would've ever had the manners to clear a lady's chair."

"How would anybody not do that?"

"The men in this town are assholes. You get used to it. You're a breath of fresh air around here. I knew you were a gentleman when you moved all that crap."

I grinned. "Well, good first impressions and all that."

Right now I stole a few sidelong glances during the offerings. I was relaxed next to an attractive woman not cussing or condemning. It was too weird but exhilarating. Aside from presuming her angular, iron lines made the case for a hard-kick I'd never get along with, I paid her little mind. I ran into her again after the presentation as frenzied suitors dashed about lining up funding for, and interest in, their business ideas. Her wide open, gumtoothed smile aimed a split second my way grabbed my attention. I moseyed over to see what she was (professionally) all about.

A wireless broadband invention, you say? Patented? Broadband through the air? Crazy. Here's my card . . . thanks for yours. See ya.

I'd previously met Dennis van Dusen, a database consultant allegedly making $200 an hour. He instantly saw me on the make and offered the chance to get involved with a new incubator company he was trying to promote using another company and its 19-year old CEO for bait.

Nineteen? Man, I'd lost a lot.

He proved of no use. Never would he pay me a dime and was entirely unclear on just how he expected me to participate. Without his $200 an hour to fall back on, I gave up his fantasies to seek work paying actual money. Making my way out of the networking event I ran into him, his 19-years *wunderkind*, and Linda politely arguing over her technology. The kid was interested.

He warned his golden ticket, "So long as you're working for me, stay away from her kooky ideas."

"There's nothing 'kooky' about it," she said. "I can prove—"

"Stay away from her. Come on, let's go."

I sidled up. "Hey, Dennis. You don't think her technology is real? I'm pretty impressed by the potential." I felt a compulsion to engage her in conversation so Dennis didn't think he controlled me. "I mean, broadband through the air?"

"You're wasting your time, Chris. Don't say I didn't warn you." He chinned me drifting away. "We'll talk later." I exited the building with Linda.

She laughed. "I meet all the dweebs. Well, I'm headed to Ballston Metro."

"Oh, you live in DC?"

"Good guess."

"Me, too. I'm driving that way . . . you want a ride?"

She laughed and sized up the potential threat of trapping herself in my car. "I'm at Dupont Circle. You know where that is?"

"I live up at Varnum and 16th, so it's on my way."

"Okay, sure. No funny stuff."

Palms out, "Who, me?"

One interesting conversation later, which I wasn't sure I wanted to end sliding out of Rosslyn over Arlington Memorial Bridge, I dropped her at a 3-storey, scruffy white condo squeezed into a congested neighborhood.

"Thanks for the ride," she said, popping the door handle. "But if I can give you some constructive criticism . . ."

My antennae flared. "Uhh, okay . . ."

"In our conversation just now, you came off as a pretty arrogant jerk." Her eyes drilled me. "I'm not a hundred percent sure you really are, it might just be how you talk, but you should work on that." She giggled. "Goodnight, thanks again!"

Her door thumped closed. "Man, that's some bold shit." I gripped the wheel stunned, appreciating her sashay up the steps to her hot-red front door. Dad waited for his drop-off to safely get indoors and I did, too. "I've only known her an hour and she thinks I'm arrogant. Damn, just like the church! What am I doing," as I wheeled out of Dupont up 16th Street, "that makes people think I'm arrogant?"

Ever since John Jones at Jack Morton first mentioned me waxing arrogant back in 1990, I'd struggled—"Figure it out yourself," he'd said—to know how I conveyed the impression. I was opinionated, sure. Passionately so. But no more than the next guy and often less so. I'd recognized how my passion in love and intellect created trouble with the less passionate, those who think a man should be eminently flexible because principles aren't rules as such but guidelines in a real politik sort of way. For me, they were inflexible. If murder's wrong, it's always wrong. No leeway. If I believe God exists and He's good, that Jesus is the Messiah then there's no give. How can there be? Church members taking a flexible view on Rev. Moon's messianism—"Well, I can't say for certain he is in fact *the* Messiah," his spokesfolks say, "but I personally believe he is"—viciously attack me for it. *Equivocate, thou snivelers!* It only ever builds doubt in others and then self-doubt. So, great job witnessers.

"Is Rev. Moon the Messiah?" we're asked.

"Yes, absolutely," the Unificationist should plainly state. "You should investigate the matter and make your stand." Christians don't pull their punches about Jesus. Why should we? Don't we *believe* it? passionately?

I'm told it's my tone of voice. The sense that maybe in my passion and conviction I don't care about their viewpoint. That they're wrong; further conversation moot. Seems a matter of diplomacy then, since conviction by its very nature considers counterargument wrong. I never equivocated on Rev. Moon's messianism. Except now. I can't say I'm a 100% certain because he can be just too much an ass to be the Messiah. That's not necessarily a disqualifier. Jesus wasn't all that subtle, kind, or quiescent in his day. Linda hadn't fathomed out that some topics were unequivocal for me. Still, it was unsettling a brand-new acquaintance so quickly pegged me an "arrogant jerk." At this rate, I'd never develop friends and allies in this town.

Even if I had a problem with arrogance, it's unconscionable for church leaders to embargo me over it. The church is replete with dictionarily defined and detestably arrogant leaders inspiring most of its members the last 20 years to vote themselves out as it devolved from "the Family" to a feudal alliance in loose, sometimes disputed, fealty to Rev. Moon. They ostracized me all the same. Arrogance—independent thinking leading one to not blindly follow Rev. Moon's *Unterführern* if not Rev. *Überführer* Himself—is one of their chief complaints with me. There's nothing I could hope to do about a charge of that nature. It meant everything and nothing; I was guilty the day I joined. Actual arrogance I could work on. With help from a caring soul, I might at last understand what it was about me lighting their wick.

A no nonsense, independent-minded, entrepreneurial go-getter running her own startup firm, Linda intrigued me. When was the last time I met a woman like that? *In my dreams.* Five days later her email invited me for a Saturday afternoon get-together at her condo. She buzzed me in through the main door and greeted me at hers in a Hawaiian *muumuu* that accentuated all her curvy curves. As she turned sideways to give me passage, my eyes couldn't help but admiringly drop the length of her figure. Truly, I wasn't looking for an illicit relationship, here. I loved Tamela—her laughter, adventurousness, quick mind, lawyerly potential— while conveniently mind-blocking everything I hated like avoiding literacy and her propensity to incessantly cross choplogic swords with no ceasefire allowed.

What I wanted was friends to help scout out job and business opportunities. Financially and professionally, it seemed I was at a nadir. I'd lost my business, money, soon my Cocoa rental; lived on the charity of frenemies; now mousily toying with seeking my millionairess sister's help whom I didn't think even liked me all that much. In my 20 enterprising years I'd never had entrepreneurial friends. My family felt no kindred spirit. A good corporate career, that's the ticket. Wealth and financial independence (especially for Dad) was something to avoid as there's no way to ethically *earn* wealth. One really *takes* it by screwing others out of their (presumedly stolen?) own. He supposed the purpose of business was to fuck everybody.

I vehemently disagreed. Commerce has its crooks, but Joe Grocer selling me an apple hardly qualifies unless he's raping on price or defrauding with rotten fruit. The church, too, had no tolerance for member-owned business or entrepreneurial effort even if some coin-dropped Vanderbilt prestige into its coffers.

Godwin said, "I persuaded Father to give me $12 million to start the country's first satellite-based newspaper. I set up *Newsworld* for simultaneous New York–Los Angeles publication in the early 1980s."

"But if it pulls you from witnessing or leadership, it's a net evil," said I.

Rev. Moon had umpteen million aspirants begging audience with his wallet. I think top leaders cultivated a cynicism that entrepreneurs were shady, fly-by-night flimflammers hamstringing their own (*deserved*) access to filching his money.

Plugging into Linda's network, I found her parties filled with interesting and successful lawyers, lobbyists, entrepreneurs, business owners, even Hawaii Senator Daniel Inouye's son, whose father she knew from Hawaii and I'd met in Nordstrom's men's wear. Saturday's frolic was ten or so folks from government and industry chatting about her wireless technology and financing prospects. As the afternoon wore on, we innocently discovered commonalities accumulating between us like there was a reason we'd met. I journaled some of over sixty things we shared:

> same right knee surgery; half Japanese and spoke it till age seven, I currently spoke it; she was born in Kodiak, I was a fisherman there; she grew up in Honolulu, I lived there a year; we had global visions to positively affect the world; hi-tech CEOs, entrepreneurs, risk takers, and journalists; she started a magazine, me a newspaper and theological journal; we loved history; cared about black-white relations; same back pain; fathers were Navy chief petty officers serving out of Pearl Harbor and photography their hobby; we played in our high school bands; read music; *Amazing Grace* was our favorite spiritual song; bank and other passwords shockingly identical to one digit; she'd worked at my favorite classical station and we loved classical music, art, architecture, and classic rock, dressing formal, Asian food, chopsticks, oceans and ships, current events, reading extensively; we produced and hosted TV shows on cable and PBS; we traveled; loved food, culture, and history of foreign lands; loved Bob Hope's "road movies," Shirley Temple, bingeing on tacos, fried rice, and banana cereal; her father and I fenced; my junior high and her senior high teams were the Rams; my senior high and her junior high teams were the Cougars; we loved scuba and bicycling; we were passionate, uninhibited.

Chills shivered up my back. Was God directing me to her? Did He understand my suffering from Tamela's bludgeoning? In spite of everything the Unification Church taught, was He stepping outside the box to save me from despairing collapse in a go-nowhere Blessing? I considered Tamela. What *did* we share, anyway? Not much. Nothing important. Our list was more what she hated:

> my traveling; Unification Church; UTS "wasted time;" business ownership over wage slavery; my white picket fence as an estate and seat of our clan over her nondescript, two-window shack lost to strangers at death; training our children to follow their dreams without forgetting humanity; growing far, far apart as I pursued my destiny albeit failing while she refused or was lackluster to achieve something as basic and critical to our children as reading.

It caused no small arguments between us; I hadn't yet cottoned on to her cognitive disability. While reading per se wasn't hard for her, it was still a mental chasm. Regardless, better effort earlier in our marriage was wanting. It was a duty she owed our family. I didn't marry a charity case but a woman I expected to *re-learn* into community college, a baccalaureate, maybe law school that she'd claimed to want. I was peeved and offended she'd gone academically unchanged for eight years while emotionally and psychologically *devolving*.

Beauty was faded like blown dust. Not physically—that suffered from a furious disposition to eat away her troubles—but spiritually. She'd shone brightest in my eye, gleaming angelically when I fell in love. The radiance of her pure, gentle heart reached out to stroke away my wrath and despair foaming at Shiori and the church. Her youthful vigor and innocence renewed my own. But unchecked rage and hate and resentment for Shiori, the church, UTS, work, business, and our knock-down-drag-out Kato-combat tsunamied through me and darkened the eyes to her soul 'neath ominous, squalling clouds reflecting her stormy, chaotic seas within.

I'd hoped all my tears and repentance at Cheongpyeong Lake would set the stage to wipe it all away, but it didn't . . . couldn't, I guess. "Please, let's go to Cheongpyeong together so you can feel my same spiritual renewal of love and affection."

"We done need real counselin' when I been say I want it, not your stupid church so-caahll spiritual retreat now. Wha' 'dat?" *Stiupp.*

By the time I reached Washington our relationship hung by a strand, our year in Florida having wrung out the last drop of love and care straining through our shipwreck of a home.

As Linda's Saturday get-together wound to a close, I didn't want to leave but get to know this woman who shared so many attributes. We gabbed the whole night through. I would've kept it going but for *her* commitment to church. Already, I couldn't have cared less about that. I was right there, in *her* cathedral! I felt God's presence. Who can know? Strictly by dogma, I was wrong. Married to Tamela, that was just that. Even so, by the compassion we take for the essence of God's heart she was destroying me as a person, tearing me down to a feral, cornered animal. The condition of my marriage and its storms and earthquakes rending my soul shorted me out as a church member, minister, UTS graduate, and a compassionate human being committed to living for God and humanity.

Surely, if God felt any concern for me at all, it would and should be for pursuing the mission He'd given me. If Tamela now—*for years!*—merited Jesus' rebuke to "Get behind Me, Satan! You are a stumbling block to Me; for you are not setting your mind on God's interests, but man's," then wasn't it provident of God to open a path to its removal? I didn't—couldn't!—know, but the difference between rationalization, justification, and reality is a damn fine line to suss.

Linda was certainly no prettier than Tamela; less so, though she boldly said, "Your wife is the definition of ugly." *Giggle.* "What were you even thinking?" But her spirit was more embracingly beautiful, more . . . well, grown up. Where Tamela seemed a wild Helen Keller, Linda was calmly adult. "Having real intellectual intercourse is intoxicating, isn't it, Chris? I can see it in your whole body." *Yeah!* I was ravenous. She was an oasis in a timeless, barren wasteland and I couldn't glug enough.

But I *was* married and sex didn't arise. For now only her intellect, global vision, kindness, and tranquility overwhelmed me. My UTS friend Rachel later said, "You have to keep your Blessing. If Tamela isn't capable of being your friend then you should find a woman who can be, without leaving Tamela."

"The problem with that logic is, once you find a woman who's a greater friend than your own wife, love grows and dies at home. It's an unsustainable duality."

"You have to make it work, Chris."

"The heart is built for singularity, Rach. Not duality. One heart, one love, one God, one spouse. Isn't that basically what Father teaches? No, it's a fool's errand to build friendships with the opposite sex not your spouse."

"Then you're stuck. Your Blessing comes first, not you."

"Ridiculous! I'm on the verge of suicide! Can't people understand that?" My duality slashed my dichotomy after a long session praising Tamela in Linda's condo. "She's no dummy. She's eventually going to law school. Look at her photo. You'll see what I mean. Here." I thrust it over.

Her reluctance was heavy. "This is your wife?" Her tone was unbelieving.

"Yeah." What a weird question. *Who's photo did you think I handed you?*

She scrutinized it in silence, her finger jabbing and bobbing at Tamela posed between our two small children. Her head tilted puppyishly puzzled and a fingertip stabbed Tamela to kids and back. A quizzical look flashed across her face. She handed it back without comment. Not even a, "Cute kids."

Now, I'd shown this very photo to plenty of folks and no one scrutinized it so cryptically. What did she mean by that? I was unwilling to dig deeper and

The portentous photo that upended everything.

blew it off. Days later it still gnawed. I found the gumption. "What's the deal with how you reacted to my wife's picture?"

She hesitated. "You sure you want to hear it?"

"I wouldn't have asked, otherwise." *Says the fool.*

In five earth-shattering minutes she laid out my marriage to perfection, divining her lack of education, that she must be an argumentative wife, and that, "You're lying when you said she'd go to law school. You already know that's never happening." My mouth fell farther open at every word. "In my opinion, this isn't a happy marriage. You should get out while you can."

I slumped back. Devastated. Horrified. Speechless. Body rigid. White-knuckled. Drained of color for all I knew—I sure felt spiked and tossed on a tusk.

In a moment of agonizing, blinding clarity scales fell from my eyes as they had Saul's on his road to Damascus. Overwhelmed, I sank wordlessly into her red, bay window sofa. I wanted to talk. Defend Tamela, my marriage, my very life. My brain locked up. Seized hot. Melted slag. I couldn't form a word. My full life was opening its hairy reality before me like *Alien*'s acidly shredding maw. I realized with sinking heart how profoundly, finally, Ahabianly I hated, loathed, and despised my life, my marriage, and Tamela.

How had this woman, on the basis of a mere photograph, pegged the reality of my life with her succinct precision? Had everyone eyeballing this photo shrouded a similar take? Was I simply too dim to catch on till feeling Linda's? Were they all laughing at me marrying an uneducated—*uneducable?*—woman from the wrong side of the hemisphere? It wasn't enough I'd alienated family and friends marrying a black woman, but one mired in ignorance, poverty, and violence, too? Solar rage erupted from every pore. Skin blistered hot. The kernel of my existence seethed in revulsion of life, myself, Tamela. I wanted to escape. I was ready to die.

No wonder the church doesn't trust me! Why Father dumped me! In the most critical decision, I'd chosen poorly. Who'd trust my judgment in anything else?

Dean Mickler's warning after my fracas with Chaz Jerman reeled up: "You know, your wife's got some problems herself. Her responses don't square up."

Was this what he'd meant? Did he see the cognitive disability, the personality disorder, the combative, unreasoning personality? Had he been trying to subtly lay into me for bringing the wrong person onto God's reservation? Shame and anger ripped through me. I wailed through my trembling mind, *How could Jerome have done this to me?* Persuading me to marry her must've been some twisted revenge he was still laughing to the bank.

"Marry her for the sake of our mission," he'd said. "Nobody will ever trust two unmarried guys from America down here. They'll always wonder what we're up to. Especially you, a white guy. They'll see you as a kid in a candy shop. How many marriage proposals have you already had down here?" though he'd known the answer was zero. "Everyone will think you're out screwing every girl in sight, because that's what they *expect* the white man to do in the black man's house."

The answer was respectable marriage. Tamela was in love with me and I liked her, was even attracted. I was gratingly miserable with Shiori who was clearly infertile and anyhow impeding my vision for her own. I suffered an enervating spiritual anxiety with her I couldn't shake, a clear sign God was displeased. Shiori had to go. A wrong choice. I never should've involved myself with a Blessed sister regardless the church kicking me out. I'd *known* that with Nanami. If I had to marry on my own because no leader would open the Blessing to me, then it was better marrying an outside woman with no church baggage. But, now, I blamed Jerome. He'd misled me. Known Tamela's disability. That she was an inappropriate, incompatible choice. Yet, he'd convinced me because it worked for *him*. And I'd bought his con.

I resented him for it. Eight more atop ten church years gone. *Wasted!* All I had to show for it was three lovely, sweet, adorable children I'd never give up nor unmake. That was another thing suddenly jerking me up short: if Tamela was such a wrong choice, how did we manage to produce such lovely, naturally sweet children? So many second-generation Blessed children are mean, rude, crude, obnoxious, and unholy, rejecting church and parents altogether. Yet despite the truculent, pugilistic madness permeating our home, ours turned out surprisingly lovely, kind, and gentle regardless pro-level training for domestic violence and a Jane Eyrean madness.

And here, confusion and doubt entered my heart. How could I trust myself? I had the worst track record with women. A malfunctioning picker. I routinely chose those Pied Pipering me into disaster, unhappiness, and despair. Linda progressively treated me as a prized gift she *cared* about. I hadn't experienced care for years with Tamela. Maybe not ever, if I was honest.

Dammit, I can't blame Jerome. The engine of my destruction, perhaps, but I'd ground it into gear. I'd made the decision. Rationalized it. Justified it. Found if not invented its logic. Built the desire. In hindsight, I perceived how I'd been too ashamed to tell my parents. I'd lied about her age and education. I knew they'd oppose me—they did anyway—and didn't want to haggle. If I knew with certainty she was God's choice (lofty pronouncements notwithstanding), I'd have proclaimed her from the rooftops, wouldn't I? Yet, for a time after our wedding I'd only referred to her as *my wife* until Dad said, "How come you never refer to her as Tamela?"

"Well . . ." *dang.* I had to wonder, too.

It was my fault. I could hate Jerome for a host of things, talking me into marriage one of them, but not for my actually doing it. I took responsibility for that. Perhaps I qualified it by noting that had the church not denied me every Blessing over ten years I'd never be in this predicament. I'd be in a different one, maybe a worse one, but not *this* one. I could've followed Malcolm X's example and devoted myself like a priest to my mission for God and let Him decide when to take a wife . . . well, shit, I thought he *had*. But I've always wanted to marry and, in truth, I'm less spiritual than I am physical. I'm more a do-er than a pray-er. Building the kingdom of heaven on earth holds far more interest for me than building it in heaven. Maybe that's why I can't get along in the church. They're less on doing and more on imagining.

All this churned my mind cringing at Linda's words, absorbing her hard blow. On the phone, Tamela later forced me to explain the vibe she was picking up.

"I'm miserable in our marriage. I don't feel any compatibility between us."

She blew a fuse in her rip-roaring Vincy vernacular. "Wha' compatibility! Who wo-maahn you be screwin' up 'der in Waahshing-tohn? Come home!"

Typical, yet scarily near the mark. "I'm not screwing anybody!" *Yet.* "I am telling you how I feel. That your endless cussing is *killing* me. Ruining our marriage."

Derision dripped honeyed vinegar. "You *mus'* be screwing some-body who be fillin' your head wi' aahll 'dat. I need you home *today*. Your chilleren are *here*!"

"I'm not leaving, this is where the jobs are."

"You fin' one yet?"

"No, I'm still—"

"How you not fin' a simple job by now? You lookin' for job or wo-maahn?"

"I may as well be for all you believe me." *And the changes erupting inside of me.* I was realizing that once you've had brain sex you can never go back to brain dead—practically necrophilia for anybody with intellect and passion. The one begs the other. When they meet, two partners' life energy spikes to where God Himself is touched. Or, so Rev. Moon says.

Tamela fumed through the phone. For weeks we'd been fighting over the wires because she hated being alone in Florida. "Bring me 'der else come back here to me an' your chilleren, job or no job."

"For God's sake, Tamela, and pay the rent how? There's no jobs. It takes time to find educated work wherever you are. I'm not looking to flip burgers here!"

"Two weeks, three weeks should be enough for any job." Her tone sharply said, *I don't believe your lying guise.* Round and round to nowhere till the line melted.

No way was I was leaving. Not only was I desperate for professional work and not a little enamored of Linda, but I loved Washington, madly wanted to be a permanent part of the local church community, frantic to avoid falling back into my marital rut, and suddenly dying for the first time in 40 years to set down roots. Florida served none of these needs. And Tamela couldn't come up at this point because I only had a small, borrowed room in a church center that refused to accept families, especially *my* no-doubt gossiped kids and boundaries-blind *nonmember* wife.

I had to hand it to her. She came up anyway on a Greyhound with our children in convoy. She spent most of our time browbeating me back into line after hearing I no longer cared about our marriage or her. I did care for her, but it no longer felt marital. In her mind, that only meant I had to be shagging somebody.

I'd crossed my Rubicon. Seen my life as it was. I wanted nothing of it except my children. She spent Christmas '99 with her cousin in Brooklyn, pressured me to show up, then spent all her time quarreling until forcing sex on me. Conveying my feelings to her was impossible. She didn't get it and I couldn't come out and say, "I want a divorce." Cowed by the same feelings that bound me to Shiori long after I should have come clean with her, I found no words to work with. I wanted to be alone. Fade into an emotional cave and come to grips with my new reality. Expressing love, affection, or care was impossible. Sex and all the affectionate intimacy it required was beyond me. I wanted to spit all my aggravation and rancor into her face like a hurricane . . . no, a sick man vomiting his sour murder onto his poisoner.

My children's presence complicated my emotions. Divorce seemed unthinkable despite my heady infatuation with Linda and my hatred for every rough moment Tamela dished out. I believed I no longer husbandly loved her. I think it happened the moment those scales fell from my eyes. All my love and affection for her—"It's just denial," Linda airily said—flipped like a tossed coin to hate and revulsion, not for *her* but for all she was and made me. I supposed divorce would come up later but no courage even to think it . . . wasn't a hundred percent sure anyway. And guilt instantly consumed me; I couldn't bear to think what divorce would put my children through. Eight years of marriage seemed a lifetime. I didn't know anything else. Tamela was my universe. Couldn't we fix it? Shouldn't we?

In sheepish humiliation, I called my sister Mona and apologized for my earlier judgmentalism over her divorce. I informed my family of my situation and intent to separate. They flipped.

Dad spoke for all. "You need to stay with Tamela. Quit fooling around."

"What fooling around? I'm *dying* under her domestic violence!"

"Oh, posh." My family's instinctive, unequivocal support bewildered me after detailing her domestic violence. "You must be imagining it, if not exaggerating." Later, Mona and my folks spent a few weeks relocating her to San Diego—imagining themselves an effective social services agency—and were staggered to discover I hadn't lied after all. Slooowly a more understanding attitude emerged.

MY DESCENT INTO emotional incoherence happened in the waning months of my fortieth year—a stereotypical midlife crisis encapsulating me spiritually, emotionally, professionally. The problem raging through me was more than my abusive marriage coming to a head. Forty years in a dysfunctional family and 21 a dysfunctional church were also climaxing. I'd reached a moment of Principled numerology. Like Jacob fighting 21 years without respite against the deceit and violence of his Uncle Laban, I struggled with the deceit and violence of my Uncle Church. It had promised me a wife and reward for my labors as Laban had Rachel to Jacob and to all he'd earned enriching his uncle. Instead, Laban The Church screwed me up the wazoo, especially blocking my Matching and Blessing eight times over 13 years.

"You're too spiritually young," Mr. Kobayashi postulated.

The Uchiyamas' take was, "You're too physically young."

"You're immature in the Principle and disobedient besides," oozed Ergela Arsch.

Wren Meyer figured, "You need a lesson in loyalty."

No respect for Rev. Moon's right to decide as he had for them. Yes, it was Laban. A self-serving, egotistical, lying old bastard concerned only with its take. If one considers the Unification Church God's own hands, then they'd turned against the very mind giving it life. A cancer in the body God slaying every healthy cell God sent until a shriveled mockery of the powerful instruments He foresaw.

I think Rev. Moon would see Satan in my words inasmuch as they imply a quid pro quo twixt us and God. He'd argue we owe God all and deserve nothing. I believe God never asks anything of a person through which they can't find happiness and satisfaction. From Christian martyrs dying with joy in their hearts in the surety of entering the kingdom of heaven to medieval monks, Catholic priests, and lonely missionaries forsaking all the goodness and intimate love which life has to offer for their greater joy and happiness leading impoverished humanity to a better future, God has always provided a way we could love our sacrifice and enjoy our tribulations. Otherwise, He'd have nothing but angry, resentful slaves on His hands. In Unificationism's indemnity course, unlike the Christian, our trials and tribulations involve preparing for the Matching and Blessing first and foremost. When church leaders ripped that salvific from my bosom they in effect told me that, "Your request for eternal life is denied . . . church amenities, too."

Fitfully letting all my hurts and anxieties out of my heart, a supreme violence boiled up in me that I'd suppressed and dominated for years. Linda forced me on the strength of her character and clarity of perception to frankly analyze and break my denial over how great was Rev. Moon and his vaunted, holy church.

"Any organization that doesn't nurture and appreciate its own members is one to stay away from," she said. "It's abusive. It'll drag you down and eventually destroy your life." Captain Obvious pointed a hard punctuation at me.

We argued it out in her apartment, up and down the streets of Washington, and in our cars like *What About Bob?* and his luckless therapist.

"You don't understand," I said. "This isn't just any old church we're talking about. If I was having an irreconcilable problem with the Presbyterians, I'd go join the Baptists. It's all the same to me. But the Unification Church is *different!* It's *messianic.* Our leader, my spiritual teacher, is the *Messiah.* Don't you get it?"

"Don't you?"

I'd always accepted a fundamental distinction between Rev. Moon and his church. However evil the latter, he was above it—a part of it yet a part distinct. I didn't blame him for the foibles of the church nor harbor resentment for him creating its mess as I did his leaders for institutionalizing and operating it . . . until this very moment, that is. I haltingly accepted he *is* the church. It reflects every aspect and nuance of his personality, from the vicious firebrand to the affectionate parent. The problem is that each member absorbs and imitates limited facets of it (as well as the Principle) like 5,000 years of religions all rolled up in a rancid meatloaf, each competing for primacy under the all-powerful eye of God, master of Divine Principle. This was the maelstrom of the Unification Church with Rev. Moon an old world Korean and new world visionary, pacifist Jesus and a Rod of Iron, the ultimate passive-aggressive pushing and pulling, pummeling and embracing.

I supposed it was normal, perhaps necessary, of a charismatic visionary founding a new religion glutted by ignorant followers unable to imbibe all that he is. His hi-fi 36 Blessed Couples are a case in point. The very core of Restoration, Rev. Moon rules his henhouse through these cockalorum. Yet, it would be safe to say each couple embraces and cognizes one, at most a few, of his aspects. Accordingly, 36-Blessed couple A runs their ship this way while 36-Blessed couple Q runs theirs that way, and so on. Like a spiritualized version of Japan's 1942 Bataan Death March, the Unification Church could be a model of religious harmony and heavenly solicitude in one place, a Soviet work gulag in another, and a medieval feudalism of gibbeted members somewhere else. The stress and strain was enormous. It showed in the breakneck abandon-ship beginning in the mid-1980s.

In fairness, this dysfunction is hardly unique to our church. Just read Paul's letters to the churches of his day. It's a problem of institutionalized religion, especially one in the grip of its charismatic founder. Catholics at least developed a bureaucracy to administer a codified canon; however unfair or tyrannical, it was foreseeable. Predictability is *ignis fatuus* in the Unification Church. I had no rights and no appeal when local leaders denied my Matching–Blessing. Our singular avenue of success was the personal relationship, as it's primarily an Asian autocracy plied by family style connections like Japan's *yakuza* and Korea's *chaebol*.

Through Linda, I gradually better understood Rev. Moon's role in the destruction and sabotage of his own church and mission. He's its autocratic control yet a victim of its chaos. The more he 'controls' it the less he *controls* it. He stifles and crushes all participation in the movement's activities because he alone, its charismatic founder on speed dial with God, Jesus, and the Saints, knows best. *He* spins its providential wheel. Why give it over to ignoramuses? Well, it's a fair point.

Except he violated his own premise the pope and king must be separate and respect the other's role. He plays both. However great a pope, he fails woefully as king. The church's financial subsidence in the wake of Asia's late 1990's currency meltdown demonstrated it with remarkable clarity. Its bureaucrats run the church according to *chaebol* rules of Korean business. The IMF and World Bank would've done well to press the same reforms on the church as they did Korea where church and business are intrinsically unstable, contradictory, and scratching—occasionally drawing blood—round the borders of the unethical, ungodly, and criminal.

This tied in with my 1998 UTS-grad argument: the pope and king in the American Unification Church improperly commingle, leading to dysfunction and wholesale abandonment by Americans. The solution was reinvigorating these positions with individuals capable of harmonizing the other and thereby the roles. He's a great proponent of the coming together of church and state to inject spiritual values into temporal concerns, but America naturally bifurcates them in our Constitutional realization that human beings can't be trusted in their integration. His latest assertion the United Nations needs add the major religions to the Security Council is about as safe as a loaded gun in the hands of a coked-up toddler. It's not organized religion we need in government or society but spiritual fidelity in the hearts and minds of individuals whom organized religion inculcates and nurtures.

Linda hammered me on Rev. Moon's culpability in the dysfunction of his church. I tongued off defense after defense her sharp wit broke down. She was practically deprogramming me . . . after all these years, what a hoot. I didn't lose my respect for and loyalty to Rev. Moon. I want to work cheek by jowl for Restoration. Global liberty and cessation of organized conflict is the next great frontier in human endeavor. Yet, I'm inimical to many of his proposals and contentions. Is there room in his heart for the loyal opposition? It doesn't seem so, though he claims to hanker for his equal. If so, would he welcome informed dissent? It's natural to brook no contradiction from those you view as inferior. My challenge, therefore, was rising to his level, gaining his respect, finally his trust—my goal throughout my church tenure and what working hand in glove meant. Linda crushed me under logic. I recursively looped through her simple and eloquent assessment of an organization refusing to nurture and appreciate its members being dangerous to me and undeserving of support. At the same time she took on my family relationships, as I was now feeling considerable venom for my millionairess sister.

"If our shoes were reversed and she was the one stuck unemployed and I had a few million in my pocket, I'd plop a hundred thou in her account to carry her the next year or two without so much as a by-your-leave." Linda cut eyes from the driver's seat as we sluiced through the District's dense traffic. "What. That's how a person treats family in crisis."

"Your sister doesn't owe you anything," she said. "Whining about her not giving you money is a cop-out so you can blame her instead of yourself."

"I don't think so." I was broke. Not even clerking at Safeway was panning out. "I feel cut off from them all. Unloved, unappreciated, unwanted . . . a barely tolerated boil on the family politic."

"So?"

"So . . . what? For the last decade or so my siblings rarely if ever call or write, much less visit. If I want to see them or just hear their voice then it's *me* has to take the initiative. Eventually, a person has to conclude the obvious and quit forcing themselves where they're not wanted."

"This isn't about them, it's about you wanting what isn't yours."

"What isn't—? Whatever. I quit because communicating was pointless."

Her head was a giant eye roll bobbling side to side at my welling tears but she kept her mouth on the road because, as she later said, "You weren't listening."

It was a bitter sadness earlier in 1999 when Tamela remarked in Florida, "How it be 'dat none o' your family ev-uhh talk to us? 'Dem spare no time goin' far place to far place to visit 'demself!"

I said, "I know, I see it. It's been—"

"It becau' you marry to me," she said, rueful words laced with spite. "An' 'dem can'a ge' ov-uhh 'dat, even to love your chilleren, 'dem own gran.'"

"No," through my own heavy sigh, "they treated me so since long before I ever met you. Since I was a kid, before I could've done anything to piss 'em all off."

We weren't imagining it. The mailbox was empty. Our phone silent. Doorbell unrung. Over my year in Florida and several in Washington I'd built considerable offense and a wizened heart of gall for their slights of a thousand cuts. I wouldn't begin to recognize and accept their limitations and mine for some time yet.

Carrying on against my sister's indifference in Linda's cramped Honda civic, she finally rebuked me. "You have no right to be angry with Mona for not helping you solve your own mess. Do it yourself!"

That stung deep and I was furious as hell to realize, even against my raging intellectual will, that she was right and I was wrong. I couldn't even understand *why* I was wrong. Just somehow, intuitively, I goddamnedly knew it. Emotions flayed me to the bone. I burst into toddler tears as we jerked around the Capitol for Dupont Circle, sobbing the hour we shoved through rush hour traffic to her condo.

In some respects she wasn't helping even if breaking my denial about my abusive marriage, abusive church, and self-abuse over my failure with CFT. She berated me for marrying "vile" Tamela in the first place and trying to build another business in Washington while not divorced. "She'll own fifty percent of whatever you do. It's unethical to draw your investors into your mess without telling them about it."

"How's my personal life and marital assets have anything to do with them?"

"Seriously? She has half your vote on anything and they didn't buy into that. She'd be a silent partner, a poison pill for your board."

"I don't see it."

"You're being stupid. You need *something* to pull your head out of your ass."

She'd pressured me into joining various Alcoholics Anonymous-style 12-step weekly programs. I faithfully tried them for months and some over a year but wearied of insatiable power and control issues, of attendees having no intention to heal but to soak up a cookies-and-donuts ambience as a crutch to whine about their (maybe fake) addictions worse than I ever did. I was *desperate* for change and a new life and they weren't helping.

Linda was falling in love. Passionately. She was manna in the desert, a cool oasis of water. I reveled in it. Drank deeply, lustily. Like those old dry bones in Ezekiel 37, I felt my broken skeleton coming together, new flesh filling me out. All I needed was the breath of life—God's *real* Word—to infuse me with new life. Where would I get *that*?

Right now it was enough to be in the mind of this vivacious, brainy woman stripping away my rusty veneer of some 20 years of denial. In

Leisure & cowboy roots entering my life for the first time in 20 years c. late 2000.

mid-December 1999 she repaired to her family's blue Pacific home for the holidays. We traded thousands of emails getting to know each other. She took on the role of therapist. We screamed, ranted, and raved through the Internet. She was never one to pull a punch and hit me with every knuckle at her command. But going into January 2000 I dimly perceived she was nearly as dysfunctional and abusive as Tamela, her top form intellect and cognitive prowess notwithstanding. While Tamela beat me up over Shiori, the church, a biblical host of errors, or to get what she wanted, Linda interminably and mercilessly dragged me over white coals for moronically marrying her at all.

"If you wanted a black woman for your Moonie black–white Restoration," she spikily said, "why didn't you at least marry an educated black woman, somebody your equal?" *Like me.*

"Well, dammit, I don't know. It seemed like a good idea at the time."

"Do you honestly think Rev. Moon would've matched you two?"

I thought about it but managed only a scrunched-up cheek.

"Dumb." *Incredulous head shake.* In her dark eyes I saw heavy pots and pans flying my way. "It's absurd. You should've done a full background check on her first. Really. Fucking. Dumb."

"Don't be so ridiculous." My Moonie mind was willing to raise up the lowest, poorest, most ignorant black woman to my level to reverse the historical sin of slavery not out of some fake liberal guilt complex but for God's Providence of Restoration as Rev. Moon articulated. I'd married in the belief she was mentally intact merely denied an education, a loving family, real opportunity. I believed the chance to grow and develop outweighed any former chains. I had no regard for where she *was* but where she could *be.* It's a purely American modus. "Like an FBI check? *Pshaw!*" But . . . perhaps? If I was rich, I might have. I'd never imagined she or her family were lying. "I mean, maybe I was naïve." *Or stupid.*

"In denial, dumbass, where you usually are."

"Dammit, Linda!" I thrilled to her anyhow. We weren't sexual but her mind had me in practical orgasm—her intellect, brilliance, global vision; a belief in me evading church abuse rolling up on Rev. Moon on my own terms being as good as anywhere for me to be. And, too, her overt excitement for my global vision and goals.

"Listening to you describe where you were going had me soaking wet on the sofa," she later revealed. "I totally wanted you. Your worthless African scorns your dreams but I love them! I want to help you accomplish them. That's my promise. Isn't that what a real woman does for her man?"

Isn't it? Should I say, "No thanks," to that? *Hell, no.*

ALL THIS APPOSITION was grinding me to splinters. We were so aggravated when Linda winged in from Hawaii in January 2000, largely over my inability to make any clean decision I could stick to, that we'd planned to not meet up. Referring to Tamela by epithets instead of her name built an ever-inflamed chasm.

"Maybe your Dad's side is engaging in some self-hatred, Linda."

"The only self-hater here is you, besotted by your African. I took one look at your book"—my UTS thesis—"and lost all interest seeing your references to her."

"You won't read it? You promised feedback before I went to a publisher."

Her head was shaking a sour, down-turned mouth. "Rewrite it. Obviously, your whole book rests on you marrying your low-class piece of shit."

"You can't skip over that? It has no academically credible argument?"

"*You* said it."

"You're so goddamned uncharitable. This is you helping me achieve my dreams?"

"Whatever. I'm not reading your tainted book."

"How do you hate somebody you don't even know? Never met? Never did you a lick of harm?"

"She ruined you. And your mess is in my life. That's harm enough."

My thoughts were a numbed, steel-shattered fist. "She is what she is. I have a right to be pissed with her but you don't. You say you love me and want to help disentangle me from her domestic violence..."

We were joyful and sweet unless Tamela cropped up. The vexation Linda's words ginned up over the church, marriage, and work were honest, denial-breaking therapy. No matter how face-slapped I felt over some of what she said, her therapeutic motivation was unquestionable. It was far from her mind with Tamela. Loathing contempt rolled off her tongue in complete disproportion to the evil I thought Tamela had done in my life. I wrote February 2,

> Without a real love for *God*, not this metaphysical shit thing called God, a person is incapable of living for the sake of others and loving their enemy...
> God, the actual *being*, is whom I love, not a bunch of metaphysical abstractness that helps me put a pretty veil over my head...
>
> I swear I see the seeds of exactly the same relationship I have with Tamela; just a more educated version of it. She criticized Tamela for not reading and helping me with my book even though it was so important to me. She made it a priority to read it. But as soon as she saw Tamela's name or references to her in my book, she quit reading it...

"I started it years ago, Linda. You're acting like it was yesterday."

"It could be today. That's how it feels looking at you like her lapdog."

"Now you're just stabbing me for fun."

Then she dropped a voicemail. "Chris, you are such an ass! You knew all along that business assets are marital property. How could you start up EET without disclosing her to your investors?" *Giggle.* "You're lucky you have me to burst your bubble and get you out of your denial and lies before they sued you."

I telephoned. "I don't know if I'm more angry with you or Tamela or *me*."

"That's what it takes to pry you out of your mess. Don't blame me. The African will never have anything to do with your real life... your vision *or* Moonie goals."

"You're so damned ruthless. Use her name, for Pete's sake!" I huffed a beat. "I know she and my family's attitude is, 'Get a job and shut the fuck up,' but why do *you* have to be that way, too?"

"Me? Why do you? I'm just the messenger."

"You purposely misinterpret my confusion over divorce with malice, thinking I'm just manipulating you for my own ends."

"Aren't you?"

"Then you drop my book because her name's in it."

"When will you decide you want a life free of your perpetrator's violence?"

I threw my head back so my eyes could roll even farther. *Can't I just disappear? See no one ever again?* "It's not that easy. I miss my children! They alone keep me tied to her when all I *want* to do is escape."

"All lies and delusion."

"My . . . vexation . . . pushes me to move on. I'm not ignoring you. But you're getting just as abusive as Tamela!"

"Don't compare me to her! I do whatever it takes to break your addiction to your low-class piece of shit. Your kids are damaged goods, Chris. They'll grow up just like their African mom. Let her raise them."

My whole being fell, my mouth the hardest. "Are you insane?" *Boy, I've fucked up my life—jumping from a searing pan into a blazing fire!* Could it be worse?

It's difficult to describe the collapse all at once of my professional, married, religious, and spiritual life along with my belief in myself and my dreams all swirling in one vicious cocktail depositing me a sniveling puddle. I bawled eyes day and night for the loss of my children, the church, my Blessing. I beat myself mercilessly during my 40-day *kyum bae* in my cluttered hovel at Varnum Street till I abruptly ended it heading into the climax, at last falling into Linda's February arms.

The morning after was a throat punch. The old bird had said, "You don't deserve the very serious responsibility and honor of being a UTS alumnus." Was he right after all? Then I remembered Ergela and . . . maybe not. Yet, had my spiritual condition opened me up to sin or did I just fail again? was God leading me out of the swamp I called my life through Linda? was I plunging deeper into Satan's quicksand in my inability to overcome my intense and irreducible need for love? would He slay me for my faithlessness? was I abandoned? Rev. Moon unstintingly warned how God would forsake us falling on Restoration's road because He wouldn't, *couldn't* wait on us to get it together. I believed him. Felt it. Resented the very notion. I wept prayer through my nights. "God! Are you leaving me? Am I too faithless even for you?"

My world was collapsing round my ears, falling in upon my body, stamping out my very life and soul. I couldn't breathe. Couldn't think. Linda was my one link to sanity, a drowning man's flotsam. I couldn't let go. She alone was helping me break through my veil to find clarity in self-awareness. How could I abandon that for something as ephemeral as sexual purity defined by a fallible church?

Godwin read my beseeching letter and phoned. I humiliatingly revealed my new situation. *Indignant.* "I feel totally betrayed after convincing Rev. Lee to give you space at Varnum Street. I gave my word you were a faithful member."

Is my every goddamned issue somebody's betrayal? "Why would he even need your assurance I wasn't a problem member? We were bosom partners at UTS less than two years ago. Did he think I betrayed the church with CFT?"

"Kind of, yes."

That hanged me. "But . . . it's bullshit, Godwin. I was following Father's mandate and waiting for Tyler to assign me a mission. Which he never did."

"I understand, I can accept, you leaving Tamela because of her abuse. But I can't accept you leaving her *for* Linda. Never."

His unexpected adamance stultified me. "I'm not leaving her for Linda. I just happened on her in the process."

"What's the difference, Chris? If you hadn't done her would you really be leaving Tamela, or trying to fix things?"

"If I'd discovered on my own what I did from Linda, then yes. Godwin, you don't know how hard—." I felt so judged and couldn't explain the whirlwind clouding every molecule of my being. "It's true my love is shifting from Tamela to Linda—what's left of it—because she's like clean air when all I've been breathing is the poison gas of Tamela's endless cussing and abuse."

"That's not an excuse to break your Blessing."

"If she hadn't violently abused me for eight years it wouldn't be happening! Didn't the church learn anything about domestic violence from Nan Sook's book?"

"Her situation's not the issue here. It's *your* relationship to Principle."

"How am I supposed to shut down my heart like you're saying? I feel like I'm at rock bottom in my devotion to the Blessing. I don't want anything more to do with her regardless how guilty or indecisive I feel," rooted in my fear of God anyhow.

"If you're feeling indecisive, then maybe that's a sign you're not—"

"My feelings *are* sincere, not some dirty lust like a few others I could mention."

"It doesn't matter. Breaking your Blessing *this* way is the wrong way to go. You should end things with Tamela and then maybe apply for a Matching."

Ugh. "That's a total crapshoot now Father's Matching Divine Principled members to unchurched, disinterested nonmembers." And I didn't want to hear that when Dr. Shimmyo's recommendation was 14 years of torn-off fingernails up the Cliffs of Insanity. "And who'll recommend me now, you?" *Pfft!*

"Yes, I'll recommend you, but you have to separate from Linda. You can't have it both ways. This is your eternal future."

"Shit, Godwin."

Second guessing divorce was a new rift forging Linda's suspicion I was only dogging her and not serious about moving on to marry her. While I wrestled with divorce, I was now forced to struggle over leaving her, too, and not merely on account of Godwin or the church. In spite of the positive effect her counseling had on me, she was simultaneously dramatically affecting me negatively in our relationship. Here I was, unexpectedly caught between the hook and the bait. *Double shit.*

Linda hated Tamela. No, I'm too charitable. She reviled her as if the fount of all her tribulations. "I hate her because she ruined your life, Chris. You're filled with promise and potential. You could be a great man but she's wrecked that and I hate her for it. Your African's nothing but a gold digger using you to support herself."

"Stop calling her that. I don't see her that way at all," howsoever the allusion might fit or fired like rubber bullets to subdue my errant delusion. "I know—well, eventually figured out—she married me in part to get out of St. Vincent and was more infatuated than in love with me."

"You see? I'm right. You know I'm always right about your African."

"No, you aren't. I think she eventually loved me—loves me—in whatever way she's capable. I'm not saying that's at all okay, I'm just saying she's no gold digger. We have three kids after all."

"That's just how she controls you so you won't leave her."

"Oh, come on. That's inane and you know it. So what if you marry somebody for money or to escape your shitty life? If you give 'em what they need then it's irrelevant, isn't it." *You're in denial and fooling yourself,* her inhospitable expression read. "If she'd brought me boundless joy, why would I care about her fake reasons for marrying me? Why should I? *I'd be fucking happy!*"

"Because she's a gold digger using you *and* a perpetrator and that's why you're broke and your life is the mess it is. Who wants to be a part of that mess?" *You, if I'm not mistaken.* "If you'd listen to me you could fix it."

Yes, Tamela's abuse called up a tremendous antipathy for her possibly suspect motives. I was feeling it now in spades. She blamed me for everything—like Linda indicting me now—and roundly condemned me for her current plight.

"If you knew you be abandon me up here," she more than once said, "wha' mek you marry to me in 'de first place an' then carry me aahll 'de way here?"

"Damn it! I didn't—" What was the point explaining? "If I knew in advance the kind of marriage you'd give me I'd have left you at the bloody altar!"

"This be aahll your doin' becau' Shiori! None o' my so-caahll cussin' would'a been happ'n but for you an' she."

"You killed all my love with your cussing. Now you want to blame me for it? That ended long ago and you *still* can't shut up about it! It's your fault for not forgiving and moving on when it's been crystal clear who I bloody well chose!"

"You broke my heart, Chris!" *Tears.* "I was afraaaid . . ."

"And you killed mine! Destroyed it! Now I'm dying for someone who can make me happy and you call that cheating? To hell with you!" Then I journaled, "Yet, I still can't bear to say I want a divorce. Why? Why?"

In March I hooked up with Peter, a kind, cordial relationship counselor, and Samantha, a pastoral counselor hostile to Moonies. Both recognized the futility of my marriage and recommended dissolution, especially when Mona sent an educational assessment exposing Tamela's severe cognitive disability and basement IQ.

Peter said, "Don't worry, man, say everything you have to say to Linda."

"That's crazy, I don't want to lose her."

"Believe me, she's not going anywhere. You can say anything you want."

"That's rather counterintuitive," yet he was dead on. The more boundaries I enforced, the more I expressed who I was and what I felt, the less she ultimately abused me. *Wow!* What a revelation to see it work on a woman.

"She's a classic enabler. You'll understand a lot when you get that."

Samantha concurred. "She's trying to remake you into the man of her dreams. She gets angry and pushes you away whenever you don't listen and ignore her advice. Then, she apologizes. Wants to be friends again. Classic pattern."

"See?" Linda cooed soothingly. "My actions speak louder than my words."

IN MID-MARCH my ex-friend In Hoi Lee chucked me out on my ass. "The house is getting too overcrowded," he said over a long talk in my room, legs comfortably stretched out on the floor, back against the loveseat sagging under cardboard boxes. "There are now three families here with small children. The nature of this house is changing, from singles to families. We need room for them." I'd been nodding out my brotherly goodwill for the house but sweating over checking into my four-wheeled Motel Taurus à la Hearst Street in Berkeley. "Anyway, you're not really a participating member anymore, are you?"

My nodding froze. "Wait. What? You said yourself not to involve myself in the church every time I asked for some opportunity to help out. 'Just concentrate on getting a job,' you said. 'Don't worry about the church right now, there'll be plenty of work for you to do later.' And now you're saying I've abandoned the church, that I've made myself a nonmember?"

"But you have no job, yet, is that right? When will you get one?"

Now *he* was sounding like Tamela. "It's been hard getting hired. It's not like I'm not trying. I can't just go to McDonald's, because then I'd trash my credibility for executive and engineering interviews. If employers see it they won't even read the next line. I'd have to *lie* on my résumé." He nodded along. "But, my interviews aren't getting offers." Maybe my traumas were in my body language or they sensed my mental instability. "I've had one CTO offer, but that's been it."

"You've been staying out very late," he unexpectedly segued, and I knew he'd been talking to Godwin. Goddamn these gossipy leaders. Even my friends! "Sometimes coming home at all hours, sometimes not at all." Did he have security cameras? He reminded me of Jonathan Spool sensing every creak and swish aboard *Ocean Hope 3.* "Where are you staying?"

"With friends," I lied through my teeth. "Out in the suburbs. Sometimes it gets too late to bother driving all the way back, so I just stay over; the floor, a sofa..."

Oh, Chris! Never one to shuck a lie if it'll save your sinning ass from unpleasant truths at inconvenient times. Linda rejected this flabby aspect of my personality. Tamela, too. And my family. And the church. *Okay! It's a flaw needs changing.*

He wasn't buying. I could tell without him saying a word. He rose up, slid into slippers. "Don't delay. A family is waiting for this room."

"Already?" *And where'll I go?* was my contrite wonder. I phoned Linda.

"Your Moonie cult kicked you out? Again? Ha ha! Well, you can stay here."

I muttered, "Thanks for making it *easier* to fall, In Hoi." *These fuckin' people.*

Despite our growing strife I carted over briefcase, clothes, laptop, and doodads. This honeymoon period was 'the happy times.' I absolutely loved living with her because even with a sea of problems raging all around she was an island of love, acceptance, kindness, service, support, and like-mind dreams... so long as Tamela didn't belly up to the bar. I might've laid down a wounded buck in a thicket to die without Linda. I loved her for the love she poured into me. I couldn't show it very well, and she complained about not receiving a Valentine's Day card and other tokens of affection. I worked at reviving my pre-Moonie habit of bestowing the tidbits of thoughtfulness and consideration so important in relationships. Thoughtless I may have been but knew she was all that kept me from sliding under icy, drowning waters in desolation. I needed and wanted her, besides.

I smarted from In Hoi's dismissiveness. What in hell had gone wrong? Like every church member, he gave the impression I was only following my lusty knob into hedonistic Bacchanalia to ramrod my way through virtuous sisters and dubious womanhood. None saw how the torturous, loveless hell sundering my heart and maddening my thoughts caged me in *love*, not sex, relationships.

Reflecting mid-March I realized I'd modeled my marriage off Rev. and Mrs. Moon. Even falling with Shiori yet keeping to the letter of the Blessing qualification was Moonish if not high-minded, shamanistic, and blood-lineaged. Tamela's mental defects perverted it. I'd figured it easily overcome but, though trying, she'd quit time and again. Rev. Moon's vain promises to fairly utilize us were a sham pinned on his victims. Meeting every shitwit leader for 21 years and no decent ones if there were any to find—maybe Godwin or Julian—burnt me to stubble. My sunk-money time and energy, distraction, suffering, and abuse confounded and ruined me as a person. A top-tier engineer cut from the herd for lack of nouveau e-commerce work, no 'recovery' job I took would support my children who should be with *me*. I had a right to my vision and was certain it supported a family in a sane scene. Tamela's soap opera could fuck off. Mona was now financially helping through June (three-quarters went to Tamela) but I felt she resented it.

I'm sooo tired of this fucking life! scrawled tirelessly through my journal entries like a Madison Avenue jingle. Could I possibly be more miserable? more a victim? more complicate my life?

Better believe it.

But not in Washington, DC. I'd have to hie off to a slim El Dorado for that.

Act XIX

The Ultimate Victim
Ostracism, Divorce, and Despair

The endgame was upon me now. The consequences of my choices these 21 years erupted from my soul like fetid puss. Tamela wallowed in her own breakdown. Her stupendous rage alternated with profound melancholy motivated in no small part by her unspeakable fear of abandonment and surviving on her own. More than anyone, she understood she suffered from a dreadful lack of comprehension. The world moved too fast and she couldn't cope. If I could've fixed her, I would've. For now, I needed fixing more.

She said to Mom, "I done reach me limit tryin' t' meet ev'rybody expecta-shuhn, especially Chris! I wan' be 'de way I am. *Who* I am. No matt-uhh whaaht."

"Who she is, is crazy, Mom." I sighed. "But I guess I can identify with that."

In early March 2000 Mona relocated her to San Diego under her protective wing believing—a product of her newfound wealth or just a tender heart—she could reform her, get her reading, and stabilize her into a daily routine in which our children could find solace. My parents, arriving at our apartment in Cocoa at the height of her dismay over my separation, had reported the children in a state of neglect. They wanted to help them more than anything, even more than me. I think Mona was motivated in no small way by their plight. It was from this time she seemed to harbor a grudge because she (incorrectly) believed I was abandoning my kids. Nothing could be farther from the truth. But I was fast coming apart at the mental and emotional seams. I had to break free of Tamela at all cost if I was to save my very life. I was no use to my children dead.

Mona bit off more Tamela than she could swallow. I'd earlier said, "Don't move her to San Diego, Mona. It's a mistake and you'll live to regret it, believe me."

"*Somebody* in this family," she piously reproached, "has to stand up for her."

"That's not—she'll be a tornado through your life. Just help her in Cocoa, she has a good apartment and support system in place. They'll be okay."

My phone waggled with her no's. "Bob and I will handle her. And her kids are better off here. We have much better schools."

"*Our* kids, you mean." Linda was complicating the picture of a man run out of his home by an abusive wife. My family and Mona especially thought Tamela the wronged party and blithely cold-shouldered my adulterous, paternal opinions. But she did regret it. Within two weeks of Tamela's arrival—her apartment still being readied—her temper and naval salvos against our children ran Mona weeping out of her own house. She vowed to stay in a hotel till Tamela was safely ensconced in a safe space. Dad mediated a shaky armistice.

In their contentious trench it occurred to Mona something might be amiss with Tamela's thinking process, something which in eight years had never occurred to me. As they chronicled their experience, something triggered. How had I never recognized her mental feebleness, instead championing to all and sundry her incisive mind and rhetorical prowess? Where was *my* perspicacity? Was I besotted? What, indeed, was wrong with *me*? Did I have a similar cognitive deficiency which Mona was now suspecting in Tamela? This wasn't merely rhetorical. How else to explain my marrying her? Suddenly, I doubted my own powers of reason, especially when Mona's investigation turned up a startling, inconceivable truth.

In late March, she posted a lengthy report to me from a cognitive specialist who'd examined Tamela's mental acuity. It was brutal and frank with an emphasis on frank and brutal. I read it aghast, hands trembling. The report demonstrated a cognitive and emotional level of a 6–10 year old and an academic achievement below first grade. With an assessed IQ of 62, the report drearily and harshly concluded that although she could learn to read effectively (she eventually did), she'd never surpass third or fourth grade (she rose to about twelfth) nor progress beyond about age ten in her emotional and cognitive capabilities.

Knuckles burned white gripping this sheaf. Dizzy, I collapsed on damaged knees in Linda's bedroom, my heart a grenade in my chest. She'd once again departed Washington to whirlwind through Israel, Turkey, Nepal, and Tibet after aggressively courting my all-expenses-paid company. I yearned to travel with her arm in arm but was too engrossed in the unraveling of my life. I couldn't find the heart for a romantic jaunt around the globe with 'the other woman.' I was very much in love with her even while the part of my heart Tamela called home ruthlessly defended itself against her homewrecker. I was a mixed-up man with a muddled heart lost in a mind fog wandering a whiteout with no compass. If there was a door out of my predicament, I couldn't see it. I was trapped in a cell with two waspish women and me dancing by the neck on an out-of-control guilt trip.

"This report can't be true! It's impossible!" How did it explain Tamela's ability to win logical arguments over educated people? Or her other, obviously adult, mental abilities? Third grade? six or ten years old? "It's preposterous! An absurdity of the highest caliber. I want a second opinion!" All but prostrate, tears shanked my eyes to wash into Linda's dusty Persian rug. I roared in anguished grief alone in the room while she gayly took in her Turkish delights or wherever.

I wept howling till my head was bursting. A sense of perfect wretchedness fell on me. "My wife is dead!" *Wailing, wailing.* "I've lost her! How can it be?" As surely as a fatal car wreck, she was done. The woman I loved, whom I thought I knew, was gone, *gone*, GONE! I keened to none but the frittering spirits of my dungeon and possibly the upstairs neighbor. "Oh, God! Most merciful father! How is this her lot? How could I have married into *this*? What have I done to myself? How can she be saved? restored? Is there no way out for her? for us? No hope?"

And Mona's bloody awful report wasn't done. One or more of our children, it droned on, could suffer the same affliction. It prattled on about the uncertainty of Tamela coming by her disability through genetics or environment.

"It *is* environmental," I assured myself. "My children *are* okay. They'll *be* okay. Kal-el is so smart, and Mona herself tells me what a firecracker Kir-el is, smart as a whip, peppering her with questions and propounding facts. Obviously, they can learn! . . . they *have* to be okay!" They'd have to be tested, absolutely. I had to know. Kal-el was too young now, but when he turned six I'd have it done.

"Chris," Dad said, wrestling himself with the implications, "I do agree the report is difficult to square with what we all know about Tamela."

"Maybe. For you." For me, it revealed a lot I wouldn't accept.

"But the more I reflect on it"—spending prolonged time in her company—"I'm realizing the report explains her, up till now, inexplicable behavior. Misinterpreting words and feelings. Problem-solving that frankly never seems to get past—and I'm sorry to say it—a child's level. Her lack of consistency . . ."

"I believed it right away," Mona said. "It perfectly matches my observations."

Dad took several weeks to absorb it's truth. I rejected every word through six stages of grief—stage 6: wring and repeat—for two months or more. In the meantime I accepted by degrees I could never go back to her. The constant drumbeat of domestic war alone was enough to keep me far, far away. Now I knew the reality of her cognitive unempowerment, I realized her wars would never diminish because she couldn't think past them. Conflict was her way of life. Pushing regardless any consequence till she got what she wanted was her *modus operandi* even though it sparked implacable, eventually hysterical, resistance from me. From her point of view, it was *me* who needed to come round to *her* way of thinking. She felt justified in every sense of the word to pummel me since I'd committed the most unpardonable sin. There was, in her mind, simply no punishment too vicious and long-lived for me—Christianity 101 learned on St. Vincent's Old Testament knee. Her lake of fire was my just desserts. Only as our marriage legally broke up did she change her tune to reconsider her rationale for infinite argument.

"It was aahll I knew how t' do," she mewled. "You done hurt me more than I e'er could ha' imagine."

"Well, you got your money's worth!"

Tamela was the undisputed master of the guilt trip and me its faithful, slavish disciple. Moth-eaten by guilt, I firmly believed if only I'd never fallen with Shiori, Tamela wouldn't have abused me all these many years. Then I remembered how she was violently abusing me within weeks of our marriage. Even in St. Vincent I'd had to play a reverse second-storey man to fly the captive coop she forced on me in her arguments. She'd descend into a maelstrom of emotion and tears till I lost all self-control. The release made me feel better, but I realized she blamed all that early fighting on Jerome and Avril and me taking Shiori's phone calls in the months following our wedding. I never called her myself but didn't hang up in her ear, either, mainly because I wanted her to understand and accept my marriage to Tamela to relieve my guilt. I carried on no lovey-dovey pillow talk à la Chaz Jermin and Trixie in our later UTS hennery, but tried to drive her toward accepting my married reality. Tamela took it for emotional adultery and figured if Shiori was in town we'd be hip-on-hip by the 'o' of *hello* and raucously abused me for it.

Okay. I had to take responsibility for that, too. I'd been foolish thinking I could maintain a friendship, however tenuous, with a prior girlfriend who wasn't letting go. If I loved Tamela, I'd have completely and irreversibly severed all ties binding me to Shiori. I didn't because I'd felt too much a heel. Tamela believed my hesitation proved I really loved Shiori, not her. And so had Shiori. I couldn't escape her logic. I'd been a cad without the slightest sensitivity. Even so, I reasoned it didn't justify years of cruelty and psychological and physical torture. It *didn't*! Plus, she brawled over my relationship with Jerome—partly her fervid fear we were slam-banging in the bushes down at Sion Hill beach—and our heavy preaching and teaching schedule in our Unification Church front and the Spiritual Baptist congregations. One of my window dives springboarded off her hysterical refusal to let me through our bedroom door for church.

Pondering and dredging up the reality of our life in St. Vincent before I fell with Shiori, Mona's report was growing more sensible by the day. Her savage quarreling and my increasingly fierce and unstable response had characterized our life almost from our vows. During a particularly harsh argument over me going out with Jerome in the early months of our marriage, she got so emotionally out of control that I slapped her remembering how, in the movies, it snapped a person back to reality and calmed their feelings. *Wrong.* When a second later the shock I'd done it wore off, she doubled her decibels and shot a slapback I only just avoided making tracks through the kitchen door and up the street at a semi-run in fear of her shrieking fury bringing a jeepload of baton-swinging constables to deal with the ever-present undercurrent of the colonialist white man Jerome ceaselessly riveted home.

"*Goddamn me!*" I thundered to a hard-boiled universe. Our marriage was a clusterfuck from the start. Sure, we'd shared so many happy, loving, intimate moments over the past eight years. Even so, the sheer deluge of our tempestuous, malignant, alienating ones were a rogue wave swamping them. I told Mona, "I don't want to—I can't!—be anywhere near her."

"You need to be here for your children, Chris. I'm very worried about them only in Tamela's care." She was unsatisfied in her belief I was abandoning them. "I'm especially troubled how Kir-el seems to be turning into a carbon copy of her mother. She's lying, deceiving, screaming, and crying to get her way worse every day."

Fuck. Tamela's range of evil feminine wiles in her had me worried, too. "It'll only be worse for them if I'm anywhere in Tamela's range. You don't understand."

Neither did Linda. "Why don't you file for divorce and walk away, Chris?"

"Umm . . . broken legs?"

"That's how I handled my violent perpetrator two years ago."

"You? Abused?" I stifled a laugh that might've only sparked a new headache.

"He beat me up. I had to go to *shelters*, for God's sake. Me! I got a civil protection order—that's what you need to do, and right now—and educated myself about perpetrators and the cycle of violence."

"Whatever. Tamela isn't some fleeting girlfriend I can just walk away from. She's my eight-year wife who carried and right now possesses our three children."

"So?"

"You serious? We're intimately, integrally connected by strong sinews of love and family and—"

"*Pshaw!*" She chirped a laugh. "Sinews. You wax so poetic about your low-class piece of shit gold digger when she's got your one foot in the grave."

"Can't you keep a civil tongue? Shit!" She snorted derision. "Regardless her trouble and strife, a cpo is out of the question. She'd break it, guaranteed, and go—"

"See? And you tell me not to worry?"

Gah. "What about my children, dammit? The government could take 'em."

"You're being a fool. And you want *me* in your mess?"

"I'm not forcing you. But, for now, I'm satisfied staying far away from her." Moving to San Diego, though, which in fear I hadn't broached, meant living in the same city however huge. Trepidation smothered me taking steps to make it happen. Linda's aggravated eye-pops over my hesitation to fast-track a divorce hit hard, making me wonder only harder which was right: divorce or rapprochement.

"Any kind of reconciliation with a domestic violence perpetrator is impossible and dangerous not to mention dumb."

"I think you're overstating the case, Linda."

"Well, I'm involved with you, and therefore on your perpetrator's shit list."

"What. You feel threatened by her? She's never even been here."

"Doesn't matter. And you're being stupid. It's suicide not to use all the protection the legal system has for victims to stop perpetrators like her."

"Stop with the 'perpetrator' shit, will you? She's not some animal. I can't sic the cops on my kids' mom."

She chuffed. "Well, I'm not going to let her kill *me*."

"Uhhgh!" It brought an eye roll despite her common sense. I had my doubts and let them guide me, instead.

In my galling time of trouble and tribulation, the Unification 'precursor-to-heaven' Church was useless. I sent a detailed, multi-page letter to leaders I knew: In Hoi Lee, church spokesman Phillip Schanker (Columbia Road's former pastor and the guy who'd bungled Blessing '97), Columbia Road's current pastor Henry Schaffler, and others elsewhere. Crickets. Surprised, but not really. Our church has a proud, North Koreanish tradition of denying aid and spiritual succor to its casualties on the providential battlefield—shoot 'em, and move on.

And life *was* our battlefield. Every day, according to Rev. Moon, we battled Satan and his minions struggling in our duty to God and True Parents. It was only natural. We were putting them out of business paying off the sin he used to keep us bound in unbreakable slavery. We Moonies constituted the greatest danger to evil since Jesus walked the earth and no defense was too low. Mrs. Kobayashi and Shiori herself vehemently denounced my marriage, claiming I'd allowed Satan to invade my life and wreck her future. They didn't accept, as I had, that God led me from her to Tamela and our eventual Blessing as a positive good. Rather, I was forever a moron following my wanker not the Principle (my dubious intentions aside).

More than a week later Godwin responded. "Sorry, Chris, it took awhile to digest your story." *Pie slice it up the chain, you mean.*

"That's a long time when you're in crisis, brother."

"Yeah. Now, tell me everything."

I retold my tale. "I desperately want a Principled solution to my situation. I'm willing to leave Linda and reconcile with Tamela if it's at all possible, but I need the church's help to make it happen. I just can't manage it on my own."

"What do you expect it can do?"

"I don't know." I sighed heavily. "I need . . . moral strength and clarity of vision to understand the real truth of my situation. I need comfort, Godwin. Understanding and love. Acceptance."

"Well . . ."

"Don't worry. I don't expect it. Leaders always denied it to me even spiritually healthy. Now I'm the equivalent of a leper. Who'd give it to me now?"

"We *are* talking, you know."

"You're the only one to respond to my letters!"

He considered that. "You sure you want it, though? It's an indemnity course."

Ugh. That brought back Julian offering me redemptive indemnity for leaving the church with Shirley's LA MFT crew. "Well, I have to make the effort. I promised God I'd faithfully attempt the high road. I've already exhausted every opportunity to get my local leaders like In Hoi or Henry Schaffler—"

"I heard," he half-chuckled. *Pfft! Of course he has.*

"—to help with this mess. I mean, it's humiliating as hell but I have to expect God will guide me. I've placed my whole life and future in His hands, man." I listened to the line hiss. "The church rejects me again and again. In Hoi especially harbors some low grade ill-will. I don't know, maybe he feels betrayed trusting my fallen, archangelic self to Principledly stay in his holy center while I hunted work to afford an apartment *outside* the center."

"That's part of it," Godwin said. "I feel pretty betrayed, too, Chris."

Now that rankled me. "Come on, Godwin, how can my spiritual struggles betray anybody? It's not like I'm backstabbing *you*. I'm just struggling and suffering!"

"I get it, but I recommended you to Rev. Lee and asked him to help you out with a place to stay. He was skeptical—"

"Why the hell would he be skeptical? I don't get his change of heart at all. We were brothers at UTS! How does that just go away?"

"—and I put my reputation on the line, and now he's pretty unhappy with me because you let yourself be invaded by some unPrincipled girlfriend action."

All I had for that was a heavy, breathy sigh into the phone. "Even so, Godwin, that's just the trials and tribulations of life. Ask half our church leaders! It's not like I invited Satan into my life just to fuck with you or In Hoi." I choked up. "I'm just under so much stress from Tamela and it just happened . . ."

"I understand that." *Do you? Truly?*

"Doesn't seem to make much of a difference, though." There's simply no greater betrayal in the Unification Church. Rev. Moon threatened Blessed couples with near eternal damnation if we fell, darkly warning, "Even Satan will be Restored back to God before a Blessed member who falls." It frightened me, aye. Even as I tramped my fiery path with Tamela and lay beside Linda's calming warmth in the night, stargazing through her narrow windows rising cathedrally alongside our bed, I contemplated my sin and its consequences. But I was taking a deep, continuing draught from her heady well of healing love and acceptance. *Though God Himself throws His thunderbolts against me, I deserve her even if in the gain I flout His heavenly law.* "The church has scorned and abused me for nigh twenty-one years. It's only now it claims some concern for my eternal life? What a joke."

"I'm not judging or condemning you, Chris. I hope you know that."

"Yeah, I do know. That's an immeasurable help more than you might know."

"But neither can I give permission to follow this course you're faltering along."

"I get that, too, dammit. And your friendship's a lifeline keeping at least one foot firmly planted in God and Divine Principle . . . even if my other one's maybe already in hell's charnel house."

Chuckle. "So, I'm good for something, then."

"You might be the only decent leader in this whole godforsaken church."

"Try not to be so morose. You'll survive this. You made it to UTS, didn't you?"

"For a no-mission mission." I forced a titter. "Even if I divorce Tamela, marry Linda, and avoid knocking myself off for some ratty, in-between existence—"

"Don't talk suicide, Chris. Don't even go there."

"—I won't forsake True Parents and the Way of Restoration . . . that's, like, the axial event of the world and my life."

"Keep up your optimism, then."

"Wish the church had some." The phone line whipped a sinusoidal brow wave from LA to DC. *Jeez, he thinks I'm tilting windmills.*

Because Linda hammered me on a regular basis for not divorcing Tamela fast enough and treating her like the violent pariah she was—the way she'd lowered the boom on her scurrile boyfriend—including abandoning my children, I felt too humiliated to tell her I was thinking of moving to California. I vacillated a week, unable to choose. And then in a sudden fit of determination I packed up my stuff. Rented a U-HAUL trailer. Collected our belongings languishing in our New York storage shed as well as our property recently boxed up in a Cocoa storage shed. Abandoned our furniture and appliances at both. Then highwayed for San Diego. A road trip might do me some good on my way to potential doom. Cruising south on I-95 for Florida, I rang up Linda with my decision. Flames burnt my ear.

"I feel totally betrayed trusting you'd talk this over like an adult, not hiding it."

"Betray, betray, betray! You sound like a church leader. You know I've been wrestling over what to do about my kids and Tamela. And I knew you'd hate it."

"You're such a fucking coward! Don't even say your perpetrator's name."

"I knew you'd react just like this. That's why I didn't want to—I didn't want a scene. I can't take any more goddamned conflict in my life! Calling you was hard enough. Can't you just be calm? Give me some encouragement?"

She surprised me in lowered tones, "I'm not saying you shouldn't go. Whatever you do with your African is your business. Just don't involve me in it. But I could've planned a goodbye event. I'd have liked that."

I burped a breath. "A goodbye event? Are you kidding?"

"No, I'm not kidding! It's what sane, normal people do. Not your perp—"

"It would've been nothing but you arguing with me to stay. The whole reas—"

"I'm not your gold digger, Chris. If you want to go, then go. But I would've liked for you to have a loving send off from the only person who cares about you . . . why I even do, I don't know."

My head was shaking down the road. "I don't think you really understand the trauma I'm living with, regardless your violent boyfriend experience."

My therapists had formally diagnosed me with severe Post Traumatic Stress Disorder (PTSD). I couldn't really distinguish Linda's potentially loving response from Tamela's certain, wildly erratic own. Domestic violence turns a person into a quivering lump of short-circuiting neurons. I was tall, big, and strong but my intestinal fortitude was all but sapped, what the Army calls a 'combat ineffective.' I was so terrified of her response to me leaving for Tamela's home turf that I delayed telling her till safe in my car, unstoppable to all but a guided missile, a thumb on the 'disconnect' button which I could only dream of having for Tamela's mouth.

"Well, it hurts you'd do it like this. It's really wounding to be so disrespected, unloved, and deceived." And then *she* hit 'disconnect.'

I growled, "Fuck!" and pitched my peeved phone to the passenger floor. I couldn't win for losing and steamed all the way to Florida.

I realized my relationship with Tamela was ruining all my relationships, new and old. How was I to avoid or transcend it when I was now consummately rooted in the moment? Tamela loomed in my foremost consciousness like a Norwegian troll, a nightmare from which I was powerless to awake.

Anxiety grew exponentially with the shortening distance to San Diego. I second-guessed my decision at practically every mile marker and then in between. Time and again I pulled up in the great deserts to let stultifying heat sink into my bones and lull me to sleep that I might reconsider the direction I was pointing my life. By the time I straggled to the coast my heart thumped ribs like a jailbreak and my shirt sopped sweat. I felt like the unlucky sod digging his own grave and reviled my predicament. Wasn't there a way out without confronting anything? anybody?

SAN DIEGO WAS the hobgoblin I'd expected. The moment I shifted into PARK at Mona's suburban home April 29, 2000, hostility ruled my every interaction. Tamela had good cause to feel hostile. I'd walked out on her and our three children. In her cognitive world, it was as unexpected as it was unjustified. On the other hand, I had my own good reason for truculence. She'd abused me near on a decade till I teetered on the edge of lunacy, a potential danger to myself and my children. Naturally, she suspected another woman behind her entirely unfair situation. But I'd learned very well my lesson regarding confessions. *Don't. Take it to the grave.* So spoke experience and therapists in one emphatic voice. She can fuck me up in the next world if that's really an option. *I'll never tell her about Linda.* But that wasn't the issue, it was her abuse. Perhaps she'd be surprised if not secretly pleased Linda was turning out to be, in some measure, similarly if differently abusive and unreasoning.

Mona put me up in her upscale, California King tract house in the hills north of San Diego where cool ocean breezes mitigated the surprisingly dry heat of the day. Her Spanish colonial neighborhood amongst cookie-cutter thousands cast a tawdry architectural uniform o'er the e'er more tarnished Golden State. *Blech.*

Her house was spacious, roomy, and overpriced but I was grateful for the tolerant hospitality as I dropped my briefcase and bag on her guest bed. Plan A was to find a job, my own apartment, and take up my parental duties. I achingly missed my children. Countless times I'd fallen bawling to Linda's home-alone Persian floor, wailing almost at the top of my lungs for their touch and laughter. It's futile describing the arrant barrels I shed or the gloomy darkness pestering my heart.

Though I appreciated Mona's support, she humiliated me over her monthly $2,000 when I asked for her May check. "How is it you don't have more left over than you do? What are you spending it on?"

"Nothing I shouldn't. I've only been frugal. Some dress shirts, ties, and whatnot for my engineering and executive job interviews—"

"I don't see you ever getting that," her fiancée Bob said. "You should look—"

"I have the skills and experience for it. Not as big as your company, obviously." I swiveled to Mona. "Besides basic bills like food, phone, and gas, I sent most of it to Tamela in Florida. Plus a thousand or so to move all our stuff 4,000 miles."

"Well . . . I'd need you to justify your expenses before I write that check."

"I'm not profligate or squandering it on Linda, if that's what you're thinking."

"We have every right to be concerned where our money was going, Chris."

"That's exactly where probably three-quarters of it goes. Wait. 'Was'?"

She and Bob roundly chastised me over . . . I wasn't even sure. "I don't think we can continue providing that support given the circumstances."

"You said you'd help through June."

"I don't think we can go that far, now."

I violently worked my jaw. So, I had what I had. I bitingly felt wronged and vowed never again to ask my family for help. I'd sooner squat under a bridge.

Bob not too unfriendlily said, "What kind of apartment are you looking for?"

"I suppose one that won't get burglarized and my car is safe." I mean, what else mattered at this point?

"Is that what you're looking for?" A scornful, querulous tone. His face posted a self-righteous scowl. "I would have thought you'd be more concerned about your children. You need something acceptable if we're paying for it."

I gawked. "What do you mean?" The disdain dripping through his sarcasm was chewable. It bit deep. Inflamed me further. "There's been no mention of the kids living with me, only with Tamela. I thought I was looking for a studio or 1-bedroom for *me*." *For chrissakes, why're you bringing me up short like this?* It didn't seem to me that Mona, accordingly Bob (or vice-versa), believed my children were even safe in my treacherous, lecherous care. I was already regretting moving to San Diego under the auspices therefore control of my sister who was clearly evincing a dominatrix glitch. She hadn't conditioned her monthly help on strings, yet now claimed control over 'her' money. I didn't think so. She gave it freely, theoretically out of the kindness of her heart. "I didn't misspend or steal a penny of that money, Mona. I've been very careful with it. Supporting Tamela and the kids has been my first priority, which is what it's mainly for. If it's receipts you want, I have all my purchases."

Now she U-turned. "No . . . that's not necessary. I believe you."

No, you damn well don't. So, I did anyway. She returned them uninvestigated. Maybe she was trying to backtrack on the distrust she'd seen sowed in my face. Regardless (and I still loved my sister if not Bob the insolent parvenu), our bleak conversation brought on a quick souring with them and my beggary.

While I stayed at her house, she'd forbidden Tamela's presence without her to hall monitor. By now, she well understood Tamela's potential violence confronting me without mediators. Her rule was the right tack but it didn't matter because it never matters. I lay sleeping early May 9. Tamela pushed 3-year old Kir-el through the pet door to unlock her entry. She burst furiously into my bedroom, rudely awakening me with her hands.

"Wake up! Wha' mek you leave me?" she said in strident Vincentian. "Tell me wha' mek you t'ink you can'a be roun' me no more. Wha' wo-maahn you wit' who be takin' you 'way from me?"

I jerked upright. "God, Tamela! You're not supposed to be here! Mona—"

"I don't care wha' Mona say! She don't rule me! Wha' 'de *hell* you doin', Chris? You ha' a *family*. Three little chilleren and *me*!" Eyes flicked to bug-eyed Kir-el.

"I'm trying to deal with all your endless, never-ending cussing. Can't you just leave me alone long enough to get my bearings?"

Her head shook violently throughout. "Who you t'ink you be, though, carryin' me up here to Ameree-cah to leave me? If you knew you be do me so—"

"Oh, my God, Tamela! Get out of here and leave me *alone!*"

Some 45 minutes of this and I managed to lock myself in the bathroom for a shower, but really to escape even if just a bare-naked minute. When I tiptoed out across her eggshells, she'd rifled through my unforethoughtedly unlocked briefcase—I'd felt safe in Mona's demilitarized zone—and hotly flung Linda's now torn-to-bits studio portrait in my face.

"Who 'de *hell* be '*dis* wo-maahn?" Flaming eyes lasered me.

"It's plainly a work photo." She could be my real estate agent for all she knew.

"Wha' work? Wha' mek you lie to me? Wha' mek you goin' wi' another wo-maahn? You miss Shiori? Wha' mek you can'a tell me? It's a simple queh-stion."

God, stop the foreplay and just kill me now.

There was no 'splaining my heart to a rabid cuckquean deaf to the sparking PTSD heaped up in me like pitchwood round a pyre. She was irrational. Not here to listen but to light off my *auto-da-fé*. She shifted from quarrel to brawl batting me backward into a glass-fronted bookcase I thought had to shatter but only toppled against the cornered wall. I tumbled into a wood rocking chair. She vented all her wronged marrow like a swelling lava dome letting go. Time to git gone.

She blocked me at every door. Knocked me down twice. Ripped my shirt off from behind, spraining my back. Scuffling through the laundry room where a door led to a fenced-in concrete path, she popped buttons on my second shirt. Slapped my sunglasses off to grind them underfoot on Mona's terrazzo in a fit of deitic wrath. I battled my way outside. Through the side gate. Broke for the car. Leapt in the driver's seat—she got both hands on the closing door. Kir-el pattered behind gaping through saucered eyes, a rictus of death by Sasquatch. Tamela struggled and cursed till I broke free and sprinted headlong down empty, suburban Riding Ridge Road—barging through the usual popcorn crowd were it St. Vincent—with her in hot automotive pursuit and wee Kir-el screaming tears. Snarling on my heels a fingers-scrabbling wraith, lungs bursting in fright and exertion, I leapt the 7-foot stone block sound barrier separating the neighborhood from the Ted Williams Freeway. I hit the slope on the other side half rolling, half bounding through sandy dirt and desert spikes. Scurrying up the nearby off-ramp to the overpass, I imagined her *stiupp!* ringing the sky. Catching my breath, I crossed it away from Mona's house and stomped far up the opposing hill into under-construction neighborhoods.

There was no way I could pop her in the mouth without *me* going to jail, much less terrorize her into docile submission à la Chaz Jermin. That by far wasn't my nature nor her weakness. I raged at her unabated abuse. Brutal force. Verbal assaults. Invasion into the deepest corners of my briefcase to destroy Linda's small executive photo. Using Kir-el to violate Mona's rules. Attacking me in my sleep.

I wanted to hike far into the badlands. Get lost in the chaparral and never found. The semi-arid environment surrounding me by noontime was uninhabited, filled with scrub and sand, old littered campfires, jeep tracks, and birds of prey wistfully winding lazily overhead hoping for brunch.

All I knew was my roiling fume and furor. Part of me just didn't care anymore. I'd come to San Diego to see about reconciling with Tamela but, if nothing else, to at least live in proximity of our children and be their dad. I was out here for their sake, not mine *or* hers. Kal-el especially was suffering without me and both were wetting their beds in suppressed eye-gouging. I couldn't endure a minute more of her temper, anger, violence, resentment, guilt trips, blame, and unpredictability. I wanted out. *Out!* Let me fly away like a bird or vanish like a wind. The children held me, of course. I couldn't desert them. I loved them more than myself. *I'll endure anything for their sake. But can I, truly?*

"Where in hell am I?" I halted to take stock. Did a three-sixty. The wild west in all directions. Ass end of the Internet. No idea where I was. My throat parched. Tongue velcroed the roof of my mouth. Face and lips reddened into a burn. "Isn't it ironic," I half muttered, "if I die of thirst on the outskirts of a huge American city for want of a little geographical knowledge."

I headed due west and landed on the beach at 7:30 PM then collapsed in Mona's violated premises at 10:30 PM. My younger sister Blair had taken my children to Santa Clarita. Mona was beside herself with Tamela and tried mightily to explain why her cross-border incursion was wrong. Hours of mostly one-sided discussion later, she was only more exasperated with our situation.

Tamela said, "I know it be wrong . . . but I will do it again tamahh-ree if I ha' to. I will do anyt'ing I ha' to."

Mona threw up her hands. "Tamela's incapable of understanding adult-level reality," she said to me.

"Ya think?"

I retreated to Blair's a few days. Then she said, "Honestly, Chris, you act more like a guest here than a father to these kids."

"If you knew how depressed and distracted I am, you'd congratulate me for *that*."

Back in San Diego May 15, Tamela came beating on Mona's doors and windows. She set up a watch while I played nobody home till Mona arrived.

"Chris," she said, "you need to make an immediate decision about what you're going to do regarding these children. Come out front and talk to Tamela."

Shit, these people don't understand domestic violence! We were warring diplomats seated in her front yard's garden area and danced bitter rivals round reality. At last I admitted, "I'm sorry, Tamela, but I don't want to stay around you. It's too much for me anymore."

"Just keep your cool, Tamela," Mona said to Tamela's stiffening quills as we tamely bickered. "This is the part where you work things out. Remember, your children need you to be calm."

She worked at it but looked unconvinced of its merits. When Mona stepped inside for a phone call—Linda! untimely voicing, among other things, "Chris loves me and wants to marry me"—Tamela pressured me to stick around for marriage counseling. She'd only boxed me in. I was browbeaten. "We work t'ing out," she gleefully advised Mona retaking her seat. "He love me. Wan' stay marry t' me."

Mona was dubious. She focused on me. "Is that what *you* really want, Chris?"

I burst into tears. "No! I want counseling, but I can't live in the same city with Tamela. I'm absolutely terrified of her." Tamela rolled her eyes. "Not for physical reasons, I just can't take her abuse any more. I feel like I'm coming completely unglued, Mona, going lock-up-time insane."

Tamela loudly scoffed. " 'Dat be ree-diculous! How you be 'fraid me? I jus' be a smaahll gyul!" She laughed at its plain absurdity.

Mona understood better and spun my head with a hug. She drew out what I really wanted. "I need to go back to my friends and support system in DC. I've been going to some 12-step meetings here the last few weeks,"—visions, codependency, and other disaster spin-offs; important, regardless my growing crop of complaints with the people in it—"but I'm having a hard time connecting with them or getting anything out of it."

Plus, I added to myself, *I want to be near Linda.* More than someone I imagined I loved—I couldn't trust any thought or feeling anymore—or wanted intimacy with, she was my lifeline to sanity and healing, my own private therapist. I needed her. We'd later decide her therapy was wrecking our relationship and jettison that function. For now, in this moment, she was the only person helping me see things clearly.

My parents and maybe a few siblings liked her in that respect. They could see she was the only one getting me to listen to sense and reason and actually grow up at age 41 where they'd found me wanting all these years. She also unabashedly trashed Tamela and sometimes our children and that really pissed off Mona and Dad. So, like me, they had contradictory feelings for Linda and the wisdom of our relationship. Mona seemed way more invested in Tamela and our children than my psychological wellbeing, which I considered a prerequisite to my children's own.

Mona briefly took her leave again and Tamela snatched the opportunity to open up a new 'discussion' over me now changing my mind on her. It quickly escalated. As usual, I was eventually on my feet winding up Mercury's wings. As I defended my decision to remain separated—"at least for the time being, Tamela, nothing's written in stone, yet"—she angrily punched me then bodily forced me backward up the walkway till I tripped over the step-up to the front stoop. I stumbled and fell hard against the front door. Tamela was crying and screaming at me, pounding my chest and cursing. Mona rushed from the garage at our rising voices and the loud thump on her door and caught the whole thing. She wrestled with Tamela.

"Tamela!" she sternly, calmly, authoritatively interjected as if to a misbehaving child. "You can't use violence. You can't hit people when you're angry at them." She struggled a moment with her on top of me until I extricated myself, then held Tamela on the ground, her own back now against the front door and apparently a little panicked. Tamela was no pushover, to be sure. "Chris, call 911!"

Incredulous. "What?!"

"Call 911. Right now!"

"But, but—"

"Right now!" she hissed. She might've realized she was in over her head. I ran inside for the cordless phone and dialed it up.

"9-1-1. What is the nature of—"

"My ex-wife's in hysterics," I said. "She's fighting me and my sister. We need an ambulance right away."

"Yes, sir. Did she hit you? Physically strike you? Is anyone injured?"

"Um . . . yes. I mean, no; nobody's injured. But, yes, she's hitting me. Was hitting me. My sister's restraining her. Send someone to calm her down. We can't!"

Mona calmed Tamela after all. They'd retreated to the open-door garage while I calculated my chances near the embattled front door. Some minutes later police arrived, not the ambulance or maybe the on-call therapeutic psychologists Mona might've fantasized 911 would dispatch to what sounded to them exactly like a violent domestic dispute. Two cops in two cars parked unseen at the neighbor's house.

Tamela wept huskily in the garage. "Chris be leavin' me, Mona! What will I dooo . . . ? Me poor chilleren . . ." *Waaaaah!*

Mona comforted her with mixed results. When Tamela spied armed heat beeline off the sidewalk and up the driveway toward her, she jumped from her stool and screamed, "No po-lice! No po-lice!"

One approached to talk. She stiff-armed him away and turned to flee into the house. He instantly immobilized her arms. Pressed her to the smooth concrete. In the echo-chamber that was Mona's garage, handcuffs loudly ratcheted round her wrists. Mona's neighbor rushed in. My first up-close and personal police action dismayed me. Mona was stupefied. Tamela wailed like a lassoed banshee. Her voice, amplified by the mostly empty garage, airhorned down Mona's peaceful, urbane suburban street. We all cried like rats watching our cheese block sink.

"She's cognitively impaired," Mona pled. "She doesn't know what she's doing."

"I understand where you're coming from," Handcuffing Cop said. "It's not in the least unusual to see it from victims of domestic violence."

"But we've arrested her for assault and have to take her in for a hearing."

"I'm sure she'll be fine when she calms down," Officer Handcuffs said. "This isn't unusual at all. You said she has kids? I'm sure court won't be a problem."

Instead of sensibly keeping her peace Tamela disconsolately blubbered, "I be kill me-self 'de mo-ment you take off 'dese eye-rons 'dem!" Her sobbing redoubled. "I don't wan' live no more . . . I jus' wan' diiieeee . . ."

That got their attention. After some calls to invisible powers Second One said, "So, we're not going to take her to jail or process the assault charge. We're taking her to county mental health for observation."

"Thank you!" Mona popped.

"For how long?" I wondered, and not a little self-interestedly, either.

"Three or four days is typical."

Three or four days! Relief washed through me. That would be enough time to calm down and figure out my next move. Unfortunately, those stupid bastards let her out the very next day as soon as her emotions cooled and she'd reasserted her faux-reasonable persona, the one that persuaded Mona, Bob, my parents, her friends, and pretty much everybody to see the problem with our marriage was me.

Back in her apartment she immediately phoned to see me. Having just got her arrested and locked in the overnight loony bin, I was having none of it. But without fleeing the state, or at least Mona's house, I couldn't avoid her. I tried more ineffectual rational discussion and attempts to convey the bandsaw emotions I was wrestling with and the effect her constant quarreling and altercations were having on me. She was oblivious. Like an ant, the only thought she marched to was my unforgivable betrayal and her insistence I reconcile, which meant living with Crazily Violent till sooner than later death do us part. Getting her agreement for any relationship I could feel safely comfortable in was impossible. We were daggers drawn.

Finally, I acted on my racking desire. Linda was in Hawaii awaiting the start of her world trip. Phoning her that I was hieing home to Washington she said, "Don't you dare sneak out on Mona the way you did me. Be a man instead. Confront her head-on with exactly what you're planning."

Damn. "Okay, fine. I will. You just don't know how hard it is to disappoint."

"Quit this cowardice crap."

"Okay, okay." She knew me well. I was indeed plotting to load up my car and skedaddle midday when Mona was away, just a voicemail to evidence my intentions after the fact. "You're right. I'll do it."

"Be brave. You'll be fine." She beefed me up enough to briefly overcome my fear of confrontation. Even the most innocuous loomed larger than life nowadays.

I phoned Mona. "I've decided to go back to DC," and explained all my reasoning. "And I'm not abandoning or deserting my children, Mona. I just need to get mentally healthy so I can parent them again."

"Well, okay, I guess. When were you planning to leave?"

"Uhh . . . right now, actually. If that's alright with you. I mean, if you prefer I wait till you get home or something, that's fine."

"No, I don't want another scene with Tamela if she finds out. And she probably will, though I don't know how. I appreciate you being forthright and telling me instead of just disappearing." That clued me in to more of her earlier phone call with Linda. But perhaps not. Minds like theirs think alike.

"I really want to thank you for your hospitality and trying to help in all this. I know it's been a mess and not easy at all, so . . . really, thanks so much."

"Just remember, we all love you regardless."

Yeah. That scary (thereon, normal) convo under my belt I cranked the engine, yanked the gear selector to DRIVE LIKE MAD, and stomped hell for election.

Confronting people with what they don't want to hear has long been a tough row. I don't know why. Mayhap two decades of scorn and denial in the church. Perhaps Tamela's decapitating pettifoggery and my inability under the pressure to defend my existence without at length screaming, punching walls, or fleeing the scene. Possibly my sense of familial rejection. I was—am—not a violent man. I've been in a grand total of two fights in my life not including Tamela's scuffles; three if you count the time I broke up a black–white fistfight in a New York City subway car in a $1,000 suit edged in cowboy hat and boots.

"You from Texas?" said a black guy when the conductor, giving up on the tardy transit cops, finally cracked the doors on our finished fracas. "Bet you're carrying, 'cause that's how they roll in Texas. I right? You carryin'?"

Pshaw. Like I wanted that gun-hating, crime-loving city sending me to Riker's Island for living my constitutional rights. I smiled in mystery.

Yet, I felt very good confronting Mona and Tamela with my real feelings. The start of a long road home, maybe. I'd said what I needed to say—"I'm sorry, Tamela, I want a divorce"—and was still breathing. There it was, plainly stated. The hardest sentence I ever uttered. Nothing was more terrifying to speak than those four words. I watched them enter her consciousness like a body blow. A knife wound to her seat of hope. Saying it, thinking it, even wanting it felt hateful. How I wished I didn't have to. But I did. I couldn't deny it. I really did. *I. Want. A. Divorce.*

Well, I wanted *separation.* To be as far from her cussing as I could get and work out the details later. Right now, I needed a total and absolute end to her contention, coercion, and combat that had so permeated the fiber of my life for eight tormentous years. I had no words to express my perfect contempt for her endless disputes. Beating my head against the floor was now preferable to talking with her.

I needed love and acceptance. Rest. Contentment. *Peace.* I didn't care where I found it. Not anymore. If not in Rev. Moon and Tamela's Blessing, then in Satan's bosom and Linda's sin. *I had to have it! Deserved it.* My children warranted a father not teetering into insanity and maybe unpredictable savagery. They needed love, acceptance, and all the rest . . . and who deserved it more? For their sake, I had to Restore myself. Heal. Stabilize my emotions and psychology. Become the self and father I thought I knew. *Domestic violence . . . you're outta here!*

TAMELA INCESSANTLY RANG my cell phone as I trekked the deserts for Washington. She so effectively paralyzed me in guilt that I halted at a truck stop on Albuquerque's fringe, unsure if I should make a Bugs Bunny left turn or right. *Back? forward? west? east? right here in Albuquerque?—why not? Maybe I can get a job fencing range, cowboying, handymanning a ranch . . .* possibly the only work I was qualified for in my mentally decrepit state. I loved the west. It was in my blood. My bones. *Maybe I'll be happier right here in this dry, searing heat.*

No . . . dammit. I need Linda. Her energy and hope kept me going. Tamela was a black hole sucking to oblivion everything in me that was good. I'd see Linda as a bit of a black hole, too, in the not so distant future. But for now, she was my light. God's hand reaching out to me. For sure I'd vise grip it come what may.

I cooled my heels two days in scorched-earth Albuquerque sparring with Tamela and seeking solace and wiser guidance from Mona, Dad, Godwin, Linda, and Silent-Bob God. I metronomed across my future and past. *Go back? forward?*

East or west dominated my thoughts. I dozed a fitful sleep, windows down to catch the flimsy breeze wafting off the torrid barrens. Ever the miser, it seemed wasteful running the air conditioner idling in the parking lot—a receipt Mona would never review—so I sweated my anxiety on the truck stop's parking oven. My night was the sleep of the damned, of those hating themselves but lacking the guts and foresight to dig themselves out. I quailed like a worm 'neath descending beaks, too resigned to my fate for even a token effort. Was there really freedom from Tamela's malevolence? *No way. There's no escape.*

Our children reached out from beyond the grave of our marriage grasping and pulling me back to my doom. I didn't believe I'd find liberty or peace. *What's the use in trying? Why not kill what's left of me and give my body over to Tamela? I can't win. Let the bird eat me.* My mind sank to the bottom of loser. A victim.

I puttered aimless around town. Suspended time. Suffered through a movie or two. Checked email at the library. Wandered a hobo.

What to do? what to do? Go east? go west?

Tamela decided for me. And thank God. I might still be rambling Albuquerque like fare-hiked Charlie trapped in Boston's MTA. Duking it out my third day, her ballistic temper launched on a shrill and unreasonable plume of damnation.

"Goddammitall!" I all but shrieked, "That's the last nail! I'm not taking—*Quit cussing me!* Goodbye"—I flung the phone across the car—"and fuck off!"

It bounced off the dashboard and popped its battery. Knotted guts burned that I still lacked the devil-may-care to say that last to her ear. Twisting the key, the engine growled. I jerked the transmission to DRIVE and tromped the gas pedal. My Taurus shot out of its parking space. Screeched around the corner to the interstate on-ramp. Flew up the highway . . . east. I brimmed with self doubt and fear despite my kettle-whistling heart. *What am I doing? the right thing or not?* My phone was firmly off but I was taking no calls regardless. Had to be on my own now. I was crazy with remorse, misery, and vexation. I detested myself as an emotional Idi 'big daddy' Amin doing to Tamela and my kids what I had to Shiori.

But wait just a goddamned minute!

I wasn't the abuser here. I'd only shagged Shiori on Tamela's time, for Pete's sake. It was Tamela who'd turned it into a denigrating, lifelong noose choking me ever to the edge. Yet . . . wasn't it still my fault? I couldn't shake it. Doubt nagged me like a hungry rat. *Damn, is there no way out?* I felt my sanity slip. I cried and screamed into the wind roaring through my four open windows. Passing through the desert mountains, I looked for a good rise to send my car careening over a cliff.

Yes, why not die now? My life is over. Tamela will never leave me in peace. She's a force of nature, a cyclone that never spins down. Isn't death so much easier?

"You have to live for the sake of your children, too, Chris," Mona had cautioned. Now her voice echoed in my head. Yeah, my sweet kids. Tamela could never safely raise them on her own. What'll become of them? *But why prolong my suffering?* I was beginning to see why people throw themselves off bridges, in front of buses, trick police into shooting them. *There's an idea!* Find a cop. Why not? He'd only be doing his job . . . no, damn it. It wouldn't be fair.

Anyway, I didn't really want to kill myself, did I? *Wait, there's a nice cliff and no guard rail. Just turn the wheel, Chris. Come on. You don't even have to turn it much at 70 MPH. It'll be quick . . . well, the end will. Take off your seatbelt to make sure; the airbag won't do squat with that off. Come on, do it!*

Maybe some Johnny-on-the-spot spirit SOB was egging me on, eager for me to make the transition . . . into . . . what? The cliff receded in my rearview mirror while I longingly agonized flying off it. *There'll be another one up ahead*, I comforted myself. Eventually, I ran out of cliffs and death wishes, too. Now I searched out billboards with big arrows to the local nut house.

That's what I need! Bedlam west. I'm practically insane now. I have no money. No job. They'll take me in. Give me a place to live. Help me deal with Tamela. Who else can do that? I am insane. I can't live in the normal world anymore. I can't control my emotions. I can't control my anger, sadness, or despair. I'm out of control. I can't do it on my own. I need help. Isn't there a mental hospital around here somewhere? *Shit! I can't even find a bughouse when I need one. Such a loser. What a victim.*

Then I realized my anxiety was receding with every mile marker eastward the way it previously puked an atrocity with each one westward. Like spent floodwaters across a devastated land, dread receded into my greater mind leaving my drenched psyche to heal. With timid joy I looked in my heart. Analyzed my feelings.

Yes! It's true. I do feel better. Lighter. More relaxed.

Not much, maybe. My essence anchored in my children, the loves of my life. As they receded, I felt my very organs dragged back, tearing free. Yet, my grinding jaw clenched less. My knuckles seemed less white on the wheel. My heart sang its first hesitant notes as miles rolled 'neath my wheels. Soon my mouth was, too. My voice burst out in thanksgiving, clamoring over the screaming wind.

"Thank you, Heavenly Father. Thank you! I did the right thing! My anxieties are lifting. I feel confident in my decision now. I regret Tamela's pain and suffering, I do. I regret going toward divorce. I'm still not sure it's the best road to walk but, at least for now, I know heading east is the right choice. Thank you for Your help . . . if I find a loony bin, I'll take that as a sign to drop in."

I didn't find one and my crisis in confidence was far from over. I had years ahead of me where I'd have to confront myself on a daily basis. Learn to set boundaries then enforce them. Fail as often as I'd succeed stepping to a higher plateau. But I'd looked my abuser in her face proclaiming my liberty. Holy shit it was hard. Nothing is more important to a domestic violence victim than to tell your abuser, "I'm tired of your smack and ain't taking it no more!" *That's right.* My own declaration of independence. Not cured by a long shot but empowered by my stiffening spine.

Joy was short-lived. Though my heart was lighter in conviction that DC was the right choice, my emotional state took a bad turn. Residing at Linda's with her halfway round the world a deep, abiding depression struck home. A miasma settled over me; a cold night air seeping into my bones. It worked remorseless into my heart. I was safely 3,000 miles from Tamela's crazed undertow, yet my shattered mind may as well have been on the same beach in her rock-grinding surf.

JUNE AND JULY 2000 I cycled my brand-new K-MART 10-speed all over the District. I slimmed down and toned up working off my rage and depression as best I could. I resumed seeing Peter. Despite his generous fee reductions, I couldn't keep it up much longer. I desperately needed someone experienced in domestic violence. I still hadn't fully accepted the truth I even was a victim. Yielding to who, or rather what, Tamela was only grudgingly percolated through my barriers. I hoped she'd change. I believed with enough love and therapy she *would* change.

"You're still deluding yourself," Linda warned. "The idea that 'love conquers all' is nothing but fantasy. Forget it."

"That's not true, sweetie. Love motivates you to aspire to what you never would without it. That's how it conquers what otherwise you couldn't. Or wouldn't."

"Perpetrators never change, Chris." She giggled in her derisively lilting way. "When are you going to learn? You're setting yourself up for her to kill you."

"*Pshaw!* You're just cynical." True love was my last Moonie cornerstone.

"And you're gullible. Not to mention stupid."

"Maybe. Not about love, though."

She snorted with extra sneer and a side of head-turning eye roll. Oh, well.

A good and dear friend who loved us both and tried her best to help.

With me gone, Tamela wiped her ass with California. Mona's help was only a means to get me back. Failing, she wanted to break her lease to flee, Kal-el's schooling be damned. Dana, her tutor from our upstate New York days and a good friend to us both, offered to take her in over a 3-year period to help her recover and live without help. I violently disagreed with Tamela dragging our kids out of cozy Carmel Valley for edgy Detroit and denounced her latest race from reality.

"I know you think you know her pretty well, Dana, but you have no idea what you're getting into."

"I appreciate what you're saying but, believe me, I understand all the abuse and trauma she's been living through." I got her crack hard upside the head as intended. *Shit, even Dana.* Like my family, she was seeing me the wronging party through Tamela's rose-colored veneer. But I also got her citing Tamela's roughshod childhood. "Everybody misunderstands her. She just needs the right help. I recognize your family's honest motives but, frankly, they're white and just don't get it."

What a forehead slapper. "What wouldn't they get? This isn't racial, Dana."

"I'm just saying, there's overtones and undertones they *can't* get, regardless."

That nettled. *Skin color ain't all that.* "You may be black but that doesn't mean you get her West Indian crazy any better than me. *I've* been living with her."

"Exactly. *I* know what she's going through which, it seems to me, *no one* does."

"Well, you don't have the whole story. I'm telling you, Dana, this is a bad decision. It's going to seriously backfire on you."

"She just needs to be around her people who know and love her. She's making the right decision. It'll be fine, you'll see."

Christ. The battle hymn of the deluded sounding its rally and every campaign a loser with Tamela. Mona and Dana's *fait accompli* shot down my every objection. Like Mona before her, Dana abundantly regretted the horse blinders she'd so excitedly strapped on and Mona her second go-round renting a single-family house in Detroit's well-to-do West Bloomfield without consulting me.

"Don't do it," I warned her when she called with the news. "It's way too pricey. When I finally get a job, I'll never be able to support Tamela's half of the rent."

"No one's asking you to pay it. It's what Bob and I decided to do for Tamela."

"Come on, Mona. Don't do that. I'm their father. I need to pay that."

"It's already done. I paid for a 2-year lease and her relocation on the condition she abides by the rules and stays the full lease." She sensed misgivings. "She promised, Chris. I trust her honesty. She says you don't know her good intentions."

"You ought to know she doesn't mean it because she *can't* mean it."

"She and the kids will be fine." *What's that about the road to hell?*

The upside was the children were only an 8-hour drive. But I was in no condition to visit because of the danger Tamela posed to my psychology. I stayed away, hated doing it, and reviled Tamela for making me. I missed my children like my own legs cut away. I wanted to hold them, squeeze their little bodies in my arms, feel the warmth of their breath on my face, kiss away their tears, sing them bedtime songs, roughhouse in the autumn leaves. Imagination soared with joy introducing them to all the places I was visiting and dreaming about them in Washington. Every bicycle trail I sweated, I pictured them pedaling beside me, behind me, before me, shouts and giggles fluttering in the wind.

Loneliness fed by our separation suffocated me under an ocean of depression I couldn't shake. A sense of hopelessness pervaded my mind. No matter how hard I tried roping some optimism, I believed I'd never find another professional job, never find freedom from Tamela's abuse, never find peace. *Life is over. My church career a dead letter. Professional life eviscerated. Spiritual life drowned in the Dead Marshes.* All perished the day I married Tamela, never seeing me a dead dream walking. Only now was I sluggishly perceiving my ghoulish reality.

Is this what it's like when you die suddenly? you don't know you're gone? you keep trying to live as though still commanding a physical body?

How I longed to pray yet couldn't. Only a whispered ditty here and there escaped bitter, dejected lips. God must've tired. I judged myself for asking His help because Rev. Moon rigorously trained us to never put ourselves before God.

"When you pray," I recall him admonishing, "you must always ask God how you can help Him, how you can heal His wounded heart. Don't you think God is so tired of listening to people demand God's help to fulfill their selfish lives?"

With Linda at one of our many congressional and diplomatic balls.

So ingrained, I felt supremely despicable falling on tearful knees regardless. "Oh, my God! Help me! I'm so sorry for the mess I've made of my life, frustrating Your efforts to lead me to fulfill your hopes for us. Help me find a job to support my babies. Help me with Tamela. To find a home to live in. Help me! *Helllp me!*" Too often I couldn't bring myself to ask. I repeated empty oaths that I'd rise from the ashes to do His will if only I might survive. Like every dying loser.

I rode my bike everywhere seeking solace in the sun and shade of the beautiful parks and trails around town, my chapel. Sweat pouring from exertion was my prayer, liturgy, and worship. The only time I felt joy or relaxation was on my bike. I reveled in the sense of freedom not even my windblown car on the open road gave me, as though my bike was the wings of eagles carrying me far from the desolate shores of my life. Every day I poured despair into my pedals till it chained onto my tire and spun off to pavement where I left it behind. For all that, my depression paralyzingly deepened. I hiked to the pay phone at Church and 17th NW.

Dad said, "You should consider prescription medication. It's obviously not going away on its own. Your depression seems like a medical problem now. I think it's clinical, Christopher. Anti-depressants will help."

"No, I refuse to cop out on drugs. It's not a brain thing, it's environmental. It's just the impossibilities of my ongoing joblessness, homelessness, divorce, my personal meltdown . . . and now I'm having so many problems with Linda's attitude over Tamela and our children."

"I'm sorry to hear that." I think he genuinely meant it. "She seems like a good addition to your life besides her attitude about Tamela. But, I think you're fooling yourself about your depression. You're way past it being problem oriented. Your mother and I aren't telling you what to do, but we think you need medical care."

I plunked in coins to keep the call going. "What're drugs going to do but cover it up? How will anti-depressants fix my domestic violence reality? Bring my kids back into my life? They'll just give me a smile sliding into death."

"That's completely the wrong perspective. You're wallowing. Medication might help you get out of your funk to find real solutions."

Might? Could? Maybe? Fucking science. *I can lick this.* "I don't need drugs, Dad. I just need to tackle each problem one by one till I transcend them all."

I heard his nose huff. "Your mother and I are praying for you."

I spurned psychiatry for therapy. Someone to hear all my confusion, hurt, and pain. Friends don't have the patience, time, or energy for that. Anyhow, I didn't have friends like . . . well, maybe Godwin, Rachel, or Julian. But you can only dump on friends so much before they need to wash you out of their mind for their own sake, and down the drain with all your shit usually goes you, too. They were important to me and I wanted to nurture, not kill, our relationships. I found Andrew through Medicaid for thrice-weekly domestic violence counseling. At least he was free.

Linda returned midsummer invigorated and inspired by the holy places in Israel, Turkey, Nepal, and Tibet. She was still miffed I'd spurned her offer—"You'd have loved it and I'd have loved sharing it"—and even more finding me lost in depression.

"It's dragging me down, too," she said. "You need to get over it."

"Ha! Easier said than done, eh."

"Only if you give up." She was happy to see me nonetheless. We figured we loved each other and worked at our relationship. But . . . shouldn't love be smoother?

Unfortunately, I was down to a couple hundred in the bank. I needed any job I could get. With luck and persistence, Rock Creek Park Horse Center hired me as barn manager. I worked 6 AM–3 PM feeding horses twice daily along with a shocking quantity of pill, capsule, and liquid medications probably quite like their pharmaceuticaled owners. I shifted hay, tractored manure into 40-foot rectangular concrete dumpsters, and handled the bric-a-brac of stables. It was hard work yet so very relaxing and peaceful. I so loved horses. Their presence offset my gnawing anxieties. It felt like Colorado amongst the trees. Maybe God *was* listening.

Working there, I was chagrined to realize I could never execute any responsible job in my agitated and distracted mental state. The barn paid $11 an hour, a far cry from the $70 I made consulting, but it was something. My responsibility for the horses wasn't taxing, though I struggled with expectations even so. I could pay some bills and Linda for utilities and groceries. The one thing I couldn't do was rent my own apartment. I hoped things would improve. It was depressing once more stuck unmonied from monied. *How the mighty always fall*, I reflected with some rancor. But now, mostly broke after dead broke energized me.

Then both feet slipped out from under me on a wet, steel staircase behind the barn, the sort of steep and narrow steps commonly used aboard ships. Though both hands firmly gripped the railings—a paragon of safety-first, I was—my feet went out from under me so fast my body plunged a weighted hangee. Muscled shoulders took a powder arresting my drop. Too sudden, maybe. I wouldn't let go and strained to support my 230 pounds. Both arms cranked violently back and up till a hand ripped free before its shoulder dislocated. I pivoted on the other hand. Slammed bodily into the steps. My neck all but snapped against a tread front. My arms went numb and my straining grip tore loose. I tumbled down the stairs and smashed ragdollish in a heap. My head bounced hard off the asphalt like it would've that time in Honolulu without my helmet. My vision blurred. For a second I thought I was knocked out. Hands burned. Shoulders and arms numbly tingled. After a minute I augured myself to a sitting position with a colossal abdominal press. Minutes more and my wits came home. I was up and thinking I'd escaped all but cuts and bruises. I staggered, dizzy. Pitched hay into a stall. My shoulder shrieked. Arm and back short-circuited, instantly numb. I knew I was in trouble and hustled for the hospital.

George Washington University Hospital's orthopedic surgeon was implausibly incompetent. His squint-eye saw nothing but a low-class laborer scamming Workers Comp. For months he obstreperously remonstrated nothing was wrong with me a little attitude change wouldn't solve. Different doctors on my second-opinion tour conclusively determined I'd torn both rotator cuffs and whiplashed my neck; nine months to heal (avoiding one's mad-eyed proposed rib resection). Debilitation forced me out of my new job and only deepened my depression. Three years and two fruitless left shoulder surgeries later, doctors pooh-poohed doing the right.

Surviving on disability payments two-thirds my $1,700 pre-tax barn wage, I'd saved enough for a gold coin in September. It might seem a waste for a pauper like me, but folks said gold brings good fortune and draws money to its owner. I needed some new luck. My $20 Double Eagle cost almost $400, but excitement surged palming it outside downtown's gold exchange. This wasn't consumer spending but an *asset*. An investment in *me*. I felt hope that life might improve.

That same day, perhaps buoyed by my golden change in affect, Linda said, "Why don't you look for a computer programming job? It's what you're good at."

Stretched out on the bed against the headboard madly crunching through my favorite angry food, I flipped eyes askance. "I don't know . . ."

"You're just sitting here injured. Anything's better than being on your butt eating through my tortilla chips glued to the TV."

I munched hard through the idea, unsure. Nagging brought me to heel and I posted my résumé on the Internet. Amazingly, I won an interview the next day. A few weeks after buying my gold coin, Carney Interactive in Old Town Alexandria, Virginia hired me as a senior software engineer for $73,000 a year, 3-½ times my barn income. Thank God for the tech bubble. Was it possible life was looking up? One thing was sure: that Liberty coin was my new BFF till a repairman stole it.

MY NEW JOB was fabulous. Good pay and they loved my work. They saw me as an expert, someone to rely on to accomplish anything no matter how difficult. If only the Moonies saw my value through their eyes.

I visited my children in Detroit over Thanksgiving 2000. Tamela's violent scenes had Dana at wits' end refereeing. It was too much. I had to scamper. Between tears of loss was always her caustic choler. She pushed me around as usual, demanding sex, more time with me, that I come back to her. I managed almost no time with the children and smoldered on our short jaunts to the sights and parks away from their tempestuous mom. I was single-minded about not falling into weekend dadding, my parenthood limited to this or that 'cool' place or thing.

How to avoid it, though? They should be home with me. Waking up together. Living life hand in hand. I needed to train and educate them, help and love them. *My* custody somehow shared with Tamela . . . I wasn't so cruel I'd take them away even if her negligent abuse argued it. But it didn't seem legally let alone practically possible. While she took excellent care of their food, clothing, and cleanliness she couldn't handle their mental, emotional, or academic needs nor their questions about the wider world. Neither could she effectively learn, according to Mona's scathing report. If she could, then certainly not soon enough to be of any use to our children. They needed her now, not in five years. Dana was picking up the slack, but it was wearing and she had her own son to raise.

Squabbling with Tamela for the right to depart, I finally made it inside my car late on a blustery day. With sudden insight she shouted, "Wait!" and dashed into the house, emerging to my suspicious frown with a comforter and sleeping bag, a pillow, and a few other things. "I t'ought you might be need 'dem."

"I ... you ... thanks." She so deeply touched me that I caught a glimpse of the woman I fell in love with and still loved despite everything. In that one moment, she almost remade our marriage. But I didn't believe for a quick tick she'd repeat the gesture nor abandon her violent habits. I didn't think she really understood the problem between us, that my hostility was rooted in her abuse not her cognitive disability or other women. I yearned to spring from my car to embrace and comfort her. But if I did, it would only produce the false impression we were reconciled, complicating matters and further breaking her heart.

I backed into the street. She yowled uncontrollably on the windblown driveway. I tried to comfort her through the window, but there was nothing to say or do except come back to her. It's all she could single-mindedly contemplate. My heart felt torn from its mount, a deep physical pain wracking my chest as my feelings broke. It was palpable, intense, and I'm keening tears just writing about it. I viciously cursed myself for the way I was treating her. And yet, if I didn't separate I'd inevitably go stark, raving mad. Her mental and emotional immaturity coupled with domestic violence was a vinegar-and-baking-soda spectacle. I burbled away with tears running down my neck, grief and sorrow pummeling me inside and out. The indelible sight of her squatting on her heels, head buried in her hands, sobs carrying across the lawn to my open window seared permanently into my self-loathing brain.

I DID CHRISTMAS 2001 with Linda in Pearl City on Pearl Harbor's northern bank with her black dad (Pearl's retired Command Master Chief) and Japanese war-bride mom who had her speaking only Japanese till age seven. She cooked up delectable Oriental vittles and I worked out my conversational Japanese. I earned my scuba certification in the open waters of Maunalua Bay (near Koko Head and Hanauma Bay) through Linda's instructor friend. I reached 60-foot depths and then 110 in the open Pacific surrounded by gigantic sea turtles. It was magical. Our holiday was peaceful and restful. No cussing. No spite.

Of course, I had to be careful not to open up Tamela or my children to discussion. Inevitably, it led to her caustic remarks that left my heart bleeding and stomping for days if not weeks. The more she let loose her dogs of war, the longer it took me to recover. She concluded "Kir-el is evil" because a photograph at age three had her glancing sidelong at the camera.

"Look at her eyes," she said. "You can see the same evil-eye as her mother. She'll be the same kind of low-class abuser when she grows up."

"You're insane." I couldn't be sure she really believed her shit or was only pissed I'd had kids before meeting her. "She's only a child. She bears no responsibility for her. If you took the time to know her, you'd love her ... if you're capable of loving anyone but yourself, that is."

On the Pacific's bottom, 110 feet.

Had to get my own digs in, I supposed. At least I could insult her without kicking off a day of close-quarters combat. A win–win. I set up boundaries, one being she never speak ill of Tamela and my children in front of me. She gunned tanks through them all. Mouthed off whenever the mood struck. If I complained, she reiterated and even embellished her slander.

"You know I'm right," she said with a giggle. "Admit it."

"I wouldn't bitch about if I thought so. Just stop. You haven't even met them."

A much later telephone therapy session in DC had her in the bedroom and me on the bay-windowed sofa. Literally opposite ends of her condo. You can see where we were by then. Her trusted, much-admired Honolulu friend and relationship counselor since our Christmas vacay remarked, "Linda, nothing Chris said leads to the conclusion you've just drawn. Your interpretation of his feelings, I have to say, is bordering on mental illness."

Harsh, in-your-face words that would've given anybody pause but didn't seem to faze her. We visited several counselors many times trying to solve her unwillingness to allow my children peacefully into her life . . . or just to exist. Even though she refused to change her mind, she refused to leave me. Peter hadn't been kidding. In March 2002 my children moved in with me. She had only kindness and a mother's tenderness for them, which I loved and appreciated. *Really, man. Fuckin' weird.*

"See?" she often said, "My actions speak louder than my words."

"But your words nullify your actions."

"That's crazy talk." Two ships passionately snogging in the night, it seemed.

Her insults weren't so frequent to merit Tamelazation, but enough to cause real psychic wounds. Until she finally met them, I had to make sure they didn't enter her conscious thoughts. In that case our life was peaceful, happy, content. She took fabulous care of me and I was a desiccated sponge. I tolerated her on–off breaches of my boundaries and we stayed together despite several painful split ups.

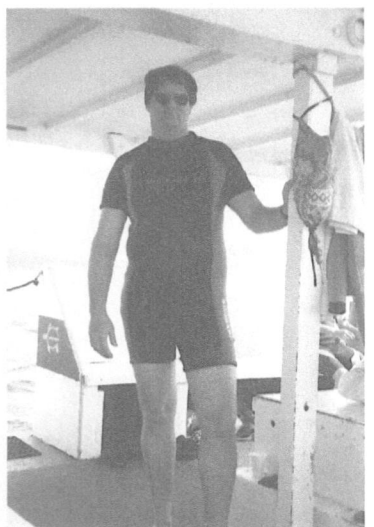

Feeling alive in Maunalua Bay.

She wanted her own family, uncompromisingly demanding I abandon mine to Tamela. "You'll visit on holidays." When that flopped she said, "We can live in separate households, you with your kids since you're so set on that. *Our* kids will live in my condo with me."

"And somehow we're happily husband and wife?" I flicked a *haha!* on the rocks in her face. "Dumbest thing ever. An ultimate absurdity."

Finally, she was feebly firm against marriage. "I want our baby out of your mess."

Yet, she wanted me her lover and she mine, plus a baby jacked up on our global visions. "I think that's a bad idea at this point, Linda."

She darkened. "That's an absolute betrayal of everything I wanted and you promised!"

"That was then. This is now. It seems we're split up more than not these days."

"You loved the idea of a global baby when we first got together."

"We argue too much. We feel too tenuous to me for a child in the mix."

"I never even wanted a baby till I met you—"

"But no way I'm giving up *my* children. You must figure I don't love them."

"—and you seemed like my child's father I always wanted."

"Look, Linda, if we have a baby, it has to be in a marriage as a blended family. All our kids together. One big, happy—"

Snigger. "Your kids will kill mine if they get the chance!"

"That is fucking crazy. How can you even imagine such a thing?"

"Because I'm a realist." She *muumuu'd* off to the kitchen. "I can't wait forever, Chris. I want our global baby. And so do you. You know I'm right."

My inner mind—perhaps the one God often tried to squeak through—was saying, *Back off while you can, dumbass.* She took my refusal as a woman scorned yet reacted in stride, tightly bottling up her grudgeful aggravation.

In spring 2001 she was snow in a sunny, clear sky. "Since you won't give me a global baby, I'm going with frozen sperm. I already found a doctor."

"That's uhh . . . What kind of genius on tap is gonna knock you up?"

She paused, some kind of mysterious look on her face. "Somebody like you."

Gah? "That's the weirdest thing you've said. I thought you hated me now."

"You're a fucking asshole, Chris! And totally dysfunctional getting involved with your low-class piece of shit perpetrator. But you're also handsome, tall, and brilliant. That's what I want for my global baby. A future president."

"Well, I, uh . . ." That made me think of Mr. Kamiyama. And boundaries. I was certainly having difficulty setting and even more upholding them. I was only just learning what they were and how to erect them. Maintaining them in the face of adversarial hatchet jobs was a master class I had yet to graduate.

WHILE I STRUGGLED on Linda's home front, Tamela's cratered. Six months into her promised 2-year Detroit resettlement, she and Dana escalated from clashing to unbounded warfare. My prescient warning had roosted. Tamela accused her 12-years son of attempting to sexually assault 4-years Kir-el. Incensed, Dana threatened to have child welfare snap our children out of Tamela's care.

Stunned and frightened by Dana's tactical nuke, Tamela phoned me the next day. "I buy a bus ticket firs' t'ing. I takin' me chilleren to Seraphina *tonight.*"

"What!" I hollered. "You're hosing Mona and abandoning—*the heck*? Absolutely, not! Do not go to Florida! I can be there tomorrow. We'll sort it out."

"She wan' tek me chilleren from me!" Tamela burned white. "I won't ha' 'dat. I ha' to leave *now.* Not you nor no-body stoppin' me!"

I muttered and cursed for a response. "Just apologize and work it out, Tamela. Jesus Christ, you can't just—"

"Yes, I can! No twelve-years boy g'wan mess wi' Kir-el. Nev-uhh!"

"Please don't drag our kids off on another half-baked—"

"I mus' protec' 'dem, Chris! No wo-maahn callin' no child service 'pon me!"

I groped with all my power for a solution she'd buy into. Mona and Dad got on the line. Nothing availed. This, in the middle of a goddamned workday. I couldn't drive nor fly to Detroit fast enough to beat her to the bus if I'd raced off that very instant. I had to swallow the dry sand of her done deal.

She shacked up with her old dope-smoking, adulterating girlfriend Seraphina to whom I'd given our furniture on my way to San Diego. I'd pressured Tamela to abandon her when we'd lived in Cocoa. Seraphina was a Pandora's box. Within two weeks she'd fingered Tamela's bank card right out of her purse to drain her account. Friendship crashed as police rolled up. Their *contretemps* forced Tamela—*with our children!*—into a city shelter. I fumed at her outlandish decision-making that greased our children's rails. Kal-el had by now been in four different schools in a single year and was collapsing mentally, emotionally, and academically. Eventually, social services found her a house in Melbourne with the $1,400 monthly support I'd been voluntarily sending since my hire at Carney. Her life settled down somewhat under the all-calming power of financial stability and private living.

But I couldn't defend my boundaries. She cast the die on belligerence by phone over Linda and our April 2001 divorce, an epic tragicomedy I couldn't hope to recount here. Driving 30 hours to visit the children, she quarreled violently in person. More than once stupid enough to enter her house, she trapped me till her rocket motor spent itself. Thanksgiving 2001 she captured me for an unrelenting 9-hour brawl, blocking me in the children's room when I tried dodging her 'discussion'. I didn't get out till so unbridled I inadvertently punched a hole in the flimsy closet wall. Frightened, she stepped aside then lit off stage three in the living room. This was when I'd taken a shot at 911 for some gunned up intervention. She'd yanked the phone out of my hand and flung it from the kitchen like a footballer.

"How dare you call po-lice 'pon me!" she snarled. "You a' need no po-lice wi' me. I is jus' a smaahll gyul. Wha' mek you so scared you need po-lice?"

Rather ineffectually I said, "I'm not scared of you but you won't stop cussing! Just leave me be! Let me out of the house!"

"No! Not till you answ-uhh me queh-stion 'bout this Linda wo-maahn."

Round and round cats chasing dogs. We darn near injured the children in the shoving match they tried to break up that finally bought my freedom. I sprinted through the front door like the hounds of hell were snatching my heels.

Tamela's shrieking "I hate you! *I hate you!*" buzzed my ears like bullets.

My entire being was a rolling boil. I slanted across the street and let fly double semi-hooks at a stop sign, severely bruising my right hand and breaking my left. Raving in all kinds of pain I tromped a mile or so to a strip mall and found the domestic violence center in a pay phone's dangling, well-abused yellow pages.

"Get your swelling hand to the hospital. We'll have someone meet you there."

"I punched a stop sign instead of her," I choked through two-days-no-sleep tears to the counselor as the nurse imprisoned my hand in a blue cast half up my arm.

"A wiser choice, even so." We talked hours, then days later three more. Tamela extorted hundreds plus my time with the kids. My fiberglassed paw slunk home frazzled to a soon-to-be disturbed Linda. All 30 hours back up my plaster pipeline I chewed her rank prophesy: "You're setting yourself up for her to kill you."

She took one head-shaking, scowling glance at my cast and put it all together in a second. "I told you. Didn't I tell you? You believe me now?"

"Let it go." She giggled her derision and swished off to whip me up a dish.

The whole event was a watershed. I'd actively resisted calling for help, but my domestic violence counselor Andrew—"She's a classic batterer and psychologically dangerous"—pushed me to ring 'em as needed. I cared about Tamela though Linda acidly scoffed. I somehow loved her, too. I simply hated—no, *loathed*—her presence. She was predictable only in the inevitability of confrontation and violence. Insane with jealousy and rejection, she couldn't control the emotions roiling her soul. But send her to jail? It wasn't in my heart. My wrath would have to churn beyond all limits before I'd lose enough compassion (and guilt) for such a drastic step.

The morning after jetting in from my Hawaiian *mele kalikimaka*, Tamela rang. "You mus' tek Kal-el and Kir-el to live wi' you. How soon can you pick 'dem up?"

"What! I couldn't manage it last December when you wanted it. Why—?"

"I ha' me reason. An' I don't ev-uhh wan' your rot-ten wo-maahn roun' 'dem."

It was anyway in accordance with our custody agreement from the shitshow that finalized our May 2001 divorce. She cussed Linda into February 2002 even as Kal-el flunked first grade, a feat I hadn't thought possible though he'd repeated kindergarten. I picked them up March 3—Ford's trashy '96 tranny blew on the way—in a hail of social services-mediated combat. We set up in a Parisian-redolent 1-bedroom third-floor walk-up at 1825 Summit Place NW (bad credit forced a 4-month advance rent to move in) overlooking a forest and DC's zoo. Screeching monkeys and animal cries wafted over tree boughs through our windows to the children's delight.

Tamela phoned. "You keepin' our pickney 'dem 'way from your wo-maahn?"

"We're not even really . . . It's all very on again off again," I temporized.

"Wha' mek? She fin' out 'de kin'a maahn you be?"

Eye roll. "No, she hates you so much even I can't take it."

"Well, you two be togeth-uhh or you not. Don't be tell me 'dis on again off again buuull-shit. I a' been born yest-uhh-day."

"Whatever. Say hi to the kids. And please be nice."

They innocently said, "Miss Linda painted Easter eggs with us, Mommy!"

It was a huge step for Linda. "Just consider it my way of saying I love you more than I hate your African perpetrator, sweetie."

"Put your fadd'uh on 'de phone!" Tamela deafeningly harassed and battered me a month over Bell Atlantic. Crumbling like a bishop backing pedo priests in court, she forced me into a civil protection order until now out of the question.

Linda said, "You don't have to answer just because it rings. I don't."

I nodded thoughtfully. She'd proved it during our breakups. "Yeah, I guess it's a human habit, like God Himself might be on the line . . . Pavlovian, isn't it?"

"I'm proud of you getting a CPO. About time."

"I've never even considered not answering. Kind of an epiphany, to be honest."

"You're welcome."

When Tamela bused up to deal with child support, she was so mad about the CPO she blocked me getting into my double-parked Taurus in front of her youth hostel to 'discuss' it. Physically whopping me right there, she knocked me against the front fender. I spied Kal-el in the back seat through the windshield literally trying to tear the hair from his scalp and bristled at Tamela.

"Look!" I jabbed a finger at the car. "See what you're doing to Kal-el? You're literally killing our son with your violence!"

That deflated her. "G'wan, then! I'll jus' tek L'or-el and go." Instead, she later wormed her way into my apartment and harangued me for hours.

"Tamela, if you don't leave I'm enforcing your restraining order. Don't make me do it." Deaf ears. I dialed 911, shielding the wireless from her batting hands.

The cops pulled her hands behind her. "Please, please don't be arres' me in front o' me chilleren!" She jabbed eyes at me. "Chris, how can you le' 'dem do me so? Wha' 'bout L'or-el? Tek 'de chilleren so 'dem don't see. Please, Chris!"

The cuffs snicked closed heedless. But like those San Diego dumbasses, they let her go the next day. Still, it sobered her up for a blessed couple months and I enjoyed a modicum of peace. In due course, the US Attorney (DC is a federal enclave) declined to prosecute because of her cognitive disability. She took that to the bank to lure me into violent confrontations over the phone. Nice work, crimebusters. I installed an answering machine, killed its volume and ringer, and restored a semblance of serenity to our home . . . not sure an unlisted number even occurred to me.

I'd struggled to explain the devastating 9-11 terrorism to 7-year old Kal-el while visiting Florida days after it. Then in March I'd gratefully traded my grungy, second-floor group-house room at 7101 Piney Branch Road near Dahlia Street NW (taken to afford Tamela's house) and a buttload of dough for my lovely, parquet-floored Parisian flat, two kids, travel costs, plus two sticks of furniture before I ran dry. Whereupon days in John Carney, having lost his anchor client's cash flow in the Trade Tower's rubble, laid me off with a month's severance right after a glowing performance review and pay raise. I'd thought my second highest-paid engineer job safe. But the tech industry was in full meltdown, the stock market crashing, the e-learning industry crushed, and clients chary. Companies in crisis don't give two shits in a Taco Bell about training, it's all panicked cost-cutting.

I phoned Tamela with trepidation. "I can't send money till I find a new job."

Teeth stiupped. "Wha' mek your job fire you becau' wha' happ'n in New Yaahk? You a good waahk-uhh. It soun' more like Lind-ahh ain' be wan' you waahk so you can spen' time on she. You tryin' to form a family wi' she an' me chilleren?"

I blew a heavy, exasperated sigh in the phone. "The idea that I'd give up six grand a month to save your thousand is just you being crazy, Tamela. I love L'or-el. You think I'm not going to support her?"

"If 'de shoe be fit, Chris, an' it don't fit me."

"You thinking I'd actually obey her even if she did . . . *pfft!* You don't even have words for your stupidness. Anyway, that's the situation. Sorry, and goodbye."

Long-dreaded, my layoff was a jolt. My boss Travis, Carney's best-paid engineer, had only days earlier reassured me. "Forget it, Chris. John is not contemplating letting you go at all. You're too valuable."

Then he barfed today's reality over the phone. "Must've lied to you, Travis."

"Well . . . he really cleaned house. He let go everybody but me and our lowest-paid engineers. Even Larita. Most of our graphic artists, too."

"Damn. I really liked her. Who's even left? He went from over fiftyish to . . . ?"

"Maybe twelve. A total slaughterhouse. Killed morale. I'm really sorry."

"It was great working with you, Travis." *And here we go again.*

Months of failed contingency hires plus Tamela's waxing abuse to ultimate arrest had me spending summer 2002 poisoning my relationship with Linda inundating her with my uncontrollable depression, self-pity, and despair. Without faith in my future, my present was a waterslide to hell.

IN EVERY WAY I was constantly forced to confront my boundaries. Often with Linda, always with Tamela. I've been conflict averse since childhood. Or maybe the church. Or Tamela. Hard to know which. I despise confrontation yet self-loathe when I don't stand up for myself. It profoundly tears up my emotions. An ever greater depression laid over me a dark, intractable fog.

Is there a way out? My eternal question for a year. *Should I just die?* Buses came and went . . . *why don't I step in front of one? It's so easy. Bam!* One and done.

Then spirit world reared up. Dr. Sang Hun Lee's *Messages From the Spirit World* widely published in the Unification Church, as well as other works by Franchezzo and Swedenborg, horrifyingly discouraged me on that front. The last place I wanted to go with all my dysfunctions, fury, and resentment was spirit world, the one place Rev. Moon says we *can't* solve our problems. I may hate life but, according to Dr. Lee, the worst it has to offer is infinitely preferable to the suffering I'd find after a suicide. Even were I killed totally by accident, my state of mind would only land me in a very unhappy spirit land. Although, without Tamela . . .

He and Rev. Moon preached our physical life governs our spiritual future. Build it of goodness centered on God's Will and you'll find yourself in a life of goodness in spirit world. Build it of evil, pain, anger, resentment, suffering, and abuse inflicted on others and you'll find that instead. I remembered Swedenborg encountering a man on a vast spirit plain standing all alone, finding out he'd made it so during his earthly life. I was already cut off from family, church, and friends. It seemed I nursed a resentful grudge for everyone. All had let me down. All conspired to hurt me. Not a single soul seemed willing to sacrifice a toenail for my sake.

Am I that lonely man? One day I'll die and be dumped in a pauper's grave with nary a soul bidding me goodbye. If I die today, will my own parents show up? I didn't think so. I felt they hated my life, my personality . . . everything about me. That all their hearts had for me was the sad fact they couldn't avoid my being their son. Perhaps I was transposing onto them the hostility I believed my sister Mona—my whole family, still less the church—held for me. *That's unfair*, I cautioned myself. Yet, I felt it in my heart, my very bones. *They just don't fucking care! Nobody does, dammit! Damn them! Damn me for ever being born!* Ah, my self-pity flew fast and furious, yes. But to me in those years it all seemed true.

"Your own actions speak louder than words," Linda loftily said over the phone.

"Theirs seem all about avoiding me. When Mona said, 'Remember, the whole family loves you,' it seems she was really saying all my family is prepared to do in my moments of harshest despair is mouth platitudes, not actually help."

"There you go, blaming your family for your own mess again."

"Shit, Linda! I need some sense I'm loved, accepted, wanted . . . cared about. How am I supposed to perceive it if they never help, visit, write, or even call?"

"Well, boo-hoo." *God, she's hardened.*

"Just a gram of my heart for their wisdom. Some help, if needed."

> For I was hungry, and you fed me. I was thirsty, and you gave me a drink. I was a stranger, and you invited me into your home. I was naked, and you gave me clothing. I was sick, and you cared for me. I was in prison, and you visited me.

"Haven't they helped you enough? What about Mona and all she's done for you? Go get welfare if you want concrete help and quit your pity party."

"Man, fuck you." But I couldn't deny it. Self-pity is nothing if not the belief your problems are made by others if not God Himself—just ask Job's friends.

"You wallow in self-pity, Chris, but it's really your refusal to recognize or accept others' inabilities. You insist their inability is actually unwillingness."

"Well, in truth isn't it? I mean, practically?"

"Why don't you give your African piece of shit whatever she's always begging for?" Her derisive giggle left marks. "You're no different than your own family."

"Ugh!" Tamela forever complained I was unwilling to help. Every crisis *she* created demanded *my* intervention. But I developed an incapacity to solve them from oversaturation and shell shock. I wanted to help. I was simply incapable. From her point of view, unwilling; from mine, unable. She thus filled up with self-pity as I was filling myself with the same savage wrath over my family. People may be evil or disinterested. My own family may not care. *Is it my fault?* No. *Theirs?* No. *People are what they are, dammit.* If they're dysfunctional (as I am) then they're incapable of caring for me in the way I want or need. *I hate it when she's right about me.*

"Maybe they scorn you because you're just an asshole. You ever consider that? It's ironic you somehow never hate your Moonie cult for doing the same shit."

My mouth might've fell open with a heavy mental sigh. "Goddammit, Linda."

"Don't blame me for your shit. Your son has glaring self-esteem issues and it's coming from watching you crumple under your African animal's onslaughts." He'd recently said, *If you call Mommy so we can say hi, she'll fight with you.* Shit! Her *animal* comment revived a raving call over me taking the kids in December 2000 (I couldn't manage it) so Tamela could work a new job. She'd said, "You've been lying, scheming, and conniving for months! You have no intention to divorce your piece of shit batterer. She's a fucking animal! You're so full of shit, Chris!"

"Stop cussing her like that! You can't just accept that I have multi-dimensional, complex emotions just like you? I've meant everything I ever said to you, but at the same time I'm torn up over divorce because of my church and children's feelings. All my faith issues are *killing me!* Can't you—?"

"They're animals just like your batterer! They should all be locked up if not institutionalized! Or else shipped back to their island." *Like Kong?* "They're *her* kids. Dragging you down, destroying *our* vision. You should dump her animal—"

I fast-balled the phone to the floor. It snapped and pieces scattered. I left it off the hook where it lay. It was a scorching memory, but she'd softened since I took custody March 2002 and now (mostly) showed me her mother's heart for them.

It would take another year to understand it all. Rudimentary realizations were under way, but I needed time to put together an *aha!* moment. As I moved ever closer my veil of depression, gall, and self-pity parted inchmeal till I discerned that, after my long nightmare of domestic violence, church abuse, and family scorn I might have the opportunity to pass from a loser victim to winning victories over my tribulations. To be the man Julian penned in my rookie *Divine Principle* book so long ago: *The way of the righteous is a life of overcoming.*

Not because anyone else changed: Tamela was still abusive; the church wanted nothing to do with me; my family scorned the life I'd scuppered. I was changing, my crippled heart and twisted mind rising above my disabilities like Stephen Hawking his withered body. It wasn't a lack of love or scorn nor abandonment dragging me into the pits of wretched desolation, indignation, and enmity but *my perception and rejection* of it and the self-pity it generated. The only way out, I was imperceptibly beginning to haply realize, was to rise above it the way I would some homeless bum cursing my success. I walk on knowing he's the crazy bastard, not me. The moment I start thinking I deserve his approbation I begin descending into the spleeny life of woe and self-loathing I was now living.

I didn't have to live like that and was beginning to discover it. The abuse, scorn, and abandonment all hurt, no doubt about it. Its perpetrators had no right to heap it on me, either. But religion, especially the Unification Church, teaches that if people really understood their sinfulness—"for they know not what they do"—they quite naturally wouldn't be so. Evil and sinfulness exist not because Satan presses it into us but because we don't understand its nature in ourselves. We think it's good, so we pursue it and inflict it on the world. *He's evil; he deserves this. He's a jerk; he deserves my scorn. He's living a life we disapprove; he deserves our abandonment till he sees the error of his ways. Americans are godless motherfuckers; they deserve airplanes flying into their unholy towers of Babel.*

We all think we're good, the hero of our story and all others the villains. That we're doing the right thing. God is on our side. No matter how much damage and destruction we instigate, somehow it's not only justified but a positive good in the world hardly different from a little tough love.

But nothing bad is ever good. Only the individual can make something good from something bad and vice versa. War, for example, is always bad. *Always.* Yet, sometimes it leads to something good. Not war itself, which is bad, but because of how those involved deal with it, learn from it, apply its lessons, and build a different life out of it where a rinse-and-repeat is less likely. That's the soil in which care and forgiveness grow. The Axis powers could forgive all the death and destruction the Allies wrought upon them in World War Two not so much because the Allies treated them with kindness and generosity at war's end, but because the Axis nations accepted the evil nature of their ways and repented. They rose above their actions that stimulated the Allied reaction to create a better world for themselves. They went from feeling victims of brutal Allied warfare to victors in a new way of thought.

It worked for them. Why not for me? From a victim to a victor. I liked the sound of that. I wanted it. I *deserved* it. And, I'd get it.

Somehow.

Act XX

An Emerging Victor
The World and I

*L*ife is all about boundaries and faith. I'm sure I knew that. I must have. There was a time when I had both and upheld them. I'm pretty sure about that, too. But somewhere in the long course of my story I gave them up. I learned to live not for the sake of others but to please them. In the process, I killed myself. That's right. Dead. The proverbial door nail. Oh, sure, my physical body was still chugging along, surviving the life. But my heart, my mind, the essence of who and what I was died a long time ago. I'm not really sure when. I just know it happened. Until Linda told me I was dead in the way she'd probed Tamela's photo, the possibility had never risen to mind.

I've read about people in spirit world who don't know they're dead; killed so violently quick or agonizingly slow that they didn't notice their transition or built a wall of denial to cope. In 1990's *Jacob's Ladder*, the soldier protagonist lives half a lifetime before discovering it's all a dream and he's dying on the operating table in a Vietnam MASH unit . . . his last conscious moment twixt life and death seemingly knowing it's coming in a bloodcurdling scream of comprehension.

Linda said, "Your whole life is a dream you built on a lie grown out of a mountain of denial and fantasy."

"That actually makes sense now. I guess I'm ready to hear it." *Boundaries, dude.* Their vaporization led me by the hand into my delusional world of self-denial.

"You're welcome. Again." This time, a pretty smile.

"Tamela's brilliant," I'd lectured myself. "She'll be a great lawyer when she finishes school. Yeah . . . she'll go to school because she's *normal*. And she loves me, too. The church is sane and godly. My career will grow and develop until Father asks me to run the American—the worldwide?—Unification Church. Because I'm the best man for the job, that's why. A sharp operational strategist. Results, baby. Okay, yeah, I fell a few times during my kick-outs—well, at UTS, too—but, they'll understand.

They'll recognize my bodacious sincerity, my commitment and dedication to Divine Principle, God, True Parents, and the Way of Restoration. It doesn't matter *how* I am so much as what I can *do* for The Mission. That's how they treat their own. Why not me? Don't I rate?"

It was all so stupidly wrong. Maybe it shouldn't have been, but it was. Tamela, the church, my family—none of them were living my romantic fable; too busy with their own. If there was a nexus where we might intersect and coexist it was too brief or confrontational for anything good to happen in my life.

Boundaries are the force protecting and nurturing individual identity. As they fall then so goes identity. Conformity is all about sacrificing individual boundaries for larger entities. While group boundaries exist at every level of human experience, they're downright dysfunctional, even dangerous, when not predicated on individual boundaries. Well-manicured personal borders form the root of a healthy interhuman relations tree the way good fences make good neighbors.

Consider the 20th–21st century's many ideological wars: Fascism, Communism, Islamism, Liberalism-cum-Statism, each an example of a group boundary squashing the very concept of the individual boundary in oppressing, globally warring, and mass murdering millions or billions without once honoring an individual's limit. Medieval religious fanaticism translates into global terrorism and progressivism using violence or political sleights of hand that deceptively lure nations along the slaughter chute of ideological conformity. Islamic fanaticists are a small minority of world Islam, yet the vast majority neither subscribing to nor identifying with them doesn't shout them down. Why? Because Islam is an overt collective championing the group over the individual. To uphold boundaries in such a group—this includes opposing taking noncombatant life by terroristic means—is to invite the group's active or passive oppression or murder. Hence, few Muslims publicly rail against terrorism the way Western Christians feel free vis-à-vis their own. *This is ideology.* For the most part and recognizing its obvious failures, the West respects individual boundaries both socially and as a practical matter through law and institutionalized rights over and above group boundaries. This is most pronounced in Constitutional America. Yet, if I lived in a world where personal boundaries predominated, I'd be as incapable of coexisting with others having equally strong boundaries as groups with groups. Conflict inevitably ensues even amongst those wishing none.

How do we maintain strong personal boundaries without losing our individual identity and the moral roots emanating from our personal experience with God? Through faith, which isn't merely believing in the existence of a God or that my religion's dogma rightly reflects His reality, but simply my acceptance of and trust in that which lies outside of me. Faith in the future, in life, in others, in God, in war, in being combative, in meekness, in my leaders, in myself. Whatever it is we invest our faith in, faith itself is that which links our personal self to something beyond self. It allows our personal frontiers to intersect another's in such a way that harmony is found in common cause and coexistence. Faith gives meaning and purpose to our personal self which our boundaries protect. Though I might have the most stringent borderlines, without faith my life is meaningless self-protection on the same psychological level as early man's animalistic struggle to survive.

Over my story's graveled road I realized I not only lost my boundaries but my faith, too. Not my faith in God, for I still believe in His existence, His goodness, His love and care for me, His desire to heal the world. God is every bit as real to me now (in 2003) as at the height of my Moonie mindset. But faith in myself vis-à-vis God suffered a grievous wound. I no longer see myself as indispensable to God. I've realized and accepted True Parents don't need me; nay, don't want me.

Though I sometimes experience guilt from my decoupled relationship with Divine Principle and the Blessing, I no longer have faith in its ultimacy. Rev. Moon says the Principle is merely a textbook on how to live our lives happily and at peace with God and the world, just like the Bible. It's not a book of judgment although it judges, nor a book of absolutes although it's absolute. It's a testament to God's effort, the hard nature of the human race, its future dreams, and the ageless human effort to change our world from its brutal reality to our familial ideal.

The mistake the Unification Church—all churches—makes is arrogating itself the power to reward 'good' and punish 'evil.' The church catalogs me in its evil bin for 'reasons' and believes it carries God's mandate to mete out justice on His behalf. Lacking the coercive power of the state it resorts to the gravest punishment any person can be made to bear: ostracism . . . individual separation from one's social and familial community. Of course, the church doesn't have such a mandate because not even God has it. It may be shocking, but this world doesn't belong to God. It belongs to itself. The Bible tells us God created human beings, the pinnacle of His creative power, *with free will.* Once given one necessarily cedes judgment, because if one can judge then the judged isn't free but a 'sinner' enslaved to the will of the judge. One is thereby judge-willed not free-willed. You have it or you don't.

We can observe the central institution of the family God created for us. If we want to understand Him, we need look no further than the healthy parent–child relationship. Prior to reaching a level of good judgment and adult independence, children are judged and punished (or rewarded) by parents training them in the way of survival and, essentially, benign or hostile interhuman relations. As judgment and punishment exceed proper levels for the particular training taking place, it's not only counterproductive but creates dysfunction in both parent and child.

Frederick Douglass remarks how slave owners were more greatly corrupted and damaged from beating their slaves than the slaves themselves. He also notes the most vicious slavers were invariably ministers and pastors. His experience paints a clear picture of the correlation between boundaries and faith. The Unification Church creates the same relationship between its leaders and members as slave-owning American Christianity did between master and slave. The judgment and punishment the Unification Church metes out often enough exceeds the requirements of its need for training that it drives away most of its membership so that today the church is the rotted carcass of beauty's youth.

Faith tells me God isn't a dysfunctional parent. That His training never exceeds what's required. That He never judges nor punishes. That He merely *is.* His standard simply the Way. Human beings *judge themselves* according to how well they perceive (via conscience) His standard. Psychology recognizes the levels to which people self-punish—the root of self-sabotage—real or imagined transgressions.

The church can't judge me, as I'm a free-willed person. What Divine Principle calls an Individual Truth Body. I naturally judge and punish myself in accord with my understanding of truth subconsciously perceived through my conscience. In spirit world we're attacked, confronted, or abused by those who feel wronged by us, but we have the power to avoid their punishment by repenting and taking steps to restore our relationships. Rev. Moon says God didn't create Hell to punish but protect humanity because His love permeates the spirit realm close to Him as air permeates the physical world. Only those with hearts developed nearer God's standard of love have the capacity to 'breathe' His 'air' without pain. For the sinful, trying to 'breathe' God's love is like sucking fire inside your lungs. To save us this excruciating pain brought on not by God—He is simply existing as He is—but by our separation from His quality of love, God created hell as a place of refuge where we could live comfortably *until we transform ourselves from so-called evil to good*. As we transform bit by bit, we rise in spirit world nearer to He.

Rev. Moon says that God never prevents evil people from coming close to Him. They simply can't endure His reality. Not only is it painful (he avows), we clearly see our own sin, too, and judge our own selves as unworthy or unwilling to enter His presence. Consider the street bum who enters the most beautiful building in the middle of a black-tie event. If he has any dignity at all, won't he feel out of place, unworthy, maybe humiliated by the reality of his life? Even if those tuxedo-clad high-rollers let him in, clap him on the back with affectations of love, he'd feel out of place . . . if not consciously then certainly subconsciously. He'd want to bathe, clean up, dress appropriately. He'd ask to come back after straightening himself out.

Like all religion, Unificationists forget this taloned reality when puffing up in righteous indignation based on a belief in moral superiority. The church invited me a guest to its banquet of the lamb like anyone. Similar in dress, word, and deed my peers, mere guests themselves, judged me unworthy of our host and cast me out perceiving *my* sin worse than how they perceived *theirs*. Yet (St. Paul remarks), "There is no one righteous, not even one . . . for all have sinned and fall short of the glory of God." How ironic that Rev. Moon says the same bleeding thing.

STRUGGLING THROUGH MY divorce from Tamela and the Unification Church, I discovered the absence of any boundaries and faith. The loss was debilitating. Why couldn't I just walk away like so many others forsaking spouse or religion? Why couldn't I rely on my own relationship with God instead of mediating through the church? It proved impossible answering these questions without understanding the reality of boundaries and faith in my life.

Enforcing my civil protection orders (CPO) marked a seminal moment in my relationship with Tamela and my sense of self. I resistantly accepted my life shouldn't be lived according to her whims: when she's happy, I can be; sad, I need endure it; angry, I must suck it up; don't do this, she won't do that. Domestic violence seems not so much about coercive force or even power and control, but *ownership*. That makes sense. According to the Bible, the very first perpetrator of domestic violence was Satan in the garden. For Rev. Moon, the Fall was all about taking possession. Satan desired Adam's position and needs possess Eve. He wanted God's love as the son rather than the servant. The struggle twixt God and Satan is over possession (ownership) of Creation, represented in humanity. If Satan can own us via behavior, boundaries, and faith then he owns Creation—vice versa for God—though it's a matter of deceptive control; for God, it's a matter of congruence. Cast this in secular terms if you prefer. It works either way. The nature of Tamela's relationship was also a matter of ownership. It clarifies her intensive effort to possess me in 'protecting' me from women, friends, the church, duty, and my own self.

I fought back. "I'm not a sofa you can own and do whatever you want with or ban others from. I'm not anybody's property!"

"You marry to me, not to no-body else. You tek me from me country and put me wi' chilleren. 'Dat mek you mine. You owe me. Wha' mek I ev-uhh le' you go? I will do whatev-uhh I ha' to!"

Such was my iron collar. As difficult as it was to involve the police and courts through obtaining and enforcing a CPO, the sun rose to reveal me repossessing thus reasserting ownership of my life. No more, "We will control the horizontal; we will control the vertical." I controlled what happened to me. I controlled my emotions. I controlled my home. I controlled *me*. You betcha.

In retaking my responsibility for these things I'd naturally inherited ownership just as Tamela inherited ownership over me. "No man loses his freedom except through his own weakness," Gandhi said. But no, it's strength through which one *gives it away* in the firm and reputedly defensible conviction it's the right choice or as a matter of principle. And so I'd done. Tamela owned me lock stock and barrel handing myself

The family I was struggling to save from domestic violence while healing from my own dysfunction.

over on demand. Taking myself back through separation, divorce, and a no-fly zone to boot put her in an uproar, and quite rightly. Her loss of control equated to loss of possession therefore ownership and, accordingly, her safety and security in life.

"I t'ought I could treat you anyhow I want," she later confessed, "and you nev-uhh be leave me, that you be aahlways mine."

"I know you love me your own way but that, there, was your own denial blowing up in your face." Her pout was Homeric.

Temporal Tamela and spiritual church went hand in hand. I'd wrestled church leaders 21 years over boundaries, i.e., conscience. The church insisted I adopt its moral standard even though it oft-conflicted in fundamental ways with my Christian heritage and even Divine Principle. In itself, the latter's not so bad. It's only natural as we attend Messiah 2.0 that we let go our old concepts just as Jesus advised us on the problem of new wine in old wineskins. Nevertheless, there are basic truths that survive age to age. The Asia-centric, Confucianistically top-down bureaucratic Unification Church obviated ageless truths like Abel loving Cain and the Golden Rule and ginned up alarming spiritual conflicts in even pious members' hearts.

Those refusing to give an inch decamped. Others delayed judgment to reconcile contradictions. In the process, we ceded self-ownership to the church in abandoning our faith-oriented boundaries to promenade along the conformational Moonie brick road of which we never truly approved, thus pinning ourselves to self-conflict in the church. Perhaps this was the unseen motive behind my typical Sunday sermons at UTS on our need to build and maintain a closer relationship with Jesus. To not forsake our ageless Christian as well as other ideals. That non-Christian members couldn't simply pole vault over 2,000 years of Messiah 1.0 into the bosom of Unificationism that Rev. Moon founded on his integral relationship with, and love for, Jesus Christ. In hindsight, I see my UTS self just beginning the process of appreciating my loss of self-ownership. That, without perceiving it, I was opening the door separating the victim from the victor and electing to walk through it. And how it took years to understand what I was doing! Dr. Shimmyo could only cringe.

~

I'M A SENTIMENTAL fellow. Probably a bit overly sympathetic if not dangerously compassionate. Linda's intensity for a global baby doped steroids when her doctor said, "You're 44, my dear. Get pregnant soon or forever hold your peace."

Because of the rivalry she plainly felt with my children for ownership of my heart, and the harsh words her fear of loss had motivated her to spit my way, I'd grown very cold to the idea of fathering her baby regardless our on-again-off-again intimacy. The last thing I needed was more paternal responsibility in a crazed maternity ward when I'd yet to stabilize the situation with my first clutch and *their* crazy mom.

Linda did frozen sperm spring and summer, 2001. It didn't take. She voiced her fear she couldn't pay for the treatments much longer and would fail in motherhood. Filled with sympathy and not a little love despite all her spasmodic venom, I agreed to spermify her not as a father but a donor. I certainly hoped I'd one day be our baby's father in heart, soul, and law too if we could make straight our relationship. For the present, it was better I follow prudence. We drew up papers protecting me from child support claims and she was quickly with child because, unlike the counterfeit deposits in her sky-high sperm bank, I wasn't shooting underpowered rounds. Although tempestuous, her pregnancy was a period of love and happiness for us both that we used to delude ourselves we'd be okay in due course.

Neither my family nor Tamela appeared capable of understanding the complexity of this arrangement rooted in my feelings and compassion for, and dreamed-of future with, Linda . . . that she not lose out on a family of her own. When Tamela found out—I bloody well didn't spill the beans; I suspected Linda forcing a wedge to pressure me into marriage and real fatherhood—vessels popped in her eyes.

"Aahll 'dis time you be lyin' 'bout 'de wo-maahn and your relationship. Wha' mek you do me so, Chris? You hate me? Wha' mek you marry me if you hate me so?"

"To avoid exactly this conversation, Tamela! We're divorced but—"

"Why not? You deserve aahll wha' you get!"

Yet, she was buttering her own bread with a black Floridian, the reason she wanted me taking the kids in December 2001. I ground teeth to dust one Saturday morning to hear Kir-el squawk over the phone, "Daddy's here now. I have to go."

I hawked up a bowling ball. Almost shouted in her ear, *The hell you just say?* "Put your mother on the phone, sweetie, there's a good girl."

She'd spent the better part of a year condemning me, threatening I'd never get custody or visitation, all of which had fallen flat at our divorce hearing. She spit through the phone, "Wha' mek you complainin' 'bout Clyde bein' here? I tell you I didn'a wan' our babies roun' your oth-uhh wo-maahn. Did you lis-ten? No!"

"Why would you think that, when billions of people do it around the world every freakin' day?" I still couldn't swear with her if I didn't want her diverging into a quarrel over "your frontin' disrespec.' "

" 'Dis Lind-ahh is no good. You know she hate our chilleren, Chris? Did she tell you? An' still you wan' bring our babies 'dem roun' her?"

"She doesn't hate our children, she's just . . ." *Ah, what's the use?*

"I'm followin' your example. Not your business anyhow tellin' me nothin.' "

"But it's yours to say it's bad around another woman because it'll confuse them? And now you have a man *living* there with the kids visiting? And they're calling him daddy!"

"So wha'? You didn'a respec' me wi' Lind-ahh. Wha' mek I respec' you now?"

"Since there's no 'mommy' with Linda, I don't know what you're talking about." And then Clyde knocked her up a month after I'd done Linda. She called with the news. "What hypocrisy, Tamela! We're totally over now. You can leave me *alone!*"

"Not hypo-crite like you!" *Click.*

I called Dad. "Her purpose was making you jealous, Christopher. Her motive is different from Monica's, but the same goal overall."

"Jes—eez." I didn't swear in front of Dad, either. "What a rationale." He might've quirked a brow.

Tamela's later admissions lent much justice to

Christmas work-break off Key West while children visited Tamela.

his assertion. And I *was* jealous, dammit . . . at first. She'd been faithful to me all through our marriage—except for her rape, whatever that really was. I'd admired her for it. Expected it. I was feeling peeved 'losing' her despite instigating the whole thing. I felt the finality of our Blessing's end. *Well, I'm truly condemned now.*

But I'd cast my lot, no going back. Even repenting and reconciling, our Blessing was wholly corrupt, not just my side of it. Yet, almost as soon as I felt these emotions, I realized I didn't care. Tamela was her own 27-years woman and I was dedicated to our divorce. Even my slightest compassion was a magnet pulling her back to derail it while increasing our confrontations and obliging me to back-pedal ever more rabidly. I was *not* going to make the same mistake I did with Shiori, where my empathy for her broken heart led me into dalliances. I ruthlessly cut myself off so I didn't lead Tamela on in any way. Though browbeating me into sex a few times visiting the children in New York and Florida before our finalized divorce, I'd prevented her threatening me into that compromising mess again. If she'd now embraced another man who also wanted to marry her, then so much the better for me. It batted her loaded gun from my head to the other sucker.

SIMULTANEOUSLY, MY ERSTWHILE Kodiak buddies Johnny and Hemi scathingly mocked me over Tamela and the church after I told Johnny, who ratted me out to Hemi. They took me unawares, each having long histories with kick outs, quitting, disparaging leaders, Blessing troubles, and a *mondai kyodai* ('problem member') renown. That's why we'd clicked in the first place. Hemi went full mullet with "you freely joined the church" rants—telegraphing he was nowadays getting, like Johnny, a church paycheck as a respectable worker bee—while condemning me for "marrying a nigger," as he had in Seattle during Jerome's and my 1991 fundraising trip. These two bitched in secret till Johnny inexplicably forwarded Hemi's email [sic]:

> After Alaska, he started hanging around this nigger named Jerome who was a fricking wierd dude. For some strange reason Chris was attracted to this nigger and tagged along with him to the nigger's island hometown. Chris later met his nigger wife Tamela there and jumped her bones, got her pregnant with a child then got Blessed. At that point the church had no choice but to Bless him. After a few years hanging with Jerome and 8 years married to the black woman Tamela, Chris has attracted a very low nigger spirit world around him full of resentment and hate. Chris actually has a slave mentality trying hard to please the Church masters and upset that he is not one of them. He now hates his masters that he served so loyal and faithful like a good nigger.
>
> Later when his masters kicked [him] out of the cottonfields Chris woke up and got angry at the fact that they could do this to him. Then like a typical nigger as in the movie *Color Purple* he took it out on his nigger wife dumping her for some white pussy. There is no doubt in my mind Chris' new lover is a white woman; he will never ever go back to another black woman. You can now see why he has this very low nigger spirit world around him making him feel the rage and anger of a former slave. Even though he is a white guy he acts like a nigger trapped in a white man's body. There is no hope for Chris other than going to Cheongpyeong lake and having Dae Mo Nim beating those evil nigger spirits living in his body by the thousands.

Yes, I wanted *acceptance* or I'd be getting bitchbucks like them. Tamela is Carib, Caucasian, Japanese–Chinese. Linda is African, Japanese, Caucasian. Johnny:

> I agree that Chris is really bitter and resentful, and yes I think he not only needs professional help, but needs God to scare the living SHIT out of him, as with a lot of ex-members the story line seems the same: blame all your problems on the Church and nothing on yourself.

With their emailed alley cat now out of the bag, Hemi wrote to me:

> A delusional person who needs professional help, you are a NOBODY in the light of the world and in Rev. Moon's church and also in GOD's providence . . . Yes, I agree with you, your last 21 years is wasted; you gained very little and lost a lot more than you gained . . . Yes, Chris that was your mistake you should have become something instead of wasting your time running around trying to find yourself in this movement . . . How could [Rev. Moon] not feel like a King and compared to him you are truly a nobody, human trash as he says . . . you

are nothing and you are a nobody. You should know your position in this life . . . No matter how much you feel the church screwed your life up nobody forced you to marry a nigger. That's right Chris you married a nigger, a former offspring of black slaves brought to the western hemisphere on slaves ships. You who once told me at JUDAH street that you come from a lineage of Irish Kings, where royal blood courses through your veins, and yet you married into a former black slave lineage. Your children will curse you later . . . why should the church want you? Ask yourself that question honestly. There is no reason for them to want you, you have to be a valuable person to be wanted. You are a nobody and you should realize your position.

Your soul is in hell . . . no way out other than another Blessing if you will not go back to your first wife. Your grounds for divorce are flimsy and nobody will respect your story of abuse by this primitive and uneducated woman you dragged out of Jamaica . . . How pathetic and weak you have become.

[speaking to Johnny] He probably thinks we are brainwashed fanatics following the Korean Bin Laden. Can you imagine he compared Father the Messiah, the King of Kings, the return of Christ to Bin Laden. If Chris had money he would write a book like that bitch Nan Sook Moon did about Hyo-jin, Chris would call it *Betrayed by the Moons*. He would go on how he was so faithful and called by God to serve the antichrist, that his real mission was to kill Moon and his family, to rid the earth of this sect.

I am sure if Chris had the money and time he would be writing book after book and telling the whole world how he was butfucked by Rev. Moon. Yes, he is full of hate, hates his ex Tamela, hates his Church, hates his Blessing, hates his old moonie pals, hates the Korean leaders, hates Rev. Moon and his wife. Chris is a very cold person to abandon [his] 3 little kids and see them only when it is conveniant for [him], shows you just how cold he is. In time when his children grow up hating him, he will already be hating them.

Like he knew the first thing about my children. Johnny:

One thing that really bothers me about all of these ex-members is, why not leave well enough alone, you joined the church, you decided to stay with the church, you left the church, nobody twisted your arm to do these things, then even after leaving you spit at the very thing you decided to join willingly. Somewhere along the way I think Chris derailed and fell in a deep chasm. I can't figure him out at all.

Hemi (to me):

Johnny and I are going to shun you from now on, you are officially shunned.

Major complainers, their emails were quite the wonder. Hemi's stung deep, hardly different from Linda at her darkest or the Ku Klux Klan at its best. Where they railed at "niggers," Linda grouched over "the African." Too polite for real execration, maybe, or remembering she was half African herself. I punched *eject* on our friendship; Rev. Moon lauds no give and take with dark hearts. Tamela may be a lot of things, but 'nigger' isn't one. *Fuck 'em.* Irish royalty marrying into Africa's lineage for historical Restoration is right up Rev. Moon's alley (if he's sincere). He Matched whites to blacks for exactly that purpose. Johnny had a point that "nobody twisted [my] arm" to join or chase the church, but Divine Principle's moral diktat sure did. I "spit at" the church like Ahab his whale, as it sold me a Divine Principled bait with a leadership switch then derailed itself with me on the train. I did write my book, Hemi.

~

IN MAY 2002 Linda delivered our global baby, Linda Makaikai, even as Tamela invaded my apartment for custody hearings, put the kids into hysterics, got arrested. In June she delivered her own baby, Brenda, in Florida. *What a soap opera.* Leading into it Linda said, "You only care about your African's kids, not *ours.*"

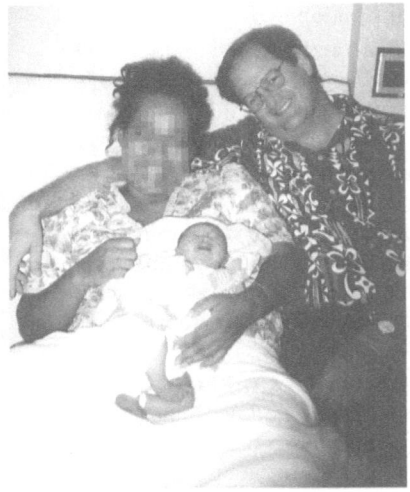

A beautiful day with the woman, daughter, and loving future I hankered after.

"If that were true," I riposted, "I wouldn't be here all the time helping take care of you, and by extension her, would I? I do want a family with you. All of our children happily living together as a family."

"Yeah, that's never gonna happen."

"It doesn't matter. I'm not abandoning them to raise a separate family with you, and that's what's really galling you."

She sneered. "Well, if you hadn't been so asinine and mentally ill to marry your low-class piece of shit in the first place—"

"I wouldn't be losing all my affection over your undying hate for Tamela—who never met you—transposed onto my children." I slumped in a heavy sigh. "I love you and you can't see it through Tamela. Or my kids, who'd be great siblings to our baby."

"They'll probably kill her. I'm not letting them anywhere near her!"

I was on my feet. "You're so fucking dramatic, Linda. They are *not* their mother! Get a grip, for God's sake. Love them for what they are: innocent children."

I took custody of Kal-el and Kir-el ten weeks before Makaikai's birth. Linda used the time to pleasantly get to know them outside her caricatures. They were bees to newborn honey helping her with feeding, diapers, playtime, and comfort.

She at last said, "I admit it, Chris. They aren't carbon copies of their perpetrator mom, I guess. It seems Makaikai is safe around them."

"Took you long enough. All you had to do was not judge 'em by their lineage."

"My actions always speak louder than my words, right? I told you. But your daughter dislikes me. Maybe hates me. It's in her face and attitude."

I barked a *ha!* "Not even a bit. The problem is that all you're seeing in her is Tamela because she's a girl. Until you quit doing that, you'll keep subconsciously alienating her. I'm sure she picks up your vibe even if she doesn't get it."

"I think you're wrong. She's probably got a headful from her mother."

"Your attitude is only creating conflict. I love all *five* of my children."

Linda's favorite therapist in Hawaii privately said to me, "Her attitude's gotten too out of control and problematic, in my view. I recommend you sever your emotional ties and move out of the relationship."

Gah! "Like she's a house? You're saying . . . wait. You're serious?"

"You have to think about what's best for all concerned."

Ugh. My domestic violence counselor Andrew (his colleague Evelyn now seeing the kids three times a week) had said for close to a year, "Linda's personality is dangerously narcissistic. You need to consider that for your kids' sake."

My pragmatic counselor over the river in Arlington said, "I agree with them, Chris. Sounds like we're all saying the same thing here."

His concurrence tilted me hard into a firmish decision. "Dammit, Peter, now I have to grieve one more soul-killing loss. I suppose . . . I'm slowly accepting the reality my relationship with Linda is, barring some miracle, mostly over."

"You'll always have problems, Chris. They just become *better* problems."

Our relationship cooled dramatically over the next year, kept together only by our force of habit and Makaikai, whom I loved. And I was dragging Marley's chains of morbid depression along my every step. All the same, we're talking and visiting heading into 2004 and our children play together and likely will into the foreseeable future. We share childcare duties and help the other as needed. We're trying to blend our lives in some fashion and make our feelings work, but we haven't been intimate in a long while. It's hard discerning just exactly where we stand.

In October 2002 two epiphanies—founded on intensive thought, reflection, and effort—demolished my so-called clinical depression like a magic wand. The reason I most probably got involved with Shiori lightbulbed while I stretched out on my Adams Morgan floor: she absolutely accepted me as I was without condition when no one else would, even if she struggled with (or hated) it. Suddenly it was plain how I'd longed for acceptance my entire life without finding it. Did I join the Coast Guard then the church because I was looking for another 'family' that, at least on paper, seemed to accept me as I was? With a stinging forehead slap, I saw how the same kind of woman attracted me over and over because each one seemed to embrace me without critique. Shiori, Tamela, Linda—all facsimiles to a degree. Later, of course, I discovered how dedicated they were to remolding me.

Second, Tamela disturbs and destabilizes me because she's always pushing me into an existential corner on money, life, love, concern for her and the children, how I use my time—my this, my that, my everything. I scribed in my journal:

> I think the root of every fight with Tamela is her forcing me to defend myself yet again—and defend the same things, over and over—which just infuriates me because it shows she doesn't ever believe me.

People discounting my feeling and desire was bad enough. Forcing me to defend them again and again was worse. As if I never meant it in the first place. That, with just a small assault, I'd change to suit. The epiphany? *Tamela is what she is.*

These were crucial revelations I instantly felt jolt me out of my rut. In a day my mood seemed normal, happy, buoyant. I viscerally felt a heavy load slough off my shoulders. I bounced lighthearted in lunar gravity. I'd struggled months to write a single page of this book, then my cumulative epiphanies had me draining ink machinelike for weeks.

Teaching Kal-el the manly arts at Summit Place.

Unemployed since my Carney layoff in March 2002, opportunities were now spring weeds. A friend offered $2,500 to pull fiber optic and comm cables for a downtown project; Kal-el joined to help and play. A women's foundation publication offered proofreading and copy editing. *Fierce Markets* magazine took me on as an editor. Washington councilwoman Carol Schwartz, now a mayoral candidate, solicited me to help her win election; her campaign manager then asked me take on his job to run the whole ball of wax. All kicking off in a single week culminating in Kir-el's eighth and Makaikai's actual birth days.

Is this the power of depression-busting self-awareness? And no drugs, Dad.

My melancholic gloom was history. Bushwhacked in March 2003 by Tamela once more invading my CPO'd apartment, hiding frowzled at Linda's (off to Hawaii) for two weeks, I was infuriated and drowning in anxiety, sure. But not depressed nor even glum. I'd realized two seemingly simple things and then those emotions permanently lifted. *Amazing!* A heady moment. I'd invested brain-breaking efforts getting there, so I saw the importance of intently and critically thinking out my problems (with a reliably good ear) if I wanted to transcend them.

With the unexpected lifting of depression, I surprisingly felt invested with a seething indignation that boiled over with my family, church, Tamela, and maybe a bit of Linda. I loathingly grudged what I felt they'd each put me through, how they'd spoke falsely to reject and abandon me. Would more epiphanies save me from this aggrievement, too? I had my answer that March when Tamela appeared on my Adam's Morgan doorstep with 3-year old L'or-el and her wee bairn Brenda. Ostensibly scouting the lay of the land in preparation for a potential relocation, she'd in truth abandoned her life in Florida. Having SWAT-styled through my front door when I'd neglected to spy out the peephole like a sensible urbanite, she intended using my apartment as a forward operating base to find herself a federal Section-8 flat and build a new life local to our children. In fact, she planned to seize sole custody. She ran me out of my home as she had Mona in San Diego when she wouldn't take no for an answer and launched a one-woman college sit-in.

I raged storming down Columbia Road toward 18th Street's cultural intersection with my Adams Morgan neighborhood and away from her, my children, and my own fucking safe space. My thoughts were a street brawl grappling over why this was continuing to happen to me. *Why don't I call the cops and enforce my fucking CPO? I did once already, why not now?* Like childbirth, shouldn't the second time be easier? Well, she's an honors graduate manipulating my sense of guilt, so, no.

I tuckered myself out wandering DC in a frenzy until realizing I couldn't crash on the streets like it was Honolulu nor did I want to. Besides, Kal-el and Kir-el must be terrified of Dad running out and maybe wondering if he'd come back. And did I want her in my house with all my stuff, alone? *I have to go back, dammit.*

"I ha' nowhere else to gooo," she wailed. "You be send your own little daught-uhh out into 'de street? An' me wi' a tiny bee-bah? How could you do we so?"

"Get a hotel! What am I sending you money for? You can't just show up here out of the blue like this. Go to that youth hostel you used before."

"I don't ha' 'de money for it after comin' aahll 'de way up here."

"Then go to a shelter!"

"No! You mus' help me, Chris. I'm your chilleren's mudd-uhh! L'or-el *need* you."

That shut me up. If the cops arrested her, would they leave L'or-el and Brenda with me for the duration or flush 'em through the gritty system while flicking me to the sidelines? My first full-time job in a year of temp work was just starting in Rockville at half my Carney pay. How would I cope with two kids plus a toddler and infant? Would Jacquelina, my charming and beautiful downstairs neighbor I was growing feelings for, help me out? *Eh, probably not, she's got her own two kids to deal*

Kir-el's favorite activity. Summit Place.

with. It's complicated enforcing a CPO against a domestic violence perpetrator when, at the same time, said perp reasons at whatever-year-old level she was really at and has your own child in hand for good measure.

"Enough's enough, Tamela! This is *my* house! I have the right to control *that.*"

"I can pay you rent. We can sleep on 'de floor. I'm fine wi' 'dat."

"No!" She'd be in my bed in two seconds, if that long. I fumed, working up to flee again to avoid being trapped with all it entailed. "This is *my* house! You *promised* when you called you were staying at the youth hostel or a shelter and we'd meet for the children in a public place. You said it was only for a week—"

"I know, I know, but—"

"—to start the social services paperwork. I threatened you over a month that I'd enforce the restraining order if you showed up here."

"I know! But don't—"

"How is it you now have the nerve to just—"

She roared, "Don't you dare taahlk to me 'bout no nerve! You wi' your—"

"Tamela! *Why. Are. You. Here?!*" Quite simple, really. She expected me to cave to whatever she wanted. And not without good cause. How incredibly annoying to know that. Her plan was as reckless as dangerous for me.

"I t'ought you could drive me 'roun' Waahshing-tohn so I can fin' me a Section-8 apaaht-men' I can afford wha' good for 'de chilleren. It be fast-uhh if you help than me takin' 'de bus." If she'd had Southern lashes they'd be batting.

"Jeez, Tamela, that could take weeks if not months. You know what that list is like. It's practically a full-time job you're wanting from me. But no way I'm getting locked in the same car with you."

"But, you could do it." She sounded expectantly hopeful.

"I finally *have* a full-time job, dammit. It's impossible! And totally outside our agreement not to mention the restrain—"

"Please? *Pleeeease?*"

Dammit. I couldn't *not* consider it, but still. "No way. And you *promised*—"

Her voice was cloying. "I *know*, but . . . "

I ran off to DV central. "My life's completely on hold with her here! I'm inhaling aspirin for headaches, neck and back—my eyes *burn* from lack of sleep!"

"You're going to have to use the police. How long can you let this go on?"

"She's out of her league, Andrew. She doesn't get her reality. Made this crisis from nothing. I want her gone! I feel shell-shocked, man. Bottom line—"

"Is, you need to enforce your CPO. Until you take control . . ."

I COMPROMISED AND went alone to places I'd considered a year earlier for the kids and me in the District's unaffluent (therefore in her price range) Southwest section. No dice on Section-8, and no thanks from her for the literature from eight potentials and my report on her options in DC. So, she berated me for my parenting.

"You call 'dis a menu for 'de chilleren food? What kin' o' per-sohn even *has* a menu?" She squalled over my ongoing if nonsexual relationship with Linda—" 'Dat be a flat out lie," she'd smirked—and her access to our kids. "I hate you abandoning me in Floree-dahh after you carry me aahll 'de way to Ameree-cah. Wha' mek you do me so, Chris? And no, it wasn'a me so-caahll violence but you chasin' pussy!"

"Watch your mouth around the kids, Tamela." I chuffed a racehorse. "But if that's what I was after then I'd have it!"

"My so-caahll abuse is nothin,' " she flatly said. "That aahll be a story you make up, nah. Ask any-body. I'm a nice per-sohn, Chris. Wha' mek you marry to me else?"

I realized two things that day. Let's call them mini-epiphanies since they didn't release me from all my madness. I told my journal:

> I realize that it's not possible to reason with her. She's incapable of reason. Trying to reason with her is simply a colossal waste of time. I've tried to reason with her over the years, but was always frustrated and then angry. I now have to give up and accept that in most respects, she's a 10-year old or less.
>
> Two, I've been talking to Dad at least three times since Tamela's arrival, and he's given me a chance to vent and talk. Today, he told me that although I've made a number of stupid decisions over the course of my life, I've coped very well and have created very smart solutions for them.

He said, "You always manage to solve your problems on your own without dragging anybody into them beyond what they choose." News to me especially after my divorce, which I felt dunked half the bloody world.

> I realized today that my parents will never understand me, and never be able to support me or understand my dreams or who I am. They can only love me within the confines, the box, of their experience or mentality. I think I'm finally beginning to come to terms with the limitations of my parents' love, and maybe my anger in that area is diminishing somewhat.

In the end my credible threats of arrest got her out of my house after 16 days. But she ended up with Mrs. Paz, Linda's and my babysitter who worked at the kids' school and bought into Tamela's sensible, wronged-woman persona. Picking them up from school at 6 PM Mrs. Paz said, "Ms. McKeon picked them up at 4:25."

Weird . . . but, okay. At home, no voicemail. *Where are my kids?* I called around but Tamela was missing in action. About 8 PM I rang the cops. Mrs. Paz told them at her door, "I don't know where they are. Their mother checked them out."

"We tracked your ex-wife to a shelter. She's only got a 7-month and 3-year old with her and denied any other knowledge. Sorry, her shelter is confidential."

"The hell?" *Where. Are. My. Kids!* I hied over to Mrs. Paz after 9 PM. She talked through her chained door. "I don't know anything. That's what I told the police."

I stomped off railing at the darkness. I felt a vibe and dialed her up. "If you know where my children are, you need to tell me before I blow this up to kidnapping and real jail time. The police say Tamela doesn't have them. She give them to you?"

"No, no, no! I don't know anything. I'm not involved." I fumed into the night.

The police called going on midnight. "We have your two children here at the station. Their mother brought them." I flamed rubber getting there. "It seems she sent them to stay with a school worker and were never in any danger."

"Mrs. Paz? She kidnapped my children! What're you gonna do about it?"

"Custody is vague. She isn't excluded from taking them from school."

"But she lied to you about it!"

Mr. Copper shrugged. "She wasn't obligated to tell us because she shares custody of some sort. The US Attorney is unwilling to charge her with anything."

Goddammit! I dragged it out of Mrs. Paz the next day. "I'm so sorry, Mr. McKeon. Your wife said it was okay. She had every authority to pick them up."

"You had no right lying they were in your house the whole damn time!"

"I know. I'm very sorry. Tamela made me think . . . I realiz—I told her to give them back. Please don't tell the school. I'll be fired! Or charged with a crime!"

"Damn right! You deserve it! Imagine coming to your door last night crying over my kids and they're right inside the whole time! You helped her kidnap my children. Now I find you're helping her get a lawyer to challenge our custody agreement! If you were a man so help me God I'd knock you flat! Twice!"

"Please, I'm so sorry! Your wife misled me."

"My ex-wife!" I forced a breath. "We trusted you, but never again." *Click.*

Tamela said, "I lie so she wouldn'a ge' fire. She could done lose her job!"

"So, you understood you were getting her to do a wrong thing, especially lying to me at her door that the kids were *right friggin' there!*"

"So, wha'? I ha' ev'ry right to me own chilleren. How dare you put po-lice 'dem 'pon me! Am I some crimee-naahl? No! I be our chilleren mudd-uhh!"

"You have no right to take them out of school and hide them from me!"

"Wha' mek you can'a spec' 'de chilleren 'dem be wi' me, 'dem mudd-uhh?"

"Are you nuts? I'm supposed to *assume* that? What kind of a shit-bucket father does that? You're out of your mind! You've burned my last bridge, Tamela. Shit!"

Then more dope to amaze: early on with Linda she'd recounted self-harming from a spiteful malice for parents who couldn't cognize her fierce drive and ambition to accomplish something important in life, to master her fate as an entrepreneur "instead of a worker bee." She'd arrived at the conclusion I just did.

"People are limited in their ability to love and comprehend you," she'd said in early 2000 over dinner. "It's ludicrous hating them just because they don't love or accept or support you the way you want or need. They have a perspective, too."

My single-dad dressmaking chops.

"Well, heck, Linda. It's all pretty disappointing. And, frankly, it hurts."

"Get used to it. Don't expect to make people what they can't be. Grow up."

My chin dropped hard. "My heart aches for them to unconditionally love and accept me *as I see myself*. The way I *need*."

"Why do you think they still talk to you?" She hit me with her typical teacher-to-stupid-student chinwagging. "They just remember you as a kid, a teenager, maybe a very young adult. *Before* you made your dumb choices to get where you are."

"All fucked up as a person?"

"Don't pity-party, Chris. Like my folks, yours love their baby. Not the entrepreneur or Moonie or dreamer or stupid victim. Whatever you are."

"That's not very helpful to me. And must you be so damned harsh about it? I mean—"

"They don't want to change your diapers."

Ugh. That was me? Maybe that's what Rev. Moon's vaunted unconditional love concept really is . . . a two-edged sword as well as a reciprocal relationship. My parents may love me for *who* I am—Chris, and only Chris—yet, all the same, can't love me for *what* I am: wandersman, Don Quixote, Don Juan, divorcé, whatever.

"Okay. Fine. I guess I can see a lot about me is too far outside their scope."

She finished her sushi. "Stop thinking it's *wrong* they're like that."

"It feels like a slap in the face."

"Pssh! From my position you're just as limited. What do you expect of people, anyhow? Don't even put me in that boat! Who else has had your back around here?" Well, I admired hers in sultry retreat to the kitchen. Followed her.

I've since grown sure that if they could, they would love and support me even if disagreeing or finding me impractical, unrealistic, or stupid. "But, would they ever say, 'You can do anything you dream, Chris. You can achieve your goal, crazy as it seems, and we'll use our experience to help you avoid mistakes you can't foresee'? Now, *that* would be acceptance, Linda. I guess they can't. At least, haven't."

"It's useless to expect it of them. Plus unfair. You don't have that right. May as well expect them to sprout wings and fly. You have a right to expect that?"

I'd rolled eyes. Felt she was prattling Greek back then. "How could you reconcile with your folks when they never accepted or supported your dreams?"

"You know, they're middle-class people, Chris. My father's an ex-Navy chief petty officer and my mother a housewife her entire life. Everything I do is so far out of their realm of life experience that to them it seems like crazy fantasy."

"As if *our* dreams simply can't exist in *their* real world?"

"In our dreamy, world-changing mindsets my mom and dad, yours, and people like them live in a black-and-white world. Our *color* is unimaginable."

"That's like living no life at all. A dusty history book. A sad story, even."

"Yeah . . . but I found a way to reconcile with them. You should, too."

"However absurd it seems? If not impossible?"

"Well, if you think it is, it usually will be."

Later, when we'd been heading crosstown for home in her Honda and I was bitterly denouncing millionairess Mona for having so little compassionate vision that it never occurred to simply provide her brother a modicum of support that was literally pocket change for her while I ferreted out professional work and extricated myself from an abusive marriage, I'd said through welling eyes, "How *doesn't* that occur to her? Or if it does, how can she decline? I remember walking a nobody homeless lady with two kids to my New York City bank and handing her a month's rent to get back into the apartment her landlord had locked her out of."

"That was your thing. How can you demand she do it, too?"

"I never imagined people would only deride my gesture. Saying my generosity was nothing but stupidity or, worse, enabling."

Linda scoffed. "You want your sister to solve the problems you created, Chris. Like it's your homeless crusade."

"I don't think so." I was in tears. "A little help, is all I'm saying."

"You have to look inside for that. Nobody lives to fix your shit."

Tamela's March invasion of my safehouse and a late April reprise for a CPO court hearing coinciding with Linda's homecoming from Hawaii forced me to confront Dad's (and Mona's) love while scrambling for advice in my predicament, to realize what my family's love *was* and especially what it *wasn't* nor *couldn't be*. Though I still wasn't bubbling beer-foaming joy for them, I felt I'd turned a corner. If I continued along my thoughtful, humbler path I'd yet find the ability to love whom I previously couldn't . . . or wouldn't. It's the essence of Jesus' admonition unreservedly endorsed by Rev. Moon that one needs love those who, to them, are unlovable.

Linda's affections nowadays were feeling mostly dead. She said, "I'm only seeing you *alone*. Your kids are too needy, too ill-mannered, and too stressful for me."

"We're a package deal, Linda. I'm not abandoning them to their crazy mother."

Face and shoulders rose to a group shrug. "If you want to see me or interact at all, you need to come over to my condo *without* your kids."

"You make me feel like a crumb for having my children. I feel so pressurized that I'm yelling at them lest they do anything wrong around you." Her eyes were flat. "I'm afrai—it's stupid and totally unfair how you might react makes me do that."

"Well, if you can't do it then don't complain like you did that you couldn't see me before I left. I'm done with your African mess."

I crossed arms. "So, are you breaking up for good?" She jetted air up her bangs. Her feelings read like hieroglyphics. *Her words say she wants no future with me. But I want a wife . . . one I don't have to constantly defend myself or my children to.*

Progress, not perfection. Tamela and Linda had me a wrathy loon. Epiphanies were important, but I needed to act on them by retraining my reflex response as each one so adroitly pushed my buttons. Reining in my passions was vein-popping. Nothing was worse than Tamela invading my life and Linda forcing me to my knees to wrest ownership. We're still at it here in 2003, but I've made productive strides slipping my choking noose calling the cops on Tamela and facing down Linda. Crucial was comprehending how my defeated boundaries and compromised faith made me like a nation who'd lost control of its borders. In rebuilding them, I'm rising to defend my personhood, my selfhood, my very essence and existence.

For Kal-el and Kir-el's sake I periodically walk them the few blocks to Sunday school in the basement of the Columbia Road Unification Church—finding Godwin there in 1997 feels so *ancien régime*—because I believe in the fundamental goodness and utility of Divine Principle. I don't generally attend Sunday service nor force it on the kids. I can't stand church, to be honest. They like Sunday school, though, and it teaches them about God and life in the way I currently understand it. I'm developing and maintaining my half-rebuilt boundaries vis-à-vis the church. I won't be sucked back into its dysfunction. I continue supporting Rev. Moon's basic vision for human Restoration from suffering along with his understanding of who and what God is, the nature of our human condition, and spirit world with which, like taxes, we all need one day deal. But as I noted in this book's preface, the only way to handle a howling wind like Rev. Moon and a treacherous, unlighted rock like the Unification Church is through upholding boundaries and maintaining faith.

My boundaries.

My faith.

My self.

My path from whence I act on *my* sense of mission without casting myself to that rapacious wind that only wants to own me. Consume me. Dictate my faith like Tolkien's Wagnerianly inimical One Ring of Power subduing all mindness.

Rock Creek Park, Washington, DC. One day in countless happily parenting my beloved Makaikai.

ON MY ROAD from victim to victor, I have to ask myself all the time where I am. We're all victims in some way. The things others do to each of us in angsty pursuit of happiness and flight from suffering, things seemingly striking out of the blue, 'acts of God,' or the stupidness we do to ourselves in the belief we're acting smartly all create a sense of victimization. Just as the Bible claims we all fall short of the glory of God, so we fall short of our own expectations and, now and again, believe and act on the belief we're victims. We can't transcend our low level existence until recognizing we *are* victims. That it's a natural part of life in a world we don't control. That we're merely one of gazillions of its parts all competing to survive and thrive. That all we *do* control is our own mind. From the snake biting us to the rock falling on us to the person abusing us to the rain falling on us when it's sunshine we want, we're none of us wrong in concluding that, besides the outcomes of our choices, unfair and uncalled-for bullshit stinks up our lives.

What's important isn't the event but how I *react*. Do I begrudge or roll with it? Rev. Moon claims historical resentment is what keeps us embroiled in generational conflict because we die yet live on in spirit world with our earthly emotions, desires, and experience. Our spirit self's loathing, malice, and revenge affects the like-minded in the physical world who act on it. We're intimately connected. The physical and spirit worlds are two planes of one existence as mind–heart, intellect–emotion, and childhood–adulthood represent two states of one individual. Resentment is a natural response, an integral part of our sense of violated boundaries and a frustrated desire for justice. Like anything in life, it can motivate the other side of the justice coin to pursue revenge. Instead of helping us seek positive love and forgiveness, it builds our road

Makaikai at Stead Park, DC c. 2007.

toward negative hate and condemnation. The former lets us free our heart of the crime while the latter makes the crime the nature of our heart.

As I walk along my road from victim to victor, I'm discovering I can slowly transform my rancorous odium to a *caring enmity*. That means I'm learning to love and accept those I find unlovable, who can't or won't necessarily love me the way I want to be loved, yet nonetheless in their own way love or at least care about me. Since unconditional love is necessarily reciprocal, those who don't love me as I want to be loved are not likely to ever grow into that ability if I'm ever unwilling or unable to love them within and regardless their limitations. Naturally, I'm not happy when people don't love me the way I need, reject who I am, or oppose my dreams. I naturally resent these perceptions. Instead of deploring it, I can choose to love or at least care about them regardless their limitations while responding positively to the interference they pose to me in living their own freedom.

This is where traditional Christian and even Unificationist thinking on the subject of unconditional love fails to adequately educate its believers. There's no such thing as unconditionally loving others in a vacuum. Without reciprocity, there's no give-and-take to generate the energy necessary to enable much less sustain it. Like electricity, love needs a completed circuit or it drains like a battery till there's nothing left. Like a real battery, a love battery can recharge but requires a completed love circuit. Hence Jesus, Rev. Moon, saints and sages—anyone striving to love the hateful or unlovable—need at least God for the boost.

Within moments of realizing the nature of my parents' love during a pay phone call with Dad while Tamela was a foreign army occupying my house, I felt more energized, more loved, and more capable of giving love and therefore dealing with her from a higher vantage. My spirit changed, and my attitude and lovability along with it. It wasn't simply a change in thinking but that my change in thinking closed a reciprocal circuit with Dad that, until then, had been open. It's the reciprocity that's important, not the intellectualism. Which brings me quite naturally back to Tamela. What about *her* love limitations? Lord knows, she (like me) has 'em. How do I learn to let her love me and I to love her within both of our significant limitations?

By respecting boundaries. Build 'em. Keep 'em. Enforce 'em.

And keep the faith in my intrinsic rightness of being *to exist as I am*. To ultimately craft a healthy relationship with her (as I'm bound to do in sharing children), it needs be defined on my side by my sense of self-protection and nurtured by personal boundaries backed up with a faith in the rightness of my task.

Family, Tamela . . . Moonies. The Unification Church is not a cult, to be sure. But it is a deeply dysfunctional bureaucratic organization that mindlessly strips members of personal boundaries and faith in a losing effort to own them heart, mind, and soul for the greater glory of God and human Restoration. The church obliterates its goodness and profound understanding of God and humanity on the rack of vicious, loveless, Confucianist beadledom much to the general loss of Divine Principle's virility. It scorns those members adequately maintaining boundaries and faith as part-time, home-member, Satan-invaded deadbeats. Yet, they're instrumental in moving the church forward in its goals and transforming it from weird Asian craze to mainstream Family Federation for World Peace and Unification however much a Christianized shell of its former self than any sort of improvement. That's an irony The Big Moon has yet to cast light upon.

DURING THIS ACT in my story, I finally stumbled through Linda across the road I've been searching for through 21 years of Unificationism, ten years of marriage, and several more of unmitigated chaos. Traveling from feeling victimized to achieving victories over it was and still is no small task though, counterintuitively, it's made easier by realizing I *am* a victim in the first place . . . not unlike recognizing one is an alcoholic before one can victoriously be *not*. For me, all that's required is opening my mind in reflection and my heart to the possibility of accepting love from others who are as limited in their lovability as my own self.

I *was* a victim.

Today in 2003 I'm not entirely a victor but walking my victorious road, its signposts my boundaries and faith. Keeping to it involves a willingness to both give and accept love even when it's not everything I need or want. Such love is the nurturing soil for my boundaries and faith to grow and develop within me.

Take that, victimizers.

Act XXI

Reverend Moon and America
Feet Shot Full of Holes

Who is Rev. Moon? Perhaps I'm hardly the one to say, but it's my perspective that he's a dichotomous dilemma. A tyrant and a friend. An old-world Korean and a new-world visionary. He's a traditionalist and a fresh-wine-new-wineskin rule breaker. A ball-buster and a comforter. Both fanatical and intellectual. Vicious and kind, tough and soft, tall and short. He's one thing and its opposite all at once, which I've despised so much yet loved so much more. He's a pain in the ass and the man I most admire here in 2003.

How does one deal with such an enigma? How has America dealt with him and he with it? Not well on both counts. Today's Unification Church and Rev. Moon are not simply scorned, they're ignored. Marginalized. At the back of America's bus.

It didn't have to be like this. From the very beginning of his American ministry he shot a big hole in his foot appalling Jesus-loving devotees with his *I'm the Second Coming and God Almighty's Vicar* yarn. His button-pushing keywords alienated the vast majority of the faithful and didn't endear him to home-team Koreans much, either. America abruptly snatched back welcoming arms digesting the true nature of his private beliefs and public dogma regarding Jesus and messianism.

"It's not bad enough he's calling himself the Messiah?" Christians lamented. "He's gotta dis Jesus as a dumb agitator practically begging the Jews to defy God?"

Ostensibly, his goal in America was restoring its faith to the moral clarity that made it great and him its core update. As *the* superpower—the ever-broken USSR-cum-Russian Federation nothing but a big gun in an impoverished and often drunk ideologue's hand—America relentlessly grinds through global culture. He had to purify this omnipotent, archangelic beast of a chosen nation. Sadly, he played up its post-fall Satanism over pre-Fall Luciferism guiding its homegrown idealism, compassion, and generally considerate foreign policy. He was less concerned to inspire America the Do-gooder than shame America the Perverse.

Rather than admiring Americanism to imbibe its unique Christian ethos and build positive relations, his Asian-centric church felt empowered by his example to mock and reject anything not codified into its liturgy—historical over operational; its personality imperially Confucianist regardless lip service—and built a dysfunctional, negative institution. Rev. Moon's own personality laid the seeds of the domestic violence that poisoned his American Family from its inception.

Most Unificationists prefer blaming America rejecting his messianism on self-centeredness, xenophobia, racism, and common cause with Satan. That misses a fundamental truth of charismatic movements: they live and die on their founder's breath. The church in 2003 is evolving into a bureaucratic institution functioning even more independently than it already does to, in its own way (like Catholicism), protect and promote its systemic interests. For now it dances, if awkwardly, to Rev. Moon's tune. It did him no good to also push the world's buttons as he claims Jesus did the Jews. At least he has America, the Great Satan of endless perversions, to thank for preserving his life, conscience, and soapbox.

The dichotomy between church idealism and reality arose in him preaching the highest ideals while inveterately unwilling to hold himself or his leaders accountable for breaching them. For all appearances, he violates his own standards in accord with the three sins he outlined while I was at UTS. He has as credible an explanation as other religious leaders but, for the average Joe, appearance matters more than fact. I accept him as a man of foibles even as he lives a trackless mission from God. Perhaps he's beyond us in his steadfast, unconditional love for the unlovable in pursuing healing for God's former angel of wisdom's sense of injury and alienation. And Divine Principle stands on its own merits.

The real question is why did tens or hundreds of thousands of Americans like me dedicated to the church, Divine Principle, and Rev. Moon quit? Moonies should pore over it for an answer. Part of a credible explanation is that they won't examine it with any seriousness. Denial speaks volumes. They find solace believing Satan blocks Americans from donning Rev. Moon's holy robes. It might be more accurate that Satan blocks Moonies from perceiving how they themselves push away this nation when, all else being equal, it might've positively responded.

In the late 1980s Rev. Moon invested considerable money and energy bringing black (over disinterested white) ministers to Korea. His personal story and Divine Principle's profound understanding of God and humanity moved many. Then they washed their hands of him because his leaders demanded they come on bended knee, mere cadets of faith. Interdenominationalism flopped. Not until the later-'90s did Rev. Kim in Chicago (promoted *bishop* by his happy black Christian flock) harvest measurable fruit marrying his outwardly warm, humble personality with an aggressive drive to recruit them into a support role.

That outreach has spread around the United States in 2003. Hundreds of black pastors proclaim him and the Missus the 'True Parents' of Mankind and, if not *the* Messiah, then *a* messiah. There's a tortuous syntactical waltz evidenced in carefully reasoning that *messiah* means 'anointed of God.' Hence, he's merely proclaiming his *anointing*. All ministers can be so anointed, making them Mini-Me messiahs in their own right and, more important, neither heretics nor apostates. Whether such dissembling wins over skeptical congregations that are fundamentally democratic in selecting paychecked leaders remains to be seen. As some of these ministers ban the cross from their churches at his behest, the sheeps and goats will find ever greater motivation to divide and conquer.

Rev. Moon backed up his Korean leaders' retreat from reality over reformative President Jim Baughman. Only years later did In Hoi Lee more adroitly revisit this question as a regional leader based out of Los Angeles before rising to Washington, DC's bigger-shot. His better respect for Americans, lesser corruption of spiritual ideals over syphilitic bureaucracy, and a smaller obsession with career and prestige won many ex-members' trust. In concert with Godwin, he built perhaps the country's most successful Moonie community in southern California. I like and admire him but he hasn't won me back on account of his unwillingness to see me as anything more than an incorrigible sinner and despoiler of sisters who icepicked his innocent hospitality in the neck, much like the permanently betrayed Kobayashis.

The membership drain arises in the damnable tendency to judge, punish, and ignore suffering. Such myopia afflicts religion across millennia. It's based on me more righteous than thee, that *my* troubles are the result of Satan's attack but *yours* from a weak and sinful nature. You can hear it in the Book of Job. Rev. Moon derides the attitude, to be sure. But refusing to put leaders' feet to fire when perjuring fidelity to Principle enhances their stature and emboldens perfidy.

I don't believe Americans fail to embrace the church—black congregations merely a stopgap on its way to the real (white) power—because we're evil, sinful, arrogant, xenophobic, or racist. This blame-the-victim mindset mirrors Rev. Moon's unseemly habit of claiming success while offloading failure, a habit all too readily employed by his leaders. He brags about unconditionally loving America in pouring billions of Japanese sweat into it; founding the *Washington Times* to guide America through its self-loathing, left-wing phase that despite his efforts is metastasizing into something worse; preaching God along its highways and byways; praying night and day for our salvation; all this and more. I've seen it. Still . . . so what?

No doubt, these are important so far as they go. But he claims it's not God we need please for Heaven but Satan's stamp of approval—"your heavenly passport"— that enables God to accept us without accusation. Recall God, with all the hallmarks of throwing Job under the bus, leaves him to the Devil. Rev. Moon's claim that he loves America doesn't matter. That's so much braggadocio. *Our* validation sets stone to mortar, and I'd say Americans think he's a weak aggregate. It's not that he doesn't exert time and energy for America's benefit. Rather, Americans don't see the relevance and smart under his denigration and airy dismissal of our intrinsic goodness for his obdurate belief in our obstinate badness. You can't love America and despise Americans. He reminds me of the tone-deaf '60s Southerner avowing to Civil Rightsters, "I don't hate niggers; some of my best friends are niggers."

As I finished this book in fall 2003, Rev. Moon proclaimed America had fulfilled its mission and earned the title of Elder Son, meaning Cain before his murderous rampage. Perhaps a grudging acceptance (I wouldn't say respect) is replacing his critical antipathy for the American person as opposed to, say, his uncritical affection for his personal American dream. In his rigorously hierarchical schema, America still pulls the duty of child to its Korean parent rather than colleague and equal. I will always find that repugnant, especially in light of him teaching we shouldn't see ourselves simply as God's children but rather His brothers and sisters; indeed, eventually His parent, as we have the inborn capacity to exceed our Creator. And that's as it should be. If you believe in God, that is. That's the premise.

Rev. Moon is a dreamer, a man of wistful fantasy in his belief that clay is divine. He's withal an old-world Confucianist who fancies himself a global emperor siring its ruling dynasty. Comparing his flamboyance to the (publicly) quiet humility of the Dalai Lama I wonder why his ego is on steroids. Only the shepherd's humility stills humanity's intrinsic distrust. His king-of-the-world events alienates and puts him in the position of taking the blame or casting it on faithless humanity or his treacherous disciples. Well, satanic Americans permit him all the freedom he needs to shout God from the mountaintops while his own Korean kinsmen tried mighty damn hard more than once to murder him these last 60 years. *You're welcome.*

Liberal with praise and humble in demeanor is seemingly Rev. Moon prior to the mid-1970s. Better than everybody who need prostrate before him is observably Rev. Moon of the last 30 years. When the Unification Church began crumbling in the early 1980s, it wasn't because Satan invaded Americans. It arose in the actions, omissions, inconsistencies, and dysfunctions of the Moon boat's captain. The church labels the assertion lies and sour grapes. Yet, every endeavor failing to achieve its goals—there's no denying that, after more than 60 years and ever bigger Blessings, he's failed to win even half a tenth of a percent to his messianism and Divine Principle's merits—begs the question: did the army or its general fail? Moonies never lacked the courage to boldly confront the fallen world, so I don't believe it's them. Leaders make or break and his are crude, selfish, self-absorbed, myopic, quarrelsome, disobedient, thievish, and disloyal. That's not me but Rev. Moon in so many speeches. In the final analysis, his prismatic leaders parroted only one or two of the many facets of their *Überführer*'s daily life. The rest was a race to the bottom.

IN EARLY JUNE 1991 Jerome was preparing to set sail on his fundraising trip across America and found me at Shiori's apartment. I'd dumped a bundle of letters I called the Great Indictment into the mailbox across from Jack Morton in winter 1991 addressed to the seminary and church leaders. They'd only recently come back half burned up from somebody throwing fire into the mailbox before pickup.

"It's disappointing only my brother received it," Jerome said.

"Maybe in the long run the arsonist was a blessing." *Sigh.*

He grunted. "Nothing will ever break the contradictions and inconsistencies of Oriental culture. You can't get into the seminary because no leader will write you a recommendation, which might even be illegal, but did you know that Toshimi—"

"That girl you fell with?"

"President Kim allowed her to stay while he ruthlessly arrested me."

"Father said ten years or so ago the Messiah was supposed to come from Ireland. But England, as Cain, failed by murdering them. Imagine an Irish messiah!"

"Funny, only Irish leaders ever gave me a chance." His eyes were pointed.

"The Messiah could've come on the Holy Roman Empire's foundation, too."

"It would've been best for the Messiah to be American. I speculate that was God's original intention. It would be much easier to unite the Adam, Eve, and Archangel nations with ethnic Americans than across nations that hate each other."

I laughed. "Korea had to be his last choice, the bottom of His list. That's why the UC is so screwed up. America has no force in the church at all, just Japanese and Korean custom running amok. Corrupting the Principle."

"Forget it, man. America's still too racist for it. Even England isn't as racist."

"They started the whole damned mess!"

"Doesn't matter. They banned it in England regardless their colonies."

I thought it over. "Maybe if we'd had colonies we might've escaped it, too."

"Pfft! WASPs hate Orientals as much as blacks. God had no good choices. The fact is, True Father has all the same problems. He selectively bends and breaks his teachings or doles out Blessings. Lets leaders persecute or disbar members with their own confessions or reject them outright. How can Principle explain that?"

"It can't, because it doesn't allow for contradictions since it preaches, as does Father, that for something to be true it must be true in all cases."

"Clearly not the case in the church."

"Well, maybe everybody's at different spiritual levels and can receive different dispensations and salvations."

His head whipped aside. "That implies original sin and the four fallen natures differ selectively among people, making some more guilty than others in the overall scheme of things. How can some filthy Korean be less guilty of original sin than an American much less an African? We all have original sin!"

"Father gives preferential treatment to Koreans regardless being a chosen-nation American or even a Blessed child. He *only* bends and breaks Principle and his own church rules for them or anybody he's close to. Plus nonmember bigshots."

"That's Hyo Jin Nim with his sexcapades, drunkenness, t'iefing, drug use—"

"Ha! Shiori told me she was right there in the room when Father made all that hushed-up shit public to a select group of closed-mouths at Tarrytown. He gets Blessed and a big position in the church with plenty of *our* pocket cash and you get thrown out of UTS for his Monday night. I'm not even Blessed but treated like I am when Wren Meyer throws me out over Shiori. No one blames her at all!"

"Just like Toshimi. I hear you, man." Jerome sucked a lip. "Koreans run it all."

I huffed a *Well!* "That's just how it is when we're the wrong race."

"It means Koreans weren't God's first choice. Father plainly operates outside Principle sometimes. On what basis can he do that? How can he remain the Messiah? Otherwise, Principle allows for preferential and racist treatment of peoples."

"We've treated Koreans and Japanese like the Chosen People, next to God, always right and holy—they're worse than us! We ruined the American UC doing that."

"I'm telling you, man, we have to rely on reason and Principle to guide us. Faith a person is following Principle and God's will won't ever get us to heaven. Only sure knowledge separates us from Satan. Acting out of faith is too risky."

"Well . . . dang, Jerome. That's—"

He braced up. "Moonies have adopted the nature of the betrayer. They think if they rat out a person to judgment or execution, they're doing right by God. That the universal principle of indemnity can't work unless they take it into their own hands to mete out. That they can manipulate universal laws to suit their own ends."

"I don't disagree." I recalled Judah Street in 1984. "History is full of Choi's good man–bad man principle. But he thought *he'd* decide who was good and bad."

"And what happened? He struck us and was himself struck, as well as all those betrayers who upheld his satanic theory of violence. Moonies think they can always manipulate any principle in the universe! Commit any crime if it's for God!"

"And break confidences, publicize confessions, ignore repentance, persecute anyone veering outside their narrow definition of Principled living . . ."

"Socrates' good life." Jerome sat back with a disgusted look. His voice rose, his tone hard. "Moonies therefore adopt Satan's same traditions and characteristics of deceit, treachery, betrayal, manipulation—all of it. They don't believe in God when they do those things but worship the devil! Thinking that universal principles can't work unless they intervene is denying God . . . setting themselves up *as* God."

"That's exactly our movement today!" I horse snorted. "Some church, eh."

"These fools think they're helping God by destroying enemies. My mentor, Dr. Jacob Needleman, taught me Plato over Aristotle, who Father stupidly prefers."

Well, the Unification Church probably won't die but continue on its wobbly way a minority faith. The pre-game show we got during Rev. Moon's mid-1980's incarceration foreshadows a savage schism after his death between Mrs. Moon and Koreans attempting to fill his mighty (rich) male shoes. After her death, I expect its zombified remains to shamble on a Sunni–Shia façade amongst those yearning for the Family's *auld lang syne*, its *théologie du jour*'s Confucianist institutionalism, and a quasi-Protestant denomination under its Jesus-anointed True Parent(s).

Perhaps it's better if it abandons religion per se for Divine Principle education within the great religions. *Unlikely.* Members all but worship Rev. Moon as the Lord's Nietzschean *Übermensch* while ignoring he's merely human pursuing the ideal of Divine Principled Man. The church is heedless elucidating Jesus as the first human reaching God's maturity yet not God Himself while snubbing the lesson. It just goes to show, denial is the ultimate hallucinogen and I should know. Absent wealth, Rev. Moon is a street preacher with delusions of grandeur. The only sure way to assess him is to rely on *Divine Principle*; though filled with profound insight and good instruction, his speeches are too meanderingly interpretive for that.

After 21 years a Moonie and 43 years a man, I've realized two things in my trials and tribulations: love is all that matters and victims can't love themselves or others, only victors can. I've wanted to change the world because I deserve a happier planet where no one, especially my children, suffer the battlefield nor their own or somebody else's torture chamber; enjoy acceptance if not love; feel their conscience and personal goals honored; experience the human dream of life, liberty, and happiness. Despite Moonworld's dysfunction, Rev. Moon taught me a singular lesson when he changed my worldview through Divine Principle and I love him for it: one person *can* make a difference.

But that person ain't the victim.

He or she is the victor.

Epilogue

The 2023 Edition

ONE HAS TO WONDER HOW AN EDUCATED, MIDDLE CLASS MAN IN THE RICHEST country in history managed to craft one experience after another that added up to playing Russian Roulette a second time after getting such a bang out of it the first. But it made me who I am over 36 Moon years into 2017. Much of that is good.

It might not seem like it, but I have no vengeful contemner for any of these characters. Everybody suffers and acts it out one way or another, and anyway my life projected into their experience as theirs did mine. Sometimes, we're just on the wrong end. Feels unfair but that's how it is in a world nobody controls. I can't master or fix you, only me. The more I try, the less I manage it . . . to my endless regret. Live and let live while protecting myself from the fallout seems better than shouldering Sisyphean rocks up interminable hills.

Life was a footslog 2003–06 healing my psyche. I wrenched my self-ownership from Tamela. The courts gave me sole custody. Life shifted to single parenting. She had a second child with Clyde and focused on raising them. I quit DC for a 3-storey townhouse and better schools in Maryland. At long last my children scattered out the front door on their own recognizance to gallivant with friends the way I did in 1960s Bowie. Happy days. I broke my spine in 2004. Airbags in a 2007 car crash inflicted hand–arm nerve damage. It killed my engineering career. Skull-melting pain aside, I adored being home for the kids' school years. Kal-el graduated and went to his older brother in Florida. In 2013 we moved to a 3-bedroom log cabin on four acres in Virginia's woods. The girls homeschooled. All smart kids.

My family relationships improved or healed. With time and help from Mona, social workers, and apparently growing up, Tamela gained literacy and education. It's still a trip when she texts me. She calmed enough to talk and visit with pleasant outcomes. Her affect drastically improved after spiritually healing within days of 2017's Big Healing (McKeon, *The Story of Life* 2022; sample below).

Kir-el said, "If I didn't know why, I'd say it's miraculous, Dad. We actually enjoy her company now."

"It's still miraculous. We can laugh together over the hell of our memories. That I can say, 'I'm gonna go now, Tamela,' and she says, 'Okay, nice talking. Next time,' was for me practically an act of God." *Read that book, y'all.*

The kids restored their relationships with her in weeks or months. It isn't perfect, but everybody's learning. Furious Kal-el calmed and recovered through his 4-year odyssey in Florida that left him a man ready to face his childhood PTSD in Navy boot camp. Kir-el is considering his footsteps. L'or-el is knocking 'em dead in New York's modeling and workaday world. Tamela's daughter joined the Marines and her brother hit adulthood. Both sojourned summers with us in Virginia. Linda relocated to Hawaii. I didn't get to parent Makaikai after that, but love her and tried to be a good dad then and now she's in college. Monica's son did his Air Force twenty and brought up two grandkids. All my children are life's greatest joy however they see my parenting or lack thereof. I'd never trade 'em for greener grass.

Friends said Shiori got reBlessed. Fervent hopes she found happiness. My heart thumped with Nanami's in the 2010s over a Maryland coffee.

She said, "I still love you same way, K'risu. But thank you for helping with Sam. You gave me good life with him. We had beautiful babies and I'm happy."

Yeah. That's what I wanted for her. Right?

Illness took her heading out of 2016. That same year Hemi apologized for his vicious emails after gorging on his own broken-Blessing crow. Jerome disappeared into San Francisco then the Big Apple.

Tamela phoned in early 2023. "Chris! Jeh-rome been die!"

Shuffled his coil, eh? "How do you know?"

"Seranie been tell me. Him brudd-uhh Ro-nald been in St. Vincent an' tell Av-ril." A chuckle surged. "He now be explainin' to he Mak-uhh aahll he sins."

I plopped my head on my chair back. Memories flooded me.

Rev. Moon preferred no contribution from me though irrevocably altering my life. Once satisfied as a geologist, Coastie, or adventurer, now his vision needs inform all I do. Then off he popped in 2012. What I predicted for the church came true in spades. It never offered nor accepted my service. UTS shrunk to a few-room school at West 43rd then as a peace and public leadership mill, Barrytown sold to maybe fund Hak Ja Han's litigious Comintern. Hats off to the holy geniuses.

MY TASK GOING forward in 2003 was to repair the wonky ship *My Life* and once more set out on the sea of spiritual growth and accomplishment I'd charted in 1977. I didn't get rich except in children. I found my boundaries and faith and worked through my trauma, PTSD, and triggers living life as I saw it without sinking into the mire of desperate acceptance by others. The vision and dedication I inherited from Rev. Moon germinated in my soul, sprouting from and nurtured in the strength of my conviction as I transformed from the victim I was to the victor I am. Mission accomplished. It all came to fruition October 13, 2017 with *The Story of Life.*

Victor onward, my friend.

Thank you for reading my story! Would you leave a review for others who might benefit? It means a lot to me. Your support makes a difference; I read all reviews for feedback to make my books even better. Just follow the QR code (books2read.com/victimtovictormemoir).

~

 Hardcover ☞ Paperback ☞ FREE Kindle

Turn the page to read a sample from Chapter 1: All Shook Up

Thursday October 12, 2017 ca. 5 PM

F ALL THE days in all the months in all the year, Friday the 13th just had to be the day the world as it was all sort of just blew up in our face. My two daughters and I . . . well, we quite lit the fuse when, about sixteen hours before that cool October morning, we'd tramped through the garage door of our woodsy rural log cabin home following an afternoon of errands and posed a simple question. Atop a wild, spiritually hectic week culminating in our long afternoon in the car talking over God, ancestry, life, and surprises from dear dead friends, my two-days-eighteen daughter El froze mid-step in our living room and blurted, "Creator, do you have a family?"

And he answered.

We all three traded surprised eyes at the *yes* response, but she was on a roll.

"Do you have a wife?"

Yes.

"Do you have children, not just us?"

Yes.

She paused a few seconds, thinking through the logic. "Do you have a *mother?*"

Yes!

While I jacked my jaw up off the floor, she looked at me. "Dad, I can literally *feel* his joy that we've just discovered this! He's really happy! Can we meet her?" she added, not to me. "Can we talk to her?"

At which point El swiveled to her right, face and eyes cranking upward as though at a much taller person. Her expression transformed, aglow with delight and excitement. A smile burst across her cheeks as her hands flew to her heart. She sucked her breath.

"*Hi,* Mother!"

Yeah. I gawped, too.

Even a wizened skeptic like me could tell my younger daughter was having a moment, an experience, a—well, a revelation. Chills, tingles, and heat shivered me timbers stem to stern. Energy and pleasure radiated from El. I could see her gleam. There was no mistaking her profound joy and rapture. We, too, felt the presence of 'Mother' fiercely blazing with happy excitement. Communicating. In our *home.* To *us.* Who were *aware* of her. My older daughter and resident spiritualist Ayako, now two days from her twenty-first year, twisted round a blue-upholstered, high-backed dining chair and plopped into it facing El with a knowing curiosity, feeling all the energy we were experiencing and more. We incessantly questioned Mother and Mina—God—into the night, all of which you'll encounter throughout this book.

That wasn't even the really exciting part. But before we got to that, our curiosity slanted us through some scary hours later in the night that left my exuberant daughters tearful and terrified, and me wondering just what can of worms we'd pulled the pop-top on. For now, though, we enthusiastically pushed our envelope of reality and the eye-popping responses snowballed. A lifelong Irish Roman Catholic, Protestant Christian, Unificationist, and now post-Unificationist, it soon registered that my worldview, my *lifeview,* was in some real distress here. Stuff needed clarifying if not a little unmitigated arguing. Yet for all that, Mina's answers were coherent, consistent, and sensible. Only good, loving, calm but excited energy bathed the room. With that, it seemed as wise a time as any to get down to the suddenly apropos nitty-gritty.

I said, "Creator, is the Bible true?"

No.

I pulled a hard breath, astonished, though as a graduate of divinity school maybe not all that surprised. Even so, a linchpin of my lifeview clattered to the wide-planked floor.

"What about the New Testament? Is Jesus' teaching in that true?"

"Dad, he said—"

No.

"*All* of it?" I gave my girls each a once over, but if you could wear a body shrug like a pantsuit, they were. *Kids*, I thought. Always jaunty at the start of a march across somebody else's Bataan.

No.

"So, some of it, then, is true."

Yes.

"How 'bout Jesus," El said, "is he a real person?"

Yes.

Well, that was a relief. I think. Anyhow, the girls looked copacetic. We quizzed Mina on this topic awhile until, inevitably, it led to the issue most pressing me.

"Is Rev. Moon's teaching in *Divine Principle* true?" I mean, I'd largely bet the farm on it in 1981.

No.

My ribs fell in. There went another linchpin. I let out a wheeze like I'd just downed a shot of two-hundred proof. Bleary eyes landed on each daughter, but saw in them none of my own jolt.

"Jeez, girls," I yawped. "That's been my lifeview purt' near forty years!"

Ever sassy, Ayako said, "Welcome to the next wave, Dad."

Unlike Jesus, I *knew* Sun-myung (he eschews titles, now). His theologically ultra-modern Divine Principle was more real to me than worn out, foggy old Christianity, its grand morsels of wisdom and Jesus notwithstanding. Sure, Divine Principle reposed upon the biblical witness, but to me it more sensibly elucidated its core truths. It underwrote the full scale of my adult life. I might be perennially at war with Sun-myung's pigheaded church institution but not his Divine Principle, not by any stretch.

I said, "*All* of it?"

I had to ask because, like everyone in spirit world communicating with a non-conversational medium in the physical world, Mina must needs be literal in our mode of communication. He has to be, really. Absent face-to-face or even just voice-to-voice conversation, it's nigh impossible to gauge what a person actually means by words alone. Consider how the misunderstanding curve rises proportionally to one's metaphorical distance from the speaker. One's words themselves—rooting in shared definitions—need convey precisely what's meant. That's a tough row to hoe for humans, wedded the way we are to contextual word play. You might think Mina could simply know our thoughts, but that creates complications of its own we discuss later. What it boils down to, Ayako pointed out, is that we had to formulate our questions thoughtfully into unambiguous inquiries and confirmations that backed up our responses.

No, Mina answered me through El.

Huh. So again, only some of my lifeview was true. Was that good? I didn't know. As with the Bible, I could only wonder, *which freaking part? Divine Principle* is a weighty *vade mecum* in its own right.

Being young, unformed, and like many in their generation rejecting religion generally though not God specifically, my daughters *looked* okay—my eldest like an old soul hearing something she'd long suspected and her kid sister charmed in high cotton—but *my* cosmology was melting apart like Icarus' wishful wax job. This conversation was sweeping away a lifetime of hard-won truths, from the nature of the universe and God to Jesus and Sun-myung's messianism and the spiritual verity and providential histories that went with them (likewise with all religions), not to mention what I'd sacrificed—wasted?—for it all. My head was spinning. I was anything *but* okay. But dammitall if that would throttle my interest; perish the thought. Come hell or high water, I'm nothing if not the cat tempting curiosity.

By and by, we worked our way to the crux of the Abrahamic religions: the Fall of Man. Original sin territory and their *raison d'être*. After some unexpected and perplexing responses from Mina, we needed to get a few things straight.

I said, "Are you saying the Fall never happened?"

Yes.

"So . . ." dittoed El, finally sounding a tad betrayed, "there *was* no Fall of Man?"

No.

"Satan never persuaded Eve to eat the 'fruit'?" she continued. "Lucifer never fell—never had a wrong sexual relationship with Eve like Rev. Moon said? People never tried to be God and 'fell' from grace or perfection, or whatever?"

No, no, no.

"Well," said I, "fuuu—!"

No.

Ayako shifted round to me with disapprobation. "That 'no' means negative energy resonates, Dad."

Great.

After more give-and-take—during which Mina recast 'the Fall' as *The Corruption* in which humans self-manifested our selfish, harmful world and self-alienated ourselves from God (I mean, Mina) without any help from anybody, including our evolutionarily left-over, full-blown-batty reptile brain—El perceptively said, "Wait. Are Adam and Eve even real people who actually lived?"

No.

Ayako and El traded stares. It seemed their own lifeviews were at last meeting some unexpected renovation. About time.

I choked. "Um, they don't exist?"

No. They don't exist.

"Then, is Satan a real being, a fallen angel, or . . . whatever?"

No. No . . . no.

"Wait, wait." Just. *Wait.* I needed a minute to *think.*

El didn't. "You mean Satan doesn't even *exist?* There's no devil, no evil force or being that—"

No, no.

"So, no war in heaven, no angel rebellion, no beings cast down to earth," she went on with obvious offense, practically ticking through Revelations (12:7–9) on her fingers and giving me, her ministerial, semi-Bible-thumping father a flinty eye, "no ancient good versus . . . *none* of these stories religion taught us are true?"

No. Sorry.

El blew off a heavy breath, threw up her hands, and tromped in a circle. Oaths welled up in my brain so fast they had to take a number.

A little hostile, I said, "What about Darwin, then?

"Not Darwin, Dad," said Ayako, ever the schoolteacher, "Darwin*ism.* Unless you mean the guy, you're talking about natural selection."

"Uh, sure . . . but is he—it—true?"

No.

"What? But then—?"

"So, evolution is *wrong?*" said El.

Yes.

"All of it?" I added, pretty much expecting the obvious.

No.

Yep. Here we go again. "So, basically, *everybody's* explanation for humanity's existence and miserable condition is total bullshit?"

"Dad . . ."

"False?"

Maybe . . . yes.

Ayako said, "Remember, Dad, he said not *every* single thing."

"Yeah, but everybody's?"

"Like, all religions and philosophies?" El said plainly.

Yes.

She let out a low, gruff whistle. "*Waaah*—when your whole existence is just a fat lie."

"So, Islam, too?" I said. "And Buddhism, Confucianism, Hinduism, Animism—"

Yes, yes, ye—

Ayako gave me an eye. "He said all religions, Dad. Come on."

Yes.

"I'm just being thorough." And not taking sides, I didn't say.

No.

"I'm not? But I . . . wait," I said toward El, who was doing our energy testing. "Are you pulling my leg?"

Yes.

"Well. Isn't he just a barrel of monkeys. Never took God for a joker," I said to Ayako, though I'd heard a medium once make the claim.

"Lots of things you never thought of, Dad," she chirped, queen of the snappy comeback and earning my tight-lipped stare-down. My mood was a little nettled, frankly.

A flurry of questions and statements followed as we plunged ever deeper down our rabbit hole. I put evolution aside for now. It only dealt with our bodies anyhow. We had *cosmic* issues on the table. But now, a few other things in my head about the human 'fall from grace' were rising to the fore and clashing with Mina's assertions. It occurred to me we'd need to pull in somebody else, the very somebody who off and on since late summer had purveyed through a local medium a seemingly clear, unambiguous spiritual reality that included a very real Adam and Eve. Archangel Michael.

Read the rest of

The Big Event, All Existence, All That's In It, And Us, and *Energy Testing*
plus ten spirit world testimonies from historical figures including
Jesus, Sun-myung Moon, Mohammad, Buddha, and Hitler in

The Story of Life

Hardcover, paperback, and FREE Kindle at
Amazon, Barnes & Noble, Lulu, Google Play,
and wherever books are sold.

Use your smartphone camera to follow the QR codes below to (L–R) visit the author at chrismckeon.com, visit toteppitpress.com for a *free* PDF with clickable cross-reference links, or purchase *The Story of Life* (or download *free* Kindle). Thank you!